MARRIAGE AND DIVORCE IN A MULTICULTURAL CONTEXT

American family law makes two key assumptions: first, that the civil state possesses sole authority over marriage and divorce; and second, that the civil law may contain only one regulatory regime for such matters. These assumptions run counter to the multicultural and religiously plural nature of our society. They are also wrong. This book elaborates how those assumptions are descriptively incorrect, and it begins an important conversation about whether more pluralism in family law is normatively desirable. For example, may couples rely on religious tribunals (Jewish, Muslim, or otherwise) to decide family law disputes? May couples opt into stricter divorce rules, either through premarital contracts or "covenant marriages"? How should the state respond when couples purport to do these things?

Intentionally interdisciplinary and international in scope, this volume contains contributions from fourteen leading scholars. The authors address the provocative question of whether the state must consider sharing its jurisdictional authority with other groups in family law.

Joel A. Nichols is Associate Professor of Law at the University of St. Thomas (Minnesota) and a Senior Fellow at the Center for the Study of Law and Religion at Emory University. His scholarship explores the relationship of theology and religion to law – especially family law, constitutional law, and international human rights. Professor Nichols holds degrees in both law and theology.

Contributors include Brian H. Bix; Michael J. Broyde; Daniel Cere; Ann Laquer Estin; Mohammad H. Fadel; Werner Menski; Linda C. McClain; Joel A. Nichols; Stephen B. Presser; Ayelet Shachar; Katherine Shaw Spaht; Johan D. van der Vyver; Robin Fretwell Wilson; and John Witte Jr.

Marriage and Divorce in a Multicultural Context

MULTI-TIERED MARRIAGE AND THE BOUNDARIES OF CIVIL LAW AND RELIGION

Edited by

JOEL A. NICHOLS

University of St. Thomas School of Law (Minnesota)

CAMBRIDGE
UNIVERSITY PRESS

CAMBRIDGE UNIVERSITY PRESS
Cambridge, New York, Melbourne, Madrid, Cape Town,
Singapore, São Paulo, Delhi, Mexico City

Cambridge University Press
32 Avenue of the Americas, New York, NY 10013-2473, USA

www.cambridge.org
Information on this title: www.cambridge.org/9780521194754

First published 2012
Reprinted 2012

A catalog record for this publication is available from the British Library.

Library of Congress Cataloging in Publication Data
Marriage and divorce in a multicultural context : multi-tiered marriage and the
boundaries of civil law and religion / edited by Joel A. Nichols.
  p. cm.
Includes bibliographical references and index.
ISBN 978-0-521-19475-4 (hardback)
1. Marriage law. 2. Divorce–Law and legislation. 3. Multiculturalism–Law
and legislation. 4. Religion and law. 5. Legal polycentricity.
I. Nichols, Joel A., 1972– II. Title.
K675.M367 2012
346.01'6–dc23   2011019706

ISBN 978-0-521-19475-4 Hardback

To Jennifer
I choose you again and again

Contents

Detail Contents

About the Editor

Joel A. Nichols is Associate Professor of Law at the University of St. Thomas School of Law (Minnesota) and a Senior Fellow at Emory University's Center for the Study of Law and Religion. He was formerly Associate Professor and Rick J. Caruso Research Fellow in Law at Pepperdine University. Professor Nichols holds degrees in law (J.D.) and theology (M.Div.) from Emory University in Atlanta. At Emory he was a Robert W. Woodruff Fellow in Law and participant in the M.Div. Honors Program; at graduation he was awarded Order of the Coif and the Herman Dooyeweerd Prize in Law and Religion at the law school and the Award for Academic Excellence at the theology school. He also holds a B.A. in interdisciplinary studies from Abilene Christian University (Abilene, TX), where he was a Jack Pope Fellow.

Professor Nichols is the coauthor (with John Witte Jr.) of *Religion and the American Constitutional Experiment*, 3rd ed. (2011). He has also authored two dozen articles and book chapters in publications including *NYU Law Review*, *Emory Law Journal*, *Vanderbilt Journal of Transnational Law*, *St. John's Law Review*, *Family Court Review*, and others. He serves in leadership roles in the American Association of Law Schools (AALS) Section on Family and Juvenile Law and the AALS Section on Law and Religion and as a referee for *Journal of Law and Religion*, among others. He is an expert in issues addressing the intersection of law and religion, including U.S. constitutional law, legal history, human rights, and family law.

List of Contributors

Brian H. Bix is the Frederick W. Thomas Professor of Law and Philosophy, University of Minnesota Law School.

Michael J. Broyde is Professor of Law, Emory University, a Senior Fellow at Emory University's Center for the Study of Law and Religion, and Rabbinical Court Judge (*dayyan*), Beth Din of America.

Daniel Cere is Assistant Professor of Religion, Law and Ethics at McGill University, Faculty of Religious Studies.

Ann Laquer Estin is the Aliber Family Chair in Law, University of Iowa College of Law.

Mohammad H. Fadel is Associate Professor of Law and Canada Research Chair in the Law and Economics of Islamic Law, University of Toronto, Faculty of Law.

Linda C. McClain is Professor of Law and Paul M. Siskind Research Scholar, Boston University School of Law.

Werner Menski is Professor of South Asian Laws, School of Oriental and African Studies, University of London.

Joel A. Nichols is Associate Professor of Law, University of St. Thomas School of Law (Minnesota) and a Senior Fellow at Emory University's Center for the Study of Law and Religion.

Stephen B. Presser is the Raoul Berger Professor of Legal History, Northwestern University School of Law.

Ayelet Shachar is Professor of Law and Canada Research Chair in Citizenship and Multiculturalism, University of Toronto, Faculty of Law.

Katherine Shaw Spaht is the Jules F. and Frances L. Landry Professor of Law, Emeritus, Louisiana State University Law Center.

Johan D. van der Vyver is the I.T. Cohen Professor of International Law and Human Rights, Emory University School of Law, and an Extraordinary Professor in the Department of Private Law, University of Pretoria.

Robin Fretwell Wilson is the Class of 1958 Law Alumni Professor of Law and Law Alumni Faculty Fellow, Washington and Lee University School of Law.

John Witte Jr. is the Jonas Robitscher Professor of Law, Alonzo L. McDonald Distinguished Professor, and Director of the Center for the Study of Law and Religion at Emory University.

Preface

The Archbishop of Canterbury, Dr. Rowan Williams, caused a substantial stir in 2008 when he called for a "plural jurisdiction" over some disputes within the United Kingdom. The Archbishop specifically proffered a system wherein Muslims could choose to resolve family law disputes (and some other civil matters) in either religious tribunals or in British courts. In July 2008, Lord Chief Justice Lord Phillips (the most senior judge in Britain) seconded the Archbishop's sentiment and, in public remarks, signaled his approval of the application of Islamic law (*shari'a*) so long as divorce rulings complied with the law of the land. These strong statements came only a few short years after public discussions in Ontario, Canada, about the propriety of religious courts operating as arbitration tribunals in family law matters. Currently in South Africa, both the legislative and judicial branches continue to contemplate the interaction between civil law and religious law with respect to marriage (especially regarding "customary marriages," polygamy, and same-sex marriage). And India and Israel lead a number of countries in delegating jurisdiction over marriage and family life to religious law or religious tribunals.

These international examples are especially interesting in light of the fact that the United States is, by all accounts, an increasingly multicultural and religiously plural society. Despite such diversity, American family law makes two key assumptions about marriage and divorce. The first is that the civil state is the sole authority for such matters, and the second is that only one regulatory regime for marriage and divorce may exist within civil law.

This book demonstrates that those common assumptions are *descriptively* incorrect. It also begins an important conversation about whether, *normatively*, more pluralism in family law is desirable and should thus be affirmatively fostered and, if so, under what conditions and qualifications.

Too often public debates about marriage and divorce overlook the dual nature of marriage for many citizens in society. That is, many citizens are bound not only to civil norms regarding marriage and divorce but also to religious norms – and often the civil and religious norms are not exactly aligned. This book tries to take seriously the dual allegiances of many citizens in society, while also hewing to the overarching norms of equality and protection for vulnerable parties that are part of the fabric of the larger civil society itself.

Rather than protecting hardened positions, the contributors to this volume draw upon their expertise in law, history, theology, political science, sociology, and feminist studies to explore difficult questions in an interdisciplinary fashion. The result is a book containing a rich scholarly conversation on the jurisdictional boundaries of marriage and divorce law in a liberal society.

Every book has its limits, and this one is surely no different. Most noticeable to some readers, perhaps, will be the relative inattention to same-sex marriage. That choice is intentional, because the topic not only receives the current lion's share of attention in academic discussions about marriage but, once raised, also frequently overshadows any other topic. The book also retells the history of marriage and divorce jurisdiction only cursorily; gives shorter shrift than may be deserved to constitutional law concerns; and treats comparative international examples selectively. While all these matters are easily defensible within the contours of the project, I recognize that more work needs to be done to continue the conversation.

The wide scope of chapters that are here, though, reveals a descriptive observation that notions of exclusive state jurisdiction of a one-size-fits-all law for marriage and divorce are more hope than reality. This owes, in no small part, to the critical role that religion plays in the individual and communal lives for many people in society. The chapters undertake a conversation about the normative implications of such pluralism in marriage and divorce law: Is more pluralism in family law desirable? If so, how should it be done to ensure adequate protections for vulnerable parties? If not, will pluralism continue to occur anyway and require interaction or regulation by the state to ensure such protections? And does attempting to avoid such pluralism run counter to the state's goals of equality and liberty?

In short, as contributor Werner Menski states, "The present volume seeks to take the debate about management of family law further than the existing literature." The reader is invited to join a conversation about the provocative and arguably inevitable question of whether the civil state must consider sharing part of its jurisdictional authority with other groups in family law matters.

* * *

Collaborative projects, by definition, do not unfold independently. Although I will undoubtedly miss some people and surely understate the relative contributions of others, it is important to acknowledge my gratitude to several people. First, thanks to the superb contributors to this volume: Brian Bix, Michael Broyde, Dan Cere, Ann Estin, Mohammad Fadel, Linda McClain, Werner Menski, Stephen Presser, Ayelet

Shachar, Katherine Spaht, Johan van der Vyver, Robin Wilson, and John Witte. It has been a great pleasure to get to know you, or to know you better, through this and to work with you. I appreciate your patience as this project has unfolded over the past few years, and several of you provided incisive criticism and also sage advice over time. Thanks. I'm also grateful to others who participated at earlier stages in this project on Multi-Tiered Marriage: Peg Brinig, Elliot Dorff, Rick Garnett, Steve Nock, and Chuck Reid. Portions of this book and my own work were presented at conferences of the International Society for Family Law and Emerging Family Law Scholars, and I am grateful to numerous participants there for useful criticism and commentary.

This book and my own contributions to it have benefited from great research assistance and other support over the years as well: thank you Elizabeth Anderson, Jesse Beier, Megan Conniff Egli, Gabriel Egli, Krista Griffith, and Mary Wells (reference librarian at St. Thomas). For additional administrative support, I am indebted to Henry Bishop, Nora Fitzpatrick, and Catherine Utrup at St. Thomas, and Novita Handoko and Carol Shadrick at Pepperdine. And I must single out Paddy Satzer at St. Thomas for her excellent and very professional work in preparing the index.

I owe a special word of thanks to John Witte, my sometime coauthor and longtime friend and mentor. One of the wisest decisions I made years ago was to move to Atlanta to study and work with John during my years as a graduate student. He has long shaped my thinking and spurred me on with encouragement, counsel, and advice. The generative ideas for this project were formed during my time in graduate school – studying under John, Michael Broyde, Abdullahi An-Na'im, and others – and have fermented and aged since then.

John was also supportive early on when I first approached him about turning my ideas into a book conversation of this nature. Our discussions encouraged me to create a proposal, which in turn led to generous financial support from Emory's Center for the Study of Law and Religion (CSLR), in partnership with Pepperdine University and the Pepperdine University School of Law and the University of St. Thomas School of Law. At Pepperdine, Provost Darryl Tippens and then-Dean Ken Starr provided strong financial and intellectual support to the project. When I moved to St. Thomas, Dean Tom Mengler was equally embracive in his backing for the project – financially, professionally, and personally. Many of my other colleagues at St. Thomas have been encouraging and helpful along the way, including Tom Berg, Mitchell Gordon, Chuck Reid, Rob Vischer, and others. And behind all this was the support of my longtime friends at Emory, especially the wonderful CSLR staff. Anita Mann and Amy Wheeler especially provided moral and administrative support.

Cambridge University Press has been very supportive of this project. I am grateful to John Berger for his faith in this project and his patience along the way. The production team at the Press has been professional, hardworking, and a pleasure to work with; I am thankful for their assistance in bringing this book into print.

Finally, I'm tremendously grateful to my wonderful wife Jennifer and to Benjamin and Natalie – for more than I could ever say. You all are the best.

Joel A. Nichols
University of St. Thomas School of Law (Minnesota)

Permissions

Ann Laquer Estin. An earlier version of this chapter appeared as Ann Laquer Estin, "Unofficial Family Law," *Iowa Law Review* 94 (2009): 449–480, although it was commissioned as part of this project. It is reprinted here, with minor modifications, with the permission of the *Iowa Law Review*.

Joel A. Nichols. This chapter draws upon Joel A. Nichols, "Multi-Tiered Marriage: Ideas and Influences from New York and Louisiana to the International Community," *Vanderbilt Journal of Transnational Law* 40 (2007): 135–196.

Stephen B. Presser. An earlier and much shorter version of this chapter appeared as Stephen B. Presser, "Marriage and the Law: Time for a Divorce?" *Chronicles: A Magazine of American Culture* (March 2004): 20–22. Portions of that article have been incorporated into this longer essay, with the kind permission of the Rockford Institute, the publisher of Chronicles.

Ayelet Shachar. This chapter was first published as Ayelet Shachar, "Faith in Law? Diffusing Tensions Between Diversity and Equality," *Philosophy & Social Criticism*, Vol. 36, Nos. 3–4 (2010): 395–411 (© Ayelet Shachar, 2010). Reproduced by permission of SAGE Publications Ltd., London, Los Angeles, New Delhi, Singapore, and Washington DC.

Robin Fretwell Wilson. This chapter draws, in part, upon Robin Fretwell Wilson, "The Overlooked Costs of Religious Deference," *Washington and Lee Law Review* 64 (Fall 2007): 1367–1383.

John Witte Jr. and Joel A. Nichols. An earlier and shorter version of this chapter appears as John Witte Jr., "Afterword," in *Shari'a in the West*, eds. Rex Ahdar and Nicholas Aroney (Oxford: Oxford University Press, 2010), 279–292.

Introduction

Joel A. Nichols

How should the civil state relate to marriage and divorce in modern society? Some, from both the left and right ends of the political spectrum, are calling for the state to extract itself from the marriage business.[1] For many proponents of this position, this presumably would leave the label of "marriage" entirely to religious or other organizations, because the state would only handle legal benefits under some sort of civil registration regime. Others pronounce that the state should be ever more involved in regulating marriage, including extending it to same-sex couples.[2] Still others contend that the state not only must remain involved in the regulation of marriage and divorce law but should adhere to a more traditional role concerning marriage and divorce.[3] This is not merely a culture-wars skirmish about same-sex marriage, though, for there are serious questions about the role of the federal government versus state governments in marriage and divorce law; there is a greater diversity in various state marriage laws than has often been the case historically; there are heightened questions about the role of premarital agreements and the ability of autonomous parties to enter such agreements; and there is continued ambiguity about extraterritorial recognition of marriage and marriage-like relationships between states as a conflict-of-laws matter.[4]

---

[1] See, e.g., Martha Albertson Fineman, "The Meaning of Marriage" in *Marriage Proposals: Questioning a Legal Status*, ed. Anita Bernstein (New York: New York University Press, 2006), 29–69; Martha C. Nussbaum, "A Right to Marry?" *California Law Review* 98 (2010): 667–696; Edward A. Zelinsky, "Deregulating Marriage: The Pro-Marriage Case for Abolishing Civil Marriage," *Cardozo Law Review* 27 (2006): 1161–1220; Stephen B. Presser, "Marriage and the Law: Time for a Divorce?" (in this volume).

[2] E.g., *Varnum v. Brien*, 763 N.W.2d 862 (Iowa 2009); Pamela S. Karlan, "Let's Call the Whole Thing Off: Can States Abolish the Institution of Marriage?" *California Law Review* 98 (2010): 697–707.

[3] See, e.g., Charles J. Reid Jr., "And the State Makes Three: Should the State Retain a Role in Recognizing Marriage?" *Cardozo Law Review* 27 (2006): 1277–1309.

[4] See, e.g., Brian H. Bix, "Pluralism and Decentralization in Marriage Regulation" (in this volume).

Why this fervent public discussion about marriage and the role of the civil state? There are a host of reasons, of course, not least of which are the many state benefits that flow from a legal marriage relationship. But even the word "marriage" itself is freighted with meaning – historically, religiously, culturally, and socially – and advocates on all sides remain eager for society and the law to embrace their preferred definition and understanding of marriage. The public discussion and disagreement about marriage also derive from the increasingly diverse and multicultural society in which we live. Even if there was a time historically when common understandings of marriage and divorce were shared in the United States, that time has passed.

The discussions about marriage and divorce are complicated by the fact that marriage is critically important to people on several levels, including access to state benefits, expression, and religion.[5] Marriage is not merely a private law contract between two individuals, but often an important familial and community event. It is not merely an avenue by which the state confers status benefits on a couple, but often serves as an entrance marker into various forms of adulthood and community. It is not merely an act to which compliance with state procedural forms of adequate notice and consent are sufficient, but often acts as the marker of union between two families requiring a religious ceremony, a qualified officiant, and capable and willing parties. Indeed, for many people marriage is more important as a religious matter than a civil matter. For them, a marriage is not valid unless it is between two similarly religious individuals who have received appropriate solemnization by qualified religious authorities. And a marital dissolution is not valid unless granted by competent religious authorities on adequate grounds via appropriate procedures. A statement by a civil authority – regarding either marriage or divorce – is simply not a conclusive statement.

This is partly because, as Ayelet Shachar and others have detailed at length, individuals exercise complex "citizenships," whereby they are simultaneously members of multiple communities at the same time.[6] Individuals frequently possess strong citizenship affiliations to a religious group at the same time that they possess a citizenship affiliation to the civil state. If those two communities lack alignment on a critical matter (such as marriage or divorce), individuals may feel competing normative pulls – and it is not a given that the civil state's normative stance will control. Instead, sometimes the "unofficial law" of the community (to use Ann Estin's phrase) has a stronger hold on individuals and communities than the sanctioned official civil law of the polity.[7]

---

[5]   Cf. Nussbaum, "A Right to Marry?" 669.
[6]   Ayelet Shachar, *Multicultural Jurisdictions: Cultural Differences and Women's Rights* (Cambridge: Cambridge University Press, 2001). See also Ayelet Shachar, "Faith in Law? Diffusing Tensions Between Diversity and Equality" (in this volume).
[7]   Ann Laquer Estin, "Unofficial Family Law" (in this volume).

The most famous recent iterations of these jurisdictional conflicts are the *"shari'a* arbitration controversy" in Ontario, Canada, in 2003–2005 and a prominent speech by Anglican Archbishop Rowan Williams in 2008, wherein he suggested that some sort of "accommodation" of *shari'a* by British common law was "inevitable." In Ontario, Canada, many Christians, Jews, and Muslims had been submitting their personal disputes to religious arbitration for years. When news broke, though, that an outspoken imam was publicly advocating a more formal procedure to promote the application of *shari'a* to Canadian Muslims in family law matters, citizens and citizens' groups complained loudly to the government. Despite a long report by the former attorney general, which recommended continued allowance of religious arbitrations if certain safeguards were followed, political leaders removed the legal option of applying any religious principles and insisted that there would be "one law for all Ontarians." One unsurprising consequence of that move is that religious arbitrations continue, but without state sanction; thus parties who are adversely affected by such proceedings do not have an appeal and further recourse in the courts.[8]

In the United Kingdom, when Archbishop Williams called for some sort of "plural jurisdiction" in the United Kingdom according to which Muslims could resolve family law disputes (and some other civil matters) in religious tribunals or in British courts, he was roundly denounced in the press.[9] Despite the cries of many critics, however, the Archbishop was not advocating a wholesale abdication of the state role in marriage and divorce jurisdiction, but rather was calling for a constructive conversation about the complex citizenships exercised by Muslim believers. Again, though, rather than engaging in productive dialogue about difficult issues, many in the popular press swiftly aired concerns about the wholesale takeover of British law (at least for some British citizens) by *shari'a* law. A few voices soon surfaced that sought a healthier discussion about how to recognize the "complex ways in which Muslims engage with sharia in the UK," and recent academic discussion has taken up the Archbishop's questions about the role of *shari'a* in the West in thoughtful and challenging ways.[10]

Such issues of jurisdictional conflict are not confined to minority Muslim communities. Jews, for example, have long struggled with the relationship between

---

[8] See Marion Boyd, Office of Canadian Attorney General, *Dispute Resolution in Family Law: Protecting Choice, Promoting Inclusion*, (2004), available at http://www.attorneygeneral.jus.gov.on.ca/english/about/pubs/boyd/fullreport.pdf [hereinafter *Boyd Report*]; see also discussion and sources in Joel A. Nichols, "Multi-Tiered Marriage: Reconsidering the Boundaries of Civil Law and Religion" (in this volume).

[9] Dr. Rowan Williams, "Archbishop's Lecture – Civil and Religious Law in England: A Religious Perspective," Feb. 7, 2008, available at http://www.archbishopofcanterbury.org/1575#.

[10] Samia Bano, "In Pursuit of Religious and Legal Diversity: A Response to the Archbishop of Canterbury and the 'Sharia Debate' in Britain," *Ecclesiastical Law Journal* 10 (2008): 283–309, 288; *Shari'a in the West*, eds. Rex Ahdar and Nicholas Aroney (Oxford: Oxford University Press, 2010).

civil law and religious law and how to live under more than one governing regime. Centuries ago they developed the important legal concept of *dina d'malkhuta dina* ("the law of the community is the law"), which meant that the minority diaspora community accepted the law of the legitimate and peaceful secular ruler who hosted them as the law of their own Jewish community, to the extent that it did not conflict with core Jewish laws.[11] But Jewish communities in Western Europe also became accustomed, over the years, to exercising a degree of autonomy over certain family law matters. This allowed them to comply with general secular law norms but also to apply their stricter, slightly different religious norms surrounding marriage and divorce.[12] Lately, however, civil law has been unwilling to accord legal effect to Jewish religious divorces, raising the need for an observant Orthodox Jew to obtain both a civil divorce *and* a religious divorce. New York has tried to ameliorate potential inequities toward Jewish women that arise from the lack of congruity between religious law and civil law by passing legislation (the *get* statutes); other states have not followed this route legislatively.[13]

But the issue of competing allegiances to the civil system and a religious system is not even confined to minority religious groups. Protestant Christians have long sought (and had the political clout) to enact their preferred definitions of marriage and divorce into the civil law in the United States. Their political power has waned in recent decades, and the attendant consonance between traditional Protestant Christian theological norms and civil marriage/divorce law has dwindled. For example, divorce was available only in cases of hard fault, if at all, for many years. But every state now has some variation of no-fault divorce – and a number of states have removed any discussion of fault even in property distribution or maintenance. One response by some Christian groups was to reinstate a more traditional understanding of marriage and divorce into the civil law itself, in the form of a "covenant marriage statute" in Louisiana and two other states. Through those statutes, couples could choose between two different legal regimes for marriage and divorce: one was easy-in and easy-out and the other was a covenant marriage, with additional premarital formalities and counseling on one end and more stringent requirements for fault grounds on the other end.[14]

This volume discusses such conflicts between civil law and religious norms in the arena of family law. Specifically, in the words of Werner Menski, "The present

[11] See Rabbi Dr. Dov Bressler, "Arbitration and the Courts in Jewish Law," *Journal of Halacha and Contemporary Society* 9 (1985): 105–117.
[12] See, e.g., Benjamin Braude and Bernard Lewis, eds., *Christians and Jews in the Ottoman Empire* (New York: Holmes & Meier Publishers, Inc., 1982).
[13] See Michael J. Broyde, "New York's Regulation of Jewish Marriage: Covenant, Contract, or Statute?" (in this volume).
[14] See Katherine Shaw Spaht, "Covenant Marriage Laws: A Model for Compromise" (in this volume).

volume seeks to take the debate about management of family law further than the existing literature. The main question [is] whether delegating authority to religious authorities would be a feasible method of meeting the challenges of increased socio-cultural pluralization and of new forms of family arrangement."[15]

Put another way, the volume lifts up examples from Islam, Judaism, and Christianity to debunk two key assumptions that lie deep within family law. The first assumption is that the civil state possesses exclusive jurisdiction over family law matters. The second is that there is a singular model that applies equally to all couples, and no deviation from that model is permitted. These two assumptions are simply incorrect, because not only do they fail to accord with the lived reality for many individuals but they also fail to recognize the decentralization and pluralism that already exists in marriage and divorce law. Instead of furthering such faulty assumptions, this book invites a conversation about whether such models of "multi-tiered marriage" provide a useful way forward. The phrase "multi-tiered marriage" is used here:

1. To describe systems whereby jurisdiction over marriage and divorce matters is shared between different authorities (such as that proposed in Canada and England); or

2. Alternatively, to refer to systems that have more than one possibility of marriage and divorce within their civil law (such as that of New York or Louisiana).

Either way, such systems are multi-tiered because they inherently recognize and explicitly reify the fact that there is more than one possible understanding of marriage.[16]

This volume strongly contends that accounts of exclusive state jurisdiction and a one-size-fits-all model are *descriptively* incorrect and simply do not accord with history, current practice, comparative law, or the lived experience of many individuals. More than that, though, the book seeks to begin a conversation about whether, *normatively*, more pluralism in family law is desirable and should be affirmatively fostered – and, if so, under what conditions and qualifications. Because conversations are not monologues, this book includes chapters by several leading scholars rather than presenting only one voice. And instead of entrenching in hardened positions, the contributors draw upon their expertise in law, history, theology, sociology, political science, and feminist studies to mine the depths of these important issues in interdisciplinary fashion. The end result is a rich discussion about the jurisdictional boundaries of marriage and divorce law in a liberal society. An explicit part of

---

[15] Werner Menski, "Ancient and Modern Boundary Crossings Between Personal Laws and Civil Law in Composite India" (in this volume).

[16] Nichols, "Reconsidering the Boundaries" (in this volume).

that discussion is whether "the civil government [should] consider ceding some of
its jurisdictional authority over marriage and divorce law to religious communities
that are competent and capable of adjudicating the marital rites and rights of their
respective adherents."[17] The contributors recognize the dual nature of marriage for
many citizens in society, whereby they are bound not only to civil norms regarding
marriage and divorce but also to religious norms. This volume takes seriously those
dual allegiances of many citizens in society while also hewing to the overarching
norms of equality and protection for vulnerable parties that are part of the fabric of
the larger civil society itself.

* * *

Although the chapters that follow are not formally broken into specific "sections"
within the volume, they do follow a progression that mirrors the shape of the opening chapter. That chapter, my own initial contribution to the volume, establishes the
scaffolding for the conversation by challenging the assumptions that exclusive jurisdiction for marriage and divorce must lie with the civil state and that a one-size-fits-all
model must apply even within the civil law. Chapter 1 argues that those assumptions
are untrue historically, untrue in modern American law, and untrue in comparative
law examples. That kind of descriptive overview leads naturally to normative questions
about whether such deep pluralism is desirable and should be affirmatively pursued.

Chapters 2 through 14, accordingly, elaborate (and at times challenge) various
pieces of the opening chapter. Those remaining chapters have been organized so
that the reader may anticipate their overall content by progressing through (a) current and past pluralism in American family law; (b) present overlap and interaction
between religious and civil content in American marriage and divorce law; (c) international examples of pluralist jurisdictional regimes; (d) theoretical reflections on
the potential and perils of moving toward more intentionally plural legal regimes;
and (e) concluding reflections on future questions. The chapters quite intentionally
do not speak with one voice on the subject, but rather enter a dialectical conversation with one another – at times reinforcing, at times challenging, and at times
questioning.

Chapter 1, described previously, is an essential cornerstone of the book, because
the remaining chapters all respond to it in some key fashion. It not only delineates
an overview of the project but also provides an entrée into many of the overarching
questions about marital jurisdiction.

Chapter 2, by Brian Bix, provides a high-level overview of the many kinds of
legal pluralism that already exist in the United States. By looking at the "de facto

[17]   Joel A. Nichols, "Multi-Tiered Marriage: Ideas and Influences from New York and Louisiana to the
International Community," *Vanderbilt Journal of Transnational Law* 40 (2007): 135–196. See also
Nichols, "Reconsidering the Boundaries" (in this volume).

pluralism and decentralization" that already exists, he sets the stage for discussing whether intentionally increasing pluralism would be advantageous. Although he tends to think the pluralism and decentralization is generally a good thing, he concludes with a recognition of the need for appropriate limits.

In Chapter 3, Stephen Presser continues the overview, but he does so by drawing the reader's attention to the historical interaction between marriage and the civil law. Presser surveys the historical landscape and compares it with the modern landscape of debates about same-sex marriage and appropriate roles for courts, individuals, and religious institutions. He concludes that the concept of marriage should be reserved (or restored) to religious institutions and the state should regulate only civil unions.

In Chapter 4, Ann Estin cautions both against further privatization and against formal pluralization of marriage, but she promptly turns the reader's attention to the "legal pluralism that already flourishes in the United States." Whereas Bix's chapter addresses the pluralism embedded in various positive laws, Estin instead focuses on the dynamic interaction between social and religious norms and positive law norms. She does so by elucidating a number of touchpoints between the two at present. Her description of the "unofficial family law" that is already operating highlights the complexity of norm interaction, and she also provides some caveats that moving toward more intentional pluralism would likely increase such complexity.

The next trio of chapters provides a set of religious overviews that differ but are all connected to specific civil laws. In Chapter 5, Katherine Spaht provides a host of details on the motivations for and the functioning of the "covenant marriage statutes" in the United States. She is well positioned to do this, as she authored the law in Louisiana and has been a prime proponent and advocate elsewhere. Implicit, if not explicit, in her chapter is an emphasis on the connection between the messages conveyed by the civil law about marriage and the need to embody strong traditional (Christian) notions of marriage within the law. She expresses discomfort about even adopting the bifurcated terminology of "civil marriage" and "religious marriage," and she cautions against using Louisiana's example as a first step toward *more* pluralism because of her perspective of the ongoing need for a strong state role in marriage.

Chapter 6 offers quite a contrast to this perspective as Michael Broyde, an Orthodox Jewish rabbi, provides a nuanced introduction to the framework of Jewish law on marriage and divorce. He is quite comfortable in differentiating between civil marriage and religious marriage, and he clearly describes the strong private contractual elements of marriage at Jewish law. Broyde also details the interplay between civil and religious marriage law for Jews, especially in New York, and then traces the history of the *get* statutes in New York – calling them the first covenant marriage laws in the United States. He is pleased with the continued interaction of civil and religious authorities in New York because, in his view, the "dance" between these two is a good model for future interactions of religious groups and civil law.

In Chapter 7, Mohammad Fadel turns the reader to Islamic law but does so from the vantage point of liberalism. Fadel makes the case that in a religiously hetero-geneous polity a "liberal family law" that allows space for "private ordering" is the "preferred means for the recognition of family law pluralism" – rather than a form of pluralism that grants greater power directly to religious bodies to administer family law. Fadel provides a helpful description of intra-Islamic pluralism to dispel notions of uniformity even within religious traditions, and he concludes that a true Rawlsian liberal family law – one that is even *more* "neutral" than current law – is the pre-ferred model.

While Fadel lifts up the New York *get* statute as a case study, he also begins to turn the book's discussion to an international perspective as he draws upon the con-troversy over *shari'a* councils in Ontario, Canada. Chapters 8 and 9 turn even more sharply to comparative law. In Chapter 8, Johan van der Vyver draws upon his deep knowledge of South African law to discuss the interaction of religious and cultural practice with positive law in South Africa. Van der Vyver describes the ongoing ten-sion in South Africa as it strives to implement the equality and nondiscrimination norms of its recent constitution with its strong concerns for group rights, both of religion and culture.

In Chapter 9, British scholar Werner Menski explores the relationship between personal (religious) law and civil law in India. Menski writes as a realist rather than a positivist, and he expresses near amusement at the "surprise" expressed by many that "supposedly strong states are not fully in control of family law regulation," as evidenced by the Ontario controversy and by Archbishop Williams's speech. He provides an introduction to Hindu law and to the legal system of India, and he also seeks to convince the reader that we must be "active, conscious pluralists, whether we like it or not." He believes that neither abandoning the state role nor ignoring the role of "the other inputs and players" is feasible in a multicultural milieu.

The next group of three chapters continues Menski's move toward the normative nature of pluralism. Although Menski advocates embracing pluralism, both as a realist and for its own inherent good of respecting different cultures and religions, others are not nearly so convinced. In Chapter 10, Robin Wilson proffers that efforts to accommodate religious minorities in family law matters are "well intentioned but naïve." She recounts the "lived experiences" of women and children in certain religious communities, highlights the family violence that occurs within religious communities (as elsewhere), and questions how notions of true voluntary consent would apply to a plural system of religious deference.

Daniel Cere, in Chapter 11, focuses on Canada and its commitment to multicul-tural diversity. Cere explores the Ontario controversy and usefully introduces the reader to multicultural theory via the "Canadian school." He laments that arguments about multiculturalism often seem to extend group rights and freedoms to certain national and aboriginal communities but stop short when claims are made by religious communities. Cere views the resolution of the Ontario debate (of precluding legal application of Islamic law by willing participants) as confirming that Canada's commitment in matters of marriage and divorce is not an embrace of multiculturalism but rather a move toward comprehensive liberalism that excludes minority religious views.

In Chapter 12, Linda McClain "train[s] a gender lens on the question of jurisdictional pluralism." She concedes the descriptive claim of legal pluralism, but she resists the normative claim that there should be more pluralism in American family law because she is skeptical that such pluralism could continue to protect women's equal citizenship. McClain reexplores specific cases from the United States and then turns again to the Ontario example, remaining focused on questions of gender equality throughout. McClain concludes, however, by suggesting that what is needed is not an all-or-nothing approach but rather a model of legal pluralism "that holds fast both to the value of religious membership and to the rights and duties of equal citizenship."

McClain's suggestion is a natural lead-in to Chapter 13, which provides the reader with a snapshot into the writings of Ayelet Shachar. Shachar's prior work and ideas featured prominently in Archbishop Williams's lecture about Islamic law in England, wherein he contended for a more accommodationist stance. In this chapter, Shachar continues to explore the idea of "regulated interaction" between religious and civil authorities and focuses on women as "both culture bearers and rights bearers." Rather than seeking to disentangle civil and religious marriage bonds (which would be futile), Shachar pursues a way to allow devout women to benefit from the protections of the liberal state while also holding onto their deep religious beliefs. She explicitly grounds her analysis both in multicultural theory and in recent legal developments in Canada.

In Chapter 14, John Witte and I conclude the book by describing possible ways forward. We focus especially on the intersection of Muslim family law and liberal democracies, investigating the claims for a different kind of interaction between religious and civil laws of marriage and divorce. We also look to the topic of education in the United States – an analogous interaction in which the state has set minimum standards but has not claimed exclusive jurisdiction – as a possible starting point for compromise. We also glance briefly at U.S. Constitutional law questions raised by proposals of marital pluralism and conclude that the involvement of religion in some aspects of family law is not as problematic as critics might suggest. Our chapter is also an afterword to the book, serving to consolidate a number of the questions raised by earlier chapters and to project avenues for further research and discussion.

This volume, in short, raises questions about the jurisdictional authority of the civil state regarding marriage and divorce. It specifically raises questions about the relationship of that state authority to any residual authority in individuals and groups, especially religious groups. From its initial chapter, the book seeks to begin rather than end such a conversation, and it does so by posing nearly as many questions as it answers. It therefore is apt to conclude this Introduction by detailing some of the "hard questions" raised by the book, as John Witte and I frame them in Chapter 14:

> What forms of marriage should citizens be able to choose, and what forums of religious marriage law should state governments be required to respect? How should ... religious groups with distinctive family norms and cultural practices that vary from those espoused by the liberal state be accommodated in a society dedicated to religious liberty and equality, to self-determination and nondiscrimination? Are legal pluralism and even "personal federalism" necessary to protect ... religious believers who are conscientiously opposed to the liberal values that inform modern state laws on sex, marriage, and family? Or must there instead be "legal universalism" with its attendant "exclusionary consequences"? Are these really the only options – or instead is something more akin to a "dance" between religious and civil law more appropriate and necessary?[18]

---

[18] John Witte Jr. and Joel A. Nichols, "The Frontiers of Marital Pluralism: An Afterword" (in this volume) (citations omitted).

1

Multi-Tiered Marriage

Reconsidering the Boundaries of Civil Law and Religion

Joel A. Nichols

I. INTRODUCTION

The U.S. Supreme Court recently remarked, "Long ago [in 1890] we observed that 'the whole subject of the domestic relations of husband and wife, parent and child, belongs to the law of the States and not to the laws of the United States.'"[1] The context for the statement was a case followed by Court-watchers for a challenge to the validity of the Pledge of Allegiance. The very way it was made, in such an off-handed way, underscores how commonplace is the basic assumption that marriage and divorce law is entirely and exclusively a state law matter.[2]

Even more basic than this federalism assumption are two further assumptions about family law, which run so deep they are virtually never even stated. The first is that the civil authority is the sole relevant authority for matters relating to marriage and divorce. The second is that within civil law there may only be one regulatory regime governing matters of marriage and divorce. Thus, there is an assumption of (1) exclusive jurisdiction, with all authority residing in the civil state; and (2) a "one-size-fits-all" model that applies to all couples, where no deviation from that model is permitted.[3]

These two latter assumptions about marriage and divorce are simply incorrect. The lived-reality for many individuals is that the civil state does not possess sole authority and jurisdiction over their marriages – usually because of deeply held religious convictions about the nature of marriage (and possible divorce). Moreover,

---

[1] *Elk Grove Unified School District v. Newdow*, 524 U.S. 1, 12 (2004) (citing *Ex parte* Burrus, 136 U.S. 586, 593–594 [1890]).

[2] See Jill Elaine Hasday, "The Canon of Family Law," *Stanford Law Review* 57 (2004): 825–900, 870 ("The family law canon insists that family law is exclusively local.").

[3] See Barbara Stark, "Marriage Proposals: From One-Size-Fits-All to Postmodern Marriage Law," *California Law Review* 89 (2001): 1479–1548; American Law Institute, Principles of the Law of Family Dissolution (2002) sec. 7.08(1).

there is already greater decentralization and pluralism in marriage law than is commonly recognized in the United States.

When Louisiana passed the nation's first "covenant marriage law" in 1997, some critics bemoaned the creation of "two-tiered system[s] of marriage."[4] Through such covenant marriage laws (in place in Arkansas, Arizona, and Louisiana),[5] couples may choose between two different statutory regimes within the same state: They may choose to enter "a contract marriage, with minimal formalities of formation and attendant rights to no-fault divorce … [or] a covenant marriage, with more stringent formation and dissolution rules."[6] Thus far, however, the public commentary about such covenant marriage laws has far outpaced both their legislative success and their usage by couples within the states.[7]

Just as the covenant marriage statutes undermine the notion that states necessarily utilize one-size-fits-all models, so the earlier experience of New York undermines the assumption that the civil state possesses exclusive authority over marriage and divorce matters. In 1983, New York sought to alleviate the harshness of civil divorce on Jewish women by passing its first *get* statute.[8] Because Orthodox Jewish women do not consider themselves able to remarry unless a religious divorce is properly issued (even if a civil divorce has already been issued), New York's legislature passed a statute that fosters cooperation between civil courts and religious courts to offset the imbalance in power at divorce between Orthodox husbands and

---

[4] Joel A. Nichols, "Louisiana's Covenant Marriage Statute: A First Step Toward a More Robust Pluralism in Marriage and Divorce Law?" *Emory Law Journal* 47 (1998): 929–1001; Katherine Shaw Spaht, "Marriage: Why a Second Tier Called Covenant Marriage?" *Regent University Law Review* 12 (1999): 1–7. See also Chauncey E. Brummer, "The Shackles of Covenant Marriage: Who Holds the Keys to Wedlock?" *University of Arkansas Little Rock Law Review* 25 (2003): 261–300, 293 ("By sanctioning covenant marriage, the state has in effect established two distinct categories of marriage, which may lead to the false impression that couples who enter one form are somehow 'more married,' and thus entitled to greater protection than those who enter into traditional marriage.").

[5] Ariz. Rev. Stat. Ann. §§ 25–901 to –906 (2007); Ark. Code Ann. §§ 9–11–801 to –811 (2009); La. Rev. Stat. Ann. § 9:272 (2008).

[6] John Witte Jr. and Joel A. Nichols, "Introduction," in *Covenant Marriage in Comparative Perspective*, eds. John Witte Jr. and Eliza Ellison (Grand Rapids, MI: W. B. Eerdmans Pub. Co., 2005) [hereinafter *Comparative Perspective*], 1–25, 1.

[7] Nichols, "Louisiana's Covenant Marriage Statute"; Witte and Ellison, *Comparative Perspective*; Steven L. Nock, Laura Ann Sanchez, and James D. Wright, *Covenant Marriage: The Movement to Reclaim Tradition in America* (New Brunswick, NJ: Rutgers University Press, 2008), 3. See also Katherine Shaw Spaht, "Covenant Marriage Laws: A Model for Compromise" (in this volume).

[8] The 1983 law (as amended substantially in 1984) may be found at N.Y. Dom. Rel. Law § 253 (McKinney 2010). The 1992 *get* act may be found at Amendments (§§ 236B(5)(h) and 236B(6)(d)) to N.Y. Dom. Rel. Law § 236B (McKinney 2010). See Michael J. Broyde, "New York's Regulation of Jewish Marriage: Covenant, Contract, or Statute?" (in this volume).

wives. Although New York's *get* laws are of a substantially different nature than the covenant marriage laws, both sets of reforms recognize greater pluralism in marriage and divorce law.

Both New York and Louisiana have thus moved in the direction of "multi-tiered marriage" – by which I mean a structure that challenges the two embedded assumptions. The phrase "multi-tiered" is here used (1) to describe systems whereby jurisdiction over marriage and divorce matters is shared between different authorities; or (2) alternatively, to refer to systems that have more than one possibility of marriage and divorce within their civil law. Either way, such systems are multi-tiered because they inherently recognize and explicitly reify the fact that there is more than one possible understanding of marriage. Such recognition is a salutary move, because the American tendency toward exclusive civil jurisdiction coupled with uniform application of a single set of laws is neither historically mandated nor uniformly accepted by the international community.

Instead of unitary notions of jurisdiction and uniform application of a single law, the idea of a multi-tiered system holds substantial promise. One finds at least two rationales for the changes in American law. The first is the "sad and serious crisis of marriage in civil society,"[9] evidenced by a wealth and welter of somber statistics about increasing divorce rates and the attendant effects on children and adult well-being.[10] This was the driving force behind the covenant marriage laws, especially in Louisiana.[11] The second is that there is more than one conception of marriage and divorce law in a plural society.[12] This rationale was part of the impetus for the New York *get* statutes.[13]

These two rationales can readily be expounded to suggest further pluralism in marriage and divorce law. First, the statistics of increasing divorce rates and the attendant consequences of divorce can be expanded to encompass a host of ongoing debates about the proper and best way to "revitalize" the institution of marriage.[14] Solutions range from the "abolition of marriage" (at least insofar as the civil state

[9] Jean Bethke Elshtain, "Marriage in Civil Society," *Family Affairs* 7 (1996): 1–5.

[10] See, e.g., Cynthia DeSimone, "Covenant Marriage Legislation," *Catholic University Law Review* 52 (2002–2003): 391–436, 403–405; James Herbie DiFonzo, "Customized Marriage," *Indiana Law Journal* 75 (2000): 875–962, 877, 909–911; Nock et al., *Covenant Marriage*, 10–20.

[11] See generally Nichols, "Louisiana's Covenant Marriage Statute."

[12] See Ann Laquer Estin, "Embracing Tradition: Pluralism in American Family Law," *Maryland Law Review* 63 (2004): 540–604; Ayelet Shachar, *Multicultural Jurisdictions: Cultural Differences and Women's Rights* (Cambridge: Cambridge University Press, 2001).

[13] See Irving A. Breitowitz, *Between Civil and Religious Law: The Plight of the Agunah in American Society* (Westport, CT: Greenwood Press, 1993), 179–185.

[14] See Alan J. Hawkins, Lynn D. Wardle, and David Orgon Coolidge, eds., *Revitalizing the Institution of Marriage for the Twenty-First Century* (Westport, CT: Praeger, 2002).

has any say in it)[15] to increased federalization of the definition of marriage[16] to all manner of things in between.

Second, the acknowledgment that there is more than one conception of the definition of marriage quite naturally expands to the recognition that we are a tremendously pluralistic society – especially with regard to religion.[17] We honor the best of our traditions when we recognize and reify our pluralistic nature – especially when we are careful to balance that pluralism with protections for women and children, with procedures to foster fairness, and with policies that advance shared societal values of nondiscrimination, free exercise, parental control, and the like.[18]

This chapter takes these twin rationales – the admitted changes in the cultural definition of marriage and divorce and the pluralistic nature of our multicultural society – as a baseline in attempting to further the conversation. Rather than continuing to assume that exclusive civil jurisdiction of a singular law is required, we should take seriously the possibility of multi-tiered marriage. We should allow for the possibility that marriage and divorce might have more than one form at law.[19] And if we open the discussion to more than one understanding of marriage, we should acknowledge the thoughtful contributions and reflections by religious individuals and groups regarding marriage and divorce law.[20] Those religious groups have an appropriate role to play in assisting the state in defining the metes and bounds of the marital relationship.

Thus, this chapter proffers the concept of promoting multi-tiered marriage in our multicultural and pluralistic society. It is unclear what form this multi-tiered marriage might take, and a variety of possibilities suggest themselves as alternatives.[21] It is possible that American law will continue on its path of viewing marriage through a strict contractarian lens, such that reforms arise as a matter of enforcing the married parties' agreement – including through designating and using religious arbitration

[15] See, e.g., Anita Bernstein, ed., *Marriage Proposals: Questioning a Legal Status* (New York: New York University Press, 2005); Daniel A. Crane, "A 'Judeo-Christian' Argument for Privatizing Marriage," *Cardozo Law Review* 27 (2006): 1221–1259; Edward A. Zelinsky, "Deregulating Marriage: The Pro-Marriage Case for Abolishing Civil Marriage," *Cardozo Law Review* 27 (2006): 1161–1220. See also Stephen B. Presser, "Marriage and the Law: Time for a Divorce?" (in this volume).

[16] See, e.g., Defense of Marriage Act, 28 U.S.C. §1738C (2000).

[17] See Shachar, *Multicultural Jurisdictions*, 17–41; Estin, "Embracing Tradition," 555–556.

[18] See Carl E. Schneider, "The Channeling Function in Family Law," *Hofstra Law Review* 20 (1992): 495–532, 497.

[19] See Shahar Lifshitz, "Married Against Their Will? Toward a Pluralist Regulation of Spousal Relationships," *Washington and Lee Law Review* 66 (2009): 1565–1634 (contending for a "pluralist approach"); Mary Anne Case, "Marriage Licenses," *Minnesota Law Review* 89 (2005): 1758–1797, 1784.

[20] See, e.g., John Witte Jr., *From Sacrament to Contract: Marriage, Religion, and Law in the Western Tradition* (Louisville, KY: Westminster John Knox Press, 1997); Nichols, "Louisiana's Covenant Marriage Statute," 979–988.

[21] See Shachar, *Multicultural Jurisdictions*, 88–113. See also Brian H. Bix, "Pluralism and Decentralization in Marriage Regulation" (in this volume).

tribunals as the selected choice of forum (and possibly choice of law also).[22] It is also possible that some variation on the state laws of New York, Louisiana, and others might be a better alternative, wherein multiple (and maybe even competing) models of marriage are available to couples through the civil law itself.[23] Or there may be other possibilities that are better for the American situation. More critical than the precise form, though, is that the broader conversation includes the possibility of the state ceding some of its jurisdictional control and hegemony. A number of religious communities are competent and capable of adjudicating the marital rites and rights of their respective adherents, and this may well be a better alternative than our current least-common-denominator notion of marriage law.[24]

To advance the conversation down this path, this chapter begins by looking backward, and then turns inward, and finally turns outward. Section II looks backward and describes the historical precedent for shared or competing jurisdiction, evidenced through the history of Western marriage law. Section III looks inward and details the modern American precedent for recognizing that citizens may have varying conceptions of marriage, evidenced primarily in the laws of Louisiana and New York. Section IV looks outward and delineates comparative precedents for multi-tiered marriages, evidenced in the laws of various countries in the international community (especially India, Kenya, South Africa, and Canada). Finally, Section V draws these strands together by elucidating their commonalities – namely their admission that there is more than one conception of marriage and divorce law. It also elucidates the potential promise of multi-tiered marriage – that plural religious communities will be able to retain and further their own understandings of the goods and goals of marriage while the state will simultaneously be able to protect the most important rights of its citizens.

II. A SHORT HISTORY OF MARRIAGE AND DIVORCE LAW JURISDICTION

The common lore of American law is that jurisdiction of marriage and divorce "has always been regulated by the civil authorities."[25] Although technically true,

[22] See, e.g., Michael A. Helfand, "Religious Arbitration and the New Multiculturalism: Negotiating Conflicting Legal Orders," *NYU Law Review* 86 (2011): __ (forthcoming); Eric Rasmussen and Jeffrey Evans Stake, "Lifting the Veil of Ignorance: Personalizing the Marriage Contract," *Indiana Law Journal* 73 (1998): 453–502, 460, 474–475.

[23] In this chapter, I have avoided discussing any Establishment Clause concerns from the potential overlap of civil and religious law and merely assumed that such objections could be overcome. For further discussion see Bix, "Pluralism and Decentralization" (in this volume), and John Witte Jr. and Joel A. Nichols, "The Frontiers of Marital Pluralism: An Afterword" (in this volume).

[24] See Witte and Nichols, "Introduction," in *Comparative Perspective*, 25.

[25] See Homer H. Clark Jr., *The Law of Domestic Relations in the United States* (St. Paul, MN: West Pub. Co., 2d ed. 1988), 31.

this broad claim elides the fact that the English common law "as received" in
the various American colonies (and then states) reveals a more complex history
and understanding of jurisdiction over both marital formation and dissolution.[26]
Moreover, the jurisdictional boundaries of marriage and divorce in the West
were far more complex and fluid than is often recounted in common public discourse – moving from custom to legal regulation to ecclesiastical regulation and
back again.[27]

The Roman Catholic Church gradually assumed jurisdiction over matters of
marriage and divorce law for believers. It initially shared jurisdiction with the civil
state, but it increasingly began to claim sole jurisdiction over such matters as it
obtained greater political strength after the Papal Revolution in the thirteenth century.[28] The Church relied on a detailed system of ecclesiastical courts and a cadre
of developing canon law as it dealt with marriages.[29] The Church believed marriage to be a sacrament – rather than merely a civil contract or a private individual
or familial matter – and thought it naturally followed (especially when bolstered
by claims from scripture) that marriage must be indissoluble. This indissolubility
was ameliorated by (1) impediments restricting the entry into marriage; (2) the possibility of annulment; and (3) the possibility of separation *a mensa et thoro* (from
bed and board) on proof of adultery, desertion, or cruelty. However, these factors
did not (and could not) mask the facts that absolute divorce remained unavailable
at canon law and that the Church claimed jurisdictional authority over matters of
marriage and divorce.

The Protestant Reformation in the sixteenth century ushered in changes in marriage and divorce law just as it ushered in changes in many other areas of life. The
reformers reconceived marriage as a social or civil estate more than a spiritual
estate, and they placed jurisdiction of marriage and divorce in civic hands rather
than clerical hands[30] – partly as a default consequence of not having ecclesiastical

---

[26] See George Eliot Howard, *A History of Matrimonial Institutions*, 3 vols. (Chicago: University of
Chicago Press, 1904); see also Witte, *From Sacrament to Contract*; Roderick Phillips, *Putting Asunder:
A History of Divorce in Western Society* (Cambridge: Cambridge University Press, 1988). See also
Presser, "Marriage and the Law" (in this volume).

[27] Mary Ann Glendon, *The Transformation of Family Law: State, Law, and Family in the United States
and Western Europe* (Chicago: University of Chicago Press, 1989), 19–34. The initial evolution of any
external jurisdiction (whether civil or ecclesiastical) over marriage and divorce was an innovation,
because matters of marriage "had largely been outside the sphere of law." Max Rheinstein, *Marriage
Stability, Divorce, and the Law* (Chicago: University of Chicago Press, 1972), 17.

[28] See generally Glendon, *Transformation of Family Law*, 19–34; Witte, *From Sacrament to Contract*,
16–41.

[29] See, e.g., Harold J. Berman, *Law and Revolution: The Formation of the Western Legal Tradition*
(Cambridge, MA: Harvard University Press, 1983), 226–230.

[30] See, e.g., John Witte Jr., *Law and Protestantism: The Legal Teachings of the Lutheran Reformation*
(Cambridge: Cambridge University Press, 2002), 232–252.

courts of their own readily at hand, and partly as a natural consequence of their theology.[31] The same aspects of the Protestant Reformation – including its shifting of jurisdiction to civil courts – did not follow the same path in England, the prime progenitor of American common law, as they had on the European continent.

In England, the Protestant Reformation led to a break between the Church of England and Rome, but there was not an accompanying break in doctrine regarding marriage and divorce.[32] The result of the English Reformation thus continued to be union of church and state – including the retention of ecclesiastical courts, which exercised jurisdiction over matters of marriage and divorce until the 1850s. Additionally in England – as at canon law – there was no judicial right to absolute divorce, although relief could possibly be gained from Parliament.[33] When the Puritans briefly took control of England in the mid-seventeenth century, they introduced the notion of civil marriage, but this was as short-lived as the Cromwellian regime itself.[34] Eventually, reform came to England with passage of legislation in 1835 and 1836 that allowed marriages to be contracted under the supervision of a civil authority rather than only by ecclesiastical authorities, and then in 1857 by the Matrimonial Causes Act.[35] The 1857 Act first allowed for absolute divorce (rather than only annulment or separation from bed and board), addressed matters of child custody, and shifted jurisdiction over issues of marriage and divorce to the civil courts rather than the church courts. Although the ecclesiastical courts were allowed to retain an internal body of canon law for voluntary use by church members, they no longer had any binding legal authority compared to the civil courts. This basic separation between civil and ecclesiastical courts has remained to this day in England, although churches continue to enjoy special rights regarding marital formation even after the state removed ecclesiastical control over dissolution issues.[36]

A parallel set of jurisdictional developments transpired in Jewish law over roughly this same time period. As set forth more fully later in this chapter, Jewish law views marriage simultaneously as a private contract between two parties (with a requisite

---

[31] See, e.g., Harold J. Berman, *Law and Revolution II: The Impact of the Protestant Reformations on the Western Legal Tradition* (Cambridge, MA: Belknap Press of Harvard University Press, 2003), 185.

[32] "[M]arriage litigation in sixteenth and seventeenth-century England continued to look much as it had during the Middle Ages." R. H. Helmholz, *Roman Canon Law in Reformation England* (Cambridge: Cambridge University Press, 1990), 69–70.

[33] See Lawrence Stone, *Road to Divorce: England, 1530–1987* (Oxford: Oxford University Press, 1990), 183–210.

[34] See Howard, *History of Matrimonial Institutions*, I: 408–435.

[35] The Marriage Act of 1836, 6 & 7 Will. 4, c. 85 (Eng); Matrimonial Causes Act of 1857, 20 & 21 Vict. c. 85 (Eng.); Mary Ann Shanley, *Feminism, Marriage and the Law in Victorian England, 1850–1895* (Princeton, NJ: Princeton University Press, 1989); Stone, *Road to Divorce*, 368–422.

[36] See Carolyn Hamilton, "England and Wales," in *Family Law in Europe*, eds. Carolyn Hamilton and Alison Perry (London: Butterworths, 2d ed. 2002), 95, 103, 113–114.

degree of community involvement) and as a covenant.[37] Over time, Jewish law has developed an elaborate set of laws governing marriage and divorce and has sought to apply those in its own religious courts. When Jews were living in predominantly Muslim territories in the Middle Ages, the Turkish authorities of the Ottoman Empire granted a measure of autonomy over certain legal matters to some religious communities known as "millets."[38] The millet system allowed Jewish law to retain jurisdiction and effective control over marriage and divorce between Jews,[39] and it allowed Jewish scholars, rabbis, and courts to continue to shape and recast and reify their conceptions of marriage into law without interference from the civil state.

In the early days of the American republic, the colonists carried marriage and divorce laws with them from their origins. This meant that in colonies (such as those in the north) settled by Puritans – heirs of the Calvinist traditions – civil authorities alone addressed matters of marriage and divorce from early on; it was only after some time that the Puritans allowed any ministers even to conduct weddings. In Virginia, however, exactly the opposite was true: A religious marriage ceremony, according to the rites of the Church of England, was prescribed by law up until the time of the American Revolution.[40]

There were similar disparities among the colonies respecting divorce, although there was never a recognition of religious authorities' power to effectuate divorce like there was for marriage. In New York, for example, divorce was within the power of the civil courts due to the Reformation heritage. But in the Southern colonies, with their stronger Anglican heritage, judicial divorce was disallowed. This derived both from the conception of marriage as an indissoluble union and also from the fact that there were no ecclesiastical courts in the new land and thus no proper judicial authority with power to grant a divorce. Parties could still appeal to the legislature for a divorce even if courts could not or would not grant a divorce; this mirrored the practice of Parliamentary divorce in England.[41]

After the American Revolution, regions on the frontier that had formerly been under Spanish control gradually came onto the American scene, including the

[37] See Michael J. Broyde, "The Covenant-Contract Dialectic in Jewish Marriage and Divorce Law," in *Comparative Perspective*, 53; David Novak, "Jewish Marriage: Nature, Covenant, and Contract," in *Comparative Perspective*, 26. See also Broyde, "New York's Regulation" (in this volume).
[38] Benjamin Braude and Bernard Lewis, eds., *Christians and Jews in the Ottoman Empire* (New York, London: Holmes & Meier Publishers, Inc., 1982), 12–13.
[39] See Jacob Katz, *Tradition and Crisis: Jewish Society at the End of the Middle Ages* (New York: Free Press of Glencoe, 1961); see also H. A. R. Gibb and Harold Bowen, *Islamic Society and the West: A Study of the Impact of Western Civilization on Moslem Culture in the Near East* (London, New York, Toronto: Oxford University Press, 1950), pt. 2, 212.
[40] Howard, *History of Matrimonial Institutions*, II: 138, 228, 366.
[41] See, e.g., ibid. at II: 349, 376; ibid. at III: 31; see also Nancy Cott, *Public Vows: A History of Marriage and the Nation* (Cambridge, MA: Harvard University Press, 2000), 49.

Louisiana territory, Florida, Texas, New Mexico, and California. Before becoming associated with the United States, these territories had been under the formal jurisdiction of Catholic bishops. Residents of those territories were thus subject to the Catholic canon law of marriage – including the notion of indissoluble marriage but with some relief via annulment. To be sure, the law on the books and the law in action were not always in harmony given the realities of daily life in sparsely populated lands, often far away from priests, bishops, and ecclesiastical courts.[42] When these territories came under control of the United States, marriage and divorce law quickly shifted to the civil authorities.

Collectively, this very short overview highlights that jurisdictional authority over marriage and divorce in the West, and even in America, has rested – at various times and places – with civil authorities, religious authorities, or both. The lines have not always been clear and uniform. History teaches that we should tread cautiously in presuming that marriage and divorce must be singular and solely under the jurisdiction of the state – and that we must be careful not to overlook the strong individual, familial, communal, and religious interests in marriage. In light of this mixed history, current advocates of exclusive civil jurisdiction bear some burden to provide justifications and rationales for their position.

III. DOMESTIC MOVEMENT TOWARD MULTI-TIERED MARRIAGE

Just as history belies the claim that the civil authority always had and must still retain sole jurisdictional authority, so too the idea that the civil law is uniform on matters of marriage and divorce is far overstated. As Brian Bix ably points out in this volume, a number of variations exist among the U.S. states at present. These include that some states recognize same-sex marriages whereas others do not (with varying levels of vehemence in opposition). In other states, same-sex couples (and sometimes opposite-sex couples) have access to alternative, marriage-like arrangements called "civil unions" or "domestic partnerships" – while the state also retains a category of "marriage." Parties may also choose to structure resolution of financial arrangements in a dispute in accordance with private ordering via premarital agreement, although the enforceability of such agreements varies by state. Then there is the fact of federalism itself – namely that among and between the states there are some differences in access to marriage and divorce, as well as differences in conflict-of-law matters regarding recognition of out-of-state marriages and divorces.[43] Other

[42] See generally Hans W. Baade, "The Form of Marriage in Spanish North America," *Cornell Law Review* 61 (1975): 1–90.

[43] See Bix, "Pluralism and Decentralization" (in this volume). See also David D. Meyer, "Fragmentation and Consolidation in the Law of Marriage and Same-Sex Relationships," *American Journal of Comparative Law* 58 (2010): 115–133.

variants of multi-tiered jurisdictional schemes exist in family law matters decided by American Indian tribal courts. Whereas "enormous uncertainties exist as to the contours of a tribe's civil jurisdiction," the tribal court's civil jurisdiction "may be at its strongest" in the realm of family law, where tribes have traditionally enjoyed a sovereign role.[44] This is especially true with regard to child custody determinations,[45] but there are also cases that indicate that jurisdiction over divorce or marital separation issues may lie with the tribal court.[46]

Even stronger examples of pluralism may be adduced, however, *within* a particular state's civil law. Under the "covenant marriage" laws of Arizona, Arkansas, and Louisiana,[47] a couple in one of these states may choose whether to marry (and divorce) under a regular marriage regime or under a covenant marriage regime. Although these laws are often hailed as the nation's first two-tiered laws, it appears that New York laid the groundwork fourteen years before Louisiana by passing state statutes regulating Jewish divorce in 1983. Such antecedent statutes arguably made New York "the first state with a covenant marriage act," as those statutes established different rules for marriage and divorce for different couples within the same state.[48]

A. *Covenant Marriage Laws (Louisiana, Arkansas, and Arizona)*

Covenant marriage laws have three key features: (1) mandatory premarital counseling that stresses the seriousness of marriage and its attendant lifelong commitment; (2) the premarital signing of a legal document (a Declaration of Intent) requiring couples to make "all reasonable efforts to preserve the marriage, including marriage counseling" in the event of difficulties; and (3) the provision of limited grounds for divorce.[49] These laws provide state-sanctioned, voluntary, and alternate forms of marriage that differ from the typical easy-entry marriage and no-fault divorce regime. Couples entering covenant marriages thus have heightened entrance requirements and more limited possibilities for exit. The theory behind such laws is that premarital counseling, combined with an advance commitment to efforts to make the marriage "work" in the face of difficult circumstances because covenant marriages are harder to exit, will lead to stronger marriages. The ultimate goal of covenant

[44] Barbara Ann Atwood, "Tribal Jurisprudence and Cultural Meanings of the Family," *Nebraska Law Review* 79 (2000): 577–656, 594–595.

[45] See, e.g., *Fisher v. District Court*, 424 U.S. 382 (1976); Barbara Ann Atwood, "Changing Definitions of Tribal Power Over Children," *Minnesota Law Review* 83 (1999): 927–996.

[46] See, e.g., *Eberhard v. Eberhard*, 24 Indian L. Rptr. 6059 (Cheyenne River Sioux Ct. App. 1997).

[47] Ariz. Rev. Stat. Ann. §§ 25–901 to –906 (2007); Ark. Code Ann. §§ 9–11–801 to –811 (2009); La. Rev. Stat. Ann. § 9:272 (2008).

[48] Broyde, "New York's Regulation" (in this volume).

[49] See generally Spaht, "Covenant Marriage Laws" (in this volume).

marriage proponents is to strengthen the institution of marriage in order to "lessen the problem of divorce."[50]

Louisiana passed the nation's first covenant marriage law in 1997.[51] Similar ideas had previously been floated in popular and academic literature and had even been introduced in a handful of state legislatures, but without sufficient traction. In Louisiana, newly elected State Representative Tony Perkins worked with Louisiana State University Law Professor Katherine Shaw Spaht to draft and introduce a covenant marriage law to "strengthen the family" by turning a "culture of divorce" into a "culture of marriage." After a series of committee hearings and a few amendments, the legislature passed the act and the governor signed it into law in mid-1997.

Louisiana's covenant marriage law introduced a fundamental change in the state's marriage law because it provided couples a choice whether to take the regular marriage option or the covenant marriage alternative. (A covenant marriage is defined as one man and one woman who agree with the proposition that "the marriage between them is a lifelong relationship" and that their marriage vows may be broken only under extreme circumstances.[52]) The covenant marriage law used the existing law of marriage and divorce as a default minimum system for marriages: Couples must explicitly choose to make their marriage (and thus potential divorce) conform to the covenant marriage standards.

Couples entering covenant marriages agree to both heightened entrance and exit requirements. The heightened entrance requirements include premarital counseling and submission of a Declaration of Intent. The couple must jointly attend premarital counseling by a "priest, minister, rabbi, clerk of the Religious Society of Friends, any clergyman of any religious sect, or a marriage counselor." This counseling must include a discussion of the nature of marriage as described by the covenant marriage law, a discussion of the legal recourse available to the parties should marital difficulties arise, and a discussion of the obligation to seek marital counseling prior to seeking legal recourse in the event of marital difficulties. The counselor must also provide the couple with an informational pamphlet published by the attorney general's office that details the rights and responsibilities in covenant marriages.[53]

---

[50] Katherine Shaw Spaht, "The Modern American Covenant Marriage Movement: Its Origins and Its Future," in *Comparative Perspective*, 243. See also discussion in John Witte Jr. and Joel A. Nichols, "More than a Mere Contract: Marriage as Contract and Covenant in Law and Theology," *University of St. Thomas Law Journal* 5 (2008): 595–615. There is some limited empirical evidence that covenant marriage laws appear to bring benefits to those married in them. Nock et al., *Covenant Marriage*, 98–140.

[51] La. Rev. Stat. Ann. § 9:272 (2008). For a history of the passage of the law, see Nichols, "Louisiana's Covenant Marriage Statute," 943–946.

[52] La. Rev. Stat. Ann. § 272(A) (2008).

[53] Ibid. at § 273(A)(2).

Following the counseling – but before the marriage ceremony – the parties must sign a Declaration of Intent.[54] This document contains the content of the parties' covenant, states their understanding of marriage as "a covenant between a man and a woman who agree to live together as husband and wife for so long as they both shall live," affirms that premarital counseling has occurred, and reiterates that the two parties understand the legal implications of entering this union. Consonant with that understanding, the parties commit themselves to seek counseling during marriage if difficulties arise.[55]

There are also heightened exit requirements for covenant marriages. In "regular" Louisiana marriages, couples may divorce for adultery, conviction of a felony, or living separate and apart for six months.[56] In covenant marriages, however, couples no longer have the option of unilateral divorce after a 180 days' separation; instead, they must wait at least two years.[57] If parties in covenant marriages have undergone the required marital counseling but have not lived apart for two years without reconciliation, divorce is obtainable upon proof of: (1) adultery of the other spouse; (2) the other spouse's commission of a felony and subsequent sentencing to "death or imprisonment at hard labor"; (3) abandonment of the matrimonial domicile for one year or more by the other spouse; (4) physical or sexual abuse directed toward the spouse seeking the divorce or a child of one of the spouses; or (5) separation for at least one year from the date of a judgment for separation from bed and board.[58]

Nonguilty spouses in covenant marriages may also benefit from a legal alternative other than divorce: separation from bed and board. This applies in only in egregious cases, such as habitual intemperance of the spouse,[59] but counseling is still required before such a separation may be granted.[60] Separation from bed and board does not

---

[54]   The law also allows already-married couples to change the status of their current marriage into a covenant marriage: The married couple must jointly execute a letter of intent to designate their marriage a covenant marriage and to subject themselves to the laws pertaining thereto. Ibid. at § 309(A)(1).

[55]   Ibid. at § 273(A)(1) (2004). This Declaration of Intent purportedly operates as a choice-of-law clause and binds the parties to Louisiana law, but it is highly doubtful that other states would give it such binding effect. Compare Katherine Shaw Spaht and Symeon C. Symeonides, "Covenant Marriage and the Law of Conflict of Laws," *Creighton Law Review* 32 (1999): 1085–1120, with Peter Hay, "The American 'Covenant Marriage' in the Conflict of Laws," in *Comparative Perspective*, 294.

[56]   La. Civ. Code Ann. Arts. 102–103 § 1 (Supp. 2010).

[57]   La. Rev. Stat. Ann. § 307(A)(5) (2008).

[58]   La. Rev. Stat. Ann. § 307(A) (2008). Section 307(A)(6)(b), concerning divorce when a minor child is involved, has another variable. The period of separation after judgment of separation from bed and board increases to one year and six months if a minor child is involved, unless the basis of the judgment of separation from bed and board was for abuse of the child or the spouse seeking the divorce. In the latter case, a divorce may be granted if the spouses have been living apart without reconciliation for only one year. Ibid. at § 307(A)(6)(b).

[59]   Ibid. at § 307(B).

[60]   Ibid. Counseling is not required if the other spouse is abusive. Ibid. at §307(D) (as added by 2004 La. Acts. No. 490).

"dissolve the bond of matrimony" because the separated spouses may not marry again in the interim.[61]

Less than one year after Louisiana's passage of its covenant marriage law, Arizona became the second state to adopt a covenant marriage law.[62] And in 2001, Arkansas joined these two by passing its own covenant marriage law.[63] "All three statutes contain the familiar three components of mandatory premarital counseling, a legally binding agreement to take reasonable steps to preserve the marriage, and restrictive grounds for divorce."[64] Arizona allows for greater flexibility in the grounds for divorce under its covenant marriage law, including that the state may grant a divorce in a covenant marriage if the parties mutually consent.[65] The grounds for divorce in Arkansas much more closely track those in Louisiana.[66] Aside from these three states, efforts to pass covenant marriage laws have failed in several states, although they have continued to be introduced on a somewhat regular basis.

Although the efficacy of covenant marriage laws is debatable, the very advent of such laws is notable for their reintroduction of more than one model of marriage in the law. These covenant marriage laws formally enact two-tiered systems for marriage and divorce law. This shift away from a unitary legal model of marriage and divorce law represents a virtual sea change in modern American law by promulgating multiple, coexisting models of marriage *within* a single state at one time rather than the typical tension caused by differences *between* various state laws. Most commentary to date, however, is still silent on this fundamental shift. And just as the literature focuses on the virtues or vices of the covenant marriage option rather than on the fact that there *is* an option, the literature also overlooks the fact that a multi-tiered system of marriage in New York pre-dated the Louisiana scheme by almost fifteen years.

B. *New York's* Get *Statutes*

New York's *get* statutes[67] have generated wide discussion in legal literature, but that discussion has been mostly limited to constitutional analysis (with most commentators believing the New York statutes to be unconstitutional).[68] What has not been

---

[61] Ibid. at § 309(A)(1).
[62] Ariz. Rev. Stat. Ann. §§ 25–901 to –906 (2007).
[63] Ark. Code Ann. §§ 9–11–801 to –811 (2009).
[64] Spaht, "Modern American Covenant Marriage Movement," 247.
[65] Ariz. Rev. Stat. Ann. § 13–3601 (2010).
[66] See Spaht, "Modern American Covenant Marriage Movement," 248–249.
[67] N.Y. Dom. Rel. Law §§ 236B, 253 (McKinney 2010).
[68] "There is no express reference to Jews in the statute in an attempt to avoid the appearance of violating the constitutional separation of church and state, but nevertheless it is highly questionable whether the statute is constitutional." Elliot N. Dorff and Arthur Rosett, *A Living Tree: The Roots and*

discussed is the fundamental change in family law wrought by the *get* statutes. And
what becomes apparent on closer investigation is that the *get* statutes introduce a
major change in American family law by acknowledging that there may be more
than one jurisdictional claim on a married couple and that there may be more than
only the singular one-size-fits-all conception of marriage typically promulgated by
the state. It is this latter principle that forms a key insight picked up by the later covenant marriage statutes.

1. Jewish Law of Marriage and Divorce

Although not explicitly mentioned anywhere in the *get* statutes, Jewish law under-
girds the rationale of the *get* statutes. According to Jewish law, a marriage may be
terminated in only two ways: through the death of a spouse or by divorce,[69] which is
effectuated by the granting of a *get*.[70] A *get* is a formal written document signifying
and stating the husband's desire to divorce.[71] The *get* has clear gender implications
in Jewish divorces because it is solely the role of the husband to give (or withhold)
a *get*; the role of the wife is limited to receiving a *get*. Further, a husband may give
a *get* and divorce his wife even against her will, "but a husband divorces only from
his own free will."[72] The power of the husband in marital relationships was furthered by the development in Jewish law of the husband's right to divorce his wife
on almost any grounds at all, no matter how frivolous. Conversely, a wife's right to
sue for divorce is much more limited and turns on the husband's willingness to issue
a *get* to finalize the divorce.[73] The issuance of a *get* is a private act, with no need for

Growth of Jewish Law (Albany, NY: State University of New York Press, 1988), 547. But see Broyde,
"New York's Regulation" (in this volume). For other examples of the voluminous literature, see,
e.g., Breitowitz, *Between Civil and Religious Law*, 179–203; Paul Finkelman, "New York's Get Laws:
A Constitutional Analysis," *Columbia Journal of Law and Social Problems* 27 (1993): 55–100; Kent
Greenawalt, "Religious Law and Civil Law: Using Secular Law to Assure Observance of Practices with
Religious Significance," *Southern California Law Review* 71 (1998): 781–843, 810–839.

[69] See M. Mielziner, *The Jewish Law of Marriage and Divorce in Ancient and Modern Times, and Its
Relation to the Law of the State* (Cincinnati: The Block Publishing and Printing Co., 1884), 108.

[70] The following discussion applies most strictly to Orthodox and Conservative Judaism, as Reform
Judaism disposed of the *get* requirement in 1869. See J. David Bleich, "Jewish Divorce: Judicial
Misconceptions and Possible Means of Civil Enforcement," *Connecticut Law Review* 16 (1984):
201–290, 232 n.96. Many Reform rabbis encourage the use of the *get* because it may avoid later legal
complications for the parties.

[71] Jewish law finds the origin of the *get* in the Torah: "A man takes a wife and possesses her. She fails to
please him because he finds something obnoxious about her, and he writes her a bill of divorcement,
hands it to her, and sends her away from his house." Deuteronomy 24:1 (JPS translation).

[72] Irwin H. Haut, *Divorce in Jewish Law and Life* (New York: Sepher-Hermon Press, 1983), 18 (quoting
Babylonian Talmud, *Yevamot*, 112b).

[73] See Michael J. Broyde, *Marriage, Divorce, and the Abandoned Wife in Jewish Law: A Conceptual
Understanding of the Agunah Problems in America* (Hoboken, NJ: Ktav Publishing House, 2001),
15–27; Haut, *Divorce in Jewish Law*, 18–25.

judicial involvement. A rabbi or rabbinical tribunal is "invariably" present, however, to ensure adherence to procedural formalities.[74]

Because the issuance of the *get* is the sole right of the husband, a difficult situation arises when a recalcitrant husband refuses, for whatever reason, to issue a *get* to his wife. Without a *get*, a Jewish woman cannot remarry according to Jewish law and she becomes an *agunah*, or "chained woman."[75] If the woman remarries without a proper Jewish divorce, she is (according to Jewish law) not married to the putative second husband and she is never allowed to marry the second man because "he is her guilty, adulterous partner."[76] Further, any children born to an *agunah* who remarries without receiving a *get* are considered bastards, or *mamzerim*, according to Jewish law. These children are "illegitimate" religiously, and they carry that illegitimate religious status with them throughout their lives. The children are effectively excluded from organized Judaism and are not even allowed to marry into Judaism for ten generations.[77] Unlike women, men are not nearly as affected by the failure to give a *get*. A man who remarries without a Jewish divorce has not committed adultery but has only violated a rabbinic decree mandating monogamy. He is nonetheless considered married to his second wife, and any children resulting from this second union are considered legitimate.[78]

Jewish law has made several efforts to protect the interests of women who lack power in divorce cases. These efforts include standardizing the *get* process to include a host of formal and technical rules that should, in part, prevent a husband from too hastily issuing a *get*. Another protection for the wife comes at the front end of marriage rather than the back end. When a couple marries, they must sign a *ketubah* ("writing") that denotes certain obligations – of money and provision for the physical needs of the wife – that a husband must undertake in the event of a divorce.[79]

These methods do not, however, address the situation of a recalcitrant husband who refuses to issue a *get*. To combat this problem, Jewish law developed a legal fiction that in certain circumstances a properly convened Jewish court acting within its jurisdiction may compel the husband to issue the *get*. Although a *get* must be issued by the free will of the husband, the legal fiction is that the husband intends to act in accordance with Jewish law and duress may thus be used to compel him to do

[74] Breitowitz, *Between Civil and Religious Law*, 6.
[75] See Broyde, *Marriage, Divorce, and the Abandoned Wife*, 15.
[76] Dorff and Rosett, *A Living Tree*, 524. See also Broyde, *Marriage, Divorce, and the Abandoned Wife*, 29–31.
[77] See Adrienne Baker, *The Jewish Woman in Contemporary Society: Transitions and Traditions* (New York: New York University Press, 1993), 57; Dorff and Rosett, *A Living Tree*, 524.
[78] See Dorff and Rosett, *A Living Tree*, 524–525 ("A man is guilty of adultery in Jewish law only if he has intercourse with a woman who is married to someone else.").
[79] See Haut, *Divorce in Jewish Law*, 27–41; Mielziner, *Jewish Law of Marriage and Divorce*, 85–89.

what his true disposition wishes to do.[80] Traditionally, the range of social pressures to encourage the issuance of a *get* spanned from public declarations in the synagogue to social excommunication and banishment from the community. These pressures met moderate success when Jewish communities were "fairly independent entities with virtually complete control over their internal affairs."[81] But in an age of increasing technology and mobility and decreasing isolation for most Jewish communities, these methods rarely effectuate the desired result. When coupled with the fact that the circumstances in which duress is proper are quite limited, this legal fiction underprotects women.

2. Effect of Dual Systems of Marriage and Divorce

Jewish law does not recognize the validity of civil divorce as effectuating the same results as a religious divorce.[82] This means that an observant Jew must obtain a Jewish religious divorce before he or she remarries.[83] When civil states delegated authority over family law to the Jewish religious authorities, as in true millet systems, such conflicts between Jewish and civil law on marriage and divorce were minimal. In recent times, however, civil courts have claimed exclusive jurisdiction over marriage and divorce and this has created increased difficulties as Jewish law seeks to assure that *gets* are given voluntarily and that *agunah* problems are minimized.

The shift to exclusive civil court jurisdiction of divorce law "raised the spectre, horrid indeed from the point of view of Jewish law, that a Jewish couple could be deemed to be divorced by the laws of the state or country in which they lived, and yet remain married in the eyes of Jewish law, unless a *get* was given and accepted."[84] In America, the exclusive civil court jurisdiction over divorce resulted in a dual law of marriage and divorce, with the civil authorities – the states – maintaining full jurisdiction over marriage and divorce while Jewish law resisted surrendering its jurisdiction over the same. The result for Jewish couples is an obligation to abide by the regulations of both civil and religious authorities.[85]

---

[80] See Haut, *Divorce in Jewish Law*, 23–25.

[81] Michael S. Berger and Deborah E. Lipstadt, "Women in Judaism from the Perspective of Human Rights," in *Human Rights in Judaism: Cultural, Religious, and Political Perspectives*, eds. Michael J. Broyde and John Witte Jr. (Northvale, NJ: Jason Aronson Inc., 1998), 77–111.

[82] See Breitowitz, *Between Civil and Religious Law*, 8 ("[J]ust as a civil divorce has no validity in the eyes of religious law, a religious divorce is not recognized civilly.").

[83] For a recent example of the opposite situation, see discussion in Josh Nathan-Kazis, "Big Love, Jewish-Style: One Divorce, Two Marriages, Lots of Questions," *Forward: The Jewish Daily*, Dec. 10, 2010, available at http://www.forward.com/articles/133568/.

[84] Haut, *Divorce in Jewish Law*, 59.

[85] See Broyde, *Marriage, Divorce, and the Abandoned Wife*, 29–32. Broyde states that "[n]ever before the twentieth century has the Jewish community been subject to a system of compulsory civil marriage

In marital formation, the dual law of marriage is not a great obstacle because most states permit marriage by either secular or religious officials. Most rabbis, empowered by the state to effectuate a civil marriage and by the religious tradition to effectuate a religious marriage, will not perform a religious ceremony without meeting the requirements of the civil marriage, and vice versa. There can never be a Jewish marriage without a civil marriage, and a civil marriage not in accord with Jewish law may nonetheless be later brought under the aegis of Jewish law. For this reason, there are not usually jurisdictional conflicts regarding formation.[86]

Marital dissolution, however, presents serious jurisdictional difficulties. Whereas the *agunah* problem is difficult enough within the Jewish tradition, it becomes even more exaggerated when civil authorities govern divorce – for if a man refuses to give a *get* to his wife, he nonetheless may obtain a civil divorce by meeting the proper civil requirements. Because Jewish law does not recognize the validity of civil divorces, the couple would thus remain religiously married even after obtaining a civil divorce. Only by complying with the strictures of Jewish law regarding the *get* procedure may a couple be divorced religiously. This anomaly allows either party to remarry according to civil law, even though doing so for the woman means that she is committing adultery and all children from the second union will be considered illegitimate. (Recall that the Jewish law consequences for the man are not nearly so dire.) This disparity decreases the incentive for a man to issue a *get* to his wife, or else encourages him to condition issuance of the *get* on certain conditions regarding custody or property distribution. In effect, "[t]he importance of the *get* to Jewish women has made it an ideal tool for blackmail."[87]

Examples abound of abuses of the inequitable bargaining position of husband and wife. For example, one recalcitrant husband agreed to issue a *get* only after receiving $15,000 and a promise that his former wife would not press assault charges against him after he broke her leg.[88] Another woman mortgaged her house for $120,000 to pay the amount demanded by her husband for issuance of a *get*, and yet another was forced to drop charges against her husband for sexually abusing their daughter so that she might obtain a *get*. And one recalcitrant husband asked for $100,000

---

and divorce law, and this requirement has had a major impact on both the contours of the agunah problem and the contours of the solutions to it." Ibid. at 30.

[86] See Dorff and Rosett, *A Living Tree*, 524. See also Ann Laquer Estin, "Unofficial Family Law" (in this volume).

[87] Shauna van Praagh, "Bringing the Charter Home: Book Review of *Religion and Culture in Canadian Family Law*, by John Tibor Syrtash," *McGill Law Journal* 38 (1993): 233–250, 243.

[88] See Peter Hellman, "Playing Hard to Get," in *Women in Chains: A Sourcebook on the Agunah*, ed. Jack Nusan Porter (Northvale, NJ: Jason Aronson Inc., 1995), 15, 16–17.

(which he received), then $1 million, and then his wife's father's pension – in addition to demanding full custody of their children.[89]

Such sordid tales of recalcitrant husbands making excessive demands in return for issuing a *get*, combined with the number of recalcitrant husbands who simply refuse to issue a *get* under any conditions, made the time ripe for reform. Prospects for reform have come both from inside and outside the religious law.

In 1954, Conservative Jewish scholar Saul Lieberman sought to add a new clause to the *ketubah*, or marriage contract. This new clause was to act as an arbitration agreement between the parties, and the Jewish Court (*beth din*) was named as the arbitrator if the parties desired to dissolve the marriage in the future.[90] The hope was that this clause would be enforceable both as a civil arbitration agreement and as a valid religious agreement between the parties to submit to the authority of the *beth din*. Orthodox rabbis reacted negatively to this Conservative proposal on halachic grounds, asserting that the agreement to pay an indeterminate sum of money is impermissible in Jewish law. Further, they contended that the *ketubah* itself – as an integral part of the Jewish marriage ceremony – is not a civil but a religious document and by its nature it is excluded from civil judicial review.[91]

The arguments about the civil enforceability of the Lieberman clause were tested in a 1983 New York case, *Avitzur v. Avitzur*.[92] In a 4–3 decision, New York's highest court held that the Lieberman clause was enforceable as an arbitration clause that could be enforced "solely on the application of neutral principles of contract law."[93] Although the *ketubah* was a document used as part of a religious ceremony, the clause in question could be culled from the document and enforced according to secular principles without excessive entanglement between religion and the state. The result of *Avitzur* is that the parties may be forced (by a civil court) to respond to a summons of the religious court; the case does *not* address the question whether a wife may later go back to civil court to compel her husband's compliance with an order by a *beth din* that has required the husband to issue a *get*.[94]

[89] See Irwin Cotler, "Jewish NGOs and Religious Human Rights: A Case Study," in Broyde and Witte, *Human Rights in Judaism*, 165–271, 264; Lisa Zornberg, "Beyond the Constitution: Is the New York Get Legislation Good Law?" *Pace Law Review* 15 (1995): 703–784, 718–720.
[90] See Shlomo Riskin, *Women and Jewish Divorce: The Rebellious Wife, The Agunah and the Right of Women to Initiate Divorce in Jewish Law, A Halakhic Solution* (Hoboken, NJ: Ktav Publishing House, 1989), 137. See also the discussion in Broyde, "New York's Regulation" (in this volume).
[91] One response to this criticism is that the couple should sign a civil prenuptial agreement in addition to the religious *ketubah*. See Riskin, *Women and Jewish Divorce*; Berger and Lipstadt, "Women in Judaism," 106.
[92] 446 N.E.2d 136 (N.Y. 1983); see also *In re Marriage of Goldman*, 554 N.E.2d 1016 (Ill. App. Ct.), *appeal denied*, 555 N.E. 2d 376 (Ill. 1990) (construing a standard Orthodox *ketubah* as an implied contract to give a *get*). But see *Victor v. Victor*, 866 P.2d 899 (Ariz. App. Div. 1 1993) (refusing to give civil validity to a similar clause in the *ketubah*, which was viewed as only a religious document).
[93] 446 N.E.2d at 114.
[94] See Breitowitz, *Between Civil and Religious Law*, 96–106.

Building on the holding of *Avitzur*, Jewish rabbis and scholars turned to the civil authorities in New York to provide assistance in the troublesome realm of recalcitrant husbands and *agunot*. The efforts culminated in the passage of the first *get* statute in 1983. Legislation had first been introduced in 1981 but was withdrawn because of possible constitutional concerns. By 1983, substantially similar legislation was reintroduced, passed by wide legislative margins, and signed into law.[95]

3. The Introduction of *Get* Statutes

The 1983 law, as slightly amended in 1984, is codified as New York Domestic Relations Law §253 ("Removal of Barriers to Remarriage"). Although facially neutral, the statute is clearly drafted to apply only to Jewish divorces. The law refrains from using the term "*get*," opting instead for the legally neutral phrase "barrier to remarriage." This phrase has a technical meaning in the statute:

> "[B]arrier to remarriage" includes, without limitation, any religious or conscientious restraint or inhibition, of which the party required to make the verified statement is aware, that is imposed on a party to a marriage, under the principles held by the clergyman or minister who has solemnized the marriage, by reason of the other party's commission or withholding of any voluntary act.[96]

The gist of the statute, applicable only to persons who were married in a religious ceremony, is that a "barrier to remarriage" (a *get*) must be removed, if within the couple's power to do so, before the state will grant a civil divorce.[97]

A more detailed analysis reveals a number of nuances and gaps, however. The statute requires two things of a party initiating an action for civil divorce or annulment: (1) an allegation in the complaint that the party has taken or will take, to the best of his or her knowledge, all steps "solely within his or her power" to remove all barriers to remarriage prior to the entry of a civil judgment; and (2) the filing of an affidavit prior to judgment that the party has indeed removed all barriers to remarriage.[98] To protect against the filing of false affidavits, the statute provides for

---

[95] New York's Senate passed the 1983 bill by a margin of 58 to 0, and the New York Assembly passed it 136 to 7. See Legislative Bill Jacket, [1983] N.Y. Laws ch. 979 (reporting results of the vote on N.Y.S. 6647, N.Y.A. 6423, 206th Sess. (1983)).

[96] N.Y. Dom. Rel. Law § 253(6) (McKinney 2010). For further discussion and sources regarding these statutes, see Broyde, "New York's Regulation" (in this volume).

[97] N.Y. Dom. Rel. Law § 253(1) (McKinney 2010). New York, like other states, recognizes religious marriages by according civil validity to a marriage ceremony performed by a duly authorized "clergyman or minister," which includes rabbis. See N.Y. Rel. Law § 11(1), (7) (McKinney 2010).

[98] See N.Y. Dom. Rel. Law §§ 253(2) and (3) (McKinney 2010), respectively. Alternately, the plaintiff may allege that the defendant has waived in writing the need for such attestations. See ibid.

criminal liability for the intentional filing of a false affidavit.[99] Further, the statute
provides that the clergyman (or rabbi) who officiated the wedding ceremony may
counter the plaintiff's affidavit with an affidavit stating that barriers to the defendant's remarriage still exist. If the clergyman so attests, the court is not authorized to
enter a judgment of civil divorce or annulment.[100] Presumably, the clergyman will
inform the court when the barriers have been removed, and the court may proceed
with the civil action at that time.

The statute was limited in its scope, however, such that not all *agunot* were covered. For example, if the woman initiated the civil divorce proceeding, the statute
did not aid her because it did not, textually, force the *defendant* to remove all barriers to remarriage. Further, the statute did not grant the civil court the power to
compel the removal of the barriers to remarriage; it only gave the power to refuse
to grant a civil divorce. Thus a husband could refuse to issue a *get*, simply forego
obtaining a civil divorce, and leave his wife stranded. Moreover, because the law
only affects weddings that were "religious" and insists that divorces conform to the
strictures of the officiating clergyman, it did not account for any change in religious
belief between the wedding and breakup of the marriage.

To fix one loophole, New York enacted additional legislation in 1992 that covers
situations in which an aggrieved wife files for divorce as a plaintiff. The result is a
more extensive law that allows the civil court to take a party's inability to remarry
into account when considering equitable distribution of property.[101] This 1992 *get*
statute applies both to plaintiffs and defendants, regardless of whether the parties
were married in a religious ceremony, and allows a court to take a husband's refusal
to issue a *get* into account when distributing the couple's assets.[102] This is critical for
an *agunah*, whose prospects at financial security through remarriage are seriously
impaired because she is religiously unable to marry until and unless her husband
issues a *get*.

[99] See N.Y. Dom. Rel. Law § 253(8) (McKinney 2010). It is unlikely that New York prosecutors would
expend time and resources to prosecute plaintiffs who had filed false affidavits in domestic divorce
cases. See Alan D. Scheinkman, *Practice Commentaries, 1999 Main Volume, McKinney's Consolidated
Laws of New York Annotated*, N.Y. Dom. Rel. Law § 253, C253:7 (McKinney 2010). But see *Kalika v.
Stern*, 911 F. Supp. 594 (E.D.N.Y. 1995) (husband had been tried and acquitted of making a false statement; there was a good faith dispute whether a *get* was required under the circumstances).

[100] See N.Y. Dom. Rel. Law § 253(7) (McKinney 2010).

[101] See N.Y. Dom. Rel. Law §§ 236B(5)(h), (6)(d) (McKinney 2010).

[102] Any "barrier to remarriage" (such as a refusal to issue a *get*) may not be considered in isolation, but is
simply one of a set of factors for court evaluation in determining equitable distribution of property and
amount and duration of maintenance. See N.Y. Dom. Rel. Law §§ 236B(5)(d), (6)(a). Common law
in New York similarly allows such consideration of the failure to give a *get*. See *Schwartz v. Schwartz*,
153 Misc.2d 789, 583 N.Y.S.2d 716 (Sup. Ct. Kings County 1992) (using the "catch-all" provision of
the equitable distribution statute, which empowered the court to consider "any other factor which the
court shall expressly find to be just and proper," to consider the failure to give a *get*).

Although the halachic validity of the *get* statutes is much debated in Jewish law circles,[103] their very existence proves that the state of New York has actively sought to provide state sanction and assistance to its citizens in fulfilling religious requirements of marriage and divorce. That the state may not have achieved its objective in the most effective manner for Jews is irrelevant in light of the fact that such a strong effort has been made.

4. New York's Laws as Precursors to Covenant Marriage Statutes

New York's *get* statutes reintroduce a seemingly radical element into American family law: an acknowledgment that there is more than one jurisdictional model and method of marriage and divorce. If the most salient characteristic of covenant marriage laws is their recognition of a greater pluralism in family law,[104] then New York's laws were not only first in this regard[105] but in fact extend farther than covenant marriage laws.

Functionally, New York's *get* statutes affect more people than the covenant marriage laws. Although reliable estimates are hard to find for either situation, sheer numbers seem to indicate a far greater impact in New York than in Louisiana. In Louisiana, only about 2 percent of those entering into new marriages chose to enter covenant marriages during each of the first five years after the law's enactment (from 1998 to 2003), although as many as 10 percent of newlyweds told researchers that they would have preferred a covenant marriage had they known about the option.[106] In New York, however, there is a substantial Orthodox and Conservative Jewish population that may be affected by the *get* statutes, and experts estimate that there are potentially thousands of *agunot* at any given time.[107]

Structurally, New York's *get* statutes outpace covenant marriage laws in the level of deference accorded to religious entities, pointing the way to a new era of increased pluralism and perhaps a return to a millet system of family law. A more robust millet system in the realm of family law would allow religious systems to function as semi-autonomous entities with the state acting as the overarching sovereign that intervenes only when basic minimum guidelines are not met. Although this type of more

[103] Compare, e.g., Chaim Dovid Zwiebel, "Tragedy Compounded: The Aguna Problem and New York's Controversial New 'Get Law,'" in Porter, *Women in Chains*, 141, with Marvin E. Jacob, "The *Agunah* Problem and the So-Called New York State Get Law: A Legal and Halachic Analysis," in Porter, *Women in Chains*, 159.

[104] See Nichols, "Louisiana's Covenant Marriage Statute," 988–994.

[105] See Broyde, "New York's Regulation" (in this volume).

[106] Nock et al., *Covenant Marriage*, 3.

[107] See Greenawalt, "Religious Law and Civil Law," 822 ("Given the large number of Orthodox and Conservative Jews that live within [New York], the statutes have a practical importance that far exceeds New York's status as one among fifty states.").

formalized millet system is still a couple of steps removed from the current status of
family law, New York and Louisiana have taken clear steps in this direction.

IV. INTERNATIONAL MODELS

In exploring the role and boundaries of the civil authority with respect to marriage
and divorce law, it is also prudent to consider contemporary international models
for comparison. Whereas there is much discussion and debate in the academy about
the "proper" role of international law for constitutional decision making, it is much
less controversial to look comparatively to other legal systems as illustrative. When
we look at other nations and their laws respecting marriage and divorce, the notion
of multiple layers of marriage law and jurisdiction and "multi-tiered" systems seems
much more plausible and workable – for several other countries already recognize
varying types of marriages and accord different groups at least limited jurisdiction
over parts of family law.

In the following section, this chapter outlines some, though certainly not all, of
the variant models of family law jurisdiction in other legal systems. This comparative approach is not intended to be comprehensive, but it casts a wide enough net
to observe that there are several other legal systems worldwide that already practice
and advocate shared jurisdiction in marriage and divorce law in more profound ways
than the current American practice. Some countries have retained systems from
precolonial times and melded those with common law regimes. But others have
recently intentionally adopted pluralistic models to deal with a host of internally
diverse cultures, as a way of facilitating modern notions of multiculturalism. This
section first looks to India (which retains a colonial model on the books and even
greater variety in practice), then to Kenya (which has a mix of residual choice of law
and choice of forum from colonial times but continues to debate whether to grant
legal recognition to Muslim religious family courts), and then to South Africa and
Canada, both of which are well-developed, progressive liberal democracies that are
seeking to balance rights of equality, liberty, group autonomy, and religious rights
in matters of family life as in other areas.[108] Whether any of these nations is a good

---

[108] For additional discussion regarding India, see Werner Menski, "Ancient and Modern Boundary
Crossings Between Personal Laws and Civil Law in Composite India" (in this volume). For South
Africa, see Johan D. van der Vyver, "Multi-Tiered Marriages in South Africa" (in this volume).
For Canada, see Daniel Cere, "Canadian Conjugal Mosaic: From Multiculturalism to Multi-
Conjugalism?" (in this volume); Mohammad H. Fadel, "Political Liberalism, Islamic Family Law,
and Family Law Pluralism" (in this volume); Linda C. McClain, "Marriage Pluralism in the United
States: On Civil and Religious Jurisdiction and the Demands of Equal Citizenship" (in this volume);
and Ayelet Shachar, "Faith in Law? Diffusing Tensions between Diversity and Equality" (in this
volume).

template for the situation in the United States is quite another matter, but the various models and approaches by these countries provide strong evidence that the civil state need not – and perhaps should not – claim and seek to exercise exclusive jurisdiction in matters of marriage and divorce.

A. *India*

Marriage and divorce law in India operates primarily through the civil apparatus, but it purports to apply religious law much of the time.[109] Indian law has specifically enacted various "religious" laws – Hindu,[110] Muslim,[111] Christian,[112] and Parsi[113] – that are intended to apply to adherents of those faiths. Additionally, there is a residual category for marriages between members of variant faiths or for citizens who simply choose secular law.[114] Under each category, civil courts explicitly claim to retain jurisdiction to resolve disputes.[115] This leads, at times, to difficulties centering on how to interpret changes within various systems of law and whether such changes should (and must) come from the civil court systems or from within the various religious communities to whom the law applies. Further, because customary religious law is permitted to supplement (though not to contradict) statutory law, divorce may

---

[109] Werner Menski skillfully discusses the intensive and intentional interactions of civil and religious law within India in his chapter in this volume. See Menski, "Ancient and Modern Boundary Crossings" (in this volume). My own brief overview is not intended to give short shrift to the actual functioning of law in communities by focusing solely on the positive law. For more on India, and Hindu and Muslim family law, see Livia Holder, *Hindu Divorce: A Legal Anthropology* (Burlington, VT: Ashgate, 2008); Werner Menski, *Comparative Law in a Global Context: The Legal Systems of Asia and Africa* (Cambridge: Cambridge University Press, 2d ed. 2006) [hereinafter Menski, *Comparative Law*]; Werner Menski, *Hindu Law: Beyond Tradition and Modernity* (Oxford: Oxford University Press, 2003) [hereinafter Menski, *Hindu Law*]; David Pearl and Werner Menski, *Muslim Family Law* (London: Sweet and Maxwell, 3d ed. 1998) [hereinafter Pearl and Menski, *Muslim Family Law*].

[110] The Hindu Code includes the Hindu Marriage Act of 1955, the Hindu Succession Act of 1956, the Hindu Minority and Guardianship Act of 1956, and the Hindu Adoption and Maintenance Act of 1956. See Robert D. Baird, "Traditional Values, Governmental Values, and Religious Conflict in Contemporary India," *Brigham Young University Law Review* (1998): 337–356, 345 (referring to these as the "Hindu Code Bill").

[111] See Muslim Personal Law (Shariat) Application Act (1937); Dissolution of Muslim Marriages Act (1939); and Muslim Women (Protection of Rights on Divorce) Act (1986).

[112] See Indian Christian Marriage Act (1872); The Indian Divorce (Amendment) Act (2001).

[113] See Parsi Marriage and Divorce Act (1936).

[114] See Special Marriage Act (1954). Additionally, Jewish personal law is not codified like other religious law is, and it is primarily governed by contract and customary law. See Paras Diwan, "Family Law," in *The Indian Legal System*, ed. Joseph Minatur (Dobbs Ferry, NY: Oceana Publications, 1978), 639–641 [hereinafter Diwan, *Legal*]; Mohammed A. Qureshi, *Marriage and Matrimonial Remedies: A Uniform Civil Code for India* (Delhi: Concept Pub. Co., 1978), 4.

[115] Marc Galanter and Jayanth Krishnan, "Personal Law and Human Rights in India and Israel," *Israel Law Review* 34 (2000): 101–133, 109.

occur at times without judicial intervention at all.[116] This is especially true of Muslim divorces but also holds true for Hindu divorces as well.[117]

Religious affiliation is the prime determinant regarding the governing statutory law for marriage and divorce issues. However, it is not religious *belief* that matters; rather, it is membership in a particular "religious" community by birth – or entrance into that community by conversion – that is decisive. So long as an individual does not denounce the religion outright and take up another, generally that person will be ruled by the personal law of the community to which she belongs.[118] Because the personal laws are national in scope in India (rather than varying state by state), this religious choice of law determination is the prime jurisdictional decision.

This practice of having multiple contiguous systems of personal laws originated with British colonial rule. In the late eighteenth century, the British authorities established a general territorial law with a common law system of courts, but they retained "enclaves of personal law."[119] This policy of retaining separate systems of personal law continued with few exceptions up until Indian independence. The shaping of the bodies of law was largely left to the religious groups, with a few exceptions to regulate practices outside the norm by British standards (such as against child marriage, against immolation of widows [*sati*], permitting remarriage of widows, and the like).[120] These bodies of "religious" law were not administered by religious authorities and courts, but rather by the civil authorities: Common law judges ruled on matters of Hindu and Muslim law, although the courts had the assistance of native law officers to advise them on the nuances of the religious laws. Beginning in 1860, the religious advisors were abolished and the judges took exclusive control in applying the personal law. This in turn began to render the "religious" personal laws less distinctly religious and instead more reflective of the views and interpretations of the common law judges themselves – such that new bodies of "Anglo-Hindu" and "Anglo-Muslim" law began to develop.[121]

---

[116] See Paras Diwan, *Law of Marriage and Divorce* (Delhi: Universal Law, 4th ed. 2002) [hereinafter Diwan, *Marriage and Divorce*]; Pearl and Menski, *Muslim Family Law*, 45.

[117] Diwan, *Marriage and Divorce*, 380–384.

[118] Ibid. at 525–530; Pearl and Menski, *Muslim Family Law*, 46.

[119] Galanter and Krishnan, "Personal Law and Human Rights," 106. For example, the Bengal Regulation of 1772 provided that with regard to "inheritance, marriage, caste, and other religious usages, or institutions" the courts should apply "the laws of the Koran with respect to the Mahometans, and those of the Shaster with respect to the Hindus." Bengal Regulation of 1772.

[120] See also Louise Harmon and Eileen Kaufman, "Dazzling the World: A Study of India's Constitutional Amendment Mandating Reservation for Women on Rural Panchayats," *Berkeley Women's Law Journal* 19 (2004): 32–105, 44. Laws permitting widow remarriage and civil marriage were available as an alternative to Hindu law, but few chose to opt out of the personal law system. Ibid.; Menski, *Hindu Law*, 290.

[121] Galanter and Krishnan, "Personal Law and Human Rights," at 106–107; Martha C. Nussbaum, "International Human Rights Law in Practice: India: Implementing Sex Equality Through Law," *Chicago Journal of International Law* 2 (2001): 35–58, 40–47. See also Menski, *Hindu Law*, 171.

Various reforms were undertaken in the twentieth century to conform Indian personal law to more modern standards and understandings of human rights. Many of these reforms originated from within the various religious communities themselves and were thereafter reified in law by the governing legislative authority.[122] For example, the Hindu law was reformed and unified in the mid-1950s, leading to the adoption of what is commonly called the Hindu Code.[123] The changes included the abolition of polygamy, the availability of divorce, and a more equitable distribution of property rights between genders. While this provided unification of Hindu law, it also rendered the law that was applicable to "Hindus" more akin to general modern civil law rather than traditional religious Hindu law.[124]

Just prior to this reform of Hindu law, India's new constitution of 1950 had come into force. Therein, there was (and still is) a hortatory provision directing the state to "endeavor to secure for the citizens a uniform civil code throughout the territory of India."[125] This provision "appears to envision the dissolution of the personal law system in favor of a Uniform Civil [personal] Code,"[126] but there has been very little movement in this direction.[127] In part, this owes to the fact that a uniform code would necessarily mean the abolition of various personal laws set forth in this section, which would especially anger the minority Muslim community because it would alter the unique characteristics of that religious group.[128] The wisdom of unification is debated within both academic literature and politics, and there remains strong opposition to a uniform code as the minority religious groups fear the new law would only represent the traditions of the majority Hindu population.[129] At present, as Werner Menski describes, "the Indian debates over the unification of family law have died down," and instead there is a "deliberate, plurality-conscious and highly sophisticated post-modern construct" that is "a new attempt to make sense of the never-ending challenges of legal pluralism."[130] The current civil legal structure

[122] See, e.g., Nussbaum, "International Human Rights Law in Practice," 41–47.

[123] See, e.g., Martha Nussbaum, *Women and Human Development: The Capabilities Approach* (Cambridge: Cambridge University Press, 2000), ch. 3. Menski is critical of this terminology. Menski, "Ancient and Modern Boundary Crossings" (in this volume).

[124] See Baird, "Traditional Values, Governmental Values, and Religious Conflict," 345.

[125] India Const. art. 44. "Uniform civil code for the citizens. – The State shall endeavour to secure for the citizens a uniform civil code throughout the territory of India."

[126] Galanter and Krishnan, "Personal Law and Human Rights," 107.

[127] Menski, *Comparative Law*, 250.

[128] See, e.g., Marc Galanter, "Remarks on Family Law and Social Change in India," in *Chinese Family Law and Social Change in Historical and Comparative Perspective*, ed., David C. Buxbaum (Seattle: University of Washington Press, 1978), 492, 494.

[129] Nussbaum, "International Human Rights Law in Practice," 46 ("In this day of growing Hindu fundamentalism, Uniform Code really does mean Hindu Code, and the resistance of the Muslim minority to losing its legal system is comprehensible.").

[130] See Menski, "Ancient and Modern Boundary Crossings" (in this volume). It may be an overstatement to say that movement has completely waned for uniformity. For example, the Hindu-nationalist Bharatiya Janata Party (BJP) used calls for a UCC (or for a reform of Muslim personal law) as part of

that remains in force has five distinct categories of personal law: Hindu, Muslim, Christian, Parsi, and a residual category of secular law.

1. Hinduism

The personal law applicable to Hindus is easily the most widely applied, because more than 82 percent of India's population of 1.19 billion self-identify as Hindu (if Sikhs are included).[131] This personal law is expansive in its reach, covering not only Hindus but also those who are Buddhist, Jaina, or Sikh by religion and "any other person domiciled in the territories to which this Act extends who is not a Muslim, Christian, Parsi or Jew by religion."[132] "Religion," for statutory purposes, is defined by the religion of one's parent or parents or by one's own explicit conversion. Because of this broad reach of those included under "Hindu law," the term "Hindu" has lost much of its religious connotation within modern Indian personal law.[133]

The Hindu Marriage Act (1955) governs marriages. Polygamy is expressly disallowed by statute, but recent analysis indicates a lack of enforcement.[134] Marriage between a Hindu and a non-Hindu is not permitted under this act, but this prohibition is not overly harsh for two reasons: first, because the definition of who is "Hindu" is so broad, any man and woman who are *not* Muslim, Christian, Parsi, or Jewish may marry under the Hindu Marriage Act; and second, a Hindu and non-Hindu can marry under the secular Special Marriage Act.

The Hindu Marriage Act attempts to abolish child marriage by establishing the legal age of marriage to be twenty-one years for males and eighteen years for females.[135] Even so, child marriage is considered neither void nor voidable (i.e., the resulting marriage is still valid), but penalties such as jail time or a fine may attach to persons who marry underage.[136] Couples seeking to enter a valid Hindu marriage may do so by either: (1) choosing to perform the Shastric rite and ceremonies recognized by Hindu law; or (2) performing customary formalities that prevail in the caste, community, or tribe to which one or both parties belong.[137] If the couple uses

---

its platform in the 2005 national elections to make the laws fit the "constitutional guarantees of equality and dignity of women." See "BJP Favours Reforms in Muslim Laws," *The Times of India*, June 29, 2005, available at http://timesofindia.indiatimes.com/articleshow/1154979.cms.

[131] All population numbers and religious percentages are from the CIA World Factbook, available at https://www.cia.gov/library/publications/the-world-factbook/index.html.

[132] Hindu Marriage Act § 2 (1955).

[133] Menski, *Hindu Law*, 7.

[134] Hindu Marriage Act § 5(i) (1955); Menski, *Comparative Law*, 54. Prior to 1955, Hindu men were permitted to have an unlimited number of wives. Diwan, *Marriage and Divorce*, 79.

[135] Hindu Marriage Act § 5(iii) (1955).

[136] Diwan, *Legal*, 57.

[137] Hindu Marriage Act § 7 (1955). See also Diwan, *Marriage and Divorce*, 145; B. P. Beri, *Law of Marriage and Divorce in India* (Lucknow: Eastern Book Co., 2d ed. 1989), 23. See generally Menski, *Hindu Law*, 283, 287.

either method, there is no national requirement for the Hindu marriage to be registered with the civil authorities.[138]

The Hindu Marriage Act provided a seminal change to prior law by introducing the availability of judicial divorce. Prior to 1955, Hindu religious law rendered marriage indissoluble, generally leaving no possibility for divorce (except for a few variations of prior customary religious law in a few areas in India).[139] This allowance for judicial divorce – as well as an alteration of male-only inheritance rules, the change of the age of capacity for marriage, and the abolition of polygamy – left Indian Hindu personal law in a quite different form from its previous condition as truly religious law.[140] In its present form (as amended in 1976), the act provides for a judicial decree of divorce on either fault grounds or mutual consent.[141] The fault grounds permit either husband or wife to sue for divorce based on adultery, cruelty, desertion for a period of not less than two years, conversion away from Hinduism, unsound mind/mental disorder, leprosy, venereal disease in a communicable form, renunciation of the world, or not known to be alive for a period of seven years.[142] Either party may also seek a divorce on the ground that there has been no resumption of cohabitation for one year or more after a decree of judicial separation or no restitution of conjugal rights for one year or more after a decree for restitution of conjugal rights.[143] There are also a few limited special grounds on which only a wife may seek divorce.[144]

The couple may also mutually consent to divorce and then seek a judicial decree. They must allege that "they have been living separately for a period of one year or more, that they have not been able to live together and that they have mutually agreed that the marriage should be dissolved." In such cases, a court must act between six and eighteen months after the petition is filed, presumably to give

---

[138] Hindu Marriage Act § 8 (1955). See also Menski, *Hindu Law*, 287.

[139] See Galanter and Krishnan, "Personal Law and Human Rights," 108; Sampak P. Garg, "Law and Religion: The Divorce Systems of India," *Tulsa Journal of Comparative and International Law* 6 (1998): 1–20, 16 n.173. As this book was in press, India continued to discuss adding a ground of irretrievable breakdown to the Hindu Marriage Act and Special Marriage Act. See "Parliamentary Panel Recommends Safeguards to Amended Divorce Law," *The Hindu*, March 7, 2011.

[140] See Galanter and Krishnan, "Personal Law and Human Rights," 108 ("Very few rules remained with a specifically religious foundation.").

[141] Hindu Marriage Act §§ 13, 13B (1955) (amended 1976); see also Menski, *Comparative Law*, 252.

[142] Hindu Marriage Act § 13(1)(i)-(vii) (1955); see also Garg, "Law and Religion," 16–18.

[143] Hindu Marriage Act § 13(1A)(i)-(ii) (1955).

[144] These include: if a previous spouse of the husband was alive at the time of a marriage conducted before the commencement of the Hindu Marriage Act; if the husband has been guilty of rape, sodomy, or bestiality since the solemnization of the marriage; if there has been no cohabitation for one year after an order of maintenance is passed under the Hindu Maintenance and Adoptions Act or the Criminal Procedure Code; or, if the marriage was solemnized before the wife attained the age of fifteen years, and she repudiated the marriage before attaining the age of eighteen. Hindu Marriage Act § 13(2)(1)-(iv) (1955).

the couple a chance to reconcile and withdraw the petition. The Hindu Marriage Act also disallows divorce within the first year of marriage except in exceptional circumstances.[145]

2. Islam

Muslims make up the largest minority group in India, comprising about 13.4 percent of the population. "Muslim Personal Law" is applied as the "rule of decision" in matters involving intestacy, dissolution of marriage, and many property cases "where the parties are Muslim."[146] Three main acts[147] provide the statutory basis for decisions, but much of Islamic law[148] in India, unlike Hindu law, remains uncodified and proceeds from case law and precedent.[149] For example, the definition of who is a Muslim for purposes of India's statutory personal law derives from such uncodified case law: Muslims are those who are born to Muslim parents, or those who convert to Islam (either by profession of faith or by a formal conversion ceremony).[150]

Marriage under the Muslim law is a contract,[151] aimed at procreation and legitimizing children. Marriage is generally accomplished by a proposal and acceptance made at the same meeting.[152] Polygamy is still permitted under Muslim personal law in India, with the husband allowed to take up to four wives at one time, although this is rarely practiced.[153] This presents a potential problem because no other Indian personal law permits polygamy, and there are charges that men may be strategically attracted to Islam simply to practice polygamy.[154] Islam itself, however, limits the practice of polygamy unless a man can treat all his wives with equity; otherwise,

---

[145] Hindu Marriage Act §§ 13B(1), 13B(2), 14(1) (1955).

[146] Muslim Personal Law (Shariat) Application Act § 2 (1937).

[147] Muslim Personal Law (Shariat) Application Act (1937); Dissolution of Muslim Marriages Act (1939); and Muslim Women (Protection of Rights on Divorce) Act (1986).

[148] The phrase "Islamic law" has a host of meanings, which are discussed in detail elsewhere pertaining to family law. See, e.g., discussion in Fadel, "Political Liberalism" (in this volume); Pearl and Menski, *Muslim Family Law*; Rex Ahdar and Nicholas Aroney, eds., *Shari'a in the West* (Oxford: Oxford University Press, 2010).

[149] See Garg, "Law and Religion," 3.

[150] See Diwan, *Legal*, 7–9, and cases cited therein. Under Indian law, if a child is born to one Hindu parent and one Muslim parent, the personal law of that child will be determined according to the faith in which the child is "brought up." Ibid., 8.

[151] Pearl and Menski, *Muslim Family Law*, 140.

[152] Beri, *Law of Marriage and Divorce*, 41–42.

[153] See Pearl and Menski, *Muslim Family Law*, 247; Nussbaum, "International Human Rights Law in Practice," 44.

[154] Indian courts have held that if one spouse changes religion, then the marriage is still ruled by the personal law under which the couple was originally married. *Lily Thomas v. Union of India & ORS and other Appeals*, 2 LRI 623 (Sup. Ct. of India, May 5, 2000).

he may only take one wife.[155] In addition, Muslim men are allowed to marry non-Muslim women, but Muslim women may only marry within their faith under Muslim personal law.[156]

There are three types of Muslim divorce in India: judicial divorce, divorce by mutual agreement, and nonjudicial unilateral divorce.[157] Muslim marriages may also be dissolved as the result of apostasy from Islam. If the husband converts away from Islam, the marriage is automatically dissolved. If the wife converts away, she must sue for divorce under of the Dissolution of Muslim Marriages Act.[158]

Judicial divorce, governed by the Dissolution of Muslim Marriages Act, requires recourse to the civil courts and is available only to females. Before passage of this act, a Muslim wife in India had virtually no right of divorce. Muslim women may now seek a judicial decree of divorce based on the unknown whereabouts of the husband; the husband's failure to provide maintenance; imprisonment of the husband; the husband's failure to perform his marital obligations without reasonable cause; impotence, insanity, or severe disease of the husband; marriage cruelty; or other grounds recognized under Muslim law.[159] The institution of civil grounds for Muslim women to seek a divorce effectively enacted a governmental preference, embodied in statutory law, for the Maliki school of interpretation over the Hanafi school, which had not recognized such grounds for divorce for women. This statutory enactment of "Muslim law" thus provided more gender equality but did so at the cost of expressing a civil law preference (indeed, potentially a mandate) for one school of interpretation.[160]

---

[155] See Quran 4:3; see also Melanie D. Reed, "Western Democracy and Islamic Tradition: The Application of Shari'a in a Modern World," *American University International Law Review* 19 (2004): 485–521, 520.

[156] See Jamal J. Nasir, *The Status of Women under Islamic Law and Under Modern Islamic Legislation* (London: Graham and Trotman, 1990), 27–28.

[157] See Diwan, *Legal*, 655; Garg, "Law and Religion," 7.

[158] See Dissolution of Muslim Marriages Act § 4 (1939) ("The renunciation of Islam by a married Muslim woman or her conversion to a faith other than Islam shall not by itself operate to dissolve her marriage."); Pearl and Menski, *Muslim Family Law*, 302–305.

[159] Dissolution of Muslim Marriages Act § 2(i)-(ix) (1939). "Cruelty" is defined in detail, including a lack of equitable treatment of multiple wives, physical mistreatment, immorality of the husband, interference in the wife's property rights, or disruption in the wife's religious observance. Dissolution of Muslim Marriages Act § 2(viii)(a)-(f) (1939).

[160] See Nussbaum, "International Human Rights Law in Practice," 43. John L. Esposito, *Women in Muslim Family Law* (Syracuse, NY: Syracuse University Press, 2d ed. 2001), 76. Prior to the passage of the 1939 law, many Muslim women were converting to other religions in order to obtain the right to divorce. Thus, more leeway for women to divorce was introduced in the Muslim law itself, and Muslim women were simultaneously disallowed to divorce solely for reasons of their own conversion. For more on the schools of interpretation, see Fadel, "Political Liberalism" (in this volume).

Spouses in a Muslim marriage may also divorce by mutual consent, although the statutory law makes no mention of this.[161] "Roughly speaking, [divorce by mutual agreement] is known as *khul'* where the aversion is on the side of the wife, and *mubara'a* where this is mutual."[162] This kind of mutual agreement rises to legal status through a form of offer and acceptance, usually through the wife paying the husband the amount of her *mahr*, a bridal gift or dower.[163] In India, the court need not be involved in this type of divorce if undertaken amicably by the parties.

The third kind of divorce is nonjudicial, unilateral divorce via *talaq* ("repudiation"), a right reserved for husbands under Islamic law. *Talaq* comes in several forms, but generally all that is required is that the husband be sane and of majority age while speaking words that indicate an intention to divorce. Some approved forms of *talaq* give the husband a period of time during which he may withdraw his repudiation. The customary form requires only that the husband say, "I divorce thee," three times and is immediately effective – without the involvement of any civil authority. The husband may generally delegate his unilateral right of divorce to any other third party, including the wife.[164]

India more recently addressed one other aspect of Muslim marriage in the Muslim Women (Protection of Rights on Divorce) Act (1986), which was passed in response to the famous *Shah Bano* case.[165] The case arose after sixty-four-year-old Shah Bano was divorced by her husband of forty-three years, who happened to be a prosperous lawyer, through his invocation of triple *talaq*.[166] Under traditional Islamic law, women divorced this way were not entitled to maintenance, but only the return of the *mahr* payment from the outset of marriage. This had led to regular and severe underfunding of Muslim women, and so women had pursued additional maintenance under section 25 of the Indian Criminal Code, which requires men "of adequate means" to provide for their ex-wives.[167] Shah Bano sued her ex-husband

---

[161] See Diwan, *Marriage and Divorce*, 587–592.

[162] Dawoud Sudqi El Alami and Doreen Hinchcliffe, *Islamic Marriage and Divorce Laws of the Arab World* (Cambridge, MA: Kluwer Law International, 1996), 27. See also Nasir, *Status of Women under Islamic Law*, 78–81.

[163] El Alami and Hinchcliffe, *Islamic Marriage and Divorce Laws*, 27–28; Lynn Welchman, ed., *Women's Rights and Islamic Family Law: Perspectives on Reform* (London, New York: Zed Books Ltd., 2004), 188. See also the discussion of *mahr*, dower, and dowry in McClain, "Marriage Pluralism in the United States" (in this volume).

[164] See Pearl and Menski, *Muslim Family Law*, 297; Esposito, *Women in Muslim Family Law*, 29–31; El Alami and Hinchcliffe, *Islamic Marriage and Divorce Laws*, 25.

[165] *Mohammed Ahmed Khan v. Shah Bano Begum & Others*, 72 AIR SC 945 (1985).

[166] Commentary abounds regarding the *Shah Bano* case and its aftermath. See, e.g., Menski, "Ancient and Modern Boundary Crossings" (in this volume); Gerald James Larson, *India's Agony Over Religion* (Albany, NY: State University of New York Press, 1995), 256–261; Shachar, *Multicultural Jurisdictions*, 81–83.

[167] See Nussbaum, "International Human Rights Law in Practice," 44.

for maintenance – as many other women had successfully done before her – and she won an award of maintenance in the lower court. On appeal, the Supreme Court affirmed and awarded her even more maintenance, in an opinion that openly criticized Islamic practices. Thus, the justices not only applied the Indian Criminal Code over the customary religious personal law, but stated that the finding was consistent with the Quran.[168] This opinion set off a storm of protest within the Muslim community, which took it as a sign that Muslim family law was being weakened by judicial reinterpretation. Muslim leaders therefore lobbied the legislature and secured passage of the Muslim Women (Protection of Rights on Divorce) Act in 1986. The act effectuates a legislative reversal of *Shah Bano* by depriving all Muslim women (but no others) of the right to seek maintenance after a Muslim divorce under the Criminal Code and shifting the responsibility for maintenance onto the wife's family.

3. Christianity

Christians constitute a much smaller minority (2.3%) of the Indian population. The laws governing Christian marriage have not been substantially updated since the late nineteenth century; the laws governing Christian divorce were revised within the past decade.

The Indian Christian Marriage Act (1872) applies to "persons professing the Christian religion" and provides for monogamous marriages between two Christians, or between one Christian and one non-Christian, who are at least twenty-one (males) or eighteen (females). Marriage is treated primarily as a contract between the parties, with attendant formalities required. Once the officiant has solemnized the marriage, it must be registered with the civil authorities to be binding.[169]

The law governing Indian Christian divorce has given commentators more pause than the marriage law. Before 2001, the law permitted divorce only in cases of hard fault. Men could initiate divorce proceedings only for adultery, whereas women could institute proceedings only for adultery coupled with some other flaw.[170] The law was amended and liberalized in 2001 so that Christian marriages may be dissolved

---

[168] *Shah Bano*, 72 AIR SC 945, 946–947 (stating, among other things, that the "fatal point in Islam is the degradation of woman").

[169] See, e.g., Indian Christian Marriage Act, preamble, §§ 4, 27ff., 60 (1872); William E. Pinto, *Law of Marriage and Matrimonial Reliefs for Christians in India* (Bangalore: Theological Publications in India, 1991), 33–35.

[170] See Indian Divorce Act § 10 (1869) (allowing for a woman to petition for divorce alleging adultery coupled with: incest; bigamy; marriage with another woman; rape, sodomy, or bestiality; cruelty; or desertion). Women could also petition for divorce if the "husband has exchanged his profession of Christianity for the profession of some other religion, and gone through a form of marriage with another woman." Indian Divorce Act § 10 (1869).

either unilaterally in cases of fault or by mutual consent.[171] Either spouse is now permitted to petition the court for dissolution on grounds of adultery, conversion by the spouse to another religion, insanity, desertion, cruelty, or other reasons. Additionally, women may petition for divorce if the husband has been guilty of rape, sodomy, or bestiality. Or, importantly, the parties may jointly petition the court for a divorce if they have been living separate and apart for at least two years and "have mutually agreed that the marriage should be dissolved."[172] Mutual consent divorce is still not immediately available, though; the parties must petition the court both initially and then again six to eighteen months later before a decree may be granted.[173]

4. Parsi (Zoroastrianism)

Parsis (also known as members of the Zoroastrian faith) first migrated to India in the eighth century because of persecution in their native Persia. They were initially governed by custom, which incorporated much of the local Hindu law and customs. In 1865, the first Parsi Marriage and Divorce Bill was passed, and it was subsequently modernized and replaced by the Parsi Marriage and Divorce Act of 1936.[174] Modern Indian Parsi personal law applies to all who are "Parsi Zoroastrians"[175] – which typically include individuals who both descended from Zoroastrian parents and continue to profess the Zoroastrian faith.[176]

Under the Parsi Marriage and Divorce Act, Parsi marriage may only be between two Parsis and must be monogamous. Like other faiths in India, the minimum age of marriage is twenty-one years for males and eighteen years for females. Marriage is a contract, but it must be solemnized by a priest with the *ashirvad* ceremony in the presence of two additional witnesses. The officiating priest must then submit a registration form to the civil authorities for the marriage to be considered valid.[177]

Fault-based divorce for Parsi marriages is statutorily permitted equally to the husband and wife.[178] Fault bases are numerous, including adultery, insanity, desertion, conversion by the other spouse to another religion, preexisting pregnancy, and others.[179] If a husband seeks a divorce based on adultery, the alleged paramour is to be joined as a codefendant (along with the allegedly adulterous spouse) and is

---

[171] See The Indian Divorce (Amendment) Act (2001).
[172] The Indian Divorce (Amendment) Act § 10A(1) (2001).
[173] The Indian Divorce (Amendment) Act § 10A(2) (2001).
[174] See Beri, *Law of Marriage and Divorce*, 48–49.
[175] Parsi Marriage and Divorce Act § 2(7) (1936).
[176] See Diwan, *Legal*, 9. Conversion into the Parsi faith is "against the usage and customs of the Parsis of India." Ibid.
[177] Parsi Marriage and Divorce Act §§ 3, 4, 6 (1936).
[178] Parsi Marriage and Divorce Act § 32 (1936).
[179] Parsi Marriage and Divorce Act § 32(a)-(j) (1936).

potentially liable for all or part of the costs of the divorce proceeding.[180] The act also allows for divorce based on mutual consent. In such cases, the parties must allege that they have lived separately for at least one year, that they are not able to live together, and that they mutually agree that the marriage should be dissolved.[181]

5. Civil Marriage and Divorce

In 1872, India established a procedure for nonreligious, civil marriage for anyone who declared that he or she was not a professing Christian, Jew, Parsi, Hindu, Muslim, or Jain. In 1954, the Special Marriage Act was modernized to eliminate the need for any such foreswearing. Parties of any religion may be married under the act, creating a true option for Indians.[182] This is especially advantageous for two Indians of different faiths who wish to marry, in the event that neither of the applicable personal laws would otherwise allow marriage (e.g., a Hindu and a Muslim).[183] Because civil marriage under the act is effectively a civil contract,[184] the parties must choose to enter the marriage and must attend to minimum formalities – including publication of banns, some form of solemnization before three witnesses and a marriage officer, recitation of a binding declaration in the presence of those parties, and registration.[185]

One notable feature of the civil marriage statute is that it provides a method for already-married parties to change the law applicable to them to that of the Special Marriage Act, effectively creating a choice of law midstream. To do so, parties must jointly petition the relevant civil marriage officer, who will post a notice akin to banns for thirty days. If there are no objections – and if the parties otherwise would have met the requirements for civil marriage – then the marriage officer registers the marriage and the parties thereafter operate under the structure and strictures of the Special Marriage Act rather than the previously applicable "religious" personal law.[186]

Parties married under the Special Marriage Act may seek a judicial divorce either unilaterally or by mutual consent. Unilaterally, either husband or wife may petition

[180] Parsi Marriage and Divorce Act § 33 (1936).
[181] Parsi Marriage and Divorce Act § 32B(1) (1936).
[182] Special Marriage Act (1954). Minimum eligibility requirements to enter a civil marriage include that the parties must be of sound mind, capable of giving consent, be of minimum age (twenty-one for males and eighteen for females), not be within degrees of prohibited relation, and not have another living spouse. Special Marriage Act § 4(a)-(d) (1954). A lack of valid consent or bigamous marriage would render a civil marriage null and void. Special Marriage Act § 24 (1954).
[183] Diwan, *Legal*, 644; Qureshi, *Marriage and Matrimonial Remedies*, 4.
[184] Diwan, *Legal*, 35.
[185] Special Marriage Act §§ 5–14 (1954).
[186] Special Marriage Act §§ 15–18 (1954).

for divorce on a number of fault grounds, including adultery, desertion for two or more years, long-term imprisonment of the spouse, cruelty, insanity, or other reasons.[187] By later amendment, there are a few additional grounds available only to a complaining wife – such as rape, sodomy, bestiality, or noncohabitation for one year after the wife has been awarded maintenance.[188] Further, either husband or wife may individually petition for divorce under the theory that the marriage has broken down if there has been no resumption of cohabitation or restitution of conjugal rights one year after an order for the resumption or restitution.[189]

The Special Marriage Act also provides for couples jointly to petition the court for divorce by mutual consent. The attestations and applicable waiting period before the court will act on the petition mirror those in the amended Indian Divorce Act (applicable to Christian marriages). There is also a requirement, akin to that in Hindu Marriage Law, that a court will not grant a divorce before the completion of one year of marriage so that the couple may have a chance to reconcile.[190]

B. Kenya

Kenya is an interesting comparative example of multi-tiered marriages, because its legal system contains both the past holdovers of (mostly colonial) personal status laws, like India, but also bears the marks of modern discussions to incorporate liberal demands for fairness and equality with competing values of group autonomy and a recognition of the limits of the civil law. While discussing Kenya, the two important ideas of multi-tiered systems need to be separated – because Kenya presents both (1) a variety of applicable personal laws (akin to India); and (2) a debate about whether a religious decisional system should have jurisdictional authority either alongside or instead of the civil courts. Thus, there is both a choice-of-law issue and also a choice-of-forum issue, although the two do not always sort themselves neatly into only one of those areas.

1. Choice of Law: Personal Laws

Kenya, like India, is a former British colony. Its colonial status led to a mixture of preexisting customary laws with Western-style statutes and common law that were introduced by the British. Kenyan statutes recognize four basic systems of civil statutory marriage: civil marriage, African Christian marriage, Muslim law, and Hindu

---

[187] Special Marriage Act § 27(1)(a)-(h) (1954).
[188] Special Marriage Act § 27(1A)(i)-(ii) (1976).
[189] Special Marriage Act § 27(2)(i)-(ii) (1970).
[190] Special Marriage Act § 29.

law.[191] Further, the uncodified category of "customary marriage" is expressly recognized by the civil law.[192]

These different categories hold differing requirements for jurisdiction (which is also discussed more in the following section). For example, Christian marriage may be celebrated either by a licensed minister or by a civil official, and the officiant must register the marriage with the proper state registry. Muslim marriages fall exclusively to the province of general (uncodified) Islamic law, but they must also be registered with the civil authority. Customary marriages, however, have no prescribed form and no requirement of registration. Jurisdiction over divorce is not much cleaner. Three forms of marriage (civil, African Christian, and Hindu) fall under the jurisdiction of the civil High Court.[193] Muslim divorce jurisdiction lies (controversially) first with religious tribunals, with recourse also available in civil courts, which are supposed to apply Islamic law. And customary marriages are subject to a mixture of tribal and civil authority. A brief overview of the various categories of marriage/divorce law reveals similarities among them, but also some notable differences.

Civil Marriage/Divorce and Christianity. Marriage under Kenya's Marriage Act is "open to all persons irrespective of race or religion."[194] Civil marriage is monogamous, and entrants must meet certain requirements such as capacity and non-affinity.[195] Further, other procedures such as banns, a proper ceremony (with two witnesses and an officiant, held at the proper time of day with proper vows), and detailed registration procedures apply.[196] Recalling civil marriages' connections to religious roots, civil marriages may occur either in the registrar's office or in a church, and they may be officiated either by a civil official or a minister.[197] Couples married under the general civil marriage statute may divorce only for fault reasons, as enumerated under the Matrimonial Causes Act. These include adultery, desertion, cruelty, insanity, or rape/sodomy/bestiality. Divorce will not be granted within

---

[191] The Marriage Act, Laws of Kenya, CAP 150 (2008); African Christian Marriage and Divorce Act, Laws of Kenya, CAP 151 (2008); Mohammedan Marriage, Divorce and Succession Act, Laws of Kenya, CAP 156 (2008); Hindu Marriage and Divorce Act, Laws of Kenya CAP 157 (2008).

[192] See Marriage Act § 37. See also Eugene Cotran, *Restatement of African Law: Kenya, Vol. 1 (The Law of Marriage and Divorce)* (London: Sweet & Maxwell, 1968), 1; Catherine A. Hardee, "Balancing Act: The Rights of Women and Cultural Minorities in Kenyan Marital Law," *New York University Law Review* 79 (2004): 712–749; Laurence Juma, "Reconciling African Customary Law and Human Rights in Kenya: Making a Case for Institutional Reformation and Revitalization of Customary Adjudication Process," *St. Thomas Law Review* 14 (2002): 459–512.

[193] Matrimonial Causes Act, Laws of Kenya, CAP 152 § 3 (2008).

[194] Cotran, *Restatement of African Law: Kenya, Vol. 1*, 1.

[195] Marriage Act, § 11.

[196] Marriage Act, §§ 3–18, 29, 32–34.

[197] Marriage Act, §§ 14, 25, 29.

the first three years after marriage except in exceptional circumstances, and there is a possibility for legal separation before divorce.[198]

African Christian marriage is very closely related to civil marriage. It is only available to African couples where at least one party is a Christian; other couples must use some other religious law, customary law, or avail themselves of the regular civil marriage procedures.[199] There is a separate statute governing African Christian marriage, but the effect of the statute is simply to relax a number of required entrance formalities (such as longer registration periods, easier preliminary notice requirements, and the like).[200] There is no separate statute for divorce; the Matrimonial Causes Act still governs the African Christian divorce.[201]

African Christian marriage contains two other distinguishing features. First, it explicitly provides for the conversion of customary marriages into Christian marriages.[202] This is a unique feature of African Christian marriage, as no other marriages can be "converted" under statutory law. Second, the statute provides additional protection for widows by forbidding the practice of widow inheritance (wherein a widow automatically becomes the wife of her deceased husband's brother) and mandating that the widow become the guardian of the children of the marriage so long as she remains a Christian.[203]

Islam. Marriage and divorce law for Kenyan Muslims is codified, but it exhibits a great amount of deference to Islamic law generally and potentially varies greatly from other forms of marriage and divorce.[204] The Muslim Act states that Muslim marriages are valid if contracted in accordance with Islamic law, and it further states that questions of validity and divorce shall be governed by Islamic law. The statute does *not* define the nature of that law, except that the burden of proof is on the party alleging that a practice is in accordance with Islamic law.[205] This allows room for polygamy, nonjudicial divorce, and other grounds of dissolution as defined by Islamic law generally. The Muslim Act does not delineate any grounds for divorce other than "any relief by way of divorce or otherwise which can be had, granted or obtained according to Mohammedan law"; Muslims do not fall under the Matrimonial Causes Act.[206] Jurisdiction in Muslim divorce cases lies both with

---

[198] Matrimonial Causes Act, Laws of Kenya, CAP 152 Part II (2008). See also Subordinate Courts (Separation and Maintenance Act), Laws of Kenya, CAP 153 (2008).

[199] African Christian Marriage and Divorce Act § 3(1).

[200] African Christian Marriage and Divorce Act. See also Hardee, "Balancing Act," 723–724.

[201] Cotran, *Restatement of African Law: Kenya, Vol. 1,* 2–4.

[202] African Christian Marriage and Divorce Act § 9.

[203] African Christian Marriage and Divorce Act § 13.

[204] Mohammedan Marriage, Divorce and Succession Act, Laws of Kenya, CAP 156 (2008).

[205] Mohammedan Marriage, Divorce and Succession Act §§ 2–3.

[206] Mohammedan Marriage, Divorce and Succession Act § 3(1).

Islamic courts (*Kadhi* courts) and civil courts – although the civil court is bound to apply Islamic law in relevant cases.

Hinduism. Marriage and divorce for Hindus bears many similarities to the African Christian Marriage Act and the Civil Marriage Act. The prime governing law is the Hindu Marriage and Divorce Act,[207] which is "largely based on the Hindu Marriage Act of India."[208] The Hindu Act expressly provides that marriages may only be between two Hindus – thereby requiring marriages to be monogamous and consequently disallowing the traditional Hindu practice of polygamy.[209] The Hindu Act allows for some variation and allowance to custom regarding marriage formation, and it similarly provides regulation regarding entrance to marriage (capacity, registration, and the like).[210]

Divorce under the Hindu Act is effectively limited to judicial divorce for cause. Like African Christian marriage, matters of divorce and separation are subject to the Matrimonial Causes Act and the Subordinate Courts (Separation and Maintenance) Act, provided there is no conflict with the Hindu Act.[211] The Hindu Act adds three additional fault grounds for divorce: religious conversion by the spouse; the spouse's entering a religious order; or judicial separation for two or more years.[212]

Customary Law. Outside of these statutory systems of marriage and divorce, Kenya's laws expressly provide for recognition of traditional, customary (or tribal) marriages.[213] The laws regarding customary marriage and divorce vary from tribe to tribe, with jurisdiction generally exercised by the elders of the community. Customary marriage is potentially polygamous, depending on the custom of any particular tribe.[214] When customary marriages break down, divorce matters are typically first heard by the tribal elders. If the dispute rises to the level of the civil judicial system, the civil courts are directed to apply the customary law of the parties.[215] Because of the reliance on custom as the driving force, there is no system for registration of

---

[207] Hindu Marriage and Divorce Act, Laws of Kenya, CAP 157 (2008).
[208] Cotran, *Restatement of African Law: Kenya, Vol. 1*, 5.
[209] Hindu Marriage and Divorce Act §§ 2, 3(a), 7(3).
[210] Hindu Marriage and Divorce Act §§ 3, 5, 6.
[211] Hindu Marriage and Divorce Act §§ 7(5), 9, 10.
[212] Hindu Marriage and Divorce Act § 10(1).
[213] See Marriage Act § 37 ("[N]othing in this Act contained shall affect the validity of any marriage contracted under or in accordance with any native law or custom, or in any manner apply to marriages so contracted."). See also Mohammedan Marriage, Divorce, and Succession Act § 6 (stating that a preexisting customary marriage is a bar to entering a Muslim marriage). For more on customary marriages, see the next section in this chapter regarding South Africa and sources cited therein.
[214] See Hardee, "Balancing Act," 727–728; Juma, "Reconciling African Customary Law and Human Rights," 477–485.
[215] See Hardee, "Balancing Act," 727–728.

marriage, for reporting of marriage or divorces, or for handing down decisions of
local tribunals regarding personal law matters.

2. Choice of Forum: *Kadhi* Courts

In addition to multiple categories of personal laws, and the effective choice of
forum for customary law mentioned in the previous subsection, Kenyan law has
long permitted decisional authority over "personal status, marriage, divorce or
inheritance in proceedings in which all the parties profess the Muslim religion" to
reside with Muslim religious courts, called *Kadhi* courts.[216] These courts developed
in Kenya's coastal areas even before the colonial British arrived, and the British
system retained them. When Kenya drafted its 1967 constitution, it specifically textually recognized *Kadhi* courts and their authority and passed a supplementary
"Kadhi Courts Act" that further spelled out their jurisdiction and capabilities as a
legitimate subordinate court.[217]

Critics of *Kadhi* courts assailed the carve-out for Islamic courts on various grounds.
They contended such courts ran counter to the separation of church and state in
Kenya, violated equal treatment of religions, and perpetuated gender inequities.
On May 24, 2010, Kenya's High Court issued a landmark ruling that the inclusion
of *Kadhi* courts in the Constitution of Kenya violated principles of nondiscrimination, constitutionalism, and separation of church and state as embodied in sections
70, 78, and 82 of the then-current constitution. Citing sources from Kenyan history,
comparative constitutionalism, and commentary and jurisprudence from the U.S.
experience, the court declared that religious courts should not form any part of the
hierarchy of courts in Kenya because that would violate the principle of separation
of church and state.[218] (The High Court cited extensively the U.S. Supreme Court
case of *Engel v. Vitale*, striking down government-led prayer in public schools, to
bolster its rationale that public funding of religious costs undermines the necessary
separation between church and state.) This was a curious ruling in that it seemingly
pitted differing parts of the constitution against each other, with a resulting holding
that one part of the constitution was, itself, unconstitutional. The High Court did
not rule on the petitioners' prayer to disallow the inclusion of *Kadhi* courts in the
new draft constitution.

In August 2010, Kenyans ratified a new constitution that legitimized *Kadhi* courts
once again. Section 170 of the new constitution repeats the jurisdictional reach

---

[216] Constitution of Kenya (rev. 2008), article 66(5), available at http://www.cabinetoffice.go.ke/index.
php?option=com_docman&task=doc_download&gid=5&Itemid=67.
[217] Ibid. See also Laws of Kenya, Chapter 11, Kadhis Courts Act.
[218] Case of *Jesse Kamau & 25 Others v. Attorney General* [2010] Kenya Law Reports, available at http://
kenyalaw.org/Downloads_FreeCases/73988.pdf.

of *Kadhi* courts from the prior constitution, and Section 24 of the constitution includes a specific statement that provisions on equality within the constitutional bill of rights shall be qualified "to the extent strictly necessary" to accommodate *Kadhi* courts.[219] Prior to ratifying the new constitution, Christian leaders and politicians (who vastly outnumber Muslims in Kenya) argued that continued recognition of *Kadhi* courts would "lead to the nullification of other religions" and created an "Islamic state within a state."[220] Muslims, in turn, argued that including *Kadhi* courts as a choice of forum for personal law matters was essential to protecting the religious freedom of the minority Muslim community, because Muslims "do not separate the secular from the sacred."[221] It is unlikely that the ratification of the new constitution has settled these concerns about *Kadhi* courts, but at present they continue to operate lawfully for Muslims with the jurisdictional authority of the state.

C. South Africa

South Africa provides the foremost example of a country intentionally structuring its laws in an attempt to protect religious and minority rights, including marriage and divorce. Its history is part of the driving force behind its institutional recognition of multi-tiered laws.[222] A former colony of the Dutch and then the British, South Africa united in the early twentieth century and soon began the policy of separation that characterized it until the 1990s. The exclusion of black South Africans (and others) from the political process under the system of apartheid left an indelible and lasting impact on the current nation. The first multiracial election was held in 1994, when Nelson Mandela was elected president, and the current constitution was ratified in 1996. That constitution, and subsequent law making, have consciously taken South Africa's history into account and have tried to ensure minority rights and equality, in part by preserving customary and religious practices of all systems. This has laid the groundwork for a multi-tiered personal law system.[223]

---

[219] The Constitution of Kenya (2010), §§ 24, 170.

[220] "Kadhi Courts and the Clamor for a New Constitution," May 2, 2010, available at http://kenyapolitical. blogspot.com/2010/05/kadhi-courts-and-clamor-for-new.html; National Council of Churches of Kenya, *Statement from Kenyan Christian Leaders*, Feb. 1, 2010, available at http://www.ncck.org/index. php?option=com_content&view=article&id=146&Itemid=29.

[221] "Kadhi Courts and the Clamor for a New Constitution."

[222] See Leonard Thompson, *A History of South Africa* (New Haven: Yale University Press, 3d ed. 2001); Rodney Davenport and Christopher Saunders, *South Africa: A Modern History* (Hampshire: MacMillan Press; New York: St. Martin's Press, 5th ed. 2000); Christa Rautenbach, "Deep Legal Pluralism in South Africa: Judicial Accommodation of Non-State Law," *Journal of Legal Pluralism and Unofficial Law* 60 (2010): 143–177.

[223] Johan van der Vyver, "Multi-Tiered Marriages in South Africa" (in this volume).

Under apartheid, there was a two-fold system of courts with jurisdiction over personal law matters, as black South Africans were subjected to a separate (and inferior) court system.[224] During the 1990s, tribal divorce courts were conclusively abolished and jurisdiction over divorce matters was transferred to newly formed civil family courts.[225] Today, customary tribal courts do not have power to issue binding decisions in marital disputes, although they retain mediation authority.[226]

Although there was duality in personal law under apartheid, it was carried forward in a way that continued to subjugate the black South African populace and continued to relegate them to second-class status. With the advent of the new constitution and subsequent laws, there is recognition not just of alternative systems of marriages, but an intentional legal movement to accord equal status to those different personal law regimes. The two statutorily recognized forms of marriage and divorce law are civil (Christian) marriage and customary marriage.[227] There is also continued discussion of passing legislation regarding Muslim marriages and maybe others, such as Hindu marriages.[228]

1. Civil/Christian Marriage

The laws relevant to civil and Christian marriage are the Marriage Act (1961) and the Divorce Act (1979).[229] Civil marriage in South Africa is similar to marriage in the United States.[230] Under the Divorce Act, couples may petition for divorce in a High Court or a family court. The only available grounds for divorce are (1) irretrievable breakdown of the marriage and (2) the mental illness or the continuous unconsciousness of a party to the marriage.[231] Irretrievable breakdown grounds may be founded on adultery, separation for one year or more, or imprisonment of the

---

[224] See T. W. Bennett, *Customary Law in South Africa* (Lansdowne: Juta and Company Ltd., 2004), 139–150.

[225] Magistrates Courts Amendment Act of 1993, Act No. 120 of 1993. If there is no family court in the area, jurisdiction lies with the High Court. Divorce Act No. 70 of 1979; Customary Marriages Act No. 120 of 1998 § 1(i). Appeals from the family courts are to the High Courts, and appeals from the High Courts are to the Supreme Court of Appeal.

[226] See Bennett, *Customary Law in South Africa*, 143.

[227] South African law also recognizes same-sex unions via its Civil Union Law (Civil Union Act 17 of 2006), but these do not alter the jurisdictional discussions in this chapter. For more discussion, see van der Vyver, "Multi-Tiered Marriages in South Africa" (in this volume).

[228] The civil law also recognizes that Jewish law has special problems operating under the state system because of the potential nonissuance of a *get*. Therefore, the Divorce Act of 1979 was amended in 1996 to require that a religious divorce be granted before a civil divorce may be granted. Divorce Act No. 70 (1979) § 5A.

[229] Act No. 25 of 1961; Act No. 70 of 1979.

[230] See David L. Chambers, "Civilizing the Natives: Marriage in Post-Apartheid South Africa," *Daedalus* 129:4 (2000): 101–124, 103.

[231] Divorce Act §§ 1, 3–5.

defendant – all of which constitute evidence that the "marriage has reached such a state of disintegration that there is no reasonable prospect of the restoration of a normal marriage relationship between [the parties]."[232]

Under the old South African government, there was a clear preference in the law for the civil/Christian form of marriage over customary marriages. Civil/Christian marriage was the form practiced by white South Africans. Black South Africans retained a choice to marry either under civil law or their customary law, but civil/Christian marriages were considered superior to customary marriages. For example, if a couple married by civil or Christian rites – that is, if they married in one of the established churches or a civil registry office – the common law applied to their marriage. And if the couple chose to combine civil/Christian ceremonies with traditional ceremonies, the marriage would be governed by common law because the law presumed dominance of the civil/Christian marriage over the customary elements.[233] This distinction matters less since the passage of the 1998 Recognition of Customary Marriages Act, but there is still a presumption in the law that the civil or Christian ceremony is the default.

2. Customary Marriage

In the early twentieth century, South Africa recognized customary marriages after the passage of the Native Administration Act (1927), but customary marriages were given inferior status at law. Five salient features typically distinguished customary unions from the otherwise prevailing civil model of marriage: (1) customary marriages permitted polygamy[234]; (2) the validity of the customary union depended on *lobolo* (a payment of bridewealth)[235]; (3) the relationship in a customary union was between two families, rather than two individuals; (4) the customary union was achieved gradually over time, rather than through a single ceremony; and (5) the customary marriage was a private affair that needed no intervention from civil or religious authorities.[236]

In 1996, the Bill of Rights in the new constitution granted Parliament the right to pass legislation "recognizing marriages concluded under any tradition, or a

---

[232] Divorce Act § 4.

[233] See Bennett, *Customary Law in South Africa*, 57–60.

[234] The potentially polygamous nature of customary marriage was a major reason for its inferior treatment by those in power. See Johan D. van der Vyver, "State Sponsored Proselytization: A South African Experience," *Emory International Law Review* 14 (2000): 779–848, 832.

[235] *Lobolo* is the practice wherein the groom and his family enter into highly stylized negotiations with the parents of the bride and agree on an amount of bridewealth; the groom then pays the *lobolo* to the bride's parents. See Chambers, "Civilizing the Natives," 103; Bennett, *Customary Law in South Africa*, 236–242.

[236] See Bennett, *Customary Law in South Africa*, 188.

system of religious, personal or family law."[237] It further imposed a duty on the government to eradicate laws that discriminated against customary marriages in order to encourage religious and cultural diversity. To this end, the South African Law Commission's Special Project Committee on Customary Law investigated the reform of customary law to implement the Bill of Rights and promote African legal heritage.[238] The committee submitted a report to Parliament, which agreed to nearly all of its recommendations and passed the Recognition of Customary Marriages Act (RCMA) in 1998.[239]

The main purposes of the RCMA are to give full recognition to existing customary marriages and to stipulate requirements for future customary marriages.[240] The RCMA also accords full legal status to customary marriages and does away with the prior favoritism for civil/Christian marriages. In the words of Deputy Justice Minister Cheryl Gillwald at the inception of the RCMA on November 15, 2000: The act "brings to an end the tyranny of dictatorial recognition of civil and other Eurocentric faith-based marriages at the expense of marriages concluded in accordance with customary law."[241]

The RCMA defines "customary marriage" as "a marriage concluded in accordance with customary law."[242] Customary law, in turn, is defined as "the customs and usages traditionally observed among the indigenous African peoples of South Africa and which form part of the culture of those peoples."[243] There are two statutory requirements for a customary marriage to be valid: (1) Both prospective spouses must be at least eighteen years old and must consent to being married to each other under customary law; and (2) "The marriage must be negotiated and entered into or celebrated in accordance with customary law."[244] Because there is no single definition of customary law, the RCMA allows a wide variation in practices and custom. Even so, there are a few common characteristics of customary marriage formation. Usually a couple is considered married by their customary or tribal community group only after the completion of a lengthy process; there is not a once-in-time

---

[237] South African Const. § 15(3)(a)(i).

[238] See Bennett, *Customary Law in South Africa*, 193.

[239] Recognition of Customary Marriages Act (1998). See also Bennett, *Customary Law in South Africa*, 194; Andrew P. Kult, "Intestate Succession in South Africa: The 'Westernization' of Customary Law Practices Within a Modern Constitutional Framework," *Indiana International and Comparative Law Review* 11 (2001): 697–729, 717–718.

[240] See Kult, "Intestate Succession in South Africa," 718; Bennett, *Customary Law in South Africa*, 194.

[241] Keynote address by Deputy Minister of Justice and Constitutional Development Cheryl Gillwald, MP, at the launch of the Recognition of Customary Marriages Act No. 120 of 1998, Nov. 15, 2000, available at http://www.info.gov.za/speeches/2000/00112110101a1006.htm.

[242] Recognition of Customary Marriages Act § 1(iii).

[243] Recognition of Customary Marriages Act § 1(ii).

[244] Recognition of Customary Marriages Act § 3(1).

ceremony as in civil or Christian marriages. The customary process usually includes payment of all or part of *lobolo* (a bride price), performance of some kind of (widely varying) ceremony, and, for some groups, a period of cohabitation or the birth of a child.[245] Under the RCMA, *lobolo* has effectively become a contractual accessory to marriage, with its payment typically signifying that a union is a customary form of marriage.[246] Many South Africans are still strongly attached to the practice, as it stands as a "symbol that the wife is valued, as a mark of the bond between families, as compensation to the bride's parents for the cost and effort to raise her, and, today, as a symbol of continuity with African traditions."[247]

One of the main purposes of the RCMA was to set up a registration system for customary marriages and divorces and thereby bring such marriages more under the aegis of the civil court system. It thus imposes a duty on the spouses to register their marriage, although failure to register does not affect the validity of the marriage.[248] The RCMA altered the customary law by adding age and consent requirements and by granting the spouses equal status and capacity[249] – but it did not abolish polygamy.[250] A husband who wishes to enter an additional customary marriage must simply apply to the court to "approve a written contract which will regulate the future matrimonial property system of his marriages."[251] This is supposed to ensure the fair treatment of the first wife/wives and will vary according to the property system that governs the marriage.[252]

The RCMA markedly changed the process and grounds for divorce. Whereas dissolution of marriage under customary law was traditionally handled by the families or the local community, the RCMA requires a civil judge to grant a divorce under codified grounds. These grounds mirror those in the Divorce Act (1979), applicable to civil/Christian marriage, and bring more uniformity to access to divorce.[253] Thus, the codification of customary marriage law has had the dual effect of legitimizing the status of customary marriage (by according it equal legal status with

---

[245] See Chambers, "Civilizing the Natives," 103–104.
[246] See Bennett, *Customary Law in South Africa*, 236.
[247] Ibid., 235.
[248] Recognition of Customary Marriages Act §§ 4 (1), (9).
[249] Recognition of Customary Marriages Act § 6; Chuma Himonga, "Transforming Customary Law of Marriage in South Africa and the Challenges of Its Implementation with Specific Reference to Matrimonial Property," *International Journal of Legal Information* 32 (2004): 260–270, 264.
[250] Recognition of Customary Marriages Act § 2(3)-(4).
[251] Recognition of Customary Marriages Act § 7(6).
[252] All preexisting marriages will continue to be ruled by the property system of customary law, and marriages entered into after the commencement of the act are in community of property unless the spouses opt out with an antenuptial contract. Recognition of Customary Marriages Act § 7(1)-(2).
[253] Recognition of Customary Marriages Act § 8.

civil/Christian marriage) but also altering it (by requiring that marriage registration and all of divorce proceed through civil channels).[254]

3. Muslim Marriage

Just as customary marriages were initially disfavored (and not recognized legally) in South Africa because of their potentially polygamous nature, so too were Muslim and Hindu marriages disfavored. Although the RCMA has given customary marriages full recognition, Muslim and Hindu marriages still have not obtained statutory status.[255] As it did with customary marriage, the South African Law Commission undertook to investigate Islamic marriage. Beginning in 1999, the commission published several documents related to Islamic marriages,[256] culminating in a July 2003 report and attached draft bill on Muslim marriages.[257] To date, this proposal has not been enacted into law.[258]

A major obstacle is the permissibility of polygamy within Islam, notwithstanding the statutory permissibility of polygamy under RCMA for customary marriages. The report and draft bill do not propose to eliminate polygamy entirely, but they would limit the circumstances under which it is legally permitted and recognized.[259] For example, (1) a spouse in a Muslim marriage would not be able to subsequently marry under any other law during the subsistence of the Muslim marriage; (2) the court would have to "grant approval [that] it is satisfied that the husband is able to maintain equality between his spouses as is prescribed by the Holy Qur'an"; and (3) polygamy without permission of the court would be punishable by a fine.[260] The draft bill further proposes to remove Muslim marriages from the community property regime and also proposes that a husband wishing to subsequently marry must apply to the court for a contract for the future regulation of matrimonial property in his marriages.[261]

---

[254] David L. Chambers, "Civilizing the Natives: Customary Marriage in Post-Apartheid South Africa," in *Engaging Cultural Differences: The Multicultural Challenge in Liberal Democracies*, eds. Richard Shweder, Martha Minow, and Hazel Rose Markus (New York: Russell Sage Foundation, 2002), 81 (stating that RCMA "inject[s] the state bureaucracy into the regulation of customary marriages").

[255] van der Vyver, "State Sponsored Proselytization," 837; Rashida Manjoo, "Legislative Recognition of Muslim Marriages in South Africa," *International Journal of Legal Information* 32 (2004): 271–282, 273.

[256] These documents include an Issue Paper (May 2000), a Discussion Paper (Dec. 2001), a Bill (Oct. 2002), and an amended draft Bill (July 2003).

[257] See South African Law Reform Commission, Project 59, Islamic Marriages and Related Matters Report, July 2003, available at http://www.justice.gov.za/salrc/reports/r_prj59_2003jul.pdf.

[258] See discussion in van der Vyver, "Multi-Tiered Marriages in South Africa" (in this volume).

[259] Draft Bill § 8(6).

[260] Draft Bill §§ 5(2), 8(6)(a), 8(11).

[261] Draft Bill §§ 8(1), 8(6).

The draft bill also proposes changes to the husband's right to irrevocable *talaq* by bringing it more into the civil registration system. A divorce would have to be registered in the nearest magisterial district within thirty days of its pronouncement and a spouse would then need to seek a legal decree within fourteen days after registration.[262] This all substantially varies from the traditional form of *talaq* divorce, which was strictly a private matter. The draft bill instead specifically provides that Muslim divorce will be under the same civil jurisdiction as other systems of marriage – beginning in the High Courts or family courts with appeals to the Supreme Court of Appeals. The draft bill proposes that the court would be assisted in an advisory capacity by two Muslim assessors who have specialized knowledge of Islamic law, and appeals would be submitted to two Muslim institutions for written comment on questions of law within sixty days. The Supreme Court of Appeals would have to give due regard to the written comments.[263] Thus, the result would be that the civil court system will be applying Islamic law – albeit with deference to the interpretation of religious authorities. Additionally, if the Muslim parties were married in a civil marriage and wish to dissolve it, the court will not grant the civil divorce until it is satisfied that the accompanying Muslim marriage has been dissolved.[264]

In sum, South Africa has moved to consolidate jurisdiction over marriage and divorce in the civil court system. It has long done so for Christian marriages. It has more recently attempted to consolidate jurisdiction of customary marriages, via the RCMA, though giving civil recognition to customary ceremonies and practices, including polygamy. But divorces for customary marriages have been altered and made more uniform with the grounds available to civil (Christian) marriages. And South Africa has not yet fully tackled the difficult questions of the intersection and overlap of Muslim (or Hindu) marriage and divorce with the protective role of the civil courts.

D. *Canada*

India, Kenya, and South Africa do not exhaust the comparative possibilities and models, of course. Commentators also frequently adduce Israel, where personal law is administered not by civil courts but primarily by religious tribunals. Rabbinical courts govern marriage and divorce law for Jews, and other "religious courts" govern adherents of other faiths; only a limited number of religious groups are recognized, however, and there is not a residual category of secular civil law

---

[262] Draft Bill §§ 9(3)(a), 9(3)(f).
[263] Draft Bill § 15.
[264] Draft Bill § 16(1).

in some subject areas (including marriage).[265] Civil courts retain a right to entertain appeals, but their grounds for reversal are essentially limited to procedural matters.[266]

Even more enlightening is the example of Canada. As several other authors in this volume elaborate, Canada has recently struggled with matters of multicultural accommodation, religious pluralism, and liberal ideals at the intersection of marriage and divorce law.[267] In 2007, the Supreme Court of Canada allowed damages on a breach-of-contract claim when an Orthodox Jewish husband failed to give his wife a *get* even though he had agreed to do so in a settlement agreement that led to the civil divorce.[268] Rather than avoiding the case entirely because of its religious aspects, the decision demonstrated how the civil and religious systems could interact in ways that "recogni[ze] that both the secular and religious aspects of divorce matter greatly to observant women"[269] and reaffirmed that the civil court had a role to play in the intersection of the two.

This 2007 case, *Marcovitz v. Bruker*, highlights a contractual model of interaction that seeks to empower individuals to incorporate aspects of religious marriage and divorce into a legally enforceable structure. In *Marcovitz*, that structure was a settlement agreement, but the more prevalent structure is an agreement containing choice-of-forum and choice-of-law clauses. In that model, individuals exercise their freedom of contract to opt into an arbitral board of their choosing to resolve disputes – including a religious arbitral board with binding authority, applying religious understandings of law. This arbitration model received substantial attention in Ontario over the past few years.

Legislators in Ontario passed the Arbitration Act of 1991 to provide an alternative to settling disputes within the court system. The act allowed parties to choose the law under which the arbitration would be conducted, and the plain language of the statute seemed to indicate that any law (not just various provincial laws) would be permitted.[270] This meant that, in practice, Christians, Jews, Muslims, and people

---

[265] Yüksel Sezgin, "A Political Account for Legal Confrontation Between State and Society: The Case of Israeli Legal Pluralism," *Studies in Law, Politics and Society* 32 (2004): 213–222; Galanter and Krishnan, "Personal Law and Human Rights," 122; Alan Reed, "Transnational Non-Judicial Divorces: A Comparative Analysis of Recognition Under English and U.S. Jurisprudence," *Loyola of Los Angeles International and Comparative Law Journal* 18 (1996): 311–337, 328.

[266] See Ruth Lapidoth, "Freedom of Religion and Conscience in Israel," *Catholic University Law Review* 47 (1998): 441–465, 462–464.; see Reed, "Western Democracy and Islamic Tradition" 499–500.

[267] See, e.g., Cere, "Canadian Conjugal Mosaic" (in this volume); Fadel, "Political Liberalism" (in this volume); McClain, "Marriage Pluralism in the United States" (in this volume); Shachar, "Faith in Law?" (in this volume).

[268] *Marcovitz v. Bruker*, 2007 SCC 54.

[269] Shachar, "Faith in Law?" (in this volume).

[270] Arbitration Act, S.O., ch. 17, 32(1) (1991) (Can.) ("In deciding a dispute, an arbitral tribunal shall apply the rules of law designated by the parties.").

of other faith traditions could arbitrate their disputes, including family law disputes, according to the principles of their faith. (In fact, this statute simply formalized what was already a settled practice, in which "family matters [had been] arbitrated based on religious teachings for many years in Jewish, Muslim, and Christian settings.")[271] In addition, the act required Ontario courts to "uphold arbitrators' decisions if both sides enter the process voluntarily and if results are fair, equitable, and do not violate Canadian law."[272]

This system functioned without much attention paid to it until the fall of 2003, when Syed Mumtaz Ali announced that the Islamic Institute of Civil Justice (IICJ) had been established "to ensure that Islamic principles of family and inheritance law could be used to resolve disputes within the Muslim community in Canada."[273] Ali's statements to the media about the IICJ created public concern that Ontario had granted special rights to *shari'a* courts to settle disputes between Muslims. Citizens and citizens' groups brought their concerns to the Ontarian government, which authorized a former attorney general, Marion Boyd, to investigate the current system of arbitration.[274] That thorough investigation led to a 2004 report endorsing the continued use of arbitration as an alternative dispute resolution mechanism in family law – albeit with certain recommendations for improvement to ensure consent and promote equality.[275]

The report was not received favorably by the public. The province adopted many of the *Boyd Report*'s procedural recommendations. But it firmly rejected the notion that a choice-of-law clause selecting religious law for the family law arbitration could be valid. Instead, all family law arbitration in the province must be conducted exclusively under Ontarian and Canadian law. This decision was proclaimed on the tell-tale date of September 11, 2005, as Premier Dalton McGuinty announced: "There will be no *shari'a* law in Ontario. There will be no religious arbitration in Ontario. There will be one law for all Ontarians."[276] Ontarian law now states that "[i]n a family arbitration, the arbitral tribunal shall apply the substantive law of Ontario, unless the parties expressly designate the substantive law of another Canadian jurisdiction,

---

[271] Marion Boyd, *Dispute Resolution in Family Law: Protecting Choice, Promoting Inclusion* (2004), 4, available at http://www.attorneygeneral.jus.gov.on.ca/english/about/pubs/boyd/fullreport.pdf.

[272] Arbitration Act, S.O., ch. 17, 34, 46 (1991) (Can.).

[273] See Boyd, *Dispute Resolution in Family Law*, 3.

[274] Ibid., 3–6.

[275] Ibid. Boyd's recommendations called for more government involvement to oversee and evaluate arbitration, education and training for arbitrators, education for the public about the arbitration process, and a requirement that parties to arbitrations obtain independent legal advice.

[276] See Prithi Yelaga and Robert Benzie, "McGuinty: No Sharia Law," *The Toronto Star*, Sept. 12, 2005, A1. Quebec has taken the same position. While Ontario was still debating its use, lawmakers in Quebec "unanimously rejected use of Islamic tribunals in its legal system." Les Perreaux, "Quebec Rejects Islamic Law," *The Toronto Star*, May 27, 2005, A8.

in which case that substantive law shall be applied."[277] This effectively not only cut off the rights of Muslims to settle disputes in family matters under Islamic law, but eliminated the rights of other religious traditions as well, including the rabbinic courts that had been present and practicing in Ontario since 1889.[278]

Although formal Ontarian law is once again uniform and civil courts will not enforce family arbitrations that purport to apply religious law, this does not mean that religious arbitrations have ceased. Rather, according to Attorney General Boyd, religious arbitrations (especially Muslim arbitrations) have "merely become invisible to official law without ceasing operations."[279] This demonstrates again that the civil law is more limited in its ability to gain the exclusive adherence of all its citizens than is sometimes believed. It is situations like this that gave rise to Anglican Archbishop Rowan Williams suggesting in 2008 that some sort of "accommodation" of Muslim family law is "unavoidable."[280] The archbishop was trying to recognize the lived-reality of individuals' religious commitments while also balancing the needs of the liberal state to protect its citizens and promote liberty and equality. It does not necessarily follow that the civil state achieves the balance it seeks when it claims to exercise exclusive jurisdiction over marriage, as some may continue their own practices but without state endorsement or enforcement. The situation of Muslims in Ontario (and that of Orthodox Jews in New York) illustrates that principle.

V. CONCLUSION

In the midst of a national debate about the meaning and definition of marriage, we would be well served to acknowledge that our multiplicity of citizens is unlikely to agree on a singular answer. This leads to at least two possible conclusions – either (1) rule by majoritarian voice or (2) allowance for variation in understandings of marriage and divorce. In recent decades and in current academic discourse, the first

---

[277] Family Statute Law Amendment Act, S.O. c.1, 32 (2006) (Can.), available at http://www.ontla.on.ca/Library/bills/382/27382.htm. In addition, the explanatory note to the amendment states that "[t]he term 'family arbitration' is applied only to processes conducted exclusively in accordance with the law of Ontario or of another Canadian jurisdiction. Other third-party decision-making processes in family matters are not family arbitrations and have no legal effect." Ibid.

[278] See Ron Csillag, "Jewish Groups Say New Bill Targets Beit Dins," *Canadian Jewish News*, Jan. 26, 2006, 5.

[279] Prakash Shah, "A Reflection on the *Shari'a* Debate in Britain," *Studia z Prawa Wyznaniowego (Studies of Ecclesiastical Law)* 13 (2010): 71–98 (citing Marion Boyd, "The Past, Present and Future of Arbitration in Religious Contexts: Reflections on Ontario Law in a Comparative Context." Lecture given at the Institute of Advanced Studies, London [July 10, 2009]).

[280] Dr. Rowan Williams, "Archbishop's Lecture – Civil and Religious Law in England: A Religious Perspective," Feb. 7, 2008, available at http://www.archbishopofcanterbury.org/1575#. See Witte and Nichols, "The Frontiers of Marital Pluralism" (in this volume); Ahdar and Aroney, *Shari'a in the West*.

option has been the theme at American law. But there are signs – in Louisiana, New York, and elsewhere – that we may be willing to consider recognizing our pluralism and reifying that into law. There are historical antecedents for recognizing different models of marriage and divorce jurisdiction. And there are also strong examples from comparative law that can serve as guides – and as warnings.

Moving toward multi-tiered marriage need not mean – indeed, *should* not mean – that we must abandon the central protections for women and children that we have assiduously worked to obtain and implement. Nor should it mean that the state must sanction actions and behavior that undermine core values of equality. But it is simply not the case that the foundational values of liberal democracy demand that the civil state institute exclusive jurisdictional control over a unitary, least-common-denominator system of marriage and divorce law.

If capable and competent parties desire to enter more binding unions under the auspices of their religious traditions, they should be free to do so. If religious communities desire to draw upon their own theological and legal resources to aid in governing their adherents, they should be able to do so. And if the civil authorities are satisfied that women and children will be adequately protected, then the civil state need not be jealous and continue to act as if alternative jurisdictional structures are not already functioning. The real question, instead, is whether the civil law can work in more cooperative and fruitful ways with those alternative, already-operating jurisdictional structures – both to recognize the state's legitimate claims as protectors and enforcers of common values and also to respect the fact that such alternative jurisdictional structures have strong normative, authoritative claims over adherents regardless of state recognition.

Despite the claim that state law is unitary and uniform, it is not. We can see bellwethers of multi-tiered marriage in current state laws – and the possibility for further reform and variation exists. We can see a history in the West of shared or complementary jurisdiction over family law – and the possibility for the reemergence of the same is just in front of us. We can see various ways to implement multi-tiered marriage through the examples of other nations in the international community – and perhaps the way forward lies in looking to and learning from those examples.

2

Pluralism and Decentralization in Marriage Regulation

Brian H. Bix

This chapter explores the role of the state in regulating marriage in the United States and what that role should be, given the growing set of alternative marriage options and the increasing decentralization of marriage regulation.[1] "State role" here is understood both broadly, as the governmental role at any level, and more specifically, as the relative roles of the federal and state governments within the U.S. federal system.

This exploration will reflect both the general sense that governments will inevitably face a growing diversity and decentralization of marriage options and the view (expressed, for example, in Joel Nichols's article,[2] in some of my own work,[3] and elsewhere[4]) that greater diversity and decentralization could be a good idea. To some extent, I will consider a level of pluralism and decentralization that may not come about (and may be unlikely ever to come about) to examine the potential attractions (and repulsions) of that alternative world. However, the fact remains that current family law doctrine, rules of federalism, and conflict-of-laws principles

---

[1]   This chapter eschews discussion of the additional complications arising from the combination of marriage pluralism *across* jurisdictions (which includes not only same-sex marriages and domestic partnerships recognized by other countries but also legally recognized polygamy, legally enforced religious marriage and divorce rules, and the like) with international travel and immigration, which, combined, raise the question of how or to what extent American governments should or must recognize the foreign marital status in such cases.

[2]   Joel A. Nichols, "Multi-Tiered Marriage: Ideas and Influences from New York and Louisiana to the International Community," *Vanderbilt Journal of Transnational Law* 40 (January 2007): 135–196; and see John Witte Jr. and Joel A. Nichols, "The Frontiers of Marital Pluralism: An Afterword" (in this volume).

[3]   Brian H. Bix, "State Interests in Marriage, Interstate Recognition, and Choice of Law," *Creighton Law Review* 38 (February 2005): 337–351; Brian H. Bix, "The Public and Private Ordering of Marriage," *University of Chicago Legal Forum* (2004): 295–318.

[4]   Eric Rasmusen and Jeffrey Evans Stake, "Lifting the Veil of Ignorance: Personalizing the Marriage Contract," *Indiana Law Journal* 73 (Spring 1998): 453–502; Larry E. Ribstein, "A Standard Form Approach to Marriage," *Creighton Law Review* 38 (February 2005): 309–335.

collectively hobble the ability of states to effectuate policies in this area. The overall consequence is a certain level of de facto pluralism and decentralization, and one might reasonably explore whether increasing that pluralism and decentralization would do more good than harm.

To a significant extent, pluralism and decentralization in this area reflect a different role for the state: primarily as supportive of individual and community ideas of marriage (within limits), rather than primarily as establishing the norms of behavior or clarifying the collective understanding of the institution.

Section I of this chapter reviews some of the sources of pluralism and decentralization in American marriage law and practice. Section II discusses possible paths to pluralism and decentralization. Section III considers the possible state and societal interests in uniformity. Section IV discusses the nature of marriage and the role of the state. Section V summarizes the limits the government might place on marriage variety. Finally, Section VI introduces some constitutional aspects of the present debate.

I. CURRENT AND GROWING VARIETY AND DECENTRALIZATION

The current legal regulation of marriage in the United States includes the following circumstances.

First, same-sex couples are able to marry in Massachusetts, Vermont, Iowa, New Hampshire, Connecticut, and the District of Columbia,[5] but they are generally unable to have those marriages recognized in (most) other states.[6] The vast majority of states are refusing to recognize same-sex marriages from other states and countries[7] through a combination of state mini-DOMAs (state-level defense of marriage acts[8]), state constitutional amendments, and classic conflict-of-laws principles (which hold that states must recognize marriages that were valid where

---

[5] The Maine legislature passed a same-sex marriage bill in 2009, but it was overturned by a state referendum. California had same-sex marriage authorized by a court decision, and 18,000 couples married under its authority, prior to the ruling being overturned by a referendum ("Proposition 8"). New York passed a same-sex marriage law as this book was in the final editorial stage.

[6] All information in this chapter is based on laws passed and cases decided as of the time of writing (June 2009), with a few updates at a later editorial stage (June 2011). This is a fast-changing area, and the information is likely to be incomplete or inaccurate relative to a later time of reading.

[7] There are exceptions: By legislation, court order, or Attorney General decision, New York, New Jersey, Maryland, Rhode Island, and the District of Columbia have indicated a willingness to recognize foreign same-sex marriages; New Hampshire recognizes foreign same-sex marriages as "civil unions."

[8] Mini-DOMAs carry the label of the federal act, which defined marriage for federal purposes as excluding same-sex unions and authorized states to refuse to recognize same-sex marriages from other states. The federal act may be found at Pub. L. No. 104–199, 110 Stat. 2419 (1996); codified at 1 U.S.C. § 7 (2006) and 28 U.S.C. § 1738C (2006).

celebrated unless those marriages are contrary to the strong public policy of the forum state).[9]

Second, same-sex couples (and, in a few jurisdictions, some opposite-sex couples as well) have access to marriage-like relationships (called not "marriage" but "civil unions," "domestic partnerships," or the like) in a number of states.[10] There is little clarity, however, about what recognition, if any, such a status will receive in other states. Likely, even less extraterritorial recognition will be given to these legal unions than will be given to same-sex marriages. The early evidence is that other state institutions will only rarely recognize same-sex unions or the incidents of such unions.

Third, "covenant marriage" is available in three states – Arizona, Arkansas, and Louisiana[11] – as a statutory option that creates a more binding form of marriage that couples can choose instead of conventional marriage, the choice coming either at the commencement of marriage or by "conversion" from a conventional marriage if the couple is already married. Those who choose a covenant marriage agree to counseling prior to marriage, and prior to divorce, as well as significant restrictions on the grounds for divorce (either fault grounds or no-fault grounds only after an extended waiting period).[12]

Fourth, even putting aside same-sex marriages, covenant marriage, and marriage alternatives like civil unions, the rules regulating marriage entrance and exit (divorce) in the states vary in small but important ways.[13] Moreover, differences in states' rules of marriage and divorce are complicated (and their policy purposes are in part undermined) by the rules and practices of interjurisdictional recognition and conflict-of-laws rules and practices. For example, when someone seeks a divorce in

[9] *Restatement (Second) of Conflict of Laws* § 283(2) (1971).
[10] A current list of states that recognize same-sex unions under a name other than "marriage" but with identical (or nearly so) state-law rights and obligations would include California, Illinois, New Jersey, Nevada, Oregon, and Washington. Hawaii, Colorado, Delaware, Maine, and Wisconsin offer a legal status for same-sex couples, but one that falls far short of the state-law rights and obligations of marriage. An up-to-date list of jurisdictions that offer legal recognition for same-sex unions can be found at http://www.hrc.org/issues/marriage.asp. These sorts of unions are also available in many other countries (especially, although not exclusively, in Europe).
[11] Ariz. Stats. §§ 25–901 to 25–904 (West 2008); Ark. Stats. §§ 9–22–801 to 9–22–808 (LexisNexis 2008); La. R. S. §§ 9:272 to 9:276 (West 2008 & Supp. 2009). See also Katherine Shaw Spaht, "Covenant Marriage Laws: A Model for Compromise" (in this volume).
[12] Some commentators have suggested that partners in other states should also be able to enter comparable unions through contract. See, e.g., Elizabeth S. Scott, "Marriage as Precommitment," in *Marriage in America: A Communitarian Perspective*, ed. Martin King Whyte (Lanham, MD: Rowman & Littlefield Publishers, 2000), 161–171. However, such a right has not been recognized in any jurisdiction to date.
[13] Just to pick two convenient examples, consider grounds for divorce and residency requirements where the differences can be significant. See "Chart 4: Grounds for Divorce and Residency Requirements," *Family Law Quarterly* 44 (Winter 2011): 5141.

a different state from where the person had lived while married, frequently that second state will apply its own laws rather than the laws of the state where the couple married or lived together while married.[14]

In general, the growing decentralization and heterogeneity in marriage laws, both across and within states, undermines efforts by either the federal or state governments to use marriage laws to promote particular interests or objectives.[15] However, I do not mean to overstate state powerlessness in implementing policy. States alone – and especially when working together or with federal government facilitation – can go far, for example, toward excluding certain groups from marriage, in particular those who want to enter polygamous marriages or same-sex marriages. However, even here the implementation of policy is incomplete, as we now deal with the complications of same-sex couples who have marriage or marriage-like status from other states and polygamous families among us who have immigrated from communities where such unions are authorized.[16]

Fifth, through premarital agreements partners entering marriage have some control over the terms of marriage. Generally speaking, premarital agreements dealing with the financial terms of the marriage itself (e.g., whether property acquired during the marriage will be covered by community-property principles or common-law principles) and the financial terms between the parties upon divorce (property division and alimony) are enforceable, at least where not unconscionable.[17] Also, some couples enter types of premarital agreements that are established by authorities within their religions; examples include the Jewish *ketubah* and the Islamic *mahr*.[18] One could view such religious agreements less as couples establishing individualized terms and more like a de facto delegation of authority to the religion by both the parties and (to the extent the agreements are enforceable) by the state.

---

[14] See, e.g., J. Thomas Oldham, "What If the Beckhams Move to L.A. and Divorce? Marital Property Rights of Mobile Spouses When They Divorce in the U.S.," *Family Law Quarterly* 42 (Summer 2008): 263–293.

[15] See Brian H. Bix, "State of the Union: The States' Interest in the Marital Status of Their Citizens," *University of Miami Law Review* 55 (October 2000): 1–30.

[16] On the last, see, e.g., Nina Bernstein, "In Secret, Polygamy Follows Africans to N.Y.," *New York Times*, March 23, 2007.

[17] See, e.g., Brian Bix, "Bargaining in the Shadow of Love: The Enforcement of Premarital Agreements and How We Think About Marriage," *William and Mary Law Review* 40 (October 1998): 145–207; see also Brian H. Bix, "The ALI Principles and Agreements: Seeking a Balance Between Status and Contract," in *Reconceiving the Family: Critique on the American Law Institute's Principles of the Law of Family Dissolution*, ed. Robin Fretwell Wilson (Cambridge: Cambridge University Press, 2006), 372–391.

[18] See Michael J. Broyde, "New York's Regulation of Jewish Marriage: Covenant, Contract, or Statute?" (in this volume); Ann Laquer Estin, "Unofficial Family Law" (in this volume); Mohammad H. Fadel, "Political Liberalism, Islamic Family Law, and Family Law Pluralism" (in this volume).

II. FOUR ALTERNATIVE PATHS TO PLURALISM AND DECENTRALIZATION

There are, roughly speaking, four different ways that the regulation of marriage can become more pluralistic and/or more decentralized[19]:

1. Delegation to religious communities;
2. Enforcement of individual premarital agreements, with the terms set (perhaps within determined limits) by the parties;
3. Establishment of "menus" of options from which couples would be required to choose; and
4. Establishment of state standards allowing couples from one state, by express choice of law, to be governed by the standards of the marriage laws from another state.

Each option has implications as to which forum will decide issues relevant to marital status and which standards will be applied. Who decides and what are the rules are obviously distinct questions, emphasized throughout law by considerations labeled "choice of law" and "conflict of laws"; but, particularly in the family law field, the two are often conflated. For example, the domicile of either married party determines which court(s) has (or have) the power to dissolve a marriage. In principle, if that court will also be deciding the division of a couple's property, it may have the obligation to apply the law of a different state (usually the state where the property was acquired). However, many state courts simply ignore such niceties of conflict-of-laws doctrine and instead apply their own laws for dividing property, even when they should be applying other states' laws.[20] The four paths, and some of their strengths and weaknesses, are discussed next.

A. *Delegation*

As Professor Nichols's article indicates,[21] many jurisdictions in the past[22] – and some still today[23] – have decentralized governance of domestic matters, with significant

---

[19] I am by no means tied to four. By variations of the themes, and by mixing and matching, as well as by options I have not even considered, I am confident that one could select a much larger number for the quantity of alternatives.

[20] See Oldham, "What If the Beckhams Move to L.A. and Divorce?"

[21] See Nichols, "Multi-Tiered Marriage."

[22] This included England. See, e.g., R. H. Helmholz, *Marriage Litigation in Medieval England* (Cambridge: Cambridge University Press, 2007), 1–2. ("Proof and enforcement of marriage contracts, annulment of invalid marriages, punishment of adultery, were all within the exclusive competence of the Church. Everything, that is, having to do with marriage except questions of property settlement and inheritance, came within the purview of the canon law courts."). See Stephen B. Presser, "Marriage and the Law: Time for a Divorce?" (in this volume). Plenary civil law control over marriage did not occur in England until Lord Hardwicke's Marriage Act of 1753.

[23] Nichols, "Multi-Tiered Marriage," 164–195. As Nichols points out, prominent examples include India, South Africa, Israel, and Kenya. One should also include Indonesia. Simon Butt, "Polygamy and

matters delegated to religious institutions that have the power to regulate the marital status of their adherents.[24] As Professor Nichols also points out, a small-scale version of this arguably occurs even in some American states to the extent that religious premarital agreements, or other religious marital laws, are affirmed by the courts or affect the decisions courts reach on domestic matters.[25]

One could imagine a greater delegation to religious groups in the United States, going to a system like those in India and South Africa, in which parties would be bound to the rules of marriage and divorce of their religious institutions if they so choose.[26] Delegating authority to religious institutions avoids current problems of believers perceiving themselves to be saddled with civil marital rules (e.g., allowing divorce, excluding polygamous marriage, or including same-sex unions) that are contrary to their sincere beliefs. One would, of course, want a purely civil option for those of no religious affiliation, and perhaps also for some marriages across religious lines. Additionally, one would probably want a system (for constitutional and other reasons) in which parties could opt out of the authority of a particular religious institution should their religious beliefs change over time.

B. Individual Contracts

As previously mentioned, it is already the case that couples can enter into enforceable agreements, prior to marriage, determining (within certain bounds) the financial terms of the marriage and the financial provisions of any divorce, although premarital agreements purporting to limit the grounds of divorce appear to be unenforceable.[27] One could consider a significant expansion on the current rights of couples to enter enforceable premarital agreements.[28] For example, couples could be allowed to set the terms of their marriage – within limits (see Section V of this chapter) – including the rules for exit.[29] Like contracts generally, the justification would be the intrinsic value of self-governance, combined with the argument that

---

Mixed Marriage in Indonesia: Islam and the Marriage Law in the Courts," in *Indonesia: Law and Society*, ed. T. Lindsey (Annandale, Australia: Federation Press, 2008), 266–287.

[24] This is sometimes called a "millet system," a label associated with a structure of regulation within the Ottoman Empire.

[25] Nichols, "Multi-Tiered Marriage," 153–164. See also Estin, "Unofficial Family Law" (in this volume).

[26] As mentioned in conferences discussing the chapters in this volume in draft form, it is far from clear that current religious institutional hierarchies in the United States would universally want this delegated authority, or be able to take on that responsibility, but that is a question and discussion for another time.

[27] See, e.g., Bix, "Bargaining in the Shadow of Love"; Bix, "ALI Principles and Agreements."

[28] The current law is itself a significant change from the law of forty years ago, when nearly all states held divorce-focused premarital agreements to be void as contrary to public policy. See Bix, "Bargaining in the Shadow of Love," 148–158.

[29] See Scott, "Marriage as Precommitment."

parties are in the best position to determine which marriage structure best meets their needs, values, and interests.

C. Menus of Options

Another possibility is for couples to have a variety of marriage/divorce regimes from which a choice must be made at the point of marriage; this is sometimes referred to as a menu of options.[30] The "menus" could be created at either the state level or the federal level. Allowing different states to create different menus would be more consistent with the current practice of state control over such matters, and this would also allow different states to create choices that better reflect the range of communities and values in their jurisdictions.[31]

D. Choice of Law

One final alternative would be for couples about to marry to be able to choose the legal regime that governed their marriage (and possible divorce).[32] The most likely version of such a choice of law would restrict party choice to rules available in (at least) one of the American states, although in principle one could imagine a system that allowed selection of a foreign legal regime.[33] The benefit of restricting the choice to the existing law of some state is that this creates greater confidence that couples (or, more precisely, the more powerful party within a couple) will not be free to choose a legal regime that is too one-sided or exploitative. (The issue of what sorts of substantive limits we might want to place on choice is discussed in greater detail in Section V of this chapter.)

A choice-of-law system would require either federal legislation or the universal (or nearly so) enactment of uniform state laws. The difference between the menus option and the choice-of-law option is the difference between choosing among options within one's state (as residents of Louisiana, Arkansas, and Arizona can currently choose between a covenant marriage and a conventional marriage) and choosing among options that range across states. Obviously, the marriage system could in principle allow both kinds of choices.

---

[30] See, e.g., Ribstein, "Standard Form Approach to Marriage"; Bix, "State Interests in Marriage."

[31] Cf. Bix, "State Interests in Marriage."

[32] See Brian H. Bix, "Choice of Law and Marriage: A Proposal," *Family Law Quarterly* 36 (Summer 2002): 255–271. See also Rasmusen and Stake, "Lifting the Veil of Ignorance"; Ribstein, "Standard Form Approach to Marriage."

[33] At the point where couples would be able to choose a "private" set of rules put forward (say) by a private organization, a religious group, or a commentator, there would be little policy or structural difference between such "choices of law" and the category of individualized premarital agreements, discussed in Section II.B of this chapter.

III. INTERESTS IN UNIFORMITY

Delegation and decentralization have the advantage of responding better to the interests and needs of individuals seeking to marry. Also, as noted previously, rules of federalism and conflict-of-laws principles already make state policy making in this area difficult at best. Additionally, there are growing doubts regarding whether the same family law policies work equally well with different communities (across class, ethnic, and religious lines), thus raising another potential reason for individualized or group-based delegations of authority.[34]

Governments commonly assert, or have ascribed to them, two prime countervailing reasons for an interest in uniformity (or at least reasons for limiting delegation and pluralism):

1. Encouraging an institution that is good for society (e.g., marital households privatize care for the young and infirm, offer a good or ideal setting for raising children, and "tame" adults – especially males); and
2. Establishing and maintaining an administratively convenient way to distribute benefits and burdens.

Regarding the first interest, one question that arises is whether, once a large variety of marriage types are allowed, some of them might not undermine social goals rather than advance them (e.g., financial arrangements that leave spouses destitute or dependent or arrangements that work to reinforce other inequalities in society). For such reasons, the government might want to place some limits on the marital forms it is willing to approve. This topic will be revisited in Section V of this chapter. As for the second interest, the desire for administrative convenience (and lower budget costs) may provide a relatively nonjudgmental basis for rejecting approval of some family forms (e.g., polygamy).[35]

One should also note that the claims and interests of individual states must sometimes yield to federalism concerns: Citizens of the individual states are also citizens of the United States, with privileges and immunities of that national citizenship, including a constitutional right of interstate travel. Some commentators have also viewed the Full Faith and Credit Clause of the Constitution as reflecting the value of national citizenship. Regardless of high principle, there are important practical problems of state-level policy making for a mobile society because a significant portion of the population moves across state lines every year and many more people travel across state lines for short-term business and recreational trips. These

---

[34] See Margaret F. Brinig and Steven L. Nock, "The One-Size-Fits-All Family," *Santa Clara Law Review* 49(1) (2009): 137–163.
[35] See Mary Anne Case, "Marriage Licenses," *Minnesota Law Review* 89 (June 2005): 1758–1797.

considerations point in the direction of some uniformity in laws, or at least the uniform recognition of rights or status that was valid where obtained.

On one hand, as expressed in the federal Defense of Marriage Act (DOMA) legislation,[36] we may be uncomfortable with the legislative choices (or judicial decisions) of one state imposing controversial marriage policy conclusions (with potential implications for state budgets)[37] on other states. On the other hand, we may be equally uncomfortable with telling people validly married in one state that they will be stripped of all marital rights and privileges if and when they should so much as travel through a state with different policy preferences. The tension of these two interests has led some commentators to suggest that states should be required to recognize at least certain aspects of legal status from another jurisdiction – in particular the rights inter se and perhaps certain third-party rights that do not involve direct financial claims on the state (e.g., rights of medical decision making for one's partner).[38]

IV. THE NATURE OF MARRIAGE AND THE ROLE OF THE STATE

Whereas marriage and family are, to a large extent, pre-legal, they appear in many forms. State involvement in marriage inevitably involves a choice among forms and a clarification of status that might otherwise remain ambiguous.[39]

Consider some alternatives and options: Over time, marriage has been monogamous and polygamous; it has had different rules regarding the ease of entry into marriage (formalities, requirements of parental permission, restrictions on who can marry, waiting periods, license fees, etc.) and exit from it (whether to allow divorce at all, on what terms, and with what mandatory waiting periods; the availability of annulment as an alternative; etc.); it has had varying property regimes during marriage and upon divorce; and it has had different rules regarding the right to remarry after death of a spouse or dissolution of the marriage. Further, state action can affect marriage indirectly. For example, the government affects marriage through the way it allows or encourages women to participate in the marketplace (thus making it harder or easier for them to leave unhappy marriages). One might speculate that

---

[36] 1 U.S.C. § 7; 28 U.S.C. § 1738C.

[37] One objection often raised against the extralegal polygamous communities of the American Southwest is that the "families" there often create a larger claim on various state benefit and educational programs.

[38] F. H. Buckley and Larry E. Ribstein, "Calling a Truce in the Marriage Wars," *University of Illinois Law Review* (2001): 561–610; Bix, "State Interests in Marriage."

[39] The role of selecting among alternatives and clarifying rules has also been played, of course, by religious institutions. This is true historically and, still, descriptively. See Presser, "Marriage and the Law" (in this volume); Joel A. Nichols, "Multi-Tiered Marriage: Reconsidering the Boundaries of Civil Law and Religion" (in this volume); and Estin, "Unofficial Family Law" (in this volume).

similar effects occur through the availability (or lack of availability) of (affordable) child care, affordable or state-provided health care or health insurance, effective protection from harassment and abuse, and so forth. These all make it easier to leave unsatisfactory marriages and thus might also, paradoxically, encourage marriage in certain circumstances (by reducing the potential risk or cost of a bad marriage decision).

Whereas the American government's role in marriage (and that of the British government in earlier times) has been mostly to standardize marriage, how could we rethink the governmental role in relation to greater diversity and decentralization? Professor Nichols's article suggests that we might consider a changed American approach to regulating marriage, in which this country, too, delegates significant portions of marriage regulation to religious groups and institutions.[40] This would have the benefit (as Mary Anne Case has pointed out)[41] of potentially defusing part of the culture wars about marriage – for even if the state could be "accused" of giving its imprimatur to same-sex unions (should it so choose), it would not be in the position it is now of seeming to impose that definition of marriage on individuals or religious groups who find it repugnant. Different groups would be able to view marriage as they see fit and recognize or fail to recognize certain unions – or dissolutions of unions – according to their own principles (as, for example, the Catholic Church refuses to recognize civil divorces).

What is, or should be, the state's role in a more plural and decentralized marital regime? Is it purely administrative (giving benefits where it thinks them most useful)? Is it offering some official (and moral?) imprimatur for certain arrangements (and not for others)? How should the state treat marital arrangements that are legitimate within certain religious traditions but disapproved by conventional majority social values (e.g., polygamy or one-sided divorce norms)? Is there a way to respect various marriage norms and choices while also expressing a preference for one structure over others (e.g., more egalitarian or more helpful for raising children)?

The role for government in the context of a more plural and decentralized marriage regime would, one assumes, include setting minimal standards and also making sure that parties were not coerced into agreeing to contracts or submitting to the jurisdiction of particular religious organizations against their will. It would of course also be permissible for government to use its power to persuade citizens regarding the marital structures it believes to be optimal, even when less optimal structures are still legal and available. Similarly, the government might offer subsidies or other inducements for the marital forms it favors.

---

[40] Nichols, "Multi-Tiered Marriage." See also many chapters in this volume discussing variants of this.
[41] See, e.g., Case, "Marriage Licenses," 1793–1797.

The idea of a general governmental structure within which individuals make choices, perhaps within broad limits set by governmental safeguards, is actually a familiar notion. One sees it in our general contract and commercial law regimes as well as in the transfer of property through estates, just to name two prominent examples. However, any approach to a government's facilitation of a more fractured and decentralized approach to marriage (or at least describing how the state could adapt to such circumstances) would need to respond to a number of challenges, two of which are summarized next.

First, Eric Posner discusses the problem of "unclear signaling."[42] Posner's argument is that it would be harder to offer strong and appropriate social support for married couples if the marriage bonds for different couples are radically different (because they are based on varying state, religious, or contractual options).

"Signaling" regarding marital status can serve a variety of purposes. For example, knowing whether another person is married can be relevant to the community's interest in supporting marital fidelity (or perhaps marital [in]equality[43]). Alternatively, marital status identification could be important to someone who is considering a commercial relationship (where joint ownership, community-property principles, or dower rights might affect an individual's right to transfer property).

Two responses come to mind initially. (1) The loss in "signaling clarity" may be offset by other corresponding gains (e.g., the benefits of allowing parties greater liberty to construct their marital lives according to individual preferences or religious traditions). (2) Even in the days of greater legal uniformity in the terms of marriage and divorce, outward uniformity hid significant differences in how marriage was experienced (e.g., traditional versus egalitarian, with a handful of "open marriages"). A variety of marital forms would echo, without entirely reflecting, the ongoing wide differences in how marriage is perceived and lived.[44]

Second, another challenge is bounded rationality. It has been argued, particularly in the context of premarital agreements, that bounded rationality limits the ability

[42] Eric A. Posner, "Family Law and Social Norms," in *The Fall and Rise of Freedom of Contract*, ed. F. H. Buckley (Durham, NC: Duke University Press, 1999), 256–274.
[43] One's beliefs on how A should treat B may turn on whether one thinks A and B are co-workers, siblings, employer/employee, friends, or spouses. If one believes that equality in marriage is an important social value, then one will want to do what one can to persuade individuals to treat their spouses accordingly. By contrast, if one believes (for religious or other reasons) in hierarchical marriage, then this will lead one to pressure individuals to treat their spouses in a different way.
[44] However clear or unclear the "signals" to one's peers, there would be a definite need for clear indications of status in dealing with governmental and private programs in which benefits turn on marital status. Thus, for example, even if marriages varied by individual contract or religious affiliation, there would be a continued need for centralized registration of marriages. (Of course, as occurred with the federal DOMA, governments and private institutions might be free to limit their benefits to only certain categories of marriages.)

of those entering marriage to make choices that are sufficiently self-protective (i.e., sufficiently "rational"). "Bounded rationality" is the label given to a variety of ways of reasoning that lead individuals to act in ways that vary significantly from the sort of rationality – the maximization of preferences – that economists and others often ascribe to (all) human beings. In real life, we systematically overestimate some risks and underestimate others, and we generally tend to be unduly optimistic. We also are more altruistic than economists assume, and our response to choices often turns on how they are framed or on extraneous options that are thrown into our consideration. We do not value an object or entitlement as much when we do not have it as when we do, and we act in many other non–preference-maximizing ways.[45]

In prior writings, I have argued that bounded rationality is a real concern but likely is overstated in the premarital agreement context.[46] However, the state's approach to a more varied and decentralized approach to regulating marriage should take this worry into account and may well justify the type of limits discussed in the next section.

V. LIMITS?

In a world of diverse marital regimes and growing decentralization of marriage regulation, there is at least one obvious role for the state: to set boundaries – namely minimum terms that will ensure that vulnerable parties (including third parties to marriage arrangements, in particular children) are not badly harmed. This would be an important potential role whether we are talking about the broad enforcement of premarital agreements affecting marital terms or the delegation of authority to religious institutions. Protecting third parties would include, but not be limited to, maintaining standards for child support and supervision over other decisions regarding children (including custody and visitation outcomes).

The need to protect vulnerable parties would likely extend to marriage formation and behavior within marriage. The government might reasonably reject recognition of a marriage of an eight-year-old[47] or a standard of marital behavior that condoned marital rape,[48] even if these standards were accepted within a particular

---

[45] See, e.g., Daniel Kahnemann, Paul Slovic, and Amos Tversky, eds., *Judgment Under Uncertainty: Heuristics and Biases* (Cambridge: Cambridge University Press, 1982).

[46] E.g., Bix, "ALI Principles and Agreements," 379–380.

[47] See Mohammed Jamjoom, "Saudi Judge Refuses to Annul 8-Year-Old's Marriage," *CNN.com*, April 14, 2009. A later news report indicates that a divorce in that case was agreed in an out-of-court settlement. "Young Saudi Girl's Marriage Ended," *BBC News*, April 30, 2009; Mohammed Jamjoom and Saad Abedine, "Report: Saudi Girl Granted Divorce," *CNN.com*, May 12, 2009.

[48] See Dexter Filkins, "Afghan Women Protest New Restrictive Law," *New York Times*, April 16, 2009. President Karzai claimed ignorance of the more controversial aspects of the Shi'ite Personal Status

religious community. Similarly, the state might reasonably not allow parties to agree to (consent to) genital mutilation or physical abuse, or having wives leave marriages with so little property that they are dependent on state benefit.

By way of example, the Islamic *mahr* (also sometimes called *sadaqa* or *faridah*), a kind of premarital agreement, involves the promise of payment of a certain sum to the wife. Occasionally this payment is made prior to the marriage, but usually it is held to be due after the termination of the marriage.[49] The majority interpretation appears to be that this post-marriage payment should be above and beyond the civil law division of property and obligation of alimony; however, a minority view argues that the *mahr* payment is in lieu of any post-marriage financial obligations of husband to wife.[50] This second interpretation, where accepted, could leave divorced women significantly impoverished.[51] (State governments already, as a matter of course, refuse to enforce premarital agreements to the extent that the financial terms leave one spouse – usually the wife – on state benefit. Whether one sees such actions as protecting vulnerable parties, setting limits on the sort of marriages that work to the social benefit, or simply protecting the public fisc, one would imagine similar limits being set in a world of delegated marriage regulation.)

Also, another variant might arise regarding covenant marriages or the possibility of recognizing individual premarital agreements creating a sort of covenant marriage for that couple. Even were a government to enforce such agreements generally, there would be arguments for limiting what parties could agree to (even beyond those limits already mentioned relating to the protection of vulnerable classes of people). For example, there would be an argument for preventing parties from entering legally binding agreements that constrain themselves *too* severely, such as agreements *never* to divorce or to pay a large sum if divorce is chosen.[52]

Law that he signed, and a review of the law was promised. Golnar Motevalli, "Karzai Signed Law Not Knowing Contents," *Reuters*, April 26, 2009.

[49] There is disagreement among scholars as to whether this payment is due if the wife initiates the divorce. Some scholars argue that it would still be due if the end of the marriage was the husband's fault. See, e.g., the discussion of intra-Islamic pluralism in Fadel, "Political Liberalism" (in this volume).

[50] See Pascale Fournier, "Flirting with God in Western Secular Courts: Mahr in the West," *International Journal of Law, Policy, and the Family* 24(1) (April 2010): 67–94, 69–70. The view of these scholars appears to be that after marriage, the (ex-)wife is to be supported by her extended family. See, e.g., Siobhan Mullally, "Feminism and Multicultural Dilemmas in India: Revisiting the *Shah Bano* Case," *Oxford Journal of Legal Studies* 24(4) (Winter 2004): 671–692, 678.

[51] Cf. Lindsey E. Blenkhorn, "Islamic Marriage Contracts in American Courts: Interpreting *Mahr* Agreements as Prenuptials and Their Effect on Muslim Women," *Southern California Law Review* 76 (November 2002): 189–234 (raising issues about the meaning, voluntariness, and enforceability of *mahr* provisions).

[52] The examples are from Scott, "Marriage as Precommitment," 161–171. See also Spaht, "Covenant Marriage Laws" (in this volume).

Some commentators have argued that the government – as a matter of both constitutional law and good social practice – should strongly encourage egalitarian marriages (rather than traditional, hierarchical marriages).[53] However, that would seem a very intrusive constraint in a pluralistic society where a number of communities and religions encourage non-egalitarian marriage.[54]

One might also ask whether there are limits that should be the providence of the state beyond protecting vulnerable parties within marriage and vulnerable third parties. For example, should the state decide what is and is not central to "marriage," such that nothing beyond is given that title and the associated status and benefits? To illustrate, there are already ongoing disputes as to whether it is proper to apply the rubric "marriage" to the union of same-sex couples, whether it should be extended to polyamorous arrangements, and whether to apply it (or a comparable status) to close companions who have no sexual or romantic ties.[55] Although the impetus of a decentralized approach to marriage regulation implies a certain laissez faire attitude, it is hard to see how the government could entirely avoid making judgments about what counts as marriage and which forms should be given state recognition.

VI. GOVERNMENT INTERACTIONS WITH RELIGION

Where the government delegates regulation of marriage to religious communities, there is both the danger and the opportunity of state interaction with the religion, particularly in regard to the processes and norms used.

Ayelet Shachar, reflecting on decentralized (religious) regulation of marriage in Israel and proposing structures of a similar sort in Canada, has considered options

---

[53] See Linda C. McClain, *The Place of Families: Fostering Capacity, Equality, and Responsibility* (Cambridge, MA: Harvard University Press, 2006), 76–84.

[54] This debate was played out in Ontario, Canada, where the government first seemed to allow, and then to draw back from, religious arbitration in family law matters. The subsequent retreat was based in part on fears that Islamic arbitration might lead to unequal treatment of women. See Marion Boyd's official report (prior to the government's retreat): Marion Boyd, *Dispute Resolution in Family Law: Protecting Choice, Promoting Inclusion* (Ontario, Canada: Ministry of the Attorney General, 2004), available at http://www.attorneygeneral.jus.gov.on.ca/english/about/pubs/boyd/. See also Fadel, "Political Liberalism" (in this volume); Linda C. McClain, "Marriage Pluralism in the United States: On Civil and Religious Jurisdiction and the Demands of Equal Citizenship" (in this volume); Ayelet Shachar, "Faith in Law? Diffusing Tensions Between Diversity and Equality" (in this volume); Robin Fretwell Wilson, "The Perils of Privatized Marriage" (in this volume); and Witte and Nichols, "The Frontiers of Marital Pluralism" (in this volume). On the possible dangers generally to vulnerable parties in deferring to religious institutions, see Shachar, "Faith in Law?" (in this volume), and Wilson, "The Perils of Privatized Marriage" (in this volume).

[55] On the last, see *Beyond Conjugality: Recognizing and Supporting Close Personal Adult Relationships* (Law Commission of Canada, 2001).

that work as a compromise between central government control and full delegation to religious communities. These include:

1. Requiring that the selection and training of religious arbitrators follow certain (government-established) standards[56];
2. Requiring that arbitration awards meet minimum standards for provision for the parties; and
3. Making challenges to arbitration awards procedurally easier, perhaps even by allowing third-party challenges (if there is concern that vulnerable parties would be under community pressure not to challenge one-sided outcomes[57]) and requiring arbitrators to establish and maintain a full(er) record of the evidence and the grounds for decision.

Shachar has further argued that these forms of regulatory interaction might also have the benefit of guiding the rules of or within the religious communities in a constructive direction.[58]

Sometimes such directed regulatory guidance is even encouraged by a religious community. As discussed extensively by Michael Broyde in this volume,[59] in the United States, in the state of New York, the legislature has worked with the local Orthodox Jewish Community to create civil laws that have the effect of modifying the laws (or at least the normal consequences of the laws) relating to marriage and divorce. Under the religious laws of the Orthodox community, only the husband can obtain or give a religious divorce, and significant sanctions are attached to any children born to a woman who tries to remarry without such a religious divorce.[60] Through state laws that withhold civil divorce and threaten one-sided monetary settlements for those husbands unwilling to grant a religious divorce,[61] New York has changed the situation from one of largely unilateral power of the husband to impose or withhold a religious divorce to a more even balance of power.

---

[56] Similar state-imposed standards on the qualifications of religious judges have occurred in Indonesia. See Butt, "Polygamy and Mixed Marriage in Indonesia," 273.

[57] For example, the plaintiff in India's famous *Shah Bano* case, under pressure from her (Islamic) community, ended up disassociating herself from the case that had been won under her name. See Mullally, "Feminism and Multicultural Dilemmas in India," 681.

[58] Ayelet Shachar, "Privatizing Diversity: A Cautionary Tale from Religious Arbitration in Family Law," *Theoretical Inquiries in Law* 9(2) (July 2008): 573–607; Ayelet Shachar, *Multicultural Jurisdictions* (Cambridge: Cambridge University Press, 2001).

[59] See Broyde, "New York's Regulation" (in this volume). See also Fadel, "Political Liberalism" (in this volume).

[60] It is a little more complicated than the simple summary in this chapter indicates. See Ayelet Blecher-Prigat and Benjamin Shmueli, "The Interplay Between Tort Law and Religious Law: The Israeli Case," *Arizona Journal of Comparative and International Law*, 26(2) (2009): 279–301, 281–283.

[61] New York Dom. Rel. §§ 236 Part B(5)(h); 253 (West 1999 & Supp. 2009).

However, it is perhaps more common for the interaction of government and religion to be more adversarial. Sometimes, it is merely a matter of the civil law overruling (or establishing limits on) the religious law. At other times (perhaps most famously in the Indian *Shah Bano* case[62]), it involves judges with no credentials within a religious tradition nonetheless purporting to make authoritative statements of what that tradition requires, and on occasion going clearly against the consensus within that tradition.[63] This seems a step too far.

VII. CONSTITUTIONAL ISSUES

A proposal that considers delegating some portion of state authority to religious organizations raises very serious First Amendment concerns under the U.S. Constitution. I mostly wish to bracket those concerns, in part because I claim no expertise in the complicated questions of the constitutional treatment of religion and in part because I wish to focus instead on whether or to what extent such delegation would be a good idea, as a policy matter, before turning to the question of whether or to what extent it would be allowed under our constitutional system.[64]

The U.S. Supreme Court has held that government may not delegate general governmental powers to a religious organization,[65] and other courts have rejected different sorts of state-church entanglements.[66] The question here would be whether authorizing and enforcing (say) religious-court arbitration in family law matters (with or without the continuing consent of both parties) constitutes a similarly improper delegation of state power.[67]

---

[62] *Mohammed Ahmed Khan v. Shah Bano Begum*, 1985 AIR SC 945.

[63] Mullally, "Feminism and Multicultural Dilemmas in India," 679–680. The court in *Shah Bano* (consisting entirely of Hindu judges) decided both that the civil general code overrides the Muslim personal law on the question of alimony and that an alimony obligation was, in any event, consistent with the personal law. Most commentators find the second decision to be as erroneous, not least because it was unnecessary to the judgment.

[64] One might view the question of constitutionality as part of a subset of the larger question of whether a plan of greater pluralism and decentralization could practicably be put into place (in the United States), regardless of one's view of the merits of such proposals. Under this rubric, one might consider not only constitutionality but whether voter majorities or political elites would ever support proposals of this sort. The answer would, of course, depend on the precise terms of the proposal, and would likely vary among different types of proposals – e.g., private contracting and menus of options would likely be more palatable to such constituencies than delegations of power to religious organizations.

[65] *Larkin v. Grendel's Den, Inc.*, 459 U.S. 116 (1982) (invalidating on First Amendment grounds a statute that gave churches and schools the right to veto liquor licenses within 500 feet of their locations).

[66] See, e.g., *Commack Self-Service Kosher Meals, Inc. v. Weiss*, 294 F.3d 415 (2d Cir. 2002) (invalidating New York's "kosher fraud" provisions).

[67] See Witte and Nichols, "The Frontiers of Marital Pluralism" (in this volume). See also *Lang v. Levi*, 16 A.3d 980 (Md. App. 2011) (upholding an arbitration decision by a Jewish court (*beth din*) grounded in a premarital agreement, while refusing to consider the claim that the arbitration decision might have been wrong as a matter of Jewish law).

In due course, the constitutional challenge needs to be faced. It may well be that certain provisions would need to be added to the proposal – provisions that might otherwise seem less than optimal – in order to make the proposal constitutional (or at least give it a tenable argument of constitutionality, although a court might still rule against it). In particular, one could consider a situation in which the delegation to religious organizations of establishing some of the terms of entrance and exit for marriage would be conditioned on the express and knowing consent of the partners both at the time of marriage and again at the time of divorce.[68] There would be policy reasons for wanting parties to be bound by an initial agreement to follow the rulings of a religious authority, even regarding later rulings on the terms of divorce, but it may be that requiring a party to be subject to religious rulings at that later time, when the party objects to being under that jurisdiction, would be contrary to establishment (and entanglement) concerns under the First Amendment.

How tight the constitutional constraints in this area are, or should be, is highly contested. It is well known that the New York Court of Appeals, in a famous 1983 case, enforced an agreement of the parties to be bound by the decisions of a religious (in this case, Jewish) authority, without need for subsequent consent.[69] Although many commentators have sided with the dissent that the majority went beyond constitutional limits, there are significant constitutional commentators who have supported the outcome.[70]

VIII. CONCLUSION

As a descriptive matter, governmental regulation of marriage – in terms of whether people can marry, how they must live their married lives, and when they can leave

---

[68] In the Israeli system, people are apparently assigned to different religious groups for the purpose of family law governance according to the religions' own rules about identity, rather than according to the individuals' own choices (thus, one could be assigned to Jewish or Islamic domestic governance even if one were entirely secular or atheistic). Blecher-Prigat and Shmueli, "The Interplay Between Tort Law and Religious Law," 280.

[69] *Avitzur v. Avitzur*, 446 N.E.2d 136 (N.Y. 1983) (4–3 vote). The Supreme Court of Canada reached a similar result in *Marcovitz v. Bruker*, 2007 SCC 54.

[70] See, e.g., Kent Greenawalt, "Religious Law and Civil Law: Using Secular Law to Assure Observance of Practices with Religious Significance," *Southern California Law Review* 71 (May 1998): 781–843, 816–822 (generally supportive of the case outcome in particular and enforcement of such agreements in general). Some courts have found creative (and frequently dubious) grounds for refusing to enforce *mahr* provisions. E.g., *Shaban v. Shaban*, 105 Cal. Rptr.2d 863 (Cal. App. 2001) (terms too cryptic, fails statute of frauds); In re *Marriage of Obaidi*, 226 P.3d 787 (Wash. App. 2010) (unenforceable because no "meeting of minds" between parties). Other courts have been more willing to enforce *mahr* provisions as premarital agreements. E.g., *Aziz v. Aziz*, 488 N.Y.S.2d 123 (1985); *Odatalla v. Odatalla*, 810 A.2d 93 (N.J. Super.Ch. 2002). On this issue, see generally Brian H. Bix, "*Mahr* Agreements: Contracting in the Shadow of Family Law (and Religious Law) – A Comment on Oman's Article," *Wake Forest Law Review Online* 1 (2011): 61–68.

marriage – is significantly lessened in the United States today. This weakening is strongly reinforced by a greater social tolerance for different domestic forms (e.g., unmarried cohabitation, single parenthood, same-sex unions, raising children outside of marriage, and egalitarian and traditional households) in most places. One question is whether one should celebrate and assist this diversity of family forms or resist it.

This chapter has tried to explore some of the ways that marriage has already become plural and marriage regulation decentralized. I have suggested that this is largely a positive development, allowing parties to structure marriages according to their individual needs and their sincere religious beliefs. Such delegation and decentralization means that the state moves to a primarily supportive role with regard to marriage, and disclaims almost entirely the role of guiding norms of and regarding marriage. However, there remains also a perceived need for limits – both to protect vulnerable parties and to reflect beliefs of what is minimally necessary for marriages to work for the social interest rather than against it.

3

Marriage and the Law

Time for a Divorce?

Stephen B. Presser

I. A ROILING POLITICAL ISSUE

In 2003, the Massachusetts Supreme Judicial Court in *Goodridge v. Department of Public Health,* by a bare one-person majority, became the first state supreme court to determine that its state constitution requires the state to allow same-sex marriages.[1] In the face of several millennia of human experience almost exclusively to the contrary, the Massachusetts Court somehow discovered that it was "arbitrary" and "capricious" and therefore legally impermissible to limit the benefits of marriage to one man/one woman couples. In the space of just six years, by 2009, five states had chosen to allow same-sex couples to marry, and the Iowa Supreme Court, in a *unanimous* decision, had essentially embraced the same arguments the Massachusetts court had elaborated.[2] Connecticut, California, Hawaii, and Iowa joined Massachusetts in establishing the unconstitutionality of limiting marriage to opposite-sex couples by court decisions.[3] The California and Hawaii decisions, however, were overturned by constitutional amendments established by popular referenda.[4] Vermont, New Hampshire, and Maine established same-sex marriage by statute.[5]

---

[1] *Goodridge v. Dept. of Public Health,* 798 N.E.2d 941 (Mass. 2003).

[2] *Varnum v. Brien,* 763 N.W.2d 862 (Iowa 2009).

[3] *Kerrigan v. Commissioner of Public Health,* 957 A.2d 407 (Conn. 2008); *In re Marriage Cases,* 183 P.3d 384 (Cal. 2008); *Baehr v. Lewin,* 852 P.2d 44 (Haw. 1993); *Varnum,* 763 N.W.2d 862.

[4] Hawaii voters in 1998 approved a constitutional amendment granting the Hawaii State Legislature the power to limit marriage to opposite-sex couples, which resulted in a law banning same-sex marriage in the state. Haw. Const. Art. 1, §23. California's Proposition 8, amending the state constitution, provides simply that "Only marriage between a man and a woman is valid or recognized in California." Proposition 8 itself was challenged in the California Supreme Court by advocates of same-sex marriage, but that court upheld it as a validly promulgated amendment even while some justices expressed regret for its effect. See *Strauss v. Horton,* 207 P.3d 48 (Cal. 2009).

[5] See, e.g., Keith B. Richburg, "Vermont Legislature Legalizes Same-Sex Marriage," *Washington Post,* April 7, 2009, available at http://www.washingtonpost.com/wp-dyn/content/article/2009/04/07/

Same-sex marriage is a roiling political issue. So far, California and Hawaii are the only states where the voters have, in effect, overturned their highest state court's decision permitting same-sex marriage, but popular action in many other states has resulted in measures designed to prevent state recognition of same-sex marriages. Following the Massachusetts *Goodridge* decision, state constitutional amendments limiting marriage to heterosexual couples were passed in Alaska, Arkansas, California, Georgia, Hawaii, Kentucky, Michigan, Mississippi, Missouri, Montana, Nebraska, Nevada, North Dakota, Oklahoma, Ohio, Oregon, and Utah. States without such constitutional provisions, but with legislation barring same-sex marriage, include Alabama, Arizona, Colorado, Florida, Idaho, Illinois, Indiana, Kansas, Maryland, Minnesota, North Carolina, Pennsylvania, South Carolina, South Dakota, Tennessee, Texas, Virginia, Washington, West Virginia, Wisconsin, and Wyoming.[6] Still, many of those state statutes are subject to constitutional challenge under state constitutions, if not the federal one. It is likely only a matter of time before every one of them will, in fact, be challenged, and, just as is likely to occur in California and Hawaii, many states will seek to remove state constitutional provisions barring same-sex marriage.[7]

Back in 1996, in what in retrospect now seems like a simpler time, the U.S. Congress passed and President Clinton signed into law the federal Defense of Marriage Act (DOMA), which defines marriage for federal law purposes as the legal union of a man and a woman. It expressly permits states to refuse to recognize same-sex marriage licenses issued by other states.[8] Whereas California's state constitutional bar on

AR2009040701663.html; Abby Goodnough, "New Hampshire Legalizes Same-Sex Marriage," *New York Times*, June 3, 2009, available at http://www.nytimes.com/2009/06/04/us/04marriage.html; "Baldacci Signs Same-Sex Marriage Into Law," *Portland Press Herald*, May 6, 2009, available at http://pressherald.mainetoday.com/story.php?id=254850. As this book was in the final editorial stage, New York's legislature passed a same-sex marriage law.

6 For tables detailing which states have which laws and which states have constitutional provisions barring same-sex marriage, and for much more data on state legislative and constitutional action on the issue, see http://www.ncsl.org/IssuesResearch/HumanServices/SameSexMarriage/tabid/16430/Default.aspx.

7 California's provision barring same-sex marriage has in fact been challenged in a lawsuit jointly brought in federal court by Ted Olson, who was a lawyer for President George W. Bush in *Bush v. Gore*, and by David Boies, who, in that same case, represented Al Gore. See, e.g., William N. Eskridge Jr. and Darren Spedale, "Sit Down, Ted Olson and David Boies: Let the States Experiment with Gay Marriage – It's Not Time Yet for a Federal Lawsuit," *Slate*, May 29, 2009, available at http://www.slate.com/id/2219252/.

8 Public Law No. 104–199, 110 Stat. 2419. Its provisions are codified at 1 U.S.C. § 7 and 28 U.S.C. § 1738C. The key provisions of the act are

(1) No State, territory, or possession of the United States, or Indian tribe, shall be required to give effect to any public act, record, or judicial proceeding of any other State, territory, possession, or tribe respecting a relationship between persons of the same sex that is treated as a

same-sex marriage is being challenged under the U.S. Constitution on equal protection grounds, it can be argued that DOMA violates the Constitution's Due Process
and Equal Protection Clauses, and, perhaps, the Full Faith and Credit Clause.[9]
Because of the possibility that the U.S. Supreme Court or other federal courts could
invalidate DOMA, there are those urging an amendment of the U.S. Constitution
to declare that marriage can only be between two people of the opposite sex. There
is also a campaign (by some of the same individuals) to get the Massachusetts legislature to do something to repudiate the reasoning of its court, although they have
so far been unsuccessful. And there are many more in American society wailing,
gnashing their teeth, and decrying the low moral state into which the culture and
the judiciary have fallen.

All of this is understandable, but the amount of political and legal energy that is
likely to be spent on advocating and fighting same-sex marriage might well be chan-
neled into something more productive. The very idea that each of the fifty states or
the federal government ought to decide what is a marriage and what is not ought
to be challenged. The truth of the matter is that, in the Anglo-American system,
marriage has always had an uneasy relationship with the secular law, and it seems
possible that the hidden meaning over the extreme reactions (on both sides) to the
Massachusetts decision, the decisions of the Iowa, California, and Connecticut
courts, and DOMA, is that perhaps the governmental role in defining marriage
ought to be less than is usually thought. This chapter will propose, as a few pundits
have also asserted,[10] that the best means of avoiding the extremely divisive political

marriage under the laws of such other State, territory, possession, or tribe, or a right or claim
arising from such relationship; and

(2) In determining the meaning of any Act of Congress, or of any ruling, regulation, or interpretation of the various administrative bureaus and agencies of the United States, the word "marriage" means only a legal union between one man and one woman as husband and wife, and
the word "spouse" refers only to a person of the opposite sex who is a husband or a wife.

See also Brian H. Bix, "Pluralism and Decentralization in Marriage Regulation" (in this volume).

[9] For the arguments against DOMA, see, e.g., Andrew Koppelman, "Dumb and DOMA: Why
the Defense of Marriage Act is Unconstitutional," *Iowa Law Review* 83 (1997): 1–33, and Andrew
Koppelman, *Same Sex, Different States: When Same-Sex Marriages Cross State Lines* (New Haven,
CT: Yale University Press, 2006), 114–136; Cass Sunstein, oral testimony at the hearings held by the
Senate Judiciary Committee, July 11, 1996, reprinted in *Same-Sex Marriage Pro & Con: A Reader*, ed.
Andrew Sullivan (New York: Vintage Book, revised and updated edition, 2004), 216.

[10] See, e.g., Steven Greenhut, "Get the State Out of Marriage: Let's Try a Thought Experiment About
Privatizing Marriage," Dec. 3, 2007, available at http://www.lewrockwell.com/greenhut/greenhut48.
html (online article reporting on various libertarian thinkers who have advocated privatizing marriage and taking away from the state the power to define a marriage); "Kmiec Proposes End of
Legally Recognized Marriage," May 28, 2009, available at http://www.catholicnewsagency.com/new.
php?n=16128 (online article reporting on the views of Douglas Kmiec, who argues that we should
turn over the concept of marriages to churches and allow any couple to get a "civil license"). See also
Camille Paglia, "What Do the Clinton's Have on Obama," Dec. 10, 2008, available at http://www.

battles over same-sex marriage is to take the state out of the business of deciding what is a marriage and to leave that question to the churches. There is historical precedent for this, and it ought now to be a matter of wise policy.

II. THE UNEASY RELATIONSHIP OF THE CIVIL LAW TO MARRIAGE

A. *The English Common Law*

Consider, to begin with, the words of Sir William Blackstone, writer of the classic *Commentaries on the Law of England* (1765–1768), the book that was second only to the Bible in influence in early nineteenth-century America.[11] Blackstone was no champion of same-sex marriage, and it seems clear that he would have been alarmed at the U.S. Supreme Court's recent decision in *Lawrence v. Texas* – cited in the opening paragraphs of the Massachusetts *Goodridge* decision – that held a state could not punish consensual homosexual sodomy.[12] (Blackstone believed that sodomy, "the infamous crime against nature," was of "a still deeper malignity" than rape.)[13] Still, Blackstone understood that the common law's relation to marriage was simply to confirm its use as a means of combining the property and personal rights of husband and wife with control placed (albeit supervised to a limited extent) in the hands of the husband. The wife was to be provided for and she was entitled to one-third profit from her husband's lands during her life if he predeceased her; the law would intervene if the husband failed to perform his duties. However, except for her "paraphernalia" (which included her ceremonial jewels), most of her property could be disposed of by her husband, and, while the marriage endured, she was incapable of entering into contracts or even of testifying against her husband in court. This did not bother Blackstone, who essentially believed that the arrangement was in the best interests of both husband and wife, but more especially the

salon.com/opinion/paglia/2008/12/10/hillary_mumbai/index2.html ("My position has always been … that government should get out of the marriage business. Marriage is a religious concept that should be defined and administered only by churches. The government, a secular entity, must institute and guarantee civil unions, open to both straight and gay couples and conferring full legal rights and benefits.").

[11] See, e.g., Richard P. Cole, Review Essay, *Indiana Law Review* 32 (1999): 1335–1381, 1339 ("The new culture was so powerful that William Blackstone's *Commentaries on the Laws of England*, published during the last half of the 1760s, 'ranked second only to the Bible as a literary and intellectual influence on the history of American institutions'." [quoting Robert A. Ferguson, *Law and Letters in American Culture* 11 (1984)]) (footnotes omitted).

[12] *Lawrence v. Texas*, 539 U.S. 558 (2003).

[13] William Blackstone, *Commentaries on the Laws of England* vol. IV, 1769 (Chicago: University of Chicago Press, reprint edition, 1979), 215. He noted that the penalty for sodomy was death by hanging, and for Blackstone this penalty was in accordance with "the voice of nature and of reason, and the express law of God." Ibid., at 216, citing Leviticus 20: 13, 15 (mandating the death penalty for sodomy and bestiality).

latter, because "[s]o great a favorite is the female sex of the laws of England." Even so, Blackstone regarded the parts of the marriage supervised by the secular law as probably not the essence of the institution. Indeed, he opened his discussion of marriage by remarking, "Our law considers marriage in no other light than as a civil contract. The Holiness of the matrimonial state is left entirely to the ecclesiastical law: the temporal courts not having jurisdiction to consider unlawful marriages as a sin, but merely as a civil inconvenience."[14] Blackstone, then, and by extension the English common law itself, saw a limited role for the state in marriage – essentially one of preserving property rights and, at that state of the law's evolution, the patriarchal character of the English family.

B. Colonial, Early Republican, and Nineteenth-Century America

In colonial and early Republican America, marriage was rarely regulated by the law. Indeed, the curiously named institution of "common law marriage" (unknown in England), whereby the law would recognize a man and a woman as husband and wife if they lived as such for an extended period of time, took hold. The consequence of this was simply to render their children "legitimate" in the eyes of the law, and to allow husband, wife, and children whatever benefits the law accorded, including especially the ability to inherit property if spouse or parent died intestate.[15] By the middle of the nineteenth century, however, probably because of the influence of some theorists who argued that the unit of loving Christian husband and wife was a basic building block in a good republic, the language of the law shifted to speak in terms of the contribution to morals rather than to property rights of the institution. For example, in *Reynolds v. United States* (1878), the U.S. Supreme Court, in the course of a decision upholding the prohibition on polygamy, declared, "Marriage, while from its very nature a sacred obligation, is nevertheless, in most civilized nations, a civil contract, and usually regulated by law. Upon it society may be said to be built, and out of its fruits spring social relations and social obligations and duties, with which government is necessarily required to deal."[16] According to

---

[14] William Blackstone, *Commentaries on the Laws of England* vol. I, 1765 (Chicago: University of Chicago Press, reprint edition, 1979), 421. For the other matters referred to in this paragraph, see ibid., at 421–433.

[15] On common law marriage in nineteenth-century America, see, e.g., Michael Grossberg, *Governing the Hearth: Law and the Family in Nineteenth Century America*, (Chapel Hill, NC: University of North Carolina Press, 1988), 83–94. See also Note, "Common Law Marriage – A Legal Anachronism," *Indiana Law Journal* 32 (1956): 99–110. For a feminist proposal to bring back common law marriage, see Cynthia Grant Bowman, "A Feminist Proposal to Bring Back Common Law Marriage," *Oregon Law Review* 75 (1996): 709–780.

[16] *Reynolds v. United States*, 98 U.S. 145, 165 (1878). Compare the criticism of the reasoning in *Reynolds* in Mohammad H. Fadel, "Political Liberalism, Islamic Family Law, and Family Law Pluralism" (in this volume).

the anthropological data the Court considered, polygamy tended to lead in most societies to despotism, and so, the Court held, it was inconsistent with the needs of America. Again, however, the Supreme Court demonstrated an understanding, also found at common law as reported by Blackstone, that "from its very nature" marriage was a sacred obligation. This obligation involved not just the parties to the marriage contract but also God – although in *Reynolds* the Court recognized the role that marriage played as a crucial intermediate association in society, bridging the gap between the individual and the state.

The period of the *Reynolds* decision was a sort of golden age for judicial as well as common law patriarchy, as judges and Justices waxed eloquent about the married state, how it was the natural one for women, and how it accorded with divine plans.[17] Mr. Justice Bradley, in famous language from a U.S. Supreme Court case upholding Illinois's power to bar women from the practice of law, said, "The natural and proper timidity and delicacy which belongs to the female sex evidently unfits it for many of the occupations of civil life." "The constitution of the family organization," Bradley continued, "which is founded in the divine ordinance, as well as in the nature of things, indicates the domestic sphere as that which properly belongs to the domain and functions of womanhood."[18]

Thus, for Bradley, "[t]he paramount destiny and mission of woman are to fulfill the noble and benign offices of wife and mother. This is the law of the Creator. And the rules of civil society must be adopted to the general constitution of things, and cannot be based upon exceptional cases."[19] This meant, then, that it was the job of the state, by barring women from the professions, to keep them under the domination of their husbands at home in, presumably, connubial bliss. But it was not just Bradley's view of the proper role of husband and wife that animated his decision. It was also his conception of what God required, and not just what the law ought to require. Bradley's views in this regard, which were probably shared by a majority of men at the time, made sense in an era when even the U.S. Supreme Court could confidently declare, as it did in *Church of the Holy Trinity v. United States* (1892) (quoting the earlier words of New York's influential Chancellor James Kent) that "[t]he people of this State, in common with the people of this country, profess the general doctrines of Christianity, as the rule of their faith and practice. ... We are a Christian people, and the morality of this country is deeply engrafted upon Christianity."[20] Moreover, quoting another case, the Supreme Court noted in *Holy Trinity* that "[i]t is also said, and truly, that the Christian religion is part of the common law. ... These, and many

---

[17] For the full story, see Grossberg, *Governing the Hearth*, and Hendrik Hartog, *Man and Wife in America: A History* (Cambridge, MA: Harvard University Press, 2000).
[18] *Bradwell v. Illinois*, 83 U.S. 130, 141 (1872).
[19] Ibid., at 141–142.
[20] *Church of the Holy Trinity v. United States*, 143 U.S. 457, 471 (1892).

other matters which might be noticed, add a volume of unofficial declarations to the mass of organic utterances that this is a Christian nation."[21] Bradley, then, was deciding the case based on Christianity as much as he was on constitutional law. This, however, is not where the law and Constitution are now.

III. WHERE WE ARE NOW

A. *The Right to Privacy*

For Justice Bradley and the *Reynolds* Court and for the Court in *Holy Trinity*, ours was a Christian nation. (Perhaps one ought to pause to realize that the Old Testament, at least, had left open the possibility of polygamy, but the New Testament appears to have been interpreted as binding on the U.S. Supreme Court [and thus the country] in its suggestion that marriage is only between *one* man and *one* woman.) These days, however, one risks universal excoriation if he or she tries to argue that the United States is a "Christian Nation," as Mississippi Governor Kirk Fordice discovered a few years ago.[22]

The story of constitutional law in the second half of the twentieth century is, in part, a repudiation of Christian concepts and their replacement by a set of notions designed to promote "self-actualization" or the maximum achievement of individual freedom, free from the regulation of the state and its imposition of traditional morals. Volumes have been written explaining how this came to be,[23] but for now it suffices to remark on the manner in which, beginning in the 1960s, the U.S. Supreme Court found in the First Amendment's Establishment Clause a license to bar mandatory prayer and Bible reading in the public schools because it believed that the state should not be in the business of coercing children in matters of religious belief.[24] Along these same lines, the states began to endorse

[21] Ibid.
[22] For that story, see Stephen B. Presser, *Recapturing the Constitution: Race, Religion, and Abortion Reconsidered* (Washington, DC: Regnery Publishing, Inc., 1994), 274–275. The outspoken Governor Fordice stated at a Republican Governors' conference in 1992 that the United States was a "Christian nation." This sparked a response seeking to have the Governor amend his remarks to suggest that the country was a "Judeo-Christian" nation. He refused. Press accounts of the controversy generally painted the governor as a bigot. He claimed he was simply accurately reporting the history of the nation, and that its tradition was not only one of Christianity, but also tolerance for other religions.
[23] See ibid. For another effort at explaining the vital role religion played in Western law and society, see M. Stanton Evans, *The Theme is Freedom: Religion, Politics, and the American Tradition* (Washington, DC: Regnery Publishing, Inc., 1994).
[24] The apotheosis of this view was reached in *Lee v. Weisman*, 505 U.S. 577 (1992), when the Supreme Court announced, in a majority opinion by Justice Kennedy, that it was unconstitutional coercion of middle schoolers to permit a prayer delivered by a clergyman selected by the principal at their graduation.

"no-fault" divorce in the name of that notion of individual freedom.[25] Formerly, marriage was thought to be an obligation both to God and to the state, and it was thought to be an unbreakable bond. (At common law, indeed, just as was true for many years in the Catholic Church, there was no divorce permitted to couples who were legally married and sought to dissolve their union.)[26] By the 1970s and 1980s, however, virtually any dissatisfied party could walk away from a personally unfulfilling marriage as states rapidly moved toward unilateral no-fault divorce. At about the same time, any social stigma to having children outside of wedlock began to evaporate, so that by the beginning of the twenty-first century more than half of the children in some ethnic and racial groups were not born to two cohabiting married parents[27] and the percentage for the entire society was hovering around 37 percent.[28] The nuclear American Christian family, as once had been endorsed by both the common law and by the U.S. Supreme Court's interpretation of the U.S. Constitution, was ceasing to exist.

In the 1960s, as part of a further embrace of this creed of individual rights, the U.S. Supreme Court began to announce that there was a "right of privacy" (as one notable decision put it) that flowed from penumbras and emanations somewhere around the First, Fourth, Fifth, and Ninth Amendments; this meant that no state could prohibit married adults from purchasing contraceptive materials.[29] This was followed, shortly, by the extraordinary *Roe v. Wade* (1973) case, which extended the right to privacy to prohibit states from criminalizing early-term abortions.[30] The right was eventually expanded to prohibit all "undue burdens" on abortions at any time during pregnancy,[31] to permit at least some "partial birth" abortions,[32] and, most recently in *Lawrence v. Texas* (2003), to bar criminal penalties for consensual

---

[25] For the history of no-fault divorce in America, see Carl E. Schneider and Margaret F. Brinig, *An Invitation to Family Law* (Eagan, MN: West Publishing, 1995) 348–349; Herbert Jacob, *Silent Revolution: The Transformation of Divorce Law in the United States* (Chicago: University of Chicago Press, 1988).

[26] Blackstone did speak of "divorce" as a term applied by the law to a marriage that was ended because of incapacity on the part of the parties to marry, and he also speaks of "divorce" *a mensa et thoro* ("from bed and board"), where the parties remain husband and wife but are permitted to live separately. The latter is to be granted "in the case of intolerable ill temper, or adultery." Blackstone explained, "For the canon law, which the common law follows in this case, deems so highly and with such mysterious reverence of the nuptial tie, that it will not allow it be unloosed for any cause whatsoever, that arises after the union is made." Blackstone, *Commentaries on the Law of England* vol. I, 428.

[27] By 1995, more than 70% of African-American children were born to unwed mothers. Harrell R. Rodgers, *American Poverty in a New Era of Reform* (Armonk, NY: M.E. Sharp, Inc., 2000), 50.

[28] See, e.g., "Almost 4 in 10 U.S. Children Born Out of Wedlock in 2005," *USA Today*, Nov. 21, 2006.

[29] *Griswold v. Connecticut*, 381 U.S. 479 (1965).

[30] *Roe v. Wade*, 410 U.S. 113 (1973).

[31] *Planned Parenthood v. Casey*, 505 U.S. 833 (1992).

[32] *Stenberg v. Carhart*, 530 U.S. 914 (2000). But see *Gonzales v. Carhart*, 550 U.S. 124 (2007), which upheld a 2003 federal statute prohibiting the practice insofar as it affects interstate or foreign commerce.

homosexual sodomy.[33] Justice Scalia, writing in dissent in *Lawrence*, stated that the U.S. Supreme Court "leaves on pretty shaky grounds state laws limiting marriage to opposite-sex couples," and that the Court was, in his words, "largely signing on to the so-called homosexual agenda."[34]

B. The "Mystery Passage"

It might be closer to the truth to say that in *Lawrence v. Texas* the majority of the Court had "signed on" to unbridled individual discretion and a refusal to allow legislators to make any moral judgments whatsoever. Thus was completed the constitutional movement away from a traditional Christian perspective on the family. This seemed to be the message implied by the Massachusetts Supreme Judicial Court in *Goodridge* when it cited the U.S. Supreme Court's dubious language from *Planned Parenthood v. Casey* (1992), invoked again in the majority opinion in *Lawrence*, that "at the heart of liberty is the right to define one's own concept of existence, of the universe, and of the mystery of human life. Beliefs about these matters could not define the attributes of personhood were they found under the compulsion of the state."[35] As Notre Dame law professor Gerard V. Bradley said of the passage, "[T]he Justices wish to be seen as affirming the right of each person to make up his own moral universe, but to affirm it without making any moral commitments of their own. As if taking the view that everybody can, or should, or should be thought to, inhabit his own world were all 'neutral' propositions." "Making up one's world," Bradley astutely notes, "is existentially impossible, no more empirically available than a unicorn. Of course, some people believe in unicorns."[36]

The majority of the Justices of the U.S. Supreme Court, and the majority of the justices of the Massachusetts Supreme Judicial Court, and perhaps the entire Iowa Supreme Court, then, are ardently unicorn hunting. As columnist John Leo remarked shortly after the Massachusetts decision was rendered, "The Massachusetts decision depicted marriage as an intimacy choice for individuals." Dazzled, perhaps by their unicorn visions, these justices had simply lost sight of the fact that marriage, for eons, had been about more than simply the carnal desires or the individual dignities of two persons. As Leo explained, "Procreation and child rearing, central to a prevailing view of marriage for most of Western history, pretty much disappeared

---

[33] *Lawrence*, 539 U.S. 558.

[34] Ibid. at 602 (Scalia, J., dissenting).

[35] For the original iteration of the "mystery passage," see *Planned Parenthood v. Casey*, 505 U.S. 833, 851 (1992). For the citation to this "liberty" language in *Casey* from the Massachusetts same-sex decision, see *Goodridge v. Dep't of Pub. Health*, 440 Mass. 309, 329 (2003).

[36] Gerard V. Bradley, "Mighty Casey at the Bat," *Catholic Dossier*, May/June 1999, formerly available at http://www.catholic.net/RCC/Periodicals/Dossier/MAYJUN99/Casey.html.

in the decision."[37] It is likely that the moral and religious basis on which marriage had rested for millennia also disappeared. By making marriage nothing more than a personal choice about "attributes of personhood" and by removing the notion that a marriage involved obligations incurred to God, the state, the culture, or one's fellows, surely the importance of the relationship became diminished, and, just as surely, the fragility of marriage as a social institution was underscored.

C. *"Landmarkism?"*

The unreflecting and likely corrosive embrace of unbridled individualism was bad enough, but, following the Massachusetts ruling, there were howls about how it was wholly improper for mere one-person majorities of state or federal courts to alter hundreds of years of belief, tradition, or morals by judicial fiat. For example, Leo lamented:

> Why do judges behave this way? One reason is "landmarkism." The loudest applause from the legal academy tends to come after a far-reaching allegedly progressive decision unsupported by public opinion, and with no real basis in the U.S. Constitution or case law. No judge gets to be admired by the legal and media elites by simply following law and precedents. No glamour there.[38]

If the *Goodridge* decision derived from a judicial search for "glamour," Leo rightly decried it as "stupefying arrogance."[39]

The *Goodridge* court also seemed to ignore the clear procreative and child-rearing functions traditionally deemed to be central to marriage. As Richard G. Wilkins, professor of law at Brigham Young University, wrote, the Massachusetts majority had forgotten the traditional purpose of marriage. "The bearing, rearing and acculturation of children are social interests of surpassing importance," he stated, echoing the nineteenth-century American view of marriage. He went further and argued (despite the advances in artificial reproductive technology) that "[p]rocreation *requires* a coupling between a man and a woman. Here, if not in constitutional law, not all sexual relationships are equal." Finally, demonstrating his refusal to bow to the Massachusetts Supreme Judicial Court's reading of the social science data, Wilkins argued, "[T]he common experience of mankind – documented by a growing mountain of research – demonstrates that the best environment for the rearing and training of a child is within a stable marriage between the child's biological father and mother. These simple facts, as true today as they were thousands

---

[37] John Leo, "Avoiding Democracy," *Jewish World Review*, Nov. 24, 2003/29 Mar-Cheshvan, 5764, available at http://www.jewishworldreview.com/cols/leo112403.asp.

[38] Ibid.

[39] Ibid.

of years ago, provide more than ample grounds for the specialized treatment – and social benefits – conferred upon [opposite-sex] marital unions." Wilkins conceded the *Goodridge* majority's view that limiting marriage to possibly conventionally pro-creative partners "confers an official stamp of approval on the destructive stereotype that same-sex relationships are inherently ... inferior to opposite-sex relationships," but Wilkins stoutly maintained that "[a] homosexual 'marriage' will *never* produce a child. Henceforth, however, we all must officially ignore this fact."[40]

Same-sex marriage advocates could counter Wilkins's argument by reference to empirical studies that have found that gay partners can raise adopted – or for that matter, cloned – children as well as heterosexual couples.[41] We can expect that counter-argument to be made with increasing frequency in the future, and, indeed, that conclusion – that gay couples can raise children just as well as can heterosexual couples – was embraced, *inter alia*, by the unanimous decision of the Iowa Supreme Court.[42]

D. The Future

The real question that now needs to be addressed is whether the decision about what marriage should become should be one for the courts or for the people. For four decades, conservatives have railed against Justices usurping the law-making function, but this seems to have had virtually no effect in the area of sexual relations, intimate association, or, if one likes, the "right to privacy." As long as a Democratic President sits in the White House, and as long as the Senate is controlled by Democrats, there will be no U.S. Supreme Court Justices placed on the bench who do not "sign on" to the "mystery passage" view of individualism and morality. It is quite possible that with one or two more Barack Obama appointments, the U.S. Supreme Court will make the extension Justice Scalia predicted, in the manner the Iowa Supreme Court has done, and find that the U.S. Constitution mandates same-sex marriage.

---

[40] Richard G. Wilkins, "Constitutional Governance and the Irrationality of Marriage," Nov. 20, 2003, available at http://www.declaration.net/news/11-20-03.asp.

[41] For one such powerful study, see Jennifer L. Wainright, Stephen T. Russell, and Charlotte J. Patterson, "Psychosocial Adjustment, School Outcomes, and Romantic Relationships of Adolescents With Same-Sex Parents, Child Development," *Child Development* 75:6 (November/December 2004): 1886–1898, available at http://people.virginia.edu/~cjp/articles/wrp04.pdf. The study concludes, "The results of the present study, which is the first based on a large national sample of adoles-cents living with same-sex couples, revealed that on nearly all of a large array of variables related to school and personal adjustment, adolescents with same-sex parents did not differ significantly from a matched group of adolescents living with opposite-sex parents." Ibid. at 1895.

[42] "Almost every professional group that has studied the issue indicates children are not harmed when raised by same-sex couples, but to the contrary, benefit from them." *Varnum*, 763 N.W.2d 874.

A "marriage amendment" to the U.S. Constitution, defining marriage as only the union between a man and a woman, is still possible, of course, but its chances of making it through the current (or even a foreseeable) Senate with the requisite supermajority required appears slim at best. Indeed, the deeper lesson of *Goodridge, Roe,* and *Lawrence* seems to be that this country may now be embarking on a few decades in which the law will not allow governmental action to be taken in the name of traditional morality. Those who would seek to preserve such morality will only be able to do it through their private associations, most notably their churches, their families, and their independent schools. This preservation can still be done. The nature of the uneasy compromise our law now permits in this regard is suggested by the fact that the same Supreme Court that declared that consensual homosexual acts could not be punished as a crime *did* recently protect the purported First Amendment right of association of the Boy Scouts of America to exclude practicing homosexuals from Scout leadership.[43] This "right of association" is bit of an extratextual creation, something like the "right of privacy," but the Court has been just as firmly committed to it over the same decades.[44]

Elite public opinion is a powerful thing in society and still holds sway even in judicial outcomes. That opinion still pays lip service, at least, to the free exercise of religion (expressly guaranteed by the Constitution)[45] and to the importance of private property and private association. Perhaps it is time to go back to the view that marriages and families and the sacred bonds that unite husbands, wives, and children can best flourish in a relationship severed from the state and not wholly dependent on a capricious judiciary or political process. Perhaps it is wrong to use the government to dictate the details of this precious institution, and perhaps marriage needs to return to the church. Cultures evolve, and not always for the best. American law follows cultural trends, but American law has wisely (at least up until now) sought to permit a maximum of individual freedom, not only for economic acts but also for spiritual ones. The Court's articulation of extreme individualism, at least for the time being, is balanced by its understanding that the most important individual right is to gather in association.[46] Taking advantage of that understanding may be the best thing that can now be done for marriage.

[43] *Boy Scouts of America v. Dale,* 530 U.S. 640 (2000).
[44] On the right of association, see the essays collected in Ellen Frankel Paul, Fred D. Miller Jr., and Jeffrey Paul, eds., *Freedom of Association* (Cambridge: Cambridge University Press, 2008).
[45] United States Constitution, Amendment I ("Congress shall make no law respecting an establishment of religion, or prohibiting the free exercise thereof …").
[46] See John Witte Jr. and Joel A. Nichols, "The Frontiers of Marital Pluralism: An Afterword" (in this volume).

We should recognize that marriage in this country is in trouble. It was put memorably recently by William Van Alstyne, one of our most distinguished constitutional scholars:

> "Marriage" is today easily entered, but then, indeed, it is also almost as easy to exit. So, too, is "marriage" a mere alternative arrangement, one not notably preferable (and, indeed, in some ways less preferable) than some other arrangements available in a number of states where, even as in California, mere "Marvin" agreements (private contracts of cohabitation) are legal alternatives to marriage itself. Not only has marriage been reduced overall in terms of any legal specialness, rather, marriage is itself frankly discouraged by some other features of our modern (or postmodern) law. So, for example, it is commonly supposed that marriage is encouraged in the structure of the federal income tax (i.e., the advantage of filing a joint return), but even this notion is substantially false. For many couples, marriage comes accompanied by a tax *penalty*. Such a couple (a "married" couple) may pay several thousand dollars *more* each year into the federal treasury than had the couple not married but stayed single, casually "cohabiting," and taking care to file separate returns. Marriage may also be discouraged for the same reason for many among the working poor as well, for they, too, may likewise be penalized by the federal tax tables such as they are.[47]

Richard Posner, perhaps America's leading legal scholar, has reached a conclusion similar to that argued here. In his 1992 book *Sex and Reason* he observed that "a sizeable fraction of heterosexual marriages in our society are not stable and are not rewarding," and further that "as heterosexual marriage becomes ever more unstable, temporary, and childless, the suggestion that it differs fundamentally from what homosexual marriages could be expected to be like becomes ever more implausible." Yet for Posner, this "is a point in favor not of homosexual marriage but of chucking the whole institution of marriage in favor of an explicitly contractual approach that would make the current realities of marriage transparent."[48]

If the institution of marriage is to be saved, if the benefits of that sacred alliance can still be seen to inure to the whole society, as Roger Wilkins, Sir William Blackstone, and William Van Alstyne all understand, we probably cannot trust in

---

[47] William Van Alstyne, "The Unbearable Lightness of Marriage in The Abortion Decisions of the Supreme Court: Altered States in Constitutional Law," *William and Mary Bill of Rights Journal* 18 (2009): 61–74. This is not the first time that the tax treatment of marriage has imperiled the institution, driving its proponents into the sacred sphere. A Jewish marriage tax in Galicia in the late 1700s "was so heavy that it was meant to discourage legal marriages of Jewish couples. It did not, however, discourage Jewish marriages because Jewish couples simply had ritual marriages and bypassed the tax regulations." Quoted in Susan Wynne, *The Galitzianers: The Jews of Galicia, 1772–1918* (Tucson, AZ: Wheatmark, 2006), 48 (quote attributed to Alice Solovy).

[48] These quotations from Posner's 1992 book *Sex and Reason* are reprinted in Sullivan, *Same Sex Marriage Pro and Con*, 186–187.

courts because, simply stated, too many judges and justices have embraced individualism and forgotten morality and community. There is a powerful argument for allowing gay couples to have all the civil benefits of the marriage relationship, but it is doubtful that such a move will save traditional marriage. The secular sphere is not the place to turn to preserve our traditional values. If there is value in thinking of marriage as a sacred institution, one that is made more stable because it is a bond forged not only by the parties but also by the Deity, marriage should be returned to the church. As Douglas Kmiec and Richard Posner have argued, as far as the state is concerned it ought to be possible for same-sex couples to make contracts that would have all the legal attributes of marriage, save the name. Anything else, especially in this day and age, will be perceived by courts as violations of equal protection or due process, as discrimination that cannot be permitted. However, because such relationships can now easily be severed by mutual desire of the parties (and frequently the unilateral desire of one party), something more – marriage – is needed. And marriage, now, ought to be the province of the churches.

IV. CONCLUSION

In the nineteenth century, in an era when it was believed that Christianity was a part of the common law, judges – governmental officials – believed that it was their job to reinforce the church's view of marriage as a sacred institution. Over time, the idea that it is the job of judges to implement religious notions lost favor, to the point at which the Supreme Court will not now even permit nonsectarian prayers at public school graduation ceremonies or student-led prayer at public school football games.[49] In the nineteenth century, there was a sort of government/church joint effort regarding marriage and morality, but in recent history the government's recognition of the sacred character of marriage has declined as the government has become increasingly involved in determining what is a marriage and what is not. But the sacred conception of marriage was something to which the founding and later American generations were committed, and now returning marriage to the church might strengthen marriage in a manner with which the framers would have sympathized. Permitting civil unions via the state as a matter of contract preserves and encourages liberty and equality; affirming the sacred character of marriage via governance by religion itself might frankly better preserve marriage. Such a move is not radical, but a conservative step quite in accordance with our traditions.

---

[49] See respectively *Lee v. Weisman*, 505 U.S. 577 (1992); *Santa Fe Independent School District v. Doe*, 530 U.S. 290 (2000).

4

Unofficial Family Law

Ann Laquer Estin

Marriage and family practices around the world are embedded in a rich matrix of cultural norms, generated by legal rules, religious traditions, and social expectations. In homogenous societies, these different normative frameworks reflect widely shared values, reinforcing a common understanding of what marriage and family life should be. In more diverse societies, the range of normative variation expands and individuals may face contrasting opportunities and constraints from official and unofficial norms of family behavior.

Some advocates of multiculturalism argue for accommodating the distinct values and traditions of religious or other minority groups through a formal legal pluralism in which governments would delegate aspects of state authority over marriage, divorce, and inheritance to separate legal authorities with power to apply their own law to members of their groups.[1] Legal pluralism, in this classic sense, is an artifact of empire and colonialism that has remained important in the contemporary world as a tool for managing deep and persistent cultural and legal differences in post-colonial nations such as India and South Africa.[2]

---

[1] See, e.g., John F. Burns, "Top Anglican Seeks a Role for Islamic Law in Britain," *New York Times*, Feb. 8, 2008, A10. For a specific proposal, see Syed Mumtaz Ali and Enab Whitehouse, "The Reconstruction of the Constitution and the Case for Muslim Personal Law in Canada," *Journal of Muslim Minority Affairs* 13:1 (1992): 156–172, 168–172; see also Mark D. Rosen, "The Radical Possibility of Limited Community-Based Interpretation of the Constitution," *William and Mary Law Review* 43 (2002): 927–1010, 929 (suggesting that the government could grant extensive powers of self-governance within territorial enclaves created on federal land to "insular communities with norms radically different from those of general society"); cf. Joel A. Nichols, "Multi-Tiered Marriage: Ideas and Influences from New York and Louisiana to the International Community," *Vanderbilt Journal of Transnational Law* 40 (January 2007): 135–196, 136 (advocating some form of "more robust pluralism" that would incorporate a greater role for religious understandings of marriage in American law).

[2] See, e.g., M. B. Hooker, *Legal Pluralism: An Introduction to Colonial and Neo-Colonial Laws* 58–84, 303–312 (Oxford: Oxford University Press, 1975). See Werner Menski, "Ancient and Modern Boundary Crossings Between Personal Laws and Civil Law in Composite India" (in this volume) and Johan D. van der Vyver, "Multi-Tiered Marriages in South Africa" (in this volume).

Over the past generation, new migration patterns have brought these questions of multiculturalism and legal pluralism from the periphery to the centers of colonial power, where the debate provokes profound uneasiness among the mainstream or majority society. In the liberal democracies of Europe and North America, the legal system (including family law) is understood to be based on universal and secular principles, affording the same rights to all citizens and rejecting any formal differentiation on cultural or religious grounds. The rules of this official family law are far from neutral, however, and define a culturally specific set of minimum requirements and expectations for family formation and behavior. This lack of neutrality creates tensions for those whose practices or traditions diverge from the predominant legal and cultural norms.

There are important reasons to facilitate multicultural accommodation in family law. All individuals are embedded in families and communities, which are important to their stability, happiness, and to the successful nurture of the next generation. A multilayered approach to family regulation builds on the notion that many families have a complex identity and experience shaped and defined by many different cultural, legal, and political ties. It supports a richer notion of citizenship in which individuals are understood not only in terms of their relationship to the state but also as members of families and religious communities.

Greater accommodation of cultural and religious diversity is possible within the framework of our legal and political system,[3] but there are also important reasons to be cautious with this project. Throughout our history, and in many places around the globe, the definition of a separate sphere of private or family life has subjected some members of the community to the risk of violence or abuse that goes unnoticed and unaddressed by any effective means of social or legal control. It has also created the risk that these group members will be prevented from participating in the wider currents of education, employment, and citizenship. Both of these risks have fallen primarily on women and girls, who are simultaneously celebrated as the carriers of culture and excluded from opportunities to exit or shape their communities.[4]

---

[3] See Ann Laquer Estin, "Embracing Tradition: Pluralism in American Family Law," *Maryland Law Review* 63 (2004): 540–604, 598–603; see also Alison Dundes Renteln, *The Cultural Defense* (Oxford: Oxford University Press, 2004). Our distinct traditions and historical experiences dictate that multicultural accommodation will likely follow a different path from the legal pluralism of Asia or Africa, for example. In the United States, the self-governance of federally recognized Native American communities extends to family law matters, but nonindigenous minority groups have no official status. See Barbara Ann Atwood, "Tribal Jurisprudence and Cultural Meanings of the Family," *Nebraska Law Review* 79 (2000): 577–656, 593–595.

[4] See Ayelet Shachar, "Faith in Law? Diffusing Tensions Between Diversity and Equality" (in this volume). See also Ayelet Shachar, *Multicultural Jurisdictions: Cultural Differences and Women's Rights* (Cambridge: Cambridge University Press, 2001), 55–57; Susan Moller Okin, *Is Multiculturalism Bad for Women?* (Princeton, NJ: Princeton University Press, 1999), 12–17.

In light of these risks, any policy that fosters multicultural or multi-tiered approaches to family law in the United States must include protections for vulnerable family members.[5] In circumstances of formal legal pluralism, the risks are substantial enough that state authorities would need to remain involved with families at some level in order to accomplish the important protective functions now performed by family law.[6]

Beyond the argument for a pluralized marriage law, other writers have argued for abolishing or "privatizing" marriage law.[7] These proposals sometimes suggest that civil marriage should be replaced with civil unions or another substitute regime, and they sometimes suggest that a status approach should be entirely rejected in favor of general principles of contract, property, and tort law. Advocates of privatization sometimes argue that these alternatives would give greater scope to the unofficial law of religious communities.[8] As with a pluralization of marriage law, however, the state would remain involved in family regulation in either of these scenarios. Most discussions never reach the more specific, pragmatic questions of how a system of pluralized or privatized marriage could be implemented.

Whereas the multiculturalism debate has become a familiar one, much less attention has been paid to the legal pluralism that already flourishes in the United

[5] Judges and other decision makers can learn to understand and respect different cultural, religious, and legal traditions, recognizing that many families are deeply connected to communities with distinct norms and practices that shape their behavior as mothers and fathers, daughters and sons, and wives and husbands. At the same time, judges and legislators have the responsibility and obligation to adhere to the fundamental norms of our legal and political system, including our commitments to equality, due process, freedom of religion and belief, and the right of access to courts for protection from serious physical and financial harm. See generally Estin, "Embracing Tradition." See also Linda C. McClain, "Marriage Pluralism in the United States: On Civil and Religious Jurisdiction and the Demands of Equal Citizenship" (in this volume) and Robin Fretwell Wilson, "The Perils of Privatized Marriage" (in this volume).

[6] This would pose substantial constitutional challenges, which are beyond the scope of this chapter. See Brian H. Bix, "Pluralism and Decentralization in Marriage Regulation" (in this volume) and John Witte Jr. and Joel A. Nichols, "The Frontiers of Marital Pluralism: An Afterword" (in this volume). Beyond the free exercise and establishment questions, a formal millet system, in which individuals are assigned to the legal and regulatory authority of distinct religious communities, also requires some method by which religious membership and affiliation are determined and regulated by the state. These are very substantial problems. See, e.g., Nadim Audi, "Egyptian Court Allows Return to Christianity," *New York Times*, Feb. 11, 2008, A11; Gershom Gorenberg, "How Do You Prove You're a Jew?" *New York Times Magazine*, Mar. 2, 2008, 46.

[7] See generally, e.g., Anita Bernstein, ed., *Marriage Proposals: Questioning a Legal Status* (New York: New York University Press, 2006); Mary Lyndon Shanley, *Just Marriage* (Oxford: Oxford University Press, 2004); Elizabeth S. Scott, "A World Without Marriage," *Family Law Quarterly* 41 (2007): 537–566; Edward Stein, "Symposium on Abolishing Civil Marriage: An Introduction," *Cardozo Law Review* 27 (2006): 1155–1159. See also Stephen B. Presser, "Marriage and the Law: Time for a Divorce?" (in this volume).

[8] E.g., Daniel A. Crane, "A 'Judeo-Christian' Argument for Privatizing Marriage," *Cardozo Law Review* 27 (2006): 1221–1259, 1222.

States. As anthropologists have observed, the official legal system in any society exists in tandem with other forms of social ordering.[9] This understanding of legal pluralism recognizes the proceedings of an ecclesiastical court, rabbinic tribunal, or Muslim dispute resolution center as a form of law, even without the backing of any official state authority. Once our lens widens to include this broader landscape of legal phenomena, other practices come into view, including religiously based marital counseling or prenuptial agreements, as well as more informal social ordering through community sanctions such as gossip or ostracism.[10] The fact that these practices may have no secular legal effect serves to begin rather than to end the inquiry.[11] One important insight from such an understanding is that state law and legal institutions have only a limited degree of control over society, and they do not necessarily dominate or displace other social systems.[12] Another is that individuals may be simultaneously subject to different systems of rules, and these systems may not be coordinated or hierarchically arranged.[13]

This chapter takes a different approach to the question of multicultural accommodation and legal pluralism in family law, beginning with the dynamics of unofficial family law as it is already practiced in the United States. Ethnographic research that would provide a rich description or understanding of these practices is not readily available, but other evidence indicates that different modes of family regulation operate here. For example, official case reports in a number of states reflect the ongoing importance of religious legal traditions, including Jewish and Islamic regulation of marriage and divorce.[14] Web sites and other literature promote the

[9] See Sally Engle Merry, "Legal Pluralism," *Law and Society Review* 22 (1988): 869–892, 872. See Menski, "Ancient and Modern Boundary Crossings" (in this volume).

[10] See generally Sally Falk Moore, "Law and Social Change: The Semi-Autonomous Social Field as an Appropriate Subject of Study," *Law and Society Review* 7 (1973): 719–746. See also Mohammad H. Fadel, "Political Liberalism, Islamic Family Law, and Family Law Pluralism" (in this volume) and Michael J. Broyde, "New York's Regulation of Jewish Marriage: Covenant, Contract, or Statute?" (in this volume).

[11] How, when, and why do participants choose to develop and pursue this form of private ordering or dispute resolution? How are religious or customary laws and norms defined, created, and enforced in these settings? To what extent do these other forms of social ordering function independently of or in some relation to state authority? See Franz and Keebet von Benda-Beckmann, "The Dynamics of Change and Continuity in Plural Legal Orders," *Journal of Legal Pluralism and Unofficial Law* 53–54 (2006): 1–44, 17–32.

[12] See generally Sally Falk Moore, *Law as Process: An Anthropological Approach* (London: Routledge & Kegan Paul Books, 1978). See also Menski, "Ancient and Modern Boundary Crossings" (in this volume).

[13] Moore, *Law as Process*, 24–25.

[14] For a survey of the American case law, see Estin, "Embracing Tradition," 569–586; Carolyn Hamilton, *Family, Law and Religion* (London: Sweet & Maxwell, 1995), 337–342 (discussing England and the United States); Asifa Quraishi and Najeeba Syeed-Miller, "No Altars: A Survey of Islamic Family Law in the United States," in *Women's Rights and Islamic Family Law*, ed. Lynn Welchman (New York: Palgrave McMillan, 2004), 177–229. See also Bix, "Pluralism and Decentralization" (in this

services of alternative tribunals for resolving disputes within the context of particular religious communities.[15] In the popular media, stories of polygamous households have become a staple of news and entertainment.[16] Beyond the United States, there is a more extensive literature on unofficial family law, particularly with respect to Muslim communities in Britain.[17] In Australia, the Law Reform Commission has studied questions of legal pluralism and multicultural accommodation,[18] and in Ontario, the prospect of "*shari'a* arbitration" in family law matters has generated significant public attention and debate.[19] From these sources, it is apparent that religious law continues to serve important purposes for many Roman Catholics, Jews, and Muslims, operating as an unofficial complement or alternative to the law of the state. The evidence suggests that members of these communities generally follow official marriage and divorce laws in order to have their family status recognized by the state, but that they also utilize unofficial law mediated by ecclesiastical courts, rabbinic tribunals, or Muslim dispute resolution centers.

Official and unofficial family law interact in three distinctive patterns. First, at the point of marriage celebration, official and unofficial law have similar goals and are often closely interwoven. Second, dissolution of marriage presents a more complex

volume); Broyde, "New York's Regulation" (in this volume); McClain, "Marriage Pluralism in the United States" (in this volume).

[15] See, e.g., Beth Din of America, http://www.bethdin.org; The Canadian Society of Muslims, Muslim Marriage Mediation and Arbitration Service, formerly at http://muslim-canada.org/brochure.htm (last visited active Nov. 9, 2008) (in Canada); Institute for Christian Conciliation/Peacemaker Ministries, http://www.hispeace.org; Islamic Sharia Council, http://www.islamic-sharia.org (in the United Kingdom); see also Adam Liptak, "When God and the Law Don't Square," *New York Times*, Feb. 17, 2008, A3 (discussing enforcement by a Texas court of an agreement to arbitrate divorce issues in local Islamic tribunal).

[16] Whereas these accounts usually focus on Mormon communities, see, e.g., Jon Krakauer, *Under the Banner of Heaven: A Story of Violent Faith* (New York: Doubleday, 2003), news accounts have also reported on polygamous households among immigrant communities from Africa. See, e.g., Nina Bernstein, "In Secret, Polygamy Follows Africans to N.Y.," *New York Times*, March 23, 2007, available at http://www.nytimes.com/2007/03/23/nyregion/23polygamy.html.

[17] See, e.g., Hamilton, *Family, Law and Religion*, 88, 302–303; David Pearl and Werner F. Menski, *Muslim Family Law* (London: Sweet & Maxwell, 3rd ed. 1998), 51–80; Sebastian Poulter, *English Law and Ethnic Minority Customs* (London: Butterworths, 1986); Ihsan Yilmaz, *Muslim Laws, Politics and Society in Modern Nation States: Dynamic Legal Pluralisms in England, Turkey and Pakistan* (Aldershot, U.K.: Ashgate Publishing, 2005), 49–81.

[18] E.g., The Law Reform Commission (Australia), *Multiculturalism and the Law*, Report No. 57, §§ 1.15–1.18 (1992); The Law Reform Commission (Australia), *The Recognition of Aboriginal Customary Laws*, Report No. 31, at 95–125, 164 (1986).

[19] See generally Marion Boyd, Office of Canadian Attorney General, *Dispute Resolution in Family Law: Protecting Choice, Promoting Inclusion* 29–68 (2004), available at http://www.attorneygeneral.jus.gov.on.ca/english/about/pubs/boyd/fullreport.pdf. See also Daniel Cere, "Canadian Conjugal Mosaic: From Multiculturalism to Multi-Conjugalism?" (in this volume); Fadel, "Political Liberalism" (in this volume); McClain, "Marriage Pluralism in the United States" (in this volume); Wilson, "The Perils of Privatized Marriage" (in this volume).

problem that has generated significant conflict between normative systems, resulting in an often intricate interaction of official and unofficial law. Third, official law
has been used as a gatekeeping tool in the substantive regulation of marriage to
define the shape of both family life and the broader social and political community.
To the extent that official law deems unacceptable certain family or marriage practices that are recognized under unofficial norms, individuals or communities with
those practices are kept outside or at the edges of law and society. Thus, although
polygamy is permitted in Islam, it may be punished by the state. The practice of
polygamy has nevertheless continued underground, regulated largely by custom or
unofficial law, leaving family members outside the boundaries of protections that
are ordinarily available under official law.

Many writers have discussed the parallel between legal prohibitions of polygamy
and the bar against same-sex marriage.[20] Like polygamists, gay and lesbian couples
in most states find that their family relationships fall outside the protection of official
law. As the debate over same-sex marriage proceeds, and as some states have moved
to establish an official legal status for same-sex couples, members of religious groups
whose marriage traditions have not previously conflicted with official marriage laws
find the prospect of a divide between official law and their unofficial norms to be
deeply unsettling.[21] One response has been the call to privatize marriage so that religious understandings will not be tainted or compromised by a secular definition that
is inconsistent with religious norms.[22]

The religious argument for abolishing civil marriage assumes the possibility of
a clear separation of the secular and religious spheres. However, as long as many
aspects of family life are legitimately of concern to the state, plural and overlapping
normative orders are unavoidable. The dynamic interplay of official and unofficial
law is a necessary attribute of social life, particularly in a multireligious and multicultural society. This reality has important consequences for both the debate over
multiculturalism and the current controversy over the definition of marriage. A privatization of marriage would not eliminate the difficulties described here. Similar
tensions would appear at the intersection of religious marriage law and contract law,
or whatever secular law was enlisted to structure and regulate family relationships,

---

[20] E.g., David L. Chambers, "Polygamy and Same-Sex Marriage," *Hofstra Law Review* 26 (1997):
53–86.
[21] Mary Anne Case suggests that this is particularly true for conservative Protestants, who "have essentially abdicated the definition, creation and, above all the dissolution of marriage to the state," leaving
them more dependent on the state's definitions of marriage and "far less able to distinguish conceptually between marriage as their religion defines it and as state law does." Mary Anne Case, "Marriage
Licenses," *Minnesota Law Review* 89 (2005): 1758–1797, 1795.
[22] See, e.g., Presser, "Marriage and the Law" (in this volume); David Novak, "Jewish Marriage and Civil
Law: A Two-Way Street?" *George Washington Law Review* 68 (2000): 1059–1078, 1077.

because the dynamic interplay of official and unofficial law is a necessary attribute of life in a multireligious and multicultural society.

I. MARRIAGE CELEBRATION: CONVERGENCE AND INCORPORATION

Laws in the United States make it relatively simple for religious clergy of all denominations to conduct wedding ceremonies that have both civil and religious effect. Civil marriage requirements are based on the Christian ecclesiastical tradition, which contributes to the common understanding of weddings as simultaneously secular and sacred. In some communities, however, secular legal norms do not fit as closely with religious traditions and law. For members of these groups, the separate demands of official and unofficial law may complicate the process of family formation and leave some family members without the protection of the state.

A. Marriage Celebrations

For most couples, very little distinction exists between the secular and religious aspects of marriage. Marriage licenses are required in almost all states, except for a few that still recognize the validity of informal marriage.[23] There is no need for two separate ceremonies, as in France, and generally no restriction on the words that must be used or the places a wedding can take place, as in England.[24] Most weddings in this country are still celebrated with a religious ceremony.[25]

In a number of jurisdictions, state statutes explicitly accommodate the practices of particular religious groups. The same New York statute that requires the parties entering a marriage to "solemnly declare … that they take each other as husband and wife" also provides that this requirement "shall not affect marriages among the people called Friends or Quakers; nor marriages among the people of other denominations having as such any particular mode of solemnizing marriages."[26] A Rhode Island statute permits Jews to marry those "within the degrees of affinity or consanguinity allowed by their religion" even if state law would otherwise prohibit

---

[23] See, e.g., Iowa Code § 595.11 (2007); New York Domestic Relations Law § 11(4) (McKinney 1999).
[24] On the French law, see Edwige Rude-Antoine, "Muslim Maghrebian Marriage in France: A Problem for Legal Pluralism," *International Journal of Law and the Family* 5 (1991): 93–103, 97–99. On the English law, see Jocelyne Cesari, *When Islam and Democracy Meet: Muslims in Europe and in the United States* (New York: Palgrave Macmillan, 2004), 59–60.
[25] Religious authorities perform an estimated 60 to 80 percent of the marriages in the United States. See Martin King Whyte, *Dating, Mating, and Marriage* (Hawthorne, NY: Walter de Gruyter, Inc., 1990), 56: Cathy Lynn Grossman and In-Sung Yoo, "Civil Marriage on Rise Across USA," *USA Today*, Oct. 7, 2003, 1A.
[26] New York Domestic Relations Law § 12 (McKinney 1999).

those marriages.[27] When statutory language is so narrow as to exclude some religious clergy or groups, courts have insisted that it be read more inclusively in order to prevent constitutional difficulties.[28]

Given the ease with which civil and religious marriage can be combined, most individuals and clergy view a wedding as simultaneously secular and religious. By incorporating unofficial law and norms into the civil rite, the state appropriates and reinforces the solemnity of the occasion for its own purposes. The twinning of secular and sacred operates to impress the couple and the community with the seriousness of the marriage commitment.

In England, with its established church and more complex requirements for solemnizing marriage, members of many minority religious groups could not readily combine civil and religious marriage ceremonies.[29] Among these groups, most couples married twice, often treating the civil ceremony as a preliminary to the religious wedding. The civil marriage may be important for immigration or other reasons, and problems may arise if one member of the couple later refuses to follow through with a religious ceremony.[30] Ihsan Yilmaz argues that Muslim communities in England do not consider a couple with only a civil marriage to be truly married, and they are "expected to abstain from all kind of intimate interactions, and by all means should most definitely not consummate the marriage" until the religious marriage is concluded.[31]

Alternatively, couples may marry in a religious ceremony without following the requirements of the civil law, generating a different set of problems. Communities often understand the potential for abuse and the risks this poses for women who have no civil status as a wife. Despite these risks, some observers report that substantial numbers of Muslim couples are only religiously married.[32] For a couple whose marriage would be valid in religious law but not in civil law, as in the case of polygamy, there are obviously additional reasons to avoid civil registration.

The same problems occur in the United States, despite the closer identification of official and unofficial marriage law. Most states broadly define who can officiate a wedding, with many state statutes providing that a marriage may be solemnized "in accordance with any mode of solemnization recognized by any religious

[27] Rhode Island General Laws § 15–1–4 (2003).
[28] See, e.g., *Persad v. Balram*, 724 N.Y.S.2d 560, 563 (N.Y. Sup. Ct. 2001); *Aghili v. Saadatnejadi*, 958 S.W.2d 784, 787 (Tenn. Ct. App. 1997).
[29] See Hamilton, *Family, Law and Religion*, 47–51 (noting that very few Muslim mosques, Hindu or Buddhist temples, or Sikh gurdwaras were registered and approved as places for civil marriages in England). See also Menski, "Ancient and Modern Boundary Crossings" (in this volume).
[30] See Pearl and Menski, *Muslim Family Law*, 73–77, 168–169.
[31] Yilmaz, *Muslim Laws, Politics and Society*, 72–74.
[32] Ibid. at 74.

denomination, Indian Nation or Tribe, or Native Group."[33] Civil courts sometimes
recognize religious or other ceremonial marriages as valid, even if they were solemnized without a license, under common law marriage doctrines and other rules
designed to uphold the validity of marriages.[34] These doctrines do not always convert unofficial marriages into official ones, however. For example, *Farah v. Farah*
involved a Muslim wedding conducted in three stages. After the couple signed a
nikah agreement in Virginia, there was a proxy ceremony in London, and then a
wedding reception and celebration in Pakistan. The couple lived together in Virginia
for a year before separating; although they had intended to have a civil marriage ceremony, they never did so. When the wife sought a divorce and equitable distribution
of property, the husband challenged the validity of their marriage and persuaded the
court not to recognize the marriage because the process of formalization did not
meet the requirements of the official law in Virginia, England, or Pakistan.[35]

B. The Interaction of Religious and Civil Law

American statutes create the opportunity for celebrating civil and religious marriage
simultaneously, but they generally do not attempt to enforce a requirement of separate civil marriage.[36] Determining how to coordinate official and unofficial law is
left primarily to the members of each religious community. Different groups take
different approaches to the interaction between religious and secular laws, but official and unofficial law function relatively harmoniously together in the celebration
of marriages.

For many centuries, Jewish communities located within non-Jewish states or
empires were treated as separate and autonomous enclaves, exercising internal
authority over marriage and divorce.[37] As David Novak explains, Jewish law developed

[33] Uniform Marriage and Divorce Act § 206(a), 9A U.L.A. 182 (1998); see also Homer H. Clark Jr., *The Law of Domestic Relations in the United States* (St. Paul, MN: West Publishing, 1988), 37–39.
[34] See, e.g., *Carabetta v. Carabetta*, 438 A.2d 109, 111–113 (Conn. 1980); *State v. Phelps*, 652 N.E.2d 1032, 1035–1036 (Ohio Ct. App. 1995).
[35] *Farah v. Farah*, 429 S.E.2d 626 (Va. Ct. App. 1993).
[36] In many civil law countries, like France, religious clergy are prohibited from marrying a couple that has not already been married in a civil ceremony. Only a few states in the United States take this approach. E.g., New York Domestic Relations Law § 17 (McKinney 1999) (defining misdemeanor offense for solemnization of marriage without a civil license). As Michael Broyde notes, any pros-ecution under this statute would raise significant First Amendment questions. Michael J. Broyde, *Marriage, Divorce, and the Abandoned Wife in Jewish Law* (Hoboken, NJ: Ktav Publishing House, 2001), 144.
   An English statute prohibits solemnizing a marriage in a place other than a building registered for that purpose, but the law has not been applied to clergy who perform only religious marriage in such a place. Hamilton, *Family, Law and Religion*, 40–41.
[37] Jews did not receive full citizenship in many Western European countries until the second half of the nineteenth century. See Pierre Birnbaum and Ira Katznelson, eds., *Paths of Emancipation: Jews,*

principles of deference to non-Jewish law in most civil and criminal matters, except for marriage and divorce.[38] As he writes, these areas "are considered to be matters too far within the interior of covenantal Jewish life to be allowed any non-Jewish jurisdiction over them whatsoever."[39] Once European Jews were emancipated, however, they lost many of their communal privileges and became simply private associations or local congregations with limited power over community members. Jewish communities accepted the new institution of civil marriage, and most Jews now marry under both civil and religious law.[40]

Novak points out the paradox of two separate jurisdictions, each asserting its own priority: "Even though the secular state has made participation in a religious marriage something *subsequent* to participation in civil marriage, traditional Jews have regarded their involvement in civil marriage as a necessity of their participation in civil society, but a necessity to which their subordination to Jewish law is *prior*." As he notes, the state requires only compliance with secular authority, and religious people can determine "whether or not such compliance is consistent with their ultimate commitment to the authority of their God as revealed and transmitted to them by their own tradition."[41]

Islamic jurisprudence concerning the obligations of individual Muslims who live in non-Muslim nations is complex, "characterised by ambivalence and great diversity of thought," but requires at a minimum that Muslims live where they can fulfill their religious obligations.[42] Indeed, David Pearl and Werner Menski describe the development of an English Islamic law, or *angrezi shariat*, as an effort to allow British Muslims "to restructure their lives in accordance with *shari'a* as well as the requirements of English law."[43]

Among Islamic communities in non-Muslim countries, there are different practices concerning marriage. While many Muslim clergy solemnize marriages under both religious and civil law, some Muslim weddings may not meet the requirements of state marriage laws.[44] Marriage in Islam, or *nikah*, is based on a contractual principle and may be formalized without religious clergy, with an exchange of consents

States, and Citizenship* (Princeton, NJ: Princeton University Press, 1995); Lois C. Duban, "Jewish Women, Marriage Law, and Emancipation: A Civil Divorce in Late-Eighteenth-Century Trieste," *Jewish Social Studies* 13 (2007): 65–92, 67–70.

[38] See Novak, "Jewish Marriage and Civil Law," 1061–1068.

[39] Ibid. at 1064. A traditional exception to this principle allows the use of civil authority to compel a man to follow the order of a Jewish rabbinical court to give his wife a *get*, or bill of divorce, discussed hereinafter. See also Broyde, "New York's Regulation" (in this volume).

[40] Novak, "Jewish Marriage and Civil Law," 1070–1071 (discussing the council of rabbis convened by Napoleon in 1807 to consider this point).

[41] Ibid.

[42] Pearl and Menski, *Muslim Family Law*, 62–65.

[43] Ibid. at 65.

[44] E.g., *Farah*, 429 S.E.2d 626; see also Cesari, *When Islam and Democracy Meet*, 57–60.

before two qualified witnesses. Couples may not be fully aware of the difference between civil and religious marriage, or of the legal benefits of marriage under state law. In France, despite laws that require completion of civil marriage formalities before a religious marriage is performed, a recent report suggests that many young Muslim couples marry only under religious law.[45] Having a religious but not a civil marriage allows a couple to have sexual relations and cohabit without violating community norms. This choice reflects a belief that compliance with religious law is more important than adherence to civil law. In some cases, a religious marriage without secular formalities may be more attractive because it allows couples to avoid the complexities of civil divorce or because it facilitates the practice of polygamy.[46]

These issues are not limited to individuals living in a few insular ethnic enclaves. Several years ago, a law student in Colorado came to my office after our discussion of the *Farah* case. He told me that he had recently signed a *nikah* agreement with a woman, and that a wedding celebration was planned to take place in California the following summer. He and his fiancée, as he referred to her, had slept together afterward, but he was having second thoughts about going through with the marriage. Were they already married?[47]

Broadening the marriage celebration rules of official law to take account of the distinct traditions of formalization in different cultural and religious groups is an important means of incorporating members of all groups into the wider social and political community. This is a useful point of convergence and consensus in a multicultural community. Here, religion and the state can speak together. Marriage is clearly understood across secular and religious frames to be a good thing, something to be encouraged, upheld, and validated. For families, the opportunity to celebrate civil and religious marriage simultaneously is beneficial at both a symbolic level and a pragmatic one: concluding marriages with a single ceremony prevents the ambiguity and potential complications of different status in civil and religious law.

II. DIVORCE LAW: CONFLICT AND ACCOMMODATION

Advocates of pluralized or privatized marriage may imagine a system in which public and private regulation dovetail in the relatively harmonious manner of marriage

---

[45] Stéphanie Le Bars, "Des Jeunes Musulmans Veulent S'affranchir du Marriage Civil," *Le Monde*, June 9, 2007.

[46] Ibid. In some traditions, couples may choose to marry after a betrothal period to allow an opportunity for courtship consistent with community norms. See, e.g., Geneive Abdo, *Mecca and Main Street: Muslim Life in America After 9/11* (Oxford: Oxford University Press, 2006), 31–32.

[47] As a matter of official law, the question was complicated by the fact that these events took place in a common law marriage state. See, e.g., *State v. Phelps*, 652 N.E.2d 1032, 1035–1036 (Ohio Ct. App. 1995) (sustaining a marriage based on Islamic ceremony as a common law marriage).

celebration rules. Civil and religious laws come into more substantial conflict at the point of marriage dissolution, however. Divorce disputes involve two individuals with different interests; these individuals may also have different rights under official and unofficial law, different understandings of their religious tradition and practice, and different motivations to seek recourse from the state. In this setting, official law operates to protect a range of individual rights that may stand opposed to religious norms, and unofficial law operates to define and defend the boundaries and membership of those communities.

Divorce presents a more complicated arena of interaction because of the conflict between civil divorce laws and the religious laws or norms of many groups. For Catholics and Hindus, whose religions prohibit divorce, secular laws that narrowly limited access to divorce were a better fit with unofficial religious norms. For this reason, the Roman Catholic Church worked strenuously for many years against the easing of official divorce laws in the United States.[48] Once no-fault divorce laws were enacted, some individuals attempted without success to resist civil divorce actions on religious grounds, arguing that entry of a no-fault divorce decree would violate their rights under the First Amendment.[49] Citing Free Exercise and Establishment Clause barriers, courts identified the central problem with this defense as a conflict between religious views: to deny a divorce based on one partner's religious convictions would impose those religious values on the other partner. One of these decisions quotes from the New Testament: "Render, therefore, to Caesar the things that are Caesar's, and to God the things that are God's."[50] Implicit in this response is the court's conclusion that civil divorce belongs to the state, as a purely secular matter, and that questions of religious belief and practice are entirely beyond its ken.

Religious communities have maintained the norms that discourage or prohibit divorce; yet as divorce rates have risen across societies, they have also increased for the membership of these groups. For groups that prohibit divorce, a civil dissolution of marriage creates the possibility of a limping marriage, terminated in official law but still binding in religious law. This is a concern for Roman Catholics who are divorced in the civil courts; they cannot participate fully in the religious life of their community if they remarry without first obtaining an annulment of their marriage under canon law.[51] To accommodate this concern, the number of annulments

---

[48] See Nelson Manfred Blake, *The Road to Reno: A History of Divorce in the United States* (New York: Macmillan, 1962), 203–225.

[49] E.g., *Sharma v. Sharma*, 667 P.2d 395, 395 (Kan. Ct. App. 1983); *Wikoski v. Wikoski*, 513 A.2d 986, 986 (Pa. Super. Ct. 1986).

[50] *Wikoski*, 513 A.2d at 989 (quoting Matthew 22:15–22).

[51] See generally Chester Gillis, *Roman Catholicism in America* (New York: Columbia University Press, 1999), 163–166.

granted by the Church has increased dramatically over the past thirty years, and this trend has been a source of internal debate.[52]

For Muslims and Jews, whose religious law has permitted divorce for many centuries, civil divorce laws create a different limping marriage problem. Both systems of law permit divorce, but just as the state does not recognize a religious divorce, the religious community does not recognize a civil divorce as ending a religious marriage. The intersection of civil and religious law is made more complicated by the fact that in these systems the legal rights of husbands are different than the legal rights of wives. These differences create opportunities for strategic behavior that frequently surfaces in civil divorce proceedings.[53]

To conclude a divorce, Jewish law requires that a husband deliver a document known as a *get* to his wife in a process carried out before a rabbinic tribunal.[54] As this requirement has been implemented in rabbinic tradition, both husband and wife must participate willingly in the process, and neither party is free to remarry until the *get* has been given and accepted. A married woman who no longer lives with her husband but has not received a *get* is known as an *agunah*, a woman "chained" or "anchored" to her husband. The consequences for a married woman who remarries without a *get* are much more serious than the consequences for a married man.[55] Many writers have described the dilemma created when a spouse refuses to cooperate in a *get* proceeding unless his or her demands for custody or a financial settlement are met.[56] Traditional Jewish communities take the *agunah* problem quite seriously, and they may attempt to pressure a spouse to participate in a *get* procedure through the use of sanctions such as shaming or ostracism.

At its core, the *agunah* problem derives from the split between religious and secular authority over marriage.[57] Local communities and Jewish courts do not

---

[52] See ibid.; Robert H. Vasoli, *What God Has Joined Together: The Annulment Crisis in American Catholicism* (Oxford: Oxford University Press, 1998). Generally, a religious annulment can be obtained only after the civil marriage has been dissolved. See generally Joseph P. Zwack, *Annulment: Your Chance to Remarry Within the Catholic Church* (New York, NY: HarperOne, 1983), 13–36.

[53] See Fadel, "Political Liberalism" (in this volume) and Broyde, "New York's Regulation" (in this volume). There are fewer opportunities for strategic behavior in the Roman Catholic context, because annulment is under the control of church authorities and does not depend on the consent of the parties to the marriage. This does not eliminate conflict between spouses over the annulment question, however. See, e.g., Sheila Rauch Kennedy, *Shattered Faith: A Woman's Struggle to Stop the Catholic Church from Annulling Her Marriage* (New York: Pantheon, 1997), xii–xvi.

[54] See Deuteronomy 24:1. See generally Irving Breitowitz, *Between Civil and Religious Law: The Plight of the Agunah in American Society* (Westport, CT: Greenwood Press, 1993).

[55] Although it is controversial, there is an alternative available under Jewish law to assist a husband whose wife has improperly refused to accept a *get*. See Breitowitz, *Between Civil and Religious Law*, 13–14 (describing the *heter meah rabbbanim* or "permission of 100 rabbis").

[56] See, e.g., ibid. at 20–23; Estin, "Embracing Tradition," 578.

[57] In Israel, where religious courts exercise jurisdiction over marriage and divorce, the *agunah* problem is much smaller and "revolves around the decision of the rabbinical courts to not impose sanctions

have sufficient power or authority to force the cooperation of a recalcitrant spouse. When *get* controversies spill over into official divorce proceedings, state judges have confronted the question of whether these disputes can be remedied under the official law, using secular principles of contract, property, or matrimonial law.

In these cases, state courts have considered whether the written agreement signed by a Jewish couple prior to their marriage, known as a *ketubah*, can be construed as a promise to cooperate in a *get* proceeding before a rabbinic tribunal should the marriage come to an end, and whether such a promise can be enforced by a secular court.[58] Courts have reached different conclusions in these cases, and the problem is made more complex by the fact that a *get* given or accepted under pressure from a civil court may be invalid as a matter of Jewish law.[59] One innovative approach, approved by the New York Court of Appeals in *Avitzur v. Avitzur*, was the inclusion of explicit language in a *ketubah* that recognized the jurisdiction of a specific rabbinic tribunal or *bethdin* over marital disputes.[60] The court viewed this provision as analogous to an arbitration clause and concluded that it provided the civil court with authority to order the parties to appear before the *bet din*. Since *Avitzur*, a broad range of Orthodox and Conservative Jewish communities have experimented with premarital and arbitration agreements intended to secure the assistance of the civil courts in bringing Jewish couples before a rabbinic tribunal.[61]

A. Legislative Responses to Religious Diversity

Jewish communities in New York and elsewhere have attempted to address the *agunah* problem by seeking civil statutes that prevent a Jewish spouse from securing a secular divorce until the *get* process has been concluded. Under New York's *get* law, enacted in 1983, a court cannot grant a divorce or annulment to any petitioner whose marriage was solemnized in the state by a religious official until the petitioner provides a sworn statement that he or she has "taken all steps solely within his or her

encouraging or mandating divorce except where it is absolutely clear that the marriage is irreconcilably over, or where there is clearly demonstrable hard fault present." Broyde, *Marriage, Divorce, and the Abandoned Wife*, 10. See also Broyde, "New York's Regulation" (in this volume).

[58] Compare *Mayer-Kolker v. Kolker*, 819 A.2d 17, 20–21 (N.J. Super. Ct. 2003) and *In re Marriage of Victor*, 866 P.2d 899, 902 (Ariz. Ct. App. 1993), with *In re Marriage of Goldman*, 554 N.E.2d 1016, 1021–1022 (Ill. Ct. App. 1990).

[59] See Breitowitz, *Between Civil and Religious Law*, 20–40.

[60] *Avitzur v. Avitzur*, 446 N.E.2d 136, 137 (N.Y. 1983). This provision, known as a "Lieberman clause," developed within the Conservative movement to attempt to prevent the *agunah* problem.

[61] See, e.g., Marc D. Stern, *A Legal Guide to the Prenuptial Agreement for Couples About to be Married*, in *The Prenuptial Agreement: Halakhic and Pastoral Considerations*, eds. Basil Herring and Kenneth Auman (Lanham, MD: Jason Aronson Press, 1996), 137. See also Broyde, "New York's Regulation" (in this volume).

power" to remove any religious barriers to the other party's remarriage.[62] A second
law, enacted in 1992, permits the civil courts to take religious barriers to remarriage
into account in determining the financial incidents of a divorce decree.[63]

Avitzur and the *get* laws exemplify the complex and dynamic relationship between
official and unofficial law that has followed the expansion of civil divorce laws.
Together, these developments have established a framework for interaction between
secular and religious courts, presenting numerous First Amendment questions that
have seen considerable discussion in the case law and other literature.[64] From this
process, a new model has emerged in which religious courts or clergy function as
arbitrators to resolve marriage and divorce disputes. After arbitration, one member of
the couple may bring the settlement or judgment to a secular court for enforcement
as an arbitration award.[65]

A number of these cases that have reached the courts raise a concern that the
applicable religious or customary laws or procedures put women at a disadvantage.[66]
Courts have set aside arbitration awards when there is evidence of undue pressure or
overreaching, and courts generally refuse to enforce agreements to arbitrate custody
or child support matters.[67] In practice, in order to ensure that their orders will be
upheld and enforced by secular courts, religious arbitrators have learned to address
these concerns.

Some Muslim groups in Canada and England have sought to go further and
establish a separate system of Muslim personal law with a semiofficial status, which
would be available to those group members who choose to invoke religious or

---

[62] New York Domestic Relations Law § 253(3) (McKinney 1999). The legislature carefully formulated the
     statute to apply only to Jews married in a religious ceremony and accomplished this despite the fact
     that the statute makes no explicit reference to Jews or the Jewish religion. Canada and England have
     enacted similar legislation. John Syrtash, *Religion and Culture in Canadian Family Law* (Markham,
     ON: Butterworth-Heinemann, 1992), 147–167; Divorce (Religious Marriages) Act, 2002, c. 27 (Eng.).

[63] The first *get* law had broad support across the Jewish community in New York, but the second law was
     more controversial because of a concern that a *get* given or accepted by a spouse in response to finan-
     cial pressure from a civil court might not be valid under Jewish law. See Broyde, *Marriage, Divorce,
     and the Abandoned Wife*, 103–117; Lisa Zornberg, "Beyond the Constitution: Is the New York Get
     Legislation Good Law?" *Pace Law Review* 15 (1995): 703–784, 703.

[64] See, e.g., Breitowitz, *Between Civil and Religious Law*, 251–276; Kent Greenawalt, "Religious Law
     and Civil Law: Using Secular Law to Assure Observance of Practices with Religious Significance,"
     Southern California Law Review 71 (1998): 781–843, 811–839.

[65] E.g., *Kovacs v. Kovacs*, 633 A.2d 425, 429 (Md. Ct. Spec. App. 1993).

[66] E.g., *Stein v. Stein*, 707 N.Y.S.2d 754, (N.Y. Sup. Ct. 1999). Cf. *Bruker v. Marcovitz* [2007] 3 S.C.R.
     607, 641 (Can.) (upholding a wife's claim for damages based on her former husband's breach of his
     agreement to provide her with a *get* and concluding that his religious freedom claim was outweighed
     by the substantial harm to the wife personally and to the public interest in protecting fundamental
     values of equality and "autonomous choice in marriage and divorce"), and see also Cere, "Canadian
     Conjugal Mosaic" (in this volume) and Shachar, "Faith in Law?" (in this volume).

[67] E.g., *Kovacs*, 633 A.2d at 431–32; *Stein*, 707 N.Y.S.2d at 758.

customary law norms.[68] According to Pearl and Menski, one important reason for the development of an informal Muslim dispute resolution process in England was the problem created when a woman sought and obtained a civil divorce but could not obtain her husband's consent to an Islamic divorce.[69]

Under Islamic law, a husband has the power to divorce his wife unilaterally by pronouncing *talaq*, but a wife's options for obtaining a divorce are more limited. Typically, she must obtain her husband's consent to a *khula* divorce, which usually requires that she relinquish her right to the marriage payment (or *mahr*) promised by the husband in their marital agreement.[70] Informal conciliation or arbitration within the Muslim community may achieve a settlement, but some disputes over *mahr* reach the official courts, where the question is whether a Muslim marital agreement can be enforced as a civil contract.[71] In countries with Islamic courts, judges have developed a judicial *khula* divorce that may be available to a wife whose husband refuses to consent to divorce.[72] Where there are no recognized Islamic courts, a wife may have no means to overcome her husband's refusal to agree to a divorce and no leverage to negotiate over keeping her *mahr* or obtaining a financial settlement.[73]

In London, the Islamic Sharia Council is a well-established organization, providing conciliation services and also acting as a court to grant such a *khula* divorce.[74] Development of this unofficial forum for dispute resolution was facilitated by the facts that the Muslim minority population in England is relatively concentrated and that it originated with South Asian immigrants with similar legal traditions.[75] The

---

[68] E.g., Ali and Whitehouse, "Reconstruction of the Constitution," 168. See also Fadel, "Political Liberalism" (in this volume) and Shachar, "Faith in Law?" (in this volume).

[69] Pearl and Menski, *Muslim Family Law*, 79–80.

[70] See ibid., 283–284.

[71] See, e.g., *Marriage of Noghrey*, 215 Cal. Rptr. 153, 155 (Cal. Ct. App. 1985); *Odatalla v. Odatalla*, 810 A.2d 93, 94 (N.J. Super. Ct. Ch. Div. 2002); see also Estin, "Embracing Tradition," 569–577; Quraishi and Syeed-Miller, "No Altars," 200–208.

[72] See Nadya Haider, "Islamic Legal Reform: The Case of Pakistan and Family Law," *Yale Journal of Law and Feminism* 12 (2000): 287–341, 316, 326–338.

[73] See Lucy Carroll, "Muslim Women and Judicial Divorce: An Apparently Misunderstood Aspect of Muslim Law," *Islamic and Comparative Law Quarterly* 5 (1985): 226–245, 226–227. Carroll is critical of the Islamic Sharia Council in London for insisting that women obtain a *khul* divorce and make financial concessions even after obtaining a civil divorce. See Lucy Carroll, "Muslim Women and 'Islamic Divorce' in England," *Journal of Muslim Minority Affairs* 17:1 (1997): 97–115, 105–111. But compare the discussion of pluralism *within* orthodox Islam in Fadel, "Political Liberalism" (in this volume).

[74] Pearl and Menski, *Muslim Family Law*, 74–80. Although unofficial, the Sharia Council also provides advice to lawyers and judges in some cases. See ibid. at 78. For more information, see The Islamic Sharia Council, http://www.islamic-sharia.org.

[75] Pearl and Menski, *Muslim Family Law*, 59–61. Muslim communities in Europe tend to be relatively homogenous, with a predominance of South Asian immigrants in Britain, Muslims from the Maghreb in France, and Turks in Germany.

Orthodox Jewish community in England also operates in a relatively centralized manner, with a chief rabbi and rabbinic court that have been based in London for two hundred years.[76] The London *beth din* is available as an arbitration tribunal for all types of civil disputes; it requires that parties sign an arbitration agreement before any hearing takes place, so that the order of the *beth din* has the force of an arbitration award enforceable in the civil courts.[77] In both the Muslim and Jewish communities, religious tribunals conduct arbitrations under religious law as a form of alternative dispute resolution within the larger framework of English law.[78]

In Canada, public controversy erupted after the announcement in 2003 that a new Islamic Institute of Civil Justice would begin conducting binding arbitration of disputes under Islamic law and Ontario's Arbitration Act, leading Ontario's attorney general to appoint Marion Boyd to review the question of religious arbitration in family disputes.[79] After extensive consultations, Boyd's report in December 2004 summarized a wide range of opinions and concerns. She recommended that religious arbitration should continue to be available as a form of alternative dispute resolution in family law and inheritance cases, subject to an extensive series of safeguards outlined in her report.[80] The province subsequently adopted many of Boyd's recommendations in legislation that permits arbitration by religious arbitrators; but the legislation rejected the prospect of arbitration based on religious law, mandating

---

[76] For more information, see The Chief Rabbinate, http://www.chiefrabbi.org and The United Synagogue: The London Beth Din, http://www.unitedsynagogue.org.uk/the_united_synagogue/the_london_beth_din/about_us.

[77] See The United Synagogue: Litigation, http://www.theus.org.uk/the_united_synagogue/the_london_beth_din/litigation.

[78] Abul Taher, "Revealed: UK's First Official Sharia Courts," *Sunday Times* (London), Sept. 14, 2008, 2. In July 2008, Lord Phillips of Worth Matravers, the Lord Chief Justice, commented in a speech:

> There is no reason why principles of Sharia law, or any other religious code, should not be the basis for mediation or other forms of alternative dispute resolution. It must be recognised, however, that any sanctions for a failure to comply with the agreed terms of the mediation would be drawn from the laws of England and Wales.

Minette Marrin, "Tolerate Sharia, Yes, But Never Respect It," *Sunday Times* (London), July 6, 2008, 20.

[79] See generally Boyd, *Dispute Resolution in Family Law*. The issues are also discussed in Jehan Aslam, Note, "Judicial Oversight of Islamic Family Law Arbitration in Ontario: Ensuring Meaningful Consent and Promoting Multicultural Citizenship," *New York University Journal of International Law and Politics* 38 (2006): 841–876, 842.

[80] Boyd made detailed recommendations for legislation and regulations that would address issues including the grounds for setting aside arbitration agreements or awards, screening for domestic violence, independent legal advice for those participating in family or inheritance arbitration, training and education for arbitrators and mediators, and mechanisms for oversight of private arbitration and mediation. See Boyd, *Dispute Resolution in Family Law*, 133–142.

instead that all family law arbitration in the province be conducted exclusively under Ontarian and Canadian law.[81]

The debate around religious arbitration in Ontario, and the details of Marion Boyd's recommendations to the Ontario attorney general, are indications of the enormous challenges involved in integrating systems of official and unofficial law. The process Boyd outlined was based on principles of contract, but her recommendations suggest that an agreement to submit to the jurisdiction of religious authorities poses particular problems not found in other arbitration agreements or marital contracts.[82] Boyd proposed that if arbitrators intended to apply a form of law other than Ontarian law to decide the dispute, that law should be identified in the written arbitration agreement and accompanied by a written "statement of principles of faith-based arbitration that explains the parties' rights and obligations and available processes under the particular form of religious law."[83] In addition, she recommended a requirement that any agreement to arbitrate in a cohabitation agreement or marriage contract must be reconfirmed in writing at the time of the dispute and before arbitration occurred.[84]

Boyd's recommendations were intended to assure the genuine consent of participants to a religious arbitration proceeding, and also to address the problem of exit rights and the risk that one member of a couple or family might have conscientious or religious objections to appearing before a religious tribunal. This is the most difficult problem in a contract-based approach to legal pluralism.

B. Consent, Dissent, and Exit

In nations with civil marriage and divorce laws, individual members of religious communities may turn to the secular legal system even when its laws are at odds with religious or other group norms. The choice to pursue a secular divorce is protected by the official family law system as well as constitutional principles of freedom of religion. Some group members make this choice even as they intend to maintain their membership in the religious community. Religious groups, which cannot use the power of the state to enforce their internal norms, are then challenged to find other means of influencing or responding to the decisions of group members.

---

[81] Family Statute Law Amendment Act, S.O. 2006, ch. 1 (Ont.) (assented to Feb. 23, 2006). The act and new regulations came into force on April 30, 2007. Ministry of the Attorney General, http://www. attorneygeneral.jus.gov.on.ca/english/family/arbitration.

[82] Boyd recommended extensive procedures and disclosures. See Boyd, *Dispute Resolution in Family Law*, 133–137.

[83] Ibid. at 136–137.

[84] Ibid. at 134.

The requirement to obtain a religious annulment or divorce as a condition of remarriage within the community is one response that is often but not always successful in maintaining the group norm. Sanctions such as shunning or excommunication are a stronger response. Thus, husbands or wives who refuse a summons to appear before a rabbinic tribunal may be subject to a *siruv*, or communal ostracism.[85] This type of sanction poses complex questions of religious law, which are not subject to the interference or regulation of civil authorities.[86]

Over time, groups may come to accommodate the choices made by their members with new institutions and practices. In the United States, this type of change is reflected in the very high rate of marriage annulments now granted by the Roman Catholic Church and the different approaches to religious divorce and intermarriage that characterize the liberal branches of Judaism.[87] In the term used by Madhavi Sunder, this is a process of "cultural dissent" that gives rise to new interpretations of religious and cultural norms and a plurality of practices within these traditions.[88] Pluralism within a broad tradition provides individuals with important alternatives to a complete exit from the group.[89]

Legal pluralism creates opportunities for forum shopping, and individuals respond creatively to these opportunities. Law becomes relevant only when people have to deal with problematic situations, and the choices individuals will make cannot be inferred in advance from the normative demands of the different legal orders within which they operate. The dialogue within and between traditions unfolds within parameters set by both official and unofficial law. It has generated interesting and

---

[85] See *Greenberg v. Greenberg*, 656 N.Y.S.2d 369, 370 (App. Div. 1997) (affirming husband's motion to vacate orders to pay spousal support, when wife signed a release because of threats from religious leaders).

[86] See *Lieberman v. Lieberman*, 566 N.Y.S.2d 490, 496 (N.Y. Sup. Ct. 1991) (holding that the threat of ostracism does not invalidate a party's agreement to religious arbitration of marital disputes). Civil courts also refuse to question the ruling of religious authorities on issues of marriage and divorce. See, e.g., *Sieger v. Union of Orthodox Rabbis*, 767 N.Y.S.2d 78, 80 (N.Y. App. Div. 2003); see also New York Domestic Relations Law § 253(9) (McKinney 1999).

   Courts typically reject tort law challenges brought by group members to shunning orders. See, e.g., *Paul v. Watchtower Bible & Tract Soc'y of N.Y., Inc.*, 819 F.2d 875, 879 (9th Cir. 1987); *Gruenwald v. Bornfreund*, 696 F. Supp. 838, 841 (E.D.N.Y. 1988). But see *Bear v. Reformed Mennonite Church*, 341 A.2d 105, 107 (Pa. 1975) (holding that excommunication from church might constitute excessive interference with areas of paramount state concern like marriage). See generally Michael J. Broyde, "Forming Religious Communities and Respecting Dissenters' Rights: A Jewish Tradition for a Modern Society," in *Human Rights in Judaism*, eds. Michael J. Broyde and John Witte, Jr. (Northvale, NJ: Jason Aronson Press, 1998).

[87] See generally Jack Wertheimer, "What is a Jewish Family? Changing Rabbinic Views," in *Marriage, Sex and Family in Judaism*, ed. Michael J. Broyde (Lanham, MD: Rowman & Littlefield Publishers, Inc, 2005), 244, 254–256.

[88] Madhavi Sunder, "Cultural Dissent," *Stanford Law Review* 54 (2001): 495–567, 498.

[89] See, e.g., Abdo, *Mecca and Main Street*, 37–43. See also Fadel, "Political Liberalism" (in this volume).

creative solutions to problems of marriage and divorce in a number of communities. These include the development of new types of premarital agreements in different Muslim and Jewish communities, designed to be enforceable in secular courts, which address some of the gender inequalities of traditional practices.[90] These developments reflect a dynamism that is typical of legal pluralism.[91]

Beyond the norms of divorce law constructed in the interactions of official and unofficial law, the process through which actors in these systems negotiate the relationship of distinct legal orders has consequences for their self-definition as a community and their authority and power within the broader society. For some participants, official recognition of unofficial law is itself a goal to be accomplished by claiming jurisdiction over families and family members.[92]

These conflicts would also exist in the context of privatized or pluralized marriage law. Just as secular family law does not map perfectly on religious or other unofficial norms, a regulatory regime based on contract or arbitration would sometimes diverge from religious rules and understandings. Debates over the context of religious and cultural traditions and the scope and meaning of group membership might shift, but they would not disappear. These conflicts would intensify if more were at stake, a phenomenon that is well known in nations with explicitly pluralist family law systems.[93] Just as there are reasons to believe that religious communities are more vibrant and that individual religious commitments are stronger in contexts where religion is not established by the state,[94] there are reasons to believe that the fluidity of belief, practice, and membership in religious communities in these circumstances may contribute to their flourishing.[95]

In conditions of official legal pluralism, there is the further need for rules by which the state defines the scope of group jurisdiction and addresses the conflict of laws

---

[90] On contemporary Muslim marriage contracts, see Yvonne Yazbeck Haddad et al., *Muslim Women in America: The Challenge of Islamic Identity Today* (Oxford: Oxford University Press, 2006), 113–119; Quraishi and Syeed-Miller, "No Altars," 188–192. On the use of new types of premarital agreements to address the *get* problem in different Jewish communities, see Broyde, *Marriage, Divorce, and the Abandoned Wife*, 66–68, 82, 86, 127–136.

[91] Benda-Beckmann, "Dynamics of Change and Continuity," 19 ("Under conditions of legal pluralism elements of one legal order may change under the influence of another legal order, and new, hybrid or syncretic legal forms may emerge and become institutionalized, replacing or modifying earlier legal forms or co-existing with them.").

[92] See ibid. at 32.

[93] See, e.g., Ruth Halperin-Kaddari, "Women, Religion and Multiculturalism in Israel," *UCLA Journal of International Law and Foreign Affairs* 5 (2000): 339–366, 347–352; Pratibha Jain, "Balancing Minority Rights and Gender Justice: The Impact of Protecting Multiculturalism on Women's Rights in India," *Berkley Journal of International Law* 23 (2005): 201–222, 209–219.

[94] See Nancy F. Cott, *Public Vows: A History of Marriage and the Nation* (London: Harvard University Press, 2000), 212.

[95] See Shachar, *Multicultural Jurisdictions*, 120–126.

between different authorities. More problematic is that these systems also require rules to assign group membership and to define the circumstances in which individuals are permitted to change their group membership.[96] Here as well, religious authorities and the civil state have different interests, and conflicts over subgroup membership and rights can undermine the sense of broader national affiliation.

III. MARRIAGE NORMS: PROHIBITIONS AND GATEKEEPING

Historically, norms of marital capacity in the United States have been strenuously contested.[97] More than a century ago, the Supreme Court denied First Amendment protection to religiously based polygamy in *Reynolds v. United States,* characterizing it as an "odious" practice that, except for Mormons, was "almost exclusively a feature of the life of Asiatic and African people."[98] A generation ago, after a twenty-year debate, the Court placed interracial marriage firmly in the ambit of constitutional right in *Loving v. Virginia,* holding that state laws limiting marriage rights on the basis of race violated the Due Process and Equal Protection Clauses.[99] By the late twentieth century, conflicts over multiculturalism and civil recognition for same-sex partner relationships had prompted a broad new debate over the official definition of marriage. As in the past, the present marriage debate reveals a close connection between marriage norms and the definition of citizenship or membership in the broader social and political community.

A. *The Gatekeeping Function of Marriage Law*

In America, marriage law has always served a gatekeeping function. Most group members adhere to these broader rules, even if their religious beliefs would allow different practices. The experience of living within a larger society, defined by different norms, may eventually lead to different practices within the tradition.[100] For

---

[96] E.g., Audi, "Egyptian Court Allows Return to Christianity" (reporting a ruling that permitted twelve Coptic Christian men, who had converted to Islam in order to be able to divorce, to return formally to their original faith).

[97] See generally Cott, *Public Vows.*

[98] *Reynolds v. United States,* 98 U.S. 145, 164 (1878). See also a critical discussion of the rationale in *Reynolds* in Fadel, "Political Liberalism" (in this volume).

[99] *Loving v. Virginia,* 388 U.S. 1, 2 (1967).

[100] See Cesari, *When Islam and Democracy Meet,* 60–61. This occurred in Europe during the eleventh century, when the Ashkenazi Jewish tradition abandoned polygamy and unilateral divorce under decrees of Rabbi Gershom. See Don S. Browning, M. Christian Green, and John Witte Jr., eds., *Sex, Marriage, and Family in World Religions* (New York, NY: Columbia University Press, 2006), 40–42.

individuals who maintain practices that deviate from prevailing expectations, family life is lived underground within the unofficial law of a small community. Official law must be evaded and manipulated, or challenged and transformed.

Even under official law, substantive limits on marriage vary notably from state to state. Although most states set the age of consent for marriage at eighteen, many permit sixteen- or seventeen-year-olds to marry with their parents' consent. In some states, younger teenagers can marry with parental consent or judicial approval, and a few set the limit as low as thirteen or fourteen.[101] States may prosecute parents who attempt to evade these limits.[102] States are also divided in their definition of what family relationships trigger incest prohibitions. All states bar marriage between ancestor and descendant or between two siblings, and most states prohibit marriages between uncle and niece or aunt and nephew. State laws vary on the legality of first-cousin marriage, and a few states retain other restrictions that trace to the traditional marriage impediments of ecclesiastical law.[103] Beyond the core prohibition of sexual or marital relationships within the nuclear family, these are questions on which different legal systems reach different conclusions.[104] These rules are significantly shaped by religious tradition and reflect a range of policy choices and historical circumstances.[105]

Because marriage laws are not uniform across the United States, we have an extensive body of case law on conflict-of-laws questions that arise after couples cross state lines in order to be able to marry.[106] Under some statutes, marriage prohibitions are unavoidable. Another of my law students once posed a question about Iowa's marriage evasion statute, which invalidates any marriage solemnized in another state that would be void under Iowa law. The student had been married the previous summer in Egypt, where his family lives, to a woman who was his first cousin.

---

[101] E.g., New Hampshire Revised Statutes Annotated § 457:4 (2007) (minimum marriage age of thirteen for girls and fourteen for boys). The age of marital capacity set by the English common law was twelve for girls and fourteen for boys; this appears to be the lower age limit in Kansas and Massachusetts. See *State v. Wade*, 766 P.2d 811, 815 (Kan. 1989).

[102] E.g., *People v. Benu*, 385 N.Y.S.2d 222, 226 (N.Y. Crim. Ct. 1976); *State v. Moua*, 573 N.W.2d 202, 206 (Wis. Ct. App. 1997).

[103] E.g., Massachusetts General Laws ch. 207, §§ 1–2 (2006). See generally Clark, *Law of Domestic Relations*, 23–24 (describing ecclesiastical law prohibitions based on age and family relationships).

[104] The American prohibition of cousin marriage contrasts with the legal practice in Europe, Canada, and many countries in Asia and Africa. See Martin Ottenheimer, "Lewis Henry Morgan and the Prohibition of Cousin Marriage in the United States," *Journal of Family History* 15:3 (1990): 325–335, 325–333. Whereas the conventional explanation for these prohibitions is a genetic one, recent research suggests that the genetic risks are smaller than is often assumed.

[105] See Clark, *Law of Domestic Relations*, 82–84. Religious legal systems impose other marriage impediments, often including prohibitions on religious intermarriage. See, e.g., Wertheimer, "What is a Jewish Family?" 245.

[106] See Clark, *Law of Domestic Relations*, 41–44, 85–88, 96–98.

The student asked if their marriage was void under the Iowa statutes that prohibit first-cousin marriages.[107]

The law governing marital capacity and consent also presents potential conflicts with practices of ethnic and religious communities. In rare instances, some conflicts are acknowledged and accommodated by state law. Historically, the practice of arranged marriage was a source of conflict between official and unofficial norms. Nancy Cott describes the growth of restrictive immigration policies targeted at single women during the late nineteenth and early twentieth centuries, designed to prevent trafficking and prostitution, which cast particular suspicion on Asian and Jewish women migrating for marriage purposes.[108] Marriages arranged by a matchmaker or the families of the bride and groom seemed to violate basic American norms of marital consent.[109] Public policies based on concern with immigration fraud, sham marriage, and human trafficking still complicate the international marriage practices of families in some religious minority groups. Conversely, young women with citizenship or residence status in the United States or similar nations may be pressed by their families to marry men seeking admission as immigrants.[110]

International human rights instruments protect the right to marry. As a corollary, they prohibit forced marriage as well as child marriages, suggesting that the minimum acceptable marriage age should be fifteen.[111] These treaties establish some baseline requirements for marriage law, but they leave other important questions open. In this debate, the hardest questions involve polygamy, which is not expressly proscribed or limited in international law and which is recognized as a valid form of marriage in dozens of nations.[112] Because polygamy is prohibited in much of the

[107] See Iowa Code §§ 595.19.2 (2007), 595.20 (2007).
[108] Cott, *Public Vows*, 132–155; see also Kerry Abrams, "Polygamy, Prostitution, and the Federalization of Immigration Law," *Columbia Law Review* 105 (2005): 641–716, 656.
[109] Cott, *Public Vows*, 149–152.
[110] See Catherine Raissiguier, "Troubling Mothers: Immigrant Women from Africa in France," *JENDA: A Journal of Culture & African Women Studies* 4 (2003): fn. 17. The distinction between arranged marriage and forced marriage is crucial in this setting, but it sometimes proves hard to draw. See generally Alison Symington, "Dual Citizenship and Forced Marriages," *Dalhousie Journal of Legal Studies* 10 (2001): 1–35.
[111] See, e.g., Universal Declaration of Human Rights, G.A. Res. 217A, at 74, U.N. GAOR, 3d Sess., 1st plen. mtg., U.N. Doc. A/810 (Dec. 12, 1948); United Nations Recommendation on Consent to Marriage, Minimum Age for Marriage and Registration of Marriages, G.A. Res. 2018, at 36, U.N. GAOR, 20th Sess., Supp. No. 14, U.N. Doc. A16014 (Nov. 1, 1965).
[112] But see, e.g., U.N. Comm. on the Elimination of All Forms of Discrimination Against Women, Gen. Recommendation 21: Equality in Marriage and Family Relations, U.N. Doc. A/49/38 (13th Sess. 1994) (concluding that the continuing practice of polygamy violates human rights norms including art. 5(a) of the Convention on the Elimination of All Forms of Discrimination Against Women). On polygamy in Muslim countries, for example, see Javaid Rehman, "The Sharia, Islamic Family Laws and International Human Rights Law: Examining the Theory and Practice of Polygamy and Talaq," *Journal of International Law, Policy, and Family* 21 (2007): 108–125, 114.

world, however, the practice goes underground when polygamous families form and migrate across international boundaries.[113]

Polygamous families of various cultural backgrounds live in many European and North American countries, presenting a complex problem in the interaction of official and unofficial law.[114] Official laws in the United States prohibit and sanction polygamy at every level, from national immigration statutes to local criminal law.[115] News reports indicate that there are substantial numbers of polygamous families in North American and European countries living beneath the radar of the official law, but nonetheless within communities and a framework of unofficial legal norms.[116]

B. Families Underground

In the United States, the largest polygamous communities are comprised of fundamentalist Mormon families found mostly in several western states. Academic and journalistic accounts describe the norms of these communities, which apparently range from ordinary-seeming, middle-class, suburban families to isolated groups regularly accused of abusive treatment of women and children.[117] In the more extreme cases, state officials pursue criminal convictions, but when there is no evidence of other crimes or fraud, state officials generally do not bring polygamy prosecutions.[118] In other countries, the issue of polygamy centers on immigrant communities. France also prohibits polygamous marriages, but it had family reunification policies in the

---

[113] North American courts have also not been willing to recognize the validity of *mut'a* (temporary) marriages, which are accepted in Shiite Islamic communities. See, e.g., *Vyronis v. Vyronis (In re Vyronis)*, 248 Cal. Rptr. 807, 815 (Ct. App. 1988); *Y.J. v. N.J.*, [1994] O.J. No. 2359 (Can.).

[114] See generally *Polygamy in Canada: Legal and Social Implications for Women and Children: A Collection of Policy Research Reports* (Ottawa: Status of Women Canada, 2005).

[115] Under the Immigration and Nationality Act, polygamists are ineligible to receive visas and are excluded from admission into the United States. 8 U.S.C. § 1182(a)(10)(A) (2000). For state criminal law, see, e.g., Utah Code Annotated § 76-7-101 (2003) (punishing polygamy as a third-degree felony). All states prohibit bigamous marriages, but not all states criminalize bigamy.

[116] See generally Pauline Bartolone, "For These Muslims, Polygamy Is an Option," *San Francisco Chronicle*, Aug. 5, 2007, E3 (describing increase of African-American Muslims practicing polygamy); Nina Bernstein, "Polygamy, Practiced in Secrecy, Follows Africans to New York," *New York Times*, Mar. 23, 2007, A1 (describing increasing prevalence of polygamy in New York); Kirsten Scharnberg and Manya A. Brachear, "Polygamy (Utah's Open Little Secret)," *Chicago Tribune*, Sept. 24, 2006, C1 (noting estimates that 40,000 people in the western United States live in polygamous relationships).

[117] See generally Irwin Altman and Joseph Ginat, *Polygamous Families in Contemporary Society* (Cambridge: Cambridge University Press, 1996) (discussing the historical background of and everyday life in polygamous families); Scharnberg and Brachear, "Polygamy (Utah's Open Little Secret)" (discussing the range of polygamous families).

[118] E.g., *State v. Holm*, 137 P.3d 726 (Utah 2006) (conviction for bigamy and unlawful sexual contact with a minor), *cert. denied*, 127 S. Ct. 1371 (2007); Jason Szep, "Fundamental Mormons Seek Recognition for Polygamy," *Reuters*, June 12, 2007, available at http://www.reuters.com/article/domesticNews/idUSN0627314820070612.

1970s and 1980s that permitted polygamous immigrants from African nations such as Mali, Senegal, and Gambia to bring multiple wives and their children to live in France. As a result, there is a large African polygamous community in France today, estimated to include as many as 15,000 households.[119] In 1993, French policy changed, and new legislation permitted immigrants with multiple wives to obtain legal residence papers for only one wife and her children. For the large numbers of polygamous households already residing in France, the new legislation created incentives and sanctions designed to break families into smaller units, including pressures to divorce (or "de-cohabit") and denials of renewed residency permits.[120] These policy changes were prompted by official concern for the overcrowded living conditions of large polygamous families and the difficult situation of women in these households, as well as rising political sentiment against immigration.[121]

In places where polygamy is practiced without official approval, families use various strategies to avoid detection or prosecution. A husband may marry only one wife under the official law, cohabiting with the others with no secular legal formality.[122] This strategy, apparently typical of Fundamentalist Mormon communities,[123] leaves subsequent plural wives without most of the protections that come from the civil marriage laws.[124] For example, an unofficial spouse would not be able to rely on the marital tie for immigration purposes, but might qualify more readily for public

---

[119] See Frank Renout, "Immigrants' Second Wives Find Few Rights," *Christian Science Monitor*, May 25, 2005, 16. See generally Edwige Rude-Antoine, "Muslim Maghrebian Marriage in France: A Problem for Legal Pluralism," *International Journal of Law, Policy and the Family* 5 (1991): 93; Adrian Pennink, "Thousands of Families in Despair as France Enforces Ban on Polygamy," *Independent on Sunday (London)*, Apr. 1, 2001, 22.

[120] Jonathan Laurence and Justin Vaisse, *Integrating Islam: Political and Religious Challenges in Contemporary France* (Washington, DC: Brookings Institution Press, 2006); see also Raissiguier, "Troubling Mothers"; Sonja Starr and Lea Brillmayer, "Family Separation as a Violation of International Law," *Berkeley Journal of International Law* 21 (2003): 213–287, 243–259.

[121] These problems have persisted despite the changes in policy, and the debate intensified in 2005 after rioting in immigrant neighborhoods. See, e.g., Molly Moore, "France Weighs Immigration Controls After Riots," *Washington Post*, Nov. 30, 2005, A14; Elaine Sciolino, "Citing of Polygamy as Cause of French Riots Causes Uproar," *New York Times*, Nov. 17, 2005, available at http://www.nytimes.com/2005/11/17/international/europe/17cnd-france.html. Polygamy communities also flourish in other European countries. See Pascale Fournier, "The Reception of Muslim Family Law in Western Liberal States" (2004), available at http://www.ccmw.com/documents/Pascalepaper.doc.

[122] In Utah, this strategy has been defeated by prosecutors using the state's "unsolemnized marriage" statute, which was initially enacted to prevent welfare fraud. See, e.g., *State v. Green*, 99 P.3d 820, 833 (Utah 2004).

[123] See, e.g., ibid. at 822 (describing how ten women considered themselves married to defendant, where defendant avoided being in more than one licensed marriage at a time by terminating each prior to obtaining a license for a new marriage).

[124] These would include property, support, and inheritance rights; rights to a share of public or private insurance coverage or benefits; and the possibility of wrongful death or other tort recovery as a spouse. Children of such a marriage would traditionally have been treated as illegitimate under the official law, but most classifications based on legitimacy have been held to be unconstitutional.

assistance payments. Alternatively, a husband might obtain a divorce under civil law from his first wife and continue to live with her, leaving their religious marriage intact, and then marry a second wife who would have a status recognized under official law. When immigration rights are at stake, this approach could allow the parties to obtain family preferences based on the new relationship. Although the first wife would not have any ongoing protections as a spouse, her legal position would be similar to that of other divorced women.

Based on these strategic choices, polygamous households formed under religious or customary law are sometimes inside and sometimes outside the scope of official marriage law. Individual household members might rely on other aspects of civil law to structure their property rights or to approximate other aspects of the secular law relating to family relationships. In this respect, they would be similar to same-sex couple families, who have worked to create parallel legal structures that mimic aspects of the work ordinarily done by official family and marriage laws. Polygamous households have a wider array of strategic alternatives, however, because civil marriage laws are available to formalize at least one husband-wife bond.

Any move toward expanding the role of religious laws and norms in regulating marriage would necessarily confront these difficult questions of definition and capacity. Because of the strong public policy interests the state has asserted in marriage, these questions are pervasive in both private and public law. General norms of contract law include rules governing capacity to contract and public policy rules that place some types of bargains off-limits. Without a specialized marriage law to regulate these questions, what rules would contract law supply? Beyond the universe of contract, our public benefit laws, immigration laws, bankruptcy laws, and tax laws are all built on commonly held marriage norms that have emerged and evolved through broad social and political debate. Here as well, our present marriage law does a lot of regulatory hard work. Privatizing marriage would require construction of new rules, a new official law, in each of these different frameworks.

IV. CONCLUSION

Proposals to remove the state from the regulation of marriage are generally framed at a high level of abstraction and suggest with no evidence, against the history and practice of several centuries, that we could cleanly separate the universe of official law from an unofficial, private sphere of human relations.[125] These are not proposals

---

[125] E.g., Stein, "Symposium on Abolishing Civil Marriage," 1157–1159 (discussing arguments for the deregulation of marriage); cf. Lawrence Rosen, "Anthropological Perspectives on the Abolition of Marriage," in Bernstein, *Marriage Proposals*, 147, 162 (arguing that removing the state from marriage would have vast and unpredictable effects).

to withdraw the state entirely from the sphere of family life, however, and these writers typically suggest that general principles of contract law, property law, tort law, and criminal law would be adequate for the tasks now performed by marriage and family law.[126]

For those who would prefer to allow religious communities to define the scope of marriage, contract law might seem to provide the basis for creating a legal space within which religious authority could flourish. Unless the state entirely relinquishes its protective role, there is no reason to believe that pluralism in this form would escape the dynamics described here. As with our present law, there would be circumstances in which official and unofficial norms converge and circumstances in which they conflict, as well as points at which religious or unofficial norms fall entirely outside the boundaries of our fundamental legal and political commitments.

Whether or not we could expect to find any benefits from a radical restructuring of the law of families, we should expect that privatizing marriage would increase the frequency and complexity of the interactions between official and unofficial family law. In a context of legal pluralism, individuals and communities find means to adapt their behaviors and norms within the spaces created by multiple normative systems. That process is unavoidable, particularly so long as the state maintains control over domains such as immigration, the allocation of social welfare benefits, and the traditional tools of property, contract, criminal, and tort law.

In our society, the dynamic relationship of official and unofficial family law serves useful purposes. At the point of marriage celebration, the convergence of official and unofficial norms expresses a powerful consensus in support of marriage and family commitments. Making room for a wide variety of religious traditions in this consensus supports an ideal of shared membership in the larger national community. State support for religious marriage celebrations also affirms the important support that religious communities provide for marriage and family life.

At divorce, conflict between family members may be expressed through a conflict between the realms of official and unofficial law. Our norms of religious freedom address individual rights as against the state and are not adapted to resolving disputes between individuals or within religious communities. Both levels of conflict are mediated in the interaction between secular and religious divorce systems. This process balances the divergent values and interests of families and groups,

---

[126] We have no legal tradition or experience in applying these general principles in the setting of families. For centuries, our law has constructed marital relationships based on the principle of coverture, which explicitly displaced property, contract, or tort law and aspects of criminal law in regulation of families. See generally Clark, *Law of Domestic Relations,* 286–289. In more recent decades, we have attempted, without making much progress, to use general principles to regulate the private law aspects of cohabitation relationships. See generally Ann Laquer Estin, "Ordinary Cohabitation," *Notre Dame Law Review* 76 (2001): 1381–1408.

and it helps preserve the vitality of religious communities and the cohesion of the state.

In our society, as in many others, the definition of marriage and the space accorded to unofficial marriage norms have been central to our self-definition as a community. Debates over marriage policy have been intensely joined because these are debates over who we are. Accommodation of the traditions and practices of different religious communities helps to define our national character, just as limitations on what family practices are acceptable helps to define the rights and meaning of citizenship. None of this is carved eternally in stone: As our shared understandings have changed and as we have moved toward a richer and more diverse conception of our national character, the boundaries of official and unofficial family law have continued to shift and transform.

5

Covenant Marriage Laws

A Model for Compromise

Katherine Shaw Spaht

Three American states – Louisiana, Arizona, and Arkansas – statutorily authorize couples to enter into a "covenant marriage."[1] These covenant marriage statutes incorporate into law, in varying degrees, the understanding of traditional marriage as historically recognized in Western countries – a sexually monogamous union between one man and one woman intended to be for life. Further, covenant marriage attempts to lessen the problems of divorce by strengthening the institution of marriage. John Witte explains the logic well:

> The Western tradition has learned, through centuries of experience, to balance the norms of marital formation, maintenance, and dissolution.... The lesson in this is that rules governing marriage formation and dissolution must be comparable in their stringency. ... Loose formation rules demand loose dissolution rules, as we see today. To fix "the modern problem of divorce" will require reforms of rules at both ends of the marital process.[2]

I. WHAT IS COVENANT MARRIAGE?

Covenant evokes a rich heritage both in the law, as a special form of contract with specific formalities and greater binding force, and in religion, as an unbreakable and perpetual agreement between the Creator and mankind. The word *covenant* added as an adjective preceding *marriage* carries with it that rich heritage from dual sources to imbue and renew our understanding of a very old, yet indispensable, social institution.[3] As Max Stackhouse describes a covenant's effect:

---

[1] Ariz. Rev. Stat. Ann. §§ 25–901–906 (2007); Ark. Code Ann. §§ 9–11–801–811 (2002, supp. 2006); La. R.S. §§ 9:272–275 (2000, supp. 2007).

[2] John Witte Jr., *From Sacrament to Contract: Marriage, Religion and Law in the Western Tradition* (Louisville: Westminster John Knox Press, 1997), 217–218.

[3] See John Witte Jr. and Joel A. Nichols, "More Than a Mere Contract: Marriage as Contract and Covenant in Law and Theology," *University of St. Thomas Law Journal* 5 (2008): 595–615.

[t]he sociotheological idea of covenant is so rich with ethical content that it gives moral meaning to all it touches.... [A] covenant shifts the terms of ... relationships. [A covenant] is not cut casually, for it entails not only celebration and sacrifice but also the incorporation of new shared duties and rights that nourish life with other meanings, and thus a sense that these duties and rights are based on an enduring law and purpose as established by a higher authority.[4]

As used in this chapter, "covenant marriage" refers to an optional, legally enforceable, statutory form of marriage, which affords each prospective spouse a stronger commitment from the other to their marriage. A covenant marriage statute ordinarily contains three unique components: (1) mandatory premarital counseling, which stresses the seriousness of marriage and the expectation that the couple's marriage will be lifelong; (2) a Declaration of Intent – a legally binding agreement that, if difficulties arise during the marriage, the spouses will make all "reasonable efforts to preserve the marriage, including marriage counseling"; and (3) limited grounds for divorce, which vary in each of the three states that have adopted a covenant marriage statute, making termination of the marriage depend on either misconduct by a spouse, which society collectively condemns, or a lengthy waiting period of living separate and apart.[5] As an optional choice for couples who marry, covenant marriage statutes effectively result in the recognition of two forms of marriage, both of which are authorized and regulated by the state.[6]

Such an idea of an optional form of marriage – existing alongside an alternative civil formulation of marriage – is rather unexceptional. As early as 1945, French law professor Léon Mazeaud proposed an indissoluble marriage option with the ringing declaration, "Let each choose! ... No one can protest, for each remains free to bind himself up to death or only up to divorce."[7] His historical description recognized divorce as "[b]orn from the fight led against the church."[8] Over the past fifteen years in this country, there have been similar suggestions, ranging from an indissoluble marriage option identical to that proposed by Mazeaud, to more vague proposed "super-vows," to more options than covenant marriage legislation allows (including allowing couples to custom-design the content of their marriage contract).[9] All of

---

[4] Max L. Stackhouse, *Covenant and Commitment: Faith, Family, and Economic Life* (Louisville: Westminster John Knox Press, 1997).

[5] Katherine Shaw Spaht, "Louisiana's Covenant Marriage: Social Analysis and Legal Implications," *Louisiana Law Review* 59 (1998): 63–130, 74–75.

[6] See Joel A. Nichols, "Multi-Tiered Marriage: Reconsidering the Boundaries of Civil Law and Religion" (in this volume). See also John Witte Jr. and Eliza Ellison, eds., *Covenant Marriage in Comparative Perspective* (Grand Rapids, MI: Eerdman's, 2005).

[7] Henri Mazeaud et al., *Leçons de Droit Civil: La Famille*, ed. Laurent Levenuer (Paris, 7th ed. 1995), bk. 1, vol. 3, no. 1415, part II, pp. 654–655.

[8] Ibid.

[9] E.g., Christopher Wolfe, "The Marriage of Your Choice," *First Things* (February 1995): 37–41; Amitai Etzioni, "How to Make Marriage Matter," *Time* (September 1993): 76. See also Amitai Etziani

these proposals bear in common the recognition of the political realities involved in solving "the divorce problem." Covenant marriage statutes put into law such an optional form of marriage via their trio of elements.

A. Premarital Counseling

A couple interested in covenant marriage must first arrange for premarital counseling; it is mandatory. However, the statute simply requires that the counseling be performed by a priest, minister, or rabbi – or the secular alternative, a professional marriage counselor. In a similar manner, the statute only requires the content of the counseling to consist of the seriousness of marriage, the intention that marriage be lifelong, and the legal obligation of covenant spouses to take all reasonable steps to preserve their marriage if marital difficulties arise.[10] The counselor then attests on a special form that the counseling was performed. Some denominations, such as Catholicism, have historically had structured and extensive premarital programs that require a few months to complete; such programs qualify as fulfillment of the mandatory premarital counseling required for a covenant marriage.

If a couple belongs to a denomination without such programs, they may not be informed of the covenant marriage option until arriving at the Clerk of Court's office to obtain the marriage license. Because a marriage license is valid in Louisiana for only thirty days, most couples wait until a week or less before the scheduled cere-mony to appear and apply for the license. The Clerk of Court is required by a 2001 statute to deliver a pamphlet prepared by the Attorney General to every couple who applies for a marriage license, explaining the availability of the option of a covenant marriage and what the law requires for entering into such a marriage.[11] Even if the couple is fortunate and does receive a copy of the pamphlet, which often does not happen due to the widespread failure by the Clerks' staff to properly implement the statute, it may be too late to complete the mandatory premarital counseling.

In a Gallup poll commissioned by the team of social scientists studying Louisiana's covenant marriage legislation, the premarital counseling component garnered the support of 81 percent of respondents who believed that it was very or somewhat important, compared to 19 percent who believed that it was not very or not at all

and Peter Rubin, eds., *Opportuning Virtue: Lessons of the Louisiana Covenant Marriage Law: A Communitarian Report* (1997); Eric Rasmussen and Jeffery Evans Stake, "Lifting the Veil of Ignorance: Personalizing the Marriage Contract," *Indiana Law Journal* 73 (1998): 453–503. See also Nichols, "Reconsidering the Boundaries" (in this volume); Brian H. Bix, "Pluralism and Decentralization in Marriage Regulation" (in this volume); Stephen B. Presser, "Marriage and the Law: Time for a Divorce?" (in this volume).

[10] La. R.S. § 9:237 (2001).
[11] La. R.S. § 9:237 A, C (2001).

important.[12] More surprisingly, Christian denominations have not universally or enthusiastically embraced the optional form of marriage. At first there were objections from the Catholic Church about requiring the religious counselor to inform the couple of the grounds for divorce; this problem was solved by curative legislation in 1999 removing that requirement from the content of the counseling. Nonetheless, the Catholic pre-Cana sessions with engaged couples still do not inform the participants of the covenant marriage option. Leaders of other denominations, such as the Methodists and the Episcopalians, object, respectively, to a tier of marriage that would have the effect of denigrating other marriages of lower legal commitment and to a return of the "bad old days" of fault-based, more difficult-to-obtain divorces.[13] Only a few Christian churches in Louisiana require their members who marry to contract a covenant marriage. Louisiana Jewish leaders have informally and without public statement rejected embracing covenant marriage.

B. Declaration of Intent

As a second step in the process of entering into a covenant marriage, the couple signs a document titled the "Declaration of Intent" that contains a "special" contract superimposed on the ordinary marriage relationship, obligating covenant couples to disclose to each other information that might affect the decision to marry. The Declaration also contains a promise to take reasonable steps to preserve the marriage if marital difficulties arise; those steps may include marital counseling or other remedial "steps."[14] The latter obligation is a legal obligation that is enforceable as any other contractual obligation of the same nature – through damages, pecuniary and nonpecuniary, rather than specific performance.[15] In the same Gallup poll undertaken by the team of social scientists described previously, it was this commitment in the form of a legal obligation undertaken in advance to try to preserve the marriage that proved the most popular: "92.3% of respondents believed that the couple agreeing in advance to seek counseling if marital difficulties arise during the marriage was very or somewhat important, whereas 7.7% believed that it was not very or not at all important."[16]

---

[12] Katherine Shaw Spaht, "What's Become of Louisiana's Covenant Marriage Through the Eyes of Social Scientists," *Loyola Law Review* 47 (2001): 709–728, 713–717 [hereinafter Spaht, "Eyes of Social Scientists"].

[13] See Joel A. Nichols, "Louisiana Covenant Marriage Law: A First Step Toward a More Robust Pluralism in Marriage and Divorce Law?" *Emory Law Journal* 47 (1998): 929–1001.

[14] Reprinted in ibid., at 996–997.

[15] For a comprehensive discussion of this obligation and its enforceability, see Spaht, "Louisiana's Covenant Marriage: Social Analysis and Legal Implications," 103–105.

[16] Spaht, "Eyes of Social Scientists," 714.

C. Restricted Grounds for Divorce

The most distinguishing feature of a covenant marriage, restricted grounds for divorce, proved to be its least popular component; only 65.7 percent of Louisiana respondents favored the restricted grounds for divorce. Nonetheless, among those Louisiana citizens polled, two-thirds supported restricted grounds for divorce. Grounds for divorce in a covenant marriage consist of four causes in the nature of fault – adultery, conviction of a felony, abandonment for one year, and physical or sexual abuse of a spouse or a child of either of the parties.[17] Absent proof of such fault, parties must live separate and apart for two years,[18] significantly longer than the six months required for a divorce in ordinary Louisiana marriages. By restoring fault grounds for divorce and a significantly longer waiting period for a "no-fault" divorce, covenant marriage

---

[17] See, e.g., La. R.S. § 9:307:

> A: Notwithstanding any other law to the contrary and subsequent to the parties obtaining counseling, a spouse to a covenant marriage may obtain a judgment of divorce only upon proof of any of the following: (1) The other spouse has committed adultery. (2) The other spouse has committed a felony and has been sentenced to death or imprisonment at hard labor. (3) The other spouse has abandoned the matrimonial domicile for a period of one year and constantly refuses to return. (4) The other spouse has physically or sexually abused the spouse seeking the divorce or a child of one of the spouses ....
>
> B: Notwithstanding any other law to the contrary and subsequent to the parties obtaining counseling, a spouse to a covenant marriage may obtain a judgment of separation from bed and board only upon proof of any of the following: (1) The other spouse has committed adultery. (2) The other spouse has committed a felony and has been sentenced to death or imprisonment at hard labor. (3) The other spouse has abandoned the matrimonial domicile for a period of one year and constantly refuses to return. (4) The other spouse has physically or sexually abused the spouse seeking the divorce or a child of one of the spouses.... (6) On account of habitual intemperance of the other spouse, or excesses, cruel treatment, or outrages of the other spouse, if such habitual intemperance, or such ill-treatment is of such a nature as to render their living together insupportable.

[18] See, e.g., La. R.S. §§ 9:307A(5)(6) and 307B(5):

> A.(5): The spouses have been living separate and apart continuously without reconciliation for a period of two years.
>
> (6)(a) The spouses have been living separate and apart continuously without reconciliation for a period of one year from the date the judgment of separation from bed and board was signed.
>
> (b) If there is a minor child or children of the marriage, the spouses have been living separate and apart continuously without reconciliation for a period of one year and six months from the date the judgment of separation from bed and board was signed; however, if abuse of a child of the marriage or a child of one of the spouses is the basis for which the judgment of separation from bed and board was obtained, then a judgment of divorce may be obtained if the spouses have been living separate and apart continuously without reconciliation for a period of one year from the date the judgment of separation from bed and board was signed.
>
> B.(5): The spouses have been living separate and apart continuously without reconciliation for a period of two years.

legislation emphasizes the importance to society of marriage and its duration. Unless there is grave misconduct by a spouse that makes the common life intolerable, either spouse must wait two years to obtain a divorce. Specified misconduct in the form of grounds for divorce implicitly defines the appropriate behavior for spouses in marriage through the use of objective societal norms, currently missing from the law of most states. Furthermore, the significantly longer waiting period of living separate and apart for covenant couples, especially when combined with the legal obligation to take reasonable steps to preserve their marriage, offers the real and distinct possibility that the marriage can be saved. The two-year period affords sufficient time for counseling or other "reasonable steps" to be pursued and to be successful.

The total number of newly married couples entering into covenant marriage in Louisiana remains exceedingly small: 2 to 3 percent. Partial explanations for the small number of such couples include the failure of the staff of Clerks' offices to implement the legislation as envisioned by the sponsors of covenant marriage and the more fundamental failure of religious denominations to encourage or insist that their congregants participate. Those who do enter a covenant marriage have a different profile from "standard" married couples, as a result of "self-selection" effects. For example, among the 250 covenant couples and 200 "standard" married couples selected by the team of social scientists to participate in their five-year study of Louisiana's covenant marriage legislation, covenant couples "received more premarital counseling, [and] were more religious and more conservative; whereas standard married couples were more likely to have cohabited, experienced more marital conflict, talked less before marriage about important issues that can cause marital problems, received less approval of their spouse from their parents, were more likely to have been previously married and were more likely to have given birth to or fathered a child previously and to bring a child into the marriage."[19]

Interestingly, "[w]omen are the leading force in a decision to get a covenant marriage.... What we are finding is, in the case of couples who elect covenant marriages, the woman is more often the leader. And with the couples who elect standard marriages, not surprisingly, [the leader] is usually the man."[20] The most obvious explanation for women leading in the choice of a covenant marriage is that women, particularly women with a vested interest in childbearing, apparently feel the need for the protection of stronger divorce laws. Covenant couples are more educated, both wives and husbands, and hold more traditional attitudes than do standard married couples.[21] Furthermore, covenant couples have a forceful conviction that their

---

[19] Spaht, "Eyes of Social Scientists," 722.
[20] Ibid., 721.
[21] Laura A. Sanchez et al., "Social and Demographic Factors Associated with Couples' Choice Between Covenant and Standard Marriage in Louisiana" (draft presented at the annual meeting of the Southern Sociological Society in Atlanta, GA, May 2002).

choice is important, a conviction not shared, naturally, by standard married couples. Covenant couples believe that they are making a powerful social statement about marriage as an institution, particularly at a time when marriage is under siege.

II. WHY COVENANT MARRIAGE STATUTES?

The most obvious answer to "why covenant marriage statutes" is that covenant marriage legislation has thus far been the *only* successful divorce reform effort. Less obvious answers focus on the current state of American culture, the moral confusion of our citizens, the failure to understand and appreciate the public character and purposes of marriage, the divisions that exist within our citizenry on salient issues, and disagreements about the most effective means to accomplish restoration of marriage as a protected, secure, and privileged sanctuary of adults and children.

With a sober understanding of the difficulty in reversing a cultural trend that developed over a two-hundred-year period, indefatigable proponents of covenant marriage legislation view its long-term potential to move the culture in a better direction as both encouraging and hopeful. Covenant marriage reform begins with a couple, the equivalent of a "grass roots" movement, and encourages that couple to participate in a social movement focused on the laudatory goal of strengthening the institution of marriage principally for the sake of children. This attitude is in fact reflected in the results of data collected by Steve Nock's research team: "Covenant couples have a forceful conviction about the importance of their choice that, of course, standard couples do not share; covenant couples believe that they are making a powerful social statement about marriage as an institution."[22] Even among the small percentage of standard married couples who had heard of covenant marriage and discussed the option, the team "found evidence that some of those currently in standard marriages, *particularly women,* had preferred covenant marriage, but perhaps faced barriers."[23] At least six reasons commend the logic of covenant marriage laws:

A. Covenant Marriage Emphasizes Strengthening Marriage, Not Merely Preventing Divorce

Unlike other divorce reform efforts, covenant marriage legislation addresses each phase of the marrying process: before, during, and at the end. By requiring premarital education that emphasizes the seriousness of marriage and the understanding

---

[22] Katherine Shaw Spaht, "Revolution and Counter-Revolution: The Future of Marriage in the Law," *Loyola Law Review* 49 (2003): 1–77.

[23] Sanchez, "Couple's Choice" (italics added).

that marriage is to be lifelong, the bride and groom are required to discuss and resolve issues not necessarily confronted without premarital counseling. Good premarital education with effective tools such as premarital inventories encourages some ill-equipped couples to postpone marriage or to reconsider their very decision to marry. For other couples, premarital education highlights areas of disagreement and explores possible conflict resolution techniques, which can prove invaluable over the duration of a marriage. Difficulties inevitably arise. The legal obligation to take reasonable steps to preserve their marriage assures that the covenant spouses' initial commitment to their marriage will continue over its duration. Covenant marriage legislation assumes that every marriage will experience its challenges and difficulties, and it provides in advance a legal commitment to take reasonable steps to preserve the marriage. At the end of the mandatory premarital counseling, which includes an explanation that the couple is legally obligated to try to preserve the marriage if marital difficulties arise, prospective covenant spouses must execute a legal document that contains their agreement to enter into a covenant marriage and all that this commitment entails, signed by each party whose signature is then notarized. A covenant couple thus begins marriage with an attitude averse to divorce, reflected in the contents of the Declaration of Intent. This attitude toward divorce, research suggests, may serve to ensure greater marital quality and thus fewer marital difficulties.[24]

In fact, data from the study of 250 covenant couples launched in 1998 confirms such findings. The everyday pattern of a covenant marriage reveals that covenant couples "are far more likely to choose communication strategies that do not revolve around attacking or belittling their partner."[25] Covenant spouses are less likely "to respond to conflict with sarcasm or hostility, two communication strategies that … are particularly strongly associated with poor marriage outcomes." As expected, covenant couples were more likely to participate in premarital classes and "address a greater number and broader range of issues in these classes." Two years after covenant couples married, they "described their overall marital quality as better than did their Standard counterparts." From the standpoint of commitment, covenant couples were more committed to their marriages two years after the ceremony than at the time of their marriage; whereas their standard counterparts had changed little in their level of commitment. In the opinion of the researchers, "a central theme that

[24] Paul R. Amato and Stacy J. Rogers, "Do Attitudes Toward Divorce Affect Marital Quality?" *Journal of Family Issues* 20 (January 1999): 69–86, 70 ("Although most Americans continue to value marriage, the belief that an unrewarding marriage should be jettisoned may lead some people to invest less time and energy in their marriages and make fewer attempts to resolve marital disagreements. In other words, a weak commitment to the general norm of life-long marriage may ultimately undermine people's commitments to particular relationships.").

[25] Spaht, "Revolution and Counter-Revolution."

discriminates between the two types of unions [is] *institutionalization of the marriage*" (italics in original). This institutionalization of the marriage reflects the view of covenant couples that "the marriage warrants consideration apart from the individualistic concerns of either partner. In regard to some matters covenant couples appear to defer to the interests of their marriage even when the individual concerns of the partners may appear to conflict. *And this orientation to married life … helps resolve the customary problems faced by newly married couples in regard to fairness and equity*" (italics added). The data collected from covenant couples who are participants in the study supports an old idea: "Two individuals do not make a strong marriage. Rather it takes the presence of a set of guiding principles around which these two individuals orient their behaviors and thinking."[26]

B. *Covenant Marriage Legislation Combines Components Appealing to Political Conservatives and Liberals*

A strategic combination of concepts attractive to both conservatives and liberals makes covenant marriage legislation more appealing than other forms of divorce reform: traditional marriage, choice, moral judgment about personal behavior, and education. Thoughtful conservatives and liberals deeply concerned about marriage and the undesirable consequences of the divorce culture can each find in covenant marriage legislation some component to support. For conservatives, the restrictive grounds for divorce in the nature of fault on the part of a spouse reintroduce objective fault, signaling that state law will once again willingly and confidently judge marital behavior by a common, objective moral code. For liberals, the components of marital education and counseling made mandatory by the legislation offer the possibility of educating citizens to make better choices rather than imposing a particular outcome on couples. Indeed, the entire regime of covenant marriage is based on choice, which in other contexts is readily embraced by liberal policymakers.

C. *Covenant Marriage Invites Religion Back Into the Public Square to Assist in Serving a Public Whose Need is to Preserve Marriages*

The premarital counseling provisions of covenant marriage statutes encourage the celebrant of a marriage to also provide required counseling. The invitation extended by the state through the legislation offers religious clerics, most of whom

---

[26] Steven L. Nock, Laura Sanchez and James D. Wright, "Intimate Equity: The Early Years of Covenant and Standard Marriages" 6 (draft presented at the annual meeting of the Population Association of America, Minneapolis, MN, May 2003), available at http://www.bgsu.edu/downloads/cas/file35380.pdf

are committed to lifelong marriage, the opportunity to counsel a couple about the value of permanent marriage. When difficulties arise, as inevitably they will, and the covenant couple is obligated to take steps to preserve the marriage, the hope exists that the couple will return to the same counselor, or his equivalent, to obtain assistance in overcoming those difficulties. Religious authorities are particularly well equipped to offer intensive one-on-one counseling for couples; they speak with moral authority yet compassionate concern for the couple and their families, all of whom are affected if the marriage ends.

Although it is appropriate for religious officials to be suspicious of governmental intrusion, covenant marriage legislation merely invites religion's assistance, as evidenced in the minimal content of premarital counseling specified in the statute. Rather than banishing religion from the public square, covenant marriage legislation invites religion back into public life to offer a service that religion is uniquely qualified to perform – preserving marriages. Restoration of a public and religious partnership for the purpose of solving one of our country's most intractable problems, sustaining marriages, offers the hope of a more secure future for our children.

D. Covenant Marriage Seeks to Persuade, Not Coerce, Citizens to Elect a Stronger Commitment to Marriage

Covenant marriage legislation depends on the effort of individual couples to change the culture, which for too long has moved toward prizing the autonomous self above all else. When that happens in marriages, it leads to disintegration of relationships based on conclusions that divorce for no good reason is an individual entitlement, as embodied in no-fault divorce statutes. Covenant marriage requires a form of "evangelizing" traditional marriage by challenging that other cultural ideal. Individual Americans need to be convinced of the value of keeping one's promises, of persevering through difficult times, of personal sacrifice for a "transcendental" cause (i.e., the marriage), and of a duty to one's children to provide a stable, warm, and loving home environment. Children deserve to be children, sheltered and protected from adult concerns and discontent. Covenant married couples in Louisiana are participating in this evangelization: The quality of their marriages confirms the rewards of living a married life that reflects the timeless virtues of duty, perseverance, and self-sacrifice.

E. Covenant Marriage Offers Traditional Communities a Refuge from the Broader Postmodern Culture

Until the dominant culture in America changes, covenant marriage legislation permits those who subscribe to a traditional set of values the ability to create an alternative legal structure for family life that social science research supports as the ideal. The legislation "allows a minority to live their desired lives without forcing a change in lifestyle on the majority."[27] According to Christopher Wolfe, the liberal ideal of autonomy is incompatible with the substantive moral ideal of marital fidelity "embraced by certain traditional communities that from one perspective are 'within' the American community and from another perspective are not."[28] One might phrase the explanation of Wolfe as being "in the world" but not "of the world." This predicament applies to people of deep religious faith or, as Gertrude Himmelfarb observes, to an entire "dissident culture" that includes "those of little or no religious faith" but who abide by traditional values and are unembarrassed by the language of morality.[29] Covenant marriage legislation offers the dissident culture the opportunity to live as a traditional community under a stricter moral code reinforced by law, within the larger dominant culture that is subject only to minimal moral constraints.

F. Covenant Marriage Offers the Promise of Surviving Migratory Divorce

No state law divorce reform effort can accomplish its goals if one spouse can simply cross state lines and, by establishing a new domicile, seek relief in another state with more liberal divorce laws.[30] Because of the unique characteristics of a covenant marriage, a court in the state with more liberal divorce laws may be compelled to reexamine the 1942 United States Supreme Court opinion in *Williams v. North Carolina I*.[31] In that decision, the U.S. Supreme Court erroneously melded together the distinct issues of judicial and legislative jurisdiction, otherwise considered separately in cases requiring the application of conflict-of-laws principles.

If a court in the more liberal state where the plaintiff spouse seeking a divorce is newly domiciled was compelled to separate the issue of jurisdiction to render a divorce from the issue of what divorce law should apply (choice of law), general choice-of-law rules would favor the application of the covenant marriage law of plaintiff's former domicile. Two reasons emerge for that favoritism: (1) the fact that the distinguishing characteristic of a covenant marriage is the parties' voluntary

[27] Jeffery Evans Stake, "Paternalism in the Law of Marriage," *Indiana Law Journal* 74 (1999): 801–818, 807.

[28] Wolfe, "Marriage," 37–41.

[29] Gertrude Himmelfarb, "The Panglosses of the Right Are Wrong," *The Wall Street Journal*, Feb. 4, 1999, A22.

[30] See Katherine Shaw Spaht and Symeon Symeonides, "Covenant Marriage and the Law of Conflict of Laws," *Creighton Law Review* 32 (April 1999): 1085–1120; Peter Hay, "The American 'Covenant Marriage' in the Conflict of Laws," in Witte and Ellison, *Covenant Marriage in Comparative Perspective*, 294–316.

[31] *Williams v. North Carolina*, 317 U.S. 287 (1942).

agreement after counseling, which is expressed in an additional contract containing an express choice of Louisiana law; and (2) the fact that the covenant marriage law does not eliminate, but simply delays, the availability of a unilateral no-fault divorce.

Covenant marriage offers the potential for reversing judicial social engineering, which as early as 1942 reduced divorce laws in the states to the "lowest common denominator." The barriers and obstacles to divorce erected by North Carolina for the protection of its citizenry crumbled in obeisance to the Supreme Court's dictate that North Carolina must give full faith and credit to a judgment of divorce rendered in Nevada, a state whose courts were willing to apply the more liberal divorce law.

III. MARRIAGE – AND "CIVIL MARRIAGE" AND "RELIGIOUS MARRIAGE"

With the looming specter of a fundamental alteration to the understanding of marriage in the law, an argument that the state should cede original jurisdiction regarding issues of marriage and divorce to faith communities (robust "pluralism")[32] comes alongside the promise (still oft unfulfilled) of these covenant marriage laws.[33] This new (and renewed) argument assumes great urgency, especially for deeply religious citizens. Taken seriously, the argument does not necessarily concede that the state has no legitimate business regulating the intimate relationships of adults and thus should relinquish the sanction and regulation of them. Instead, the argument appeals at least superficially to a religious person's deepest and most profound beliefs about marriage and family. What religious person could strenuously object to the regulation of marriage and divorce ceded by the state to her own religious community? After all, she follows these tenets without the imposition of law.

The possibility of religiously pluralistic marriage appeared in the wake of a shift in legal terminology in the public square that occurred over a decade ago. The shift was occasioned by the addition of the adjective "civil" before the word "marriage." The purpose of the addition was to introduce a dichotomy not then recognized in this country – "civil" versus "religious" marriage. The intention of those who added "civil" was to deny that the structure of marriage was normative and reflective of the natural moral law. Natural moral law applies equally to the religious and non-religious alike, of course, accessed through the use of conscience and reason. The

---

[32] See Nichols, "Reconsidering the Boundaries" (in this volume). See also Joel A. Nichols, "Multi-Tiered Marriage: Ideas and Influences from New York and Louisiana to the International Community," *Vanderbilt Journal of Transnational Law* 40 (2007): 135–196.

[33] The lack of passage of covenant marriage statutes outside of Arkansas, Arizona, and Louisiana – and the low number of couples entering covenant marriages in those states – dampens a bit of the early hope but does not alter their importance or possibility.

dichotomy was intended to sever from "civil marriage" – that is, legally recognized marriage – any connection to what could be considered its religious foundation. The dichotomy evidenced by these two adjectives prevents one from speaking simply of *marriage* to communicate a monogamous union of one man and one woman intended to last for life. The dichotomy prevents the recognition of marriage as a social, pre-legal institution privileged by the law to channel heterosexual couples into it for the purpose of rearing and protecting children.[34]

Instead, the dichotomy between "civil" and "religious" marriage more closely reflects the history in Europe of the struggle between secular governments and the Catholic Church in asserting legislative and judicial authority over marriage. The Catholic Church was triumphant in wresting that authority from secular governments in the tenth century, and the secular governments wrested authority from the Church by the end of the eighteenth century.[35] The separate secular and religious authoritative realms resulting from these historical struggles remain especially influential in Europe. The strict division between civil authority over marriage as distinguished from religious practice regarding marriage has never been of the same ilk in the United States, where most states permit religious officiants to perform the ceremony required by law as a representative of the state.[36]

Essentially, the state's ceding legislative and judicial jurisdiction over marriage to some other authority, with minimal restrictions assuring some basic protections for women[37] and children,[38] privatizes marriage. Marriage becomes a purely private relationship based on an emotional commitment between two adults[39] and thus loses its public character. In some cases it may even lose its name.[40] Public relinquishment of marriage confirms that intimate relations between at least two consenting adults is no one else's business. But is that true? As a social, pre-legal institution marriage is society's, or the public's, business. Covenant marriage statutes in no way constitute a privatization of marriage; instead, they maintain and protect the public purposes of marriage. They in no way cede the institution of marriage to the private

---

[34] Carl E. Schneider, "The Channelling Function in Family Law," *Hofstra Law Review* 20 (1992): 495–532. But see Linda C. McClain, "Love, Marriage, and the Baby Carriage: Revisiting the Channelling Function of Family Law," *Cardozo Law Review* 28 (2007): 2133–2183. See also Presser, "Marriage and the Law" (in this volume).

[35] Marcel Planiol, *Traité Elementaire de Droit Civil* [francais] I No. 699–702 (12th ed. 1939) (La. State Law Institute transl. 1959).

[36] See, e.g., La. R.S. §§ 9:201 *et seq*. See also Ann Laquer Estin, "Unofficial Family Law" (in this volume).

[37] See Linda C. McClain, "Marriage Pluralism in the United States: On Civil and Religious Jurisdiction and the Demands of Equal Citizenship" (in this volume).

[38] See also Witte, *From Sacrament to Contract*.

[39] David Blankenhorn, *The Future of Marriage* (Encounter Books: New York, 2007).

[40] Jennifer A. Drobac and Antony Page, "A Uniform Domestic Partnership Act: Marrying Business Partnership and Family Law," *Georgia Law Review* 41 (2007): 349–429. See also Presser, "Marriage and the Law" (in this volume).

realm of religious authority – but quite the opposite. They invite religion into the public sphere to assist in accomplishing the very purposes of marriage that affect the public – ensuring that children will have an enduring emotional, moral, and legal relationship with the parents who are responsible for their existence.[41]

If marriage has a public purpose that is truly essential, there are limits to how much of marriage can or should be privatized. If marriage is converted into a private relationship between consenting adults, rather than a social institution for creating and protecting children, it imposes one narrative about marriage on the whole society – a new narrative that is both false and destructive. It is false because marriage is not simply a private relationship between two people without a public interest in how that relationship functions. Marriage is a relationship with the responsibility for acculturating the next generation, which is a lengthy, expensive, and inefficient process. It is destructive because the characterization of marriage as private ignores the fact that this relationship is not simply one between the contracting parties that affects no one else directly.[42] Children move from center stage of the public institution to the fringes of a "private" adult relationship. They become nothing more than a by-product of this private relationship between adults.

Despite the clear religious reference contained in "covenant marriage," covenant marriage statutes were never intended by their advocates to represent the first step in the ceding of state jurisdiction over marriage to religious authorities. Instead, advocates of covenant marriage statutes envisioned that couples, when "informed" of the option, would choose covenant marriage. Thus, by their own choices over time, Louisiana couples would shift the public paradigm of marriage from a "no-fault" marriage to a stronger, more enduring institution. After more than ten years of experience with the statute in Louisiana, that vision remains frustrated and unfulfilled.[43] Part of the frustration derives from the failure of religious authorities to embrace and thus require of its members a state-authorized and regulated vision of marriage more compatible with the traditional Judeo-Christian understanding of the institution. Considering Louisiana's disappointing experience with religious authorities' refusal to encourage covenant marriage, it is difficult to entertain confidence in their ability to accept the solemn responsibility of jurisdiction over marriage and divorce.

---

[41] Blankenhorn, *The Future of Marriage*. See also Robin Fretwell Wilson, "Evaluating Marriage: Does Marriage Matter to the Nurturing of Children?" *San Diego Law Review* 42 (2005): 847–880.

[42] Maxine Eichner, "Marriage and the Elephant: The Liberal Democratic State's Regulation of Intimate Relationships Between Adults," *Harvard Journal of Law & Gender* 30 (Winter 2007): 25–66.

[43] For a final compilation of the data accumulated from the empirical study of Louisiana's covenant marriage law, see Steven L. Nock et al., *Covenant Marriage: The Movement to Reclaim Tradition in America*, (New Brunswick, NJ: Rutgers University Press, 2008).

IV. WHY NOT OTHER OPTIONS?

In the United States, a country with a fluid, multireligious society, there are only a few religious denominations or sects with historical, much less current, experience exercising jurisdiction over marriage matters. If an established procedure for regulating the marriage relationship is an essential element of asserting original jurisdiction in marriage formation and dissolution, then only a few religions or denominations would, in varying degrees, have that capability. They are the Catholic Church, Orthodox Judaism, and possibly, the Episcopal Church (relying on its historical affiliation with the Anglican Church of England).[44] With only two Christian denominations, at most, possessing such an established procedure and infrastructure, large segments of the United States population would be foreclosed from the possibility of religious jurisdiction over their marriages. Many of these Americans are deeply religious and are among the most concerned about the undermining of marriage, such as evangelical Protestants. Yet they have no historical experience with exercising legislative and judicial jurisdiction over marriage and, generally, have no hierarchical structure that would facilitate such jurisdiction. Even the Catholic Church, which has had such experience and infrastructure historically, would be overwhelmed by the sheer number of cases in this country if it were to assume such authority over marriage issues.

To the extent that there is recognition that the public has at least some minimal interest in marriage[45] and other intimate relationships, what limits will be imposed on the exercise of jurisdiction by religious authorities? Will other constitutional protections trump the free exercise of religious "practices," as distinguished from beliefs, concerning marriage and divorce? Is it conceivable that a state's relinquishment of jurisdiction over marriage to religious authority would insulate the religious authority's laws and practices from constitutional scrutiny? Is this a delegation of state authority to religious authorities subjecting the latter to constitutional protections against actions of the state?[46] Or, is it instead an abandonment of state regulation and literally nothing more than an agreement between two parties to be bound by religious laws and practices concerning marriage and divorce? Constitutional protections as limits on religious authority are only part of the range of legal issues raised by state-imposed "minimal" restrictions.

---

[44] For Muslim groups, see Mohammad H. Fadel, "Political Liberalism, Islamic Family Law, and Family Law Pluralism" (in this volume).

[45] See, e.g., *United States v. Reynolds*, 98 U.S. 145 (1878). See also Charles J. Reid, "And the State Makes Three: Should the State Retain a Role in Recognizing Marriage?" 27 *Cardozo Law Review* (2006): 1277–1307.

[46] See Bix, "Pluralism and Decentralization" (in this volume) and John Witte Jr. and Joel A. Nichols, "The Frontiers of Marital Pluralism: An Afterword" (in this volume).

Will the law continue to protect children born out of wedlock to the same extent as children born of the marriage? Consistent with the present legal understanding of the rights and obligations of parents to children and vice versa, that is, that they exist independently of marriage, the relinquishment of jurisdiction over marriage need not affect the legal relationship of parent/child. However, what if under a particular religious law paternal rights and responsibilities are assigned solely on the basis of marriage? What if a particular religious law also permits the father to use extreme corporal punishment? Would there be a distinction between religious law that in the former case assigns rights and responsibilities but does not affect the child's physical well-being (private law) and a religious law that permits a result prohibited by "public" law?[47]

If the answer is "yes" to the distinction between private and public law, the first religious law referenced in the preceding paragraph assigns parental rights to the father alone, hence the use of the word "paternal." Would there be a limit on the relinquishment of jurisdiction over marriage to religious authorities that would prohibit the application of any religious law that discriminated against women?[48] Religious law may well discriminate against women. Would the distinction between private and public law permit such discrimination only if the area of the law affected was purely private law, rather than public law? If so, the private law of husband and wife encompasses a body of law enacted to eliminate such discrimination and to protect women. For example, what if only the husband had the right to seek a divorce under religious law? What if, as to marital or community property under the private law, the property accumulated during marriage belonged to both husband and wife but under religious law belonged solely to the husband?

In the same vein, would the limits imposed on religious jurisdiction over marriage include prohibiting incest, bigamy, polygamy, polyandry, and "open" marriage (one in which the spouses agree not to be monogamous)? Any of these practices could be permitted or compelled under a particular religious law. To the extent that any of these practices are prohibited by criminal law, the same public versus private law distinction could be made to limit the application of religious law. But what if the criminal law does not explicitly punish a practice such as polyandry or adultery – then should limits on these religious practices exist in the realm of private law for the purpose of protecting the public interest?

Religious law could also prohibit the intermarriage across religious denominations and sects, which would arguably constitute a form of discrimination. Assuming that at least as to this form of discrimination there would be less constitutional concern,

---

[47] See Robin Fretwell Wilson, "The Perils of Privatized Marriage" (in this volume).
[48] See Ayelet Shachar, "Faith in Law? Diffusing Tensions Between Diversity and Equality" (in this volume) and McClain, "Marriage Pluralism in the United States" (in this volume).

what rules would religious authorities have to devise to accommodate or prohibit marriage across religious lines? What happens if, after marriage, one of the spouses changes religious affiliation – a common occurrence in this country? If husband and wife were Catholic at the time of marriage, would the Catholic Church retain some form of "continuing jurisdiction" to rule on annulment? What if the spouse's new religious affiliation does not prohibit divorce and neither does the private law? Would we permit the Catholic Church to rule on marriages of a Catholic and a non-Catholic when the non-Catholic seeks the protection of his own religion or of the state?

Relinquishing jurisdiction over marriage, both legislative and judicial, threatens to undermine marriage as a critical public social institution and creates a myriad of practical, as well as legal, problems for resolution. In a multireligious society like that of the United States, resolution of the problems would result in a highly complex and arguably unworkable patchwork of systems. A shared cultural understanding of marriage would be lost, and with it the clear signaling that occurs between partners. Some practices permitted by religious law would be harmful to societal interests, even if state and federal constitutional guarantees precluded the most egregious of such practices. At least covenant marriage as a sole, optional alternative to "no-fault" marriage recognizes a stronger form of union between a man and a woman, which is intended to afford greater protection to children born of that union. It would be irresponsible to recognize a form of union through relinquishment of jurisdiction to religious authorities that posed harm to children, the participants, or society at large.

V. CONCLUSION

If marriage is recognized and regulated in the law only by minimal constraints protecting the public's health and welfare (and if "health" and "welfare" are narrowly defined), the retreat of law from more comprehensive regulation communicates the idea that society has little interest in the formation and the duration of marriage.[49] This retreat conveys the idea that marriage, the most fundamental of human relationships, is strictly a private matter about which the two (or more) parties may contract, even if that contract conveys jurisdiction over the parties' marriage to religious authorities. Widespread personalization of marriage through individuals' contracts[50] ultimately destroys the common cultural understanding and meaning of marriage

---

[49] Katherine Shaw Spaht, "The Last One Hundred Years: The Incredible Retreat of Law from the Regulation of Marriage," *Louisiana Law Review* 63 (2003): 243–308.

[50] Jamie Alan Aycock, "Contracting Out of the Culture Wars: How the Law Should Enforce and Communities of Faith Encourage More Enduring Marital Commitments," *Harvard Journal of Law & Public Policy* 30 (2006): 231–281.

shared by a people, often disadvantages the less sophisticated or worldly partners, and affords no protection to noncontracting parties like children.

What covenant marriage statutes represent, however, is a reasonable compromise between religious authority over marriage and a single state version of "no-fault" marriage that offends the religiously orthodox. A covenant marriage statute retains recognition of the public interest in marriage reflected in the law, incorporates a version of marriage that more closely conforms to natural moral law, and utilizes law to exhort and express an ideal of human behavior. Covenant marriage is a remnant of the received, natural understanding of marriage, its purpose, and its function. Louisiana's version is especially complete and comprehensive.[51] Legal remnants, of course, have biblical analogues; and remnants have always served an indispensable, and in some cases even divine, purpose.

---

[51] La. R.S. §§ 9:293 *et seq.*

6

New York's Regulation of Jewish Marriage

Covenant, Contract, or Statute?

Michael J. Broyde

I. INTRODUCTION

Is Jewish marriage and divorce law essentially covenantal or contractual? The answer to this ancient question – and the extent to which the answer is an amalgamation of the two choices – has changed over time. Different authorities have disagreed about this question in profound ways, and the answer is still in flux today.

On the one hand, Jewish tradition is replete with references to the sacred nature of the marital relationship. The Talmud recounts that a person is not complete until he or she marries, and he or she is not even called a person until two are united.[1] Further, the classical sources recount the profound Divine hand in the creation of marriage. One Talmudic source goes so far as to state, "Forty days prior to birth, the Holy One, Blessed be He, announces that so-and-so should marry so-and-so."[2] Marriages appear to be holy relationships that embrace and are embraced by the Divine. For example, the earliest commentaries on the Bible posit that God performed the wedding ceremony between Adam and Eve.[3] Indeed, the blessings recited at Jewish weddings recount that it is God who "commanded us with regard to forbidden relationships, forbade [merely] betrothed women to us, and permitted wives [to husbands] through the Jewish wedding ceremony."[4]

On the other hand, the incorporation of godliness, sanctity, and covenant into the union is but one facet of marriage in the Jewish tradition. The tradition also presents a countervailing set of factors that provide insight into the nature of Jewish marriage: The Jewish law mechanics of entry into and exit from marriage are rooted in private contractual rights. Central to this model is the rabbinic tradition of the *ketubah*,

---

[1] Babylonian Talmud [hereinafter BT], *Yevamot* 63a.
[2] BT *Sotah* 2a.
[3] Louis Ginzberg et al., *The Legends of the Jews* (Philadelphia: Jewish Publication Society, 1968), 68.
[4] See, e.g., Rabbi Nosson Scherman, ed., *The Complete Artscroll Siddur, Rabbinical Council of America Edition*, (New York: Mesorah Publications, 1995), 202–203.

the premarital contract to which a couple agrees, which spells out the terms and conditions of both the marriage and its termination. This tradition, discussed in dozens of pages of closely reasoned Talmudic texts (including an entire tractate in the Talmud devoted to the topic titled *"Ketubot"* [the Hebrew plural of *ketubah*]), describes marriage as a contract that is freely entered into by both parties and dissolvable by divorce – with little sacred to it. Further refinements to marriage in the immediate post-Talmudic period kept with the spirit of this contract or partnership model of marriage.

These two perspectives on marriage in the Jewish tradition are not merely variant strands of Jewish law and lore, nor are they parallel courses that never cross paths. Around one thousand years ago, European Jewish legal authorities worked – particularly by enacting significant restrictions on exit from marriage – to minimize the contractual view of marriage found in the earlier Talmudic *ketubah* literature. This backlash against the long-running Talmudic tradition moved marriage closer to a covenantal scheme and also established the normal mode of marriage as one husband and one wife for life. In the past fifty years, however, Jewish law has reemphasized and restored some elements of the contractual view of marriage. It has also added another model – the statutory paradigm.

This shifting between marriage as covenant and contract in Jewish tradition, coupled with a lack of authority of rabbinical courts in the United States to enforce even equitable divorce settlements, created a situation in which Jewish law in the United States was unable to regulate (or even determine) its own marriage constructs. This, in turn, led to an absolutely unique situation – the regulation of Jewish marriage by the state of New York since 1983 through the creation of the first "covenant marriage statute" in the United States – to solve the problems created by Jewish marriage doctrines.[5]

This chapter describes the covenant-contract conflict and interplay. Section II briefly leads the reader through the Talmudic history of family law, emphasizing its contractual roots. Section III then explains the post-Talmudic developments in family law and the rise of the marriage as covenant. Section IV examines the dialectic tension of Jewish covenant and contract marriage in the laws of New York, and it explains how New York effectively created the nation's first covenant marriage act. Section V explores the practicalities of how this secular regulation of marriage has impacted Jewish marriage and divorce. Finally, Section VI concludes with some observations about living under two legal systems in the modern age.

---

[5] Compare Katherine Shaw Spaht, "Covenant Marriage Laws: A Model for Compromise" (in this volume).

II. JEWISH MARRIAGE LAWS: MOVEMENT FROM
CONTRACT TO COVENANT

Jewish law differs from other mainstream legal or religious systems in that it views entry into marriage and exit from marriage through divorce as private contractual rights rather than public rights. In the Jewish view, one does not need a governmental "license" to marry or divorce. Private marriages are fundamentally proper; a political and even a religious official's regulation of marriage or divorce is the exception rather than the rule.[6]

According to the Talmudic understanding of Biblical law concerning remarriage of one's divorcee,[7] the husband has a unilateral right to divorce even though marriage requires the consent of both parties; the wife has no right to divorce except in cases of hard fault.[8] Exit from marriage thus differed fundamentally from entry into marriage in that it did not require the consent of both parties. Moreover, because there is a clear biblical concept of divorce, no stigma has historically been associated with its use.[9] The marriage ended if and only if the husband wished to end it by his executing a writ of divorce (in Hebrew called a *get*, plural *gittin*).

As soon as Jewish law was first redacted, the notion of the dower (*ketubah*) was developed for all brides. The dower was payable upon divorce or death of the husband, and this became, by rabbinic decree, a precondition to every marriage. Whereas the right to divorce remained unilateral, it was now restricted by a clear contractual financial obligation imposed on the husband to compensate his wife if

[6] This stands in contrast to the historical Anglo-American common law view, which treats private contracts to marry or divorce as quintessential examples of illegal and void contracts; the Catholic view, which treats marriage and annulment (divorce) as sacraments requiring ecclesiastical cooperation or blessing; and the European view, which has treated marriage and divorce as an area of public law. Jewish marriage does have many sacramental parts also, but the contractual view predominates in the beginning-of-marriage and end-of-marriage rites. See J. David Bleich, "Jewish Divorce: Judicial Misconceptions and Possible Means of Civil Enforcement," *Connecticut Law Review* 16 (1984): 201–289.
[7] Deuteronomy 24:1–4. Incidental mention of divorce is also found in Genesis 21:10, Leviticus 21:7, and 22:13.
[8] The Talmud records a three-sided dispute as to when divorce was proper. The school of Shammai recounted that divorce was only proper in cases of fault. The school of Hillel asserted that divorce was proper for any displeasing conduct. Rabbi Akiva maintained that a man could divorce his wife simply because he wished to marry another and could not support both wives. See BT *Gittin* 90a-b. As is always the rule in Jewish law, the school of Shammai is rejected as incorrect.
[9] The exception is the case that proves the rule. There are a small number of cases where marriage is not discretionary but ethically mandatory. See, e.g., Deuteronomy 22:19. These cases involve either fault or detrimental reliance by the other. In the case of seduction, the Bible mandates that the seducer is under a religious duty to marry the seduced, should she wish to marry him. That marriage does not require the same type of free-will consent to marry, in that the religious and ethical component to the Jewish tradition directs the man to marry this woman; indeed, in certain circumstances he can be punished if he does not marry her. No divorce is permitted in such cases.

he exercised his right to engage in unilateral divorce absent judicially declared fault on her part.

The wife, as a precondition to entry into the marriage, could insist on a dower higher than the minimum promulgated by the rabbis.[10] Further, the wife or husband could use the *ketubah* as a forum for addressing other matters between them that ought to be regulated by contract, such as whether polygamy would be permitted or what would be the response to childlessness or other potential issues in the marriage. These *ketubah* documents followed the standard formulation of contracts and openly contemplated divorce.[11] They said little about marriage as sacred or covenantal.

The Talmud clearly set out – and the *ketubah* would reiterate – the wife's right to sue for divorce if her husband was at fault. Grounds would include not only hard faults such as adultery but also softer faults such as repugnancy, impotence, unlivability, cruelty, and others. In such cases, the husband had to divorce his wife (and in most instances pay his wife the dower, too). The wife's access to fault-based divorce was expanded into a clear and concrete legal right in the Talmud. She even had a right to have children, and her husband's refusal to have children was grounds for divorce by her.[12] Thus, although she could not sue for divorce as a general rule, she could restrict his rights through a *ketubah* provision.[13]

Soon after the close of the Talmudic period, the rabbis of that time (called *Geonim*) changed or reinterpreted[14] Jewish law to vastly increase the right of a woman to sue for divorce, but that change had little impact on the basic nature of marriage as essentially contractual. (This is true even though the marital bonds were weaker and the penalty for the breach of contract was somewhat reduced.)[15] Among European Jews, this contractual tradition did not continue much beyond the end of the first millennium of the common era, for a decree was enacted under the leadership of Rabbenu Gershom that moved Jewish law toward a covenantal model of marriage. Rabbenu Gershom held that it was necessary to restrict the rights of the husband

---

[10]   See Michael Broyde and Jonathan Reiss, "The Ketubah in America: Its Value in Dollars, its Significance in *Halacha* and its Enforceability in American Law," *Journal of Halacha and Contemporary Society* 47 (2004): 101–124.

[11]   For an excellent survey of the *Ketubot* from Talmudic and the immediate post-Talmudic time, see Mordechai Akiva Friedman, *Jewish Marriage in Palestine* (Tel Aviv: Tel Aviv University, 1983). The second volume contains dozens of actual *ketubahs* from before the year 1000 C.E.

[12]   See BT *Yevamot* 64a, *Shulhan Arukh, Even Haezer* 154:6–7 and *Arukh HaShulhan, Even Haezer* 154:52–53.

[13]   BT *Yevamot* 65a; but see the view of Rav Ammi.

[14]   Through a mechanism called *takanta demitivta*, or decree of the academy, whose exact mechanism is unclear. See Irving A. Breitowitz, *Between Civil and Religious Law: The Plight of the Agunah in American Society* (Westport, CT: Greenwood Press, 1993), 50–53.

[15]   See Michael Broyde, *Marriage, Divorce and the Abandoned Wife in Jewish Law: A Conceptual Approach to the Agunah Problems in America.* (Hoboken, NJ: Ktav, 2001).

and prohibit unilateral no-fault divorce by either husband or wife.[16] Divorce was limited to cases of provable fault or mutual consent, and fault was vastly redefined to exclude cases of soft fault such as repugnancy. In only a few cases could the husband actually be forced to divorce his wife, or the reverse.[17] Equally significant, these decrees prohibited polygamy, thus placing considerable pressure on the man and woman in a troubled marriage to stay married.[18] Because neither could divorce without the other's consent, divorce was exceedingly rare and possible only in cases of dire fault. The basis for Jewish marriage changed when the refinements of Rabbenu Gershom were implemented. Together, the decrees severely restricted the likelihood of divorce and essentially vacated the economic provisions of the *ketubah*. Marriage, in effect, became a covenant between the parties, and not a contract.

Rabbenu Gershom's ban against divorcing a woman without her consent or without a showing of hard fault[19] called into question the value of the marriage contract itself. The Talmudic rabbis had instituted the *ketubah* payments to deter the husband from rashly divorcing a wife. But now, because the husband could not divorce his wife without her consent, there seemed to be no further need for the *ketubah*.[20] As Rabbi Moses Isserles (Rama), the leading codifier of European Jewry, wrote at the beginning of his discussion of the laws of *ketubot*:

> See *Shulhan Arukh, Even Haezer* 177:3, where it states that in a situation where one only may divorce with the consent of the woman, one does not need a *ketubah*. Thus, nowadays, in our countries, where we do not divorce against the will of the wife because of the ban of Rabbenu Gershom ... it is possible to be lenient and not write a *ketubah* at all.[21]

---

[16] The decree of Rabbenu Gershom was enacted under penalty of ban of excommunication (*herem*). The collective decrees of Rabbenu Gershom are thus known as *Herem deRabbenu Gershom*. See *Herem deRabbenu Gershom, Encyclopedia Talmudit* (Yad Harav Herzog, 1996) 17:378.

[17] This insight is generally ascribed to the eleventh-century Tosafist Rabbenu Tam in his view of the repugnancy claim (Heb.: *ma'is alay*). In fact, it flows logically from the view of Rabbenu Gershom, who not only had to prohibit polygamy in order to end coerced divorce, but even divorce for soft fault.

[18] The decree restricting the right to divorce would not work without prohibiting polygamy, for the husband who could not divorce would simply remarry and abandon his first wife.

[19] In cases of hard fault where the woman was at fault, the value of the *ketubah* did not need to be paid. What exactly is hard fault remains a matter of dispute, but it generally includes adultery, spouse beating, insanity, and frigidity. See *Shulhan Arukh, Even Haezer* 154.

[20] Thus, for example, *Shulhan Arukh, Even Haezer* 177:3, states that "a man who rapes a woman ... is obligated to marry her, so long as she ... wish[es] to marry him, even if she is crippled or blind, and he is not permitted to divorce her forever, except with her consent, and thus he does not have to write her a *ketubah*." The logic seems clear: Because he cannot divorce her under any circumstances without her consent, the presence or absence of a *ketubah* seems to make no difference to her economic status or marital security. When they both want to divorce, they will agree on financial terms independent of the *ketubah*, and until then, the *ketubah* sets no payment schedule.

[21] *Shulhan Arukh, Even Haezer* 66:3.

The *ketubah* did remain a fixture of Jewish weddings after the tenth century,[22] but it was transformed from a marriage contract (which governed a contractual marriage) to a ritual document whose transfer initiated a covenantal marriage. The *ketubah* held no economic or other value as a contract. Indeed, the contractual model of marriage ended for those Jews – all European Jews – who accepted the refinements of Rabbenu Gershom. Rabbi Moses Feinstein, the leading American Jewish law authority of the last century, commented on this matter:

> The value of the *ketubah* is not known to rabbis and decisors of Jewish law, or rabbinical court judges; indeed we have not examined this matter intensely as for all matter of divorce it has no practical ramifications, since it is impossible for the man to divorce against the will of the woman, [the economics of] divorce are dependent on who desires to be divorced.[23]

The contrast between those Jewish communities that accepted the enactments of Rabbenu Gershom and those that did not can be clearly seen in the juxtaposed comments of the European and Oriental authorities, which comprise the classic law code of the *Shulhan Arukh* in the area of family law. Rabbi Moses Isserles (of Poland) accepts these refinements and values the essence of marriage as a covenant, but Rabbi Joseph Karo (of Palestine), who does not incorporate them, portrays a less lofty ideal of marriage. Consider the opening discussion of marriage, which states:

> Karo: Every man must marry a woman in order to reproduce. Anyone who is not having children is, as if, they are killers, reducers of the place of people on this earth, and causing God to leave the Jewish people. Isserles: Anyone who is without a wife lives without blessing and without Torah and is not called a person. Once one marries a woman, all of one's sins are forgiven, as it states, "One who finds a wife finds goodness, and obtains the favor of God." Proverbs 18:22.[24]

Rabbi Karo subscribes to a view that marriage, although mandatory, is but a necessary precondition to the fulfillment of the Jewish law obligation to have children. The marriage is a means to an end and is governed by mutually agreeable contractual provisions. Rabbi Isserles, by contrast, sees inherent value in the very act of taking a wife. One who marries moves beyond a state of incompleteness, and it is the union of marriage itself that "obtains the favor of God." This is a marriage of covenantal nature.

The covenantal model of marriage set out by Rabbi Isserles, however, suffers from a grave defect: It eliminates the clear rules that are the foundation of Jewish divorce law. In the Talmudic period and beyond, Jewish divorce law was contractual.

---

[22] See Broyde and Reiss, "The Ketubah in America."
[23] Moses Feinstein, *Iggrot Moshe, Even Haezer* 4:91. (This *responsum* was written in 1980.)
[24] *Shulhan Arukh, Even Haezer* 1:1.

Women and men protected themselves from the consequences of divorce by contractually agreeing to the process and costs of divorce. Although that approach had failings, it led to predictable results that the parties had negotiated in their *ketubah*. After Rabbenu Gershom's decrees, Jewish divorce law lacked clear rules to follow. Except in cases of fault (where a Jewish law court could order a divorce), all Jewish divorces became negotiated exercises between a husband and a wife. Jewish decisors could not force a divorce, nor could they direct its financial arrangements. At best, Jewish law courts could enact a settlement based on the principles of equitable authority conferred or vested in them by the civil authorities. Any such decisions were not based on the *ketubah*, however, but rather derived from the later negotiation between the estranged parties. Contractual divorce law ceased to exist except in cases of fault, and divorces became negotiation exercises resolved only by consent.

This covenant understanding of marriage and divorce has proved difficult to maintain. It was workable only in premodern Europe because divorce was not common and was limited, given the social and economic reality of that time and place, to cases of hard fault.[25] Moreover, Jewish law courts in these communities had authority to provide equitable relief when the parties appearing before the court desired to divorce but could not agree on the terms. The modern American Jewish experience, with divorce increasingly common and with religious courts not legally empowered to offer equitable resolutions enforceable by the state, has brought the vacuousness of the *ketubah* contract to the forefront and has raised serious issues about the continued functioning of Jewish law in the United States. Three basic solutions have been advanced, all of which involve the innovative use of secular law to enforce Jewish law.

III. JEWISH MARRIAGE CONTRACTS AND AMERICAN LAW

The use of the secular legal system to produce Jewish law solutions is unique and represents a noteworthy break from the Jewish tradition, which has long resisted allowing a secular legal authority into the details of Jewish law.[26] Such innovative collaboration with the secular legal system was perceived as necessary by many, because Jewish law was confronting a central challenge to its vision of family law.

Until the massive migration to the United States, there was clear equitable authority in rabbinical courts to resolve matters of divorce fairly as needed – even

---

[25] For a discussion of the problems posed in pre-emancipation Russia by this construct of Jewish law, see ChaeRan Y. Freeze, *Making and Unmaking the Jewish Family: Marriage and Divorce in Imperial Russia, 1850–1914*, (Ph.D. Dissertation, Brandeis University, 1997) (noting that Jewish divorce was more common than Orthodox Christian divorce but still relatively uncommon).

[26] See Michael Broyde, "Informing on Others for Violating American Law: A Jewish Law View," *Journal of Halacha and Contemporary Society* 41 (2002): 5–49.

though no substantive Jewish family law could substantiate rabbinical court decisions except in cases of hard fault. The laws of nearly all European states recognized
the authority of Jewish law courts in many matters to be binding and enforceable.
The American states did not, however, and the coercive jurisdiction of the rabbinical courts that had been a fixture of European Jewish communal life disappeared.
American rabbinical courts ceased to be a significant source of authority in the
American Jewish community. They only regained authority when the individuals in
a particular marriage not only empowered the rabbinical court to resolve their dispute but also refused to challenge the outcome in a secular court. In America, the
Jewish marriage covenant was – in essence – unenforceable.

Three distinct solutions have been advanced to preserve the centrality of the legal
status of Jewish marriage within the Jewish tradition.[27] Each of them involved the
secular law of the United States in some form, but none has worked very well.

A. *The Enforceability of the* Ketubah *as a Contract*

The earliest effort to engage secular law sought to have the provisions of the *ketubah*
enforced as a matter of American contract law.[28] This was litigated in a number of
cases. For example, in 1974 a widow tried to collect the amount of her husband's
ketubah and claimed that the *ketubah* superseded her prior waiver of any future
claims pursuant to a prenuptial agreement between herself and her husband. (The
ketubah had been signed after the prenuptial agreement, and thus, if it were a valid
contract, would have superseded it.) The New York Supreme Court denied the
claim, concluding that even for an observant Orthodox Jew the *ketubah* had become
more a matter of form and ceremony than a legal obligation.[29] The basic claim of
the litigant seemed reasonable from a Jewish law view: She had entered into a marriage, which was bound by Jewish law, and the courts ought to enforce it. The New
York courts did not agree.

In no case has a secular court enforced the *ketubah* provision mandating
payments,[30] in part because the financial obligations described in the *ketubah* – in
zuzim and *zekukim*, which require determinations of Jewish law to ascertain their

---

[27] Reform Judaism in America abandoned such efforts and accepted civil marriage and divorce as
preeminent.

[28] See, e.g., *Hurwitz v. Hurwitz*, 215 N.Y.S. 184 (NY App. Div. Second, 1926), where the court referred to
the *ketubah* by the term "koshuba" and had no context to examine it.

[29] *In Re White's Estate*, 356 N.Y.S.2d 208, 210 (NY Sup. Ct. 1974).

[30] An Arizona court suggested in dicta that financial obligations described in a *ketubah* could perhaps
be enforceable if described with sufficient specificity, *Victor v. Victor*, 866 P.2d at 902 (Ariz. 1993),
but Jewish law in practice has never sought to conform the text of the *ketubah* to the requirements of
American contract law.

proper value – are not considered specific enough to be enforceable.[31] Moreover, the absence of an English text (where either the husband or wife are not fluent in Aramaic and Hebrew) and the absence of signatures of both husband and wife would seem to render the *ketubah* invalid as a contract under American law.

The New York Court of Appeals, in a subsequent case, did enforce a *ketubah* provision in which the parties agreed to arbitrate future marital disputes before a rabbinical court, but the court did not revisit the actual issue of the enforceability of the *ketubah*'s financial obligations.[32] Although it has not been tested, it is conceivable that a *ketubah*'s financial provisions might be enforceable in the United States if it is executed in a country (such as Israel) where it is recognized as a binding contract. In such a case, American conflict-of-laws rules might determine that the rules governing the validity of the *ketubah* are found in the location where the wedding was performed, where the *ketubah* is a legally enforceable document.[33]

However, to the best of this writer's knowledge, no American court has ever directly enforced the financial component of a *ketubah* written in America in a case of divorce. Thus, court-ordered enforcement of a Jewish marriage contract seems unlikely in the United States.[34]

B. Rabbinic Arbitration Agreements to Construct Jewish Marriages

The second method to provide American law support for Jewish marriage has been the use of private arbitration law. Although attempts to use prenuptial agreements to enforce the covenantal aspect of Jewish marriage date back more than three hundred years and can be found in a standard book of Jewish legal forms from seventeenth-century Europe,[35] the earliest use of arbitration agreements in America to govern Jewish marriages was in 1954 under the direction of Rabbi Dr. Saul Lieberman. These arbitration agreements were included in an additional clause to the *ketubah*:

> [W]e the bride and the bridegroom ... hereby agree to recognize the Beth Din of the Rabbinical Assembly and the Jewish Theological Seminary of America or its duly appointed representatives, as having the authority to counsel us in the light

---

[31] Whether the language of a *ketubah* forms a basis for compelling a *get* according to secular law doctrine is beyond the scope of this chapter.

[32] *Avitzur v. Avitzur*, 459 N.Y.S.2d 572 (1983).

[33] This principle was first noted in *Montefiore v. Guedalla*, 2 Ch. 26 Court of Appeals, England (1903), where a British court enforced the *ketubah* of a Sephardic (Moroccan) Jew who had moved to England, because the law of Morocco would have enforced this *ketubah*. These same conflict-of-laws principles could well enforce an Israeli *ketubah* in America. It has been followed in many American cases where the parties were married in another jurisdiction. See *Miller v. Miller*, 128 N.Y.S 787 (NY Sup. Ct. 1911) and *Shilman v. Shilman*, 174 N.Y.S. 385 (NY Sup. Ct. 1918).

[34] For more on this, see Broyde and Reiss, "The Ketubah in America."

[35] Shmuel ben David HaLevi, *Nahlat Shiva* 9:14.

of Jewish tradition which requires husband and wife to give each other complete love and devotion and to summon either party at the request of the other in order to enable the party so requesting to live in accordance with the standards of the Jewish law of marriage throughout his or her lifetime. We authorize the Beth Din to impose such terms of compensation as it may see fit for failure to respond to its summons or to carry out its decision.[36]

This exact formulation was upheld as a valid arbitration agreement by the New York Court of Appeals in the now famous case of *Avitzur v. Avitzur*.[37] Under normal circumstances, it is generally understood as a matter of secular law that binding arbitration agreements undertaken to enforce religious values in a marriage are binding on the parties so long as they follow the procedure and forms mandated by New York (or whatever local jurisdiction governs procedure).[38]

Although the particular form used in the Lieberman clause (as it became known) has been subject to intense criticism[39] and ultimately not accepted by the vast majority of the Jewish law community, the idea of using binding arbitration agreements to enforce the promises and expectations of Jewish marriage has taken firm hold. Over the last fifty years, many different Jewish-law-based arbitration agreements have been composed in an attempt to create a legal construct in which Jewish law has a significant stake in the outcome of a divorce and cannot simply be ignored when one of the parties wishes to ignore it. Indeed, there is an organization with a section of its Internet site devoted to sharing such agreements.[40] The version currently widely used in the Orthodox Jewish community incorporates a binding arbitration agreement into a prenuptial agreement, such that one who signs this form of an agreement integrates Jewish law into the divorce process in a legally binding manner according to American law.[41]

Although Jewish-law-based binding arbitration agreements designed to mandate adherence to Jewish law are quite common in the community that observes Jewish law, such agreements suffer from a number of defects. First, they require forethought. They must be composed, executed, and filed in anticipation of difficulty in the pending marriage. Second, they require – prior to the commencement of the marriage – a clear comprehension of the process of divorce and the various

---

[36] *Proceedings of the Rabbinical Assembly of America XVIII* (1954), 67.

[37] 459 N.Y.S.2d 572 (1983).

[38] See, e.g., Linda Kahan, "Jewish Divorce and Secular Court: The Promise of Avitzur," *Georgetown Law Journal* 73 (1984): 193–224; Lawrence M. Warmflash, "The New York Approach to Enforcing Religious Marriage Contracts," *Brooklyn Law Review* 50 (1984): 229–253.

[39] See Norman Lamm, "Recent Additions to the Ketubah," *Tradition* 2 (1959):93–119, and A. Leo Levin and Meyer Kramer, *New Provisions in the Ketubah: A Legal Opinion* (New York: Yeshiva University Press, 1955).

[40] See http://www.theprenup.org/

[41] See http://www.theprenup.org/prenupforms.html.

options available to the couple in terms of divorce. Such foresight is rare in newlyweds. Finally, they are subject to litigation that can hinder their effectiveness.
Thus, whereas such agreements are clearly a part of the process of returning the
legal covenant of Jewish marriage to its place among couples who seek a genuinely
Jewish marriage, they are not the global solution they were thought to be when first
developed. Indeed, the fact that the community sought statutory assistance is itself a
measure of the failures of the prenuptial agreements.[42]

C. The New York State Jewish Divorce Laws

There has been one serious – and successful – attempt to introduce Jewish law as
a foundation in secular marriage law in the United States. Indeed, although it is
commonly asserted that the first covenant marriage statute was passed by Louisiana
in 1997,[43] it actually seems that the changes to New York's marriage laws in 1983
(revised in 1984 and 1992) make New York the first state with a covenant marriage
act.[44] These New York laws were designed to accommodate the needs of those Jews
who observe Jewish law; the covenant referred to here is one grounded in the Jewish
marriage tradition.

New York, because of its concentrated population of Jews deeply observant of
Jewish law, has a lengthy history of secular courts interacting with the Jewish legal
traditions and its conceptions of marriage and divorce. Especially in the last thirty
years, Jewish women have appealed to the state of New York to address the pressing
problem of recalcitrant husbands who were refusing to participate in Jewish divorces
or who were using the requirements of Jewish divorce to seek advantages in the division of finances in the secular divorce proceedings.

In essence, unlike the situation under the previously self-contained Jewish law
system, observant Jews in America who wish to be divorced now must effectuate
a divorce in a manner that is valid according to both secular and Jewish law.[45]
(Alternatively, they can choose not to marry according to secular law and thus not be
bothered by secular divorce law at all.)

Every system of law that ponders divorce and marriage recognizes that there are
two basic models for marriage and divorce law: the public law model and the private

---

[42] For more on arbitration agreements, see Breitowitz, *Between Civil and Religious Law.*
[43] See Joel A. Nichols, "Multi-Tiered Marriage: Reconsidering the Boundaries of Civil Law and
Religion" (in this volume) and Spaht, "Covenant Marriage Laws" (in this volume).
[44] By this I mean a law that provides a religious framework for marriage, especially in restricting its termination. Whereas covenant marriage laws may have secular or religiously neutral motivations for
limiting easy access to divorce (such as to protect children's well-being), the use of the term covenant
clearly indicates the influence of religious values.
[45] One for religious reasons, and one for cultural, social, and secular law reasons.

law model.[46] In the public law model, marriage and divorce are governed by soci-etal or governmental rules and not exclusively by private contract or right. There is no "right" to marry and no "right" to divorce,[47] for both are governed by the rules promulgated by society. One needs a license to be married, and one must seek legal permission (typically through the court system in America) to be divorced. Were society to rule that divorce be prohibited, divorce would cease to be legal.[48] Indeed, there were vast periods of time when divorce essentially never happened in the Western legal world.[49] The American legal tradition, in the laws of the various states, including New York, exemplifies the public law model.[50]

In the private law model, marriage and divorce are fundamentally private activ-ities. Couples marry by choosing to be married and divorce by deciding to be divorced; no government role is needed. Law is employed only to regulate the pro-cess to the extent that there is a dispute between the parties, or to adjudicate whether the proper procedure was followed. Government is not a necessary party in either marriage or divorce.

Jewish law in its basic outline and contours adheres to the private law model for both marriage and divorce, and it recognizes that divorce in its essential form requires private conduct and not court supervision. Thus, private marriages and private divorces are valid in the Jewish tradition, so long as the requisite number of witnesses (two) is present.[51] Indeed, the Jewish tradition does not mandate the

[46] Compare the discussion in Ayelet Shachar, "Faith in Law? Diffusing Tensions Between Diversity and Equality" (in this volume).

[47] Whereas the U.S. Supreme Court has declared that freedom to marry is one of the vital personal rights essential to the orderly pursuit of happiness, *Loving v. Virginia*, 388 U.S. 1, 12 (1967), it has never asserted a right to divorce as a fundamental right. The Supreme Court has additionally never found a constitutional right to remarry. (The closest it has come is *Zablocki v. Redhail*, 434 U.S. 374 (1978), which held as unconstitutional a state statute that denied a person the right to remarry if he had failed to pay child support.) If the Court had done this, a right to divorce could be inferred.

[48] Indeed, for many years divorce was simply illegal in many Western jurisdictions. Some states did not permit divorce at all until the late 1950s, and Ireland did not permit divorce until 1997. Some of these jurisdictions did permit some form of Jewish divorce ritual. See Alan Reed, "Transnational non-Judicial Divorces: A Comparative Analysis of Recognition under English and R.S. Jurisprudence," *Loyola International and Comparative Law Review* 18 (1996): 311–337.

[49] There were only 291 civil divorces in all of England from 1669 to 1850, an average of 1.6 divorces every year for the whole country, or less than one divorce per one million individuals. See Susan Dowell, *They Two Shall be One* (London: Flame, 1990), 139. The current divorce rate in America is 4,800 per one million individuals, nearly a 5,000-fold increase from the English statistics of 150 years ago. For statistics for the United States, see *Vital Statistics of the United States*: Marriage and Divorce Table 1–1, at 1–5, and Table 2–1, at 2–5 (1987).

[50] See also Mohammad H. Fadel, "Political Liberalism, Islamic Family Law, and Family Law Pluralism" (in this volume); Linda C. McClain, "Marriage Pluralism in the United States: On Civil and Religious Jurisdiction and the Demands of Equal Citizenship" (in this volume); Robin Fretwell Wilson, "The Perils of Privatized Marriage" (in this volume).

[51] This is different from the Jewish law approach to Levirate separation (*halitzah*), which the codes clearly state is a court function and cannot be validly done absent a proper Jewish court. Marriage

participation of a rabbi in either the marriage or divorce rite, although the custom always has been to include a rabbi.[52]

New York has pondered the plight of those Jews who consider themselves bound by both legal systems: What are they to do, and how should divorce law be constructed so that the process of leaping through both hoops – Jewish divorce and secular divorce – does not harm weaker parties? The two New York Jewish divorce laws and the controversy they have engendered embody, at core, an acknowledgment of the ultimate (lack of) power of the secular divorce law.[53] The purpose of the 1983 statute was not, however, to compel a secular vision of marriage and divorce on the Jewish community – but rather to bend the model of divorce employed by the state of New York to the needs of those Jews who already had an alternative model grounded in the Jewish marriage covenant.

The first New York law that addresses Jewish marriages, titled "Removal of Barriers to Remarriage," makes this clear.[54] A close and detailed read of the statute is important, even though many aspects of the statute are quite cryptic. (Some have claimed that this unclarity is because the legislature wanted to make no mention of its actual purpose, lest the statute be struck down on church-state grounds.)[55] The statute states, in part:

1. This section applies only to a marriage solemnized in this state or in any other jurisdiction by a person specified in subdivision one of section eleven of this chapter.[56]

and divorce do not need a proper court; the role of the rabbi is merely as a resident expert aware of the technical law. This is indeed reflected in the common Hebrew terms used. One who performs a marriage is referred to as the *mesader kiddushin*, merely the "arranger of the marriage," and one who performs a divorce as the *mesader gittin*, "arranger of the divorce," as a rabbi is not really needed. The participants in a levirate separation (*halitzah*) are, in contrast, called judges (*dayanim*).

[52] As demonstrated in Bleich, "Jewish Divorce," the term "rite" is a misnomer; "contract" would be more accurate.

[53] See Edward S. Nadel, "New York's Get Laws: A Constitutional Analysis," *Columbia Journal of Law and Social Problems* 27 (1998): 55–100; Patti A. Scott, "New York Divorce Law and the Religion Clauses: An Unconstitutional Exorcism of The Jewish Get Laws," *Seton Hall Constitutional Law Journal* 6 (1996): 1117–1189.

[54] See McKinney's Consolidated Laws of New York Annotated Domestic Relations Law (Refs & Annos.) § 253.

[55] See, e.g., Michelle Greenberg-Kobrin, "Civil Enforceability of Religious Prenuptial Agreements," *Columbia Journal of Law and Social Problems* 32 (Summer 1999): 359–394; Kent Greenawalt, "Religious Law and Civil Law: Using Secular Law to Assure Observance of Practices With Religious Significance," *Southern California Law Review* 71 (1998): 781–843; Scott, "New York Divorce Law and the Religion Clauses," 1117–1189; Lisa Zornberg, "Beyond The Constitution: Is The New York Get Legislation Good Law?" *Pace Law Review* 15 (Spring 1995): 703–784; Edward S. Nadel, "A Bad Marriage: Jewish Divorce and the First Amendment," *Cardozo Women's Law Journal* 2 (1995): 131–172; Paul Finkelman, "New York's Get Laws: A Constitutional Analysis," *Columbia Journal of Law & Social Problems* 27 (1993): 55–100.

[56] New York Domestic Relations Law § 253 (McKinney 1999).

This section limits this law to clergy marriages, as opposed to secular marriages performed by a judge or mayor. The reason for this is obvious – Jewish-law-based marriages, as a matter of practice, require clergy solemnization.

The statute continues:

2. Any party to a marriage defined in subdivision one of this section who commences a proceeding to annul the marriage or for a divorce must allege, in his or her verified complaint: (i) that, to the best of his or her knowledge, that he or she has taken or that he or she will take, prior to the entry of final judgment, all steps solely within his or her power to remove any barrier to the defendant's remarriage following the annulment or divorce; or (ii) that the defendant has waived in writing the requirements of this subdivision.

3. No final judgment of annulment or divorce shall thereafter be entered unless the plaintiff shall have filed and served a sworn statement: (i) that, to the best of his or her knowledge, he or she has, prior to the entry of such final judgment, taken all steps solely within his or her power to remove all barriers to the defendant's remarriage following the annulment or divorce; or (ii) that the defendant has waived in writing the requirements of this subdivision.[57]

Although these sections are linguistically cryptic, their intent and purpose is to require that a husband give and a wife receive a Jewish divorce prior to the granting of a civil divorce.[58] The words "solely within his or her power" were put in intentionally to exclude reference to the annulment process used in the Catholic rite; this is made clearer in subsequent statutory sections. Also, these sections were enacted because men (and some women) were marrying in the Jewish tradition but were refusing to end their Jewish marriages when it was time. They would instead seek only a civil divorce, thus leaving their wives forever chained to the dead marriage as matter of Jewish law.[59] The solution was simple: prevent such people from having access to the secular divorce process.

---

[57] Ibid.
[58] *Golding v. Golding*, 581 N.Y.S.2d 4, 176 A.D.2d 20 (N.Y.A.D. 1 Dept. Feb 18, 1992); *Perl v. Perl*, 512 N.Y.S.2d 372, 126 A.D.2d 91 (N.Y.A.D. 1 Dept. Mar 03, 1987).
[59] Sections four and five of the statute deal exclusively with form and timing of the affidavits that need to be filed.

> 4. In any action for divorce based on subdivisions five and six of section one hundred seventy of this chapter in which the defendant enters a general appearance and does not contest the requested relief, no final judgment of annulment or divorce shall be entered unless both parties shall have filed and served sworn statements: (i) that he or she has, to the best of his or her knowledge, taken all steps solely within his or her power to remove all barriers to the other party's remarriage following the annulment or divorce; or (ii) that the other party has waived in writing the requirements of this subdivision.

The statute then continues with its most crucial section – defining those barriers to remarriage regulated by the state of New York:

> 6. As used in the sworn statements prescribed by this section "barrier to remarriage" includes, without limitation, any religious or conscientious restraint or inhibition, of which the party required to make the verified statement is aware, that is imposed on a party to a marriage, under the principles held by the clergyman or minister who has solemnized the marriage, by reason of the other party's commission or withholding of any voluntary act. [60]

The "barrier to remarriage" is a reference to a religious principle that derived from the process of solemnization in a religious marriage. The further text of section six makes clear that it is not a reference to a Catholic annulment process.[61] Further, should there be any dispute between the parties to this divorce about what qualifies as substantive requirements of divorce in any given faith, the statute forbids judicial determination of the substantive rules employed by the faith. It instead directs that:

> 7. No final judgment of annulment or divorce shall be entered, notwithstanding the filing of the plaintiff's sworn statement prescribed by this section, if the clergyman or minister who has solemnized the marriage certifies, in a sworn statement, that he or she has solemnized the marriage and that, to his or her knowledge, the plaintiff has failed to take all steps solely within his or her power to remove all barriers to the defendant's remarriage following the annulment or divorce, provided that the said clergyman or minister is alive and available and competent to testify at the time when final judgment would be entered.[62]

---

5. The writing attesting to any waiver of the requirements of subdivision two, three or four of this section shall be filed with the court prior to the entry of a final judgment of annulment or divorce.

New York Domestic Relations Law § 253 (McKinney 1999).

[60] Ibid.

[61] Indeed, other sections of this statute make clear that this section does not apply to the Catholic annulment process. For example, section six of the statute states: "All steps solely within his or her power shall not be construed to include application to a marriage tribunal or other similar organization or agency of a religious denomination which has authority to annul or dissolve a marriage under the rules of such denomination." Ibid.

[62] Ibid. Section eight imposes a penalty for perjury with regard to such affidavits, and section nine is a conclusory statement with regard to certain first amendment issues.

8. Any person who knowingly submits a false sworn statement under this section shall be guilty of making an apparently sworn false statement in the first degree and shall be punished in accordance with section 210.40 of the penal law.

9. Nothing in this section shall be construed to authorize any court to inquire into or determine any ecclesiastical or religious issue. The truth of any statement submitted pursuant to

To put this in plain English – something the statute does not seek to do because a full millet marriage system would be fraught with constitutional challenges[63] – if one marries in a Jewish ceremony in New York and one seeks a civil divorce in New York without providing a Jewish divorce, New York will not grant such a divorce. New York is handing the keys to civil divorce to the rabbi who performed the religious ceremony – that is certainly a covenant marriage.

To recast this slightly, one could say the 1983 New York Jewish divorce law recognized that a fundamental wrong occurred when secular society allowed a person who had been married in a Jewish ceremony to be civilly divorced while the spouse of that person considered herself still married until a Jewish divorce was executed. The 1983 law fixed this problem by preventing the civil authorities from exercising their authority to civilly divorce a couple who still needed a religious divorce. Importantly, the law prevented a splitting of the civil and religious statuses by precluding the civil authorities from acting, absent the religious authorities. The law thus harmonizes civil law with Jewish law, in that Jewish law maintains that the couple is married until a *get* is issued and New York now commits itself to not issuing a civil divorce in such cases until a *get* is issued. It contains no incentive for a person actually to issue a Jewish divorce unless that person is genuinely desirous of being divorced. To put this differently, the divorce process employed by the state of New York is different for those married in the Jewish faith than anyone else. Fundamentally, *that is a covenant marriage*.

Although the 1983 New York Jewish divorce law addressed certain cases, it had one obvious limitation – it was written to be applicable only in cases where the plaintiff is seeking the secular divorce and failing to provide a religious divorce. Only the *plaintiff* is obligated to remove barriers to remarriage under the 1983 law – and a defending spouse who does not desire to comply with Jewish law need not do so. To remedy this one-sidedness, the 1992 New York Jewish divorce law took a quite different approach. Although the problem it confronted remained substantially the same, the solution advanced by the 1992 law was different. It permitted a judge applying the secular divorce law regarding equitable distribution of assets to impose penalties on the recalcitrant spouse in order to encourage participation in the religious divorce.[64] The law sought to prevent the splitting of the religious and

this section shall not be the subject of any judicial inquiry, except as provided in subdivision eight of this section.

[63] See, e.g., Elizabeth R. Leiberman, "*Avitzur v. Avitzur*: The Constitutional Implications of Judicially Enforcing Religious Agreements," *Catholic University Law Review* 33 (1983): 219–243. See also John Witte Jr. and Joel A. Nichols, "The Frontiers of Marital Pluralism: An Afterword" (in this volume).

[64] Domestic Relations Law §236 was modified in 1992 to add: "In any decision made pursuant to this subdivision the court shall, where appropriate, consider the effect of a barrier to remarriage, as defined in subdivision six of section two hundred fifty-three of this article, on the factors enumerated in paragraph (d) of this subdivision." This allows a judge to change the equitable distribution in a situation

civil marital statuses by encouraging the issuance of the religious divorce when a civil divorce was to be granted. This law functions in the opposite manner than the 1983 law – it harmonizes Jewish law with New York law by committing state authorities to a policy of encouraging a Jewish divorce to be issued. That, too, is a form of covenant marriage, albeit one with a different focus on the relationship between Jewish and secular law.

The technicalities of both these laws have generated a considerable amount of scholarly debate, both within the Jewish tradition[65] and within the secular legal community,[66] because they were an attempt to impose a vision of religious marriage on a subset of the population through the vehicle of secular law. The 1983 law did so by restricting access to secular divorce when the rules of religious divorce were not followed. The 1992 statute did so by compelling religious divorce through financially penalizing recalcitrant spouses. Both approaches, however, are grounded in the centrality of Jewish marriage to its adherents and the simultaneous desire to respect access to civil divorce.

One could thus claim that New York had not only the first covenant marriage law, but it had the first two such laws – the 1983 Jewish divorce law and the 1992 Jewish divorce law, each with a different approach to Jewish marriage. Granted, New York does not offer a covenant marriage option to all citizens, because, practically speaking, Jewish clergy will not allow non-Jews to opt into Jewish marriage. However, in terms of reframing or superimposing secular and religious definitions of marriage and divorce and offering a state-sanctioned model of religious union and dissolution, these statutes pave the way.[67]

IV. JEWISH MARRIAGE AND DIVORCE IN PRACTICE IN NEW YORK

The previous section outlined three basic approaches used by American Jews to create Jewish marriages within a secular state. On analysis, only two of the options were

where the husband or wife will not give or receive a Jewish divorce. Section 253(6) limits "barriers to remarriage" to situations where a *get* is withheld.

[65] For an examination of the issues raised in the Jewish tradition, see Michael Broyde, "The New York State *Get* [Jewish Divorce] Law," *Tradition: A Journal of Jewish Thought* 29:4 (1995): 3–14; this article was followed by Michael Broyde and Chaim Malinowitz, "The 1992 New York *Get* Law: An Exchange," *Tradition: A Journal of Jewish Thought* 31:3 (1997): 23–41; and concludes with "The 1992 New York *Get* Law: An Exchange III," *Tradition: A Journal of Jewish Thought* 32:1 and 33:1 (1999): 99–100, 101–109.

[66] See, e.g., Greenberg-Kobrin, "Civil Enforceability of Religious Prenuptial Agreements," 359–394; Greenawalt, "Religious Law and Civil Law," 781–843; Scott, "New York Divorce Law and the Religion Clauses," 1117–1189; Zornberg, "Beyond The Constitution," 703–784; Nadel, "A Bad Marriage," 131–172; Finkelman, "New York's Get Laws," 55–100.

[67] The question of the applicability of this statute to Islamic marriages (a result never contemplated by the New York State Legislature) is a fascinating one that merits further analysis. See Ghada G. Qaisi,

found to be viable: prenuptial agreements and the New York *get* laws. This section explores what Jewish divorce law looks like in practice when either of these options is employed. I am not interested in writing a "practice manual" for Jewish divorces, but an exploration of the realities of the system explains much that theory alone simply cannot. Accordingly, this section strongly reflects my practical experience working in a rabbinical court.

Legal analysts involved in the New York community of adherents to Jewish law are aware that both the New York State *get* laws and the *Avitzur* appellate decision are vulnerable to constitutional challenge. Many communal resources have been invested in defending these laws and rulings when challenged in the lower state courts. Further, there has been significant communal pressure within the Orthodox community to prevent a plaintiff husband from presenting a "free exercise" claim to a court. (Such a claim, which I sense would have considerable legal merit, would be that it violates the husband's free exercise rights in being pressured into engaging in a religious act – a Jewish divorce ritual – to which he objects on religious grounds.) Such pressure is applied by implicitly threatening to exclude from the Orthodox Jewish community any person who files such a claim, with attendant religious and social consequences from the exclusion. So far, there has not been a single challenge to the constitutionality of either *get* law, nor a single case since *Avitzur* raising such issues (and it is commonly believed in the legal community that *Avitzur* was an arranged test case).

The reason for the absence of a challenge derives from the nature of the religious Jewish (mostly Orthodox) community in New York. A free exercise challenge to the *get* laws would entail a community member – someone married by an Orthodox rabbi – maintaining in court that the giving or receiving of a *get* is a violation of his or her right to practice religion as he or she sees fit, and that New York law is, in essence, coercing them by statutory means into participating in a religious ritual. Although an argument has been put forward to explain why coerced participation in a Jewish divorce ritual might not be a free exercise violation,[68] this argument is hard to accept as correct as a matter of First Amendment jurisprudence. Even if the Jewish legal tradition views the Jewish divorce ritual as civil,[69] there is little doubt that American law views participation in a Jewish divorce rite as an activity that cannot be compelled as a matter of law. Thus, for example, a man or woman who married under the Orthodox Jewish rite and then subsequently converted to Catholicism would have a substantial claim that the statutes in question violate

---

"Religious Marriage Contracts: Judicial Enforcement of Mahr Agreements in American Courts," *Journal of Law & Religion* 15 (2000–2001): 67–81.

[68] Bleich, "Jewish Divorce."

[69] It is, for example, without blessings or invocation of the deity.

his or her free exercise rights.[70] Yet no husband has sought to make such a claim because doing so would lead to exclusion from the community through formal or informal excommunication, demonstrating the powerful cohesion of the Orthodox community.[71]

In practice, vast segments of the traditional Orthodox community in New York use three mechanisms to ensure (or at least seek to ensure) that traditional Jewish values are predominant during the divorce proceedings. These three are prenuptial agreements, the use of the *get* laws, and opting out of the secular legal system.

A. Prenuptial Agreements

The first practical mechanism is the use of mutually signed prenuptial agreements. These agreements set out the basic framework under which the parties will end their marriage, providing that such a determination will be made by the Beth Din of America. The most popular of these prenuptial agreements is one circulated by the Beth Din of America, the largest rabbinical court in the United States.[72] Its purpose is threefold. First, the agreement ensures that a Jewish divorce is given in a timely fashion by assigning a penalty of $150 per day for delay in the delivery of a *get*. Second, the agreement, as a matter of binding arbitration, assigns the authority to resolve disputes about rights to a Jewish divorce to a named rabbinical court (usually the Beth Din of America). This forces secular courts both to recognize such assignment of jurisdiction as a matter of secular arbitration law and to compel the husband and wife to appear in front of the rabbinic arbitration panel if necessary. Finally, the agreement gives couples who are engaged at the time of its drafting the ability to choose to assign all matters of their divorce – financial dissolution and custody, as well as Jewish divorce – to the rabbinical court if they wish.

In practice, this agreement forces a close and tight interrelationship between the civil and Jewish divorce processes if the couple fails to conduct themselves in a manner consistent with the obligations of both Jewish law and secular law. It is not unusual for hotly contested divorces to shuttle back and forth between secular and rabbinical courts, with individuals seeking rulings from each on various matters in the divorce proceedings. Sometimes rabbinical courts will agree to hear Jewish divorce proceedings on referral from a judge handling the secular divorce, and sometimes the secular judge will direct that the parties may appear

---

[70] See, e.g., Witte and Nichols, "The Frontiers of Marital Pluralism" (in this volume).
[71] See Michael J. Broyde, "Forming Religious Communities and Respecting Dissenters' Rights," in *Human Rights in Judaism: Cultural, Religious, and Political Perspectives*, eds. Michael Broyde and John Witte Jr. (Northvale, NJ: Jason Aronson, 1998), 35–76.
[72] It is reproduced at http://www.bethdin.org.

in their court only after receipt of a letter from the rabbinical court certifying compliance with the mandates of the rabbinical court (consistent with the arbitration agreement). In other cases, rabbinical courts will seek assistance from the secular courts in compelling adherence to arbitration rulings, and in yet other cases, secular court judges will enlist the rabbinical courts to help ensure compliance. This is because, for couples who sign this type of an agreement, the ending of marriage civilly does not accomplish the wishes of the parties unless accompanied by the giving or receiving of a Jewish divorce. At the same time, the secular government has an interest in allowing both parties to part ways and not be married – but civil divorce absent a Jewish divorce does not accomplish that objective. (The same would be true for a religious divorce without a civil divorce being issued concurrently.)[73]

(I first grasped the magnitude of this cooperation ten years ago when I spent my sabbatical as the director of the Beth Din of America, and I saw the regular interaction between the dictates of Jewish law and the mandates of the civil legal system. As but one example, I returned to Emory for one day in February to give some lectures while I was in the midst of a particularly complex Jewish divorce case. Throughout the day, my cell phone was ringing, but I simply could not answer it due to the schedule of the day. Finally, at about 2:30 in the afternoon, I was sitting in the dean's office speaking with him about my sabbatical when the secretary knocked on the door and asked to speak to me. She told me that a New York State Supreme Court [trial court] judge was on the phone and needed to ask whether I thought that holding a particular husband in jail overnight would help facilitate the Jewish divorce process. The dean listened closely and asked me, "What are you really doing during this year off?!")

The Jewish law court has considerable civil authority, particularly if one allows the named rabbinic arbitration panel such as the Beth Din of America to serve in the capacity of a full arbitration panel. Even without such naming, the agreement signed by the parties consenting to a hearing before the Beth Din of America grants the rabbinical court the authority to assign civil penalties of up to $950 per week if the parties defy the direction of the rabbinical court. The close relationship between civil and rabbinic courts can sometimes produce complexities, and it is not surprising that there are dozens of reported appellate division cases dealing with rabbinic arbitration.[74]

---

[73] For this reason, the Beth Din of America notes on its writ of Jewish divorce that the parties are not, in fact, free to remarry (even as a matter of Jewish law) until a civil divorce is issued.

[74] It is also not surprising that there are more reported cases in New York that discuss Jewish law than Canon law, even though there are many more Catholics than Jews in New York, because of this interrelationship between civil and religious courts.

B. *New York's* Get *Statutes*

The second mechanism employed by the observant community is the New York State *get* laws. In New York, as explained previously, the statutory regime directly regulates the giving and receiving of a Jewish divorce even though the statutes make no reference to any religion in particular. New York family law judges are quite familiar with the *get* laws and their application, and they do not hesitate to apply them. Indeed, practicing lawyers inform their clients that, when the husband is the plaintiff in a divorce action, the judge will explicitly ask if a *get* has been given and, if so, at what rabbinical court. The husband should expect considerable difficulties, he is told, if he has not complied with the requirements of the 1983 New York *get* law by the time the final civil divorce decree is to issue.

The application of the 1992 *get* law is much more complex. Jewish law has raised serious questions about whether it is possible to apply the *get* law consistent with the demands of Jewish law that a Jewish divorce be given only through the free will of the husband or after an order of compulsion issued by a rabbinical court (and not a secular one). The problem has proved difficult.

New York has a real interest in ensuring that all of its citizens are in fact free to remarry after they receive a civil divorce, and it thus has an interest in the resolution of the Jewish law issue. If a group of its citizens will not, in fact, conduct themselves as if they are divorced unless they are also divorced according to Jewish law, the state becomes legitimately concerned, for the purpose and function of the secular divorce law are defeated by the absence of a religious rite. Thus, New York wishes to provide statutorily that its Jewish residents are entitled to a *get* if they wish. Jewish law and the Jewish community share that basic concern: They also wish that couples be Jewishly divorced when they are civilly divorced. In particular, they recognize that once a couple has in fact separated and are no longer living together, it is wise to ensure that a Jewish divorce is issued.

Either secular law or Jewish law alone could easily attempt to resolve this problem, but only to the dissatisfaction of the other. On the one hand, Jewish law could seek to act autonomously, as in premodern Europe. Given full freedom, rabbinical courts sometimes compelled the giving and receiving of a bill of divorce through the use of physical force. In lesser cases, the rabbinical courts imposed fines in the form of support payments to the wife in order to entice the husband to give a Jewish divorce. These two methods of judicial coercion rendered cases in which the husband refused to give a Jewish divorce exceedingly rare. However, American law is loathe to give religious tribunals such authority.

On the other hand, state legislatures could attempt to do away with religious divorce (and perhaps even religious marriage) entirely. This would, of course, be anathema to the religious community. Legislatures or courts could also choose to compel religious divorce when they saw fit. However, Jewish law unswervingly holds that when a Jewish divorce is compelled by a secular court or by private citizens, the act of compulsion voids the entire Jewish divorce.

In light of this tension, the reality in New York is an extremely complex and mostly invisible dance between the New York judges who enforce state law and the rabbinic court judges who ensure that the religious divorces are valid as a matter of Jewish law. If the New York state courts were to apply direct coercion without some involvement of a rabbinical court, the rabbinical courts would likely refuse to issue a Jewish divorce in such a case, for it would be deemed coerced as a matter of Jewish law. On the other hand, the rabbinical courts acknowledge that the keys to coercion will never be placed directly in the hands of the rabbinical courts in the United States. Jewish leaders thus acknowledge that if the problem of men withholding Jewish divorces from their wives is to be adequately addressed, it must involve the rabbinical courts working hand in hand with the family courts to craft solutions.

Four examples from my own involvement in the rabbinical courts help illuminate this cooperation.

1. Case One

A husband and wife were married for many years and had a number of children. They wished to be divorced. There was no prenuptial agreement between the parties. The husband and wife had a very intense disagreement over how to divide the marital estate, worth nearly $5 million. The husband consented to give a Jewish divorce at the conclusion of the civil divorce; the wife agreed. The wife filed for divorce. She essentially triumphed in the civil divorce and was afraid that the husband would refuse to give a Jewish divorce. The judge directed that the Jewish divorce be written, signed, and given in his chambers during the processing of the civil divorce, and he delayed issuing the civil divorce until the Jewish divorce was granted.

2. Case Two

A husband and wife were married for only a short period of time – less than ten days – when the wife filed for an annulment on the grounds that the husband is inclined to physical violence and hit her twice in the first week of marriage. An annulment is not – by statutory lacuna – included in the jurisdiction of the New York *get* laws. The judge asks the parties, who are clearly observant of Jewish law, what a secular annulment will do to the ability of either the husband or wife to remarry as a matter of Jewish law. The husband's lawyer responds by stating that the question is beyond the statutory purview of the judge in deciding whether to allow the annulment to proceed. The judge responds by ordering the parties to contact the Beth Din of America to request written confirmation that, after a civil annulment, the parties will be free to remarry as a matter of Jewish law, and then the judge adjourns the proceedings. The Beth Din of America writes a letter to the court stating that Jewish law would not accept an annulment issued by New York in lieu of a Jewish divorce, and that Jewish law has an annulment procedure but it is disfavored. The judge then issues an order allowing the annulment on the condition that the husband gives and wife receives a Jewish divorce before a specific date.

3. Case Three

The husband has refused to give his wife a Jewish divorce for a number of years; a judge has refused to issue a civil divorce decree because of that refusal. The wife came to the Beth Din of America to ask how to encourage the husband to give a Jewish divorce; the Beth Din of America advised her to seek an increase in her pre-divorce payments. The wife requested that the judge increase the *pendente lite* support for the wife to the rate of $1,750 a month, which was nearly $900 more per month than the husband was previously ordered to pay. The judge told the husband that the keys to releasing himself from this higher support obligation are in his own hands: All the husband must do is finish his civil divorce (which would happen after the husband issues the *get*), and then payments go back to $850.

4. Case Four

The husband and wife have been civilly divorced since 1996, when they both lived in New Jersey, but no Jewish divorce was ever issued. The wife moves to Brooklyn and files for an increase in maintenance, citing her inability to remarry religiously as grounds for increased maintenance. The husband declines to appear, and the judge orders an increase in maintenance. The husband refuses to pay and is held in contempt of court. The husband is ultimately arrested in New York and incarcerated for civil contempt. The judge tells the husband at a court hearing that the judge will waive the contempt citation if the husband will issue a Jewish divorce now. This leads to a lively courtroom discussion as to whether such a divorce is valid as a matter of Jewish law. After the decision is made that such a divorce is valid, the Jewish divorce is written in the Brooklyn detention center that afternoon.

In each of these cases, the outcomes were successfully reached only because the civil courts and the rabbinical courts in New York worked closely together to accomplish a goal that neither could meet on its own.

C. Opting Out of the Secular Legal System

Finally, rather than relying on prenuptial agreements or the New York State *get* laws, many members of the Orthodox community opt out of the secular legal system entirely and resolve all their disputes before rabbinical courts. This solution is the most complex of the three mechanisms to retain traditional Jewish practice in divorce proceedings because secular law does not really allow the arbitration of child custody disputes outside of family court; such determinations can always be reviewed *de novo* by the secular courts.

Many such arbitration hearings do take place, however, and they entail the substantive application of Jewish law to the area of divorce. These rules include fault-based adjudication in some instances, evaluation of parental fitness as suitable religious role models in certain situations, and the placement of children consistent with their religious needs in deciding matters of child custody. There are dozens of such cases a month in the United States.

V. OTHER MODELS OF JEWISH AND SECULAR MARRIAGE LAW

There is a complex dance between the rabbinical courts and the secular court in the state of New York, reflecting the so-to-speak balance of power. Try as they might, the secular courts cannot order a Jewish divorce, and as much as they wish to the contrary, the rabbinical courts do not control many financial aspects of divorce or the custody of children. In successful dealings, both courts freely and informally interact with one another, referring matters back and forth with each respecting the limits of its authority. The system does not always work smoothly, however, and there have certainly been cases in which a family court judge has sought to "order" a Jewish divorce and even to hold rabbinical court judges in contempt for declining to write one. So too, rabbinical courts have on occasion sought to religiously sanction litigants for exercising their legal rights in secular court, all to little avail. Neither legal system can control the other, and everyone has to know that for the system to work.

This dynamic has emerged in New York because of the particularly high concentration of observant Jews seeking to live in consonance with both Jewish and secular law. In almost no other diasporal Jewish community is there a large enough critical mass for such a fluid interaction between the legal systems to develop. In New York, the rabbinic and secular courts interact with one another in these matters countlessly and continuously. In other U.S. states, for instance, Georgia, there is not nearly enough traffic in Jewish divorces to allow the two courts to cultivate an informal, fluid relationship.

The one other locale where this church-state dynamic might be relevant, the modern State of Israel, avoids this problem completely. In Israel, marriage and divorce law are completely delegated to the various religions. Jewish marriage falls completely and solely under the rabbinical courts, and there is no secular state intervention. Israel thus falls under the covenant model of Jewish marriage. The mechanisms are similar to those in medieval Europe, but they are officially backed by the secular authorities rather than flying under (or completely off of) their radar screen. The main concern of this chapter is how Jews deal with the interaction of the state in marital affairs; in Israel, there is effectively no interaction of the state.

VI. CONCLUSION: THE PROBLEM OF OBEYING TWO LEGAL SYSTEMS

This chapter highlighted an ongoing dialectic patterning within the Jewish marriage tradition: The basic elements of Jewish marriage law seem in contest and have shifted over time. What started as equality in contract in Talmudic times reverted to covenant for vast segments of the European Jewish community in the next millennium. Even the contours of secular interference into Jewish law during the last twenty years have been whipsawed by this conflict. The 1983 New York *get* law sought to harmonize New York law with Jewish law, as if to emphasize the primacy of the sacred covenant. The 1992 New York *get* law, however, sought to force Jewish law to mimic New York law, giving the covenant far less emphasis.

One of the issues unique to the American modern Jewish divorce problem is the presence of a secular civil divorce law that governs the process of divorce for all members of society. Unlike the norm of civil law throughout the world a hundred years ago, when matters of family law were left to religious authorities within each community and when "secular" marriage and divorce were, at best, reserved for those who were not a member of any religious community, modern American divorce law (and to a lesser extent, marriage law) mandates being married and divorced in accordance with the neutral, secular principles of law established by society. Thus, each person who marries in America, even with the intent that the marriage be governed exclusively by Jewish law, must be divorced by the secular legal authorities and secular law.

Secular law can and will impose its own values on divorce, from its ethical perception of the proper place for children to reside, to its understanding of the respective rights of spouses in cases of divorce, to the tax ramifications of divorce. On some of these issues the state will impose its values even against the wishes of both spouses, and in others it will do so at the request of one spouse. Absent a prenuptial agreement, it is rare that the state will not seek to adjudicate every area of a divorce, even if the parties would not have wanted that at the time of their marriage.

This overarching civil divorce system is nearly unique historically. Never before the twentieth century has the Jewish community been subject to a system of compulsory civil marriage and divorce law, and this requirement has had a major impact on both the contours of the *agunah* problem and contours of solutions to it. This has led to a continued dance between religious and civil authorities. Variations of that dance are sure to continue as people seek to comply with the dictates of both their religious obligations and civil obligations.

7

Political Liberalism, Islamic Family Law, and Family Law Pluralism

Mohammad H. Fadel

Western democracies in recent years have witnessed dramatic (and often highly charged) debates regarding Islamic law, women, and the limits of pluralism in a liberal polity. Perhaps the most relevant of these for the issue of family law pluralism was the "Shari'a Arbitration controversy" of Ontario, Canada, of 2004–2005. Although Jewish, Christian, and Isma'ili Muslim (a relatively small sect of Shi'a Muslims who follow the Agha Khan) residents of Ontario had long made use of private arbitration for the resolution of intracommunal family disputes, when a group of Sunni Muslims announced their intent to establish a mechanism to allow orthodox Muslims to arbitrate their family law disputes in accordance with their understanding of Islamic law, a transatlantic controversy erupted that was resolved only when Ontario took the drastic step of prohibiting the arbitration of all family law disputes in which the arbitrator purported to apply non-Canadian law.[1] Great Britain, too, experienced its own moment of Islamic law anxiety when the Archbishop of Canterbury suggested that British commitments to pluralism might require the English legal system to recognize certain aspects of Islamic law.[2] That controversy was subsequently heightened

---

[1] Numerous academic articles in response to the Shari'a Arbitration controversy have been published. See, e.g., Jean-Francois Gaudreault-DesBiens, "The Limits of Private Justice? The Problems of the State Recognition of Arbitral Awards in Family and Personal Status Disputes in Ontario," *Perspectives* 16:1 (Jan. 2005): 18–31; Natasha Bakht, "Family Arbitration Using Sharia Law: Examining Ontario's Arbitration Act and Its Impact on Women," *Muslim World Journal of Human Rights* 1:1 (2004); Ayelet Shachar, "Privatizing Diversity: A Cautionary Tale from Religious Arbitration in Family Law," *Theoretical Inquiries in Law* 9:2 (July 2008): 573–607; Anver Emon, "Islamic Law and the Canadian Mosaic: Politics, Jurisprudence, and Multicultural Accommodation," *Canadian Bar Review* 87:2 (February 2009): 391–425; and Melissa Williams, "The Politics of Fear and the Decline of Multiculturalism," in *The Ties that Bind*, eds. John Erik Fossum, Johanne Poirier, and Paul Magnette (Brussels: P.I.E. Peter Lang, 2009), 53–77. For a critical overview of the reaction to the controversy related to Islamic arbitration, see Natasha Bakht, "Were Muslim Barbarians Really Knocking on the Gates of Ontario?: The Religious Arbitration Controversy – Another Perspective," *Ottawa Law Review* 40 (2006): 67–82.

[2] See, e.g., John F. Burns, "Top Anglicans Rally to Besieged Archbishop," *New York Times*, Feb. 12, 2008 (discussing the controversy that erupted in Britain as a result of Archbishop Rowan Williams'

when it was revealed that British Muslims had already set up judicial councils that engaged in legally binding arbitration of family law disputes pursuant to British law permitting binding arbitration.[3]

Given the general anxiety surrounding Islamic law in Western democracies, the fact that fear of Islamic law should be a substantial stumbling block to increasing legal pluralism in the domain of family law is ironic given the pluralistic nature of Islamic law's regulation of the family. At the same time, legal recognition of family law pluralism is not without its genuine risks: The rules of Islamic family law, as well as the rules and traditions of other subcommunities within a liberal polity, are not substantively equivalent to the generally applicable rules of civil law. Any system of family law pluralism within a liberal polity, therefore, must establish institutional mechanisms to ensure that legal pluralism does not become a tool to deprive individuals of their rights as citizens.[4]

This chapter will attempt to explain how the Islamic religious and legal commitments of "orthodox"[5] Muslims can reinforce and promote Islamic conceptions of the family within the general legal background provided by a liberal system of family law. Indeed, this chapter will make the perhaps surprising case that for orthodox Muslims, a liberal family law – at least in the context of a religiously heterogeneous polity – represents the preferred means for the recognition of family law pluralism, in contrast to other arguments in support of family law pluralism that would give greater power directly to religious bodies in the administration of family law.[6] Orthodox Muslims have their own profound disagreements on the nature of marriage and its legal and religious consequences, a fact that gives them strong Islamic reasons to support family law pluralism. Orthodox Islam also has a well-established historical commitment to the recognition of non-Islamic conceptions of marriages, a fact that also contributes to Muslim comfort with family law pluralism. At the same

comments that recognizing certain elements of Islamic law would be consistent with British law). A copy of the speech is available at http://www.archbishopofcanterbury.org/1575.

[3] Abul Taher, "Revealed: UK's First Official Shari'a Courts," *The Sunday Times*, Sept. 15, 2008. For more information on the operation in the United Kingdom of the Muslim Arbitration Tribunal, see http://www.matribunal.com.

[4] See Linda C. McClain, "Marriage Pluralism in the United States: On Civil and Religious Jurisdiction and the Demands of Equal Citizenship" (in this volume).

[5] Any reference to "orthodox" Muslims in this chapter should not be taken to refer to any specific group of Muslims living in any contemporary society, but rather refers to a theoretical category intended to capture individuals who affirm the truth of the historically accepted theological doctrines of Sunni Islam and grant at least prima facie authority to historically accepted Sunni ethical and legal doctrines.

[6] For one argument as to why democratic states should be willing to cede regulatory authority over marriages to religious authorities, see Joel A. Nichols, "Multi-Tiered Marriage: Ideas and Influences from New York and Louisiana to the International Community," *Vanderbilt Journal of Transnational Law* 40 (January 2007): 135–196.

time liberal family law, because of its commitments to autonomy, contemplates the legitimate use of private ordering within the family subject to certain limits. The space liberalism creates for private ordering within the family is sufficient for robust manifestations of Islamic family life that are also consistent with the minimum requirements of liberalism. Accordingly, there is no need, from an Islamic perspective at least, for a system of family law pluralism beyond that already implicit within liberalism itself.

In exploring the interaction of Islamic religious and legal conceptions of the family with liberal family law, this chapter accepts as normative a version of liberal family law derived from Rawls's conception of political liberalism (focusing in particular on Rawls's remarks on the family in "The Idea of Public Reason Revisited") rather than on other versions of family law that might adopt a more comprehensive form of liberalism.[7] This chapter will argue that despite orthodox Muslims' religiously grounded understanding of marriage, a politically liberal family law along the lines espoused by Rawls – because of its neutrality with respect to metaphysical conceptions of the family and its commitment to provide a qualified form of autonomy for the family – is entitled to the support of orthodox Muslims even if it would exclude as impermissible certain norms of the family that orthodox Muslims would deem morally permissible or even just.

The chapter begins with a brief account of the role of the family in political liberalism and the limits political liberalism places on both the public regulation of the family and the family's internal autonomy within those limits (Section I). To determine whether Islamic conceptions of the family can satisfy political liberalism's limitations on the family's autonomy, Section II provides a general description of how orthodox Islam understands the relationship between the legal and moral spheres and the role of individual conscience in that relationship. Section III explains why the difference between objective law and subjective moral obligation generates pluralism in Islam, a fact that in the context of family law generates competing legal doctrines of the family, relatively broad contractual freedom within the marriage contract, and competing religious visions of the family. Not all manifestations of Islamic conceptions of the family will be consistent with the requirements of political liberalism, however, and for that reason it is appropriate that any system of legal pluralism that permits Muslim citizens to use Islamic law to adjudicate their family law disputes be conducted pursuant to institutional

---

7   For the significance of the differences between a comprehensive liberal's approach to matters of family law and gender equality and their relationship to religion, and the approach of a political liberal, see Susan Moller Okin, *Is Multiculturalism Bad for Women?*, eds. Joshua Cohen, Matthew Howard, and Martha C. Nussbaum (Princeton, NJ: Princeton University Press, 1999), 7–26, and Martha C. Nussbaum's reply, "A Plea for Difficulty," in *Is Multiculturalism Bad for Women?*, 105–114.

arrangements that can confirm that the results of such adjudication are in conformity with the minimum requirements of a liberal legal order. Section IV gives examples of some salient historical differences in Muslim understandings of family law and their relationship to Islamic religious conceptions of marriage. Then Section V turns to why, from an Islamic perspective, a politically liberal family law could very well be attractive to orthodox Muslims; it further investigates whether the use of Islamic law to conduct family law arbitration, from the perspective of political liberalism, could be consistent with political liberalism's approach to regulating the family. Section VI discusses cases from New York involving family law arbitration in the context of Orthodox Jewish law to demonstrate that, as a practical matter, courts in a liberal jurisdiction have the institutional capacity to give effect to the autonomy of nonliberal citizens as evidenced by their desire to abide by their own family laws while simultaneously protecting successfully those aspects of family law that are mandatory from the intrusion of nonliberal norms. This suggests, as Section VII concludes, that courts in liberal jurisdictions could do the same in the case of Muslim family law arbitrations, despite the contrary outcome in Ontario.[8]

I. FAMILY LAW PLURALISM AND POLITICAL LIBERALISM

One of the central objections to the legal recognition of Islamic family law arbitrations raised at the time of the Shari'a Arbitration controversy in Ontario was that Islamic law would conflict with Canadian commitments to gender equality within the family.[9] The meaning of equality within the family, however, remains deeply contested, even among liberals. And even religions that are commonly viewed as endorsing a patriarchal family structure have their own conceptions of gender equality: Islam, for example, teaches the equal moral worth of men and women, and the New Testament states that men and women are "all one in Christ Jesus."[10]

Equality, therefore, can mean radically different things, especially in connection with its application to particular disputes. Numerous plausible (though incompatible) theories could be advanced regarding the family that are consistent with some

---

[8] Compare Daniel Cere, "Canadian Conjugal Mosaic: From Multiculturalism to Multi-Conjugalism?" (in this volume) (suggesting that Canadian family law has, in recent years, taken a decided turn toward comprehensive rather than political liberalism).

[9] See, e.g., Anna C. Korteweg, "The Sharia Debate in Ontario," *ISIM Review* 18 (Autumn 2006): 50–51.

[10] Quran, *Āl 'Imrān*, 3:195 ("And so their Lord answered their prayers, saying 'I suffer not the loss of the deeds of any of you, whether male or female; you are of one another.'") and *Al-Nisā'*, 4:124 ("Whosoever does a righteous deed, whether male or female, and is a believer, they shall enter Paradise."); Galatians 3:28 (New International Version).

theory of liberal equality. For example, one could take the view that gender equality in marriage should be viewed as a matter of distributive justice, in which case equality means that men and women should receive an equal share of the benefits of married life. One potential drawback of such a conception, however, is that it would not exclude marriages organized around a gendered division of labor, if such a marriage resulted in fact in an equal (or relatively equal) sharing of the burdens and benefits of marriage.[11] Alternatively, equality within the family could produce a conception of marriage as "an egalitarian liberal community" that "resists individual accounting" of desert.[12] Such a conception would preclude traditional homemakers from receiving any tangible rewards for nonmarket services they perform in the household. Some feminists, however, argue that marriage should be treated in a manner analogous to a partnership, in which case equality would require valuing the individual contributions of each spouse to the family, including the nonmonetary contributions historically provided by wives in the form of child rearing and housework.[13] If "care work" is monetized, however, it might encourage women to continue to specialize in household rather than market production.[14] This would have the (unintentional) effect of reinforcing the gendered division of labor that many feminists have traditionally sought to eliminate.

Political liberalism does not attempt to determine which of these liberal (or nonliberal) conceptions of equality is correct. It instead regulates the family from the perspective of what is required "to reproduce political society over time" in a manner consistent with its ideal of treating all citizens as "free and equal."[15] Because the family is part of political society's basic structure, labor inside the family is "socially necessary labor."[16] On Rawls's account, however, the family is an association[17] and therefore "the principles of justice – including principles of distributive justice – [do not] apply directly to the internal life of the family."[18] They are relevant only in a

[11]　Empirical evidence in fact suggests that traditional marriages are more likely to produce this result than most two-wage earner couples. Amy L. Wax, "Bargaining in the Shadow of the Market: Is There a Future for Egalitarian Marriage?" *Virginia Law Review* 84 (May 1998): 509–672, 519.

[12]　Carolyn J. Frantz and Hanoch Dagan, "Properties of Marriage," *Columbia Law Review* 104 (January 2004): 75–133, 77–78.

[13]　Cynthia Lee Starnes, "Mothers, Myths, and the Law of Divorce: One More Feminist Case for Partnership," *William and Mary Journal of Women and the Law* 13 (Fall 2006): 203–233, 232–233.

[14]　Philomila Tsoukala, "Gary Becker, Legal Feminism, and the Costs of Moralizing Care," *Columbia Journal of Gender and Law* 16 (2007): 357–428, 421–422, 425.

[15]　John Rawls, "The Idea of Public Reason Revisited," *University of Chicago Law Review* 64 (Summer 1997): 765–807, 779–780.

[16]　Ibid., 788.

[17]　John Rawls, *Political Liberalism* (New York: Columbia University Press, expanded ed. 2005), 40–43 (describing "association" as a kind of voluntary ordering within political society that, because of its voluntary nature, is entitled, among other things, to offer different terms to different persons in the association).

[18]　Rawls, "The Idea of Public Reason Revisited," 790.

negative sense, meaning that the basic rights of women as citizens place limits on permissible forms of family organization.[19] The public constraints of justice on matters of internal associational life must not be so severe, however, as to constrain "a free and flourishing internal life [of the association]."[20]

Rawls's analysis of the family effectively places it in a median position between public institutions (to which the principles of justice apply directly) and associations (to which the principles of justice require only a right of exit). On the one hand, the family, because of its essential role in the reproduction of political society over time, is part of the basic structure of society; on the other hand, it is a voluntary association and thus the principles of justice do not apply to it in the same way that the principles of justice constrain a wholly public institution such as the legislature or courts. Rawls's analysis of the family within political liberalism has important implications for equality within a system of family law that is politically liberal: It tolerates the continued existence of inequality within the family, but on the condition that such inequality "is fully voluntary."[21] Religiously justified hierarchies of the family, therefore, are consistent with the principles of justice if the background conditions of political justice are met.

The only gender-based inequality that must be abolished as a matter of the principles of justice is that which is involuntary.[22] Religiously justified inequality satisfies the voluntariness requirement because adherence to religion in a politically liberal regime is, by definition, voluntary. Although Rawls appears indifferent as to whether the burdens of labor in the family should be shared equally between men and women or whether it is enough for women to be fairly compensated for taking on a disproportionate share of such labor, he insists that justice requires that one of these two possibilities be satisfied.[23]

Family law, therefore, plays a secondary role for Rawls in guaranteeing gender equality because women enjoy all the basic rights of citizens and also have access to the material means necessary to allow them to make effective use of their liberties and opportunities.[24] In such circumstances, any residual gender-based inequality can be assumed to be voluntary. From a Rawlsian perspective, therefore, as long as women are being fairly compensated for any additional work they take on with respect to reproductive labor (measured against a hypothetical baseline of

---

[19] Ibid., 789–790.
[20] Ibid., 790.
[21] Ibid., 792 (stating that a liberal conception of justice "may have to allow for some traditional gendered division of labor within families"). Rawls further explains that an action is only "voluntary" if it is rational from the perspective of the actor and "all the surrounding conditions are also fair." Ibid. n. 68.
[22] Ibid.
[23] Ibid., 792–793.
[24] Rawls, *Political Liberalism*, 469–471.

reproductive labor that reflects a gender-neutral division of labor) and the background political conditions are otherwise just, political liberalism has nothing to say about the internal organization of the family, even one explicitly endorsing a gendered division of labor.[25]

II. THE RELATIONSHIP OF ISLAMIC LAW TO ISLAMIC ETHICS

Despite the oft-repeated claim that Islamic law is a "religious" law, Islamic law in fact regularly distinguishes between the moral or ethical consequences of human actions and their legal consequences.[26] As a general matter, Islamic ethics is scripturalist in orientation: It claims to derive its moral judgments from an examination of Islamic revelatory sources that are believed, in principle, to provide morally conclusive knowledge.[27] The goal of Islamic ethical inquiry is to classify all human acts into one of five ethical categories: forbidden, obligatory, indifferent, disfavored, or supererogatory. Because these categories represent God's judgment of human acts, they are primarily theological categories and are not necessarily rules of law.[28] Muslim theologians refer to these categories as "the rules of obligation" because they apply to the conduct of a morally responsible person and represent ethical judgments regarding the conduct of such a person.[29]

Revelation itself yields conclusive answers for only a limited set of moral questions, thus giving rise to the need for good-faith interpretation of revelation. Interpretation is an equivocal enterprise, and consequently Islamic ethics, despite its scripturalist commitments, recognizes that Muslims acting in good faith will have different views of the contents of God's commands. In the absence of a temporal authority that can conclusively resolve these ethical and theological disputes, individual Muslims

---

[25] One might object to this conception of the family on the grounds that it does not sufficiently take into account the effect on children of growing up in a family organized around principles of gender hierarchy. Presumably Rawls's reply would be that children, too, are exposed to the principles of justice through mandatory public education, and therefore a family organized around principles of gender hierarchy would not be free to insulate their children from the egalitarian norms of public reason. Rawls, *Political Liberalism*, 199–200.

[26] For example, the Ḥanafī school of Islamic law provides that a mother has a religious obligation (*diyānatan*) to nurse her infant child, but that such an obligation cannot be enforced by a court (*qaḍā'an*). 2 'Umar b. Ibrahim Ibn Nujaym, *Al-Nahr al-Fā'iq Sharḥ Kanz al-Daqā'iq* (Beirut: Dar al-Kutub al-'Ilmiyya, 2002), 518–519. For a more detailed description of the relationship of Islamic ethics to Islamic law, see Mohammad H. Fadel, "The True, the Good and the Reasonable: The Theological and Ethical Roots of Public Reason in Islamic Law," *Canadian Journal of Law and Jurisprudence* 21:1 (January 2008): 5–69, 19–29.

[27] The three revelatory sources are the Quran, Islam's holy book; the *sunna* – the normative statements and practices of the Prophet Muhammad; and consensus.

[28] See Bernard G. Weiss, *The Spirit of Islamic Law* (Athens, GA: University of Georgia Press, 1998), 20.

[29] Fadel, "The True, the Good and the Reasonable," 68.

satisfy their moral obligations to God by adhering to that rule that they in good faith believe best represents the divine will as evidenced by Islamic revelatory sources.[30] Ethical conduct requires also that a human must direct his actions for the purpose of pleasing God rather than self-interest.[31] Islamic ethics, therefore, consists of a combination of theoretical knowledge regarding the status of one's action in the eyes of God, conformity of one's conduct to that theoretical judgment, and the intention by an individual to perform the act in question for the sake of God. For example, the valid discharge of the obligation to pray prescribed Islamic prayers five times daily requires (1) knowledge that to do so is obligatory, (2) knowledge of the manner by which the prayer is to be performed, (3) performance of the prescribed ritual acts in accordance with the rules for ritual prayer, and (4) an intention to perform the prayer solely for the sake of God. Whereas all ritual acts require a religious intention, secular acts – such as entering into contracts, including a contract for marriage – are valid without the requirement of a religious intention.[32]

Islamic law, in contrast to Islamic ethics, is concerned solely with determining the secular consequences of human conduct within a system of temporal justice that, although certainly related to the ethical norms of Islamic revelation, is never wholly determined by it.[33] Moreover, Islamic law, as a secular system of justice, does not attempt to determine the subjective states of human actors, even though in the absence of such data it is impossible to know the true moral status of any act.[34] Because of rule indeterminacy and fact indeterminacy,[35] the judgments of courts, viewed from a moral perspective, can only produce valid (*ẓāhir*) judgments rather than morally true (*bāṭin*) judgments. Whereas a judge's verdict is sufficient to terminate the dispute that gave rise to the litigation in the secular world, it is not enough

---

[30] Ibid., 41–43.

[31] This principle is set forth in a statement attributed to the Prophet Muhammad in which he is alleged to have said, "Actions [are judged] solely by intentions, and each individual shall only receive what he intends. Therefore, whoever immigrated [to Medina] for the sake of God and His prophet, then his immigration was for the sake of God and His messenger. As for the one who immigrated for the sake of a worldly gain or to marry a woman, then his immigration was for that [and not God]." "Hadith Number One: Actions are but by Intentions," *Ibn Rajab's Commentary on Imam Nawawi's Forty Hadith*, trans. Mohammed Fadel, available at http://www.sunnah.org/ibadaat/alamal_bilniyyat.htm.

[32] Shihab al-Din al-Qarafi, *al-Umniyya fi Idrāk al-Niyya*, ed. Musa'id b. Qasim al-Falih (Maktabat al-Haramayn: Riyad, 1988), 112.

[33] A more accurate conception of the relationship of Islamic ethics to Islamic law is that the latter exists within certain boundaries established by the former. Fadel, "The Good, the True and the Reasonable," 23–29, 48–49.

[34] Baber Johansen, "Truth and Validity of the Qadi's Judgment. A Legal Debate among Muslim Sunnite Jurists from the 9th to the 13th centuries," *Recht van de Islam* 14 (1997): 1–26.

[35] "Rule indeterminacy" arises from the impossibility of knowing whether the judge has applied the "correct" rule of law to the case (correct in the sense of corresponding with God's rule for the case); "fact indeterminacy" refers to the risk that the evidence provided by the litigants to the court may not correspond to the actual facts of the case.

to discharge the conscience of the prevailing litigant unless she acted in good faith. Good faith means two things: first, that the successful litigant did not deceive the court as to the facts of the case;[36] and second, that the successful litigant did not advance a rule of law that he or she subjectively rejects.[37] If these two conditions are met, the judge's ruling grants the prevailing party not only a legal entitlement but also a moral entitlement to that which had been previously in dispute, and it categorically moots the prior moral controversy with respect to that particular case.[38]

However, legal rules cannot be viewed as entirely separate from a Muslim's moral obligations. For example, an invalid contract of sale may result in a defective transfer of title, with the result that the recipient of the property is deemed to be holding the object of the sale not as an owner but rather as a trustee with corresponding moral and legal obligations to return the item to its true owner without making any use of it for himself.[39] Or, in the case of family law, "if a man and a woman enter into a marriage in a manner that does not conform to the basic requirements of a marriage contract, the couple may not be considered to be truly married, and sexual intercourse between them will be illicit."[40] Moreover, legal rules do not derive exclusively from jurists' interpretations of revelation: State officials may promulgate legally binding rules under a doctrine known as *siyāsa shar'iyya* on the condition that such rules do not contradict Islamic norms, that is, that they do not command an act that would be religiously forbidden or prohibit an act that would be religiously obligatory.[41]

Two sets of regulations, therefore, are relevant to the ethical decisions of an orthodox Muslim: his subjective perception of his religious obligations and the legal system's objective regulation of his conduct.[42] Where a discrepancy exists between the two sets of norms, an individual Muslim faces the moral problem of determining

---

[36] Johansen, "Truth and Validity of the Qadi's Judgment," 12–13; Mohammad Fadel, "Adjudication in the Maliki Madhhab: A Study of Legal Process in Medieval Islamic Law," 114–116 (unpublished Ph.D. dissertation, University of Chicago, 1995).

[37] An example would be one in which a defendant asserts the validity of his marriage to a woman despite the fact that it was contracted without the approval of the wife's father, who was alive and present, in reliance on a Ḥanafī rule recognizing the validity of such marriages, even though the defendant is a Mālikī and subjectively believes that a marriage in such circumstances is invalid in the absence of the father's consent. Fadel, "Adjudication in the Maliki Madhhab," 115 n. 223.

[38] Ibid., 116.

[39] Weiss, *Spirit of Islamic Law*, 21; 2 Aḥmad b. Muḥammad b. Aḥmad al-Dardīr, *al-Sharḥ al-Ṣaghīr*, ed. Mustafa Kamal Wasfi (Cairo: Dar al-Ma'arif, 1986), 110.

[40] Weiss, *Spirit of Islamic Law*, 21.

[41] Fadel, "The True, the Good and the Reasonable," 58 n. 234.

[42] The problems arising from the duality of ethical/legal regulation that an orthodox Muslim faces would exist even if this Muslim lived in a perfectionist Islamic state. See Johansen, "Truth and Validity of the Qadi's Judgment." See also Haider Ala Hamoudi, "Baghdad Booksellers, Basra Carpet Merchants, and the Law of God and Man: Legal Pluralism and the Contemporary Muslim Experience," *Berkeley Journal of Middle Eastern and Islamic Law* 1 (2008): 1.

whether he will abide by the legal rule in question or his own moral opinion. If the legal rule in question is a mandatory rule of law, that is, either commanding an act or an omission, Muslim jurists are of the view that a Muslim can, in good faith, comply with a legal rule that he rejects as unjust provided that compliance with that rule does not entail disobedience to God. In other words, mere moral disagreement with the inherent rightness of a legal rule does not excuse compliance – only a true conflict between fidelity to the rule of law and fidelity to God could excuse compliance with a mandatory law.[43] A Muslim's obedience in such a context does not imply his or her moral agreement with the command in question or that it is just, only that he or she can comply with it without committing a sin.

The distinction between the moral and the legal in the context of permissive rules creates for observant Muslims what can only be described as a moral quandary: The person may be objectively entitled under prevailing law to press a certain claim or raise a certain defense, but unless he or she subjectively assents, as a moral matter, to that right or defense, that person is not religiously entitled to avail himself or herself of that particular rule because to do so would be to act in a manner that he or she subjectively understands to be unjust.[44] This moral problem is especially pressing in the case of certain rules of family law regarding a Muslim woman's right to remarry and rules regarding the distribution of marital property on termination of a marriage.

III. THE SCOPE OF ISLAMIC FAMILY LAW AND ITS RELATIONSHIP TO ISLAMIC ETHICS[45]

To understand the dynamics of Islamic family law[46] and the interaction of ethical and legal claims in the life of an orthodox Muslim, one must keep in mind that Islamic

---

[43] For this reason, a government agent that unlawfully killed another could not raise as a defense that he was merely acting on the instructions of his superior on the theory that he has a moral duty to resist an immoral command. See, e.g., 5 Muḥammad b. Muḥammad al-Khaṭib al-Shirbīnī, *Mughnī al-Muḥtāj ilā Maʿrifat Maʿānī Alfāẓ al-Minhāj*, eds. ʿAli Muhammad Muʿawwad and ʿAdil Ahmad ʿAbd al-Mawjud (Beirut: Dar al-Kutub al-ʿIlmiyya, 1994) (holding an executioner personally liable if he knows that the victim was unjustly executed and jointly liable with his superior if he pleads duress).

[44] Mālikī, for example, routinely cite the example of the Ḥanafī principle giving neighbors a legal right of first refusal in the event of a sale of land as a rule for which it would be immoral for a Mālikī to act on, given their belief that a legal right of first refusal only accrues to partners in land, not neighbors.

[45] References to Islamic law in this chapter do not refer to any system of positive law enacted or given effect by a state, but rather to the doctrines of Islamic family law in pre-nineteenth-century legal treatises by Muslim jurists. Although many of these rules are no longer politically salient because they have been replaced or modified by positive legislation in states that have incorporated Islamic family law as part of their legal system, their authority is independent of any state command, and therefore they remain highly relevant to orthodox Muslims' understandings of their rights and obligations, especially in liberal jurisdictions where there is no state-established system of Islamic law adjudication.

[46] For overviews of classical and contemporary interpretations of Islamic family law, see John L. Esposito with Natana J. Delong-Bas, *Women in Muslim Family Law* (Syracuse, NY: Syracuse University Press,

family law operates principally at two different levels. First, Islamic law regulates sexual intimacy and the lawful reproduction of children, where the most important rule is that sexual intimacy (including intimate contact not involving intercourse) is illicit in the absence of a valid marriage; it in fact constitutes a mortal sin and, in certain cases, a capital crime.[47] Only children conceived pursuant to a recognized marriage contract are considered legitimate.[48] The legal validity of marriage contracts is generally a matter of strict liability: Even good-faith mistakes can result in the contract being defective, in which case the parties are generally required to separate, at least until a valid contract is concluded.[49] The Islamic law of divorce also regulates sexual intimacy by rendering sexual intimacy between the former spouses illicit, immoral, and potentially subject to criminal sanction.[50] Divorce does not affect the relationship of the parent to the child, however; a legitimate child remains permanently part of each parent's kin group even after dissolution of the marriage.

Second, Islamic law introduces a broad new set of economic relationships, primarily within the nuclear family but also within the extended family. A valid marriage contract creates new economic relationships within the family requiring, for example, periodic transfers of property from the husband to his wife; from the father to any minor children; and from adult children to their parents, if the parents become indigent. Such transfers are mandated both during the lifetimes of the individuals concerned (in the form of mandatory maintenance obligations) and after death (in the form of a mandatory scheme of inheritance). Maintenance obligations

2d ed. 2001); Dawoud S. El Alami, *The Marriage Contract in Islamic Law in the Shari'ah and Personal Status Laws of Egypt and Morocco* (London: Graham and Trotman, 1992); Jamal J. Nasir, *The Status of Women Under Islamic Law and Under Modern Islamic Legislation* (London: Graham and Trotman, 2d ed. 1994).

[47] Illicit intercourse constitutes the crime of *zinā*, which, according to traditional doctrines of Islamic law, is the subject of a mandatory penalty (one of the so-called *ḥudūd* [sing. *ḥadd*] penalties). The penalty set forth in the Quran for adultery is 100 lashes. *Al-Nūr*, 24:2. Muslim jurists, however, limited this punishment to illicit intercourse between persons who were legally virgins (*bikr*), that is, had not experienced *marital* intercourse. The punishment for individuals who had the experience of marital intercourse (*muḥsan*) was stoning to death, which, although not mentioned in the Quran, was believed to have been practiced by the Prophet Muhammad.

[48] Children born outside of a lawful relationship are lawful descendants of the mother but can never be lawful descendants of the father, even where the biological father admits paternity or subsequently marries the mother. Daniel Pollack et al., "Classical Religious Perspectives of Adoption Law," *Notre Dame Law Review* 79 (February 2004): 693–753, 734–735.

[49] 2 al-Dardir, *al-Sharh al-Saghir*, 384 (stating that the general rule is that invalid marriages must be annulled); 2 Ibn Nujaym, *Al-Nahr al-Fa'iq Sharh Kanz al-Daqa'iq*, 252 (stating that it is obligatory to annul an invalid marriage contract). Children born of an invalid marriage, however, are nevertheless deemed to be legitimate. Ibid., 254. Other incidents of a lawful marriage, for example, the right to inherit, are present until the marriage is annulled. 2 al-Dardir, *al-Sharh al-Saghir*, 388.

[50] David S. Powers, "From Almohadism to Malikism: The Case of al-Haskuri, the Mocking Jurist, *ca.* 712–716/1312–1316," in *Law, Society and Culture in the Maghrib, 1300–1500* (Cambridge: Cambridge University Press, 2009), 53–94.

between parents and legitimate children are mandatory by virtue of the relationship itself.[51] A husband's obligation to support the wife is contingent on the continued existence of the marriage. Once the marriage is dissolved by divorce or death, any ongoing maintenance obligation terminates after a limited time.[52]

Although universal agreement exists with respect to certain aspects of family law, such as the impermissibility of sexual intimacy in the absence of a valid marriage contract, for example, not all Islamic ethical or legal rules regulating family life enjoy such universal recognition. In particular, because the background rules governing property relations are more permissive than those involving sexual intimacy, there is substantially wider scope within Islamic ethics and law for the organization of a household's economic relations than would be contemplated for the organization of sexual relations. The next section will discuss the practical consequences of intra-Muslim differences of opinion regarding both the ethical and legal rules governing family life and how such differences, as a historical matter, helped sustain an Islamic version of family law pluralism.

IV. ISLAM AND FAMILY LAW PLURALISM

Four factors lie behind pluralism of family regulation in societies governed by Islamic law. First, intra-Islamic pluralism arises by virtue of the role of human interpretation in the law-finding process and the impossibility of resolving resulting differences of opinion. Second, Islamic family law is a mix of mandatory and permissive rules, resulting in potential departures of Islamic marriage contracts from the default terms of Islamic law (and at times in a manner that appears to subvert the religiously normative "ideals" of marriage). Third, there is nonjudicial religious and moral regulation of the family. Fourth, Islamic law is willing to give partial recognition to non-Islamic systems of family law.

A. *Intra-Islamic Legal Pluralism and Islamic Family Law*

As a result of the relationships between and among Islamic ethical theory, moral epistemology, and law, four distinct systems of substantive law (commonly referred to as "schools of law") arose among Sunni Muslims: the Ḥanafī, the Mâlikî, the Shâfi'î, and the Ḥanbalî. Although each system of law is considered equally "orthodox" from an ethical perspective, they nevertheless often have material differences in

---

[51] Pollack et al., "Classical Religious Perspectives of Adoption Law," 733–735.

[52] Maintenance is required until the divorce becomes final upon expiration of the applicable waiting period (*'idda*), which in the case of a woman who is not pregnant is approximately three months. *Al-Baqara*, 2:228. For a pregnant divorcée, the husband's maintenance obligation continues until she delivers. *Al-Talāq*, 65:6. The widow's waiting period is four months and ten days. *Al-Baqara*, 2:234.

their substantive legal doctrines, including their approaches to the regulation of the family. To illustrate the range of substantive disagreement, consider a few salient differences between the Ḥanafī and Mâlikî schools.[53]

Whereas both the Ḥanafī and the Mâlikî schools of law recognize the right of an adult woman to marry without the consent of her father (or her father's male relatives in the absence of the father),[54] the Ḥanafīs give the father (or the father's male relatives) the right to annul a daughter's marriage if it was contracted without his consent and if the bridegroom was not the wife's social equal (*kuf'*).[55] Although the Mâlikîs also recognize the doctrine of social equality (*kafā'a*) in marriage, they restrict it to religion and freedom, and, accordingly, the father (or a male relative of the father) has no right to annul the marriage of his adult daughter if contracted without his consent (or even in defiance of his will) on the grounds that her husband is not her social equal. Significantly, the relatively greater independence Mâlikî law gives women to contract their own marriages results in a correspondingly *weaker* claim to maintenance against their extended kin group relative to the Ḥanafī rule. Whereas the Ḥanafī law of maintenance obliges the father or the father's male kin to maintain even adult unmarried or divorced daughters (or daughters whose husbands fail to provide for them), the Mâlikî law of maintenance does not recognize intrafamilial maintenance obligations other than those between a parent and a child.[56]

Another important difference between the two schools of law pertains to the law of spousal maintenance. Whereas both agree that it is the husband's duty to support the wife, the Ḥanafīs understand the maintenance obligation to be more akin to a gift rather than a contractual undertaking. Accordingly, the failure of a husband to honor this obligation does not give rise to an enforceable legal claim for money on the part of the wife.[57] Only after the wife complains to the judge and the judge reduces the maintenance obligation to a sum certain (whether payable as a lump sum, monthly, or yearly), or after the wife enters into a specific contractual agreement with her husband regarding the amount of her maintenance, does the wife

---

[53] Historically, both the Ḥanafī and the Mâlikî schools of law have been closely associated with dynasties in the Islamic world. In the modern era, Ḥanafī doctrines largely prevail in the field of family law in much of the Arab world with the exception of North Africa, where Mâlikî influence on modern family law codes is greater. For a discussion of some of the differences between the Mâlikîs, the Ḥanafīs, and modern Arab family law codes, see Lama Abu-Odeh, "Modernizing Muslim Family Law: The Case of Egypt," *Vanderbilt Journal of Transnational Law* 37 (October 2004): 1043–1146.

[54] Mohammad Fadel, "Reinterpreting the Guardian's Role in the Islamic Contract of Marriage: The Case of the Maliki School," *Journal of Islamic Law* 3 (1998): 1–26, 12–14.

[55] Farhat J. Ziadeh, "Equality (*Kafā'a*) in the Muslim Law of Marriage," *American Journal of Comparative Law* 6 (1957): 503–517, 510.

[56] 2 al-Dardir, *al-Sharh al-Saghir*, 750–751; 2 Ibn Nujaym, *Al-Nahr al-Fa'iq Sharh Kanz al-Daqa'iq*, 510.

[57] 2 Ibn Nujaym, *Al-Nahr al-Fa'iq Sharh Kanz al-Daqa'iq*, 512 (unpaid maintenance is not enforceable by a judge because it is in the nature of a gift, not a debt).

have an enforceable claim against the husband.[58] Moreover, repeated failures of a husband to meet his maintenance obligation do not give rise to a right of divorce; instead, the wife may borrow money on the credit of the husband in order to satisfy her needs,[59] or the judge may imprison the recalcitrant husband as he would imprison any other recalcitrant debtor in order to induce him to perform his financial obligations.[60] For the Mālikīs, however, the maintenance obligation is a debt owed by the husband to the wife that she is free to enforce legally at any time.[61] In addition, the Mālikīs deem a husband's failure to maintain his wife a fundamental breach of the marriage contract, giving her a right to divorce as a result.[62]

The Ḥanafīs and the Mālikīs also differ on the law governing consensual divorce (khulʿ). Both schools agree that if the husband is at fault, that is, the wife is not in a state of disobedience (nushūz) to the husband, then a husband is prohibited from receiving any consideration from his wife in exchange for divorce.[63] The Ḥanafīs characterize this prohibition as only a religious and not a legal obligation. Thus, an innocent wife's agreement to pay her husband consideration in exchange for a divorce is legally binding and she has no right to seek repayment of that amount.[64] The Mālikīs, however, treat this prohibition as creating both religious and legal obligations. They therefore grant a divorced woman a cause of action for the recovery of any sum wrongfully paid to her ex-husband if she can prove that she had been entitled to a divorce from her husband (if, for example, he had been abusing her).[65] Indeed, even a cuckolded husband is not permitted by the Mālikīs to harass his wife into accepting a separation by khulʿ.[66] The contrasting positions of the Ḥanafīs and Mālikīs on this issue reflect, in turn, a deeper disagreement on judicial divorce: The Ḥanafīs only grant a judicial divorce on extremely limited grounds whereas the Mālikīs permit the judge to divorce a wife whenever she proves harm.

Finally, the Ḥanafīs and Mālikīs have substantially different understandings of the financial consequences of a wife's disobedience. For the Ḥanafīs, the wife loses her right to maintenance simply by virtue of her disobedience, and it is not restored until she submits again to her husband's authority.[67] For the Mālikīs, however, a

[58] Ibid.

[59] Ibid., 510.

[60] Muhammad b. ʿAlī al-Ḥaddād, al-Jawhara al-Nayyira, 246.

[61] 2 al-Dardir, al-Sharh al-Saghir, 754.

[62] Ibid., 745–746.

[63] 2 Ibn Nujaym, Al-Nahr al-Faʾiq Sharh Kanz al-Daqaʾiq, 436.

[64] 3 ʿAlāʾ al-Dīn Abū Bakr b. Masʿūd al-Kasānī, Badāʾiʿ al-Sanāʾiʿ fī Tartīb al-Sharāʾiʿ (Beirut: Dar al-Katub al-ʿIlmiyya), 150.

[65] The husband's return of property unlawfully received from his wife in exchange for the divorce does not vitiate the divorce's effectiveness. 2 al-Dardir, al-Sharh al-Saghir, 530.

[66] 3 Muhammad b. Yūsuf al-Mawwāq, al-Tāj wa al-Iklīl li-Mukhtaṣar Khalīl (Beirut: Dar al-Fikr, 1992), 491.

[67] 2 Ibn Nujaym, Al-Nahr al-Faʾiq Sharh Kanz al-Daqaʾiq, 507.

husband's maintenance obligation persists until the husband exhausts all legal avenues to secure the submission of the rebellious wife to his authority.[68]

The schools' abstract and general agreements on certain fundamental points[69] should not obscure the often profound differences regarding how to give concrete effect to such principles within a general system of rights and remedies. Although none of the historical schools of Islamic law directly provides grounds for a liberal conception of marriage (such as a partnership of equals), some are more consistent with a politically liberal family law than others. As the preceding examples indicate, Mâlikî rules appear substantially more favorable to women, both from the perspective of distributive justice and protecting a woman's right to exit an undesirable marriage. Accordingly, the default rules of Mâlikî family law may provide greater doctrinal resources for fashioning Islamic marriage contracts that satisfy the minimum substantive requirements of political liberalism relative to the default rules of Ḥanafî family law.

B. *The Contractual Nature of Islamic Family Law*

Islamic marriage law permits tailor-made agreements (if drafted using the proper contractual formula) that may deviate, within specific bounds, from the legally provided terms of the marriage contract. Parties are not free, however, to include terms that are "repugnant" to the Islamic conception of marriage, that is, terms that purport to alter fundamentals of the Islamic marriage contract. If such a term is sufficiently "repugnant," it could render the contract void in its entirety. An example of such a repugnant term, from the Sunni perspective, is a marriage contracted for a specific period of time (*mut'a*). The Mâlikî school also considers "repugnant" an agreement to marry on condition that the parties will keep the marriage a secret or an agreement that the husband will not spend the night with the wife or will visit her only during certain specified times (e.g., the day time).[70] Other terms, although not repugnant to the marriage contract, may not be judicially enforceable by specific performance, such as a promise by a husband to refrain from marrying another woman or from causing her to settle in another town. The non-enforceability of such a term does not, however, vitiate the validity

---

[68]   2 al-Dardir, *al-Sharh al-Saghir*, 740.

[69]   Lama Abu-Odeh has observed that the historical schools "tend to pull toward a particular position" in certain basic questions regarding the family. For example, they generally endorse a family structure that is both gendered and hierarchical and that accrues "to the benefit of the husband ... but with a strong underlying element of transactional reciprocity of obligations ... in which husbands provide money, in the form of maintenance, and women provide conjugal society in return." Abu-Odeh, "Modernizing Muslim Family Law," 1070, 1073.

[70]   2 al-Dardir, *al-Sharh al-Saghir*, 382–384.

of the marriage[71] nor does it imply that the husband is morally free to ignore it.[72] The enforceability of other terms, for example, a marriage on the condition that the wife possesses a unilateral right to divorce at any time, is controversial: the Mâlikîs do not recognize it, but the Ḥanafîs do.[73]

The breach of a contractual term may give rise to monetary damages even if it is not enforceable through specific performance. The Ḥanafîs, for example, hold that if a woman agrees to a reduction in her dowry in consideration for the groom's promise to perform or to refrain from an act that is beneficial to her or another and is otherwise lawful (e.g., a husband's promise not to take another wife), then a subsequent breach by the husband entitles her to receive compensation. Damages would be calculated as the difference between the dowry she would have ordinarily received (*mahr al-mithl*) but for the husband's promise and the dowry she actually received pursuant to the contract.[74]

More important than the availability of damages, however, is the ability of parties to transform what would be a non-enforceable term into one that is enforceable by including an express remedy for breach. For example, a contractual clause granting the wife a unilateral right to divorce in the event that her husband marries a second wife is enforceable, even if a general promise by the husband not to take a second wife is not. Because Islamic law views such a provision as an oath or a conditional divorce, the right to divorce becomes available to the wife simply by virtue of the occurrence of the specified contingency without regard to whether the wife offered a financial concession in exchange for that contingency. The conditional structure of this device allows it to protect the wife from all sorts of contingencies for which the law does not provide a remedy, for example, a prolonged absence of the husband from the marital home. Accordingly, even the Ḥanafî school, which is the most restrictive in terms of allowing judicial divorces to women, provides women greater access to divorce as a matter of the spouses' contract than the school's default rules would otherwise permit.

As a matter of both social and legal history, we know that Islamic marriage contracts routinely departed from the legally provided default rules; examples of standard

---

[71]   Such conditions are viewed as legally unenforceable promises that ought to be kept as a matter of morality.

[72]   Abū al-Walīd Muḥammad b. Aḥmad Ibn Rushd (the Grandfather), 4 *al-Bayān wa-l-Taḥṣil* (Beirut: Dar al-Gharb al-Islami, 1984), 377 (explaining that a husband is morally but not legally bound to fulfill a promise to his wife not to prevent her from attending the mosque).

[73]   2 al-Dardir, *al-Sharh al-Saghir*, 386; 2 Ibn Nujaym, *Al-Nahr al-Fa'iq Sharh Kanz al-Daqa'iq*, 371–372.

[74]   2 Ibn Nujaym, *Al-Nahr al-Fa'iq Sharh Kanz al-Daqa'iq*, 245–246. See also Lucy Carroll Stout, "Muslim Marriage Contracts in South Asia: Possibilities and Limitations," in Harvard Law School, Islamic Legal Studies Program: Conference on the Islamic Marriage Contract, January 1999 (unpublished manuscript on file with the author).

form marriage contracts with terms that depart from legal default rules appear as early as the late tenth and early eleventh centuries. One such model from Andalusia includes provisions providing the wife the option of divorce in the event her husband took a second wife, left the marital home beyond a contractually defined period of time, or demanded that the wife leave her home town for another.[75] Such provisions were enforced in courts.[76]

Likewise, in the urban centers of fourteenth- and fifteenth-century Mamluk Egypt and Syria, monetization of the marriage contract had become sufficiently widespread as to undermine the "patriarchal ideal of conjugal harmony ... [pursuant to which] a household should constitute one indivisible economic unit ... [un]contaminated by the monetary transactions taking place outside the household."[77] Far from condemning these contractual innovations, Islamic law gave them legitimacy through the development of new contractual clauses[78] that came to be inserted routinely in marriage contracts even though some religious authorities condemned such clauses as contrary to normative Islamic conceptions of the family.[79]

Islamic law thus furthered an internal system of family law pluralism by promoting the use of nonstandard contractual terms to replace default legal terms, with the result that Islamic family law is best understood as a mixed system of mandatory public rules and contractual private rules.

C. Religious Regulation of the Family in Islam

At the same time that Islamic contractual legal principles provide parties with significant opportunities to depart from the default terms of Islamic law, so too religion

---

[75] Muḥammad b. Aḥmad al-Umawī, "A Father's Marriage of His Virgin Daughter Who is Under His Authority," appendix in Fadel, "Reinterpreting the Guardian's Role in the Islamic Contract of Marriage," 24–25.

[76] David S. Powers, "Women and Divorce in the Islamic West: Three Cases," *Hawwa* 1:1 (2003): 29–45, 39.

[77] Yossef Rapoport, *Marriage, Money and Divorce in Medieval Islamic Society* (Cambridge: Cambridge University Press, 2005), 52.

[78] Two new clauses were particularly important in these developments. The first transformed the husband's maintenance obligation from one payable in kind – food, clothing, and shelter – to one payable only in cash at regular intervals. The second transformed the husband's obligation to pay a dowry from an obligation payable only upon a fixed schedule or upon death or divorce to an obligation payable at the demand of the wife. Ibid., 52–53, 56.

[79] Ibid., 57 (quoting Ibn Qayyim al-Jawziyya, a famous Syrian jurist from the fourteenth century, as complaining that "[i]f a husband scolds his wife for her housekeeping, or prevents her from stepping out or leaving his house, or does not let her go wherever she wishes, the wife then demands her marriage gift. The husband is sent to prison, while she goes wherever she wants.").

and religious rhetoric impact the regulation of Muslims' marital life,[80] especially in light of strains of (especially historical) religious rhetoric that value an ethic of female sacrifice[81] – sometimes to the point of self-abnegation[82] – over individual rights. Different religious conceptions of marriage may account for the different approaches taken by the Mâlikîs and the Ḥanafîs here.[83] Whereas both the Ḥanafîs

[80] Reform of the pre-Islamic Arabian family (both at a moral level and at a legal level) was an express goal of numerous verses of the Quran. See, e.g., Quran, *al-Takwîr*, 81:8–9 (condemning the pre-Islamic Arabian practice of female infanticide); *al-Nisâ'*, 4:19 (prohibiting the pre-Islamic practice of "inheriting" women for remarriage, prohibiting men from harassing women in order to extort property from them, and admonishing them to live with women in kindness); *al-Baqara*, 2:229 (calling on men to live with their wives in kindness or to divorce them in a spirit of generosity); *al-Baqara*, 2:233 ("The mothers shall nurse their children for two years, if the father desires to complete the term. But he shall bear the cost of their food and clothing on equitable terms. No soul shall have a burden laid on it greater than it can bear. No mother shall suffer an injury on account of her child, nor [shall the] father on account of his child [suffer an injury].... If they mutually agree to wean the child and after they consult with one another, there is no blame on them. If ye decide on a foster-mother for your offspring, there is no blame on you, provided ye pay (the mother) what ye offered, on equitable terms. But fear Allah and know that Allah sees well what ye do.").

[81] Abu Hamid Muhammad b. Muhammad al-Ghazali, *The Proper Conduct of Marriage in Islam*, trans. Muhtar Holland (Al-Baz Publishing, 1998), 61 (attributing to the Prophet Muhammad the statement that a woman who endures a bad husband will receive heavenly reward); and Aḥmad b. Muḥammad Ibn Ḥajar al-Haytamī, *al-Ifṣāḥ 'an Aḥādīth al-Nikāḥ* (Baghdad: al-Maktaba al-'Alamiyya, 1988), 87 n.3 (attributing to the Prophet Muhammad the statement that a woman, even if her husband is oppressive, should not disobey him) and 93 (attributing to the Prophet Muhammad the statement that a woman who demands a divorce from her husband without just cause will be deprived from even the "scent of Paradise"). For an example of a modern manifestation of this ethic among Turkish Muslims in Thrace, Greece, see Robin Fretwell Wilson, "The Perils of Privatized Marriage" (in this volume).

[82] The expectation that a wife should completely subordinate her individual desires to the service of her husband was periodically expressed by medieval Muslim (male) writers on marriage. For example, the well-known medieval Muslim theologian, jurist, and philosopher al-Ghazali described the virtuous wife in the following terms:

> She should stay inside her house, and stick to her spinning wheel. She should not go up too often to the roof and look around. She should talk little with the neighbors, and visit them only when it is really necessary to do so. She should look after the interests of her spouse in his absence and in his presence, seeking to please him in all that she does. She must be loyal to him in respect of herself and of her property. She should not go out of her house without his permission. When she does go out with his permission, she should be disguised in shabby attire, keeping to out-of-the-way places far from the main streets and markets. She should be careful not to disclose her identity to her husband's friends; indeed, she should avoid recognition by anyone who thinks he knows her, or whom she recognizes. Her only concern should be to keep things right and to manage her household.

Al-Ghazali, *Proper Conduct of Marriage in Islam*, 92–93.

[83] Hina Azam argues that the different legal approaches taken by the Ḥanafîs and the Mâlikîs reflect a deeper disagreement on the nature of human sexuality and ownership of the body, with the Ḥanafîs adopting a "theocentric" view of the body and sexuality whereas the Mâlikîs took a more "proprietary" view of the body and sexuality. Hina Azam, "Identifying the Victim: God vs. the Woman in Islamic

and the Mâlikîs treat marriage as a contract that is supererogatory, the Ḥanafîs give marriage greater devotional weight than the Mâlikîs. One later Ḥanafî author, for example, states that aside from faith in God, marriage is the only religious obligation that began with Adam and Eve, persists for the entirety of human history, and continues into the afterlife.[84] This kind of religious rhetoric surrounding marriage is largely absent from Mâlikî sources, which are simply content to state that all things being equal, marriage is a religiously meritorious act on account of the secular benefits it provides.[85]

This does not mean, however, that religious ideals do not inform Mâlikî family law. For example, Malik, the eponymous founder of the Mâlikî school, reportedly discouraged contractual stipulations in marriage contracts on the theory that their inclusion is inconsistent with the relationship of trust at the heart of marriage.[86] Further, religious conceptions of marriage manifest themselves even in strictly legal matters. Islamic law treats marriage contracts differently from commercial ones. To illustrate, the norms of arm's-length bargaining permit each party to seek its maximum advantage (*mushāḥḥa* or *mukāyasa*) in commercial contracts. Marriage contracts, however, are construed according to the principal of mutual generosity (*musāmaḥa* or *mukārama*), pursuant to which the norms of magnanimity and sharing prevail over individual welfare-maximizing interpretations of the contract.[87] For that reason, the Mâlikîs do not permit a husband to annul his marriage in the event that certain contractual representations, for example, actual virginity, were breached, even if such representations were explicitly demanded by the husband.[88] This interpretive principle also meant, however, that a woman's economic contribution to the household can easily be recharacterized as a gift to the husband rather than as a loan that the husband must repay.[89] In short, tension exists between the values of Islamic law

Rape Law," lecture delivered at the 2008 Annual Meeting of the Middle East Studies Association (unpublished manuscript on file with the author).

[84] 3 Ibn ʿĀbidin, *Ḥāshiyat Radd al-Muḥtār* (Cairo: Mustafa al-Babi al-Halabi, 1966), 4.

[85] 2 al-Dardir, *al-Sharh al-Saghir*, 330.

[86] Abū al-Walīd Muḥammad b. Aḥmad Ibn Rushd (the Grandfather), 4 *al-Bayān wa-l-Taḥṣīl* (Beirut: Dar al-Gharb al-Islami, 1984), 311–312. According to Ibn Rushd the Grandfather (twelfth century), however, Malik disliked such conditions, not for religious reasons as such, but because they are bad deals for women: In most instances a woman will never have an opportunity to exercise her contingent rights, yet she agrees in advance to a reduced dowry in consideration for these additional stipulations.

[87] Ibid., 263.

[88] 3 al-Mawwaq, *al-Taj wa al-Iklil*, 491.

[89] Mâlikî law required a wife to swear an oath that she intended to treat her contributions to the household as a debt payable in the future in order for her to receive compensation for such contributions in the future. 4 al-Mawwaq, *al-Taj wa al-Iklil*, 193; see also Ibn Rushd, 4 *al-Bayan wa-l-tahsil*, 345–346. Moreover, a wife's failure to timely claim amounts that her husband owes her would result

as a legal system and traditionalist Islamic religious discourse: The former protects and vindicates the individual rights of the parties to the marriage contract (even rights that go beyond those proscribed by law), whereas the latter promotes an ethic of sacrifice, trust, love, and female subordination to their husbands.

To the extent that individual Muslims internalize the traditional religious discourse regarding marriage, the prospect that they will use their ability to opt out of the default terms of Islamic law would seem, necessarily, to be diminished, and to that extent giving effect to family law arbitrations that reflected such a discourse would be inconsistent with political liberalism. Traditional religious discourse, however, does not exercise a monopoly over Islamic religious conceptions of marriage and gender relations.[90] Islamic discourse on gender and the family over the last one hundred and fifty years has generally stressed egalitarian religious themes at the expense of the traditionalist doctrines described earlier in this chapter.[91] To the extent contemporary Muslims internalize this discourse, one would expect that they would be more willing to take advantage of the contractual structure of Islamic law to opt out of its default terms in favor of a more egalitarian marriage contract that could in principle be consistent with the requirements of political liberalism.

In short, religious beliefs, at least in the contemporary context, operate as a wild card in determining the behavior of individual Muslims: Some religious Muslims may be traditionalist in their views of marriage, whereas other religious Muslims may adopt a much more egalitarian view of the family. The prevalence of divergent subjective religious beliefs among Muslim citizens further exacerbates the problem

in a dismissal of her claim. *Al-Ḥadīqa al-Mustaqilla al-Naḍra fī al-Fatāwā al-Ṣādira 'an 'ulamā' al-Ḥaḍra* 24b (unpublished manuscript, containing legal opinions from fourteenth- to fifteenth-century Granada, on file with the author).

[90] Even among conservative groups that are typically labeled "Islamist," important shifts in the religious discourse toward a more egalitarian understanding of marriage and gender relations have taken place. See Gudrun Krämer, "Justice in Modern Islamic Thought," in *Shari'a: Islamic Law in the Contemporary Context*, eds. Abbas Amanat and Frank Griffel (Stanford, CA: Stanford University Press, 2007), 20–37, 33. Indeed, the translator of al-Ghazali's *The Proper Conduct of Marriage in Islam* described the difficulties he had in finding an Islamic publishing house willing to publish the entire translation, presumably because they found some of Ghazali's statements regarding women's role in marriage to be an obsolete relic of the middle ages, if not an outright embarrassment.

[91] See, e.g., Qasim Amin, "The Emancipation of Woman and the New Woman," in *Modernist Islam 1840–1940: A Sourcebook*, ed. Charles Kurzman (Oxford: Oxford University Press, 2002), 61–69; Nazira Zein-ed-Din, "Unveiling and Veiling," in *Liberal Islam: A Sourcebook*, ed. Charles Kurzman (Oxford: Oxford University Press, 1998), 101–106; Fatima Mernissi, "A Feminist Interpretation of Women's Rights in Islam," in Kurzman, *Liberal Islam*, 112–126; Amina Wadud-Muhsin, "Qur'an and Woman," in Kurzman, *Liberal Islam*, 127–138; Muhammad Shahrour, "Islam and the 1995 Beijing World Conference on Women," in Kurzman, *Liberal Islam*, 139–144; Khaled Abou el Fadl, *Speaking in God's Name: Islamic Law, Authority and Women* (Oxford: One World Publications, 2001); Kecia Ali, *Sexual Ethics & Islam: Feminist Reflections on Qur'an, Hadith and Jurisprudence* (Oxford: One World Publications, 2006).

of family law pluralism within the Muslim community because it reinforces the gap between the norms of an objective legal system (whether or not nominally Islamic) and the subjective moral norms of individual Muslims.

D. Marriages of Non-Muslims and Islamic Family Law

Another important historical cause of family law pluralism is Islamic law's historical willingness to afford limited recognition to marriages conducted under non-Islamic law, pursuant to the principle that non-Muslims enjoyed autonomy over their religious affairs.[92] Islamic law did not view such recognition as an endorsement of the specific moral conceptions underlying non-Islamic marriages; rather, it was a function of the political agreement between the Islamic state and the particular group of non-Muslims permanently residing in an Islamic state (*dhimmīs*). Thus, Islamic law was willing to tolerate marriages that it would condemn as incestuous if the marriage at issue was believed to be permissible according to the parties' own religion.[93] Non-Muslims, according to the Ḥanafīs (but not the Mālikîs), could avail themselves of Islamic family law, but only if both parties agreed to submit their dispute to an Islamic court.[94]

Whereas Islamic law took a strong hands-off position respecting the standards that governed the formation and dissolution of non-Muslim marriages, Muslim jurists did not feel such restraint regarding intrahousehold transfers of wealth. Accordingly, a non-Muslim husband was subject to the same legal duty to maintain his wife as was a Muslim husband. If that husband breached or could not fulfill those duties, the extended family had to take on those maintenance obligations to the same extent a Muslim family would have.[95] Similarly, whereas Islamic law gave non-Muslim parents the right to raise their own children (including teaching them a non-Islamic religion),[96] they could not take actions that would endanger the *secular* well-being of their children (such as agreeing to send them to enemy territory where they could be enslaved).[97] Thus, to the extent that a family law dispute appeared to implicate a norm that Muslims believed was nonreligious, sectarian identity did not shield non-Muslims from the jurisdiction of an Islamic court.

[92] The Ḥanafî principle was expressed in the rule that "they are to be left alone in matters that pertain to their religion (*yutrakūn wa ma yadinūn*)."

[93] Fadel, "The True, the Good and the Reasonable," 58–59.

[94] 2 Ibn Nujaym, *Al-Nahr al-Fa'iq Sharh Kanz al-Daqa'iq*, 285.

[95] 3 Ibn ʿAbidīn, *Hashiyat Radd al-Muhtar*, 159; 2 Ibn Nujaym, *Al-Nahr al-Fa'iq Sharh Kanz al-Daqa'iq*, 266 (both noting that rules governing maintenance, descent, inheritance, and the option of a minor to annul his or her marriage upon puberty all apply to non-Muslims).

[96] Pollack et al., "Classical Religious Perspectives of Adoption Law," 746–747.

[97] 5 Muḥammad b. Aḥmad al-Sarakhsī, ed. Muḥammad Ḥasan Muḥammad Ḥasan Ismāʿil al-Shāfiʿī, *Sharḥ Kitāb al-Siyar al-Kabīr* (Beirut: Dar al-Kutub al-ʿIlmiyya, 1997), 46.

E. Conclusion

Islam, as a religious and a legal system, systematically contributes both to the social fact of family law pluralism (by sustaining numerous ways in which families can live) and a normative system of family law pluralism (by legally recognizing the existence of different legal rules that can apply to issues of family and by allowing individuals to create their own "rules" via inclusion of express contractual terms in their marriage contracts that depart from legally provided default rules). As a matter of religious doctrine, traditional Islamic religious teachings endorse a hierarchical relationship with a strong emphasis on female subordination and sacrifice. The rules of Islamic law, which permit women to insert favorable provisions into the marriage contract that strengthen their positions with respect to their husbands and which emphasize a rights-based approach to marriage, have mitigated this ethic. Even the Ḥanafī school, which has produced legal doctrine substantially increasing the vulnerability of married women to domestic abuse, has recognized the legal validity of these contractual provisions. Moreover, in the modern period, even traditional Islamic religious rhetoric has itself taken a turn toward egalitarianism, even if it has not embraced gender blindness as a norm within the family.

Islamic religious and legal tradition thus gives broad support to a robust system of family law pluralism. The dynamic aspect of religious understandings of marriage and gender, as well as Islamic law's support for individualized marriage contracts, further support the notion that orthodox Muslims have sufficient Islamic resources to generate both religious and legal norms of family law that are consistent with politically liberal limits on family law pluralism. The next section discusses why orthodox Muslims may find a politically liberal system of family law to be normatively attractive, even if it might foreclose some kinds of legitimately Islamic families.

V. THE ATTRACTIVENESS OF A POLITICALLY LIBERAL FAMILY LAW TO MUSLIMS

Because of Islamic law's distinction between a legitimate rule of law and moral truth, an orthodox Muslim's decision as to whether she can comply in good faith with non-Islamic norms will entail two judgments: first, whether the conduct demanded of her would require her to act in a manner that is sinful, and second, whether she is required to endorse a doctrine that she believes to be false.[98] This Islamic reticence

---

[98] Fadel, "The True, the Good and the Reasonable," 58 n.234; Andrew F. March, "Islamic Foundations for a Social Contract in Non-Muslim Liberal Democracies," *American Political Science Review* 101:2 (May 2007): 235–252, 251 (stating that for Muslims, "the *rhetoric* employed by a state … is crucial – are Muslims being asked to *profess* something contrary to Islam or even to endure quietly the glorification of a contrary truth?" [italics in original]).

to endorse false metaphysical reasoning suggests that political liberalism's agnosticism with respect to the truth of various nonpolitical metaphysical doctrines makes it more palatable to orthodox Muslims than a "Christian" or "Jewish" or a "Judeo-Christian" state (or even a state based on a comprehensive secular philosophy for that matter), despite the many shared practical norms that Judaism or Christianity have with Islam but some of whose metaphysical foundations Muslims find objectionable. Because political liberalism only requires Muslims to endorse non-Islamic conceptions on political rather than metaphysical grounds, nothing more is at stake from the perspective of an orthodox Muslim than the political recognition of non-Muslim marriages, something not fundamentally different from premodern Islamic law's recognition of non-Islamic marriages on political but not moral grounds.[99] Political liberalism's refusal to endorse any specific metaphysical foundation for the family, provided it continues to do so, has the potential of solving many Islamic objections to features of contemporary family law in the United States and Canada.

A few examples may clarify why orthodox Muslims could find the metaphysical neutrality of a politically liberal family law attractive. Consider the historical prohibition on polygamy in common law jurisdictions.[100] Numerous reasons have been advanced to justify the historical ban on polygamy in common law jurisdictions, some of which could be viewed as implicitly racist.[101] Some common law courts asserted that polygamy is socially dangerous as evidenced by its draconian punishment in common law,[102] is politically incompatible with democracy,[103] and is contrary to the norm of "Christendom."[104] Given the strong historical connection between the teachings of Christianity and the common law's regulation of the family,[105] it ought to be no surprise that Muslims may consider the prohibition

[99] 2 Ibn Nujaym, *Al-Nahr al-Fa'iq Sharh Kanz al-Daqa'iq*, 283–284.

[100] The anti-polygamy provisions of the common law took an especially extreme form in South Africa, where the legal system refuses to recognize the validity of any marriage that is "potentially polygamous" even if the marriage is in fact monogamous. Rashida Manjoo, "Legislative Recognition of Muslim Marriages in South Africa," *International Journal of Legal Information* 32 (Summer 2004): 271–282, 276. See also Johan D. van der Vyver, "Multi-Tiered Marriages in South Africa" (in this volume).

[101] *Reynolds v. United States*, 98 U.S. 145, 164 (1878) (describing polygamy as a practice that is "odious among the northern and western nations of Europe" and that is "almost exclusively a feature of the life of Asiatic and of African people").

[102] Ibid., 165 (stating that English law, and later the laws of her American colonies, including Virginia, punished bigamy and polygamy with death).

[103] Ibid., 165–166 (quoting an expert for the proposition that polygamy leads to "stationary despotism," whereas monogamy prevents it).

[104] *Hyde v. Hyde and Woodmansee*, L.R. 1 P&D 130, 133 (HL) (1866) (stating that "marriage, as understood in Christendom, may for this purpose be defined as the voluntary union of life of one man and one woman, to the exclusion of all others").

[105] *Reynolds*, 98 US at 165 (stating that "ecclesiastical [courts] were supposed to be the most appropriate for the trial of matrimonial causes and offences against the rights of marriage"); see also Nichols,

of polygamy to be a reflection more of religious policy than the views of a neutral lawmaker. Orthodox Muslims could hardly be expected to endorse a ban on polygamy on the historical grounds articulated by these common law courts because to do so would require them to abandon their belief that the Quran is an inerrant source of moral truth.[106] Muslims could, however, endorse legal regulation or even prohibition of polygamy if the justification for such a ban was morally "neutral," that is, it did not condemn polygamy as morally odious or inherently degrading to women but instead justified the regulation or prohibition of polygamy on the grounds that it unjustifiably injured the interests of children, that the ex ante availability of polygamy inefficiently raised barriers to marriage, or that it prevented women in polygamous marriages from enjoying equal rights as a citizen.[107]

Another problematic example from the perspective of an orthodox Muslim would be the definition of marriage included in "covenant marriage" legislation appearing in certain U.S. jurisdictions. In Louisiana, for example, a couple who desires to choose covenant marriage must "solemnly declare that marriage is a covenant between a man and a woman who agree to live together as husband and wife for so long as they both may live."[108] This conception of marriage, to the ears of an orthodox Muslim, smacks of a legislative endorsement of a peculiarly *Christian* ideal of marriage as a lifelong commitment between one man and one woman.[109] If the

---

"Multi-Tiered Marriage," 142–147 (discussing influence of Roman Catholic and Anglican churches in the substance of American family law).

[106] According to orthodox interpreters, the Quran expressly allows a qualified form of polygamy. Quran, *Al-Nisā'*, 4:3 ("So marry women as you please, two, three or four, but if you fear that you will not be just [among them] then [marry only] one.").

[107] See Mohammad H. Fadel, "Public Reason as a Strategy for Principled Reconciliation: The Case of Islamic Law and International Human Rights Law," *Chicago Journal of International Law* 8 (Summer 2007): 1–20. See also Rawls, "The Idea of Public Reason Revisited," 779 (stating that the prohibition of polygamy must be justified solely in terms of women's rights as citizens and not in terms of the value of monogamy as such). The fact that such arguments are consistent with public reason does not necessarily mean that they are persuasive. For an argument that a liberal political order can tolerate polygamy, see Andrew F. March, "Is There a Right to Polygamy? Marriage, Equality and Subsidizing Families in Liberal Public Justification," *Journal of Moral Philosophy* 8(2) (2011): 244–270.

[108] La. Rev. Stat. Ann. § 9:273(A)(1) (2006). On the relationship of religion to covenant marriage, see Nichols, "Multi-Tiered Marriage," 147–152. See Katherine Shaw Spaht, "Covenant Marriage Laws: A Model for Compromise" (in this volume).

[109] Since the middle ages, Muslims have identified the conception of marriage as a lifelong relationship as a specifically Christian conception of marriage as distinguished from that of Sunni Islam, which characterized the relationship as one of indefinite duration. See, e.g., 2 Abu Ishaq al-Shatibi, *al-Muwafaqat fi Usul al-Shari'a* (Cairo: al-Maktaba al-Tijariyya al-Kubra, 1975), 389 (stating that permanence, even if it is one of the legal goals of marriage, is not a necessary element of a lawful marriage in Islam; and rejecting the requirement of permanence in marriage as an unreasonable restraint [*tadyiq*]). See also ibid., 398–399. D.S. D'Avray provides a compelling historical account of the relationship between Christian metaphysical conceptions of the relationship of the Church

justification of covenant marriage, however, were more along the lines suggested by Professors Robert and Elizabeth Scott – a means to allow couples to opt out of the no-fault regime in order to encourage greater marital-specific investments by prospective spouses – then no theological norms from an Islamic perspective would be implicated.[110]

The implicit norm of marital permanence that still infuses much of current family law does not simply amount to an expressive injury to Muslims that can be dismissed as lacking practical consequence[111]; the historical ideal of marital permanence, despite its clear sectarian roots in Christian theology and despite lip service to the ideal of the "clean break" following the adoption of no-fault divorce, continues to have a profound impact on the law of spousal support as evidenced by the continued salience of "need" in fashioning spousal support awards.[112]

Need-based spousal support awards broadly conflict with Islamic conceptions of maintenance obligations in numerous respects. The most significant area of conflict is the gender-blind approach to the law of spousal support, for a wife never has an obligation to support her husband in Islamic law – and if she does support him, she has the right to treat such support as a debt for which she can demand repayment.[113] Moreover, although a wife could agree to forego her present right to maintenance in favor of supporting herself from her own property, or to forgive accrued maintenance debts,[114] she cannot prospectively waive her right to maintenance because Islamic law deems such a condition repugnant to an essential term

---

to Jesus Christ and the historical origins of the legal doctrine of marriage indissolubility in the Latin middle ages in *Medieval Marriage: Symbolism and Society* (Oxford: Oxford University Press, 2005).

[110] Elizabeth S. Scott and Robert E. Scott, "Marriage as a Relational Contract," *Virginia Law Review* 84 (October 1998): 1225–1334, 1331–1332.

[111] In cases involving religious sentiment, sometimes expressive injury *simpliciter* is the greatest injury imaginable. See, e.g., Martha C. Nussbaum, "India: Implementing Sex Equality Through Law," *Chicago Journal of International Law* 2 (Spring 2001): 35–58, 44–45 (describing the tone in the opinion of the *Shah Bano* case as "contemptuous" of Islam, with the result that large segments of the Indian Muslim community abandoned previous openness to greater gender egalitarianism).

[112] See, e.g., Carol Rogerson, "The Canadian Law of Spousal Support," *Family Law Quarterly* 38 (Spring 2004): 69–110, 71–73 (describing persistence of "need" as basis for spousal support orders in Canada decades after the no-fault divorce revolution rendered traditional justifications of alimony obsolete); *Divorce Act*, R.S.C. 1985 c. 3 (2nd Supp.), § 15.2(4) (requiring Canadian courts, in fashioning a spousal support order, to take into account the "needs … of each spouse"); Uniform Marriage and Divorce Act § 308, 9A U.L.A. (West 2008) (permitting court to grant an order for maintenance to either spouse based on the spouse's need). The sectarian roots of marital permanence as an ideal receives further circumstantial support in the historical split between European and Middle Eastern Jewry's approaches to family law. See Michael J. Broyde, "New York's Regulation of Jewish Marriage: Covenant, Contract, or Statute?" (in this volume).

[113] See 4 al-Mawwaq, *al-Taj wa al-Iklil*, 193.

[114] 2 Aḥmad b. Muḥammad al-Ṣāwī, *Bulghat al-Sālik* (on the margin of 2 al-Dardir, *al-Sharh al-Saghir*), 385–386.

of the marriage contract – the husband's duty to provide support.[115] In the secular law of the United States and Canada, however, a Muslim wife can find herself saddled with both her equitable share of the marital household's debts at divorce and also a prospective obligation to provide financial support to her ex-husband in circumstances where she is better prepared for life post-divorce than her husband.[116]

These contradictory outcomes in spousal support (between the default civil law of an equitable distribution or a community property scheme and the default rules under Islamic family law) create an opportunity for strategic forum shopping on the part of both Muslim spouses. Such post hoc strategic behavior, relative to a Muslim couple's ex ante expectations regarding their economic rights and obligations by virtue of their marriage under Islamic law, is most acute in circumstances where the wife is saddled with household liabilities, prospective support obligations, or both. It is also present, however, when the Muslim wife is the beneficiary of the jurisdiction's default laws, particularly with respect to a claim for prospective support on the basis of need.

The basic norm of gender blindness with respect to distribution of the economic burdens and benefits of the marriage derives from the liberal conception of marriage as a community based on sharing.[117] Such a norm of spousal sharing in an intact marriage is consistent with Islamic law and Islamic religious teaching, but Islamic law does not apply the same norms at dissolution. Instead, Islamic law assumes that the divorcing parties maintain separate "accounts" for their property, and it is the task of the court to determine precisely the "contents" of each spouse's account at dissolution, with no right of redistribution of those assets between the spouses. To illustrate, consider Islamic Law's treatment of the bride's dowry (*mahr* or *ṣadāq*) and her trousseau (*jihāz* or *shuwār*). The former is a gift from the husband to the wife at the time the parties agree to marry, whereas the latter is a gift from the bride's parents to the bride at the time of her marriage. Both are legally the bride's property,[118] but while the marriage remains intact, Islamic law states that her individual ownership right to both the dowry and the trousseau is qualified. For example, a bride is customarily obligated to bring to the marital home a trousseau commensurate with the size of the dowry she received from her husband.[119] This is because the groom has the right to use the bride's trousseau in an intact marriage, even though it is nominally her exclusive property.[120] Only upon the dissolution of the marriage does the wife receive unfettered control of her dowry and trousseau.

[115] Ibid., 386.
[116] American Law Institute, *Principles of the Law of Family Dissolution* § 4.09(1) (2002).
[117] See Frantz and Dagan, "Properties of Marriage."
[118] Rapoport, *Marriage, Money and Divorce*, 14–15.
[119] 2 al-Dardir, *al-Sharh al-Saghir*, 458.
[120] Ibid., 735.

The fact that Islamic law has its own conception of the requirements of distributive justice at dissolution does not in itself explain why orthodox Muslims should object to the application of a different civil norm, given that Islamic law generally does not object to positive legislation unless it commands disobedience to God. The issue, rather, is that although compliance with the secular command to redistribute assets from one spouse to another may not be morally problematic for the spouse from whom assets are being redistributed (because it does not command disobedience to God), the recipient spouse may not be morally entitled to bring such a claim based on her subjective Islamic conception of justice. Orthodox Muslim spouses will thus recognize that there are potential conflicts at divorce between the default civil laws regarding marital assets and their private Islamic conceptions of what constitutes a just distribution. They will individually need to consider whether these material differences are consistent with their Islamic conceptions of justice. There are three possible responses from the recipient spouse: (1) *No Conflict*: The recipient spouse believes in good faith that the jurisdiction's default norms are consistent with Islamic norms of justice and thus can present his or her legal claims consistent with his or her subjective Islamic ethical commitments; (2) *Conflict with Opt-Out*: The recipient spouse believes that the jurisdiction's default rules are inconsistent with his or her Islamic conception of justice, and thus he or she does not make a claim to his or her full "legal" entitlement, resulting in such a Muslim spouse opting into an Islamic distributive scheme, even though it makes him or her economically worse off than he or she would have been under the jurisdiction's rules; and (3) *Strategic Opt-In*: The recipient spouse believes that the jurisdiction's default rules are inconsistent with his or her Islamic conception of justice, but because the jurisdiction's default laws would make him or her better off, he or she chooses to apply the jurisdiction's rules in contradiction to his or her own conception of what justice requires out of self-interest.

These last two cases illustrate that because of the potential conflict between a jurisdiction's default norms and those of Islamic law, orthodox Muslims have an important ethical stake in the debate on family law pluralism. However, orthodox Muslims can resolve the conflict by endorsing a form of family law pluralism that allows an opt-out of generally applicable civil norms and a precommitment to an Islamic conception of distributive justice. A more general delegation of powers to religious authorities, even if such authorities could be conclusively identified would be both unnecessary and undesirable – both from an Islamic perspective (because such authorities could impose their own subjective understandings of Islamic norms on the parties) and from a politically liberal perspective (because it would make citizens' rights contingent on their religious community). As a further rationale for this position, historical experience suggests that when Muslims find themselves as a minority and are governed by a mandatory system of Islamic family law, the integrity of Islamic family law becomes fused with the minority's Islamic identity, making it more difficult to achieve internal reform of Islamic family law.

Binding arbitration agreements executed in advance of marital breakdown are perhaps the most and maybe even the only effective means of giving orthodox Muslims who worry about the possibility of strategic behavior a way to solve this problem. Binding arbitration agreements also have the potential to solve the particular problems facing Muslim women who obtain a civil divorce but are unable to procure an Islamic divorce from their husbands.[121] In such a case, an orthodox Muslim woman might not believe she is eligible for remarriage, especially if her Muslim husband openly denies having divorced her Islamically. Or, even if she believes she is eligible to remarry, some consequential proportion of her religious community may not recognize her divorce as valid, therefore creating a substantial obstacle to her ability to remarry. Unlike Jewish law, Islamic law (except for the Ḥanafīs) provides a remedy for women whose husbands refuse to divorce them: a judicial divorce. Because an Islamic court is theologically empowered to resolve morally controversial cases, a judgment from an Islamic court that a woman is divorced conclusively establishes her legal and moral entitlements within the Muslim community. In the absence of the establishment of Islamic courts in liberal jurisdictions, only arbitration conducted pursuant to Islamic law can fulfill this important function of generating moral certainty. Indeed, from a purely religious perspective, it is critical that the law assures specific performance of a Muslim couples' obligation to appear at arbitration even if the jurisdiction is unwilling to respect the results of the arbitration.[122]

Contemporary family law in Canada and the United States already largely provides a structure that should enable orthodox Muslims to opt out of conflicting family law provisions,[123] including affording them the right to arbitrate their family

---

[121] Compare the situation in Jewish law with obtaining a *get*, described in Broyde, "New York's Regulation" (in this volume).

[122] See, e.g., 4 al-Dardir, *al-Sharh al-Saghir*, 199 (stating that an arbitrator cannot rule against an absent party).

[123] See, e.g., ALI *Principles of the Law of Family Dissolution* § 7.04 (permitting parties to use premarital agreements to opt out of default state law marital property distribution principles if procedural requirements are met); ibid., § 7.09(2) (separation agreements); *Uniform Premarital Agreement Act* § 6 (2001) (providing for the enforcement of premarital agreements subject to certain requirements); *Canadian Divorce Act* § 9(2) (1968) (encouraging parties to "negotiate[e] … the matters that may be the subject of a support order"); *Family Law Act*, R.S.O. 1990, c. F.3, § 2(10) (2006) (making provisions of Ontario Family Law Act subject to parties' agreement "unless this Act provides otherwise") and § 52(1) (permitting marital parties to contractually regulate "their respective rights and obligations under the marriage or on separation"); and Carol Rogerson, "Case Comment: *Miglin v. Miglin* 2003 SCC 24 'They Are Agreements Nonetheless,'" *Canadian Journal of Family Law* 20 (2003): 197–228. Compare the chapters by Brian H. Bix, "Pluralism and Decentralization in Marriage Regulation" (in this volume) and Ann Laquer Estin, "Unofficial Family Law" (in this volume).

law disputes (with the exception of Ontario and Quebec).[124] Given the flexibility of Islamic family law in both legal doctrine and its recognition of parties' right to depart from the default terms of the marriage contract, one cannot assume that orthodox Muslims would not contract Islamic marriages and regulate the legal incidents of their dissolution (using binding arbitration) in a manner that would inevitably violate the limits of a politically liberal regime's mandatory law. In other words, state enforcement of binding family law arbitration agreements (subject to the state's right to confirm that such arbitration agreements were validly entered into and that the results of such arbitrations do not violate public policy) should be sufficient to meet orthodox Muslims' religious commitments with respect to family law within a politically liberal polity. A liberal regime should also be satisfied that its public policy boundaries are sufficient to police such arbitral awards.

This does not mean that orthodox Muslims might not have legitimate complaints regarding certain details of the actual rules in particular jurisdictions (rather than the rules of an idealized politically liberal family law). For example, given the role the state has assigned to intact couples for the distribution of various public benefits, the state may be justified in refusing to recognize polygamous unions for these distributive purposes.[125] This would not, however, at least in circumstances where there has been a broad deregulation of consensual sexual relations between adults, justify the continued criminalization of polygamy or punishment of an officiant of such a marriage.[126] Similarly, Muslims can legitimately criticize the continued incorporation of need in spousal support determinations, despite its theoretical inconsistency with no-fault divorce, as a tacit endorsement of a sectarian view of marriage as a lifelong commitment.[127]

---

[124] But see Bakht, "Were Muslim Barbarians Really Knocking on the Gates of Ontario?," 80–81 (suggesting that arbitration of family law disputes pursuant to religious norms is still permitted in Ontario despite the Family Law Amendment Act of 2005 that purported to prohibit such arbitrations).

[125] Mary Anne Case, "Marriage Licenses," *Minnesota Law Review* 89 (June 2005): 1758–1797, 1783.

[126] Polygamy is prohibited by statute in both the United States and Canada. See, e.g., N.Y. Penal Law § 255.15 (2008) (criminalizing bigamy and classifying it as a class E felony); R.S.C. 1985, c. C-46, § 290 (criminalizing bigamy). Canada also punishes any person who "celebrates, assists or is a party to a rite, ceremony, contract or consent that purports to sanction a [polygamous] relationship." R.S.C. 1985, c. C-46, § 293(1). Aiding and abetting liability might apply to reach a similar result in U.S. jurisdictions, at least according to some nineteenth-century cases. See, e.g., *Boggus v. State*, 34 Ga. 275 (1866). Other features of Canadian law, however, are quite permissive with respect to polygamous unions, such as recognizing the validity of polygamous marriages if they were contracted in a jurisdiction that recognizes polygamous marriages. R.S.O. 1990 c. F3, § 1(2). Likewise, the Family Law Act's definition of "spouse" can result in a person having numerous spouses for support purposes. See Marion Boyd, *Dispute Resolution in Family Law: Protecting Choice, Promoting Inclusion* (December 2004), 24, available at http://www.attorneygeneral.jus.gov.on.ca/english/about/pubs/boyd/fullreport.pdf.

[127] Recognizing the anomalous nature of need-based spousal support orders, the ALI's proposed *Principles of the Law of Family Dissolution* expressly seeks to substitute "*compensation for loss* rather than *relief*

As the outcome of the Shariʻa Arbitration controversy in Ontario and the continued controversy regarding Islamic family law arbitration in the United Kingdom[128] reveal, the recognition of Islamic family law arbitration remains extremely contentious. The next section will use the example of New York and how its courts have monitored family law arbitrations conducted pursuant to orthodox Jewish law to demonstrate the practical ability of courts in a liberal jurisdiction to ensure that the results of religious arbitrations are consistent with public policy and individuals' rights as citizens. The success of New York in this regard ought to dispel much of the reasonable (and not irrational) concern that family law arbitration conducted pursuant to Islamic law could systematically deprive individuals of their rights.

VI. FAMILY LAW ARBITRATION, RELIGIOUS LAW, AND PUBLIC POLICY: THE CASE OF NEW YORK

As stated previously, arbitration of family law disputes is conceptually consistent with the structure of a politically liberal family law. Because liberal family law must allow parties the right to opt out of at least some legal provisions out of respect for the parties' autonomy,[129] it is difficult to understand why arbitration of disputes within family law that are governed by permissive rather than mandatory law (e.g., division of marital assets and post-divorce support agreements) should be forbidden as a normative matter. If, however, there are practical reasons (e.g., the fear that the judicial system is incapable of ensuring that arbitrations are conducted in accordance with mandatory law, or that individuals who would make use of family law arbitration are ignorant of their rights), then these are defects in the background conditions of justice that should be, from a Rawlsian perspective, addressed directly rather than used as reasons to restrict an otherwise permissible liberty.

As a practical matter, arbitration also appears to be the most promising institutional tool for reconciling liberal and nonliberal conceptions of the family.[130] From

---

of need" (italics in original) as the justification for post-divorce spousal support orders. ALI *Principles of the Law of Family Dissolution,* § 5.02, comment a. Unlike need, "compensation for loss" is broadly consistent with Islamic conceptions of distributive justice, and for that reason their adoption as law in the United States would result in a law of spousal support that would be more consistent with both public reason and Islamic law.

[128] See Ayelet Shachar, "Faith in Law? Diffusing Tensions Between Diversity and Equality" (in this volume).

[129] The recent Canadian Supreme Court decision of *Bruker v. Marcovitz,* [2007] 3. S.C.R. 607, 2007 SCC 54, gives support to the notion that religiously motivated contracts, to the extent that they are valid contracts, are equally amenable to enforcement under Canadian law as a contract entered into with a secular motive.

[130] The procedures governing the enforceability of an arbitrator's orders provide a practical mechanism for creating a dialogue between the mandatory norms of a liberal regime and the internal norms of a nonliberal community. See Patrick Macklem, "Militant Democracy, Legal Pluralism and the Paradox

a liberal perspective, the permission to use arbitration to resolve family law disputes can only be tolerated if it is not used to shield parties from the reach of family law's mandatory elements.[131] However, adherence to liberal principles of autonomy would seem to require a reviewing court to enforce an arbitrator's decision in permissive areas of family law to the same extent a reviewing court would enforce a private agreement between those parties covering the same issues.[132]

This is the path family law arbitration has taken in numerous decisions of New York courts involving disputes between Jewish couples who had submitted or agreed to submit some or all of their family law disputes to Jewish religious courts for resolution. The New York case law is clear that, as a threshold matter, a court is to determine whether the dispute is amenable to arbitration, that is, that the dispute does not involve some matter of mandatory public law.[133] Because matters such as division of marital assets and post-divorce spousal support are not, as a general matter, subject to public policy restraints, they are presumptively amenable to arbitration (provided the procedural requirements for a valid arbitration are met)[134] and an arbitrator's decision in these matters must be enforced.[135] Decisions regarding child custody are not amenable to arbitration, because that would violate mandatory public policy, which in New York requires a court to determine custody arrangements in the "best interests of the child."[136] New York courts also specifically enforce the obligation to arbitrate the dispute, even if the arbitration agreement provides for

of Self-Determination," *International Journal of Constitutional Law* 4 (July 2006): 488–516, 512–513 (arguing for the need to initiate a "jurisprudential dialogue between [liberal] and Islamic legal orders, where the individual tenets of one system are tested against those of the other" rather than dismissing a commitment to the values of Islamic law as indicative of the wholesale rejection of democratic values).

[131] Gaudreault-DesBiens, "Limits of Private Justice," 18.

[132] This is consistent with the Supreme Court of Canada's reasoning in *Miglin v. Miglin*, 1 S.C.R. 303, 2003 SCC 24 (2003), which upheld a spousal support agreement against a challenge that it was inconsistent with the terms of the Divorce Act by holding that vindicating the spouses' autonomy as reflected in their agreement takes precedence over the Divorce Act's provisions regarding spousal support.

[133] *Glauber v. Glauber*, 192 A.D.2d 94, 96–97 (N.Y. App. Div. 1993).

[134] *Stein v. Stein*, 707 N.Y.S.2d 754, 759 (N.Y. Sup. Ct. 1999) (declining to confirm arbitrator's order where there was no evidence that procedural requirements of the arbitration statute were satisfied); *Golding v. Golding*, 176 A.D.2d 20 (N.Y. App. Div. 1992) (refusing to enforce an arbitrator's award where the court found that the wife was compelled to participate as a result of the husband's threat to refuse to grant her a Jewish divorce).

[135] *Hirsch v. Hirsch*, 37 N.Y.2d 312 (N.Y. 1975) (upholding agreement to arbitrate spousal support claims); *Hampton v. Hampton*, 261 A.D.2d 362, 363 (N.Y. App. Div. 1999); *Lieberman v. Lieberman*, 566 N.Y.S.2d 490 (N.Y. Sup. Ct. 1991).

[136] *Glauber*, 192 A.D.2d at 97–98. New York courts, moreover, follow a principle of severance in the event that an arbitrator's decision included both permissible objects of arbitration and nonpermissible objects of arbitration. *Lieberman*, 566 N.Y.S.2d 490 (upholding decision of rabbinical tribunal granting a religious divorce, dividing marital assets, and awarding child support, but vacating order for joint parental custody).

religious norms to govern the arbitration.[137] More controversially, perhaps, they have refused to find that an agreement to arbitrate could be set aside on the grounds of duress where a woman was subjected to the threat of "shame, scorn, ridicule and public ostracism" by the members of her religious community if she did not agree to participate in the arbitration.[138] In short, the jurisprudence of New York courts with respect to family law arbitration seems to be to enforce agreements to arbitrate and to enforce the results of such proceedings to the same extent that the court would enforce the parties' own private agreements.

This approach of New York courts (policing arbitral results on a case-by-case basis for conformity with public policy and only striking down those elements of an order that actually violate public policy) is consistent with Rawls's conception of a politically liberal family law: This approach understands that the function of public law in the context of the family is to ensure that the internal governance of the family does not deprive any of its members of their fundamental rights as citizens, and as long as that condition is satisfied a family should enjoy autonomy. The approach contrasts with the categorical approach taken by Ontario, which simply states that an arbitrator's decision, if it is based on non-Canadian law, violates public policy *simpliciter*, without a need to determine any actual substantive conflict between the arbitrator's decision and Ontarian law.[139]

Ontario law in this regard mimics the suggestion of Professor Gaudreault-DesBiens, who argues against a policy of legal recognition of arbitrators' awards in the context of family law while at the same time allowing believers to continue to submit their disputes to arbitrations.[140] Although he cites many reasons why he believes that legal recognition of arbitral decisions in the family law context is misguided and perhaps even dangerous,[141] Professor Gaudreault-DesBiens's primary argument is that because family law affects the status of the person, it raises "the potential application of constitutional values such as dignity and equality, over which the State may still legitimately insist upon retaining some normative monopoly."[142] Even though he recognizes that recognition of faith-based arbitration – whether based on Islam or

---

[137] *Avitzur v. Avitzur*, 446 N.E.2d 136 (N.Y. 1983) (upholding order compelling husband to appear before a rabbinic tribunal pursuant to an agreement contained in his *ketubah*, a Jewish religious marriage contract).

[138] *Lieberman*, 566 N.Y.S.2d at 494.

[139] *Family Law Act*, R.S.O. 1990, c. F.3, § 59.2(1)(b).

[140] Gaudreault-DesBiens, "Limits of Private Justice," 23.

[141] Ibid., 21 (recognition of faith-based arbitration in family law disputes could lead a minority group to demand "the creation of separate institutions exercising some form of *imperium* over a segment of the population" [italics in original]).

[142] Ibid., 20. Compare McClain, "Marriage Pluralism in the United States" (in this volume) and Wilson, "The Perils of Privatized Marriage" (in this volume) concerning equality and the potential for negative outcomes in faith-based arbitration.

another religion – will not inevitably result in "outcomes that undermine the dignity or the equality of the individuals involved,"[143] he nevertheless concludes that nonrecognition is the best policy choice because it minimizes the risk that "fundamental constitutional values could be undermined."[144]

Gaudreault-DesBiens's approach can best be described as a comprehensive liberal approach in which the boundaries of mandatory law – here the Canadian Charter of Rights and Freedoms – are applied to matters of family governance directly, rather than in the indirect fashion that Rawls endorsed. To the extent that Gaudreault-DesBiens justifies this approach on a controversial normative conception of equality, however, he is advocating the use of state power to impose a comprehensive rather than a political doctrine, and thus on Rawlsian terms, his proposal is unreasonable.[145] To the extent that his objections are prudential,[146] it is not clear why those prudential concerns should not be addressed directly instead of taking the drastic step of eliminating a normatively justified method for the resolution of family law disputes.[147]

VII. CONCLUSION

Muslims have a keen interest in preserving and even enhancing a pluralistic system of family law. Muslims are interested in maintaining a political system (and a family law) that is neutral with respect to both religious and secular comprehensive doctrines. Some kinds of family law pluralism, such as that implicit in the covenant marriage statutes, appear to endorse a sectarian religious understanding of marriage rather than foster a family law pluralism that is consistent with a metaphysically neutral family law. At the same time, a politically liberal family law along the lines Rawls describes is sufficiently respectful of family autonomy to permit orthodox Muslims to structure their family life within some (but not all) Islamic conceptions of the family. The current regime of family law in the United

---

[143] Gaudreault-DesBiens, "Limits of Private Justice," 20.

[144] Ibid., 22.

[145] Rawls, *Political Liberalism*, 37 (stating that society cannot remain united on a version of liberalism without "the sanctions of state power," something he refers to as "the fact of oppression"). See also Cere, "Canadian Conjugal Mosaic" (in this volume) and Shachar, "Faith in Law?" (in this volume).

[146] That is, based on the empirical conditions, whether there are particular defects in the Canadian legal system that make it implausible for Canadian courts to regulate arbitrations in the manner undertaken by New York courts or whether there are unique sociological circumstances involving the Canadian Muslim community that render its members particularly vulnerable to the involuntary loss of their rights in the context of arbitration.

[147] Indeed, a former attorney general of Ontario, Marion Boyd, suggested a reform of the Arbitration Act that would preserve the right of religious arbitration while including greater procedural protections to ensure that the results of arbitrations would be consistent with Canadian law. See Boyd, *Dispute Resolution in Family Law*. See also Shachar, "Faith in Law?" (in this volume).

States and Canada is broadly consistent with Rawls's conception that principles of justice apply to the family indirectly, especially to the extent that faith-based arbitration is permitted. Accordingly, within the bounds required by these principles, orthodox Muslims should have adequate resources to adjust their doctrines in a manner that is faithful to their own ethical commitments while also respecting the public values of a liberal democracy.

For these reasons, orthodox Muslims' interests in family law pluralism are better served through marginal reforms to the current family law regime (such as decriminalization of polygamy and replacement of spousal need with compensation for loss as a basis for post-divorce spousal awards) that render it closer to the Rawlsian ideal of neutrality in contrast to more robust proposals that would award religious institutions greater jurisdiction over family life. Even if the state were to cede such jurisdiction equally to all religious groups and thus ameliorate Muslims' concerns about the state endorsing a sectarian conception of marriage, orthodox Muslims in a liberal state would still worry about the state ceding power over family law to a Muslim religious institution. Because orthodox Islam is inherently pluralistic, the state would inevitably have to privilege one group of Muslims and their interpretation of Islam over another group, with the result that some otherwise permissible conceptions of family life (both from the perspective of political liberalism and Islam) could be excluded. Accordingly, arbitration of family law disputes, at least for Muslims, is an ideal institution. Because arbitration is essentially contractual and therefore voluntary from a political standpoint, it respects the autonomy of individual Muslims both as religious believers (against the views of other believers) and as citizens (by allowing them to opt out of general default rules). Arbitration does not, as its critics often assume, amount to a kind of delegation of state power to an imagined Muslim collectivity.

The most substantial fear in applying the New York model of state supervision of religiously motivated family law arbitration to Muslim communities may be that U.S. courts lack sufficient capacity regarding Islamic law to perform this task effectively.[48] As evidenced by the U.S. cases discussed by Linda McClain in this volume, American courts have reached wildly divergent interpretations of the meaning of the *mahr* (a sum paid or payable from the husband to the wife, which is included in the Islamic marriage contract).[49] More sinisterly, there is the risk that anti-Islam bias could infect judicial interpretations of Islamic law in a fashion that exacerbates

---

[48] Compare Estin, "Unofficial Family Law" (in this volume).

[49] Different interpretations of the *mahr* reflect, in part, the strategic behavior of parties once they are involved in litigation. They are also a reflection of parties' conflation of cultural norms, Islamic law norms, and even legal confusion resulting from the fusion of Islamic and common law conceptions of divorce. See McClain, "Marriage Pluralism in the United States" (in this volume).

rather than reduces Muslim alienation from public law.[150] Arbitration reduces both of these problems. To the extent that disputes arising from Muslim marriages are resolved through arbitration rather than civil court proceedings, civil courts will avoid thorny issues arising out of the interpretation of Islamic law. Questions that currently bedevil civil courts, such as the "true" meaning of *mahr*, whether *mahr* is a religious or legal obligation, or whether a woman who initiates divorce is entitled to retain her *mahr*, would simply be moot in a proceeding for the enforcement of an arbitral award.

Although Muslim communities in the United States and Canada have much work to do if they wish to transform the premodern Islamic legal tradition into a workable body of rules that satisfies the requirements of political liberalism, some of the structural features of Islamic family law will be especially helpful in this regard. The first is the contractual nature of the marital relationship. Orthodox Muslim communities could prepare standard premarital agreements, for example, that are drafted to conform to both the requirements of the local jurisdiction and Islamic law.[151] The second is more doctrinal: Building on the notion that a woman is generally not obligated to contribute to the economic welfare of the household, Islamic law could take the view that contributions by the wife to the household remain debts unless the husband proves that she intended them to be gifts. This change, even though doctrinally marginal (essentially consisting of only a shift in the burden of proof), would substantially enhance a traditional wife's economic position within the family while also respecting Islamic law's policy of treating intrahousehold transfers within an intact marriage as undertaken in a spirit of liberality rather than expectation of profit.

At the same time, one should not underestimate the possibility that large numbers of Muslims – even religiously committed Muslims – will accept the default norms of applicable family law as consistent with their religious values. Given the relative flexibility of liberal family law, as well as Islamic family law's general willingness to respect parties' agreements and its respect for intra-Muslim pluralism, it should not be surprising that even orthodox Muslims might not feel the need for substantial changes to the present family law regime. Viewed in this light, incidents such as the Shari'a Arbitration controversy overstate the tension between Islamic family law and that of a liberal regime. With hindsight, they may very well appear to have been little more than tempests in the proverbial teapot. Although it is of course possible that bad-faith religious fanaticism and deeply held anti-Muslim sentiments (or some

---

[150] See, e.g., Mohammad Fadel, "German Judge and Legal Orientalism," March 29, 2007, formerly available at http://www.progressiveislam.org/german_judge_and_legal_orientalism (discussing the tendency of judges in Western jurisdictions to ascribe exotic positions to Islamic law based on its assumed "otherness").

[151] Compare the discussion of Jewish agreements in Broyde, "New York's Regulation" (in this volume).

combination thereof) will come together again in the future to produce an even more noxious brew than was served in Ontario during the Shariʻa Arbitration controversy, the example of New York shows quite clearly that liberal jurisdictions have sufficient resources to manage the interaction between religious and public norms. Hopefully, this lesson will be remembered the next time the issue of Islamic family law becomes a political football in a liberal jurisdiction.

8

Multi-Tiered Marriages in South Africa

Johan D. van der Vyver

South Africa is committed to upholding the international law directive proclaiming the rights of ethnic, religious, and linguistic communities to promote their indigenous culture, to practice their religion, and to speak their language without undue state interference.[1] Throughout its history, it sought to afford legality to customary law practices of its rich variety of peoples. However, affording full recognition to multi-tiered marriages[2] was problematic from the outset due mainly to the persistence of a typically Western perception of marriage and the dictates of predominantly Christian principles relating to matrimonial affairs.

Marriage law in South Africa reflects an evolving fusion of historical and current developments. The ample diversity of peoples, religions, and cultures colors the multidimensional approaches to marriage in both official and unofficial marriage law. In striving to reconcile the various forms of marriage and union with constitutional principles of equality and nondiscrimination, South Africa faces a Herculean challenge that will not be fully conquered any time in the near future.

Civil marriage formation under South African law is fairly straightforward. The challenge arises in dealing with marriages formed under customary marriage laws that vary from culture to culture and community to community. Historically, the common law definition of marriage excluded such customary marriages from any sort of official status. Although courts deferred to customary law on some matters, that deference was sharply restricted to those provisions that were deemed consistent

---

[1] As to the right of peoples to self-determination, see Johan D. van der Vyver, "The Self-Determination of Minorities and Sphere Sovereignty," in *The American Association of International Law: Proceedings of the 90th Annual Meeting: Are International Institutions Doing Their Job?* (Washington DC: The Society, March 27–30, 1996), 211–214.

[2] See Joel A. Nichols, "Multi-Tiered Marriage: Reconsidering the Boundaries of Civil Law and Religion" (in this volume). See also Joel A. Nichols, "Multi-Tiered Marriage: Ideas and Influences from New York and Louisiana to the International Community," *Vanderbilt Journal of Transnational Law* 40 (January 2007): 135–196, 135.

with "the principles of public policy or natural justice."[3] Such exclusion of customary law, the product of a racist ordering of society, was tempered by key provisions that afforded recognition and protection to aspects of customary marriages.[4]

The progressive 1996 Constitution established a new paradigm that enshrines "[h]uman dignity, the achievement of equality and the advancement of human rights and freedoms."[5] The far-reaching societal and political transformation reverberated throughout family law, resulting in broader acknowledgment of the diversity of marriage forms and customs. Yet such acknowledgment was heavily tinted by a concern to uphold the constitutional principles of equality and nondiscrimination. Accordingly, the Recognition of Customary Marriages Act 120 of 1998 sought to offer official status to customary marriages while retaining protections for the equality and rights of participants.[6] More recently, the Civil Union Act 17 of 2006 provides official legal status, either as a civil union or marriage, for same-sex couples.[7]

Yet tensions remain in dealing with the intricate and problematic relationship between civil and customary marriage law. Where the substantive nature of some customary marriage laws conflicts with constitutional principles, as in instances of polygamous unions, primogeniture, or other occurrences of gender inequality, courts and Parliament struggle to afford customary marriages a place in law while maintaining consistency with foundational constitutional principles. Unique problems arise in polygamous unions where two of the spouses enjoy official civil marriage status but others do not. Islamic law presents another facet of tension between upholding customary marriages and eliminating gender discrimination. Courts have used a variety of approaches to reconcile such conflicts, including applying contract law principles and prioritizing a stance against discrimination. A cross section of cases discussed throughout this chapter highlights specific instances of those tensions and a variety of responses.

The recent recognition of same-sex marriage exemplifies a further step toward the diversification of official marriage law.[8] Yet its incipience was not without dissidence; the Civil Union Act implicated questions of church and state separation and the

---

[3]   Native Administration Act 38 of 1927, § 11(2): "What Law to be Applied in Native Commissioner's Courts" (repealed).

[4]   E.g., Native Administration Act 38 of 1927, §§ 11(1) and 22(7); Bantu Laws Amendment Act 76 of 1963, § 31, discussed later in this chapter.

[5]   Constitution of the Republic of South Africa, Act 108 of 1996, ch. 1, § 1(a) [hereinafter 1996 SA Const.].

[6]   E.g., Recognition of Customary Marriages Act 120 of 1998, § 6: "Equal Status and Capacity of Spouses," ensures the "full status and capacity" of the wife in a customary marriage.

[7]   Civil Union Act 17 of 2006.

[8]   Compare Daniel Cere, "Canadian Conjugal Mosaic: From Multiculturalism to Multi-Conjugalism?" (in this volume) and Stephen B. Presser, "Marriage and the Law: Time for a Divorce?" (in this volume).

protection of minorities from the will of the majority. Those issues invoke broader constitutional questions regarding the nature of South Africa's "consultative democracy" and the source of its foundational constitutional principles.

The following exploration of South African marriage law probes those tensions, their roots, and the various approaches to their resolution. Section I gives a brief summary of the state of South African law dealing with marriages. Section II discusses historical steps toward broader legalization and acknowledgment of customary marriages. Section III turns to one method courts have utilized to reconcile customary law and constitutional principles: the application of contract law principles. Section IV involves the recent advent of same-sex marriages in the growing diversity of marital forms. Finally, Section V discusses the foundational constitutional principles and their implementation from the top down in the context of a consultative democracy.

I. BASIC PRINCIPLES OF THE SOUTH AFRICAN LAW
OF HUSBAND AND WIFE

The mainstream South African law regarding formalities for the creation of a marriage has always been quite simple: A marriage can only be solemnized by an official marriage officer. To become a marriage officer, one must register with the governmental Department of Home Affairs under the Marriage Act 25 of 1961. The clergy of any denomination may apply, and automatically qualify, to be registered as marriage officers.[9] Magistrates (lower court judges) and certain other public officers are ex officio marriage officers.[10] Marriages are therefore solemnized either in a religious ceremony officiated by a member of the clergy who has been registered as a marriage officer, or by a magistrate. If the person conducting the religious ceremony is not a registered marriage officer, the marriage will be null and void, even if the person who signs the required documentation and registers the "marriage" is a marriage officer.[11]

For marriages entered outside South Africa, the conflict-of-laws rules as applied in South Africa denote the *lex loci celebrationis* (the law of the place where the marriage was concluded) to govern the formalities required for the marriage to be regarded as valid in South Africa.

However, South African law comprises much more than merely the "mainstream" rules just mentioned. Since early times, South Africa has recognized and enforced

---

[9] Marriage Act 25 of 1961, § 3.
[10] Ibid., § 2.
[11] *Ex Parte L (Also Known as A)*, 1947 (3) SA 50, 58 (CPD); *Santos v. Santos*, 1987 (4) SA 150, 152 (WLD).

the rules of African customary law in regard to persons living under, and conducting their affairs according to, any one of the various systems of tribal law operative within traditional African communities. Such customary law was subject to one overriding principle, however: South African law did not recognize, and would not enforce, any rule of African customary law perceived to run counter to "the principles of public policy or natural justice."[12] Until almost the turn of the century, the South African legislature and courts refused to recognize as a marriage any conjugal union that was, or could potentially be, polygamous.[13] As was said by C. J. Innes in *Seedat's Executor v. The Master (Natal)*:

> Bearing in mind the essential characteristics of marriage, it is clear that the union in question was not a marriage as we understand it. It was a relationship recognized no doubt by the legal system under which the parties contracted, but forbidden by our own and fundamentally opposed to our principles and institutions.[14]

This applied to African customary marriages as well as those concluded under Muslim and Hindu rites.

Because under conflict-of-laws rules the nature of a legal relationship or institution was governed by the *lex fori* (the law of the place where the nature of the legal relationship or institution is being adjudicated) rather than the *lex loci celebrationis*, polygamous or potentially polygamous unions concluded on foreign soil were also not recognized as marriages within South Africa.[15]

II. LEGALIZATION OF CUSTOMARY AFRICAN MARRIAGES

Because the family, founded on marriage, was the centerpiece of the entire legal system of African communities, nonrecognition of "customary unions" as marriages resulted in all kinds of anomalies. For that reason, the South African Parliament from time to time enacted legislation to afford protection to partners in customary unions as if they were lawfully married – but always without affording the status of "marriage" to the customary union. For example:

---

[12] Native Administration Act 38 of 1927, § 11(2): "What Law to be Applied in Commissioner's Courts" (repealed).

[13] As to the nonrecognition of marriages concluded under indigenous African systems of law, see *Kaba v. Ntela*, 1910 TS 964, 965–969 (per De Villiers, J. P.) and 970 (per Bristowe, J.); *Seedat's Executors v. The Master (Natal)*, 1917 AD 302, 309; J. D. van der Vyver, "Human Rights Aspects of the Dual System Applying to Blacks in South Africa," in *The Individual Under African Law: Proceedings of the First All-African Law Conference*, ed. Peter Nanyenye-Takirambudde (University of Swaziland Law, 1982), 130, 136–137.

[14] *Seedat's Executor*, 1917 AD 302, at 309.

[15] *Kalla and Another v. The Master and Others*, 1995 (1) SA 261 (TPD) 266 (applying the norm to a foreign polygamous Muslim marriage). For analogous developments in the United States, see Brian H. Bix, "Pluralism and Decentralization in Marriage Regulation" (in this volume).

1. A provision in the Native Administration Act of 1927 provided that it was unlawful for any court to declare the custom of *lobola* or *bogadi* or other similar custom (the payment of dowry) to be repugnant to the principles of public policy or natural justice and therefore unenforceable[16];

2. Section 22(7) of the same act protected the property rights of the female partner or partners in a customary union in the event of a subsequent civil marriage of the husband with someone other than the customary law wife[17];

3. The Bantu Laws Amendment Act of 1963 afforded to the female partner(s) in a customary union the dependant's action to claim damages from a person held legally responsible for the death of the "husband."[18]

The political transformation of South Africa in 1994 from a racist oligarchy to "an open and democratic society based on human dignity, equality and freedom"[19] brought about radical changes in regard to almost every aspect of the prevailing legal arrangements, including family law.

The transitional 1993 (interim) Constitution authorized legislation that would afford legal recognition to religious systems of personal and family law and would acknowledge the validity of marriages concluded under such systems, subject to specified procedures.[20] Such legislation was authorized notwithstanding other provisions in the chapter on fundamental rights in the Constitution and was therefore unaffected by considerations of gender equality and nondiscrimination.[21] The 1996 Constitution remedied this latter cause for concern by providing that recognition of marriages and systems of personal and family law must be consistent with other provisions of the Constitution.[22] It also extended the reach of the envisioned legislation by authorizing the recognition of marriages concluded under "any tradition,"[23] thereby making provision for the legalization of polygamous or potentially polygamous unions concluded under African customary law.

In 1998, the South African Parliament enacted legislation that afforded recognition to all existing (African) customary marriages as well as future customary marriages

[16] Native Administration Act 38 of 1927 §11(1): "What Law to be Applied in Native Commissioner's Courts," reenacted in Law of Evidence Amendment Act 45 of 1988, § 1(1).

[17] Native Administration Act 38 of 1927, § 22(7): "Marriages of Natives: Property Rights."

[18] Bantu Laws Amendment Act 76 of 1963, § 31: "Rights of a Partner to a Customary Union to Claim Damages from Person Unlawfully Causing Death or Other Partner."

[19] 1996 S.A. Const., ch. 2, § 39(1)(a): "Interpretation of Bill of Rights"; see also ch. 1, § 1: "Republic of South Africa"; ch. 2 § 7(1): "Rights"; ch. 2 § 36(1): "Limitation of Rights."

[20] Constitution of the Republic of South Africa, Act 200 of 1993, ch. 3, § 14(3): "Religion, Belief and Opinion."

[21] Ibid. ("Nothing in this Chapter shall preclude legislation recognizing …").

[22] 1996 S.A. Const., ch. 2 § 15(3)(b).

[23] Ibid., ch. 2 § 15(3)(a)(i): "Freedom of Religion, Belief and Opinion."

that comply with the substantive requirements and formalities of the act.[24] Polygamy is no longer an obstacle to the recognition of such customary unions as marriages. Recognition of African customary marriages (including polygamous and potentially polygamous marriages) was accompanied by far-reaching conditions designed to uphold principles of human rights proclaimed in the Constitution, notably to eliminate the most glaring practices of gender discrimination inherent in customary law decrees. For example, Section 6 of the act provides:

> A wife in a customary marriage has, on the basis of equality with her husband and subject to the matrimonial property system governing the marriage, full status and capacity to acquire assets and to dispose of them, to enter into contracts and to litigate, in addition to any rights and powers that she might have at customary law.[25]

In 1984, Parliament abolished the marital power of the husband in a marriage in community of property and removed legal restrictions that limited the capacity of the wife under common law to enter into a contract, to act as plaintiff or defendant in a civil action, and the like.[26] Parliament generally afforded the wife the same powers with regard to the management and disposal of assets of the joint estate as those of the husband.[27] The act initially did not apply to marriages of Africans, but this instance of racial discrimination was remedied in 1988 when the act was extended to apply also to marriages of Africans by civil rites.[28]

The question whether Section 6 of the Recognition of Customary Marriages Act suffices to secure gender equality between wife and husband in a customary (polygamous) marriage, as required by the enabling provision in the Constitution, is debatable. The Promotion of Equality and Prevention of Unfair Discrimination Act of 2000 was enacted to flesh out the equal protection and nondiscrimination provisions of the 1996 Constitution, and "to give effect to the letter and spirit of the Constitution."[29] It prohibits unfair gender discrimination, such as "any practice, including traditional, customary or religious practice, which impairs the dignity of women and undermines equality between women and men, including the undermining of the

---

[24] Recognition of Customary Marriages Act 120 of 1998, §2: "Recognition of Customary Marriages," entered into force on November 15, 2000. Requirements for a valid customary marriage are (1) consensual agreement between two family groups as to two individuals who are to be married and lobolo to be paid; and (2) transfer of the bride by her family group to the family of the man. See *Mabena v. Letsoalo*, 1998 (2) SA 1068 (TPD); *Fanti v. Boto & Others*, 2008 (5) SA 393 (CPD); *Ndlovu v. Mokoena*, 2009 (5) SA 400 (GNP).
[25] Recognition of Customary Marriages Act 120 of 1998, § 6: "Equal Status and Capacity of Spouses."
[26] Matrimonial Property Act 88 of 1984, § 11: "Abolition of Marital Power," and § 12: "Effect of Abolition of Marital Power."
[27] Ibid., § 14: "Equal Powers of Spouses Married in Community."
[28] African Matrimonial Property Amendment Law 3 of 1988.
[29] Promotion of Equality and Prevention of Unfair Discrimination Act 4 of 2000, ch. 1, § 2(a): "Object of the Act."

dignity and well-being of the girl child."[30] African customary marriages, however, are essentially founded on practices of patriarchy and male dominance.[31] This includes polygamy, which, according to one analyst, "gives one a sense of unease" because "it … detract[s] from the dignity and independence of women."[32] In traditional African customary law, husbands and fathers had exclusive rights over the property of their households; and under the Recognition of Customary Marriages Act, such property-related consequences of customary marriages concluded before the entry into force of that act remained governed by customary law.[33]

These remnants of gender discrimination were declared unconstitutional by the Constitutional Court in *Gumede v. President of the Republic of South Africa*.[34] The case concerned discrimination on grounds of gender and race of women married under customary law in the province of Kwa Zulu-Natal, and, more specifically, the case concerned access to and control of family property by women upon dissolution of their customary marriage. Deputy Chief Justice Dikgang Moseneke, who delivered the unanimous decision of the Court, referred to "the stubborn persistence of patriarchy and conversely, the vulnerability of many women during and upon termination of a customary marriage."[35] At issue in the case was:

1. Section 7(1) of the Recognition of Customary Marriages Act 120 of 1998, which provided that the property consequences of customary marriages entered into before the commencement of the act will continue to be governed by customary law;

2. Section 7(2) of the same act, which provided that a customary marriage entered into after the commencement of the act will be a marriage in community of property (subject to certain exceptions that were not in issue in the case);

3. Section 20 of the Kwa Zulu Act in the Code of Zulu Law 16 of 1985, which proclaimed the family head as owner (with control) over family property in the family home; and

4. Section 22 of the Kwa Zulu Act, which provided that "inmates" of a kraal are in respect of all family matters under the control of and owe obedience to the family head.[36]

---

[30] Ibid., ch. 2, § 8(d).
[31] See J. Bekker and C. Boonzaaier, "How Equal is Equal? A Legal-Anthropological Note on the Status of African Women in South Africa," *De Jure* 40 (2007): 277–289, 278.
[32] Ibid., 286.
[33] Recognition of Customary Marriages Act 120 of 1998, § 7(1): "Proprietary Consequences of Customary Marriages and Contractual Capacity of Spouses."
[34] *Gumede v. President of the Republic of South Africa*, 2009 (3) SA 152 (CC).
[35] Ibid., ¶ 1.
[36] Ibid., ¶ 4.

The Constitutional Court upheld the decision of the Durban and Coast Local Division of the High Court, proclaiming these statutory provisions to be unconstitutional.[37] It recognized that the Recognition of Customary Marriages Act of 1998 "represents a belated but welcome and ambitious legislative effort to remedy the historical humiliation and exclusion meted out to spouses in marriages which were entered into in accordance with the law and culture of the indigenous African people in the country,"[38] but it nevertheless concluded that "the government has advanced no justification for the discrimination to be found in the impugned legislation."[39]

The customary marriage of the plaintiff in *Gumede* was monogamous,[40] and the Constitutional Court expressly decided that invalidation of Section 7(1) of the Recognition of Customary Marriages Act of 1998 is limited to monogamous marriages "and should not concern polygamous relationships or their proprietary consequences."[41] This state of affairs created a certain anomaly. By declaring Section 7(1) constitutionally invalid, there seems to be no legislative provision regulating polygamous marriages concluded prior to the entering into force of the Recognition of Customary Marriages Act. The Constitutional Court decided in this regard that "it is sufficient to do no more than draw the legislature's attention to this possible lacuna, if any."[42]

Courts of law have indeed applied their substantive review powers to outlaw certain practices, otherwise sanctioned by African customary law, that violate constitutional norms for the protection of human rights and fundamental freedoms. Thus, for example, the Constitutional Court held that the practice of primogeniture as applied in the customary law of succession cannot be reconciled with the current notion of equality and human dignity as contained in the Bill of Rights, because primogeniture excludes women and extramarital children from inheriting property.[43]

Gasa v. Road Accident Fund & Others is instructive for how South African courts have addressed problems from the earlier nonrecognition of African customary marriages. That case highlights problems resulting from the subordination of customary marriages to civil marriages, particularly when a party to a customary law marriage enters into an additional polygamous civil marriage. The case concerns a

---

[37] Ibid., ¶¶ 49, 58, with reference to *Gumede v. President of the Republic of South Africa*, Case No. 4225/2006 (D&CLD) (unreported).
[38] *Gumede*, 2009 (3) SA 152 (CC), ¶ 16.
[39] Ibid., ¶ 49.
[40] Ibid., ¶ 6.
[41] Ibid., ¶ 58(e).
[42] Ibid., ¶ 56.
[43] *BHE and Others v. The Magistrate, Khayelitsha and Others; Shibi v. Sithole and Others; South African Human Rights Commission and Another v. President of the Republic of South Africa and Another*, 2005 (1) SA 580 (CC), ¶ 95.

claim for damages by two surviving spouses against the Road Accident Fund based on the death of their husband, one David Siponono Gasa, in a motor car accident. During the trial, it turned out that the second wife, Makhosazana Virginia Gasa, was married to the deceased under the Marriage Act but the first wife (Nontobeko) was not. Makhosazana was paid out by the Fund, but Nontobeko was not, because the civil law did not recognize the legality of her customary marriage. The matter eventually came before the Supreme Court of Appeal. The applicant (Nontobeko Virginia Gasa) claimed that affording primacy to the civil marriage did not accord proper respect for the customs and traditions of people living under customary law and reduced customary marriages to the status of unions. The Supreme Court of Appeal, by agreement of the parties, abandoned the lower court's judgment. It held that the applicant, as "the spouse of a customary marriage existing at the time of the death of the deceased," was entitled to compensation even though the other spouse in "the customary marriage was, at the time of that marriage, a spouse in an extant civil marriage."[44] The Court also recorded that the Minister of Home Affairs (third respondent in the case) agreed to review a provision in the Black Laws Amendment Act 76 of 1963 that rendered a customary marriage invalid if the husband entered into a civil marriage with another woman. The review would take into account the "genesis [of that provision] in [a] racially discriminatory legal regime."[45]

However, as previously noted, this still leaves many questions unanswered. In the Venda tribe, for example, a woman may marry a woman.[46] This has nothing to do with sexual orientation but derives, exactly, from the inferior status of women in African customary law. If a Venda woman is of noble descent, she can take wives for herself and she will then enjoy the capacities of head of the household. She will not bear children but can require her wife or wives to have children. To that end, a male member of the tribe, called an *ukungena*, will be appointed to impregnate the concerned wife.

Under African customary law, the death of a husband does not dissolve the marriage.[47] Here, too, the services of an *ukungena* may be summoned for the purpose of procreating children for the "widow's" household – but only if she is still relatively young and has given her consent.

[44] *Nontobeko Virginia Gasa v. Road Accident Fund and Others*, Case No.579/06 SCA, ¶ 2 of the Court Order (November 19, 2007).
[45] Ibid., ¶ 4 of the Court Order. In South African constitutional law, a court of law may afford the legislature a prescribed period of time to amend a law to bring it into conformity with the Constitution (as interpreted by the Court) rather than merely declaring the law unconstitutional.
[46] J. C. Bekker, *Seymour's Customary Law in Southern Africa* (Cape Town/Wetton/Johannesburg: Juta & Co. Ltd., 5th ed. 1989), 125.
[47] Ibid., 176.

III. APPLYING PRINCIPLES OF CONTRACT TO SOME MARRIAGES NOT RECOGNIZED UNDER SOUTH AFRICAN LAW

No legislation has been enacted in South Africa to legalize Muslim or Hindu marriages, and this can raise questions of equal protection and nondiscrimination.

Courts still apply the common law (Roman-Dutch) position to Muslim and Hindu conjugal alliances by denying the status of marriage to all polygamous and potentially polygamous unions.[48] If one accepts the premise that a marriage is essentially a union between one man and one woman, one could perhaps argue that nonrecognition of Muslim and Hindu marriages, though amounting to "unfair discrimination," is not unreasonable. However, the South African legislature has discredited that line of reasoning through the legalization of polygamous and potentially polygamous African marriages[49] and more recently, having been instructed to do so by the Constitutional Court,[50] of same-sex marriages.[51] However, given the discriminatory practices inherent in Islamic and Hindu family law, it would be extremely difficult for Parliament to recognize marriages based on those religious systems while maintaining consistency with "other provisions of the Constitution."[52]

Parliament finds itself on the horns of a dilemma regarding Muslim marriages. The Muslim community is deeply divided internally regarding the desirability of bringing Muslim marriages within the confines of South African law and thereby bringing it under constraints dictated by the constitutional Bill of Rights.[53] There are some who want Muslim marriages to be afforded the sanction of law for the very reason of subjecting them to the norms of gender equality and nondiscrimination.[54] For example, an insightful law review article by a Muslim feminist proposes that Muslim personal law should be recognized in terms of Section 15(3)(a) of the 1996

---

[48] *Docrat v. Bhayat*, 1932 TPD 125, 127; *Ismail v. Ismail*, 1983 (1) SA 1006 (A) 1019–1020; and see Firoz Cachalia, "Citizenship, Muslim Family Law and a Future South African Constitution: A Preliminary Enquiry," *Tydskrif vir Hedendaagse Romeins-Hollandse Reg* 56 (1993): 392, 398–399; Johan D. van der Vyver, "Constitutional Perspective of Church-State Relations in South Africa," *Brigham Young University Law Review* 1999 (1999): 635–672, 659–664; Johan D. van der Vyver, "State-Sponsored Proselytization: A South African Experience," *Emory International Law Review* 14 (Summer 2000): 779–848, 781–799.
[49] Recognition of Customary Marriages Act 120 of 1998.
[50] *Minister of Home Affairs and Another v. Fourie and Another*, 2006 (1) SA 524 (CC), ¶ 114.
[51] Civil Union Act 17 of 2006.
[52] See 1996 S.A. Const., ch. 2, § 15(3)(b): "Freedom of Religion, Belief and Opinion."
[53] Compare the discussion of intra-Islamic pluralism about internal rules of Islamic family law in Mohammad H. Fadel, "Political Liberalism, Islamic Family Law, and Family Law Pluralism" (in this volume). See also the discussion about the interaction of Islamic law and civil regimes in John Witte Jr. and Joel A. Nichols, "The Frontiers of Marital Pluralism: An Afterword" (in this volume).
[54] Compare, e.g., Linda C. McClain, "Marriage Pluralism in the United States: On Civil and Religious Jurisdiction and the Demands of Equal Citizenship" (in this volume) and Robin Fretwell Wilson, "The Perils of Privatized Marriage" (in this volume).

Constitution, precisely so that its provisions can be brought into conformity with the constitutional Bill of Rights as required by Section 15(3)(b).[55] Women experience discrimination under Islamic law, and the new constitutional dispensation in South Africa provides an opportunity for reform:

> Even though the final Constitution promotes and protects the human rights of women through national machinery, their powers do not extend beyond the Constitution. Gradual social reform within the Muslim community, along with active participation by Muslim women, appear to be more realistic safeguards and long term solutions for effective improvement to the status of Muslim women.[56]

In July 2003, the South African Law Reform Commission submitted a report titled "Islamic Marriages and Related Matters (Project 59)" to the Minister for Home Affairs. The Minister took no further action to convert the proposal of the law commission into legislation. The Women's Legal Centre Trust consequently applied to the Constitutional Court for an order of court to compel the legislature to enact legislation, pursuant to the law commission's report, to legalize Muslim marriages. (In South African law, the Constitutional Court can, in exceptional circumstances relating to matters of great urgency, be approached directly.) Action taken by the Women's Legal Centre Trust provoked strong opposition from thirty-four traditional Muslim bodies. The affidavit of a school teacher, Farhan Patel, submitted to the Constitutional Court in support of an Interveners Notice of Motion, maintains that legislation intended to legalize Muslim marriages within the confines of South African law "falls foul of the Koran." Mr. Patel added: "Muslims in their overwhelming majority do not engage in civil marriages, in an attempt to avoid the legal consequences arising from them." On July 22, 2009, the Constitutional Court rejected the Application of the Women's Legal Centre Trust to approach the Constitutional Court directly.[57] Justice Edwin Cameron, delivering the unanimous decision of the Court, noted that direct access to the Constitutional Court has only rarely been granted in the past, and for good reason. Because the Constitutional Court in such instances is a court of first and final instance, it would deprive an applicant of a right to appeal; and, absent multistage litigation, it would furthermore deprive the Constitutional Court of the benefit of other courts' insights. Justice Cameron went on to say:

---

[55] Najima Moosa, "The Interim and Final Constitutions and Muslim Personal Law: Implications for South African Muslim Women," *Stellenbosch Law Review* 9:2 (1998): 196–206.

[56] Ibid., 205. Compare the discussion of "unofficial law" in Ann Laquer Estin, "Unofficial Family Law" (in this volume); see also Werner Menski, "Ancient and Modern Boundary Crossings Between Personal Laws and Civil Law in Composite India" (in this volume).

[57] *Women's Legal Centre Trust v. President of RSA*, 2009 (6) SA 94 (CC).

The application elicited an intense response from a wide range of organizations concerned with the position of women in the Muslim community, the application of Islamic law and the interests of the Muslim community as a whole.... It is clear ... that not only the legal issues, but also the factual issues, are much in dispute. They may require the resolution of conflicting experts and other evidence. It is not appropriate for this court to attempt that task as a court of first and final instance.[58]

The Promotion of Equality and Prevention of Unfair Discrimination Act of 2000 outlaws, among other things, female genital mutilation[59] and, as noted earlier, also prohibits "any practice, including traditional, customary or religious practice, which impairs the dignity of women and undermines equality between women and men, including the undermining of the dignity and well-being of the girl child."[60]

South African courts, conscious of their constitutional obligation to develop the common law and customary law with a view to promoting "the spirit, purport [sic] and objects of the Bill of Rights,"[61] have sought to remedy the discriminatory treatment of Muslim marriages by upholding the consequences of such marriages on the basis of contract law. For example, in *Ryland v. Edros* the Court enforced contractual arrangements pertaining to maintenance and a compensatory gift, which according to Islamic custom accompany a Muslim marriage.[62] Because the parties in that case were married according to Muslim rites (but not according to South African law), and because their union was de facto monogamous, the Court found nothing morally repugnant in their conjugal relationship. The Court was not called on to proclaim the marriage valid, however, and expressly confined the binding effect of its judgment to a potentially polygamous union that was in fact monogamous.[63]

In *Amod v. Multilateral Motor Vehicle Accident Fund*, the Supreme Court of Appeal went one step further by also making the contractual obligations of a Muslim marriage effective against third parties.[64] The plaintiff in that case claimed damages

---

[58] Ibid., at 104–105.

[59] Promotion of Equality and Prevention of Unfair Discrimination Act of 2000, ch.2 § 8(b): "Prohibition of Unfair Discrimination on Grounds of Gender."

[60] Ibid., ch. 2, § 8.

[61] 1996 S.A. Const., ch. 2, § 39(2): "Interpretation of Bill of Rights."

[62] *Ryland v. Edros*, 1997 (2) SA 690 (C); and see also *Lawrence, Negal and Solberg v. State*, 1997 (4) SA 1176 (CC) § 101. The Constitutional Court overruled an earlier judgment of the Appellate Division of the Supreme Court (as it was then called) in which the latter held that contractual obligations attending an invalid Muslim marriage, as well as consequences intrinsic to the marriage (such as maintenance), were unenforceable. See *Ismail*, 1983 (1) SA 1006 (A), 1019–1020; and see also *Docrat v. Bhayat*, 1932 TPD 125, at 127.

[63] At least one commentator views this judgment as possibly a step toward affording legality to potentially polygamous marriages. See I. P. Maithufi, "Possible Recognition of Polygamous Marriages, Ryland v. Edros," *Tydskrif vir Hedendaagse Romeins-Hollandse Reg* 60 (1997): 695.

[64] *Amod v. Multilateral Motor Vehicle Accident Fund*, 1999 (4) SA 1319 (SCA).

for loss of support, in terms of the third-party insurance law of South Africa, from the person responsible for the death of her husband in a car accident. Chief Justice Ismael Mahomed noted that the "new ethos" that prevails in contemporary South Africa "is substantially different from the ethos which informed the determination of the *boni mores* of the community when the cases which decided that 'potentially polygamous' marriages which did not accord with the assumptions of the culturally and politically dominant establishment of the time did not deserve the protection of the law for the purposes of the dependant's action."[65] Whereas the deceased had "a legally enforceable duty to support" the plaintiff, and because that duty arose from "a solemn marriage in accordance with the tenets of recognized and accepted faith" and "it was a duty which deserved recognition and protection," the plaintiff's action for damages was upheld.[66] As in the previous cases, the marriage was in this instance de facto monogamous. The Court expressly left open the possibility that the principle enunciated in the judgment might also apply to de facto polygamous Muslim marriages.[67]

In *Daniels v. Campbell*, the Constitutional Court held that the term "spouse" in the Intestate Succession Act 81 of 1987 includes the surviving spouse to a monogamous Muslim marriage, and that the term "survivor" as used in the Maintenance of Surviving Spouses Act 27 of 1990 includes the surviving spouse of a monogamous Muslim marriage.[68] In *Khan v. Khan*, the Transvaal Provincial Division of the High Court went even further and held that the Maintenance Act 99 of 1998, which applies "in respect of the legal duty of any person to maintain any other person, irrespective of the nature of the relationship between those persons giving rise to that duty,"[69] applies to inherently polygamous marriages concluded under Islamic rites.[70]

In another case, the Cape Provincial Division of the High Court applied the Maintenance of Surviving Spouses Act 27 of 1990 to a surviving member of "a permanent life partnership" between a man and a woman. The partnership was not solemnized as a marriage in accordance with the law of South Africa or any other country. The Court held that failure to afford the surviving partner the status of "surviving spouse" for purposes of the act amounted to discrimination based on marital status in violation of the nondiscrimination provisions of the 1996 Constitution.[71]

The judgment was overruled by the Constitutional Court.[72] Speaking for the majority, Justice Skweyiya noted that marriage and family are "important social

[65] Ibid., ¶ 21.
[66] Ibid., ¶ 26.
[67] Ibid., ¶ 24.
[68] *Daniels v. Campbell N.O. and Others*, 2004 (5) SA 331 (CC).
[69] Maintenance Act 99 of 1998, ch. 1, § 2(1): "Application of the Act."
[70] *Khan v. Khan*, 2005 (2) SA 272 (T).
[71] *Robinson and Another v. Volks & Others*, 2004 (6) SA 288 (C).
[72] *Volks N.O. v. Robinson and Others*, 2005 (5) BCLR 446 (CC).

institutions in our society."[73] He held that the purpose of the Maintenance of Surviving Spouses Act was to extend an invariable consequence of marriage beyond the death of a spouse. Thus, the distinction drawn in this regard between a married and unmarried person could not be perceived as unfair if considered in the larger context of the rights and obligations uniquely arising from marriage.[74] In a dissenting opinion, Justice Albie Sachs accepted the "legal logic" of the majority judgment but maintained that the matter should be decided on the basis of fairness and equity and not on exclusively legalistic grounds.[75] Where a woman has given her all for the family and the father of her children, it is not only socially harsh but also legally unfair to leave her without means of subsistence just because she has no marriage certificate.[76] In their dissenting opinion, Justices Mokgoro and O'Regan emphasized that "the institution of marriage is an important social institution which has extensive legal consequences."[77] However, ensuring that one surviving member of cohabiting partners is not left destitute after the death of the other does not undermine the sanctity of marriage. To the contrary, failure to extend such protection amounts to discrimination and is unfair and unjustifiable in an open and democratic society.[78]

Courts have been less accommodating of Hindu marriages. In January 2007, Judge Chiman Patel of the Durban High Court refused the application of university lecturer Suchitra Singh to have her unregistered Hindu marriage recognized so that she could get a divorce. The judge held that nonrecognition of Singh's marriage did not offend her dignity, nor could any purported offence against her dignity be remedied by granting a divorce decree.[79] More recently, though, the Durban and Coast Local Division of the High Court decided that the word "spouse" in the Intestate Succession Act 81 of 1967 must be interpreted to include a partner in a monogamous Hindu marriage.[80]

IV. SAME-SEX MARRIAGES

South African common law defines marriage as "a legally recognized voluntary union for life of one man and one woman to the exclusion of all others while it

---

[73] Ibid., ¶ 52.
[74] Ibid., ¶ 56.
[75] Ibid., ¶ 151.
[76] Ibid., ¶ 220.
[77] Ibid., ¶ 106.
[78] See ibid., ¶¶ 135–136.
[79] *Singh v. Ramparsad*, Case No. 564/2002 (DCLD) ¶ 53 (January 22, 2007) (unreported), available at http://www.saflii.org/za/cases/ZAKZHC/2007/1.html.
[80] *Govender v. Ragavayah N.O & others*, 2009 (3) SA 178 (DCLD).

lasts."[81] In view of this principle, South African courts have refused to recognize the validity of a marriage between persons of the opposite sex where one of the parties had undergone a sex-change operation.[82]

The South African Constitution prohibits unfair discrimination by the state,[83] and by other persons,[84] based on sexual orientation. In May of 2005, the Constitutional Court held that failure to recognize same-sex unions as marriages constitutes discrimination based on sexual orientation. The Court instructed Parliament to amend a provision in the Marriage Act that was based on the common law definition of marriage as "a union of one man with one woman, to the exclusion, while it lasts, of all others," in order to place such unions on equal footing with marriages.[85]

The Constitutional Court was confronted in that case with *amici* briefs claiming, with reference to texts from the Old and New Testaments and with references to the Koran, that from a religious perspective "the institution of marriage simply cannot sustain the intrusion of same-sex unions."[86] Justice Albie Sachs, delivering the near-unanimous decision,[87] noted the many difficulties attending "the relationship foreshadowed by the Constitution between the sacred and the secular."[88] He went on to say:

> Religious bodies play a large and important part in public life, through schools, hospitals and poverty relief programmes. They command ethical behaviour from their members and bear witness to the exercise of power by state and private agencies; they promote music, art and theatre; they provide halls for community activities, and conduct a great variety of social activities for their members and the general public. They are part of the fabric of public life, and constitute active elements of the diverse and pluralistic nation contemplated by the Constitution. Religion is not just a question of belief or doctrine. It is part of a people's temper and culture,

---

[81] *Ismail*, 1983 (1) SA 1006 (A), at 1019–1020.

[82] W v. W, 1976 (2) SA 308 (WLD); *Simms v. Simms*, 1981 (4) SA 186 (D&CLD).

[83] 1996 S.A. Const., ch. 2, § 9(3): "Equality."

[84] Ibid., ch. 2, § 9(4).

[85] *Minister of Home Affairs and Another v. Fourie and Another*, 2006 (1) SA 524 (CC), at ¶ 3 (quoting *Mashia Ebrahim v. Mahomed Essop*, 1905 TS 59 at 61); see also *Lesbian and Gay Equality Project and Others v. Minister of Home Affairs and Others*, 2006 (3) BCLR 355 (CC).

[86] *Minister of Home Affairs and Another*, 2006 (1) SA 524 (CC), at ¶ 88. See also Elsje Bonthuys, "Irrational Accommodation: Conscience, Religion and Same-Sex Marriages in South Africa," *South African Law Journal* 125:3 (2008): 473–483, 473–474 (noting that "there were fundamental differences of opinion" among the religious groups that presented their views).

[87] Justice O'Regan dissented in part with regard to the remedy; she thought the court should effectuate the immediate availability of same-sex marriage by reading it into the statute. Ibid., ¶¶ 165–169.

[88] Ibid., ¶ 89.

and for many believers a significant part of their way of life. Religious organizations constitute important sectors of national life and accordingly have a right to express themselves to government and the courts on the great issues of the day. They are active participants in public affairs fully entitled to have their say with regard to the way law is made and applied.[89]

Even so, the Court must recognize the distinctive spheres of the secular and the sacred and "not ... force the one into the sphere of the other;"[90] it must "accommodate and manage [the] difference of intensely-held world views and lifestyles in a reasonable and fair manner"[91] and not impose the religious views of one section of the population on the other. In doing so, it must protect minorities against discrimination resulting from majority opinions.[92] The Court concluded "that acknowledgment by the state of the right of same sex couples to enjoy the same status, entitlements and responsibilities as marriage law accords to heterosexual couples is in no way inconsistent with the right of religious organisations to continue to refuse to celebrate same sex marriages."[93]

For the government, the instruction of the Constitutional Court presented a dilemma because a considerable percentage of South Africans – perhaps in excess of 80 percent of the population – do not approve of same-sex marriages. As Elsje Bonthuys noted, "Members of Parliament were so divided on the issue that the [African National Congress (ANC)] party took the relatively unusual step of compelling all its members to attend Parliament and vote in favour of the Bill becoming law.... It is of course ironic that ANC Members of Parliament were not allowed a conscience vote on the Civil Union Act, while the civil servants who administer the Act may object on grounds of conscience."[94] The legislature consequently did not change the Marriage Act as it was instructed, but opted instead for the "separate but equal" alternative. It enacted the Civil Union Act 17 of 2006, which grants a civil union the legal consequences contemplated in the Marriage Act but "with such changes as may be required by context" – whatever that might mean.[95] The parties to a civil union can decide whether they want their union to be known as a marriage or a civil partnership.[96] A religious denomination or organization can apply

---

[89] Ibid., ¶ 93.
[90] Ibid., ¶ 94.
[91] Ibid., ¶ 95.
[92] Ibid., ¶ 94.
[93] Ibid., ¶ 88.
[94] Bonthuys, "Irrational Accommodation," 474.
[95] Civil Union Act 17 of 2006, § 13: "Legal Consequences of a Civil Union."
[96] Ibid., § 11(1): "Formula for Solemnisation of Marriage or Civil Partnership."

to solemnize civil unions in terms of the act.[97] Except for officials of such denominations or organizations registered as marriage officers, no other marriage officer, including state officials who act as such under the Marriage Act, can be compelled to solemnize a civil union.[98]

Given these peculiarities, doubts remain as to whether the legislature substantively complied with the instructions of the Constitutional Court. This question has thus far not been raised in the Constitutional Court.

V. IMPOSING PRINCIPLES OF EQUITY AND JUSTICE FROM THE TOP DOWN

The South African constitutional system is in many respects quite unique. For example, the 1996 Constitution mandates that legislation dealing with matters of general public interest will be unconstitutional if the enactment has not been preceded by adequate consultation with the people affected by, or with a special interest in, such legislation.[99] In light of that important provision, South Africa is not only a representative democracy but also a consultative democracy. To the best of my knowledge, this state of affairs renders the constitutional system of South Africa unique in the entire world.

The consultative component of the constitutional system does not mean that the legislature is bound to give effect to public preferences. Nor would refusal of the legislature to uphold popular perceptions pertinent to constitutionally protected values violate the democracy prong of the constitutional system. Democracy deals with the designation of persons in authority and is not implicated by bona fide efforts of the repositories of political power to uphold a constitutionally protected value system. The people must be consulted, and their views must be considered, but in the end the constitutional Bill of Rights remains the supreme law of the land. As stated by President Chaskalson in a death penalty case: "The question before us ... is not what the majority of South Africans believe a proper sentence for murder should be. It is whether the Constitution allows the sentence."[100]

---

[97] Ibid., § 5: "Designation of Minister of Religion and Other Persons Attached to Religious Denomination or Organisation as Marriage Officers."

[98] Ibid., § 6: "Marriage Officer Not Compelled to Solemnise Civil Union."

[99] 1996 SA Constitution, § 59(1)(a): "Public Access to and Involvement in National Council"; § 72(1)(a): "Public Access to and Involvement in National Council"; and ch. 6, § 118(1)(a): "Public Access to and Involvement in Provincial Legislatures." See, e.g., *King and Others v. Attorneys' Fidelity Fund Board of Control and Another*, 2006 (1) SA 474 (SCA); *Doctors for Life International v. Speaker of the National Assembly and Others*, 2006 (6) SA 416 (CC).

[100] *State v. T. Makwanyane and M. Nchunu*, 1995 (3) SA 391 (CC), § 87.

However, there are also distinct discrepancies between the lofty constitutional principles embodied in the Bill of Rights and actual perceptions and practices of segments of the South African community. Those discrepancies are evident at three levels. First, supporters of the racist oligarchy of yesteryear maintain a persistent skepticism with regard to human rights protection, because their previously privileged status in apartheid South Africa was at odds with, and challenged by, the human rights ideology. Second, remnants of discrimination remain in the facilities, services, and support available to past victims of racial discrimination, for example, in the area of public education.[101] Third, cultural practices of certain indigenous communities are incompatible with the human rights ideology of our time.

The systems of human rights protection in the world today can be divided into two main categories: those that have grown from the bottom up and those that have imposed human rights values on the political community from the top down. In countries belonging to the former category, the values embodied in a Bill of Rights are based on, and keep track with, an existing and evolving public ethos. Drafters and law-creating agencies simply endorse moral perceptions entertained by a cross section of the peoples comprising the nation. The United States Constitution, proclaimed in the name of "We, the people...," belongs to this category. The U.S. Supreme Court may well feel constrained to interpret and reinterpret the constitutional Bill of Rights to coincide with the will of the people.

South Africa, on the other hand, belongs to the category of political communities where the Bill of Rights has been imposed from the top down. That is, the rights and freedoms protected by the Constitution have been dictated by internationally recognized norms of right and wrong, which, in many instances, are not in conformity with the moral perceptions and customary practices of large sections of the South African population. Some of the laws drafted to implement human rights principles occasionally provoke strong voices of protest from groups within the country whose age-old customs may fall prey to the legal reform measures. The daily lives of those group members and the customs they observe are in many instances far removed from the nice-sounding ideologies written into the Constitution and reflected in judgments of the courts. In one of the early judgments of the Constitutional Court, Justice Mokgoro referred to the "delicate and complex" task of accommodating African customary law to the values embodied in the Bill of Rights. She noted that "[t]his harmonization exercise will demand a great deal of judicious care and sensitivity."[102]

---

[101] See, e.g., *Ex parte Gauteng Provincial Legislature: In re Dispute Concerning the Constitutionality of Certain Provisions of the Gauteng School Education Bill of 1995*, 1996 (3) SA 165 (CC).

[102] *Du Plessis and Others v. De Klerk and Another*, 1996 (5) BCLR 658 (CC), § 174.

Effective nationwide implementation of the human rights-based laws and judgments will, in the final analysis, be conditioned on the cultivation of a strong human rights ethos among all peoples and in all tribal communities of the South African "rainbow nation." In its aim to accommodate multi-tiered marriages on a basis that recognizes values held sacred in all factions of its extremely divergent plural society while simultaneously upholding the principles of equality and gender justice, South Africa still has many more miles to run.

9

Ancient and Modern Boundary Crossings Between Personal Laws and Civil Law in Composite India

Werner Menski

I. INTRODUCTION: THE REALITIES OF PLURALISM

The starting point of this chapter is somewhat different from that of most contributors to this volume, in part because of my late-comer status to the project, as well as my outsider perspective. Some European legal systems, but also Canada and the United States, have over time developed highly regulated state-centric methods of family law management that seemed to leave little or no room for religious and other authorities to make any input. Today's agonized debates over the emergence of some eighty-five Sharia Councils and Muslim Arbitration Tribunals in Britain thus reflect surprise, to put it mildly, that supposedly strong states are in fact not fully in control of family law regulation.

Such debates (if one can call them that) show that it is not sufficiently well known in a global context that European and North American models of regulatory framework are not universally replicated all over the globe. Colonialism never fully achieved its ambitious civilizing missions. In particular, it did not wipe out most preexisting sociocultural (and thus legal) traditions, but it did influence them. Today there is certainly no single, global method of managing family relations through state intervention. Rather, there are many ways of handling family law. Individual states have gradually developed patterns that suit their country-specific needs and national identities. In many cases, however, colonial intervention and other interferences imposed certain patterns that are not even close to what one may call "indigenous." Hybridity of legal regulation is thus a global fact everywhere; pluralism of methods, specifically in the management of family relations, is a global reality.

For many scholars, this raises the question (in my view quite misguided) of whether it is possible to conceive of and develop an ideal model suitable for all. In this respect, it seems that the grass is always greener on the other side of the fence. Hence many countries with state-centric regulation mechanisms, including the United States and Canada, are now debating whether there should be less state control or a more sophisticated method of state-driven intervention such as a revised multi-tiered system of legal regulation.[1] At the same time, many legal systems that have retained less state control have been engaged in equally tortuous discussions over increasing state involvement.

In the world as a whole, I see today three types of legal systems[2]: (1) those that claim to have state-centric regulation through all-encompassing general laws for all citizens or residents, with France being a somewhat extreme example; (2) countries like the United States, Canada, Australia, New Zealand, and many others that maintain a fairly centralized system but allow a unique legal position for one particular group of people, often the original inhabitants of the land; and (3) countries and legal systems that incorporate an explicitly pluralistic combination of "general law" and various country-specific "personal laws" for different groups of people, not necessarily on the basis of religion. The third category is much larger than Eurocentric scholars seem to be aware. It certainly includes countries like South Africa[3] and actually comprises most countries of Asia and Africa. For example, the Indian legal system has had to manage religious and legal pluralism for thousands of years. It has coped with the presence of Muslim personal law for centuries and today covers more than 150 million Muslims within an officially secular legal framework.[4]

Various personal law methods of legal regulation apply to the majority of the world's population today and are not historical remnants from Roman or Ottoman times. These powerful legal realities deserve respect for their capacity to operate intricate regulatory frameworks for billions of people. Assuming that one's own system, or any one particular system for that matter, is somehow the norm is a fatal methodological error. We must acknowledge that no legal system in the world has managed to maintain perfect justice at all times before we pass judgment on distant "others."

On the one hand, it is evident from this volume that state-centric types of legal systems in the first and second categories currently face debates about pluralization;

---

[1]   On governability, see Katherine Osterlund, "Love, Freedom and Governance: Same-Sex Marriage in Canada," *Social & Legal Studies* 18:1 (March 2009): 93–109. See also Joel A. Nichols, "Multi-Tiered Marriage: Ideas and Influences from New York and Louisiana to the International Community," *Vanderbilt Journal of Transnational Law* 40 (January 2007): 135–196; and Joel A. Nichols, "Multi-Tiered Marriage: Reconsidering the Boundaries of Civil Law and Religion" (in this volume).

[2]   Werner Menski, "Law, Religion and South Asians in Diaspora," in *Religious Reconstruction in the South Asian Diasporas: From One Generation to Another*, ed. John R. Hinnells (Basingstoke: Palgrave Macmillan, 2007), 243–264, 252–257.

[3]   See Johan D. van der Vyver, "Multi-Tiered Marriages in South Africa" (in this volume).

[4]   In India, "secular" means equidistance of the state from all religions, which is not quite the same as the U.S. system, although there are remarkable overlaps. See Gerald James Larson, ed., *Religion and Personal Law in Secular India: A Call to Judgment* (Bloomington, IN: Indiana University Press, 2001).

relaxation of state control; less rigid formality regarding marriage, aspects of divorce, and related matters; and post-divorce maintenance law.[5] They face pressure to adopt pluralization and more explicit recognition of various interactive boundary crossings between state regulation and other normative orderings. On the other hand, states in the third category have found themselves under various pressures to modernize, impose uniform rules, and effect more centralized state control, specifically to reform and control "religious" personal law systems. Often explicitly portrayed as an urgent matter of justice, these pressures aim for what in India is called a "Uniform Civil Code." Found in Article 44 of the Indian Constitution of 1950 and framed as a program for the future, it envisages a new civil law structure that would apply to all people.[6]

Although pulling the state out of marriage and family law altogether is rightly considered risky and is probably not really sustainable, de facto pluralization, particularly as a result of new sociocultural developments and recent migrations from other parts of the world,[7] has become a part of social reality in the Western world.[8] Such developments – nothing new in countries outside the Western hemisphere – have given rise to whole new sets of literature that largely agonize over fears of state-centric mechanisms losing control to religious authorities and other forces right in our midst. This loss of control is perceived as undermining various forms of human rights protections and is portrayed as particularly negative for women and children.[9] Somehow, it is never questioned in depth whether state regulation does not also pose risks of certain kinds of violence and infringements of basic rights. In South

---

[5] See, e.g., Brian H. Bix, "Pluralism and Decentralization in Marriage Regulation" (in this volume); Daniel Cere, "Canadian Conjugal Mosaic: From Multiculturalism to Multi-Conjugalism?" (in this volume); Ann Laquer Estin, "Unofficial Family Law" (in this volume); Nichols, "Reconsidering the Boundaries" (in this volume).

[6] As shown in this chapter, this anticipated development did not materialize. An astute early critic of excessive positivism quite rightly called this "no more than a distant mirage." Antony Allott, *The Limits of Law* (London: Butterworth, 1980), 216.

[7] Rather than treating this as a form of legal transplant, I speak about reverse colonization and call this private importation of ethnic minority legal concepts "ethnic implants." See Werner Menski, *Comparative Law in a Global Context: The Legal Systems of Asia and Africa* (Cambridge: Cambridge University Press, 2d ed. 2006), 58–65.

[8] For Britain, much before the Archbishop of Canterbury made his comments and caused a storm, I devised the concept of British Muslim law (*angrezi shariat*) as a hybrid entity to indicate that state control over family law can never be absolute. Various communities and individuals in their daily lives, rather than states, face the challenges of navigating the boundaries of official and unofficial laws. For details, see David Pearl and Werner Menski, *Muslim Family Law* (London: Sweet & Maxwell, 3d ed. 1998). On the U.S. scenario, see Saminaz Zaman, "*Amrikan Shari'a*: The Reconstruction of Islamic Family Law in the United States," *South Asia Research* 28:2 (July 2008): 185–202.

[9] See, e.g., Linda C. McClain, "Marriage Pluralism in the United States: On Civil and Religious Jurisdiction and the Demands of Equal Citizenship" (in this volume) and Robin Fretwell Wilson, "The Perils of Privatized Marriage" (in this volume).

Asia, at any rate, states are well known as the worst violators of the law. Moreover, secular civil law regulation is certainly not value-neutral, but scholars often seem to "know" what is good and bad, prejudging the entire field through preconceived notions. Scholars thereby exhibit various forms of amnesia and myopia, specifically when it comes to assessing developments in non-European legal contexts. As someone with one foot in the East and one in the West, I find myself having to write one article after the other about such issues.[10]

The present volume seeks to take the debate about management of family law further than the existing literature. The main question appears to be whether delegating authority to religious authorities would be a feasible method of meeting the challenges of increased sociocultural pluralization and of new forms of family arrangement. New patterns often go well beyond the standard norm of marriage as a lifelong bond between one man and one woman to the exclusion of all others; they comprise both the retraditionalizing effects of global non-Western migration in all directions and also the recent manifestations of modern Western sociocultural changes. I find the focus of analysis a little too narrowly put on the competition of state law and religion, when in fact the field is much more complex and plural than mere binary pairings of these elements – of East and West, or North and South, or of tradition and modernity. Reality almost everywhere is increasingly marked by super-diversity.[11] Whereas the focus in this volume is largely on U.S. law and whether a multi-tiered marriage system would be a suitable form of legal regulation, my contribution to this debate aims to show that a sophisticated pluralistic regulatory system has already existed in India for thousands of years, only more recently supplemented by stronger and more explicitly targeted state control. This indicates that abandoning the state altogether does not seem feasible, but ignoring the other inputs and players is not a feasible solution either. So perhaps we must be active, conscious pluralists, whether we like it or not.

Starting from ancient pluralistic roots of legal self-regulation, Indian law offers a model that has always respected various competing religious and cultural normative patterns while gradually developing increasingly fine-tuned overall state control, albeit with notable limits to positivist intervention. This Indian method of managing "good governance" has turned into a specific form of a social welfare state. However, in this system of partial regulation, the state is neither willing nor able to devote sufficient resources to rescue disadvantaged citizens; it mainly aims to create supportive conditions for self-controlled ordering of human actions. This is also true when

---

[10] See, e.g., Werner Menski, "Beyond Europe," in *Comparative Law: A Handbook*, eds. David Nelken and Esin Örücü (Oxford: Hart Publishing, 2007), 189–216.

[11] On Britain still overlooking the legal dimensions of such super-diversity, see Steven Vertovec, "Super-Diversity and its Implications," *Ethnic and Racial Studies* 30:6 (November 2007): 1024–1054.

it comes to social welfare arrangements.[12] With many more than a billion citizens today, the flip side of state respect for religious and social self-control in India is now increasingly manifesting itself as explicit reliance on family and communal support mechanisms, especially among women, children, and the elderly.[13] As a result, the state calls on men and other persons who have control over resources to operationalize enhanced obligations rather than enjoy superior rights. This responsibility arises from the basic foundations of traditional value systems in Indic cultures, which are built on presumptions of interconnectedness and duties toward others rather than on individual rights.

Managing this particular method of family law regulation has never been easy or uncontroversial. The Indian state today largely continues to sit back and let people decide the details of how to lead their lives. The state offers merely a symbolic safety net through somewhat symbolic fundamental rights guarantees, and little more. However, these minimal guarantees undergird Indian state interventions if there are unsustainable or blatantly unjust or imbalanced developments within various societies and religious normative orders. For example, the definition of "wife" in Indian law has since 1973 included "divorced wife."[14] It took decades for this deliberate manipulation of social relations to occur, yet this subtle move has proven powerful in the long run. These seemingly symbolic state interventions probably now also influence private interactions between individuals in their homes. (Laborious fieldwork would be necessary to ascertain that.) Formal interventions may take the form of such symbolic legislation or significant judicial pronouncements, reflecting the fact that India is not just a traditional common law system but an extremely hybrid jurisdiction. This intricate interplay of various judicial and legislative elements creates powerful legal dynamisms with remarkable outcomes.

It should surprise no one that the traditional Indian method of relying on self-controlled ordering in society was never fully effective on its own. However, it is a mistake to dismiss it as too problematic rather than seeing its intrinsic ameliorative potential. Before jumping to conclusions about certain perceived crises of the state or significant alleged maldevelopments,[15] one first needs to understand what has

[12] Recent evidence of bureaucratic abuses of India's meager welfare program strengthens doubts over the feasibility of state-centric welfare mechanisms. See Subhash Mishra, "Ghosts in the Darkness," *India Today*, August 20, 2009, available at http://indiatoday.intoday.in/site/Story/57748/States/Ghosts+in+the+darkness.html (detailing how women connive with officials under a new Widow Pension Scheme to declare their husbands dead).

[13] See Werner F. Menski, *Modern Indian Family Law* (Richmond, UK: Curzon, 2001).

[14] India Code of Criminal Procedure § 125 (1973).

[15] Attractive-looking books such as Rajeshwari Sunder Rajan, *The Scandal of the State: Women, Law and Citizenship in Postcolonial India* (Durham, NC: Duke University Press, 2003) are political manifestos rather than factually reliable legal analyses. Such writing must be treated with caution, because even basic legal facts are misrepresented.

actually been going on in Indian law "on the ground" and how such intricate pluralistic regulatory methods, grounded in thousands of years of experience handling
legal conflicts, pan out today.[16]

Remarkably, this complex story is hardly ever told because too few legal scholars
are also trained as Indologists, historians, or social scientists. Indian textbook writers
are mostly sterile "black letter" lawyers who typically list one judgment after another
and fail to analyze what they report. Most damaging, much writing on Indian law
these days comes from scholars, often Indian scholars based abroad, who are highly
politicized commentators and self-appointed social reformers. Ideological blinders
and often personal agendas prevent them from giving global readership a comprehensive account of Indian legal developments. As a result, selective and highly par-
tisan reporting on Indian family law (and many other non-Western legal systems in
the world, especially neighboring Pakistan and Bangladesh) has not allowed us to
gain a full picture of the various methods of legal management that exist in the interplay between so-called religious laws and civil laws in various jurisdictions around
the globe and specifically in South Asia.

In this chapter, I seek to show that India's long-tested method of handling family
law intricately combines overall state control with ongoing deep respect for – and
explicit recognition of – social and religious authorities. In such explicitly pluralist
scenarios, no one form of authority is ever beyond criticism. No entity is allowed to
control the entire field autonomously. Legal monism is restrained and every component, as Sally Falk Moore suggested decades ago, is "semi-autonomous."[17] Hence,
all players in South Asian legal scenarios have had to be somewhat altruistic in their
interactions with other legal actors to maintain stability and continuity. Legal pluralism has long been a fact in South Asia, and such complex management is not
easy to achieve; it may become unbalanced or uprooted, as can be seen from the
unfortunate developments in Afghanistan and Pakistan, and to a lesser extent in
Bangladesh and Sri Lanka. India appears to have reached reasonably stable democratic standards in pursuing sustainable methods of family law regulation. Recent

A prominent example is the persistent global misrepresentation of the *Shah Bano* saga in Indian
law. The story of how an old Muslim lady was thrown out of marriage, deprived of her legal entitlements by an unscrupulous lawyer-husband, and then let down by a gender-insensitive legal system is
brilliant scholarly fiction. This fiction has been used to support familiar allegations that "religious law"
is bad for women and that modern secular state intervention in India has been totally ineffective. The
real story will be discussed further in its wider context later in this chapter.

[16] For a sample of excellent fieldwork-based study, see Sylvia Vatuk, "Divorce at the Wife's Initiative in
Muslim Personal Law: What are the Options and What are Their Implications for Women's Welfare?"
in *Redefining Family Law in India*, eds. Archana Parashar and Amita Dhanda (London: Routledge,
2008), 200–235.

[17] Sally Falk Moore, *Law as Process: An Anthropological Approach* (London: Routledge & Kegan Paul,
1978).

historical scholarship suggests, however, that this may have been achieved at a cost: allowing the Pakistanis to have their own neighboring state only to find that Muslim law remains a critical component in India's legal scenario.

My coverage of recent Indian developments in marriage law and post-divorce maintenance arrangements is prefaced by a brief historical overview to inform readers on the remarkable cultural and conceptual continuities in South Asian legal systems. These continuities are embedded with ancient concepts of self-controlled ordering and accountability for one's own actions, ideas originally developed outside state-centric legal regulation in various Hindu, Buddhist, Jain, and Muslim religio-cultural contexts. These multicultural building blocks are now subtly incorporated into – and ultimately supervised by – officially "secular" and religiously equidistant formal legal structures. A clear reflection of such "soft" duty-based approaches is embodied in the new Article 51A of the Indian Constitution, which comprises a set of Fundamental Duties. These include the duty "to promote harmony and the spirit of common brotherhood amongst all the people of India transcending religious, linguistic and regional or sectional diversities; to renounce practices derogatory to the dignity of women";[18] and "to value and preserve the rich heritage of our composite culture."[19]

Although modern Indian law thus looks at first sight like a Western legal system and even seems to resemble U.S. law,[20] the trajectory of Indian legal developments and outcomes is in fact very different from what we find in Europe or North America. Lessons from the Indian experience are therefore not directly transposable to our contexts. However, by showing how the Indian law of marriage and post-divorce maintenance has developed in recent times, I seek to illustrate that an intricate pluralist combination of state control and socioreligious management can and does work. This model offers sustainable solutions, even though it remains subject to never-ending manipulations and fine-tuning. Law, after all, is a culture-specific, dynamic process and not merely a set of rules.

II. ANCIENT ROOTS OF PLURALISM AND BOUNDARY CROSSING

India's so-called composite culture has manifestly ancient roots.[21] Diversity management has been an integral element of South Asian social and legal systems for centuries. Examples include the much-maligned and heavily abused caste system,

---

[18] *Constitution of India*, Article 51A(e) (1950).
[19] Ibid., Article 51A(f).
[20] Larson, *Religion and Personal Law in Secular India*.
[21] It seems the word "multiculturalism" – which perhaps suggests polluting mélanges – has become disfavored.

which evinces the basic recognition that humans have different functions in life, and also the enormously important ancient ethnic encounters that specialist scholars are still struggling to unravel.[22] Very few lawyers, Western or Indian, are able to perceive these basically cultural Indic roots as potent and intrinsically plural growth stimulants for an amazingly versatile system of gradually developing legal regulation.[23] "Hinduism" may well be a more recent term and a constructed entity, but Indic culture itself has unquestionably ancient pedigree and is manifestly more than a religious tradition.[24]

Indic cultural traditions include ancient textual evidence, dating to circa 1000 BCE, that explicitly and intimately connects human marriage rituals to macrocosmic phenomena.[25] These texts laid conceptual foundations that have receded into the past and tend to be forgotten and ignored today. They are deliberately omitted by many scholars today because of their allegedly suspect religious provenance. However, such deep-rooted concepts within the subconscious of Indic people of all kinds, including now many South Asian Muslims and Christians, continue to exert much invisible and indeed some visible influence. Many legal systems in Asia have been influenced by the migration of such early Indic concepts, especially throughout Southeast Asia and into the Far East, extending from Japan west past Afghanistan and Iran.[26] Excavating these ancient pluralisms helps to explain why India is so different from other jurisdictions today regarding management of family law regulations.

Given such ancient Indic foundational concepts, it is not surprising that modern Indian family law struggles with implementing state control of marriage. Marriage was, first of all, a new relationship of a man and a woman, linked to family, clan, and community and ritually connected through the solemnization of increasingly elaborate rituals directed toward the Universe. It was not primarily a matter for the state.[27] Interconnectedness was the key element of early Indic thought, conceptually embedded in dynamic terms like *karma* (action and its consequences) and *dharma* (the duty of everyone to do the right thing at any moment of one's life). This concept

---

[22] A key issue here is whether Indic cultures were significantly influenced by early European or Central Asian models ("the Aryan question") as a result of migrations. A related issue is the relative input of non-Aryan cultures, specifically Dravidian and various tribal models. The latter would bring Indians closer to Africans, which is widely resented.

[23] For details, see Werner F. Menski, *Hindu Law: Beyond Tradition and Modernity* (New Delhi: Oxford University Press, 2003).

[24] Werner Menski, "Hindu Law as a 'Religious' System," in *Religion, Law and Tradition: Comparative Studies in Religious Law*, ed. Andrew Huxley (London: Routledge Curzon, 2002), 108–126.

[25] Menski, *Hindu Law*, 86–93.

[26] Ibid.

[27] See Stephen B. Presser, "Marriage and the Law: Time for a Divorce?" (in this volume) (concerning the nature of marriage and its connection to the state in the Western common law tradition).

was manifested in the expectation that microcosmic entities and processes should perennially be harmonized with visions of macrocosmic Order.[28]

The failed imperial and colonial efforts – by Muslims and especially by the British – to restructure Indian personal laws and to privilege state control are simplistically characterized by many post-colonial scholars as mischievous actions that afforded unwarranted prominence to religion. As a result, even the most recent studies on Indian family law are content to presume that Indian personal laws are just religious constructs. This intellectually impoverished approach completely ignores the intense interaction and constant border crossing between various forms of law within Hindu and Indian law and precludes even analyzing interactions between secular "general laws" and allegedly religious "personal laws."[29]

Ignorance of Indic cultural traditions and unwillingness to accept and interrogate the complex subsequent developments within India's deeply plurality-conscious family law are also reflected when surprised legal observers note and/or are forced to admit that in India today a Hindu (or indeed Muslim) marriage still becomes legally valid not through an act of state-ordained registration but through performance of requisite religious and social ceremonies. It is worth emphasizing that both religious *and* social aspects exist, underscoring the fact that manifestations of legal pluralism are not restricted to struggles between law and religion; they comprise every aspect of human existence. Marriage registration documents are not unknown, but they are normally not the appropriate final proof that a legally valid marriage exists, especially because documents can be purchased and forged.[30] Scholars, including many South Asian lawyers, became brainwashed by legal positivism and focus solely on "the law" and therefore struggle to understand what is really going on in the complex field of South Asian laws.

Moreover, many scholars, as this volume confirms, have deep-seated ideological problems with legal pluralism and thus tend to advise that state-centric control mechanisms promote good governance and rule of law better than allegedly limitless pluralism.[31] This shows that we still live in the age of positivism, which

---

[28] Ibid., 71–130; Menski, *Comparative Law in a Global Context*, 196–234.

[29] See Parashar and Dhanda, *Redefining Family Law in India*. Notably, the very first sentence of the editors' introduction decrees conceptual blindness and tolerates no dissent: "Family law is synonymous with religious personal laws in India." Ibid., ix.

[30] This was illustrated in the Workshop on Informal Marriages and Dutch Law, held in Amsterdam on March 13, 2003, under the guidance of Dr. Leila Jordens-Cotran. Although the proceedings from that Workshop are unpublished, unfortunately, they include papers explaining why Dutch immigration officials had wrongly assumed for some time, simply on the basis of marriage documents, that many marriages between foreign Muslim men and Dutch women were legally valid.

[31] See, e.g., McClain, "Marriage Pluralism in the United States" (in this volume); Katherine Shaw Spaht, "Covenant Marriage Laws: A Model for Compromise" (in this volume); Wilson, "The Perils of Privatized Marriage" (in this volume).

proudly claims to have developed out of earlier stages of legal theorizing that were focused on more or less religio-centric natural law. Such misguided evolutionary thinking among lawyers and other observers is simply not maintainable in the long run. Revision is reflected in the currently growing attention at last given to legal pluralism as an ever-present phenomenon,[32] expressed in various ways as the ubiquitous nature of law[33] (which is a simple word with many meanings).

This trend toward more open-minded acceptance of the law as internally plural, and thus always as its own other, was reflected in my earlier studies of legal pluralism as a global phenomenon.[34] My analysis has recently further considered the current expectation that international human rights norms are new forms of natural law that need to be built into global pictures of law. The result of such plurality-conscious theorizing has been the emergence of new, complex models of envisaging law and pluralism.[35] The messy realities of legal pluralism do not comport neatly with popular obsessions with legal certainty and will therefore irritate "black letter lawyers."

Whereas strong Indian legal pluralism, in the sense that John Griffiths uses the term,[36] is partly a postmodern phenomenon, recent research has uncovered important lessons about the ubiquity of legal pluralism in time and space. It appears that Indic laws always operated beyond the boundaries of tradition and modernity. For example, evidence of acute consciousness of patterns of legal pluralism existed already in Vedic times (circa 1500 to 1000 BCE). This consciousness was characterized by heavily contested and competing truth claims in relation to law (in the wider sense of cosmic Truth – that is, natural law rather than state law) along patterns quite akin to today's struggles over the "war on terror."[37] State law was certainly not absent, but it also was clearly not dominant. Emerging concepts of the state (particularly of rulers as sponsors of certain elaborate ritual performances) remained subservient to higher forms of order, particularly macrocosmic Order. But in this heavily contested

---

[32] Brian Z. Tamanaha, "Understanding Legal Pluralism: Past to Present, Local to Global," *Sydney Law Review* 30 (September 2008): 375–411.

[33] Emmanuel Melissaris, *Ubiquitous Law. Legal Theory and the Space for Legal Pluralism* (Farnham and Burlington, VT: Ashgate, 2009).

[34] Menski, *Comparative Law in a Global Context*, 82–192.

[35] *See* Masaji Chiba, ed., *Asian Indigenous Law in Interaction with Received Law* (London and New York: KPI, 1986), excerpted in Menski, *Comparative Law in a Global Context*, 119–128; Werner Menski, "Flying Kites: Banglar Ghuri – Iccher Ghuri. Managing Family Laws and Gender Issues in Bangladesh," *Stamford Journal of Law* 2:1 (2009): 23; Werner Menski, "From the Amoeba to the Octopus. Socio-Legal Analysis of Plural Perspectives," Osaka Symposium Paper, 2009 (to be published in Japanese) (forthcoming).

[36] See John Griffiths, "What is Legal Pluralism?" *Journal of Legal Pluralism and Unofficial Law* 24 (1986): 1–56.

[37] Werner Menski, "Sanskrit Law: Excavating Vedic Legal Pluralism," paper for the 14th International Sanskrit Conference in Kyoto, September 2009 (to be published in the Conference Proceedings) (forthcoming).

field, "religion" was also clearly not the sole or unquestionably dominant force. There were many religions and competing philosophies and visions, including atheism and agnosticism. Everything was contested among the people that lived at that time, just as we see today.

Because fine conceptual distinctions of invisible religious truth and macrocosmic Order (*rita*) are recorded as coexisting with secular visible truth (*satya*) in such early textual sources, I can now firmly deduce that struggles over law and religion are actually much older than previously imagined. However the later concept of *dharma* developed – both as a central Hindu law term and as an idea of microcosmic ordering – it is evident that Indian law today remains influenced by such early key concepts,[38] which we see in the Indian Constitution of 1950 and in many current laws.

The most recent legal developments in Indian family law, with which this chapter is mainly concerned, are also invisibly but deeply influenced by ancient cultural notions that link religion, society, law, and everything else into a giant web of normative elements that humans have at their disposal to arrange their day-to-day affairs. That this inevitably introduces "religion" into "secular" patterns of law making and management is a lesson that Americans should find relatively easy to understand and accept. Many South Asian scholars and others who are deeply influenced by the post-Enlightenment ideal of strict separation of law and religion sometimes find it difficult to grasp the basic meaning of "secularism" in Indian law and misunderstand it to be French-style separation of law and religion. This creates a huge obstacle for a plurality-conscious analysis of how today's Indian family law handles competing claims among more than a billion citizens.

In such a complex field as family law, aiming for state-centric legal regulation would never lead to realistic and just outcomes and would run diametrically counter to ancient Indic principles of self-controlled ordering. These include, among others, *dharma* – the expectation to do the right thing at the right time at any point of your life.[39] Some fifteen years ago, the self-appointed social reformer Madhu Kishwar rightly highlighted that modern Indian legislators, conscious of such powerful ancient legal history and concepts, did not completely abolish "tradition" but rather presented ancient customs and normative patterns in a new, statutory form.[40] Even the flavor of this old wine in new bottles irritates many modernity-focused

---

[38] There are ongoing debates about whether the term *dharma* has more Buddhist rather than Hindu antecedents. See Patrick Olivelle, "Hindu Law: The Formative Period, 400 B.C.E. – 400 C.E.," in *The Oxford International Encyclopedia of Legal History*, vol. 3, ed. Stanley N. Katz (New York: Oxford University Press, 2009), 151–155.

[39] For details see Menski, *Hindu Law*, 198–237.

[40] See Madhu Kishwar, "Codified Hindu Law: Myth and Reality," *Economic and Political Weekly* 29:33 (August 13, 1994): 2145–2161.

scholars who are still desperately arguing for the abolition of tradition and seeking to segregate law and culture. They constantly attempt to hide from public view what is actually going on in Indian family law in this impossible endeavor. Seeking to redefine the whole field on their own terms, they claim to search for justice,[41] but they fail to remember Derrida's famous message of legal dynamism and innate plurality – namely, that justice is always à venir.[42] In reality, such efforts are merely attempts to inject certain value judgments into ongoing global debates and to deliberately silence other voices. Such scholars disregard the voices of hundreds of millions of Indians who continue to live by what I call "slumdog law," a law aware that its people live in atrocious conditions, are desperately poor, and face rights deprivation every second of their lives.[43]

A legal system that knows most citizens struggle to feed themselves and their children can nevertheless endeavor to promise people fundamental rights that may then be claimed in situations of dire emergency. For most Indian legal scenarios, however, informal regulations and self-controlled ordering are much more effective remedies than formal litigation, resulting in what has now become known as "law-related outcomes."[44] These outcomes are not based on strict adherence to the letter of state law, which is often too contemptuous of the average citizen to be able to offer just and acceptable solutions. To analyze such multilayered phenomena, multiple lenses are required and even open-minded analysts must be prepared for surprises. If formal laws do not always mean what they seem to say, open-eyed observation is only a first step.[45] Many preconceived notions of what "law" is really about are challenged by evidence of strong and deep Indian forms of legal pluralism.

In such a hotly contested and ideologically poisoned field as family law, how does one analyze the significant boundary crossings and ongoing interactions between India's personal law systems and the country's general laws? This is the major challenge for the remainder of this chapter. The next section will first outline what the legal system appears to look like, and then following sections detail various examples of plurality-conscious interaction and purposeful boundary crossings.

---

[41] Parashar and Dhanda, *Redefining Family Law in India.*

[42] See Melissaris, *Ubiquitous Law*, 20, 93.

[43] Werner Menski, "Slumdog Law, Colonial Tummy Aches and the Redefinition of Family Law in India," *South Asia Research* 30:1 (February 2010): 67–80.

[44] This term surfaced in conversation with Professor Mohan Gopal, former Director of the Bangalore National Law School of India and Head of the National Judicial Academy in Bhopal.

[45] An important recent example is the Prohibition of Child Marriage Act of 2006, which makes child marriages in India voidable but not outright void. Additional reform proposals by the Indian Law Commission in 2008 seem to have been stalled by the realization that invalidating all child marriages would cause havoc among the very people the law seeks to protect. Such considerations did not arise from blind respect for any one religion, but owe to broader social concerns. The same goes for reform efforts to introduce compulsory registration of all Indian marriages.

III. HINDU FAMILY LAW WITHIN COMPOSITE INDIA

India inherited an extremely complex legal system characterized by a remarkable plurality of laws when the country gained independence in 1947. Even though Pakistan was carved out at the same time as a separate state for Muslims, India (as the major successor state of the colonial Empire) knew it would need to cater to an extremely diverse population, including many Muslims. In the short-term, this meant that the traditional personal law system would need to be retained. However, India employed a common tool of nation building – also a hallmark of modern legal reform in South Asian states – to tackle personal law reforms first, beginning with the respective majority personal law. Hindu law was thus subjected to vigorous reform efforts in India, whereas Pakistan was introducing legal reforms to Muslim family law. Both countries initially ignored the minority laws altogether.

The trend of modernizing and unifying Hindu family law was first promoted by the British during the nineteenth century, and it was then carried forward by some sections of the Indian elite. These elites were instrumental in securing further legislative reforms, particularly the Hindu Women's Right to Property Act of 1937, which gave Hindu widows a "limited estate" in the share of the deceased husband to help ensure their dignified maintenance. Heated debates about various aspects of Hindu law reforms continued during the 1950s.[46] They were closely linked to tortuous ongoing discussions about the position and future of India's various personal laws.[47] The official Anglo-Hindu law at that time was mainly based on case law and precedent, whereas the major source of post-colonial Hindu law has been prominent legislative interventions.[48] Modern India clearly went much further than the colonial rulers in seeking to modernize and secularize Hindu law.[49]

Immediately after independence, vigorous debates about the future of Hindu law in India resulted in the preparation of what is often misleadingly called the "Hindu Code." This ambitious project of comprehensive codification, which also involved much proclaimed secularization and Westernization, was driven by a reform-focused

---

[46] They are well documented in J. D. M. Derrett, *Hindu Law Past and Present* (Calcutta: A. Mukherjee & Co., 1957). See also J. D. M. Derrett, *A Critique of Modern Hindu Law* (Bombay: N. M. Tripathi, 1970).

[47] See Tahir Mahmood, *Personal Laws in Crisis* (New Delhi: Metropolitan, 1986); Archana Parashar, *Women and Family Law Reform in India: Uniform Civil Code and Gender Equality* (New Delhi: Sage, 1992); Flavia Agnes, *Law and Gender Inequality: The Politics of Women's Rights in India* (New Delhi: Oxford University Press, 2000).

[48] For details, see Marc Galanter, *Law and Society in Modern India* (New Delhi: Oxford University Press, 1989).

[49] However, modernist reformers still did not attempt to abolish the traditional joint Hindu family altogether. This happened, formally, only in the southern Indian state of Kerala through the Kerala Joint Hindu Family System (Abolition) Act of 1975.

London-trained barrister, Dr. B. R. Ambedkar, who became a Buddhist to signal his disgust with Hindu caste discrimination. He was ultimately defeated, however, because his agendas were too radical. Instead, Indian lawmakers constructed an uneasy compromise between tradition and modernity: a typical pluralist assemblage in the form of four separate acts of Parliament regulating most aspects of modern Hindu family law.[50]

At first blush, especially to outside observers, the result appears modern, reform-focused, and uniform. However, this fragmented, state-made family law system often merely codified customary law.[51] On paper, polygamy was banned for Hindus,[52] but this reform has never been vigorously implemented. Polygamy among Hindus continues to exist and quite appropriately gives rise to rights for any affected women and children.[53] Numerous fault grounds for divorce were introduced in the Hindu Marriage Act.[54] However, the reformers not only retained the traditional law on Hindu marriage solemnization in Section 7 of the Hindu Marriage Act (discussed later in this chapter) but also allowed traditional Hindu customary patterns of divorce to continue.[55] This shows that India's lawmakers in the 1950s still knew the old Hindu law fairly well and were acutely aware that it would continue to apply even after the formal statutory reforms. This underscores that effective law reform clearly does not – and cannot – happen overnight or at the stroke of a pen – a fact that Indian legislators know well.

Today, most Hindu divorces do not have to go through formal proceedings in state courts, contradicting the widespread presumption that earlier supposedly religious Hindu law did not accept or even know divorces.[56] In socio-legal reality, divorce was always possible. Yet because it was thought to be a serious deviation from the ideal of everlasting sacramental marriage, it was downplayed and hidden. Although reformist euphoria ruled the roost for some time during the 1960 and 1970s,[57] and in

---

[50] These are the Hindu Marriage Act (1955), the Hindu Succession Act (1956), the Hindu Adoptions and Maintenance Act (1956), and the Hindu Minority and Guardianship Act (1956).

[51] Kishwar, "Codified Hindu Law."

[52] For details, see Menski, *Modern Indian Family Law*, ch. 3; Menski, *Hindu Law*, ch. 10.

[53] This means that if husbands wish to engage in polygamous arrangements, they now have to pay for the privilege, as the extremely brief but powerful Supreme Court verdict in *Sumitra Devi v. Bhikhan Choudhary*, AIR 1985 SC 765, establishes.

[54] Specifically in Section 13. For details, see Menski, *Modern Indian Family Law*, ch. 2; Menski, *Hindu Law*, ch. 11.

[55] Hindu Marriage Act § 29(2).

[56] Today, the picture "on the ground" remains extremely pluralistic, and Indian courts appear to give increasing recognition to customary divorces. Excellent fieldwork-based evidence on this, including reference to an instructive documentary film, is found in Livia Holden, *Hindu Divorce: A Legal Anthropology* (Aldershot and Burlington, VT: Ashgate, 2008).

[57] J. D. M. Derrett, *The Death of a Marriage Law* (New Delhi: Vikas, 1978), makes reference to earlier field studies about the impact of state-driven relaxations in divorce law for middle-class Hindu

1976 divorce by mutual consent was introduced, there have been no major statutory reforms to Hindu matrimonial law since then.[58]

Post-colonial Indian lawmakers were unable to enact fully codified, state-centric Hindu law reforms. Postmodern Indian lawmakers, including many far-sighted judges and a silently active class of bureaucrats, seem to have covertly cultivated a new "slumdog law."[59] Middle-class Indians detest such a term, but my students readily adopt it as an analytical tool to cut through myopic middle-class rhetoric. Cheap, simple, and efficient self-controlled ordering processes that utilize informal methods of settling disputes remain an important component of India's family law regime. Strong evidence is found in several significant facts and developments analyzed in this chapter: (1) Indian marriage laws largely do not require formal state registration to establish the legal validity of a marriage, but they rely on evidence of customary solemnization rituals; (2) Indian divorces do not always have to go through formal court proceedings, and Indian divorced wives, in such a potentially perilous and hostile climate, came to benefit from special protective measures in the mid-1980s onward; and (3) the overall picture is not one of total state control through official laws, but rather a pluralistic scenario in which the constant navigation of boundaries between state law and non-state law is a central systemic factor. Because Indian matrimonial law has been multi-tiered for a very long time, its analysis might indicate some significant perils and potential benefits of plurality-conscious navigation for other jurisdictions.

IV. THE TORTUOUS AGENDA OF LEGAL UNIFORMITY IN INDIAN LAW

Before turning to substantive family law, it is important to examine the more general issue of India's continued refusal to develop Western-style state-centric legislation in the form of the projected Uniform Civil Code. As discussed previously, the four acts on Hindu family law are not a comprehensive code and do not purport to abolish or completely supersede the old Hindu law. Rather, they serve as a tool for further sociocultural, religious, and legal negotiations. Beyond Hindu law, the gradually restructured plurality of family law regulation for India has maintained much space for the concurrent system of traditional personal laws. This worked well even for some small minorities – including the Parsis, who lobbied successfully

women, raising doubts about the usefulness of modern matrimonial reforms. See Rama Mehta, *Divorced Hindu Woman* (Delhi: Vikas, 1975).
[58] Indian judges, among others, have voiced the sentiment that legislative intervention has had deeply dangerous side effects, that divorce has become too easy, and that "we are not America."
[59] By "slumdog law" I mean to describe the actual ordering structures that are applied by and govern, apparently with official sanction, the numerous millions of people in India that live far below the poverty line.

during the mid-1980s for modernizing reforms to retain their ethnic identity.[60] Just
as Hindu law (the majority personal law system) was continuously subjected to
reforms, we also find separate Muslim, Christian, Parsi, and Jewish laws. The much-
overlooked optional secular family law, critically important as an exit route from
religious restrictions and as an alternative for foreigners, was also further reformed.[61]
Buddhists, Jainas, and Sikhs have also been governed by the modern codified Hindu
law since the 1950s, officially to reduce communal diversities. Because of the large
space granted to customary traditions within the codified Hindu law, however, the
inclusion of these communities has actually in practice increased the internal plurality within modern Hindu law regulation.

Although it retained the personal law system and granted much space for non-
state law, India also put the agenda of state-centric national unification of laws
into the Constitution. Article 44 of the Indian Constitution is an uncomfortable
compromise between traditional self-controlled ordering within a personal law
structure and reform-focused, state-centric legal regulation. The wording of Article
44, namely that "[t]he state shall endeavour to secure for the citizens a uniform
civil code throughout the territory of India," indicated a long-term program for
development of the nation, through a Directive Principle of State Policy rather
than a guaranteed and justiciable Fundamental Right. This article, however, has
remained an empty declaration despite constant rhetoric from scholars and many
judges about the supposed advantages of legal uniformity and the desirability of a
Uniform Civil Code.

The diverse Hindu foundations of modern Indian law, as well as the massive
demographic presence and considerable conceptual input of Muslim law, preclude
an easy path for formal, uniform legal development in accordance with Western
models. Modern Indian law thus remains and will remain a culture-specific Asian
legal system in its own right rather than an imperfect copy of some Western model.
Legal plurality in Indian law will never disappear because it makes sense to retain it
in a vast country that is conscious of its composite legal culture. From this perspective, too, pluralism is definitely an asset rather than a liability. Yet much agitated
scholarly writing remains in favor of legal uniformity.[62]

---

[60] The result is the Parsi Marriage and Divorce (Amendment) Act of 1988, which contains provisions
that are harmonized with the rules of the Hindu Marriage Act of 1955, as amended in 1976, and the
similarly amended Special Marriage Act of 1954.

[61] The main provisions of this are found in the Special Marriage Act (1954), which remains an optional
secular law for most spouses. Under this act, a marriage becomes legally valid when the official registration documents are signed. Significantly, this act is not used by many couples, and its provisions
and cumbersome procedures are now increasingly criticized as outdated.

[62] See Narmada Khodie, ed., *Readings in Uniform Civil Code* (Bombay: Thacker, 1975); Vasudha
Dhagamwar, *Towards the Uniform Civil Code* (Bombay: Tripathi, 1989); Madhu Deolekar, *India
Needs a Common Civil Code* (Mumbai: Vivek Vyaspeeth, 1995); Kiran Deshta, *Uniform Civil Code:*

India's concept of secularism also strengthens strategies to use law as a tool for creating a more cohesive composite nation. In modern Indian law, secularism does not have the same meaning as the Western concept of separation between law and religion or between church and state.[63] Rather, Indian law guarantees the state's equidistance from all religions (and is somewhat akin to U.S. law in that respect)[64] and clearly seeks to prevent India from ever declaring itself a majoritarian Hindu Republic. This notion of equidistance proved important when Indians, some years ago, elected a Hindu nationalist government of the Bharatiya Janata Party. More people then began to understand that calls for a Uniform Civil Code would actually mean advancement of Hinduization and vigorously maligned culture-specific *hindutva* tendencies.

The nuanced Indian concept of secularism arose from historical awareness of internal pluralities among and within religions and of their ancient coexistence in the sociopolitical and legal fields. Hence, the new leaders of independent India (initially even of Pakistan) used this concept to promise religious minorities that they would not be treated as second-class citizens. In India, "secularism" posits equidistance – that is, the state's equal respect for all religions – as a *Grundnorm* of the Indian Constitution; it protects "others" against undemocratic majoritarian excesses and annihilation. Many are still haunted by the lived experience and memory of the massive ethnic cleansing conducted on the basis of religion that followed the achievement of independence in August of 1947. History demonstrates that the multiethnic, multireligious nature of the Indian polity needs vigilant protection because allegedly nonviolent Indic people can and often do use violent means of self-preservation. Even today, we hear of communal riots and virtual pogroms against certain groups of people in parts of India: the destruction of the Babri Masjid mosque in Ayodhya in 1993; the 2002 riots in Gujarat that left a disproportionate number of Muslims dead; and more recent killings of Christians in Orissa, to name a few. Managing a plural nation remains a major challenge. Simply blaming either pluralism or religion for such problems is not a sensible

In Retrospect and Prospect (New Delhi: Deep & Deep, 1995); Dina Nath Raina, *Uniform Civil Code and Gender Justice* (New Delhi: Reliance, 1996); Madhukar S. Ratnaparkhi, *Uniform Civil Code: An Ignored Constitutional Imperative* (New Delhi: Atlantic, 1997); Virendra Kumar, "Uniform Civil Code Revisited: A Juridical Analysis of *John Vallamattom*," *Journal of the Indian Law Institute* 45:3–4 (July–December 2003): 315–334.

[63] See T. N. Madan, "Secularism in its Place," *Journal of Asian Studies* 46:4 (November 1987): 747–759; T. N. Madan, ed., *Religion in India* (Oxford: Oxford University Press, 2d ed. 1994); Robert D. Baird, ed., *Religion and Law in Independent India* (New Delhi: Manohar, 1993); Arun Shourie, *A Secular Agenda* (New Delhi: ASA, 1993).

[64] For U.S. law, see John Witte Jr. and Joel A. Nichols, *Religion and the American Constitutional Experiment* (Boulder, CO: Westview Press, 3d ed. 2011); see also John Witte Jr. and Joel A. Nichols, "The Frontiers of Marital Pluralism: An Afterword" (in this volume).

academic approach, and secular fundamentalism is not a useful guiding principle in such culture-conscious surroundings.

While awaiting the implementation of a Uniform Civil Code, modernists pushed for the gradual creation of a more secularized, modernized Hindu law regarding families. Currently, there is pressure to bring about certain further reforms as evidence of modern secularity, specifically requiring compulsory registration of all marriages and making divorces available on the basis of irretrievable breakdown. Such reformist approaches, initially pursued in a spirit of post-colonial euphoria, are today pressed with seemingly desperate and stubborn determination despite evidence that they would be bad for many "slumdog citizens." Such culture-blind prescriptions ignore the enormous tension between uniformity and diversity, failing to appreciate that any new legal regulation would influence the nature of the interaction between official laws and unofficial laws, between state law and the various forms of people's law. To understand this legal labyrinth from a plurality-conscious perspective, one must look well beyond official law reports and statutes. The lived differences between the converged personal laws are currently rather small, but politicized sloganeering continues to exaggerate them by employing simplistic models and concepts of law to gain adherents to an allegedly progressive cause.

This leads to a depressing picture, and it seems remarkable how easily scholars get away with such games. The most prominent examples cited are that Muslims in India may have up to four wives (and thus, of course, many children) and their men can pronounce instant *talaq*. Few writers admit that far too many Hindu families continue also to have large numbers of offspring and that Hindu men are not exactly restrained from metaphorically throwing their wives to the wolves. Hindu polygamists openly benefit from the persistent nonimplementation of laws that would send Hindu polygamous males to jail for up to seven years. (And, of course, it seems unfair that Muslim polygamists would not face such penalties.) Indian courts have thus continued to administer the consequences of Hindu polygamy rather than enforce its abolition.[65] In reality, because Hindu men have found it much easier over the years to procure divorces,[66] and because South Asian Muslim women can – and increasingly do – abandon and divorce their husbands,[67] there are no significant legal differences between codified Hindu law and uncodified Muslim law. Even the extremely outdated Christian divorce law of India was quietly harmonized two weeks after 9/11 in the Indian Divorce (Amendment) Act of 2001, which introduced ten different grounds for divorce virtually overnight. Scholars thus use purported

---

[65] Menski, *Modern Indian Family Law*, ch. 3.
[66] Derrett, *The Death of a Marriage Law.*
[67] Vatuk, "Divorce at the Wife's Initiative."

legal contrasts between personal laws as political footballs without taking account of the application of the law itself.

The secular framework of the Indian Constitution, in its disavowal of religiously colored legal discourse, creates additional areas of underexplanation.[68] The extensive reform of modern Hindu law during the 1950s, for example, was, in reality, partly designed to make it acceptable to all Indians. This hidden uniformizing agenda, later reinforced by the Hindu Marriage (Amendment) Act of 1964 and particularly the Marriage Laws (Amendment) Act of 1976, created further convergence with the formal provisions of the secular Special Marriage Act of 1954. This strategy of artificial uniformization soon turned out to be hostile to women and children in practice, however. Merely assuming gender equality within a patriarchal setting actually advantaged men, creating new legal problems for women and other disempowered individuals.[69] Finally, as indicated earlier, the modernist ideology of legal uniformization collapsed as soon as the Hindu nationalist party rose to prominence in the 1990s and more people realized that insisting on a Uniform Civil Code might mean imposing Hindu law on all Indians. Since then, the Indian debates over the unification of family law have died down and scholars now openly refuse to discuss this issue.[70]

The desired uniformization strategy was bound to fail for other reasons as well. One of these is directly relevant to the present analysis. Postmodern Indians somehow began to remember fragments from their ancient legal past and realized the impossibility of total legal uniformity within Hindu law itself, let alone between the various personal laws and their partly religious identity markers. Recent recourse to old Hindu concepts suggests that legal reformers have at least partly overcome modernist myopia and have become more aware that modern statutory law could never completely replace the historically rooted, multi-tiered regulation mechanisms. Ridding this region of ancient cultural practices and its rich range of customs by ignoring the socio-legal and religious aspects of such mechanisms would mean depriving India's own people of their legal identity. Perhaps Indian lawmakers have also wisely realized the unsustainability of promoting laws tending toward extreme individualism, especially for a massive "slumdog" population. Postmodern legal positivism in India therefore now often explicitly accounts for socioreligious norms and local values within legislative provisions and in case law, even from the highest courts. The policy of harmonization or convergence, as some scholars

---

[68] See S. P. Sathe and Sathya Narayan, eds., *Liberty, Equality and Justice: Struggles for a New Social Order* (Lucknow: EBC Publishing (P) Ltd., 2003).
[69] Derrett's 1978 study, *Death of a Marriage Law*, marks the beginning of the end of specialist scholars' belief in following English legal developments through modernizing reforms in Indian family law.
[70] E.g., Parashar and Dhanda, *Redefining Family Law in India*, ix.

prefer to call it,[71] of India's personal laws is not a meek surrender to outdated concepts of non-state authority. Rather, it is a deliberate, plurality-conscious and highly sophisticated postmodern construct; it is a new attempt to make sense of the never-ending challenges of legal pluralism. This policy is virtually impossible to appreciate through applying only a state-centric lens and a superficial positivist analysis. It is increasingly evident that only pluralistic methodologies and techniques can open our eyes to what is really going on in Indian family law and can help the country fine-tune a sustainable system of family law regulation that straddles state and non-state laws.

V. POSTMODERN INDIAN AND HINDU MARRIAGE LAW

Although major Indian legal scholars seem bored with the perennial prominence of Hindu law, it constantly brings new surprises. The existing Hindu marriage law in India is a good example of a recycling of old substantive rules in the shape of modern statutory regulation. For example, at first sight modern Hindu law on marriage solemnization, codified and written in English, looks Westernized. However, the statutory law almost completely preserves the diversity-conscious, situation-specific methods of traditional Hindu law. Section 7 of the Hindu Marriage Act of 1955 provides for the solemnization of Hindu marriages:

7. Ceremonies for a Hindu marriage. –

(1) A Hindu marriage may be solemnized in accordance with the customary rites and ceremonies of either party thereto.
(2) Where such rites and ceremonies include the *saptapadi* (that is, taking of seven steps by the bridegroom and the bride jointly before the sacred fire), the marriage becomes complete and binding when the seventh step is taken.

Subsection 1 confirms unambiguously that the legal validity of a Hindu marriage in India is not determined primarily through state-controlled procedures such as formal registration, but rather the relevant criterion remains performance of customary marriage rituals. The modern state has thus chosen to put the old shastric law into statutory form without even attempting to change the law's substance or challenge its universal validity (provided that both parties to the marriage are Hindus). In cases of doubt, such as interreligious marriages solemnized according to Hindu rituals, Hindu litigants must simply prove that they followed the respective customary norms of marriage solemnization of either family. Although the statute seems to

---

[71] See Narendra Subramanian, "Legal Change and Gender Inequality: Changes in Muslim Family Law in India," *Law & Social Inquiry* 33:3 (Summer 2008): 631–672.

presume that customs are fixed and certain, observation in practice shows that every marriage solemnization can be treated as a uniquely constructed sequence of rites and rituals whose totality is then simply perceived and treated as customary. This is legal pluralism "on the ground," with enormous and often highly meaningful variations in ritual patterns from case to case. Nobody, it seems, knows enough about these practices today to make final judgments about details.[72] Helpfully, the role of custom as a source of Hindu marriage law has been explicitly respected in general terms by statutory Hindu matrimonial law, as the statute defines custom as a usage "followed for a long time."[73] How this squares with the perception of every ritual as an ad hoc construct eludes precise analysis. The most relevant issue here, however, is that a legally valid custom under the newly codified Hindu law need no longer be a custom observed "since time immemorial" (as was required under the earlier strict and hostile Anglo-Hindu law), but merely "for a long time." This leads to some instructive cases addressing how long is "long."

Two lines of judicial decisions address this question. The first reflects a type of patriarchal interference with basic gender justice through positivism, and it condones deliberate misuse of state law, in most cases to let polygamous husbands "off the hook." *Bhaurao Shankar Lokhande v. State of Maharashtra*, in my view a misguided precedent, is still misused more than forty years later.[74] In that case, a Hindu husband successfully claimed that he was not validly married to his wife. The whole ceremony was held to be legally invalid merely because some element of the rituals was allegedly not "customary." Few people realize that this case was about the emergence of new Buddhist customs, and many authors and cases blindly rely on this gender-insensitive decision.

The second line of cases better accounts for customary plurality and displays sensitivity to sociocultural factors, gender justice, and situation specificity. In *Sumitra Devi v. Bhikhan Choudhary*, a polygamous Hindu husband tried to claim that he was not validly married.[75] The court held for the wife by applying a presumption of

---

[72]   On the problems of determining prohibited degrees of marriage among Hindus and the issue of custom, see Patricia Uberoi, "Saving Custom or Promoting Incest? Post-Independence Marriage Law and Dravidian Marriage Practices," in Parashar and Dhanda, *Redefining Family Law in India*, 54–85.

[73]   This, too, recycles tradition. Section 3 of the Hindu Marriage Act of 1955 provides:

3. Definitions

In this Act unless the context otherwise requires,
(a) the expressions "custom" and "usage" signify any rule which, having been continuously and uniformly observed for a long time, has obtained the force of law among Hindus in any local area, tribe, community, group or family: Provided that the rule is certain and not unreasonable or opposed to public policy; and provided further that in the case of a rule applicable only to a family it has not been discontinued by the family…

[74]   AIR 1965 SC 1564.
[75]   AIR 1985 SC 765.

Hindu marriage, in part because there had been a Hindu marriage ritual and there was also a child. Where local practice can be proved to exist over a few decades, especially among a large number of people, those new rituals are entitled to official legal recognition per this line of cases.[76]

Feminist, modernist observers argue that people should register their marriages, and then women would simply not have such problems. However, this state-centric remedy does not work in the "slumdog" conditions of India (a fact recognized by the statutory law).[77] The key issue thus is not whether judicial interpretations will privilege state law over social norms or religion, but whether there will be a fair hearing for both parties. More specifically, the question is whether judges will be gender-sensitive enough to resist the temptation to privilege men and their perspectives by relying exclusively on positive law. In a patriarchal setting, with very few senior women judges, there is no assurance that gender justice will be achieved. However, to abolish the existing law as a result of such problems seems an inadequate and rather excessive form of state intervention.

The potential conflict, moreover, is not actually between "law" and "religion," because the modern Hindu law on marriage solemnization measures the legal validity of a Hindu marriage by recourse to traditional sociocultural norms rather than "religion" as a superior entity. I highlight this to emphasize that a multi-tiered system of family law regulation does not necessarily pit formal state law against religious authority. In the Indian case, formal state law is normally primarily opposed to countervailing social norms, not to religion as such. So the critical criterion for achieving better gender justice is how flexibly decision makers interpret socio-legal facts, and not whether they give in to religious authority.

This argument can be further strengthened. A more apparently religious element does exist and has caused some havoc, but only because gender-insensitive, tradition-focused judges have allowed it to dominate. Subsection 7(2) of the Hindu Marriage Act, cited previously, states that "[w]here such rites and ceremonies include the *saptapadi* … the marriage becomes complete and binding when the seventh step is taken." The statute itself thus indicates that this ritual may not always be performed. The ritual of *saptapadī* – the taking of seven steps by bride and bridegroom together, which in its pristine ancient form is a wonderfully dramatized friendship

---

[76] See the neo-Buddhist case of *Baby v. Jayant*, AIR 1981 Bombay 283, which is instructive even though only a High Court case.

[77] Section 8(5) of the Hindu Marriage Act of 1955 provides that "[n]otwithstanding anything contained in this section, the validity of any Hindu marriage shall in no way be affected by the omission to make the entry." This means that the modern Indian state (like many states in Asia and Africa) accepts that the ultimate legal criterion of legal validity of a Hindu marriage remains a matter for society and depends on societal norms and facts rather than religious doctrine or bureaucratic criteria provided by state law, such as registration formalities.

ritual near the end of the ceremony as the spouses walk away from the fire – is not performed in most Hindu marriages. The assumption of the modern statutory wording clearly reflects that the Hindu ritual of *saptapadī* may be executed in many different ways – or not at all, depending on custom. The rest of the section indicates that its completion on the seventh step shall be the precise point at which the ritualized solemn contract of Hindu marriage becomes legally valid and binding.[78] This rule was copied directly from the ancient text of *Manusmriti* 8.227, where it had the obvious function of determining the precise point at which a Hindu marriage was legally binding.[79] The sacramental Hindu contract of marriage, according to the *Manusmriti* as well as Section 7(2) of the Hindu Marriage Act, may thus be completed on the seventh step of this particular ritual, but the *saptapadī* may be omitted entirely and the marriage will nonetheless still be treated as legally valid. However, some judges have failed to read the statute accurately and thus quite unfairly hand down adverse decisions to women.

Significantly, allegations by some Hindu husbands (or after their death by their male relatives) that a woman was not validly married mainly arise in disputes over property or maintenance or when husbands are faced with criminal prosecution for polygamy. In such cases, devious lawyers and tradition-fixated judges facilitate legal mischief of depriving women of property entitlements and status, regrettably even in the Supreme Court.[80] The battle over this issue continues in India today.

Plurality-conscious legal positivism, informed by culture-sensitive modern statutory Hindu law, has the capacity to take account of specific sociocultural factors to achieve situation-specific justice. This is done in Indian law by increasingly liberal use of powerful presumptions of marriage, as authoritatively stated in a leading handbook for practitioners:

> Where it is proved that a marriage was performed in fact, the court will presume that it is valid in law, and that the necessary ceremonies have been performed. ...

---

[78] Contrary to almost exclusive emphasis on the sacramental nature of Hindu marriage in almost every textbook, a Hindu marriage is both a solemn contract and a sacrament.

[79] The verse suggests that the performance of certain rituals and use of *mantras* are an indication that Hindu marriage rituals are being performed, but the decisive ritual element shall be the seventh step of the *saptapadī*. One can envisage distressing situations where it might be crucial to know when precisely during the lengthy marriage rituals the parties were actually husband and wife: What if the groom died during the extended rituals? Was the bride to be treated as a widow, or could she undergo a further marriage to another man?

[80] *Bhaurao Shankar Lokhande v. State of Maharashtra*, AIR 1965 SC 1564, asserted that every Hindu marriage must involve a *saptapadī* and invocation of the fire to be legally recognized. Injustice was also done in *Surjit Kaur v. Garja Singh*, AIR 1994 SC 135, where apparent male chauvinist contempt for a remarried Sikh woman – specifically, slandering her to grab her deceased husband's property – did not strike the judges as a blatant abuse of the modern law. For excellent examples of judicial alertness, see *M. Govindaraju v. K. Munisami Gounder*, AIR 1997 SC 10 and *P. Mariammal v. Padmanabhan*, AIR 2001 Madras 350.

There is an extremely strong presumption in favour of the validity of a marriage and the legitimacy of its offspring, if from the time of the alleged marriage, the parties are recognised by all persons concerned as man and wife and are so described in important documents and on important occasions. The like presumption applies to the question whether the formal requisites of a valid marriage ceremony were satisfied.[81]

This legal position reinforces another important observation about multi-tiered Hindu matrimonial litigation. Modern Hindu law, like the old system, relies ultimately on judicial alertness – the skill of judges in dispute processing (described as "extracting the thorn" [*vyavahāra*]). The primary function of India's modern judges continues to involve the removal of particular social hurts, including gender injustices, and not simply the slavish application of statutory law. Application of the *dharmic Grundnorm* on a case-by-case, situation-specific basis remains pertinent in Hindu law today. Reading modern Hindu family law through the pluri-focal lenses of the old law thus offers important lessons for global comparative lawyers and serves the ultimate aim of justice. Regrettably, most modernist observers cannot perceive Hindu law in this way because they too quickly presume that anything "Hindu" is necessarily (and unhelpfully) "religious."

In India today, then, even in the absence of formal registration documents, a married woman's legal status is protected by law if she can show through other evidence that she was in fact married. Indian state law has carefully crafted mechanisms to account for such claims and clearly remains conscious of "living law." Given the public nature of Hindu marriage rituals, there will likely always be some witness to a marriage ritual who could speak in support of an individual faced with denial of her marriage. Applying presumptions of marriage offers a socially meaningful and effective remedy.[82] Significantly, some recent Indian reports suggest that unmarried cohabitation should now be recognized as equivalent to marriage. This modernist turn seeks to rename unregistered marriage as "unmarried cohabitation." However, that renaming effort, seeking to copy Western models and apparently anticipating eventual recognition of same-sex relationships in Indian law, does significant cultural violence to many millions of Indians by treating traditional cultural patterns and legal practices with typical modernist contempt by failing to accord them the definition of marriage.

Modern Hindu and Indian law itself, however, quietly admits that there are limits to state-centric positivism, and it does not fuss about strictly preserving and following, let alone obeying, religious tradition. The question arises whether to interpret this

---

[81] Satyajeet A. Desai, ed., *Mulla's Principles of Hindu Law* (New Delhi: Butterworths, 2004), 770–771.

[82] Presumptions of marriage are now also applied in some cases among Asians in Britain. See *Chief Adjudication Officer v. Kirpal Kaur Bath*, [2000] 1 Family Law Reports 8 [CA].

as giving in to *hindutva*, that is, a blanket recognition of Hindu tradition as evidence of continued self-controlled ordering or instead more as a consequence of resource limitations in "slumdog territory." Probably all these factors (and others) play some role. The continuing legal recognition of unregistered marriages in Indian law is not an oversight or a slippage, however; it is a systemic necessity. Although modern Indian state law could dream of developing comprehensive socio-legal control, reliable records of how several hundred millions of people marry in their homes will never be produced.[83] India's post-colonial positivists employed the ancient model of customary self-regulated order as a useful ingredient for reconstructing modern Hindu law. The real challenge today is to navigate gender-sensitivity and justice across the boundaries of state law and non-state law when contested cases come up before courts. Another challenge, and probably a more difficult one, is to persuade scholars that this multi-tiered system can be trusted to deliver justice to the people who need it most – women and children.[84]

Legal scholars today tend to argue that if individuals have a legal problem, they should turn to state law for help. They should not access traditional sources and certainly should not use religious authorities. However, evidence from Britain's eighty-five Sharia Councils and Muslim Arbitration Tribunals confirms that such centralist claims overlook social reality and do not match with what is happening around the world. The Indian evidence clearly shows that most people do not turn straight to lawyers or courts; they first negotiate within their respective sociocultural spheres. Even if warring parties eventually turn to modern Hindu law mechanisms, the official law itself refers Hindus swiftly back to custom and lower-level processes for dispute settlement and ascertainment of what is appropriate. Superior Indian courts are far too busy, and seriously plagued by arrears, to become involved in airing "dirty laundry" in public, especially in divorce law.[85] The ancient Sanskrit term of *vyavahāra*, inadequately and too narrowly translated for centuries as "court proceedings," in fact comprises all these various forms of dispute settlement, both

---

[83] Formal marriage registration remains an option for the elite and for those who require official documentation (e.g., to facilitate travel abroad). It is important to be aware that registered Hindu marriages are not automatically treated as legally valid in India. Indian law still requires proof that the requisite customary rituals were followed, a fact that causes much surprise in European embassies and courtrooms. See *Joyita Saha v. Rajesh Kumar Pandey*, AIR 2000 Calcutta 109, and the interesting case studies of Perveez Mody, "Love and the Law: Love-Marriage in Delhi," *Modern Asian Studies* 36:1 (February 2002): 223–256.

[84] See McClain, "Marriage Pluralism in the United States" (in this volume) and Wilson, "The Perils of Privatized Marriage" (in this volume).

[85] Disgust over such warmongering is elaborately expressed in *V. Bhagat v. D. Bhagat*, AIR 1994 SC 710. This decision modified the Indian judicial approach to irretrievable breakdown of Hindu marriages as a ground for divorce, allowing it in exceptional circumstances, but without opening the floodgates because the case is not taken as a precedent. Significantly, the husband was a senior lawyer.

formal and informal, and is in itself a multi-tiered entity.[86] It is striking that such
realizations are only evident to us now, in the postmodern age of reinventing the
wheels of Indian justice.

VI. POST-DIVORCE MAINTENANCE LAWS, THE INDIAN
CONSTITUTION, AND HINDU LEGAL CONCEPTS

Although postmodern Indian state law happily allows self-ordering in matrimonial
matters, it has purposefully intervened to protect basic social welfare frameworks
that continue to rely on traditional family structures for delivery. Rather misleadingly, this has been portrayed in most writing as a battle between state law and
religion, and specifically between the secular Indian state and Islamic authorities
(as epitomized in the world-famous *Shah Bano* affair and its aftermath). But this
complex saga, too, is actually a contest between state-centric legal regulation and
sociocultural delegation of important aspects of India's matrimonial law rather than
simply a battle over "law" and "religion." Middle-class analysts conveniently forget
that the Indian state actually seeks to avoid recourse to its formal support mechanisms as a critically important aspect of its "slumdog law" strategy, particularly when
that would implicate state financial resources.[87] It is thus important to review how
informal support mechanisms in Indian matrimonial law have evolved in the recent
past and how they continue to contribute a vital element to India's multi-tiered marriage regulation by working to subjugate so-called religious dogma to the sophisticated social welfare agenda of the Indian state.

India's radically activist post-divorce maintenance law apparently seeks to protect
"pre-existing rights" of divorced or widowed women.[88] As in earlier traditional patriarchal contexts, married women are entitled to receive support from their husbands
during marriage, and they remain entitled to maintenance after the marriage ends,
whether by death or otherwise. As indicated earlier, this neatly matches the redefinition of "wife" under Indian law after 1973, which explicitly includes "divorced
wife" and presumes the inclusion of widows.[89] In brief: Postmodern Indian state law
is clearly not afraid to confront, tackle, and co-opt other forms of law, including religious law, to construct a revised, gender-sensitive legal framework that protects and

---

[86] See Werner Menski, "On Vyavahāra," *Indologica Taurinensia* 33 (Turin: CESMEO, 2007), 123–147
     (proceedings of the "Law and Society" Section of the 13th World Sanskrit Conference in Edinburgh,
     July 10th–14th, 2006).
[87] See Menski, *Modern Indian Family Law.*
[88] This concept is found hidden in fierce litigation during the 1970s over the succession rights of Hindu
     widows under Section 14 of the Hindu Succession Act of 1956. See *V. Tulasamma v. V. Sesha Reddi,*
     AIR 1977 SC 1944, and *Bai Vajia v. Thakobhai Chelabhai*, AIR 1979 SC 993.
[89] Code of Criminal Procedure § 125 (1973).

helps impoverished individuals, especially women, to "keep body and soul together" (as a famous judicial phrase goes).[90]

This remains an under-analyzed phenomenon in legal circles, even though I have written about it in some detail.[91] Significant Indian legal developments can be closely linked to 9/11, and Indian legal developments today are significantly influenced by the presence of a large Muslim minority that seeks to assert "religion" as an alternative legal authority. My analysis of politically sensitive issues along these lines has resulted in blacklisting by several Indian legal publishers, for it seemingly upsets the presuppositions of many scholars and lawyers about gender and law, law and religion, and especially about the political football of legal uniformity in India. I have nonetheless continued such writing and analysis because it comports with what actually goes on in Indian law today, even if it is not politically popular because it addresses the reality of "slumdog law."

As a legal realist who conducts his own fieldwork, I observe that the Indian state today does not shy away from employing sociocultural and religious concepts to navigate and redefine, where necessary, the boundaries of state law and non-state law. Because such skillful navigation takes place on several levels at the same time, and because much other literature wrongly claims that the Indian state has surrendered power to religious dogma, a few extra words are needed here.

In essence, the Indian state employs two methods (often conceptually contradictory) to improve the financial position of potentially vulnerable individuals. First, since colonial times there have been efforts to strengthen the legal rights of women regarding property entitlements. These have given rise to some notable but piecemeal reforms. The Hindu Succession Act of 1956 went much beyond the earlier Hindu Women's Right to Property Act of 1937 and its provision of a "limited estate" to Hindu widows. It secured, on paper at least, greater rights for Hindu women as

---

[90] *Bai Tahira v. Ali Hussain Fissalli Chothia*, AIR 1979 SC 362 (Mr. Justice V. R. Krishna Iyer (as he then was). *Bai Tahira* was an important case before the more famous *Shah Bano* case, *Mohd. Ahmed Khan v. Shah Bano Begum*, AIR 1985 SC 945.

[91] See Werner Menski, "Asking for the Moon: Legal Uniformity in India from a Kerala Perspective," *Kerala Law Times* 2006(2), Journal Section: 52–78; Werner Menski, "Double Benefits and Muslim Women's Postnuptial Rights," *Kerala Law Times* 2007(2), Journal Section: 21–34; Werner Menski, "Literate Kerala, Bribes and a New Case of *Mata*: On the Limits of Judicial Patience and Legal Realism," *Kerala Law Times* 2008(4), Journal Section: 21–31; Werner Menski, "The Uniform Civil Code Debate in Indian Law: New Developments and Changing Agenda," *German Law Journal* 9:3 (March 2008), available at http://www.germanlawjournal.com; Werner Menski, "Indian Secular Pluralism and its Relevance for Europe," in *Legal Practice and Cultural Diversity*, eds. Ralph Grillo et al. (Aldershot: Ashgate, 2009), 31–48; Werner Menski, "Law, State and Culture: How Countries Accommodate Religious, Cultural and Ethnic Diversity: The British and Indian Experiences," in *Cultural Diversity and the Law: State Responses From Around the World*, eds. Marie-Claire Foblets, Jean-François Gaudreault-DesBiens, and Alison Dundes Renteln (Brussels: Bruylant, 2010), 403–446.

absolute owners of property that earlier used to be joint family property. Section 14
of the 1956 act immediately made such Hindu widows the absolute owners of any
share they previously held as a "limited estate," leading to thousands of cases filed
by enraged males, including many Sikhs.[92] The transition from joint family ownership to individual property rights was, however, never fully completed. Postmodern
Indian law has gradually begun to rediscover the role and value of the family, particularly the joint family, as a most basic element of social welfare.

At the same time, Indian law has tenaciously pursued modernist tendencies and
seeks to strengthen women's property rights at the individual level. Most evidently
for Hindus, this was finally achieved by amending the Hindu Succession Act in
2005 to grant equal birthrights in joint family property to Hindu sons and daughters
throughout India. Such reform had gradually been implemented earlier in several
southern states, which often – although not always – tend to be a little more enlight-
ened when it comes to gender sensitivity. Concurrently, however, and to the cha-
grin of modernists and feminists, Indian law has also continued to make vulnerable
individuals dependent on various welfare duties toward them delivered by those
(mostly male) individuals who hold the purse strings and control property rights.
This means not only that all parents have to pay for their children's upbringing and
welfare, but also that children have a legal duty to maintain their parents, when
necessary, in accordance with the Maintenance and Welfare of Parents and Senior
Citizens Act of 2007.

Further, in a move that upset some feminists, either Hindu husbands or wives
may officially have to pay maintenance to their indigent spouse under Sections 24
and 25 of the Hindu Marriage Act of 1955. Whereas a Hindu husband who seeks to
live off his wife in this way is publicly ridiculed in several reported cases, women
who go to court claiming maintenance can today increasingly count on the state's
support for such gendered claims. The results have been truly amazing. Recent
legal changes are now beginning to create new gender imbalances. A highly significant movement in the navigation of India's multi-tiered maintenance laws occurred
two weeks after 9/11 when the Code of Criminal Procedure (Amendment) Act of
2001 (Act No. 50 of 2001) removed the maximum allowable monthly maintenance
payment (500 Rupees) that had been in place under Section 125 of the Criminal
Procedure Code of 1973. The new law now permits all Indian wives (and ex-wives,
by definition) to claim appropriate post-divorce maintenance. The principle is by
now firmly entrenched in case law.

However, some recent cases suggest risks of new transgressions of gender balance
when women attempt to misuse such rightly protective provisions.[93] The relative

92 See *Partap Singh v. Union of India*, AIR 1985 SC 1695.
93 See Menski, "Double Benefits and Muslim Women's Postnuptial Rights" and Menski, "Literate
    Kerala, Bribes and a New Case of *Mata*." Both articles concern cases in which divorced Muslim

scholarly silence about such emerging imbalances evinces either ignorance of case law developments at the High Court level (a familiar problem for Indian legal scholarship) or disgust that many Indian women ask for handouts from men rather than making claims in their own right. Either way, gender relations and marital expectations rather than matters of religious authority still occupy the center stage of Indian marriage dramas.

Silence about such significant recent legal developments also hides the fact that under current Indian law women can abuse the system in the precise manner that a leading Muslim scholar, Tahir Mahmood, warned of in 1986.[94] The strategy is simple. Marry a prosperous man, then divorce him or bring about a divorce (it does not really matter how), and then proceed to demand the considerable legal entitlements to post-divorce maintenance that Indian state law quietly introduced two weeks after 9/11. Such developments illustrate the concurrent contradictory moves of strengthening individual property rights for women, particularly through succession laws, on the one hand and reconnecting women to male authority through maintenance arrangements on the other. It is possible that this bifurcated, multi-tiered approach is actually designed to cater to elite women through one strategy while providing for India's millions of "slumdog women" through the other route. Nobody talks about this; legal developments just seem to happen. Here again, sophisticated official policies disclose lawmakers' plurality consciousness and acute awareness about an enormously different range of expectations among Indians when it comes to social welfare mechanisms.

Ultimately, the underlying agenda can be linked to protection of the constitutionally guaranteed right to life under Article 21 of the Indian Constitution as well as several other constitutional provisions. India's method of implementing such guarantees is to hold social actors accountable and restrain religious authority, where necessary, to ensure the survival of vulnerable individuals. This is, in my analysis, a solution based primarily on the ancient Indian concept of limited state regulation of the private sphere. The development of India's radical post-divorce maintenance law thus confirms that Hindu law has remained a much more important ingredient of Indian constitutional law than modernist writers would wish to know. The realities of such "soft legal positivism" in Indian family law influence the entire legal system as a whole and thus offer a blueprint for more sophisticated and culture-specific legal development in this internally pluralistic jurisdiction.

The focus of scholarly agitation, however, has distractingly been on Muslim law. Such agitation depicts a gender war between the supposedly secular post-colonial

---

women were able to rely on pro-women approaches. Another way to phrase this analysis, however, is that men have been unsuccessful in their attempts to avoid responsibilities.

[94] Tahir Mahmood, *Personal Laws in Crisis* (New Delhi: Metropolitan, 1986), 127–130.

Indian state and the medieval-rooted Muslim authorities who seek to deny Muslim wives basic entitlements from an ex-husband after divorce. Verse 2.241 of the Quran itself, typically vague, merely suggests that a divorcing husband should be kind to the woman he divorces. Early Islamic scholar-jurists interpreted this verse to impose responsibility on the husband for maintenance of an ex-wife until it was clear that any child she might bear was the child of the ex-husband. Then she could, and should, move on. This means that a Muslim woman who has just given birth cannot even rely on the traditional *iddat* rule for one day;[95] she is instantly without support, even though the father has an obligation to maintain the child. There is strong evidence that Muslim men everywhere manipulate such rules to their advantage, and it is clear that Muslim jurists agreed over time to limit the *iddat* payments to roughly three months. This is also unjust.

Under Indian law, however, a guiding principle has been established since 1979 that maintenance arrangements must be sufficient to "keep the woman's body and soul together."[96] In the infamous *Shah Bano* case of 1985, this development was dramatically challenged by a senior Muslim lawyer through reliance on Islamic religious authority.[97] Terminating his marriage to Shah Bano after some forty years, he had offered her some small amounts of payment that technically complied with Muslim law but violated the emerging principles of Indian general law. On appeal before the Supreme Court, Shah Bano won a crucial victory and secured maintenance for life. Five Hindu judges interpreted the relevant Quranic verses and held that there was no conflict between the Quran and India's secular Criminal Procedure Code of 1973 (which overrode the religious personal law in any event). Because the Indian Supreme Court further needled Muslims by suggesting that India should introduce a Uniform Civil Code, widespread public unrest followed almost instantly.

The rest is much-misunderstood recent legal history. The Indian government quickly promulgated an act that seemed to take away the right of divorced Muslim wives to post-divorce maintenance beyond the three-month *iddat* period.[98] However, despite the assertions of irate scholars and many others, the Indian government did not let Muslim women down. It cleverly hid within the 1986 act a wording that became, in due course, a silver bullet for all Indian ex-wives. Section 3(1)(a) states that a divorced Muslim wife shall be entitled to "a reasonable and fair provision and

---

[95] The *iddat* period is basically a woman's menstrual cycle of three months, or about ninety days.

[96] *Bai Tahira v. Ali Hussain Fissalli Chothia*, AIR 1979 SC 362.

[97] *Mohd. Ahmed Khan v. Shah Bano Begum*, AIR 1985 SC 945. See also Bix, "Pluralism and Decentralization" (in this volume) and Nichols, "Reconsidering the Boundaries" (in this volume).

[98] The Muslim Women (Protection of Rights on Divorce) Act (1986) actually does what its name suggests, however: It protects the rights of divorced Muslim wives. This was authoritatively confirmed by the Indian Supreme Court in *Danial Latifi v. Union of India*, 2001 (7) SCC 740.

maintenance to be made and paid to her within the *iddat* period by her former husband." Since 1988, this provision has been authoritatively interpreted to mean that divorced Muslim wives are entitled to two types of support: maintenance during the *iddat* period and reasonable provision for her life after that. Both types of support must be made during the *iddat* period, so that a wife who finds herself virtually on the pavement in "slumdog land" has instant access to the courts. The Supreme Court, in *Danial Latifi*, calmly confirmed that position, albeit after fifteen years of studied silence – and no riots ensued at that particularly well-chosen moment, two weeks after 9/11.

Worldwide scholarship, however, continues to misguidedly assert that Indian law gave in to religious fundamentalism from 1986 onward. Nothing could be further from the truth. India's multi-tiered post-marriage law has clearly subjugated allegedly religious doctrine, and it works assiduously for better gender justice by remembering and actively co-opting religious and social normative orders. Navigation of the boundaries of general laws and personal laws has been a remarkable success. Now the challenge is to protect such achievements and to avoid turning gendered rebalancing into gender war.

VII. CONCLUSION

The conceptually mature nature of postmodern Indian family law as a harmonized personal law system is beginning to become more apparent today. There is solid evidence that the Indian state has managed to regulate the majoritarian Hindu family law in a uniquely hybrid manner, navigating the boundaries of past and present, tradition and modernity, state law and non-state laws. Additionally, by overriding traditional and "religious" dogma when necessary, postmodern Indian family law has created an increasingly strong social welfare net through combining old principles of socioeconomic responsibility with newly worded and socialism-inspired constitutional principles.[99] Indian state law's strategically wise and financially prudent reliance on traditional self-control mechanisms within society illustrates the extent of navigation between the multiple tiers of general law and personal laws. It also makes sophisticated use of internal tiers of pluralism within the various personal laws.

This analysis confirms that today's modern-looking Indian family law system is not just "modern," but consciously postmodern. It is definitely no longer built on a primary assumption that total legal control of society can be exercised by state-made laws. New methods of "soft legal centralism" or "soft positivism" illustrate that India's state law has again learned to delegate much legal authority to society, but not – I must reiterate here – to religious authority. Linking concepts

---

[99] See Menski, *Modern Indian Family Law.*

like *hindutva* (Hinduness) with theocracy is merely ideological scaremongering. Crucially, the "soft positivism" of Indian law today is able to trust the social sphere, while co-opting it ever more closely. After all, both have been sharing the same social space and awareness of ancient legal tradition and are deeply sensitized to each other's presence. The mutually beneficial collaboration between old and new in Indian matrimonial laws is clearly a plurality-conscious reconstruction, a multi-tiered arrangement that works with increasing efficiency for more than a billion people. It is protected by an umbrella of powerful constitutional guarantees, some of which have acquired increasingly direct relevance. The inevitable result of this strategic alliance is that state law thereby delegates a considerable amount of legal authority to the social sphere and to non-state laws. This is, at least for me, not only a good and sustainable form of managing positive law, but it also evidences the living reality of legal pluralism as a superior technique in today's multi-tiered world for handling the immense, never-ending challenges in the search for justice.

My pluralistic analysis also supports the argument that the so-called religious personal laws of Asian and African countries today are themselves multilevel mechanisms of governance that are crucial to the maintenance of appropriate standards. They are largely secular, not just "religious," and they not only show remarkable resilience but are also essential for good governance and maintenance of the nation's identity. These "traditional" laws and their sociocultural norms are now clawing back territory that seemed lost earlier. Meanwhile, to many skeptical observers, they seem to have infiltrated, undermined, and subverted modern state laws in Asia and Africa, causing consternation and surprise among modernists and positivists. However, these "traditional" forces are not coming back to rule absolutely; they never did so in the first place. Rather, they are actually making their customary contributions as support mechanisms for governance within postmodern systems that we can observe and study as intrinsically multi-tiered and internally pluralistic.

In India, state-centric positivism of the colonial and early post-colonial type has clearly lost credibility and stands on increasingly questionable moral authority. Similarly, insistence on simple universal "rule of law" arguments or on globally uniform standards of human rights sounds increasingly absurd for a legal system that fails to provide direct welfare remedies for hundreds of millions of people living below the poverty line. Speaking and writing about "slumdog law" seems to irritate some of my colleagues as well as Indian lawyers, but how does one protect the rights of those people who have no means to assert them? India knows many ancient answers to such burning questions and has been experimenting with various methods. When a leading Indian scholar argues that human rights are not gifts of the West and highlights instead that the local, and not the global, "remains the crucial site for the enunciation, implementation, enjoyment, and exercise of human rights,"[100] we should realize that India still needs a sensible state – but it has to be a soft and yet strong central state, prepared to listen to other voices than its own.

This retraditionalization of post-colonial Indian laws and their transformation into postmodern laws is partly built on vague memories and sketchy knowledge of ancient legal concepts. It has gone hand in hand, however, with a conscious and gradually more vocal rejection of state-centric Western models and legal rules. This development was foretold in the 1970s when Derrett observed that prominent Supreme Court judges like V. R. Krishna Iyer were turning their backs on the "Anglophilic bias in Bharat's justice, equity and good conscience," arguing that "free India has to find its conscience in our rugged realities and no more in alien legal thought."[101]

Indira Gandhi must have thought about *dharma* rather than positive law when she engineered the Indian Emergency during the 1970s, partly to remind Indians that legal developments were not going in the right direction. Of course her self-serving actions overshadow much of the analysis. However, her most famous electoral slogan, *garībī hatāo* (banish poverty), anticipates concern for "slumdog law." It contains a manifesto of development that cannot be implemented unless the ancient concepts of inevitable interconnectedness and responsibility for "the other" are remembered and practiced. This restructuring, based on ancient Hindu concepts of *rājadharma*, includes the ruler's duty to maintain a sustainable balance in a deeply heterogeneous society. Recent Indian phenomena like public interest litigation show that recycling ancient concepts can promote badly needed forms of justice today.

Using such borrowings from the legal past, it has become possible for secular Indian constitutional law to develop a new culture-specific style of plurality-focused legal positivism that remains closely related to Hindu principles and elements of other personal laws, including Muslim law. Rather than constituting evidence of the state giving in to religious claims, as some modernists suggest, this sophisticated strategy of reconnection makes society and religion work for the overarching agenda of the state. Relying on ancient holistic concepts of duty, it seems that Indian public and private law can actually make somewhat larger claims on individual citizens than can Western-style laws. Politician-lawmakers of modern India, as well as many judges, are now appealing more openly to such duty consciousness, asking for greater moral integrity and even *dharma* sensitivity.

My observations suggest that Indian law has been moving toward further indigenization in two other major ways. First, through increased awareness of the continued relevance of traditional sociocultural concepts, Indian state law is acutely sensitive to legal pluralism and its manipulative and dynamizing potential. Second, there

---

[100] Upendra Baxi, *The Future of Human Rights* (New Delhi: Oxford University Press, 2002), vi and 89.
[101] J. Duncan M. Derrett, *Essays in Classical and Modern Hindu Law: Anglo-Hindu Legal Problems*, vol. 3 (Leiden: E. J. Brill, 1977), xxi.

is stronger realization that the application of foreign-style laws and Western legal concepts like individualism and privileged treatment of contract law and private property do not suit Indian socioeconomic and legal "slumdog" conditions; instead, readjustment by strengthening duty-based normative systems is necessary.

It is prudent (and realistic) to be constantly alert to the never-ending expectations of justice to face the existing enormous challenges. The lessons learned by post-colonial India in this respect point to serious dissatisfaction with positivistic modernity. There is nothing religious or fundamentalist about this, as the search for appropriateness and justice within the composite pluralistic structure of Indian legal systems is not a doctrinal matter of religious belief or social dictate. It is instead an endeavor to establish a somewhat idealistic approach in which religion and ethics, society and state (and really all aspects of life) are intimately interconnected.

Indian legal realism, today no longer in its embryonic stage, has managed to cultivate the customary plurality of traditional Hindu family law. It has not abandoned reformist agendas and human rights ideals by listening to such tradition. But neither is it blinded by intellectual dogmatisms. Rather, Indian law is desperately searching for sustainable practical justice and appropriateness, not for an ideal Hindu ideology as opponents of the personal law system constantly insinuate. Taking a holistic, plurality-conscious approach to the development of Indian personal laws, one can therefore see that the postmodern Indian state values substantive reforms more than ideology and rhetorical uniformity, especially when financial implications are involved.

This exceptionally sophisticated legal rearrangement, outwardly engineered by swift positivist lawmaking but inspired by deeply considered socio-legal and ethical concerns, may eventually be understood as a key example of postmodern legal reconstruction. It demonstrates a spirit of plurality consciousness, helps us to understand plurality of law as a global phenomenon, and suggests that all legal systems are culture-specific constructs that need to match their respective populations. Because the population of the United States, as an immigrant country, is composed of so many different elements and entities, it is hardly surprising that multi-tiered methods of regulating family law have been developing over time.[102] It is thus necessary, it seems to me, to acknowledge that exclusive state control of the wide domain of family law is not a realistic possibility in our postmodern times. That message, an ancient and almost forgotten truth, is evidently being remembered and now applied in Indian family law. It is a globally valid message that countries need to translate into suitable legal arrangements to fit the culture-specific needs of their respective populations. Trying to exile religion from this pluralistic scenario appears to be, in light of the Indian experience, an entirely futile endeavor.

---

[102] See Estin, "Unofficial Family Law" (in this volume) and Nichols, "Reconsidering the Boundaries" (in this volume).

10

The Perils of Privatized Marriage

Robin Fretwell Wilson

Governments around the world continue to struggle with how to accommodate religious minorities in an increasingly pluralistic society. In February 2008, the Archbishop of Canterbury called for a "plural jurisdiction" in which Muslims could choose to resolve family disputes in religious tribunals or in British courts.[1] A firestorm of controversy erupted in response. The Bishop of Rochester, Dr. Michael Nazir-Ali, protested: "It would be impossible to introduce a tradition like *Shari'a* into [the] corpus [of British law] without fundamentally affecting [the] integrity" of British law.[2] Prominent Islamic scholar Sheikh Ibrahim Mogra called these fears "Islamophobic," but observed, "[T]he vast majority of Muslims do not want to see a parallel ... system for Muslims in our society."[3]

Lawmakers responded to the Archbishop's comments. Nick Clegg, Britain's Liberal Democrat leader, stated: "Equality before the law is part of the glue that binds our society together. We cannot have a situation where there is one law for one person and different laws for another."[4] The Prime Minister proclaimed that "British law should apply in this country, based on British values."[5] On the heels of the Archbishop's comments, British authorities reported that 17,000 women were

---

[1]   Dr. Rowan Williams, "Civil and Religious Law in England: A Religious Perspective," Royal Courts of Justice, Foundation Lecture, Feb. 7, 2008, available at http://www.bishopthorpepalace.co.uk/1575.

[2]   Ruth Gledhill and Philip Webster, "Archbishop of Canterbury Argues for Islamic Law in Britain," *The Times*, Feb. 8, 2008, available at http://www.timesonline.co.uk/tol/comment/faith/article3328024. ece. Nazir-Ali served as Bishop of Rochester from 1994 to 2009. See Jonathan Wynne-Jones, "Bishop of Rochester Resigns to Become Defender of Persecuted Christians," *The Telegraph*, March 28, 2009, available at http://www.telegraph.co.uk/news/religion/5067202/Bishop-of-Rochester-resigns-to-become-defender-of-persecuted-Christians.html.

[3]   Gledhill and Webster, "Archbishop of Canterbury Argues for Islamic Law in Britain."

[4]   Ibid.

[5]   Jonathan Petre and Andrew Porter, "Uproar over Archbishop's Sharia Law Stance," *Telegraph.co.uk*, Feb. 9, 2008, available at http://www.telegraph.co.uk/news/uknews/1578019/Uproar-over-Archbishop's-sharia-law-stance.html (reporting comments made by Prime Minister Gordon Brown).

victims of honor-related violence annually, raising caution flags about how women, and children, will fare in such a system[6] – the subject of this chapter.

These concerns echo those of Ontario Premier Dalton McGuinty, who, two years before, faced the prospect of binding family law arbitrations for religious adherents. Like British officials, McGuinty declared that there should be "one law for all Ontarians."[7] This position prevailed. In 2006, the Ontario legislature amended its laws to permit religious arbitration in family law matters "only in accordance with Canadian law."[8]

Unlike Ontario, Great Britain "quietly sanctioned the powers for *Shari'a* judges to rule on cases ranging from divorce and financial disputes to those involving domestic violence."[9] Under Great Britain's Arbitration Act, the judgments of eighty-five *shari'a* courts may be civilly enforced through the British courts provided both parties agreed to binding arbitration.[10] These tribunals build on the experience of Jewish *beth din* courts, which have resolved civil cases for Orthodox Jews "for more than 100 years."[11]

Questions of pluralism also arise before courts, regardless of legislation.[12] For example, in March 2007 German Judge Christa Datz-Winter denied a fast-track divorce to a German citizen of Moroccan origin. The woman's husband beat her during their marriage and threatened to kill her.[13] Rejecting an expedited divorce, the judge cited the husband's "right" in the Quran "to castigate" his wife. She explained that these circumstances do "not fulfill the hardship criteria" for a speedy divorce in Germany.[14]

6   "A Question of Honour: Police Say 17,000 Women are Victims Every Year," *The Independent*, Feb. 10, 2008, available at http://www.independent.co.uk/news/uk/home-news/a-question-of-honour-police-say-17000-women-are-victims-every-year-780522.html.

7   "Sharia Law Move Quashed in Canada," Sept. 12, 2005, available at http://news.bbc.co.uk/2/hi/americas/4236762.stm.

8   See "No Religious Arbitration Law Passes," *Ontario Womens' Justice Network*, Feb. 24, 2006, available at http://www.owjn.org/owjn_new/index.php?option=com_content&view=article&id=159&Itemid=107.

9   Abul Taher, "Revealed: UK's First Official Sharia Courts," *The Times*, Sept. 14, 2008, available at http://www.timesonline.co.uk/tol/news/uk/crime/article4749183.ece.

10   Steve Doughty, "Britain has 85 Sharia Courts: The Astonishing Spread of the Islamic Justice Behind Closed Doors," *The Daily Mail*, June 29, 2009, available at http://www.dailymail.co.uk/news/article-1196165/Britain-85-sharia-courts-The-astonishing-spread-Islamic-justice-closed-doors.html.

11   Taher, "Revealed: UK's First Official Sharia Courts." See also Werner Menski, "Ancient and Modern Boundary Crossings Between Personal Laws and Civil Law in Composite India" (in this volume).

12   See, e.g., Ann Laquer Estin, "Unofficial Family Law" (in this volume).

13   Mark Landler, "Germany Cites Koran in Rejecting Divorce," *New York Times*, March 22, 2007, available at http://www.nytimes.com/2007/03/22/world/europe/22cnd-germany.html?ex=1332216000&en=3d013a9c6e9714d6&ei=5088&partner=rssnyt&emc=rss.

14   Veit Medick and Anna Reimann, "A German Judge Cites Koran in Divorce Case," *Der Spiegel*, March 21, 2007, available at http://www.spiegel.de/international/germany/0,1518,473017,00.html. The judge was subsequently removed from the case. See Mark Lander, "Judge Who Cited the Quran in

The ruling sparked a heated debate over the use of *shari'a* law and what, precisely, it allows. Feminists believed the ruling provided husbands with the right to beat their wives. Islamic scholars disputed whether the Quran authorizes spousal abuse. Legislators expressed outrage at the ruling, with one calling it a "sad example of how the conception of law from another legal and cultural environment is taken as the basis for our own notion," whereas another saw it as an "extreme violation of the rule of law."[15] As this debate has unfolded across the world stage, scholars have offered concrete proposals to accommodate religious minorities in the family law arena. As this volume illustrates, such proposals would confer considerable latitude in family matters, not only on adherents of Islam, but also on Christians, Jews, and members of other faiths.[16]

This chapter argues that such efforts are well intentioned but naïve. Although there might be religious understandings of family matters that are not at odds with ordinary civil law,[17] in places where religious arbitration is occurring there are striking breaks between civil law norms and the outcomes demanded by religious understandings. Indeed, as detailed in Section I, the lived experiences of women and children demonstrate poignantly that removing state protections from the family is fraught with peril. In some systems of religious deference, the cost of exiting a marriage, even an abusive one, for women is unconscionable – leading to a substantial risk of poverty and sometimes the loss of child custody after divorce.[18]

Wife-Beating Case Ousted," *Religion News Blog*, March 23, 2007, available at http://www.religion-newsblog.com/17796/judge-who-cited-the-quran-in-wife-beating-case-ousted.

[15] Medick and Reimann, "A German Judge Cites Koran in Divorce Case." Ironically, if the woman had been a Moroccan citizen living in Germany, the judge would have applied Moroccan law. See Marion Boyd, *Dispute Resolution in Family Law: Protecting Choice, Promoting Inclusion* (Ontario, Canada: Ministry of the Attorney General, 2004), 83, available at http://www.attorneygeneral.jus.gov. on.ca/english/about/pubs/boyd/fullreport.pdf. Under Moroccan Law, the wife would be entitled to a divorce due to recent reforms. See "The Moroccan Family Code (Moudawana) of February 5, 2004: An Unofficial English Translation of the Original Arabic Text," Global Rights Partners for Justice, Preamble, § 7.

[16] See, e.g., Joel A. Nichols, "Multi-Tiered Marriage: Reconsidering the Boundaries of Civil Law and Religion" (in this volume); Mohammad H. Fadel, "Political Liberalism, Islamic Family Law, and Family Law Pluralism" (in this volume); Michael J. Broyde, "New York's Regulation of Jewish Marriage: Covenant, Contract, or Statute?" (in this volume); Daniel Cere, "Canadian Conjugal Mosaic: From Multiculturalism to Multi-Conjugalism?" (in this volume); Stephen B. Presser, "Marriage and the Law: Time for a Divorce?" (in this volume).

[17] Compare Figure 10.1 (discussing Hanbali norms for child custody, which permit children to choose between parents) with Uniform Marriage and Divorce Act §402(2) (providing that the court shall determine custody in accordance with the best interest of the child, considering all relevant factors, including "the wishes of the child as to his custodian").

[18] This chapter focuses primarily on whether to give deference to religious understandings of divorce, custody, and the duty to treat children. Religious and societal norms also diverge on other family law questions, such as inheritance and how to treat polygamous marriages. See Robin Fretwell Wilson, "Privatizing Family Law in the Name of Religion," *William and Mary Bill of Rights Journal* 18 (2010): 925–952.

Society should not rob women and children of the state's protection in its attempt to support a diverse community.[19] The state plays an important role for traditionally vulnerable groups, who are themselves minorities within a minority.[20] Binding women who want to exit a marriage to a religious community's norms – whether by enforcing judgments arrived at in religious arbitration or ceding jurisdiction over family disputes to religious authorities[21] – will raise the costs of exiting, undermine a woman's ability to exit, and prevent her from privately regulating conduct toward herself and her children.

Governments should be especially wary of authorizing barriers to exit in cases of family violence. Although family violence is less prevalent in religious communities than elsewhere, it nonetheless occurs (Section II). More importantly, some religious leaders tolerate family violence, further frustrating a woman's ability to exit (Section III).

The foreseeable inequities to women and children in systems of religious deference cannot be justified on grounds that a woman voluntarily chooses to participate. Unlike prenuptial agreements, which must be in writing and are policed for duress and unconscionability, existing systems of religious deference offer no such safeguards to women (Sections IV and V). This chapter concludes that policymakers should give serious consideration to the risks before ceding authority for family disputes to religious bodies.

[19] This is true regarding the application of religious norms to family law matters, but need not counsel concerns for vulnerable persons against deference to religion in all other contexts. Rather, society should accommodate individual religious beliefs in a range of contexts, from the wearing of beards by Muslim prisoners to the respecting of holy days in employment. See, e.g., Kent Greenawalt, *Religion and the Constitution: Free Exercise and Fairness*, chs. 9, 10 and 13; Robin Fretwell Wilson, "Matters of Conscience: Lessons for Same-Sex Marriage from the Healthcare Context," in *Same-Sex Marriage and Religious Liberty: Emerging Conflicts*, eds. Douglas Laycock, Anthony R. Picarello Jr., and Robin Fretwell Wilson (Lanham, MD: Rowman & Littlefield Publishers, Inc., 2008), 77–102 (arguing for religious exemptions to same-sex marriage laws where no hardship results for same-sex couples).

[20] Ayelet Shachar, "The Puzzle of Interlocking Power Hierarchies: Sharing the Pieces of Jurisdictional Authority," *Harvard Civil Rights-Civil Liberties Law Review* 35 (Summer 2000): 385–426, 386 ("Well-meaning accommodation policies by the state … may unwittingly allow systematic maltreatment of individuals within the accommodated minority group – an impact, in certain cases, so severe that it nullifies these individuals' rights as citizens.").

[21] Religious arbitration and shared jurisdiction with religious authorities stand in sharp contrast to other experiments in multiple forms of marriage in the United States, like covenant marriage. Covenant marriage generally makes it more difficult both to get into the marriage and to exit the marriage – requiring extensive premarital counseling and imposing lengthened waiting periods before receiving a no-fault divorce. See Katherine Shaw Spaht, "Covenant Marriage Laws: A Model for Compromise" (in this volume). Whereas covenant marriage provides a vehicle for a certain vision of marriage that may be attractive to certain religious adherents, the understandings being applied have been democratically agreed on and then memorialized in state law. In this sense, the state's provision of this alternative track does not rob women and children of state's protection because covenant marriage has safeguards in the event of domestic violence. Ibid.

I. LIVED EXPERIENCES

Several contributors to this volume advocate greater accommodation of religious understandings of family relationships.[22] Although different in key respects,[23] each proposal shares a dangerous assumption: that protections for women and children can be preserved *without* significant state oversight in systems of religious autonomy for all kinds of faith groups, including Muslims, Christians, Jews, and other sects.[24] Experiences of women and children around the globe provide a cautionary tale about the costs of removing state oversight from family relationships.

This section summarizes empirical evidence from three systems of religious deference operating today. In the first system, the state cedes control of an entire sphere of traditional oversight – the medical care of children – to religious groups, exempting them from rules that apply to everyone else. In the second system, the state delegates authority to decide family disputes to certain religious groups with nominal oversight by the state. In the third system, the state authorizes religious groups to arbitrate family disputes using religious law rather than state law.

In each, religious understandings of the duties and prerogatives within the family break sharply from civil understandings.[25] This has important consequences for women and children. In the first system, allowing religious beliefs to govern the

[22] See, e.g., Nichols, "Reconsidering the Boundaries" (in this volume); Fadel, "Political Liberalism" (in this volume); Broyde, "New York's Regulation" (in this volume); Presser, "Marriage and the Law" (in this volume); Cere, "Canadian Conjugal Mosaic" (in this volume).

[23] In one proposal, the state would cede some jurisdiction over family disputes to religious groups. See Joel A. Nichols, "Multi-Tiered Marriage: Ideas and Influences from New York and Louisiana to the International Community," *Vanderbilt Journal of Transnational Law* 40 (January 2007): 135–196, 140–141. Other proposals would abolish state-sponsored civil marriage, leaving a purely contractarian form of domestic relationships. Edward A. Zelinsky, "Deregulating Marriage: The Pro-Marriage Case for Abolishing Civil Marriage," *Cardozo Law Review* 27 (January 2006): 1161–1220, 1219; Daniel A. Crane, "A 'Judeo-Christian' Argument for Privatizing Marriage," *Cardozo Law Review* 27 (January 2006): 1221–1259, 1250.

[24] Nichols would accommodate religious understandings only if "balance[d] ... with protections for women and children." See Nichols, "Multi-Tiered Marriage," 140. Zelinsky would not invalidate agreements "except upon very compelling grounds, e.g., to protect minor children." Zelinsky, "Deregulating Marriage," 1184. Crane would require standard-form religious agreements to reflect "minimal norms of [a] liberal democratic society." Crane, "A 'Judeo-Christian' Argument for Privatizing Marriage," 1253. Because each proposal would refuse to enforce an agreement only in the most egregious cases, each gives religious believers considerable latitude and religious autonomy.

[25] Litigants have also attempted to apply religious norms to block the application of civil rules in their own divorce proceedings. Doug Rendleman, "Collecting a Libel Tourist's Defamation Judgment?" *Washington & Lee Law Review* 67 (2010): 467–487 (discussing *Aleem v. Aleem*, 947 A.2d 489, 502 (Md. 2008), in which the husband tried to beat his wife to the courts by running to the Pakistan embassy and performing a *talaq* in order to religiously dissolve the marriage; the Maryland court rejected the *talaq* as a proper method of divorce because it went against public policy and stripped the wife of adequate due process).

care of children leaves them vulnerable when they are most in need of protection, in times of medical crisis. In the second and third systems, the state retains some authority to oversee family relationships, but it faces a number of hurdles in policing dangerous family situations. Child abuse and neglect systems are reactive and have a woeful track record of *preventing* violence.[26] Consequently, a woman's primary ability to protect herself and her children from family violence rests with her ability to exit an abusive relationship. Removing state oversight from the marital relationship virtually guarantees that some women will be trapped in abusive homes, because religious understandings about custody arrangements and financial matters upon dissolution would strip women of their children and plunge them into poverty. Many women likely would see no avenue of escape on such terms.

A. *Faith-Healing Communities in the United States*

In a majority of U.S. states, religious understandings of family duties currently govern in one significant context: the medical treatment of children. The state's choice to turn a blind eye to parental refusals to treat dying children has yielded tragic results.

Although parents generally have a duty to provide necessary medical treatment for their children,[27] many states shield parents from both civil and criminal liability for their failure to treat. States do this with exemptions that "allow religious parents … to refuse medical care for their sick children."[28] These exemptions are tied to the two principal mechanisms for discouraging parental failures to treat: civil child abuse and neglect laws and criminal statutes, such as manslaughter. Thirty-nine states provide exemptions from civil laws, and thirty-three states allow religious defenses to criminal charges. The costs of this wholesale delegation of the choice to treat are chilling.[29]

---

[26] See generally Robin Fretwell Wilson, "Sexually Predatory Parents and the Children in Their Care: Remove the Threat, Not the Child," in *Handbook of Children, Culture and Violence*, eds. Nancy E. Dowd, Dorothy G. Singer, and Robin Fretwell Wilson (Thousand Oaks, CA: Sage Press, 2006), 39–58.

[27] See Ann M. Haralambie, *The Child's Attorney: A Guide to Representing Children in Custody, Adoption, and Protection Cases* (Chicago: American Bar Association, 1993), 173.

[28] Richard A. Hughes, "The Death of Children by Faith-Based Medical Neglect," *Journal of Law and Religion* 20 (2004–2005): 247–265, 248. The federal Child Abuse Prevention and Treatment Act (CAPTA) originally required states to exempt faith-based denials from child abuse laws in order to receive federal funding. Congress later amended CAPTA to permit, but not require, such exemptions.

[29] Others have also argued that religious exemptions imperil children. Marci A. Hamilton, *God vs. the Gavel: Religion and the Rule of Law* (Cambridge: Cambridge University Press, 2005), 32–33 ("The result [of exemptions and parental failure to treat] is suffering, unnecessary death, and the martyrdom of children who have not been permitted to reach adulthood when they could make an informed choice to live or die for their religious beliefs.").

A 1998 study in *Pediatrics* reviewed 172 child deaths in the United States from 1975 to 1995 in which parents denied their children medical care because of their belief in faith healing.[30] (Faith healers use prayer to encourage healing through divine power.[31]) Of 172 children studied, 146 would have had a 90 percent chance of survival with medical intervention, and 16 others would more probably than not have lived.[32] Thus, 162, or 94 percent, would more probably than not have survived if they had received medical treatment.

Because the prognosis for cancer is especially hard to predict, the study separated cancer and noncancer deaths, with equally sobering results. Of ninety-eight children who died from noncancer deaths, only two "would not have clearly benefited from [commonly available medical] care." Ninety-two would have had "an excellent prognosis" with such care and four would likely have had a good outcome.[33] In other words, ninety-six of ninety-eight children likely would have survived if their parents had provided medical treatment.

The *Pediatrics* study did not capture the deaths of seventy-eight additional children in Oregon (between 1995 and 1998) or twelve children in Idaho (between 1980 and 1998). These deaths resulted from "faith-healing practices ... within the Oregon-based Followers of Christ Church." Whereas it is unclear whether the Idaho children would have survived, twenty-one of the Oregon children "could have lived if they had received medical treatment."[34]

Of course, even when the state exempts faith healers from the duty to treat, the state may intervene to authorize treatment for specific children in need.[35] In practice, however, the state rarely knows about a denial until a child dies because the family does not seek medical treatment. This places a premium on civil and criminal charges as the vehicle for changing behavior in insular communities.[36] Here, Oregon's experience is illustrative. After seventy-eight children died, Oregon amended its laws in 1999 to permit the prosecution of parents who fail to seek

---

[30] Seth M. Asser and Rita Swan, "Child Fatalities from Religion-Motivated Medical Neglect," *Pediatrics* 101:4 (April 1998): 625–630. Although Swan is a former Christian Scientist whose son died after non-treatment, the study appears in *Pediatrics*, a peer-reviewed journal that is the most cited in the field. See Mike Larabee, "Parents Turn Grief into a Mission: Change the Laws," *The Oregonian*, Nov. 28, 1998, available at http://www.rickross.com/reference/foc/foc6.html.

[31] Followers of the Christian Science denomination utilize "practitioners," who "[o]ffer spiritually-based treatment – a specific kind of prayer ... which results in physical healing." Christian Science Practitioners, available at http://www.tfccs.com/healingresources/practitioners.jhtml.

[32] Asser and Swan, "Child Fatalities," 625 (discussing children with better than a 50/50 chance of survival).

[33] See ibid., 626.

[34] Hughes, "The Death of Children by Faith-Based Medical Neglect," 247.

[35] See Joan H. Krause, "Freedom or Responsibility: When Spiritual Healing Fails," 32 (unpublished paper on file with author).

[36] Ibid.

medical care for a sick child. Between 1999 and 2003, no children in the Followers of Christ Church died from medical neglect.[37]

Religious exemptions also send the wrong message to those outside faith communities. Child protective services caseworkers and other officials often believe they cannot intervene to protect a child even when they know about a treatment denial. As Doctors Asser and Swan explain, "Believing they were powerless in the face of the parents' wishes, some teachers ignored obvious symptoms and sent lessons home to bedridden children. Some social workers and law enforcement officers allowed parents to decline examinations of children reported to be ill."[38]

The death on March 23, 2008, of eleven-year-old Madeline Kara Neumann exemplifies the continued need of children for the state's protection. Her death also shows that exemptions from child abuse laws send mixed signals to parents. Kara died from "too little insulin," a treatable condition.[39] Kara's parents, who do not "'believe' in" medical intervention, "just thought it was a spiritual attack and … prayed for her."[40] Following Kara's death, her mother contended that "we did not do anything criminal."[41] Her father "told investigators that 'given the same set of circumstances with another child, he would not waiver in his faith and confidence in the healing power of prayer.'"[42] Although Wisconsin law exempts faith healing from child abuse charges, it does not exempt parents from homicide charges. In May 2009, a jury convicted Kara's mother of second-degree reckless homicide, and in August 2009, her father was convicted of the same charge.[43]

Kara's death demonstrates the horrific consequences that result when the state prizes religious deference over a child's welfare. Kara, like the children in the studies

---

[37] Hughes, "The Death of Children by Faith-Based Medical Neglect," 247 (attributing this change to fears of prosecution).

[38] Asser and Swan, "Child Fatalities," 628.

[39] Associated Press, "Wisconsin Parents Didn't Expect Daughter to Die During Prayer," *Fox News*, March 26, 2008, available at http://www.foxnews.com/story/0,2933,341869,00.html.

[40] Bill Glauber, "Parents Charged in Diabetes Death, They Didn't Get Medical Help for Sick Daughter, 11," *Milwaukee Wisconsin Journal Sentinel*, April 29, 2008, available at http://www.jsonline.com/news/wisconsin/29556929.html.

[41] Associated Press, "Wisconsin Parents Didn't Expect Daughter to Die During Prayer."

[42] Glauber, "Parents Charged in Diabetes Death, They Didn't Get Medical Help for Sick Daughter, 11."

[43] See ibid.; Liz Hayes, "Jurors Weigh Opening States in Dale Neumann Trial, Leilani to Testify," *WASW.com*, July 25, 2009, available at http://www.wsaw.com/home/headlines/51699457.html; Colby Robertson, "After two days, jury finds Dale Neumann guilty," *WASW.com*, Aug, 1, 2009, available at http://www.waow.com/Global/story.asp?S=10832105. Dale and Leilani Neumann were subsequently sentenced to "serve 30 days in jail each year for the first 6 years of a 10 year probation term." WSAW Staff, "Dale and Leilani Neumann Sentenced To Spend Time In Jail, On Probation, and Serve Community Service," *WSAW.com*, Oct. 6, 2009, available at http://www.wsaw.com/karaneumann/headlines/63630282.html.

discussed previously, was no more disease-riddled than other children. Instead, her preventable death arose almost certainly because society removed its protection from some of its most vulnerable citizens.[44]

B. Family Law in Western Thrace

Shared jurisdiction over family issues exists in Western Thrace because of the Treaty of Lausanne, signed in 1923 to accommodate Turks living in Greece and Greeks living in Turkey. A Muslim minority of 110,000 lives in Western Thrace, which enjoys unique independence from the Greek government. They maintain their own religious and legal institutions, headed by three Muftis, who "conduct all matters related to civil law" using *shari'a* law.[45] Whereas Islam recognizes seven distinct schools of

[44] Whether criminal liability will serve as a deterrent is a complex issue. See Kent Greenawalt, "The Rule of Law and the Exemption Strategy," *Cardozo Law Review* 30 (2009): 1513–1534, 1529. As Greenawalt notes, "[p]arents convinced that faith healing will work may not be much deterred by criminal sanctions, especially since the possible death of their child will probably seem much more threatening to them than remoter criminal penalties after that occurs. But for parents who are already ambivalent about what to do, the prospect of criminal penalties may exert a push toward seeking ordinary medical treatment." Indeed, the "main deterrence" may be "more indirect. Highly publicized instances of Christian Scientists being carted off to jail because their children have died may reduce the attractiveness of Christian Science (and other similar religions) for people who might otherwise be inclined to embrace that faith." Ibid.

Medical neglect exemptions are only one instance of religious exemptions that may imperil the health and safety of children. Forty-eight states also provide religious exemptions to mandatory vaccination laws, with Mississippi and West Virginia the lone holdouts permitting an exemption only for medical reasons. Anthony Ciolli, "Religious & Philosophical Exemptions to Mandatory School Vaccinations: Who Should Bear the Costs to Society?," *Missouri Law Review* 74 (2009): 287–299. Proponents "argue that the free-exercise clause of the First Amendment mandates state accommodation for members of religious groups who object to the vaccinations on religious grounds." Shaun P. McFall, "Overview: Vaccination & Religious Exemptions," First Amendment Center, available at http://www.firstamendmentjournal.com/rel_liberty/free_exercise/topic.aspx?topic=vaccination. As with medical neglect exemptions, critics argue that "these nonimmunized children are exposed to the risk of acquiring these sometimes serious diseases." Stephen P. Teret and Jon S. Vernick, "Gambling with the Health of Others," *Michigan Law Review First Impressions* 107 (2009): 110–113. Unlike medical neglect exemptions, however, these exemptions foster a greater number of nonimmunized people and threaten the "herd immunity" that helps to prevent the spread of diseases in a given community. Ciolli, "Religious & Philosophical Exemptions to Mandatory School Vaccinations," 287–289. Further, critics argue exemptions impose significant costs as "vaccine-preventable diseases impose $10 billion worth of healthcare costs and over 30,000 otherwise avoidable deaths in America each year." Ibid. at 290.

[45] The text above describes Western Thrace up to the latest edits on this chapter in June 2011. As this book was in press, Greece reformed its family laws to ban the application of *Shari'a* law. Lia Pavlov, "Shariah Abolished for Greek Muslims," *Greek Reporter*, Aug. 21, 2011, available at http://greece.greekreporter com/2011/08/21/shariah_abolished_for_greek_muslims. Irini Lagani, "Greece's Muslim Minority in Western Thrace," *Briefing Notes on Islam, Society, and Politics* 3:1 (Center for Strategic and International Studies, June 2000): 8–9.

law,[46] which differ on substantive questions,[47] the Hanafi school predominates in the Balkans, which includes Greece.[48]

Shari'a law, as practiced in Western Thrace, departs significantly from Greek law in four important areas: polygamy, the age of marriage for minors, the husband's repudiation of the wife (known as *talaq*), and child custody after divorce.[49] The disadvantages for women are severe:

> [U]nder Islamic law the wife must compensate her husband for the termination of the marriage. In a way she has to buy herself out of the marriage, usually by returning the dower (*mahr*) she had received for the formation of the marriage, by waiving her right to alimony or even her right to the custody of the children.[50]

If the husband does not agree to the divorce, the wife can only terminate the marriage by reason of his fault.[51] Fault-based reasons include his desertion, adultery, change of religion, failure to provide financial support, bigamy, or violent behavior – in short, a marital breakdown due to the husband's behavior. Although women in violent relationships technically may divorce, the Muftis often reject their divorce applications, trapping them in "non-functioning marriages."[52]

Although the Muftis' decisions in Western Thrace are not final until declared enforceable by the Greek courts, the decisions are rarely reviewed or overturned. Almost no one disputes the Muftis' authority to decide family matters. Even when

---

[46] Kristine Uhlman, "Overview of Shari'a and Prevalent Customs in Islamic Societies – Divorce and Child Custody," July 21, 2009, available at http://www.expertlaw.com/library/family_law/islamic_custody.html#10 (describing four schools of law within the Sunni sect – Hanafi, Hanbali, Maliki, and Shafi'i – and three schools of the Shia sect – Ithna-Ashari, Zaidi, and Ismaili, but noting that "the Hanafi school is the most widespread and widely applied in modern Sharia-based legislation").

[47] See Fadel, "Political Liberalism" (in this volume) (noting that "Muslims have their own profound disagreements on the nature of marriage" and describing among the four Sunni schools "material differences in their substantive legal doctrines").

[48] Aspasia Tsaoussi and Eleni Zervogianni, "Multiculturalism and Family Law: The Case of Greek Muslims," in *European Challenges in Contemporary Family Law*, eds. Katharina Boele-Woelki and Tone Sverdrup (Antwerp, Belgium: Intersentia, 2008), 209–242, 217–218.

[49] Ibid., 209, 215–219.

[50] Ibid., 216–217. Many Islamic schools follow this rule. See Jamal J. Nasir, *The Islamic Law of Personal Status* (The Hague, The Netherlands: Kluwer Law International, 3d ed. 2002), 115–116 (noting that "[m]arriage may be dissolved by mutual consent by the wife giving the husband something for her freedom," which is known as *khula, mubaraat*, or "ransom," but that the *talaq ala mal*, "does not deprive the wife of her rights under the marriage contract, e.g., deferred dower or maintenance"); Mosa Sayed, "The Muslim Dower (*Mahr*) in Europe – With Special Reference to Sweden," in Boele-Woelki and Sverdrup, *European Challenges in Contemporary Family Law*, 187–208; M. Hashim Kamali, "Islamic Law: Personal Law," in *Encyclopedia of Religion*, ed. Lindsay Jones (Detroit, MI: MacMillan Reference Books, 2d ed, 2005), 4705, 4708.

[51] Nasir, *The Islamic Law of Personal Status*, 120–121. In Syria, "[i]f the injury, or most of it, is on the part of the husband, the arbiters, having failed to reconcile the spouses, shall award an irrevocable divorce." Ibid., 121.

[52] Tsaoussi and Zervogianni, "Multiculturalism and Family Law: The Case of Greek Muslims," 217.

School of Law	Custody Outcome:
Hanafi	Mother retains custody of boys until age 7 or 9 and girls until 9 or 11; father receives custody after this age
Shafi'i	Child chooses custodial parent upon the child's attainment of discretion, which has no set age limit
Maliki	Mother retains custody of boys until puberty and girls until marriage
Hanbali	Mother retains custody of boys and girls until age 7, after which the children may choose between parents

FIGURE 10.1. "Child Custody Rules in Islamic Schools of Law"

a party faces an unfavorable outcome or is the weaker party, "the vast majority of cases are brought before the Mufti."[53] On the rare occasion that someone disputes a Mufti's decision, the Greek court is likely to find it enforceable. One study found that Greek civil courts "denied enforceability in only 11 cases out of 2,679 or less than one-half of 1%."[54] The nearly nonexistent possibility of invalidation follows from limiting civil review to "whether the Mufti remained within his field of competence and whether the law applied contravenes the Constitution."[55] Moreover, because no higher religious authority reviews the decisions made by an individual Mufti, the Muftis are largely unchecked.[56] Without review, there is no guarantee that the Muftis will reach consistent decisions.

Such deference has real consequences. Consider the effect of enforcing Islamic understandings about custody. In some schools, there is a "strong presumption … that the husband will get custody of the children in the event of a divorce,"[57] as Figure 10.1 illustrates.[58]

Imagine the Catch-22 that will result for some women if Hanafi custody rules govern upon divorce. If a father harshly disciplines his adolescent son – even discipline that might constitute child abuse – and the Mufti enforces this religious norm as to custody, the mother is powerless to help her child. If she stays with her husband her

[53] Ibid., 219–221.
[54] Ibid., 219–220.
[55] Ibid., 214.
[56] Ibid., 221.
[57] Caryn Litt Wolfe, "Faith-Based Arbitration: Friend or Foe? An Evaluation of Religious Arbitration Systems and Their Interaction with Secular Courts," Note, *Fordham Law Review* 75 (October 2006): 427–469, 448.
[58] Adapted from Nasir, *The Islamic Law of Personal Status*, 170.

child will be beaten – and if she exits, her child remains with her husband. By contrast, in the Hanbali, Shafi'i, and Maliki schools, women do not necessarily jeopardize custody of their children upon divorce.

Whereas contributors to this volume would draw the line at respecting religious understandings about custody because of the state's paramount interest in protecting children,[59] this is not the practice in Western Thrace. Moreover, in some Islamic schools, the rules governing financial affairs at divorce may trap women in nonfunctioning marriages. A woman who ends the marriage must pay back her *mahr* and forfeit the right to any deferred *mahr* that would otherwise be due. Moreover, the Quran limits the husband's duty to provide maintenance, or alimony, to the *iddat* period, which ends months after the divorce.[60] The Muftis in Western Thrace sometimes require a wife to waive even this time-restricted amount before they will grant a *khul*, or divorce of mutual consent.[61] Enforcing religious understandings about finances leaves a woman in the same bind as forfeiting custody – the prospect of certain poverty may tether a woman to a marriage as surely as losing her children would. Although courts in some countries, such as Egypt, have at times rejected rigid applications of *shari'a* law, even these more "liberal" courts remain committed to *shari'a*.[62] By deferring to religious understandings of custody arrangements *or* financial consequences, society increases the cost to women who seek a divorce for their own safety or the safety of their children.

C. *Controversy Over* Shari'a *Courts in Great Britain*

Great Britain's eighty-five *shari'a* courts serve a Muslim population of more than 1.5 million people, the overwhelming majority (96%) of whom are Sunni.[63] The furor

---

[59] See, e.g., Nichols, "Reconsidering the Boundaries" (in this volume); see also Zelinsky, "Deregulating Marriage"; Crane, "A 'Judeo-Christian' Argument for Privatizing Marriage."

[60] Nasir, *The Islamic Law of Personal Status*, 135 (citing to 2:228 of the Quran, stating that the *iddat* lasts for "three monthly courses," but noting that individual countries have required additional compensation – *mutat* – in cases of "arbitrary repudiation" of the wife to mitigate the rule's harshness); David Pearl and Werner Menski, *Muslim Family Law* (London: Sweet & Maxwell, 3d ed. 1998), 182–184.

[61] Tsaoussi and Zervogianni, "Multiculturalism and Family Law: The Case of Greek Muslims," 216–217.

[62] See Clark B. Lombardi and Nathan J. Brown, "Do Constitutions Requiring Adherence to Shari'a Threaten Human Rights? How Egypt's Constitutional Court Reconciles Islamic Law with the Liberal Rule of Law," *American University International Law Review* 21 (2006): 379, 418, 423 (noting that "[i]n dicta, the SCC [Egyptian Supreme Court] has argued that Islamic law is, for constitutional purposes, a source of general moral principles that must be interpreted anew in every day and age and must take evolving notions of human welfare into account" but that the Egyptian Supreme Court interprets Egyptian law "to require the state to develop laws that … must be consistent with universally applicable scriptural rules of Islamic Shari'a").

[63] See *The World Fact Book*, July 27, 2009, available at https://www.cia.gov/library/publications/the-world-factbook/geos/uk.html; "Muslims in Great Britain," available at http://guide.muslimsinbritain.org/

arising from the operation of these tribunals in Great Britain stems from whether *shari'a* law is reconcilable with British law and how women will fare in this system.[64] Although Muslims are leveraging the same processes that Jews have used for a century to arbitrate family matters, critics argued to the European Commission that "women are particularly vulnerable as they're forced to submit to [Muslim arbitration] tribunals and Islamic law treats women less favorably than men."[65] Dr. Suhaib Hasan, secretary of the Islamic Sharia Council, denies "an inherent conflict between *shari'a* and British law." He also defends Islamic understandings on the merits, believing that "[i]n matters of divorce, the right of ending a marriage lies with the man because 'women have emotions, whereas a man thinks first before he speaks.'"[66]

Wading into the debate, Sadiq Khan, then Great Britain's minister for community cohesion and a Muslim himself, remarked that although he has "seen good examples of Jewish courts" he "would be very concerned about *shari'a* courts applying [*shari'a* law] in the UK. I don't think there is that level of sophistication that there is in Jewish law." He warns that *shari'a* courts may "entrench discrimination against women" because "'there is unequal bargaining power [so that] women can be abused and persuaded to do things that they shouldn't have to do.'"[67]

In both Judaism and Islam, men and women occupy different positions in bargaining power. In Judaism, the husband alone holds the prerogative to issue a *get* or religious divorce; by contrast, the wife's failure to secure the *get* makes her "anchored." This means that any children she subsequently bears in a later secular marriage become illegitimate *mamzerim* and are unable to marry other Jews.[68] In some Islamic traditions, women lack the ability to seek a divorce for reasons other than fault by the husband, unless she compensates him.[69] Women may also be barred from receiving custody of adolescent children and receive scant financial support upon exit.[70]

---

guide3.html#_ftn1. A majority of British mosques are controlled by one Hanafi sect, the Deobandis. Denis MacEoin, *Sharia Law or 'One Law for All'*, (Trowbridge, UK: The Cromwell Press Group, 2009), 30.

[64] Gledhill and Webster, "Archbishop of Canterbury Argues for Islamic Law in Britain."

[65] Edna Fernandes, "Sharia Law UK: Mail on Sunday Gets Exclusive Access to a British Muslim Court," *The Daily Mail*, July 4, 2009, available at http://www.dailymail.co.uk/news/article-1197478/Sharia-law-UK – How-Islam-dispensing-justice-side-British-courts.html.

[66] Ibid. (quoting Dr. Suhaib Hasan).

[67] Jonathan Oliver, "Muslims Rebuffed Over Sharia Courts," *The Times*, Oct. 12, 2008 (quoting Sadiq Khan), available at http://www.timesonline.co.uk/tol/news/politics/article4926612.ece.

[68] See Shachar, "The Puzzle of Interlocking Power Hierarchies: Sharing the Pieces of Jurisdictional Authority"; see also Broyde, "New York's Regulation" (in this volume).

[69] See Nasir, *The Islamic Law of Personal Status*, 120–121.

[70] See Figure 10.1. The woman's family may have a duty of support, although cultural norms have "probably been modified by the impact of the welfare state." Pearl and Menski, *Muslim Family Law*, 235. See also Fadel, "Political Liberalism" (in this volume).

Muslim women also face unique procedural hurdles when divorcing. In some British *shari'a* courts, a woman seeking a divorce must pay £250 to initiate the proceeding, whereas a man pays £100. The increased fee reflects the requirement that a woman must provide corroboration, something men need not supply: "It takes more work to process a woman's application as her word has to be corroborated … by other witnesses – preferably male."[71]

Muslim women may feel compelled to participate in *shari'a* courts because of their religious and cultural upbringing. "[G]ender norms that prescribe passivity and compliance make it difficult for women to enact resistance."[72] Because many women had little choice in marrying,[73] it seems unlikely they would exercise more control over their exit. Moreover, in tight-knit religious cultures, collective norms are more likely to influence group members than persons in "individualist cultures."[74] Outright coercion may also occur, and women often face ostracism and community backlash if they do not obtain an Islamic divorce.[75]

Women in *shari'a* courts report pressure to reconcile with abusive husbands,[76] as the experience of a woman identified as "Ameena" illustrates. Ameena sought assistance from the Islamic Sharia Council to divorce her husband. Backed by testimony of her daughter and two women's shelter workers, Ameena told the imam, Dr. Suhaib Hasan, that her husband "'beats me and the children, he doesn't give us our rights.'" Hasan documented the abuse: "He beat her. Then he asked her to massage his shoulders and legs. … One time her nose was broken and an operation was carried out. Another day, because of the beating there was a miscarriage." Because Ameena's husband refused to grant a divorce, Ameena needed the imam's

---

71 Fernandes, "Sharia Law UK: Mail on Sunday Gets Exclusive Access to a British Muslim Court."

72 Heidi M. Levitt and Kimberly Ware, "'Anything With Two Heads Is a Monster': Religious Leaders' Perspectives on Marital Equality and Domestic Violence," *Violence Against Women* 12 (December 2006): 1169–1190, 1170.

73 Whereas Great Britain's Forced Marriage Unit deals with 300 cases annually, police estimate that "the total number [forced marriages] is much higher." James Brandon and Salam Hafez, *Crimes of the Community: Honour-Based Violence in the UK* (Trowbridge, UK: The Cromwell Press, 2008), 9. "[T]hreats of violence" by a woman's family, "substantial physical violence," and removing women "abroad," are all used to force women to marry. Parents also use "emotional blackmail," "isolation from the community," and withdrawal from school to force children to accept marriages. Ibid., 16–18.

74 Ron Shor, "The Significance of Religion in Advancing a Culturally Sensitive Approach Towards Child Maltreatment," *Families in Society: The Journal of Contemporary Social Services* 79 (1998): 400–409.

75 Brandon and Hafez, *Crimes of the Community: Honour-Based Violence in the UK*, 99 ("Until [an Islamic divorce] is obtained, the woman risks being socially ostraci[z]ed by her family, neighb[o]rs and religious community.").

76 Ibid. ("Keeping families together therefore can often take precedence over protecting women from violence."). Concededly, the Islamic Sharia Council itself is under pressure not to grant a woman's divorce. Ibid., 101 (discussing "family members who believe that they will suffer shame if the council grants a divorce to their female relatives").

blessing. Finding her case "sufficiently serious to merit [further] consideration," Hasan referred it to the seven imams, who "decided that [Ameena's husband] will be given another opportunity to respond." If they grant Ameena a divorce, the imams will decide how to divide the couple's assets and "who will care for the children." Of course, if the imams apply Hanafi law, Ameena would receive no maintenance after the *iddat* period, would lose custody of her adolescent children, and depending on whether she shared any fault, would have to pay "ransom" to leave the marriage. As of July 2009, "Ameena's fate remains in limbo."[77] Even in more progressive jurisdictions, women like Ameena would still be at the mercy of judges who are bound to follow *shari'a* law.[78]

Under British law, Ameena would receive considerably more protection. There is no question that she would be entitled to divorce. She would be entitled to equitable division of the couple's assets and perhaps alimony. Most importantly, custody of Ameena's children would be determined by the childrens' best interests.[79] Ameena's case vividly illustrates the risks for women and children if the state permits religious understandings to substitute for the state's more protective rules.[80]

In *EM v. Secretary of State for the Home Department*, the British House of Lords recognized the obvious collisions between *shari'a* law and British law.[81] The case involved a question of asylum for a Lebanese woman, EM, whose husband beat her, tried "to throw her off a balcony," strangle her, "ended her first pregnancy by hitting her on the stomach with a heavy vase," and had not seen their son since birth. Without asylum, EM would be returned to Lebanon, where her husband would receive custody of their twelve-year-old son. Under "Islamic law as applied in Lebanon," unless the husband agrees otherwise, "the transfer [of custody] to the father at the stipulated age is automatic: the court … may not consider … the best interests of the child."[82]

As the House of Lords noted, "[t]he place of the mother in the life of a child under [Lebanon's] system is quite different … from that which is guaranteed in the

---

[77] Fernandes, "Sharia Law UK: Mail on Sunday Gets Exclusive Access to a British Muslim Court."
[78] See Lombardi and Brown, "Do Constitutions Requiring Adherence to Shari'a Threaten Human Rights?," 433 (noting that some rulings of the Egyptian Supreme Court would appear to liberalize certain principles of *shari'a* law but acknowledging that Egyptian appellate courts have acted to temper these progressive leanings).
[79] Alison Diduck and Felicity Kaganas, *Family Law, Gender and the State: Text, Cases and Materials* (Portland, OR: Hart Publishing, 2d ed. 2006), 312, 507–526, 596–599.
[80] Fernandes, "Sharia Law UK: Mail on Sunday Gets Exclusive Access to a British Muslim Court."
[81] [2008] UKHL 64, available at http://www.parliament.the-stationery-office.co.uk/pa/ld200708/ldjudgmt/jd081022/leban-1.htm. The House of Lords also described *shari'a* law as "wholly incompatible" with human rights law. See Afua Hirsch, "Sharia Law Incompatible with Human Rights Legislation, Lords Say," *The Guardian*, Oct. 23, 2008, available at http://www.guardian.co.uk/world/2008/oct/23/religion-islam.
[82] Ibid., 10–11 (Lord Bingham of Cornhill).

[European Convention on Human Rights]. There is no place in [Lebanon's system] for equal rights between men and women." *Shari'a* law in Lebanon is both "arbitrary and discriminatory" – arbitrary because it "permits no exceptions to its application, however strong" and discriminatory "because it denies women custody of their children [after the stipulated age] simply because they are women."[83] Because of the sharp divergence between *shari'a* law and human rights guarantees promised by Great Britain, the House of Lords granted EM asylum. Her experience underlines the risks facing Muslim women and children as *shari'a* courts spread throughout Great Britain.

D. Summary

These experiences of religious deference demonstrate the difficulty in protecting traditionally vulnerable groups. The next section poses a number of questions that must be addressed before allowing religious principles to govern family disputes.

II. REASONS FOR CAUTION

A number of concerns immediately arise from these sketches, including: Will religious communities protect women and children from family violence? If family violence occurs, how would a scheme of deference impact the state's ability to police such violence?

Deference to religious understandings of family relationships would not be troubling if society could say with confidence that the safety and welfare of traditionally vulnerable groups would not be impaired. Yet the triumvirate of family violence – domestic violence, child physical abuse, and child sexual abuse – is more likely to occur in insular, patriarchal communities.[84] Based on these markers, one should wonder whether women and children will suffer if society hands over greater authority to religious groups.[85]

---

[83] Ibid., 3 (Lord Hope of Craighead).

[84] David Finkelhor, "Risk Factors in the Sexual Victimization of Children," *Child Abuse and Neglect* 4:4 (1980): 265–273, 269 (finding in a study of 796 college undergraduates that "[w]hen a father has particularly Conservative family values, for example, believing strongly in children's obedience and in the subordination of women, a daughter is more at risk"); Emerson Dobash and Russell Dobash, *Violence Against Wives: A Case Against the Patriarchy* (New York: Free Press, 1983), 33–34 ("[T]he seeds of wife beating lie in the subordination of females and their subjection to male authority and control.").

[85] Muhammad M. Haj-Yahia, "Wife Abuse and Battering in the Sociocultural Context of Arab Society," *Family Process* 39:2 (Summer 2000): 237–255, 252 ("In Arab societies, power in marital relations is based on patriarchal principles, and equality is not considered a central value."); Virginia Ramey

This section reviews an emerging empirical literature concerning intimate partner and child abuse in religious communities.[86] Two conclusions can be drawn:
First, religious observance does weakly protect individuals from family violence;
but, second, family violence still occurs in religious communities.

A. Domestic Violence

Domestic violence affects five million Americans each year, more than 85 percent of
whom are women.[87] Simple rates of domestic violence across demographic groups
suggest that religious adherents experience domestic violence in much the same
way as the rest of the nation. In 2000, the U.S. Department of Justice found in a
large sample that 24.8 percent of women and 7.6 percent of men report being the
victims of rape or physical assault by an intimate partner during their lifetimes.[88] In
a smaller study of randomly sampled members of the Christian Reformed Church
in North America, 28 percent of respondents had been a victim of domestic violence
at some point during their lives.[89]

Studies of domestic violence risk factors report that religion is weakly protective
against domestic violence. A 1999 study found that men and women who attend
religious services regularly are less likely to commit acts of domestic violence than
persons who attend rarely or not at all.[90] A second study, using the second National
Survey of Families and Households (NSFH2), found a similar phenomenon:

Mollenkott, *Women, Men, and the Bible* (New York: Crossroad Publishing Co., 1989) (acknowledging that, although the Bible promotes mutual submission, Roman Catholicism and many Protestant
churches lend support to patriarchal dominance and repressive authoritarianism).

[86] Researchers have found it difficult to measure the incidence of family violence within religious groups.
See Anahid Dervartanian Kulwicki and June Miller, "Domestic Violence in the Arab American
Population: Transforming Environmental Conditions Through Community Education," *Issues in
Mental Health Nursing* 20:3 (May 1999): 199–215, 204 (using home interviews to study domestic violence among Arab-Americans, "[b]ecause of the high percentage of illiteracy … [and] the reluctance
of Arab Americans to discuss sensitive questions outside their homes").

[87] See Tricia B. Bent-Goodley and Dawnovise N. Fowler, "Spiritual and Religious Abuse: Expanding
What is Known About Domestic Violence," *Affilia: Journal of Women and Social Work* 21:3 (Fall
2006): 282–295, 282.

[88] Patricia Tjaden and Nancy Thoennes, *Extent, Nature, and Consequences of Intimate Partner Violence,
Findings From the National Violence Against Women Survey* (Washington, DC: U.S. Department of
Justice, Office of Justice Programs, 2000), 19 [hereinafter *DOJ Study*].

[89] "Highlights of Abuse Questionnaire," available at http://www.crcna.org/pages/safechurch_
questionnaire.cfm.

[90] See Christopher G. Ellison, John P. Bartkowski, and Kristin L. Anderson, "Are There Religious
Variations in Domestic Violence?," *Journal of Family Issues* 20 (January 1999): 87–113, 104 ("[T]he
frequency of attending religious services bears an inverse relationship to the likelihood of perpetrating
abuse for both men and women.").

"[A]ctive conservative Protestant husbands are significantly less likely to commit domestic violence compared to active mainline Protestant husbands as well as nominal conservative Protestant husbands."[91]

Although religious participation in some sects confers some limited protection, empirical studies also show that domestic violence and child abuse occur in religious communities, as they do in any other.[92] Countless anecdotes report that domestic abuse "is on the rise in Muslim communities,"[93] prevalent among conservative Protestants,[94] and visible in Jewish communities as well.[95] An empirical literature is also emerging. Studies of domestic violence among conservative Protestant husbands reveal that domestic violence is a reality for many families. Using NSFH2, Professor Brad Wilcox found that "4.8 percent of conservative Protestant married men with children committed domestic violence in the year prior to NSFH2, compared to 4.3 percent of mainline Protestant married men with children and 3.2 percent of unaffiliated married men with children." Although differences among these groups were not "statistically significant," significant differences emerged when Wilcox took church attendance into account. Wilcox found that "[n]ominal conservative Protestants husbands have a domestic violence rate of 7.2 percent and are significantly more abusive than unaffiliated husbands, active conservative Protestant husbands, and nominal mainline Protestant husbands."[96]

A study by Dr. Muhammad Haj-Yahia sheds light on the degree of intimate violence in Arab religious communities. In a study of 291 married Arab women in Israel, "[81%] of the participants knew of women who had experienced verbal and psychological abuse by their husbands; 78% knew of Arab women who had experienced 'moderate physical violence' (slapping, pulling hair or clothes, pushing)."

---

[91] William Bradford Wilcox, *Soft Patriarchs, New Men: How Christianity Shapes Fathers and Husbands* (Chicago: University of Chicago Press, 2004), 182. "Active" is defined as those who attend church three times a month or more, and "nominal" as those who attend church less frequently. Ibid.

[92] See, e.g., *DOJ Study*.

[93] See Fatima Agha Al-Hayani, "Arabs and the American Legal System: Cultural and Political Ramifications," in *Arabs in America: Building a New Future*, ed. Michael W. Suleiman (Philadelphia: Temple University Press, 1999), 69–83, 74, 80 ("Almost all lawyers have admitted that cases of domestic violence among Arabs are on the rise.").

[94] See Ellison et al., "Are There Religious Variations in Domestic Violence?," 89 ("[I]f some popular images are accurate, Conservative Protestant (i.e., fundamentalist and evangelical) affiliation and belief may be linked with an elevated risk of domestic violence, particularly by men.").

[95] Linda L. Ammons, "What's God Got To Do With It? Church and State Collaboration in the Subordination of Women and Domestic Violence," *Rutgers Law Review* 51 (Summer 1999): 1207–1288, 1269 ("Now I see a connection between religion and violence.... He beat me more after going to synagogue"), quoting Beverly Horsburgh, "Lifting the Veil of Secrecy: Domestic Violence in the Jewish Community," *Harvard Women's Law Journal* 18 (Spring 1995): 171, 183.

[96] Wilcox, *Soft Patriarchs, New Men*, 181–182. Wilcox classified any denomination that "adhere[s] to a theologically conservative worldview as conservative," including Pentecostal, Baptists, Anabaptists, Southern Baptists, Church of God in Christ, and Reformed Churches. Ibid., 15–16.

Nearly two-thirds (64%) knew Arab women "who had experienced 'severe physical violence,'" defined as "hard pushing at frequent intervals, attacking the wife and throwing her body against the wall, or attacking the wife with a hard object such as a chair, belt, or stick."[97]

B. *Child Physical Abuse and Corporal Punishment*

Like domestic violence, child physical abuse also afflicts religious communities. Professors Christopher Dyslin and Cynthia Thomsen explored the issue of whether religious affiliation or religiosity is related to child physical abuse risk. They distinguished mere spanking from child physical abuse, which they defined as "entail[ing] more extreme forms of physical aggression," such as "being hit with a fist, burned, or choked."[98]

Although the results showed that "conservative Protestant"[99] religious affiliation was *not* related to child physical abuse risk,[100] "[i]ndividuals with high levels of *extrinsic religiosity* had higher [child-abuse tendencies]" than those with lower extrinsic religiosity.[101] (Extrinsic religiosity is akin to wearing one's religion on one's sleeve; it places an emphasis on religion as membership in a "powerful in-group,"[102] providing protection, consolation, and social status.[103])

Whereas Dyslin and Thomsen and other researchers have restricted their inquiry to more severe acts such as choking and burning, some researchers have

[97] See Haj-Yahia, "Wife Abuse and Battering," 242–244 (reporting that 72% of those surveyed were Muslim, 18% were Christian, and 10% were Druze). Because the study asked about knowledge of other Arab women who experience certain kinds of violence, it cannot give a meaningful sense of the prevalence of violence in these communities, which measures the total number of abuse victims in a given population.

[98] Christopher W. Dyslin and Cynthia J. Thomsen, "Religiosity and Risk of Perpetrating Child Physical Abuse: An Empirical Investigation," *Journal of Psychology and Theology* 33:4 (Winter 2005): 291–298, 292, 293 (measuring participants' attitudes toward abuse with the Child Abuse Potential Inventory rather than self-reports of behavior).

[99] Dyslin and Thomsen classified the following as conservative Protestants: Adventists, Assemblies of God, Baptists, Church of God in Christ, Evangelical Free Foursquare Gospel, Full Gospel, Holiness, Missouri or Wisconsin Synod Lutheran, Nazarene, Nondenominational (Evangelical), Pentecostal, and Wesleyan. Ibid., 293 n.2.

[100] But see Bette L. Bottoms et al., "Religion-Related Child Physical Abuse: Characteristics and Psychological Outcomes," *Journal of Aggression, Maltreatment & Trauma* 8 (2003): 87–114, 88–89 (finding in a survey of nearly 650 members of the Christian Reformed Church that "church attendance was inversely related to reported perpetration of child abuse").

[101] Dyslin and Thomsen, "Religiosity and Risk of Perpetrating Child Physical Abuse," 296 (italics added).

[102] Vicky Genia and Dale G. Shaw, "Religion, Intrinsic-Extrinsic Orientation, and Depression," *Review of Religious Research* 32:3 (March 1991): 274–283, 274.

[103] Gordon W. Allport and J. M. Ross, "Personal Religious Orientation and Prejudice," *Journal of Personality and Social Psychology* 5 (1967): 432–443, 441.

examined links between religion and simple corporal punishment or spanking.[104] The overwhelming weight of evidence indicates that certain religious adherents resort to corporal punishment more often than other parents.[105] Multiple studies report that conservative Protestants[106] "support and use physical punishment more than other Americans."[107] Specifically, "conservative Protestants are clearly more likely than other parents to spank or slap young children,"[108] even by their own reports.[109]

This is especially true of more rigid adherents.[110] "Theological conservatism is one of the strongest predictors of spanking. … [Its] magnitude … is substantially greater than that of other common predictors of corporal punishment and parenting practices, such as parental education and race/ethnicity."[111] Corporal punishment, considered by some to be a form of child abuse, often posits scriptural

[104] A 1995 study of religion-related child abuse surveyed mental health professionals who encountered religiously motivated "child abuse … medical neglect, and severe forms of abuse and even murder perpetrated by parents and religious groups who believed they were ridding children of evil." According to the study, forty-three percent of reported cases involved "fundamentalist or fringe Christian religions, 38% involved other Protestants, and 16% involved Catholics." Across all religions, a parent was the perpetrator in 85% of the cases. Nearly two-thirds (66%) of the cases included physical abuse, nearly half involved sexual abuse, and almost a third involved neglect. Many cases of physical abuse were quite extreme. Even though the abuse was often "quite violent … less than a fifth of the cases involved police, and only 6% involved prosecutors." Bottoms et al., "Religion-Related Child Physical Abuse," 90–91.

[105] See Christopher G. Ellison, "Conservative Protestantism and the Corporal Punishment of Children: Clarifying the Issues," *Journal for the Scientific Study of Religion* 35:1 (March 1996): 1–16, 2 (discussing "conservative Protestant [i.e., fundamentalist and evangelical] denominations"). See Wilcox, *Soft Patriarchs, New Men*, 129 (finding that "Conservative Protestant fathers are more likely to report using corporal punishment" but also "are more likely to praise and hug their children and less likely to yell at them than are mainline Protestant and unaffiliated fathers").

[106] See Christopher G. Ellison, John P. Bartkowski, and Michelle L. Segal, "Do Conservative Protestant Parents Spank More Often? Further Evidence from the National Survey of Families and Households," *Social Science Quarterly* 77:3 (September 1996): 663–673, 666 (defining conservative Protestants as "Southern Baptist, Independent Baptist, other fundamentalist Baptist [Primitive, Foursquare Gospel, etc.], Church of Christ, Church of God, Independent or Open Bible Churches, Adventist, Alliance Church, Church of God in Christ, Assemblies of God, Pentecostal, Holiness, Apostolic, and various other fundamentalist or evangelical churches").

[107] Ellison, "Conservative Protestantism and the Corporal Punishment of Children," 14 (cautioning, however, that these practices may not "translate[] into widespread physical abuse" and that it is unclear how much harm these child-rearing practices inflict). See also Christopher G. Ellison and Darren E. Sherkat, "Conservative Protestantism and Support For Corporal Punishment," *American Sociological Review* 58:1 (February 1993): 131–144. The majority of U.S. parents report using corporal punishment. More than 70% of parents in the National Survey of Families and Households with at least one child under age twelve in the household reported using corporal punishment on some occasion. Ellison et al., "Do Conservative Protestant Parents Spank More Often?," 663, 666.

[108] Ellison, "Conservative Protestantism and the Corporal Punishment of Children," 5.

[109] Ellison et al., "Do Conservative Protestant Parents Spank More Often?," 666–668.

[110] Ibid., 663–664.

[111] Ibid., 670.

grounding in the Old Testament.[112] In one study of religion-related child abuse, perpetrators in 31 percent of the cases justified the "punishment or discipline ... with religious texts."[113]

C. Child Sexual Abuse

Child sexual abuse mars religious communities as well. Studies of sexual abuse have found pockets of elevated risk in adolescence, although religious affiliation mutes child sexual abuse risk in early childhood. One study found that Protestant and Catholic children were much less likely to be sexually abused when compared to children with no religious affiliation. However, the study further found that Protestant children "were more likely to be abused during adolescence" than their unaffiliated counterparts.[114] Indeed, the increase in their relative risk rivals other risk factors that intuitively impact a child's risk of sexual abuse, such as living with a male in the household.[115]

A 1997 survey of 397 freshmen students at a Southern university found that, among individuals sexually abused as a child, persons from "fundamental Protestant" religious family backgrounds – defined as Baptist, Southern Baptist, Church of Christ, Church of God, Pentecostal, and Holiness – were more at risk of sexual abuse by a relative. The authors concluded that "the type of religious affiliation and involvement in religious activities (measured as frequency of church attendance and practice of religious beliefs at home) affect the nature and extent of child sexual abuse."[116]

D. Summary

Evidence of domestic abuse, child physical abuse, and child sexual abuse demonstrates that religious communities are not immune from family violence. The question then becomes what recourse will women and children have under schemes of deference *when* family violence occurs. As the next section documents, many

---

[112] Bottoms et al., "Religion-Related Child Physical Abuse," 88–89 (observing that certain Biblical passages may encourage child abuse, including Proverbs 13:24 and Proverbs 23:13–14).

[113] Ibid., 99, 96 (defining punishment and discipline as being reprimanded "with a belt, cord, or other hard object").

[114] See Rebecca M. Bolen, "Predicting Risk to Be Sexually Abused: A Comparison of Logistic Regression to Event History Analysis," *Child Maltreatment* 3:2 (1998): 157–170, 167, 164 fig. 6.

[115] Robin Fretwell Wilson, "Children at Risk: The Sexual Exploitation of Female Children After Divorce," *Cornell Law Review* 86 (January 2001): 251–326, 255.

[116] Ruth Stout-Miller, Larry S. Miller, and Mary R. Langenbrunner, "Religiosity and Child Sexual Abuse: A Risk Factor Assessment," *Journal of Child Sexual Abuse* 6:4 (1997): 15–34, 23, 30–31.

victims of family violence receive little support for exiting the relationship from community members and religious leaders.

III. TOLERANCE OF FAMILY VIOLENCE

Although religion "is a powerful, regulating force,"[117] it is not always a force for good. Domestic violence experts note that "leaving an abuser is difficult for women who hold either to traditional religious beliefs about gender roles or who accept doctrinal distortions about suffering and forgiveness."[118] Whereas victims of domestic violence often look to their faith communities for support, studies across multiple faiths reveal that victims are likely to find cold comfort in their religious communities. Religious groups often acquiesce in or, worse, condone family violence.

"[D]omestic violence is probably the number one pastoral mental health emergency," according to Professor Nancy Nason-Clark.[119] When abused, religious women are:

> less likely to leave, are more likely to believe the abuser's promise to change his violent ways; frequently espouse reservations about seeking community-based resources or shelters for battered women, and commonly express guilt – that they have failed their families and God in not being able to make the marriage work.[120]

Such traits make religious adherents more vulnerable than their secular counterparts, and this vulnerability is compounded by religious notions about the value of suffering and the role of women.[121] For instance, "Jewish women tend to stay in abusive relationships longer th[a]n non-Jews," largely because of community pressure to maintain peace in the home or "*shalom bayit*."[122] Consequently, it is "especially difficult for religious victims to see the full extent of their suffering or to sound out the call for help."[123]

Religious victims sometimes interpret "their guilt and blame as the voice of God, and this only serve[s] to further excuse and enable their husband's abuse."[124] One

---

[117] Ammons, "What's God Got to Do With It?," 1268.

[118] Ibid., 1268–1269.

[119] Nancy Nason-Clark, "When Terror Strikes at Home: The Interface Between Religion and Domestic Violence," *Journal for the Scientific Study of Religion* 43:3 (September 2004): 303–310, 303.

[120] Ibid., 304.

[121] Ibid.

[122] Ammons, "What's God Got to Do With It?," 1269 n. 377.

[123] Nason-Clark, "When Terror Strikes at Home," 304.

[124] Norman Giesbrecht and Irene Sevcik, "The Process of Recovery and Rebuilding Among Abused Women in the Conservative Evangelical Subculture," *Journal of Family Violence* 15:3 (September 2000): 229–248, 236 (conducting in-depth interviews with five women from conservative evangelical communities).

woman explained that "not only was I failing in my marriage, I was failing in my faith and belief in God. I began to feel like I was completely going against the will of God." This mindset does not come only from within. In one woman's words, "as people found out that we were separated, the pressure was there.... [M]y place was at home with my husband." Another woman reports that community members thought she "had divorced and remarried without proper grounds (i.e., adultery) ... (and so had) written [her] ticket to hell."[125]

A 1999 study by Professors Anahid Kulwicki and June Miller evidences the tacit acceptance of domestic violence by some Muslims in the United States.[126] Their survey of Arab-American immigrants, nearly all of whom were Muslim, asked women and men when it would be appropriate for husbands to slap their wives.[127] Women were more accepting of slapping than men in a number of circumstances, ranging from when a wife disrespects her husband when no one else is around,[128] to when the husband discovers that his wife is committing adultery.[129] Perhaps most shocking, 18.2 percent of women would "approve" of a husband killing his wife if he discovered adultery.[130]

Other studies across the globe mirror such results. A study by Haj-Yahia of 356 Jordanian women, 92 percent of whom were Muslim, found that "Jordanian women have a strong tendency to justify wife-beating."[131] In the study, one-third (33.4 percent) agreed or strongly agreed that a husband had the right to beat his wife if she challenged his manhood, and 46.6 percent agreed that a husband had the right to beat his wife if she constantly disobeyed him. Moreover, 68.5 percent agreed or strongly agreed that a husband had a right to beat his wife if she did not respect his parents or siblings.[132] Indeed, Jordanian women often blamed the wife for violence against her. Almost half agreed that in most cases "a husband beats his wife due to her mistaken behavior," or that "the wife's behavior toward her husband or children is the cause of violence against her."[133]

[125] Ibid.
[126] Kulwicki and Miller, "Domestic Violence in the Arab American Population," 209 tbl. 1 (reporting that 97.51% of survey respondents were Muslim).
[127] Ibid., 207 tbl. 3.
[128] See ibid. (showing that 34.8% of female respondents and 33.3% of male respondents would approve of a man slapping his wife if she insults him when they are at home alone).
[129] See ibid. (showing that 48.4% of female respondents and 22.5% of male respondents approve of a man slapping his wife if he learns that she had an affair).
[130] Ibid. The sample was not large enough to present parallel statistics for male respondents on this question.
[131] Muhammad M. Haj-Yahia, "Beliefs of Jordanian Women about Wife-Beating," *Psychology of Women Quarterly* 26:4 (Winter 2002): 282–291, 285.
[132] Ibid., 286.
[133] See ibid. (reporting 41.8% and 47.5%, respectively).

Men also share these views. In 1998, Haj-Yahia surveyed Palestinian men from the West Bank and Gaza Strip, the majority of whom were Muslim.[134] Nearly a quarter, and sometimes more than two-thirds, justified wife beating because of sexual infidelity, insulting the husband in front of friends, challenging his manhood, disobeying him, failing to meet his expectations, refusing to have sex with him, disrespecting his parents and relatives, and reminding him of his weaknesses.[135]

Beyond tacit acceptance, some religious groups actually discourage women from seeking help. For example, Professor Ruksana Ayyub explains that the Muslim community "condemns any woman who seeks legal protection from an abusive spouse."[136] Haj-Yahia notes that an Arab woman who seeks removal of her husband from the home "may be ostracized by [her] community and blamed for undermining family stability and unity."[137] Preserving the marriage is of such great importance that physical violence is viewed as "preferable to divorce."[138]

Christian groups are not immune from this phenomenon. One church-funded survey of an evangelical denomination found that a majority of members believed that "[c]hurch leaders are not prepared to help members of their churches who are victims of abuse," and "Christians too often use the Bible to justify abuse."[139]

Just as some community members accept family violence, so do some religious leaders. Among South Asian Muslims in the United States, "[v]iolence in marriage is generally condemned but when it does happen the religious community gives no clear consequences for the violent behavior."[140] In fact, acquiescence is so pervasive

[134] See Muhammad M. Haj-Yahia, "Beliefs About Wife Beating Among Arab Men From Israel: The Influence of Their Patriarchal Ideology," *Journal of Family Violence* 18:4 (August 2003): 193–206, 196 ("82% of the respondents were Muslim ..., 13% were Christian ..., and 5% were Druze").

[135] Compare Muhammad M. Haj-Yahia, "A Patriarchal Perspective of Beliefs About Wife Beating Among Arab Palestinian Men from the West Bank and the Gaza Strip," *Journal of Family Issues* 19 (September 1998): 595–621, 604–605 with Haj-Yahi, "Beliefs About Wife Beating Among Arab Men From Israel," 199 ("[A] substantial proportion of the [male] respondents justified wife beating. Fifty-eight percent strongly agreed or agreed that 'there is no excuse for a man to beat his wife' ... whereas about 28% strongly agreed or agreed that 'sometimes it is OK for a man to beat his wife.' ... Moreover, between 15 and 62% strongly agreed or agreed that wife beating is justified on certain occasions.").

[136] Ruksana Ayyub, "Domestic Violence in the South Asian Muslim Immigrant Population in the United States," *Journal of Social Distress and the Homeless* 9:3 (2000): 237–248, 239, 243.

[137] Haj-Yahia, "Wife Abuse and Battering in the Sociocultural Context of Arab Society," 238–240 (attributing ostracism to "the prevailing belief that the children's best interests [and the reputation of the wife's family] take precedence over her own well-being and safety").

[138] S. Douki, F. Nacef, A. Belhadj, A. Bouasker, and R. Ghachem, "Violence Against Women in Arab and Islamic Countries," *Archives of Women's Mental Health* 6:3 (2003): 165–171, 169.

[139] See Bottoms et al., "Religion-Related Child Physical Abuse," 88–89 (discussing a study of Christian Reformed Church members).

[140] Ayyub "Domestic Violence in the South Asian Muslim Immigrant Population in the United States," 242.

that "Islamic Centers themselves fail to impart any information on domestic violence protection and prevention programs, ... seeing them as too radical."[141]

This tolerance is shared by many Christian religious leaders. A 2000 study of 158 Christian religious leaders found that many believed "marriage must be saved at all costs" – even when domestic violence occurs – and that a realistic solution was "forgiving and forgetting the abuse."[142] Earlier studies show that an overwhelming number of female victims received this type of advice from clergy. A 1981 study of abused women found that of the 28 percent who asked clergy for advice, 80 percent received only religious advice or, because it is a wife's duty to forgive, were told to return home or to seek marriage counseling.[143] A 1988 survey of conservative Protestant pastors found that 92 percent would "never advise a woman to divorce an abuser."[144] These leaders felt that "the victim's lack of submissive behavior was in part responsible for the violence."[145] A 2006 study of religious leaders across different religious traditions found that most "expressed concerns related to balancing the sacredness of marriage with the urgency of divorce in cases of [interpersonal violence]. Many suggested that divorce be considered only as a 'last resort' and would urge reconciliation if possible."[146]

This tolerance of family violence stems both from sharply contested readings of religious texts[147] and from the belief that "the marriage [must] be maintained" at

---

[141] Ibid.

[142] Al Miles, *Domestic Violence: What Every Pastor Needs to Know* (Minneapolis: Fortress Press, 2000), 149–150.

[143] See Mildred Daley Pagelow, "Secondary Battering and Alternatives of Female Victims to Spouse Abuse," in *Women and Crime in America*, ed. Lee H. Bowker (New York: Collier Macmillan, 1981), 277–300, 287–288.

[144] Colleen Shannon-Lewy and Valerie T. Dull, "The Response of Christian Clergy to Domestic Violence: Help or Hindrance?" *Aggression and Violent Behavior* 10:6 (September–October 2005): 647–659, 651 (citing J. M. Alsdurf and P. Alsdurf, "A Pastoral Response," in *Abuse and Religion: When Praying Isn't Enough*, eds. A. L. Horton and J. A. Williamson (Lexington, MA: Lexington Books, 1988), 165–172, 168).

[145] Ibid., 651. Importantly, attitudes may have moderated among Christian or other religious leaders since these studies were conducted. But even if the percentage of religious leaders who tolerate domestic violence dropped to 50%, this would still suggest a considerable potential for overt or unconscious coercion of battered spouses.

[146] Heidi M. Levitt and Kimberly N. Ware, "Religious Leaders' Perspectives on Marriage, Divorce and Intimate Partner Violence," *Psychology of Women Quarterly* 30:2 (June 2006): 212–222, 212 (surveying 22 religious leaders in Memphis, Tennessee).

[147] E.g., some scholars note that portions of the Quran "clearly imply that obedience and respect for husbands is the Muslim wife's duty and that in some situations wife-beating is justified," citing Sura 4:34 – which provides that "Men are the maintainers of women ... the good women are therefore obedient ... and (as to) those on whose part you fear desertion, admonish them, and leave them alone in the sleeping-places and beat them." Haj-Yahia, "Beliefs of Jordanian Women about Wife-Beating," 283. Under this reading, "a refractory wife has no legal right to object to her husband's exercising his

all costs.[148] For example, some scholars trace the acceptance of family violence in the Christian tradition to two primary themes – the idea that suffering is Christ-like and the historical role of men as the natural head of the household.[149] Not only do some Christian leaders struggle with Biblical commands about marriage, but abusers commonly "quote scripture to justify their treatment of the women they beat, and to give reasons to them why they must endure the violence."[150]

The emphasis on family privacy, reputation, and solidarity makes maintenance of the marriage of paramount importance in many religious communities, as a result of which, "abusiveness almost becomes invisible."[151] For religious women, the stakes in maintaining a marriage may simply be much higher than for other women.

States face significant challenges in policing family violence. The best hope for safeguarding family members is to empower women to act as private attorneys general, regulating conduct with respect to themselves and their children. Providing a financial safety net at divorce – as the state's off-the-rack rules do – is essential to a woman's ability to exit.[152]

disciplinary authority." Douki et al., "Violence Against Women in Arab and Islamic Countries," 168. Other scholars argue that the Quran allows only a "symbolic beating of a wife if she disobeys." Ayyub, "Domestic Violence in the South Asian Muslim Immigrant Population in the United States," 242. A "selective preference of one verse from the Quran over many other verses that talk about kindness and justice toward women has created an atmosphere that tolerates and allows violence toward women." Ibid. See further discussion of intra-Islamic interpretive pluralism in Fadel, "Political Liberalism" (in this volume). Similar disputes arise about Biblical passages. See, e.g., Dyslin and Thomsen, "Religiosity and Risk of Perpetrating Child Physical Abuse," 295.

[148] Ayyub, "Domestic Violence in the South Asian Muslim Immigrant Population in the United States," 243.

[149] Nancy Eileen Nienhuis, "Theological Reflections on Violence and Abuse," *Journal of Pastoral Care and Counseling* 59: 1–2 (Spring-Summer 2005): 109–123.

[150] Ibid., 120.

[151] Ayyub, "Domestic Violence in the South Asian Muslim Immigrant Population in the United States," 243. See also Douki et al., "Violence Against Women in Arab and Islamic Countries," 166 ("Arab families tend to emphasize mutual support, and individual members are expected to sacrifice their own needs, well-being and welfare for the benefit of the family as a unit.").

[152] Importantly, raising the costs of exit for women in cases of family violence undercuts the power that the state has not ceded and will not cede to religious courts: the decision to prosecute domestic violence. For instance, many states have instituted "no drop" policies for domestic violence, which "mandate prosecution of abusers, even if the victims do not wish to proceed." Aya Gruber, "Rape, Feminism, and the War on Crime," *Washington Law Review* 84 (2009): 581–660, 649. The objective of these policies is to take offenders out of the home and community. By removing the offender's opportunity to convince a victim to dismiss the charges, such policies serve to empower victims, who can feel confident that domestic violence will not be tolerated by the state. See J. Alex Little, "Balancing Accountability and Victim Autonomy at the International Criminal Court," *Georgetown Journal of International Law* 38 (2007): 363–397, 384–385. If a legally enforceable religious tradition hobbles a battered spouse's ability to leave the relationship, many women likely will not report family violence, undercutting the state's scheme for sanctioning family violence.

IV. DOES RESPECT FOR AUTONOMY TRUMP
FORESEEABLE INEQUITIES?

As Section I of this chapter illustrates, women face significant inequities in systems of deference.[153] Despite these inequities, some scholars maintain that respect for women's autonomy can justify a system of deference. They argue that prenuptial agreements have long permitted spouses to privately order their affairs.[154] Others, like Mohammad Fadel in this volume, argue for a "family law pluralism" that would allow religious adherents to "opt out of generally applicable civil norms and [make] a precommitment to a [particular religious] conception of distributive justice."[155] Implicit in both ideas is the notion that the state should not impose protections on those who do not wish to be protected. Yet the state often protects individuals from themselves and exercises especially vigorous oversight when the relationship is an intimate one.[156]

The state polices the content of prenuptial agreements, asking whether the agreement is so odious as to be unconscionable or a bargain that no reasonable person would accept. In twenty-six U.S. jurisdictions, an agreement's fairness is evaluated "relative to the time the agreement was signed," but in other jurisdictions fairness is evaluated "relative to the time of enforcement."[157] Given the staggering financial and custodial consequences of divorce for women in some religious traditions, one wonders whether any court would enforce a prenuptial agreement with terms like those routinely accepted in systems of deference today.[158]

[153] Some scholars have argued that autonomy affords the less powerful an opportunity to "transform" their communities from within, giving those traditionally vulnerable groups greater power in the long run. See, e.g., Ayelet Shachar, "Faith in Law? Diffusing Tensions Between Diversity and Equality" (in this volume). Other scholars suggest that granting greater autonomy to cultural groups places the less powerful in those groups, often women and children, at a further disadvantage. See, e.g., Natasha Bakht, "Family Arbitration Using Sharia Law: Examining Ontario's Arbitration Act and Its Impact on Women," *Muslim World Journal of Human Rights* 1:1 (2004): 1, 18 (arguing that a "regressive interpretation of *Shari'a* will be used to seriously undermine the rights of women").

[154] See generally Zelinsky, "Deregulating Marriage," and Crane, "A 'Judeo-Christian' Argument for Privatizing Marriage."

[155] See Fadel, "Political Liberalism" (in this volume).

[156] See Brian H. Bix, "The ALI Principles and Agreements: Seeking a Balance Between Status and Contract," in *Reconceiving the Family: Critique on the American Law Institute's Principles of the Law of Family Dissolution*, ed. Robin Fretwell Wilson (Cambridge: Cambridge University Press, 2006), 372–391, 373–374 (noting that most U.S. states employ a more "paternalistic and substantive test for enforceability" of prenuptial agreements than would be used for a "commercial agreement").

[157] Ibid.

[158] See Section I of this chapter. See also Ann Laquer Estin, "Embracing Tradition: Pluralism in American Family Law," *Maryland Law Review* 63 (2004): 540–604, 557 (discussing substantive limitations on enforcement of prenuptial agreements that affect child welfare or other public policies, but noting that courts have enforced some financial terms). Some courts limit enforcement to agreements

In addition to substantive review, ordinary prenuptial agreements are subjected to exacting review for procedural fairness. Courts require voluntariness, full financial disclosure, representation by separate counsel, and other procedural protections before the agreement may be enforced against a party.[159] One crucial safeguard to ensure that the parties have knowingly bound themselves to a specific, shared understanding in advance is that the agreement be reduced to writing. Fadel urges in this volume that religious deference allows believers to precommit to certain conceptions of the good. Yet, as Section I details (and even Fadel's chapter discusses), Islamic understandings of family relationships are not a monolithic whole and can differ in nuanced but material ways from place to place and group to group. Because the "ethical conceptions" of the good are not always committed to writing in advance, questions immediately arise about the congruence between the parties' understandings ex ante and the rules applied ex post by religious arbitrators. Questions also arise about whether like cases will be treated alike.

Publicly available documents from Great Britain's Islamic Sharia Council do not explain how the council ensures that the decision to arbitrate religiously is voluntary and not coerced.[160] Ontario, which recently curbed religious arbitration, recommended forty-six safeguards and reforms to protect vulnerable parties.[161] These included public education "aimed at creating awareness of the legal system, alternative dispute resolution options, and family law provisions"; screening parties "separately about issues of power imbalance and domestic violence, prior to entering into an arbitration agreement"; and protections like those used with prenuptial agreements.[162]

All the ordinary concerns that courts have over the ability of prospective spouses to bargain at arm's length and appreciate the consequences are exacerbated when a religious body acts as the arbitrator. Religious groups can exert considerable influence on their members, and the systems of deference described in Section I provide no evidence that women can, or have, resisted such powerful influences.

---

that are capable of specific performance under "neutral principles of law." *Odatalla v. Odatalla*, 810 A.2d 93 (N.J. Super. Ct. Ch. Div. 2002).

[159] See Bix, "The ALI Principles and Agreements," 372, 373–374.

[160] See Islamic Sharia Council, http://www.islamic-sharia.org/. A separate body, the Muslim Arbitration Tribunal (MAT), also conducts arbitrations using *shari'a* law in Great Britain. *See* John Bingham, "Non-Muslims Turning to Sharia 'Courts' in Britain to Resolve Disputes, Claim," *The Telegraph*, July 21, 2009, available at http://www.telegraph.co.uk/news/religion/5876577/Non-Muslims-turning-to-sharia-courts-in-Britain-to-resolve-disputes-claim.html. A report by Civitas, a British think tank, faults the MAT for not having "any system of record keeping" and lacking transparency both "within their own community [and] the outside community." Afua Hirsch, "Dozens of Sharia Courts are Giving Illegal Advice, Claims Civitas Report," *The Guardian*, June 29, 2009, available at http://www.guardian.co.uk/uk/2009/jun/29/sharia-courts-illegal-advice-claims.

[161] Boyd, *Dispute Resolution in Family Law*, 83.

[162] Ibid., 136, 138.

Family violence only exacerbates the risks to vulnerable parties. Given the routine acceptance of family violence by some religious communities discussed earlier, it seems unlikely that these communities will relax the application of harsh financial understandings in cases of violence – as courts sometimes do when there is a material change of circumstances after a prenuptial agreement's execution.[163] Neither is it clear that women will be allowed to exit abusive relationships at all, as Ameena's case illustrates.

Ayelet Shachar observes that violations of individual rights "within an identity group" are often justified by a supposed "right of exit" from the group.[164] As she notes, "the right of exit rationale forces an insider to a cruel choice of penalties: either accept all group practices – including those that violate your fundamental citizenship rights – or (somehow) leave." Shachar notes that "this 'solution' never considers that obstacles such as economic hardship, lack of education, skills deficiencies, or emotional distress may make exit all but impossible for some."[165] This claim about exit also ignores the reality that women in need of protection are embedded in a culture that tolerates significant family violence, views that they themselves may share. As a consequence, many women may not even know that they do not have to accept this group practice.[166] Just as women cannot easily exit the community as a means to protect their interests, they cannot easily resist the "choice" to arbitrate. More fundamentally, the state should not subject these women to such impossible choices.

V. EVALUATING POSSIBLE REGULATORY RESPONSES

The concerns raised here powerfully indict the entire enterprise of permitting religious norms to govern family matters. Perhaps most problematic is the ceding of jurisdiction to religious bodies over family questions because the risks to vulnerable women and children are so great. Western Thrace demonstrates not only that applying religious norms will significantly disadvantage women, but that there will be few checks on the decisions reached by religious leaders at the back end. Likewise, the wholesale withdrawal of state oversight from an area of decision making within the family – medical treatment of children in need – underscores the real human costs when the state walks away.

The harder question here is whether to allow religious arbitration if a woman wants her pastor, imam, or priest to arbitrate family matters using religious norms. Two overarching concerns require a regulatory response: first, the possibility of

---

[163] Bix "The ALI Principles and Agreements," 373–374.
[164] Ayelet Shachar, *Multicultural Jurisdictions: Cultural Differences and Women's Rights* (Cambridge: Cambridge University Press, 2001), 41.
[165] Ibid.
[166] Kulwiki and Miller, "Domestic Violence in the Arab American Population."

"forced," not truly voluntary, participation; and second, the possibility of harsh or unconscionable outcomes. As with any enterprise, the state can address these concerns ex ante or ex post. If the state regulates ex ante, it could police the circumstances under which arbitration may occur or police entry into arbitration. It might, for example, follow the Ontarian model and permit arbitration by religious figures using only civil law.[167] That regulatory approach mutes the concern about unconscionable outcomes for women but does not remove it entirely. The significant tolerance for violence in the family by fundamentalist religious believers and leaders means that the state would nonetheless have to police the substantive judgments reached in those proceedings to prevent overreaching. On the entry side, the state might require proof that a woman voluntarily elects to participate in arbitration. This safeguard seems grossly inadequate in the face of cultural and religious norms that define "good believers" as ones who accept unconscionable outcomes.[168] It may suffice, however, if paired with substantive restrictions barring the application of religious norms. Presumably, however, very few religious leaders and adherents would embrace religious arbitration on those terms.

The state could also address the possibility of harm from religious arbitration ex post. In this scheme, for example, it could police the substantive judgments reached in arbitration with robust public policy limitations that bar certain substantive outcomes.[169] This approach imposes a duty to trigger this substantive review on parties

[167] In the United States, some questions are not capable of arbitration because mandatory law applies. See Edward Brunet et al., *Arbitration in America: Critical Assessment* 43 (Cambridge: Cambridge University Press, 2006) (suggesting that "antitrust or securities laws, Title VII of the Civil Rights Act, or claims for punitive damages ... probably arise under mandatory law, in that the parties cannot affect the law by agreement" and discussing the U.S. Supreme Court's approach to determining the "arbitrability of statutory claims"). Just as legislators may dictate the law to be applied in arbitration, legislators could also proscribe arbitration of family matters entirely. Compare the discussion of constitutional questions in Brian H. Bix, "Pluralism and Decentralization in Marriage Regulation" (in this volume) and John Witte Jr. and Joel A. Nichols, "The Frontiers of Marital Pluralism: An Afterword" (in this volume).

[168] Boyd, *Dispute Resolution in Family Law*, 3. See also Rabia Mills, coordinator, "Interview: A Review of the Muslim Personal/Family Law Campaign," Interview with Syed Mumtaz Ali, (August 1995), available at http://www.scribd.com/doc/24286845/A-Review-of-the-Muslim.

[169] Compare Brunet et al., *Arbitration in America*, 25 (noting that "the lengthy history of the public policy exception represents a perception that society would oppose an arbitration system in which courts would enforce awards blatantly inconsistent with public policy") with Thomas E. Carbonneau, *The Law and Practice of Arbitration* (Huntington, NY: Juris Publishing, 2d ed. 2007), 30 (discussing the availability of judicial relief from unjust arbitral awards and concluding that such relief is only available in cases involving "flagrant and fundamental procedural deficiencies"). Even if a court possesses the right to review, it may be loathe to set aside an arbitral award. Consider the 2006 case of a Hmong couple who voluntarily arbitrated their divorce with Hmong elders in accordance with Hmong beliefs. (The Hmong are an ethnic group from Laos.) The couple had independent counsel and signed an arbitration agreement that provided for civil court review in limited circumstances, such as if the arbitrators exceeded their power or if the arbitral award was obtained by fraud. Arbitration proceeded over the following year, with seven meetings of the panel. After settlement, the husband moved to vacate

who are already disadvantaged. Yet the same people that the state would require to trigger this review – divorced women – may not understand that they have been disadvantaged by the application of religious norms. Neither may these women understand or be empowered to resist those norms given the importance of religious identity to them in their lives. This approach would also require a series of judgments by the state about when women can be made too poor as a result of divorce or be too trapped in an abusive marriage or be too threatened by the possibility of losing access to their children. Obviously some of these judgments have already been made in the context of prenuptial agreements – for instance, that decisions regarding children cannot be removed from state oversight – but a robust theory of substantive floors, below which the state will not allow religious arbitration to go, means that questions of financial and physical vulnerability would have to be addressed as well.[170]

VI. CONCLUSION

Efforts to respect religious understandings in family disputes seem at first blush innocuous: They would allow religious groups to define their own norms and celebrate the rich diversity of society. However, the experience of women and children of multiple faiths across the world demonstrates that religious deference extracts an unconscionable price. Religious communities are not immune from family violence, and religious norms place women at significant financial and custodial disadvantages. When these two phenomena collide, many women will face near certain poverty and may lose their children by exiting their marriages. Some will surely be forced to remain in households that are unsafe, not only for themselves, but also for their children. These costs of giving deference to religious understandings of family relationships must seriously be considered before pulling the state out of marriage and the family.

the award, claiming that the arbitration was against public policy and resulted in an inequitable settlement. Because the civil court could "discern no public policy that prohibits the parties from agreeing to have their legal issues decided by an arbitration panel according to Hmong culture and tradition," it refused to set aside the judgment. *Vue v. Vue*, 2006 WL 279070 (2006).

[170] Bix, "The ALI Principles and Agreements," 375. In such a system, it would be useful to collect data about arbitral judgments so that the state can monitor outcomes across cases as well as on a case-by-case basis. Such monitoring would not only surface any inequities against women, but would also incentivize incremental improvement in substantive outcomes for women in *shari'a* courts. That is, if religious arbitrators know they are operating in the shadow of state law generally hostile to certain Islamic legal precepts, this knowledge may lead to gradual liberalization of the precepts' application.

11

Canadian Conjugal Mosaic

From Multiculturalism to Multi-Conjugalism?

Daniel Cere

The "Canadian school" of social and political theory has been at the forefront of theoretical reflection on the problem of multicultural diversity.[1] These theoretical contributions, some claim, have built on Canada's proven political capacity to accommodate deep diversity.[2] Canada was the first nation in the world to adopt multiculturalism as its official state policy, a landmark venture that was wedded to an equally strong commitment to the modern rights revolution.[3] The historic 1982 constitutional act that established the Canadian Charter of Rights and Freedoms also entrenched multiculturalism, gender equality, aboriginal rights, and bilingualism – as well as reaffirming confessional educational rights of Catholics and Protestant minority communities. This is a classic Canadian constitutional mix.

---

[1] Canada has been widely hailed as a leader in both the theory and practice of dealing with the intersections of multicultural identities, law, and citizenship. Major theorists in this school include Charles Taylor, Will Kymlicka, James Tully, Joseph Carens, Margaret Moore, Alan Patten, and David Weinstock, among others. Amy Gutmann acknowledges Canada as "the theoretical home of group rights." Amy Gutmann, "Identity and Democracy: A Synthetic Perspective," in *Political Science: The State of the Discipline*, eds. Ira Katznelson and Heln V. Milner (New York: W. W. Norton and Company, 2002), 550. Sujit Choudhry explores the prominence of both Canadian political experience and Canadian political theory in contemporary debates about multiculturalism and law in "Does the World Need More Canada? The Politics of the Canadian Model in Constitutional Politics and Political Theory," in *Constitutional Design for Divided Societies: Integration or Accommodation?*, ed. Sujit Choudhry (Oxford: Oxford University Press, 2008), 141–172.

[2] Will Kymlicka, *Finding Our Way: Rethinking Ethnocultural Relations in Canada* (Oxford: Oxford University Press, 1998), 2–4. See also Will Kymlicka, "Marketing Canadian Pluralism in the International Arena," *International Journal* 59:4 (2004): 829–852.

[3] The commitment came late. Canada was the only Western country to abstain from endorsing the Universal Declaration of Human Rights in the first round of voting. (The nine countries that abstained included Canada, Saudi Arabia, South Africa, and six Soviet bloc nations.) For the first century of its national history, the record of Canadian courts in defending basic human rights and freedoms was checkered, at best. See Thomas R. Berger, *Fragile Freedoms: Human Rights and Dissent in Canada* (Toronto: Clarke Irwin, 1982).

How does marriage fare in this land of multiculturalism, rights, and deep diversity? Canadian couples dwell in a complex array of political intersections, cultural fissures, and ideological divides when it comes to questions of gender, sexual orientation, and conjugality.[4] In the last decade, Canada has been at the forefront of a number of innovative developments in the domain of conjugality. After a relatively tame public debate, Canada redefined marriage to include gay and lesbian couples. Canadian courts and legislatures have been advancing our constitutional commitments to gender equality in areas of conflict between civil and religious family law. Moreover, Canadian and provincial governments have launched a public debate over the question of decriminalizing polygamy. By 2003, Canada's growing "boldness in social matters" was earning it a "rather cool" rating from global public pundits.[5] It remains an open question, however, whether these developments have uniformly caused gains in advancing Canadian commitments to deep diversity in the domain of conjugality.

I. CONSTITUTIONALITY AND CONJUGALITY: THE CIVIL AND RELIGIOUS

In Canada's constitutional framework, marriage and family are parsed out into a multi-tiered order that entangles married couples in a juridical maze of provincial and federal authorities.[6] The power to define marriage resides in the federal government,[7] but the power to solemnize marriage lies in provincial hands.[8] The power to dissolve marriage is given to the federal government, but jurisdiction over matrimonial property, spousal support, custody, succession, adoption, guardianship, and affiliation rests with the provinces.[9] This situation is further complicated by courts' expansive interpretation of federal power over divorce (Section 91:26 of the

---

4   For a Foucauldian feminist approach to these intersections, see Rebecca Johnson, "Gender, Race, Class and Sexual Orientation: Theorizing the Intersections," in *Feminism, Law, Inclusion: Intersectionality in Action*, eds. Gayle MacDonald, Rachel L. Osborne, and Charles C. Smith (Toronto: Sumach Press, 2005), 21–37.

5   "Canada's New Spirit," *The Economist*, Sept. 25, 2003.

6   Compare Joel A. Nichols, "Multi-Tiered Marriage: Reconsidering the Boundaries of Civil Law and Religion" (in this volume). See also Joel A. Nichols, "Multi-Tiered Marriage: Ideas and Influences from New York and Louisiana to the International Community," *Vanderbilt Journal of Transnational Law* 40 (2007): 135–196.

7   British North America Act (BNA Act), art. 91:26.

8   BNA Act, art. 92:12.

9   BNA Act, art. 92:13. For discussions of constitutional jurisdiction over marriage in Canada, see Peter Hogg, *Constitutional Law of Canada*, (Toronto: Carswell, 5th ed. 2007), "The Family" ch. 27; Neil Boyd, *Canadian Law: An Introduction* (Toronto: Thomson & Nelson, 2007), "The Changing Family and Family Law," 265; Mary Jane Mossman, *Families and Law in Canada: Cases and Commentary* (Toronto: Carswell, 1997), 52–54; and Hogg, *Constitutional Law of Canada*, 655–667.

BNA Act), allowing federal legislation to address matters of alimony, maintenance, and custody directly related to the dissolution of marriages.

In addition to these overlapping civil jurisdictional claims, civil and religious laws also make competing claims. The parallel and sometimes overlapping claims of civil and religious law have become a marked feature of the Canadian conjugal experience. The divide between the two developed slowly but has become more sharply pronounced in the last few decades.

For much of Canada's history, marriage, religion, and law seemed to intermingle seamlessly.[10] This fusion was particularly evident in the predominantly Catholic province of Quebec where, for more than a century after Confederation, no legal form of civil marriage "profaned" Quebec's family law.[11] Thus, until 1969, all solemnized marriages had to be performed by recognized religious authorities. This comfortable alliance of religious and civil law was due, in part, to the federal government's reluctance to exercise its jurisdictional authority in the domain of marriage and divorce law. For the first century of Canadian family law, there was no federal divorce law. However, this federal deficiency was corrected with sweeping legislative changes introduced by Pierre Trudeau. In 1968, the Divorce Act passed, establishing fairly uniform procedures for divorce across Canada. In addition, homosexuality was decriminalized and abortion legalized. Trudeau's famous dictum that "there's no place for the state in the bedrooms of the nation" underscored his conviction that criminal law has no place in the domains of conjugality and sexuality, even though, he noted, there may be valid moral and religious normative concerns that could have effect in civil society.[12]

The insistence on establishing a clear divide between civil and religious law was formally proclaimed when the Canadian parliament exercised its constitutional authority to define marriage in the historic 2005 Civil Marriage Act (Bill C-38), extending the definition of marriage to include same-sex unions.[13] Bill C-38 insists on a bifocal view of marriage as operating within two radically distinct frames, civil and religious.[14] The legislation introduces itself as "an Act respecting certain aspects of legal capacity for marriage for civil purposes," and the formal title of the legislation is the "Civil Marriage Act." The phrase "marriage *for civil purposes*" is the

---

[10] Robert Leckey, "Profane Matrimony," *Canadian Journal of Law and Society/Revue Canadienne Droit et Société* 21:2 (2006): 1–23, 11–13.

[11] Ibid., 12.

[12] A video clip of Trudeau explaining his historic legislation can be found on the CBC Digital Archives, "Trudeau's Omnibus Bill," 1967, available at http://archives.cbc.ca/politics/rights_freedoms/topics/538/.

[13] The Civil Marriage Act, Bill C-38 (2005).

[14] Compare the discussion of civil and religious marriage in Katherine Shaw Spaht, "Covenant Marriage Laws: A Model for Compromise" (in this volume). See also Stephen B. Presser, "Marriage and the Law: Time for a Divorce?" (in this volume).

conceptual frame used throughout the legislation.[15] The central operative clause of the legislation reads: "Marriage, for civil purposes, is the lawful union of two persons to the exclusion of all others."[16]

Despite the rhetorical resolve of Bill C-38, the religious past still blends and fuses with the autonomous civil present. Provincial solemnization protocols continue to allow religious and civil marriages to coexist in deeply symbiotic ways. Most marriage ceremonies are solemnized in a religious context with the minister officiating both as a religious celebrant and an officer of the state. The religious rite of solemnization is still recognized as having "civil effect."[17] For most Canadians, clear distinctions between the two regimes become quite fuzzy due to the complex ways these two regimes intersect in actual practice. In the discussions leading up to the redefinition of marriage, some legal experts did float the idea of a strict separation that would require a civil solemnization of marriage in addition to any religious solemnization. This path was not taken, however, for fear of contributing to "feelings of marginalization by religious groups" due to the fact that they would be "no longer receiving civil recognition of their religious marriages."[18]

This overlay of religious and civil marriage breaks down at various critical points in Canadian law, but there is no clear rule to determine how or when merger, fragmentation, or conflict will occur. For example, religious legal systems typically impose more complex impediments to marriage than civil law. Catholic same-sex couples are able to access civil marriage but are strictly prohibited from religious marriage. Marriages, in many cases, are dissolved by quite separate civil and religious procedures. However, such seeming dichotomies regarding dissolution will fade for religious traditions that readily accept civil divorce as a valid dissolution of the religious "covenant" of marriage (e.g., the United Church of Canada). Even in cases where there is a sharp divide between civil and religious procedures for marriage dissolution, there can be a tuning of civil law to religious law. For example, the interface between Canadian civil law and religious law is complex and still evolving regarding Jewish divorce.[19]

---

[15] The lengthy preamble mandates that "couples of the same sex and couples of the opposite sex have equal access to marriage for civil purposes." C-38 argues that "*only* equal access to marriage for civil purposes" would satisfy the demands for "equality without discrimination" (italics added).

[16] Civil Marriage Act, art. 2.

[17] Lorraine P. Lafferty, "Religion, Sexual Orientation and the State: Can Public Officials Refuse to Perform Same-Sex Marriage?" *Canadian Bar Review* 85 (2006): 287–316, 291. For discussion of such overlap of religious and civil law in the United States, see Ann Lacquer Estin, "Unofficial Family Law" (in this volume).

[18] Lafferty, "Religion, Sexual Orientation, and the State," 292.

[19] See Lisa Fishbayn's discussion in "Gender, Multiculturalism and Dialogue: The Case of Jewish Divorce," *Canadian Journal of Law and Jurisprudence* 21:1 (2008): 71–96. For Jewish divorce in the United States, see Michael J. Broyde, "New York's Regulation of Jewish Marriage: Covenant, Contract, or Statute?" (in this volume).

So why does the Civil Marriage Act insist so emphatically on a civil–religious divide? In part, it relates to Bill C-38's equally adamant insistence on the freedom and autonomy of religious communities to adhere to, proclaim, and solemnize forms of marriage "in accordance with their religious beliefs."[20] The Preamble states:

> [N]othing in this Act affects the guarantee of freedom of conscience and religion and, in particular, the freedom of members of religious groups to hold and declare their religious beliefs and the freedom of officials of religious groups to refuse to perform marriages that are not in accordance with their religious beliefs.[21]

In the operative clauses of the legislation, the bulk of the text is dedicated to reassurances that the redefinition of "civil marriage" will not impose constraints on those who adhere to an alternative understanding of marriage:

> For greater certainty, no person or organization shall be deprived of any benefit, or be subject to any obligation or sanction, under any law of the Parliament of Canada solely by reason of their exercise, in respect of marriage between persons of the same sex, of the freedom of conscience and religion guaranteed under the *Canadian Charter of Rights and Freedoms* or *the expression of their beliefs in respect of marriage as the union of a man and woman to the exclusion of all others* based on that guaranteed freedom.[22]

In short, Bill C-38 accomplishes more than just the extension of marriage to same-sex couples. The legislation seems to have five goals: (1) to establish the distinct juridical nature of civil marriage as a union of two persons; (2) to highlight the discriminatory nature of the heterosexual constraint on marriage and highlight the need to extend marriage to same-sex couples in order to meet Canada's constitutional commitments to equality; (3) to guarantee the freedom of religious marital regimes to operate freely and without constraint; (4) to affirm the freedom of Canadians to adhere to an alternative public discourse on marriage as a union of man and woman; and (5) to underscore the mutual autonomy of the intersecting domains of civil and religious laws on marriage.[23] To strike this balance, Bill C-38 strongly asserts the rights of individuals and communities to affirm and entrench diverse conceptions of marriage.

The precarious balance of these several goals was the result of a lengthy public consultation in which religious, cultural, legal, and academic voices raised serious

---

[20] Civil Marriage Act, art. 3.

[21] Ibid., preamble. The point is repeated in even more expansive terms: "It is not against the public interest to hold and publicly express diverse views on marriage." Ibid.

[22] Ibid., art. 3.1 (italics added).

[23] An additional important component of the legislation is the deletion of all references to "natural" or "biological" parenthood in federal law. This component surfaces in the consequential amendments, not the operative clauses.

concerns about the implications of the legislation. Article 3.1 on freedom of conscience and religion was added to the original draft legislation toward the very end of the legislative process to address these nagging concerns. However, the logic of the Civil Marriage Act, as it stands, still poses a dilemma that is more than just theoretical. The act offers broad assurances for the freedom to speak to and promote a conception of "marriage as the union of a man and woman to the exclusion of all others." However, it simultaneously repudiates this more restrictive conception of marriage as discriminatory and a violation of Canadian Charter commitments to equality.[24] In fact, in its reference questions to the Supreme Court, the government pressed the court to confirm its view that the historic definition of marriage violated Canadian constitutional commitments to equality.[25] (The Supreme Court deliberately did not answer this question.)

Bill C-38's insistence on the divide between civil and religious marriage was an integral part of the legislative attempt to settle the public debate over marriage. The debate had coalesced into two distinct public conceptions of marriage vying for recognition. On the one hand, there was the historic conception of marriage as a union anchored in the social ecology of opposite-sex pair-bonding, procreation, and genealogical affiliation of parents and children.[26] On the other hand, there was a new conjugal imaginary that viewed marriage as a close interpersonal union of two persons devoid of any reference to gender or procreation. The legislators perceived the debate to be an either-or contest. The result was that the historic conjugal conception of marriage was banished from the domain of civil law and relocated to the domain of religious law. The contestation between the two public languages of marriage was resolved by allocating each language to distinct spheres: the civil and the religious. The result was that the historic language of marriage no longer received recognition as an official or legal conjugal language.

Was this solution the only option if one wanted to extend civil marriage to same-sex couples? The initial framing of this debate by courts appeared to make the redefinition of marriage the only logical option. The initial Ontario Superior Court judgment that set the legislative process into motion declared that the preexisting legal framework (recognizing only opposite-sex marriage) was discriminatory.[27] The Court gave the federal government two years to remedy this problem. It tentatively proposed three possible legislative remedies: (1) to redefine marriage as a union of two persons; (2) to establish a federal "civil unions" category that would extend legal recognition and benefits to same-sex unions; or (3) to abolish marriage as a category

---

[24] Civil Marriage Act, preamble.
[25] *Re: Same-Sex Marriage* [2004] 3 S.R.R.
[26] One statement of this position can be found in "The Statement on the Status of Marriage in Canada," *Globe and Mail*, June 18, 2003, available at http://www.marriageinstitute.ca/pages/stmt.htm.
[27] *Halpern v. Canada* (Attorney General), 2002 CanLII 49633 (ON S.C.).

in law and replace it with a civil registration system for adult close relationships.[28] Given this selection, only one remedy could meet the demand to extend civil marriage to same-sex unions. The Court noted difficulties with all of these remedies and concluded that the crafting of a legislative response was not its domain of competence.[29] However, despite the Court's warnings about its limited capacity to frame a creative legislative response, when parliamentary hearings began the government announced that these three court-created options would be the exclusive focus for public deliberation.[30]

Nonetheless, some commentators proffered other proposals to try to address the quest for recognition of same-sex couples while respecting the diversity of views on conjugality. One proposal was to simplify the bill by eliminating the excessively long preamble and then rewriting the operative clauses to recognize both conceptions of marriage as valid legal conceptions.[31] The unusually long preamble is argumentative and advances a contested rights argument designed to stigmatize the historic conjugal conception of marriage while simultaneously insisting on the expressive rights of this discriminatory language of marriage. There was no need to defeat one language in order to advance another, however. Bill C-38 could have recognized the existence of *two* legally valid, though distinct, conceptions of marriage within Canadian law.

Embedding the historic conception of marriage in the law, alongside the new close relationship conception of marriage, would have rectified the one-sidedness of the legislation. It would have recognized in law that current social conceptions of marriage now coalesce around two distinct public languages of conjugality. Entrenching both visions of marriage in the law would have extended marriage to same-sex couples while continuing to give legal recognition to the historic conjugal conception of marriage and affording it a rightful place within public law. In many ways, this solution would have been a quintessential Canadian solution. Canada is a country of dualities, bilingual and bicultural. Canada even operates with dual legal systems – civil law in Quebec and common law in the rest of Canada. Canada's well-worn traditions of official multiculturalism and bilingualism would seem nicely positioned to slide into a form of official bi-conjugalism.

---

[28] Ibid., ¶ 132.

[29] Ibid., ¶¶ 103–109.

[30] Department of Justice Canada, "Marriage and Legal Recognition of Same-Sex Unions: A Discussion Paper" (Nov. 2002), 21–27, available at http://www.justice.gc.ca/eng/dept-min/pub/mar/index.html.

[31] See Daniel Cere, "Brief to the Senate of Canada on Bill C-38" (July 12, 2005). A transcript of the edited oral submission to the Senate hearings on Bill C-38 can be found in the "Proceeding of the Standing Committee on Legal and Constitutional Affairs," Senate of Canada, Issue 20, Evidence – Afternoon Meeting (July 12, 2005), available at http://www.parl.gc.ca/38/1/parlbus/commbus/senate/com-e/lega-e/20evb-e.htm?Language=E&Parl=38&Ses=1&comm_id=11.

However, the legislature saw no need to recognize the historic conjugal conception of marriage as an official language of marriage in the eyes of the law. Some
observers worried that the effect of the legislation, despite the warm reassurances of
Article 3.1, placed the historic conjugal conception of marriage under a legal cloud,
which would ultimately drive it from the public square until it remained confined
to religious sanctuaries.

Developments since Bill C-38 may confirm these fears. Some provincial marriage
commissioners in Saskatchewan held fast to their convictions concerning the historic
conjugal understanding of marriage and were peremptorily fired as soon as Bill C-38
was passed. The assurances of Bill C-38 regarding religious beliefs and conscience
did little to protect them.[32] The civil–religious divide that was partially designed
to protect the historic conception of marriage seemed to provide the rationale for
removing all traces of such language from the civil sphere. In his commentary on
this, Robert Leckey insists that there is no need to accommodate "religious" convictions of marriage commissioners if one appreciates the sharp divide between civil
and religious marriage. Civil marriage is civil because it is "a secular institution
framed in rejection of religious rules." Allowing a "religious rule" (i.e., the commitment to the historic opposite-sex conception of marriage) to inform the response of a
marriage officer undermines the integrity of "civil marriage."[33] In advancing this line
of argument, Leckey, with a touch of irony, cites a few scriptures for the dissenters
from the newly crafted doctrine of marriage.

The plight of a few marriage commissioners might seem fairly innocuous,[34] but
many constituencies, both religious and nonreligious, who identify with or adhere
to the historic conjugal language of marriage may be increasingly vulnerable. For
example, in December of 2009, Quebec's Justice Department launched a major
public policy initiative designed to wage "war against homophobia" (*Politique
Québéqoise de lutte contre l'homohobie*).[35] Fighting homophobia is a laudable

---

[32] Bruce MacDougall argues in support of the decision to force the resignation of marriage commission-
ers refusing to perform same-sex marriages in "Refusing to Officiate at Same-Sex Civil Marriages,"
Saskatchewan Law Review 69 (2006): 351–374. For critiques of the decision, see Lafferty, "Religion,
Sexual Orientation and the State"; Geoffrey Trotter, "The Right to Decline Performance of Same-
Sex Civil Marriages: The Duty to Accommodate Public Servants – A Response to Professor Bruce
MacDougall," *Saskatchewan Law Review* 70 (2007): 365–392. Bruce Ryder suggests that there needs
to be temporary accommodation of existing marriage commissioners in "The Canadian Conception
of Equal Religious Citizenship," in *Law and Religious Pluralism in Canada*, ed. Richard Moon
(Vancouver: UBC Press, 2008), 87–109.

[33] Leckey, "Profane Matrimony," 21.

[34] Further, it is not self-evident that a policy of official bi-conjugalism could protect their uni-conjugal
approach.

[35] *Politique Québéqoise de lutte contre l'homohobie [Québec Policy Against Homophobia]*, Department
of Justice (Dec. 2009), available at http://www.justice.gouv.qc.ca/FRANCAIS/publications/rapports/
pdf/homophobie.pdf.

project, and one that is, in principle, supported by the conservative Roman Catholic
faith community that has defined the spiritual landscape of Quebec.³⁶ However,
the project defines an extremely broad front along which this proposed "war" is to
be fought. Following a line of argument popularized by Gregory Herek, the policy diagnoses homophobia as a symptom of a more fundamental social pathology,
"heterosexism."³⁷ Heterosexism, in turn, is defined as the "[a]ffirmation of heterosexuality as a social norm."³⁸ The goal of the government initiative is to launch a broad
range of government actions designed "to eliminate heterosexism at [its] source."³⁹
The document outlines the government's commitment to "deal with" all manifestations of heterosexism including "heterosexist values," "heterosexist schemas and
mindsets," "heterosexist assumptions," "heterosexist attitudes," and "heterosexist
stereotypes."⁴⁰

It may seem difficult to square the aggressive moral edge of this war against "heterosexism" with Bill C-38's assurances of the right to free expression with respect
to historic heterosexual conceptions of marriage. However, government initiatives
to root out heterosexist conceptions can be viewed as fully consistent with Bill
C-38's view that the historic definition of marriage is inherently discriminatory.
Once the state has decided to opt for one comprehensive doctrine of marriage on
the grounds that its main competitor is inherently discriminatory, then it seems
reasonable to push for the elimination of all vestiges of this alternative conjugal
language in the civil sphere. Given the breadth of the civil sector, it becomes difficult to draw any meaningful limits to the scope of this kind of action. Accordingly,
the reach of this initiative must include the array of civil society sectors that the
government partners with and the "general population" as a whole, as well as
"public institutions."⁴¹

The logic of these developments appears to be fostering increasing closure on
forms of public discourse that attempt to affirm the historic language of marriage.
Margaret Somerville's recent experience illustrates this drift toward closure both
within the academy and in the public forum. Somerville is an internationally
acclaimed ethicist, winner of the first UNESCO prize in science and ethics, and
recipient of the "Order of Australia." Her progressive approach to ethics won her

³⁶ This principle of social justice is articulated in a number of church documents, including the
Catechism of the Catholic Church, which asserts that "men and women who have deep-seated homosexual tendencies" must be "accepted with respect" and that "every sign of unjust discrimination in
their regard should be avoided." *Catechism of the Catholic Church*, no. 2358.
³⁷ See Gregory Herek, "The Context of Anti-Gay Violence," *Journal of Interpersonal Violence* 5 (1990):
316–333.
³⁸ *Québec Policy Against Homophobia*, 12.
³⁹ Ibid., 28.
⁴⁰ Ibid., 18, 20, 28.
⁴¹ Ibid., 18–22, 30–31.

acclaim in the early 1990s as she fought for a responsible health care response to the AIDS crisis. Somerville is also a strong advocate of children's rights in the domain of new reproductive technologies. In recent years, this commitment has evolved into a complex argument for the role of marriage as an institution safeguarding the birthrights of children.

As the legal and political debate on marriage unfolded, Somerville soon found herself occupying the role of Canada's foremost public intellectual arguing in defense of the historic conception of marriage as a conjugal union of man and woman. She became the target of a remarkable stream of public abuse, including continuous hate mail, university petitions condemning her work, and demands to have her tenured position terminated.[42] Her nomination to the "Order of Canada" was dismissed by the nominating committee on the grounds that she was too controversial.[43] Over the course of her career, Somerville has consistently disavowed any personal interest in religion. Ironically, the absence of any sacred canopy for her public arguments in defense of the historic language of conjugality appears to have left her more exposed.

These developments suggest that the particular strategy Canada has adopted to entrench its legal and political commitment to a nondiscriminatory doctrine of marriage may be posing problems for Canadian commitments to inclusion and deep diversity. Currently, this trajectory appears to require the public enforcement of a comprehensively "liberal" language of conjugality and the public suppression of an alternative language of conjugality widely shared by many sectors of the Canadian community.[44] Some may welcome this result, but how does this outcome square with Canada's strong commitments to liberal multicultural values?

II. FROM MULTICULTURALISM TO MULTI-TIERED CONJUGALITY?

Canada's evolving discourse on multicultural liberalism has a number of peculiar features. In the 1960s, Pierre Elliott Trudeau led the charge to redefine Canadian liberalism. As a public intellectual and Prime Minister, Trudeau's work wove together contributions in political theory, major public policy initiatives, and historic constitutional reforms. The fact that Canadian multiculturalism is now viewed as a thick

---

[42] Ryerson University's decision to grant her an honorary doctorate provoked such intense controversy that elaborate security measures were required to ensure her safety during the event. Somerville offers her own account of this controversy in "Incorrectly Labelled," *MercatorNet*, Feb. 24, 2009, available at http://www.mercatornet.com/articles/view/incorrectly_labelled/.

[43] During the same year, however, the committee awarded the "Order of Canada" to Henry Morgenthaler, Canada's most controversial proabortion advocate.

[44] Compare the discussion of comprehensive liberalism in Canadian marriage law in Mohammad H. Fadel, "Political Liberalism, Islamic Family Law, and Family Law Pluralism" (in this volume).

reality shaping Canadian political ideologies, policies, and practices is, in part, a testimony to the decisive impact of Trudeau's contribution.[45]

Trudeau promoted a unique form of political liberalism forged from his engagement with the work of a number of leading Catholic political thinkers including Lord Acton, Joseph Delos, and Jacques Maritain.[46] At a time when most Western democracies were committed to a "mono-national" concept of the liberal state, Trudeau launched a sweeping theoretical and political assault on this conception.[47] In his 1962 essay "New Treason of the Intellectuals," Trudeau argued for a clear distinction between the nation and the state.[48] To the Lockean achievement of the disestablishment of religion, Trudeau added a call for a historic disestablishment of nationality as the basis for the liberal state. Trudeau claimed that the fusion of nationality and the state had corrupted liberal political order and led to more severe forms of conflict, violence, and repression:

> [R]eligion had to be displaced as the basis of the state before the frightful religious wars came to an end. And there will be no end to wars between nations until in some similar fashion the nation ceases to be the basis of the state.[49]

Trudeau's multicultural imagery attempts to tame and relativize the political aspirations of national and cultural communities, to remove them from the domain of politics, and to firmly relocate them in the sphere of civil society.

Sujit Choudhry argues that Canada's most influential contemporary political theorists, Charles Taylor and Will Kymlicka, have "picked up and further developed" Trudeau's vision of the multicultural liberal state.[50] Choudhry is partially correct, but Taylor and Kymlicka's reading also misrepresents critical tensions in Canadian political thought and practice. Taylor and Kymlicka are deeply committed to a robust multicultural diversity within the liberal state, but they take issue

---

45 See Hugh D. Forbes, "Trudeau as the First Theorist of Canadian Multiculturalism," in *Multiculturalism and the Canadian Constitution*, ed. Stephen Tierney (Vancouver: University of British Columbia Press, 2007), 27–42; see also Augie Fieras and Jean Leonard Elliott, *Engaging Diversity: Multiculturalism in Canada* (Toronto: Nelson Thomson, 2002), ch. 2.

46 See the citations of Catholic social thinkers (Lord Acton, Jacques Maritain, and J. T. Delos) in support of his argument for the separation of nationality and statehood in Pierre Elliott Trudeau, *Federalism and the French Canadians* (New York: St. Martin's Press, 1968), "New Treason of the Intellectuals," 151–181, 159, 169, 177–181. His argument echoes a longstanding Catholic critique of nationalism, namely that the fusion of nation and state can seriously distort the pursuit of the "common good" by conflating it into the interests of "an ethnic group." Ibid., 169. Trudeau's critique of the fusion of state and nationality leans heavily on Lord Acton's analysis in *Essays in the History of Liberty*, vol. 1 (Indianapolis: Liberty Classics, 1985), "Nationality," 409–433, 431–433.

47 Will Kymlicka, *Multicultural Odysseys: Navigating the New International Politics of Diversity* (Oxford: Oxford University Press, 2007), 64.

48 Trudeau, "New Treason of the Intellectuals," 151–181.

49 Ibid., 157–158.

50 Choudhry, "Does the World Need More Canada?" 162.

with Trudeau's approach to diversity. The conflict is rooted in deeper philosophical and political disagreements about liberal multiculturalism. Trudeau's affirmation of the multicultural texture of Canadian society rejects all forms of any extension of legal or political power to cultural communities. The state celebrates, supports, and affirms diversity within civil society but refuses to allow cultural diversity any structural expression in the legal or political order. Taylor and Kymlicka argue that liberal societies can and should allow for more robust public expressions of communitarian identities. They critique "procedural" visions of liberalism that advance conceptions of citizenship cleansed of deep communal commitments to shared goods and aspirations. Trudeau's framework of "symbolic" multiculturalism is wrenched open to include various forms of "structural" multiculturalism that affirm and support diversity through legal and political empowerment.[51]

The conflict between these two visions came to a head in a constitutional crisis. Should the Canadian Federation accommodate francophone aspirations to forge a Quebec political community within Canada empowered to promote their collective "national" concerns for language and culture? Taylor and Kymlicka stressed the need to recognize and accommodate these aspirations. Trudeau strongly repudiated any political empowerment of cultural nationality. The conflict crystallized in a constitutional battle over the Charlottetown Accord, a major constitutional amendment that attempted to entrench recognition of Quebec as a "distinct society" with a "distinct identity" and recognition of aboriginal rights to self-government.[52] The defeat of the Charlottetown Accord was a Pyrrhic victory for proponents of the Trudeau vision of multiculturalism. It resulted in the near loss of the 1995 Quebec referendum on separation by federalist forces. The trauma of the 1995 referendum shifted Canadian discourse on multiculturalism toward the Taylor-Kymlicka vision of "deep diversity."[53] This approach argues that liberal societies should create legal and political space for communities with "strong collective goals" and "ways of belonging" and allow for forms of citizenship anchored in affiliation to particular communities.[54] This form of multiculturalism does not require the internal fabric

---

51 See Joseph Eliot Magnet, *Multiculturalism and the Charter: A Legal Perspective* (Toronto: Carswell, 1987), 145–153.

52 The Charlottetown Accord (1992) was a revised version of the original Meech Lake Accord (1987) that triggered the constitutional debate. The text of the Charlottetown Accord is available at http://www.thecanadianencyclopedia.com/index.cfm?PgNm=TCE&Params=A1ARTA0010099.

53 This development stands in marked contrast to the pessimism expressed by Taylor in the wake of the failure of the Meech Lake Accord. See Charles Taylor, "Deep Diversity and the Future of Canada," in *Can Canada Survive? Under What Terms and Conditions?* Transactions of the Royal Society of Canada, ed. David M. Hayne (Toronto: University of Toronto Press, 1997), 29–35.

54 Charles Taylor, "Shared and Divergent Values," in *Reconciling the Solitudes: Essays on Canadian Federalism and Nationalism* (Montreal and Kingston: McGill-Queens University Press, 1993), 155–186, 177, 183–184.

of political order to be carefully partitioned off from communitarian identities. Multicultural diversity can be afforded legal and political accommodation within the liberal state. Communitarian identities can find expression in diverse forms of multi-tiered legal and political culturalism. The growing recognition of Quebec's distinct status in the federation and the greater accommodation of First Nations' self-government signal a decided shift away from Trudeau's multiculturalist vision to a different form of "deep diversity."[55] By 2001, Will Kymlicka could confidently declare that the terms of public debate has been successfully redefined by those who had fought for the recognition of minority group rights.[56]

The push toward the political recognition and accommodation of diversity feeds into the Canadian discourse on "legal pluralism."[57] The evolving tradition of modern legal pluralism is marked by a "decentring [sic] theme" that displaces the claim of the state to be "the sole or even the privileged source of law."[58] It emphasizes the existence of multiple legal orders, each with their own claim to legitimacy.[59] Some sectors of society, such as religions, corporations, commercial enterprises, and educational institutions, have somewhat formal legal systems with written codes, tribunals, disciplinary procedures, and, in some cases, security forces.[60] Other sectors such as families, kinship groups, or ethnic communities may operate at more informal levels with unwritten codes and customary practices.[61] Legal pluralism challenges the notion that law should be viewed solely through the lens of codified state law. It views the complex world of law as a "muddy, gothic sort of an affair."[62]

[55] Katherine Fierbleck suggests this shift away from the Trudeau vision may be short-lived. See "Minority Rights and Multiculturalism," in *Political Thought in Canada: An Intellectual History* (Peterborough, ON: Broadview Press, 2006), 133–151.

[56] Will Kymlicka, *Politics in the Vernacular: Nationalism, Multiculturalism, and Citizenship* (Oxford: Oxford University Press, 2001), 32–33; Anne Phillips, *Multiculturalism Without Culture* (Princeton, NJ: Princeton University Press, 2007), 11.

[57] Roderick Macdonald, the first president of the Law Commission of Canada, is one of Canada's most prominent exponents of critical legal pluralism. See, e.g., R. A. Macdonald, "Metaphors of Multiplicity: Civil Society, Regimes and Legal Pluralism," *Arizona Journal of International and Comparative Law* 15 (1998): 69–91.

[58] Jeremy Webber, "Legal Pluralism and Human Agency," *Osgoode Hall Law Journal* 44:1 (2006): 167–198, 189.

[59] Roderick A. Macdonald and David Sandomierski, "Against Nomopolies," *Northern Ireland Legal Quarterly* 57 (2006): 610–633. According to Leopold Pospisil, "[E]very functioning subgroup in a society has its own legal system which is necessarily different in some respects from those of the other subgroups." *The Anthropology of Law: A Comparative Theory of Law* (New York: Harper and Row, 1971), 107.

[60] See John Griffiths, "What is Legal Pluralism?" *Journal of Legal Pluralism* 24 (1986): 1–56, 38.

[61] Sally Merry Engle, "Legal Pluralism," *Law & Society Review* 22:5 (1988): 869–896, 870–871.

[62] Margaret Davies, "Pluralism and Legal Philosophy," *Northern Ireland Legal Quarterly* 57 (2006): 577–596, 583 (quoting William James, *A Pluralistic Universe* [Cambridge, MA, and London: Harvard University Press, 1977], 26). See also Werner Menski, "Ancient and Modern Boundary Crossings Between Personal Laws and Civil Law in Composite India" (in this volume).

However, some forms of legal pluralism go a step further and argue for the recognition and incorporation of diverse regimes of law into state law in order to address areas of legal concern central to the survival and development of diverse communities within society. Given the centrality of conjugal life to the identity and survival of religious and cultural communities, it comes as no surprise to find that the legal accommodation of diverse religious regimes of marriage or family law has been one of the major expressions of legal pluralist systems of law.[63]

In recent years, multicultural conflicts have centered on religion, gender, family, and marriage, rather than on national and cultural identities. According to Kymlicka, the increasing "salience of religion" in liberal debates over pluralism is one of the most notable shifts in the discourse on diversity in recent years.[64] The Canadian brew of multiculturalism, deep diversity theory, and legal pluralism has allowed for multi-tiered constitutional accommodations of linguistic, cultural, and aboriginal communities. It has also provided constitutional space for multi-tiered systems of education that include various forms of public confessional educational institutions. Does it offer a prime setting for experiments in multi-tiered systems of conjugal law? This question was raised, and to some extent answered, in the heated debate over family arbitration boards in Ontario.[65]

The *shari'a* courts debate was sparked in 2003 with the announcement by the Islamic Institute of Civil Justice (IICJ) of its intention to establish a Muslim family law arbitration tribunal. Marion Boyd's 2004 government report on "Dispute Resolution in Family Law" notes that the IICJ's declaration "raised acute alarm throughout Ontario and Canada" and beyond.[66] However, the public alarm seemed curiously belated, for Christian, Jewish, and Islamic (Ismaili) communities had established and operated faith-based family arbitration tribunals since the passage of the Ontario Arbitration Act in 1990. Public outrage only flared with the announcement and publicity of a project to establish an arbitration tribunal that would draw on principles from Sunni religious law. The proposal was immediately branded as an attempt to impose the harsh disciplines of *shari'a* law on vulnerable Muslim women. The president of the IICJ, Syed Mumtaz Ali, was portrayed as a hard-line fundamentalist Muslim leader determined to exploit Ontario's Arbitration Act as a

[63] The integration of indigenous law by Western colonial regimes is the standard historical example of this form of juridical legal pluralism. See Engle, "Legal Pluralism"; John Griffiths, "What is Legal Pluralism?" 869–896.

[64] Will Kymlicka, "Introduction," in *Canadian Diversity/Diversité Canadienne* 2:1 (2003), 4, available at http://canada.metropolis.net/publications/Diversity/Diversity.Spring2003.pdf.

[65] See also Fadel, "Political Liberalism" (in this volume) and Ayelet Shachar, "Faith in Law? Diffusing Tensions Between Diversity and Equality" (in this volume).

[66] Marion Boyd, Office of Canadian Attorney General, *Dispute Resolution in Family Law: Protecting Choice, Promoting Inclusion* (2004), 3, 29–68, available at http://www.attorneygeneral.jus.gov.on.ca/english/about/pubs/boyd/fullreport.pdf.

Trojan horse to smuggle the sword of *shari'a* law into Canada's naively good-natured multiculturalism.[67]

This account does not do justice to the biographical complexity of Ali, however, nor to the theoretical and political sophistication of the faith-based arbitration proposals that he and his colleagues advanced. Ali studied law at the University of London and the Osgoode Hall School of Law at York University. In 1962, he became the first Muslim to be appointed to the Canadian Bar Association and served as a corporate lawyer in the Ontario government for twenty-five years. Throughout his legal career, he was an advocate for Canada's Charter of Rights and Freedoms and a keen proponent of Canadian multiculturalism. In addition, he was active in the Toronto Muslim community and a faithful devotee of the Sufi mystical tradition, a fairly inclusive brand of Islam. In some ways, Ali could be viewed as a "poster boy" for Canadian multiculturalism.[68]

In his retirement, Ali decided to dedicate himself to enriching the Canadian multicultural experience by working to integrate the Muslim community more fully into the Canadian mosaic. In 1992, Ali and Anab (Bill) Whitehouse published an essay in the *Journal of Muslim Minority Affairs* that voiced a classic Canadian lament, namely that Canada was still falling short of its "promise and potential" as a "truly multicultural society." It then proceeded to issue a predictable call for a more generous expansion of Canadian principles of diversity, multiculturalism, minority rights, and legal pluralism.[69] Ali and Whitehouse sided with theorists of deep diversity in challenging hegemonic conceptions of the nation-state sovereignty. They argued that the growing recognition of the distinct character of Quebec and Aboriginal communities underscores the fact that Canadian multiculturalism has been evolving toward recognition of the collaborative coexistence of multiple sovereignties

[67] This line of interpretation was common in mainstream media accounts as well as more nuanced responses. For example, see the position paper of one of Canada's prominent human rights organizations, the government-established Centre for Human Rights and Democratic Development: Karin Baqi, "Behind Closed Doors: How Faith-Based Arbitration Shuts Out Women's Rights in Canada and Abroad," International Centre for Human Rights and Democratic Development (2005), available at http://www.dd-rd.ca/english/commdoc/publications/women/arbifaith.htm.

[68] "Syed Mumtaz Ali, 82 ... Muslim Visionary 'Believed in the Promise of Multiculturalism,'" *The Toronto Star*, July 21, 2009, available at http://www.thestar.com/article/669288; "Syed Mumtaz Ali, First Muslim Lawyer in Canada, Dies at 82," *CBC News*, July 17, 2009, available at http://www.cbc.ca/canada/story/2009/07/17/syed-mumtaz-ali.html.

[69] Syed Mumtaz Ali and Enab Whitehouse, "The Reconstruction of the Constitution and the Case for Muslim Personal Law in Canada," *Journal of Muslim Minority Affairs* 13:1 (1992): 156–172, 156. Whitehouse's expertise is in the area of educational theory and policy. He has been active in the Sufi community for more than thirty years. An earlier and more extended version of their argument can be found in *Oh! Canada: Whose Land? Whose Dream? Sovereignty, Social Contracts and Participatory Democracy*, Canadian Society of Muslims (1991), available at http://www.scribd.com/doc/34252345/ocanada.

within a liberal federal system. Diverse communities should be empowered to "govern their own affairs" in domains vital to their existence. In their view, two spheres of social life were of critical concern to religious communities: education and family law.[70]

Ali and Whitehouse argued that Canadian constitutional commitments to multiculturalism and religious freedom can only be met through a more robust form of legal pluralism that recognizes religious communities as comprehensive forms of identity that touch on the diverse facets of an individual's life.[71] They noted that the capacity for a religious community to operate effectively within its legal order is particularly acute for traditions that view religious law as integral to their identity and practice. If Muslims are seriously constrained from the free exercise of their religious law, then they are "prevented from freely pursuing and committing themselves to the Islamic religious tradition, since adhering to the various aspects of Islamic family and personal law are all acts of worship."[72]

The IICJ's arguments for multi-tiered conjugal law tap into longstanding traditions of Islamic legal pluralism that accent of the role of religion in the domain of personal and family life.[73] But they also converge with vectors of Canadian multiculturalism that call for structural as well as symbolic accommodation of diversity. Strong versions of structural accommodation may fall into forms of "non-interventionist accommodation" or "reactive culturalism," critiqued by Ayelet Shachar.[74] Noninterventional forms of accommodation grant full jurisdiction over family law to religious groups with minimal state intervention. Shachar warns against maximizing identity group rights at the expense of individual rights, particularly the rights of vulnerable sectors within the group.[75]

The expert appointed to examine the question of faith-based arbitration, Marion Boyd, was a respected feminist legal reformer who shared Shachar's concerns about noninterventionist forms of legal pluralism.[76] However, Boyd also argued that a "secular absolutist" approach dismissive of any form of accommodation would

---

[70] Ali and Whitehouse, "Reconstruction of the Constitution," 162, 165–170.

[71] Ibid., 171.

[72] Ibid., 166, 167–168.

[73] For a discussion of Islamic legal pluralism, see Baudouin Dupret, Maurits Berger, and Laila Al-Zwaini, eds., *Legal Pluralism in the Arab World* (The Hague: Kluwer Law International, 1999).

[74] Ayelet Shachar, "Reshaping the Multicultural Model: Group Accommodation in Individual Rights," *Windsor Review of Legal and Social Issues* 8 (1998): 83–112, 94ff. Shachar labels this approach "reactive culturalism" in *Multicultural Jurisdictions: Cultural Differences and Women's Rights* (Cambridge: Cambridge University Press, 2001), 35–37.

[75] Shachar, *Multicultural Jurisdictions*, 17–62.

[76] Marion Boyd, "Religion-Based Alternative Dispute Resolution: A Challenge to Multiculturalism," in *Belonging? Diversity, Recognition and Shared Citizenship in Canada*, eds. Keith G. Banting, Thomas J. Courchene, and F. Leslie Seidle (Montreal: The Institute for Research on Public Policy, 2007), 469.

be "equally contentious, given the religious and multicultural rights enshrined in the Charter of Rights and Freedoms."[77] Modern liberal democracies must create space for those who want to "live their lives in a manner more closely aligned to their faith."[78] Boyd's report deliberately leaned toward a third option, namely the "transformational accommodation" approach advocated by Shachar. This approach attempts to achieve a "balancing" or "institutional dialogue" between "group religious and cultural freedoms with individual rights and freedoms."[79] Communities would be given an institutional forum for the expression of their religious law with constitutional commitments to basic rights and gender equality built into the arbitration procedures. Religious law would be invited, not compelled, to dance with secular law.[80] However, if the invitation were accepted, this dance would be shaped by Charter commitments to rights and gender equality. Shachar argues that this approach would have a transformative impact on the internal development of religious legal traditions.

Despite the claims of some that the IICJ was wedded to a hard-line strategy of noninterventionist accommodation, in fact Ali responded to Boyd's model of "transformative accommodation" with considerable enthusiasm. He had consistently argued that Muslims were required to work within the law of the land and expressed complete satisfaction with an approach that ensured that "Canadian laws prevail" as *shari'a* law "takes a back seat."[81] He concluded that the approach advanced in Boyd's report was "a model for the whole world to see how sharia law can be used in a Western society."[82] Canadian multiculturalism seemed poised to take a few steps toward multi-tiered conjugalism. However, that line of development was brought to an abrupt halt with the proclamation by the Ontario government on September 11, 2005, that all forms of faith-based family arbitration would be abolished.[83]

Some scholars argue that the negative public and political reaction was largely driven by forms of Orientalist discourse that viewed Islam as inherently patriarchal and Muslim women as immured in a culture of domination and subordination.[84]

---

[77] Ibid.

[78] Ibid.

[79] Ibid., 470–471.

[80] See Shachar's discussion of the voluntary nature of these arrangements in "Privatizing Diversity: A Cautionary Tale from Religious Arbitration in Family Law," *Theoretical Inquiries in Law* 9:2 (2008): 573–607. See also Shachar, "Faith in Law?" (in this volume).

[81] Caroline Mallan, "Report Called 'Betrayal' of Women: Proposal Backs Use of Islamic Principles in Settling Disputes, Ontario Heading in 'Dangerous Direction', Opponents Say," *Toronto Star*, Dec. 21, 2004.

[82] Ibid.

[83] "Ontario Premier Rejects Use of Shariah Law," *CBC News*, Sept.11, 2005, available at http://www.cbc.ca/canada/story/2005/09/09/sharia-protests-20050909.html.

[84] See, e.g., Anna C. Korteweg, "The Shariah Debate in Ontario: Gender, Islam, and Representation of Muslim Women's Agency," *Gender and Society* 22:4 (2008): 434–454.

The swift and successful defeat of Boyd's fairly modest multi-tiered conjugal proposal may also illuminate another problem, however – the ambiguous place of religion in Canadian multicultural discourse. For a variety of reasons, Canadian multiculturalism, in both policy and theoretical discourse, has systematically excluded any reference to religion. Throughout the 1970s, 80s, and 90s, Canadian multicultural discourse rarely referred to religion or included religious communities in its policy deliberations. Some argue that this omission has been a "critical flaw" in Trudeau's multicultural model.[85] Religion was not completely ignored, but rather completely subsumed under the category of ethnicity and culture. The communal or institutional face of religion could find a place in the Canadian multicultural mosaic as an expression of culture. However, in the Trudeau vector of multiculturalism, religion (like culture or ethnicity) must undergo a thoroughgoing depoliticization in order to find its place in the Canadian mosaic.

The "deep diversity" vector of multiculturalism and legal pluralism has also proven to be suspicious of the communal rights of religion. Despite their emphasis on deep diversity, both Kymlicka and Taylor seem to side with this strict relegation of religion in the domain of civil society. Kymlicka insists that liberalism "can and should endorse certain group-differentiated rights for ethnic groups and national communities," but this endorsement does not extend to religious communities.[86] He places two major restrictions on the extension of group rights to religious communities. First, a liberal conception of group rights does not cover communities that place "internal restrictions" on its members that are inconsistent with liberal values. The internal life of the community must be governed by liberal values, and its members must have the "freedom and capacity to question and possibly revise the traditional practices of their community."[87] Second, liberalism cannot allow forms of group rights that would privilege one group in ways that could facilitate the oppression or exploitation of other groups. Liberalism demands "freedom within" the rights-holding community as well as freedom between communities.[88]

The second requirement poses no major problem for religious communities and represents a fairly longstanding consensus within liberal societies. However, the first requirement poses serious concerns. Kymlicka recognizes the controversial nature of his argument insofar as his "unrelenting commitment" to liberal values may appear

[85] John Biles and Humera Ibrahim, "Religion and Public Policy: Immigration, Citizenship, and Multiculturalism – Guess Who's Coming to Dinner?" in *Religion and Ethnicity in Canada*, eds. Paul Bramadat and David Seljak (Toronto: Pearson Longman, 2005), 154–177, 164.
[86] Will Kymlicka, *Multicultural Citizenship: A Liberal Theory of Minority Rights* (Oxford: Oxford University Press, 1995), 152.
[87] Ibid. See also Linda C. McClain, "Marriage Pluralism in the United States: On Civil and Religious Jurisdiction and the Demands of Equal Citizenship" (in this volume).
[88] Kymlicka, *Multicultural Citizenship*, 152.

to foster a stance of intolerance toward "non-liberal groups."[89] Religious traditions loom large in Kymlicka's discussion as they are the prime examples of groups organized along illiberal lines. These communities often pose unique challenges for liberal democracies "since they often demand internal restrictions that conflict with individual civil rights."[90]

But are these internal restrictions protected by a fundamental liberal principle, namely religious freedom? Not quite, according to Kymlicka. His insistence on the limits of liberal tolerance involves some serious work on the question of religious freedom. Kymlicka argues for a strictly individualistic conception of religious freedom. He contends that the modern liberal affirmation of religious freedom has taken "a very specific form – namely, the idea of individual freedom of conscience."[91] Religious freedom, in this formulation, reinforces liberal commitments to autonomy and freedom as it asserts the fundamental subjective right to define one's basic conception of life, the right to dissent from shared religious or nonreligious conceptions of the good, and the right to engage in ongoing "radical revision" of one's fundamental religious, philosophical, or ethical values.[92] Religious freedom is not about rights linked to communal commitments. On the contrary, religious freedom underscores and highlights the basic liberal "commitment to autonomy – that is, the idea that individuals should be free to assess and potentially revise their existing ends."[93]

This conception of religious freedom was endorsed by Canada's Supreme Court in its landmark *Amselem v. Northcrest Syndicat* decision (2004).[94] Writing for the majority, Justice Iacobucci puts forward "a personal or subjective conception of freedom of religion – that is integrally linked with an individual's self-definition and fulfillment and is a function of personal autonomy and choice."[95] Charles Taylor, Canada's most prominent "deep diversity" theorist, also embraces this view. In the Quebec commission report on reasonable accommodation, Charles Taylor and Gerard Bouchard argue on behalf of *Amselem's* "subjective conception of religious freedom."[96] Canada's Charter of Rights and Freedoms affirms both freedom of conscience and religion (in Article 2), but Taylor and Bouchard argue

[89] Ibid., 154–155.
[90] Ibid., 164.
[91] Ibid., 156.
[92] Ibid., 82.
[93] Ibid., 158.
[94] *Syndicat Northcrest v. Amselem*, [2004] 2 S.C.R. 551, 2004 SCC 47.
[95] Ibid., ¶ 42.
[96] Gérard Bouchard and Charles Taylor, *Building for the Future: A Time for Reconciliation* (Québec: Bibliothèque et Archives Nationales du Québec, 2008), 175–177, available at http://www.accommodements.qc.ca/documentation/rapports/rapport-final-integral-en.pdf.

that "freedom of religion" should be viewed merely "as an aspect of freedom of conscience."[97]

Proponents of this view emphasizing freedom of conscience see this formulation as an advance in two ways. First, they argue that it represents "an expansive definition of freedom of religion" because any deeply held conviction of conscience can be viewed as equivalent to a religious conviction.[98] Second, and "more fundamentally," as Taylor and Bouchard emphasize, "it is not religious convictions in themselves that enjoy special status in liberal democracies but instead all deep-seated convictions or convictions of conscience that allow individuals to shape their moral identity."[99] Taylor wants to ensure the proper weight is accorded to "questions of identity" and the "deep-seated convictions that dwell in the human heart."[100]

There is a valid concern to this viewpoint. However, it is not clear why blurring meaningful distinctions between religion and subjective conscience are required in order to accord due weight to claims of conscience. Historically, conscience and religion have typically been linked in human rights talk but have not been conflated. In part, this seems due to the fact that religion involves a critical nexus of communal relationships and traditions that are not adequately captured in the concept of conscience. By collapsing religion into the category of conscience, rights talk is rendered incapable of speaking to these communitarian dimensions of religion and religious freedom.

This trade-off seems to be a particularly steep price to pay for an evolving school of social theory celebrated for its attention to the communal, contextual, and situated dimensions of the self. Nonetheless, Kymlicka emphasizes the contrast between his modern liberal conception of religious freedom and communitarian versions of religious freedom that defend the right of religious groups to organize their community life as they see fit, even "along non-liberal lines."[101] He labels these communitarian conceptions as variations of the "millet system" of the Ottoman Empire. Under that system, religious communities are left free to govern large sectors of their personal, communal, and familial life. This approach to religious freedom, in Kymlicka's view, creates a "federation of theocracies" with little room for liberal commitments to freedom, equality, dissent, and ongoing reform in the internal life of these communities.[102] Revised variations of the millet system can be found in

[97] Ibid., 144–145.
[98] *Syndicat Northcrest v. Amselem,* ¶ 40. Taylor and Bouchard cite the example of a prisoner who has embraced vegetarianism due to secular convictions of conscience. These convictions merit accommodation as much as religious convictions. *Building for the Future,* 145.
[99] Ibid., 145.
[100] Ibid., 144.
[101] Kymlicka, *Multicultural Citizenship,* 156.
[102] Ibid., 156–157.

current communitarian conceptions of religious freedom. Liberal multiculturalism, Kymlicka insists, must resist these communitarian accounts of religious freedom.

Whereas the leading exponents of the "Canadian school" press for multi-tiered legal pluralism in arguing for the extension of group rights and freedoms to certain national and aboriginal communities, they firmly put the foot to the brake in the face of claims by religious communities. In fact, some Canadian liberals head in the opposite direction, arguing for more aggressive intervention by the liberal state into the internal illiberal practices of religious communities. Janice Stein is particularly concerned with patterns of gender inequality and homophobia that infect religious approaches to marriage, family, and sexuality. She suggests the possibility of a variety of disciplinary measures such as court intervention, stripping communities of charitable tax status, and the removal of other public benefits for religious traditions that violate liberal norms in the sensitive areas of gender equality and family law.[103] Stein is advocating state confrontation with, not multi-tiered accommodation of, diverse religious marriage regimes.

Kymlicka is sympathetic to Stein's concerns, but he contends that the rights issue must be kept distinct from the strategic question of best practices in negotiating conflicts between a liberal state and illiberal groups within their jurisdiction. Kymlicka suggests a softer strategy. He argues that attempts at external coercive intervention typically backfire and provoke communal entrenchment and resistance, especially in the case of minority traditions that have been the victims of a history of discrimination and disempowerment by the majority culture.[104] However, turning down strategies of strong interventionism does not mean that the state should remain neutral. Kymlicka recommends a variety of public strategies that foster softer forms of persistent pressure rather than hard, decisive interventions. He contends that the more effective investment is to actively promote liberal values through education, persuasion, incentives, and concrete support for reformers and movements of reform internal to these communities.[105]

In gentle disagreement with Stein, Kymlicka argues that the critical problem is not the tension between multiculturalism and the culture of rights, but the tension between flawed conceptions of religious freedom and human rights. He defends multiculturalism as "an integral part of the rights revolution" but firmly rejects the notion that religious traditions should be accorded any group rights protection under the banner of multiculturalism. Religions, Kymlicka acknowledges, continue

---

[103] Janice Gross Stein, "Living Better Multiculturally," *Literary Review of Canada* 147 (Sept. 2006): 3–5. A revised version of this essay was published as "Searching for Equality" in *Uneasy Partners: Multiculturalism and Rights in Canada*, eds. Janice Gross Stein, David Robertson Cameron, John Ibbitson, and Will Kymlicka (Toronto: Wilfrid Laurier Press, 2007), 1–22.

[104] Kymlicka, *Multicultural Citizenship*, 167.

[105] Ibid., 166–168.

to claim such rights by invoking "the pre-modern doctrine of *libertas ecclesiae*."[106] However, this premodern approach is no longer tenable given the decisive modern shift toward an individualistic conception of religious freedom accenting autonomy and choice.

Kymlicka's dismissive approach to the communal character of religious freedom offers a troubling reading of the history of liberal discourse on religious liberty. First, by anchoring his critique of communal conceptions of religious freedom in an analysis of the Ottoman "millet system," Kymlicka clearly implies that this approach finds its origins in premodern, authoritarian, non-Western traditions. More specifically, he implies that the advocacy of communal religious rights finds its true ideological home in medieval Islamic law. Labeling communitarian accounts of religious rights as "*shari'a*-made" is surely, in the current context of debate, a not-so-subtle exercise in discrediting.

Second, Kymlicka dismisses the longstanding emphasis on communal dimensions of religious freedom in the Western tradition as a "pre-modern" perspective inconsistent with modern liberal commitments to personal autonomy and choice. It is true that this communitarian perspective does have premodern roots. The first major rights document of the Western tradition, the Magna Carta (1215), begins with an affirmation of communal religious freedom, the rights and freedom of the church in relation to the state. Religious freedom, in this decidedly communal form, stands out as the "first freedom" in the Western narrative of human rights. In Canada, the discourse on religious freedom begins with eighteenth-century treaties and legislation offering robust recognition of the institutional freedom of the Roman Catholic Church under the British conquest. The extension of confessional educational rights in the 1867 BNA Act continues this line of communal religious rights talk. However, such discourse carries forward well into the modern era. Some of the major watershed court decisions in the late twentieth-century jurisprudence on religious freedom continued to work with this "pre-modern" understanding.[107] Not surprisingly, Kymlicka finds himself deeply at odds with these historic court decisions defending the communal texture of religious freedom.[108] It appears that the drift of contemporary Canadian legal and social theory seems to be following Kymlicka's lead.

---

[106] Will Kymlicka, "Disentangling the Debate," in Stein et al., *Uneasy Partners*, 147.

[107] One example is the *Hofer v. Hofer* decision, which dealt with the authority of a Hutterite community over its members (*Hofer v. Hofer*, [1970] S.C.R. 958). See Chief Justice Beverley McLachlin's discussion of the pre-Charter history of religious freedom in Canada, in "Freedom of Religion and the Rule of Law: A Canadian Perspective," in *Recognizing Religion in a Secular Society*, ed. Douglas Farrow (Montreal: McGill-Queen's University Press, 2004), 12–34.

[108] Kymlicka, *Multicultural Citizenship*, 161–162.

In short, despite a rich body of Canadian multicultural theory and praxis, there seems to be little or no appetite for any meaningful recognition or multi-tiered legal accommodation of religion, especially when it comes to the contentious areas of marriage and family law. The final resolution of the debate over Islamic religious arbitration boards in Ontario only seems to underscore this aversion.

III. CONCLUSION

Monogamy and consent now seem to be the last markers of marriage in Canadian law. However, it remains an open question whether Canada's new doctrine of "conjugality" ("the lawful union of two *persons* to the exclusion of all others") can be stabilized in the face of new challenges. In spite of Canada's extended legal and political debate on the civil law definition of marriage, the substantive meaning of conjugality has become increasingly elusive. Conjugal unions can exist without sexual intimacy, shared residence, pooling of assets or domestic tasks, or even a common understanding of conjugality.[109] Susan Drummond concludes that the concept of conjugality in Canadian law is "collapsing into uncertainty and incoherence" – it has "become fluid and open-ended to the point of having no legal meaning at all."[110]

A series of court judgments prepared the way for the Civil Marriage Act. These decisions denounced as discriminatory the longstanding legal definition of marriage established in *Hyde v. Hyde* (1866): "Marriage as understood *in Christendom* is the voluntary union for life of one man and one woman, to the exclusion of all others."[111] In the debates over the redefinition of marriage, much was made of the fact that *Hyde's* "Christendom" conception of marriage entrenched a heterosexual concept of marriage. However, the defense of heterosexuality was not the intent of *Hyde*. *Hyde* was grappling with the issue of polygamy, and its direct appeal to Christianity served to anchor its argument for the monogamous nature of marriage, not sex difference. Bill C-38 does nothing to challenge this core Christian conviction. In fact, it simply pares marriage down to this "Christendom" principle that *Hyde* deliberately invokes to rebut polygamy.

But even this pillar seems shaky. Immediately after the passage of Bill C-38, the federal government launched a legal research project to examine the grounds for the criminalization of polygamous unions under Section 293 of the Criminal Code of Canada. The reporters recognize that the "pressing and substantial objective"

---

[109] Susan D. Drummond, "Polygamy's Inscrutable Criminal Mischief," *Osgoode Hall Law Journal* 47 (2009): 317–369, 323; see also Brenda Cossman and Bruce Ryder, "What is Marriage-Like Like? The Irrelevance of Conjugality," *Canadian Journal of Family Law* 18 (2001): 269–326.

[110] Drummond, "Polygamy's Inscrutable Criminal Mischief," 324, 368.

[111] *Hyde v. Hyde and Woodmansee*, 1 L.R.P& D. 131 (1866) (italics added).

pursued by the criminalization of polygamy serves a "religious purpose," namely the suppression of Mormon polygamy.[112] The reporters conclude that the law can be saved only by substituting a secular purpose, namely our constitutional commitment to gender equality.[113] However, this line of argument meets with considerable legal skepticism. First, Canadian courts frown on legislation originally designed to serve a religious purpose and have been reluctant to entertain "shifting purposes."[114] Second, because monogamy has been wedded to patriarchy for most of its history, the strict application of gender equality to polygamous unions appears to be both "under-inclusive" and "arbitrary."[115] Third, according to one reporter, field research into Canada's best-known polygamous sect, the FLDS Bountiful community, challenges the dominant narrative that depicts polygamous women as submissive, silent, oppressed, and isolated. This "counter-narrative" portrays Bountiful women as thoughtful, articulate, engaged with the wider world, and capable of wielding authority in their social context.[116] This reporter questions "why their lifestyle should trigger a risk of incarceration while 'ours' (i.e., monogamous unions) … is not only tolerated, but actively promoted by the state."[117] Finally, even if widespread concerns for women's equality and the protection of women and children in polygamous communities deserve attention as "pressing and substantial," the reporters argue that these objectives can be met more effectively by laws and social policies "more rationally connected" to these goals than the criminalization of polygamy.[118]

If the pillar of monogamy eventually falls, it will not be due to the working out of a Canadian ethos of deep diversity intent on finding a place for the curious conjugal practices of religious communities like Bountiful. The drift of Canadian law appears to be in the direction of legal arrangements that allow for increasing diversity in the private ordering of conjugal relationships. Multi-tiered conceptions of marriage envisage a respectful dance between state law and other forms of normative conjugal ordering. The drift toward private ordering seems bent on marginalizing or eroding all forms of normative ordering in order to maximize individual choice.

Canadian legal theorist Brenda Cossman celebrates this evolution toward the legal deregulation of the family and argues for the ongoing "bundling, unbundling and rebundling [of family forms] in ways that may have previously been

---

[112] Martha Bailey, et al., "Expanding Recognition of Foreign Polygamous Marriages: Policy Implications for Canada," Legal Studies Research Paper, *Status of Women Canada* (2005): 22–23, available at http://papers.ssrn.com/sol3/papers.cfm?abstract_id=1023896.

[113] The reporters conclude that gender equality is "the only argument available to establish a secular objective for s. 293." Ibid., 22.

[114] Ibid., 23.

[115] Ibid., 24.

[116] Angela Campbell, "Bountiful Voices," *Osgoode Hall Law Journal* 47 (2009): 183–234, 183.

[117] Ibid., 228.

[118] Drummond, "Polygamy's Inscrutable Mischief," 325, 361.

unimaginable."[119] This approach to conjugal and familial diversification rejects multi-tiered approaches that might provide some legal support for, and stabilization of, specific conjugal or familial forms. In this view, the goal of the law is not to strengthen or institutionalize normative orders. On the contrary, the law works to dissolve restrictive bonds and extricate marriage and the family from the traditional normative constraints imposed by legal or religious codes. The law becomes a creative solvent that continually lubricates and loosens up normative constraints so that there can be an ongoing "reimagining of the possibilities and realities of Canadian families."[120] Charles Taylor anglicizes a somewhat untranslatable French term *fragiliser* (literally, "to render fragile") to speak to pressures within modernity that destabilize, pluralize, and relativize normative orders.[121] If Cossman is right, then the trajectory of Canadian family law is not toward multi-tiered legal accommodations of diversity, but toward the legal weakening or "fragilisation" of diverse forms of conjugal ordering. This vision of pluralism does not work to legally stabilize and shore up conjugal cultures, but to render them more contingent, conditional, fragile, and malleable to the evolving interests and aspirations of the autonomous self.

[119] Brenda Cossman, "Parenting Beyond the Nuclear Family: *Doe. v. Alberta*," *Alberta Law Review* 45:2 (2007): 501–514, 513.
[120] Ibid.
[121] See Charles Taylor, *A Secular Age*, (Cambridge, MA: Belknap Press, 2007), 303–304.

Marriage Pluralism in the United States

On Civil and Religious Jurisdiction and the Demands of Equal Citizenship

Linda C. McClain

I. INTRODUCTION: THE CALL FOR MORE PLURALISM AND SHARED JURISDICTION IN U.S. FAMILY LAW

"Legal pluralism" is hot. Indeed, "legal pluralism is everywhere."[1] As Brian Tamanaha observes, not only is there "in every social arena one examines, a seeming multiplicity of legal orders, from the lowest local level to the most expansive global level," but, in the last few decades, legal pluralism itself "has become a major topic in legal anthropology, legal sociology, comparative law, international law, and socio-legal studies."[2] But problems with defining and understanding legal pluralism continue to "plague" its study.[3]

What of legal pluralism in family law? Is such pluralism already "everywhere," if we just look closely? A common observation is that family law – and family law practice – in the United States have become global due to "the globalization of the family."[4] As people form families across geographic and national boundaries, lawyers and courts routinely deal with complex questions of jurisdiction and comity with respect to marriage, divorce, child custody, and the like.

Has the time come, at the normative level, to embrace more legal pluralism in family law within the United States? If so, what form should it take? To answer these questions, clarifying what is meant by "legal pluralism" in family law is crucial. Broadly defined, legal pluralism acknowledges that there are multiple sources of normative ordering in every society. Such sources include not only the "official"

---

[1] Brian Z. Tamanaha, "Understanding Legal Pluralism: Past to Present, Local to Global," *Sydney Law Review* 30 (September 2008): 375–411, 375.
[2] Ibid.
[3] Ibid.
[4] Ann Laquer Estin and Barbara Stark, *Global Issues in Family Law* (St. Paul, MN: Thomson-West, 2007), 1.

legal system, embodied in civil cases, statutes, and constitutions, but also, as Ann Estin describes in this volume, the "unofficial family law" of religious tribunals, rules, customs, and the like.[5] This unofficial family law has a formative effect on persons and communities even if it is not buttressed by binding state authority.

More narrowly defined, legal pluralism refers not to this broader normative pluralism but to questions of jurisdiction and juridical power.[6] Sally Engle Merry explains that "state law" is "fundamentally different" than non-state forms of ordering because "it exercises the coercive power of the state and monopolizes the symbolic power associated with state authority." She urges that the study of legal pluralism attend to the interaction of state law with these other forms of ordering.[7]

The Multi-Tiered Marriage Project calls for a national conversation on this interaction between state and non-state power with respect to jurisdiction over marriage and divorce. It answers "yes" to the "ought" question about whether there should be more jurisdictional pluralism. Project convenor Joel Nichols proposes that, in the United States, "civil government should consider ceding some of its jurisdictional authority over marriage and divorce law to religious communities that are competent and capable of adjudicating the marital rites and rights of their respective adherents."[8] He finds, already within the United States, some forms of a multi-tiered system, described elsewhere in this volume: covenant marriage, available in three states, and New York's *get* statutes.[9] In Louisiana, for example, key proponents of covenant marriage self-consciously sought to instantiate a covenant model of marriage in keeping with "God's intended purpose for marriage."[10]

To usher in more legal pluralism in the United States, Nichols proposes to learn from other legal systems. He spins the globe and finds many instructive ways to share jurisdiction over marriage and divorce law, such as multiple systems of personal law, in which religious tribunals have jurisdiction; legal recognition of customary marriage; and allowing religious bodies to arbitrate family law matters.[11]

What form would a new jurisdictional pluralism in U.S. family law take? Nichols proposes a "more robust millet system."[12] The analogy is to the Ottoman Empire's millet system, in which personal law (including marriage) was administered by

[5] Ann Laquer Estin, "Unofficial Family Law" (in this volume).
[6] Tamanaha, "Understanding Legal Pluralism."
[7] Sally Engle Merry, "Legal Pluralism," *Law and Society Review* (1988): 869–896, 869, 879.
[8] Joel A. Nichols, "Multi-Tiered Marriage: Ideas and Influences from New York and Louisiana to the International Community," *Vanderbilt Journal of Transnational Law* 40 (January 2007): 135–196, 135. See also Joel A. Nichols, "Multi-Tiered Marriage: Reconsidering the Boundaries of Civil Law and Religion" (in this volume).
[9] Nichols, "Multi-Tiered Marriage," 148. The three states are Arkansas, Arizona, and Louisiana.
[10] Katherine Shaw Spaht, "Covenant Marriage: An Achievable Legal Response to the Inherent Nature of Marriage and Its Various Goods," *Ave Maria Law Review* 4 (Summer 2006): 467–496, 470.
[11] Nichols, "Multi-Tiered Marriage," 164–195.
[12] Ibid., 164.

religious tribunals, a system still operating to varying degrees in some countries that Nichols canvasses. His model, which envisions "semiautonomous" religious entities and the state acting as the overarching sovereign that intervenes only when basic minimum guidelines are not met, seems to reject a model of complete autonomy of religious tribunals. However, the reference to "basic minimum guidelines" suggests a thin supervisory role for the state.

In this chapter, I will concede the descriptive point that "legal pluralism is everywhere" and challenge – or at least raise cautions about – the normative claim that there should be more of it in U.S. family law. An exercise in comparative law readily does reveal many different ways of allocating jurisdiction over family law. This does not, however, answer the normative question of whether these are good models for U.S. family law.

One normative concern over civil law ceding authority to religious and other tribunals to regulate marriage and divorce regards the place of key commitments, values, and functions of civil family law. What authority will civil government have in the modified system to advance family law's functions of protecting the best interests of children and other vulnerable parties? What will happen if its model of marriage as an equal partnership premised on gender-neutral and reciprocal (rather than complementary and hierarchical) rights and duties conflicts with religious models? What will happen if there is a gap between religious law on marital dissolution and civil law's norm of equitable distribution of marital property and rationales for spousal support?

Another pressing concern is whether such a millet system can adequately protect the equal citizenship of women. I am skeptical that it can, for reasons I elaborate in this chapter. Nearly every foreign example that Nichols offers of jurisdictional pluralism concerning family law raises the troubling question about how to reconcile sex equality with religious freedom.[13] Feminist scholars highlight the importance of claims of national and constitutional citizenship – or "public citizenship" – as a strategy for redressing sex inequality, even as they affirm the value of membership in religious and cultural groups.[14] Will a new jurisdictional pluralism accommodate this dual membership? Training a gender lens on the question of jurisdictional pluralism would better inform the national conversation that the Multi-Tiered Marriage Project invites.

[13] On clashes between religious liberty and sex equality in India, see Martha C. Nussbaum, *Women and Human Development: The Capabilities Approach* (Cambridge: Cambridge University Press, 2000), 167–240. For a critical evaluation of the millet systems in Canada, India, Israel, and Kenya, see Ayelet Shachar, *Multicultural Jurisdictions: Cultural Differences and Women's Rights* (Cambridge: Cambridge University Press, 2001). In this volume, Werner Menski posits "postmodern Indian family law" as a realistic, functioning model of legal pluralism. Werner Menski, "Ancient and Modern Boundary Crossings Between Personal Laws and Civil Law in Composite India" in this volume.
[14] See Audrey Macklin, "Particularized Citizenship," in *Migrations and Mobilities: Gender, Citizenship, and Borders*, eds. Seyla Benhabib and Judith Resnik (New York: New York University Press, 2009) 276–303.

Nichols assures readers that "[m]oving toward multi-tiered marriage" is compatible with family law's protective functions and with "core values of equality."[15] His international examples contradict this reassurance, however. They call into question whether the proper model should be "ceding" authority or recognizing plural forms of authority, but only subject to constitutional and civil limiting principles. When government forms a partnership with religion, we might contrast two competing models of this relationship: unleashing, in the sense of turning loose or freeing, versus harnessing, in the sense of utilizing by yoking or restricting in light of important constitutional and public values.[16] This distinction between unleashing and harnessing may prove useful when considering calls for shared, or multiple, jurisdiction.

Family law, to be sure, already allows persons to opt out, to some extent, from its protective "default rules" through private ordering (such as premarital agreements and arbitration). Thus, in assessing the demand for jurisdictional pluralism, it is important to consider the place family law already accords to individual choice and freedom of contract.[17]

This chapter first asks precisely what form of marriage pluralism in the United States is sought and what might be motivating this demand. It examines differing views about the relationship between religious and civil marriage and notes how public norms of sex equality in the family may be in tension with religious traditions. It then examines some of the case law in which state courts within the United States have dealt with religious and foreign family law in resolving civil disputes about marriage and divorce. It asks what this case law suggests about the prospects for a multi-tiered marriage law in the United States and what tension points might arise. Finally, it takes up one of Nichols' comparative examples: the controversy over religious family law arbitration (or "*shari'a* arbitration") in Ontario. Guided especially by Canadian feminist commentary on this controversy, I ask what lessons this example might teach about the possibilities for more pluralism in U.S. family law.

II. WHITHER THE DEMAND FOR MORE MARRIAGE PLURALISM IN THE UNITED STATES?

A. An Initial Question: Should Religious and Civil Family Law Be Congruent?

Is there a demand, within the United States, for "multi-tiered marriage"? It may clarify matters to distinguish two types of demands for more legal pluralism. First,

---

[15] Nichols, "Multi-Tiered Marriage," 195.
[16] Linda C. McClain, "Unleashing or Harnessing 'Armies of Compassion'?: Reflections on the Faith-Based Initiative," *Loyola University Chicago Law Journal* 39 (Winter 2008): 361–426, 363–364.
[17] See Brian H. Bix, "Pluralism and Decentralization in Marriage Regulation" (in this volume).

particular religious communities might challenge the authority of the state to regulate marriage and argue either for sole or shared authority. This demand could arise either from religious communities that are long-established within the United States or, as a part of multicultural accommodation, from newer immigrant religious communities. A solution that Nichols floats is a millet system in which religious tribunals have jurisdictional autonomy with minimal state oversight. Second, religious communities might express discontent with the substance of civil marriage law and desire to instantiate, with more binding force in civil law, religious understandings of marriage so that the two are congruent. If this latter strategy is preferred, the question arises: Which religious understandings? That of majority religious institutions? What place will there be for the many minority religions practiced in America? And what place for minority views within the respective religious traditions?

The political and legal battles over same-sex marriage seem to be one motivating factor in the demand for both forms of legal pluralism. One response to the prospect of states redefining civil marriage to permit same-sex couples to marry (as Massachusetts and now five other states have done) is to propose that the state "get out of the marriage business" and leave it to religious institutions to define and regulate marriage. Offering a "Judeo-Christian" argument for "privatizing marriage," legal scholar Daniel Crane proposes that civil law permit couples to make civil contracts assigning jurisdiction over their marriage to religious authorities.[18] That way, religious believers and institutions would not cede the power to define marriage to the state. Edward Zelinsky offers a different "pro-marriage case" for abolishing civil marriage: Government should shed its monopoly on marriage in favor of a "market for marriage" in which civil marriage competes with other models of marriage offered by religious and other sponsoring institutions.[19]

Given the role of religious understandings of marriage in opposition to extending civil marriage to same-sex couples, another way to clarify that religious and civil marriage are distinct would be to cede the term "marriage" to religious traditions and replace it with a new status like civil unions or civil partnerships, to which the new status would attach various benefits and obligations now linked to civil marriage.[20] More typically, religious opponents of same-sex marriage seek *congruence* between religious and civil law. Appeals to religious tradition have animated efforts by religious institutions and lawmakers to "defend" marriage by enshrining in state and

---

[18] See Daniel A. Crane, "A 'Judeo-Christian' Argument for Privatizing Marriage," *Cardozo Law Review* 27 (January 2006): 1221–1259.

[19] Edward A. Zelinsky, "Deregulating Marriage: The Pro-Marriage Case for Abolishing Civil Marriage," *Cardozo Law Review* 27 (January 2006):1161–1220, 1164.

[20] See also Stephen B. Presser, "Marriage and the Law: Time for a Divorce?" (in this volume). This option was considered but rejected in the Law Commission of Canada's report, *Beyond Conjugality* (2001).

federal constitutions a definition of marriage as one man and one woman. The argument for congruence is that if the legal definition of marriage is so altered that it no longer recognizes the goods and purposes of marriage as understood in religious traditions, marriage law will not rest on a true conception of marriage.[21] A comparative example may be found in Canada. After Parliament passed a law redefining marriage as being "between two persons," a group of religious leaders issued a "Declaration on Marriage" urging members of Parliament and Canadian citizens to reconsider such redefinition because it severed marriage from its "nature and purpose," and faith communities could not promote an institution "when the identifying language has been stripped of its real meaning."[22] These opponents of redefining marriage seek greater congruence between religious and civil marriage, not marriage pluralism.

Covenant marriage also reflects a congruence strategy: It harnesses state power to instantiate an ideal of marriage in keeping with Christian traditions about permanence and mutual sacrifice.[23] In this volume Katherine Shaw Spaht, an architect of Louisiana's covenant marriage law, defends covenant marriage as offering a "dissident culture the opportunity to live under a stricter moral code reinforced by law." In effect, this introduces pluralism into the law of marriage and divorce, because the state recognizes "two forms of marriage." In establishing covenant marriage, she argues, the state invites religion into the public square to help preserve marriages; by contrast, privatizing marriage – the state "ceding jurisdiction" to other authorities – risks marriage losing its "public" character and purposes. She also acknowledges that advocates of covenant marriage statutes envisioned that if couples widely embraced it, the paradigm would shift from no-fault to covenant marriage.[24] (For this reason, Spaht and some proponents of covenant marriage express disappointment that religious authorities have not embraced it and required members to enter into this model of marriage.)[25] Moreover, requiring premarital counseling and specifying that it may be performed by religious functionaries draws attention to the unique capacity of religious communities to preserve marriages.[26] Congruence is

---

[21] See, e.g., The Witherspoon Institute, *Marriage and the Public Good: Ten Principles* (Princeton, NJ: The Witherspoon Institute, 2006).

[22] *Declaration on Marriage*, Nov. 9, 2006, available at http://www.cccb.ca/site/Files/Declaration_Marriage_En.pdf.

[23] See Spaht, "Covenant Marriage: An Achievable Legal Response" (discussing how covenant marriage is closer to God's purpose for marriage). Spaht reports that the Catholic Bishops of Louisiana, although agreeing with the ideal of permanence, disagreed with the law's allowance of divorce. Katherine Shaw Spaht, "Louisiana's Covenant Marriage: Social Analysis and Legal Implications," *Louisiana Law Review* 59 (Fall 1998): 63–160, 76.

[24] See Katherine Shaw Spaht, "Covenant Marriage Laws: A Model for Compromise" (in this volume).

[25] Ibid.

[26] Spaht, "Louisiana's Covenant Marriage," 75–77.

evident in Spaht's argument that conceding a difference between civil and religious marriage fails to recognize that "[n]atural moral law applies equally to the religious and nonreligious alike" and is accessible through the exercise of reason.[27]

If covenant marriage is a way for religion to harness state power, the state also harnesses – and does not simply unleash – religion. Civil officials issue marriage licenses and civil courts adjudicate divorces and rule on custody, property distribution, and the like. Covenant marriage proponents are not making the argument that the state should cede this authority to religious tribunals so that civil courts no longer have jurisdiction in such matters.

In the U.S. family law system, civil and religious authorities already share jurisdiction over marriage to a degree, as other chapters in this volume explain. In contrast to some legal systems (like France or the Netherlands), in the United States religious leaders may perform marriage ceremonies that will be recognized as civil marriages provided the couples comply with civil formalities. Through this "simultaneously … secular and … religious event," which incorporates "unofficial law and norms into the civil rite" and "reinforces the solemnity of the occasion," the state might be said to harness religious power for its own ends.[28] If religious leaders or couples do not follow these civil formalities, however, the resulting religious marriage generally will not have civil effects. This highlights the status of religious marriage as independent of the secular government but also carries risk for the participants in such a marriage. It shuts them off from the protections of civil family law with respect to the incidents of marriage and procedures for marital dissolution, property distribution, spousal support, and the like.[29]

Within the United States, certain religious faiths (e.g., Catholicism, Judaism, and Islam, but notably not the Protestant traditions) have their own system of courts that handle certain family matters.[30] Parties to such proceedings already ask civil courts to enforce or decline to enforce religious marriage contracts, divorce orders, arbitration agreements, and custody and support orders.[31] One motivating factor for the demand for "multi-tiered marriage" might be the perception that such courts are failing at this task, either out of a lack of understanding of the particular religious tradition at issue or out of an overzealous view of separation of church and state. Some Islamic scholars, for example, critique civil courts in the United States and

---

[27] Spaht, "Covenant Marriage Laws" (in this volume). See also Charles J. Reid, "And the State Makes Three: Should the State Retain a Role in Recognizing Marriage?", *Cardozo Law Review* 27 (2006): 1277–1307.

[28] Estin, "Unofficial Family Law" (in this volume).

[29] See Lynn Welchman, ed., *Women's Rights and Islamic Family Law: Perspectives on Reform* (London, New York: Zed Books Ltd., 2004), 188.

[30] See Ann Laquer Estin, "Embracing Tradition: Pluralism in American Family Law," *Maryland Law Review* 63 (2004): 540–604.

[31] Ibid., 35.

Canada for ignorance about Islamic traditions and for failure to properly adjudicate claims arising from Islamic marriage contracts.[32] But these analyses generally call for civil courts to do a better job when they confront Islamic family law, rather than to cede authority to religious courts and cease exercising jurisdiction over family law.[33] Thus, in this volume, Mohammad Fadel asserts that Muslims have a "keen interest" in a pluralistic system of family law, but he concludes that "orthodox Muslims are better served through marginal changes to the current family law regime" than by "any proposals that would award religious institutions greater jurisdiction over family life."[34] Notably, in the recent controversy in Ontario over so-called *shari'a* arbitration of family law, many Muslim groups stressed the religious obligation of Muslims to obey civil authority and urged that any religious arbitration should be subject to proper civil law norms.

The demand for a more "robust" millet system in the United States, therefore, is not evident. What is evident is that some religious groups seek greater congruence between civil and religious family law. Others seek greater accommodation of or at least appreciation by civil courts of religious law.

A complicating factor in considering calls for congruence between civil and religious marriage is that although civil marriage, as distinct from religious marriage, is in a sense a creature of state law and regulation,[35] America's history reveals the strong influence of Christian conceptions of marriage on the secular law.[36] As the late Lee Teitelbaum observed: "For most of American history ... the law of marriage was consistent with and supported – if not created – by the views of dominant religious communities."[37] The incompatibility of polygamy with Western Christian understandings of marriage animated governmental campaigns against Mormons and Native Americans. Thus, "to the extent that the majority faith communities

[32] See Pascale Fournier, "The Erasure of Islamic Difference in Canadian and American Family Law Adjudication," *Journal of Law and Policy* 10 (2001): 51–95, (critiquing *Kaddoura v. Hammond*, 168 D.L.R. (4th) 503 (Ont. Gen. Div., 1999)); see also Asifa Quraishi and Najeeba Syeed-Miller, "The Muslim Family in the USA: Law in Practice," in Welchman, *Women's Rights and Islamic Family Law*, 199–212 (offering praise and criticism of how civil courts in the United States have handled Islamic family law).

[33] Quraishi and Syeed-Miller, "Muslim Family in the USA," 199–212.

[34] Mohammad H. Fadel, "Political Liberalism, Islamic Family Law, and Family Law Pluralism" (in this volume).

[35] Most vividly, *Goodridge v. Dept. of Public Health*, 798 N.E.2d 941 (Mass. 2003), repeatedly refers to "civil marriage" and describes it as a "wholly secular institution." For a critique of *Goodridge* on this point, see Perry Dane, "A Holy Secular Institution," *Emory Law Journal* 58 (2009): 1123–1194.

[36] See John Witte Jr., *From Sacrament to Contract: Marriage, Religion, and Law in the Western Tradition* (Louisville, KY: Westminster John Knox Press, 1997).

[37] Lee E. Teitelbaum, "Religion and Modernity in American Family Law," in *American Religions and the Family: How Faith Traditions Cope with Modernization and Democracy*, eds. Don S. Browning and David A. Clairmont (New York: Columbia University Press, 2006), 227–243, 229.

were oppositional, it was to value sets that argued for change in the formation of families," whether it be polygamy in the nineteenth century or, in the late twentieth, the values of secular humanism.[38] Even today, as Estin observes, although U.S. family law is thought to be secular and universal, traces of its religious roots are apparent in aspects of the law of marriage and divorce, which may look Christian, exclusive, or sectarian to people of other faiths.[39]

Once again, the issue of same-sex marriage is a crucible for sorting out marriage's dual status. Some religious authorities and lawmakers oppose extending marriage to same-sex couples because such a redefinition would be contrary to "millennia" of cultural and religious tradition as well as to the created order.[40] However, a dissenting theological view is that insisting on congruence by calling for a national definition of marriage risks "reifying marriage as a legal, rather than religious, construct" and concedes to the state – rather than religious traditions – the power to say what marriage is.[41]

I will not attempt to resolve this theological debate about congruence. I believe that, notwithstanding the religious roots of contemporary civil law, distinguishing religious and civil marriage is necessary to clarify government's interest in recognizing and regulating marriage. Indeed, state legislatures and governors that have opened up civil marriage to same-sex couples stress this distinction as they declare support both for equality in civil marriage and for protecting religious freedom.[42] Making this distinction follows from constitutional principles and from liberal political principles about the fact of reasonable moral pluralism and toleration of religious difference.[43] Furthermore, the nature of civil marriage has evolved over time. As Mary Anne Case observes, what "marriage licenses" today is quite different from what it licensed in an earlier era, when marriage entailed a hierarchical set of rights and duties of husband and wife (*baron* and *feme*) and the criminal law prohibited nonmarital, nonprocreative, and nonheterosexual sexual expression.[44] Today, much of that criminal law has given way to understandings of a realm of constitutionally protected liberty and privacy. Moreover, pursuant to the transformation of family law spurred by the Supreme Court's series of Equal Protection Clause rulings, the rights and obligations of civil marriage are stated in

---

[38] Ibid., 229–230.

[39] Estin, "Embracing Tradition: Pluralism in American Family Law," 543–546.

[40] See Linda C. McClain, "God's Created Order, Gender Complementarity, and the Federal Marriage Amendment," *Brigham Young University Journal of Public Law* 20 (2006): 313–343.

[41] Crane, "A 'Judeo-Christian' Argument for Privatizing Marriage," 1221–1222.

[42] Examples include Maine, New Hampshire, and Vermont.

[43] On these tenets of political liberalism, see John Rawls, *Political Liberalism* (New York: Columbia University Press, 1993, 1996).

[44] Mary Anne Case, "Marriage Licenses," *Minnesota Law Review* 89 (June 2005): 1758–1797, 1765–1768.

gender-neutral terms. Spouses are much freer to choose how to live their marital life, and the rules of exit are far less strict.[45]

B. Tensions Between Civil and Religious Law: Gender Roles and Gender Equality

Civil marriage law is at odds with at least some religious conceptions of marriage. Considerations of a more pluralistic approach to legal regulation should attend to these possible tension points. One example is sex equality and gender roles in the family. Contemporary family law rejects the common law's model of husbandly rule and wifely obedience. Sex equality is also an important political value and constitutional principle.[46] Civil family law's model of equal spousal and parental rights and responsibilities may be in tension with religious conceptions of proper gender ordering.

In the recent book *American Religions and the Family: How Faith Traditions Cope With Modernization and Democracy*,[47] nearly every religious tradition examined includes a tenet that men are to exercise authority and leadership in the home (and, often, in the broader society) and that women have special duties in the home including (in some traditions) submission to or respect for male authority. In coping with modernization, religious leaders and adherents confront how to reconcile such traditional religious beliefs with contemporary American values about equality of the sexes and marriage as a partnership.[48] Similarly, another recent book, *Muslim Women in America: The Challenge of Islamic Identity Today*, identifies a central tension between support in Muslim cultural and religious traditions for male authority in the home and in society and "the general climate of American discourse about equality and justice between the sexes," including equal responsibility and decision making in the family.[49] (The fact that American social practice may vary from these ideals is not the point; the discourse and public attitudes themselves serve as identifiable contrasts to religious and cultural traditions.)

---

[45] Indeed, some argue that these legal changes create a "vacuum ... of legally mandated meaning" of marriage precisely because individuals have more latitude to decide or negotiate the content of marriage. Martha Albertson Fineman, *The Autonomy Myth: A Theory of Dependency* (New York: New Press, 2004), 99.

[46] Linda C. McClain, *The Place of Families: Fostering Capacity, Equality, and Responsibility* (Cambridge, MA: Harvard University Press, 2006).

[47] Browning and Clairmont, *American Religions and the Family*.

[48] Examples of this tension are found in Browning and Clairmont, *American Religions and the Family*, in the chapters on mainline Protestantism, evangelical Christianity, Hinduism, Islam, Confucianism, and Buddhism.

[49] Yvonne Yazbeck Haddad, Jane I. Smith, and Kathleen M. Moore, *Muslim Women in America: The Challenge of Islamic Identity Today* (Oxford: Oxford University Press, 2006), 90–91.

Religious communities have diverse responses to this challenge. Some religious traditions (for example, mainline Protestantism) have moved away from teachings about male dominance and female submission, fixed gender roles, and the marital, nuclear family to more egalitarian and pluralistic visions of marriage and family forms.[50] In various religions, women – and men – have engaged in efforts to generate less patriarchal interpretations of religious texts and to critique subordinating practices that have been justified by religious teaching. By contrast, some religious groups embrace traditional gender roles as part of an "oppositional" stance to American culture and the perceived weakening of family values.[51] Various immigrant communities contrast the morals and family values of their own societies of origin favorably with perceived American values, similar to how many religious conservatives in America view feminism and challenges to traditional gender roles as part of a longer litany of forces (e.g., individualism and secularism) that threaten strong families.[52]

Muslim communities in America illustrate this diversity of responses to ideals of equality. On the one hand, "[m]uch of the contemporary discourse, joined by both men and women, portrays the liberal Western model of 'equality' between the sexes as unrealistic, unnatural and leading ultimately to many Western women trying to raise children alone and below the poverty level."[53] On the other, women and men attempt to "reinterpret Qur'anic texts that seem to support male dominance over women, trying to argue that the justice of God affirmed in the holy text cannot allow women to be subordinated in any way to men."[54] Generational differences are also a relevant factor. One study reports that "[y]oung Muslims in America struggle both to respect the honor of the family and to break free of expectations it imposes on them. Muslim girls are becoming more articulate about their own frustrations at the double standards that their parents seem to apply to the girls and their brothers."[55]

This diversity of views and these generational tensions are pertinent to the proposal for multi-tiered marriage. They raise questions about how to define and interpret religious family law and whose voice will prevail if there are conflicting interpretations.

---

[50] See W. Bradford Wilcox and Elizabeth Williamson, "The Cultural Contradictions of Mainline Family Ideology and Practice," in Browning and Clairmont, *American Religions and the Family*, 37–55, 42.

[51] See Paul D. Numrich, "Immigrant American Religions and the Family," in Browning and Clairmont, *American Religions and the Family*, 20–34; Margaret Bendroth, "Evangelicals, Family, and Modernity," in Browning and Clairmont, *American Religions and the Family*, 56–69.

[52] Numrich, "Immigrant American Religions," 27.

[53] Haddad, Smith, and Moore, *Muslim Women in America*, 91.

[54] Ibid.

[55] Jane I. Smith, "Islam and the Family in North America," in Browning and Clairmont, *American Religions and the Family*, 211–224, 215.

III. PLURALISM IN U.S. FAMILY LAW: JURISDICTION,
LOCATION, AND CITIZENSHIP

Some likely tension points in moving to a multi-tiered marriage system may be
evident from reasoning by analogy from case law in the United States in which
courts already consider the relationship between civil and religious family law
and are asked to enforce terms of a religious marriage contract, recognize a foreign or religious marriage or divorce, or assume jurisdiction over child custody
disputes. The case law suggests a certain capaciousness already at work as courts
have embraced pluralism to a degree. However, it also suggests important limiting
principles about when courts will not and should not cede authority to religious
or foreign courts or apply religious family law. At issue also are questions of how
to relate membership and location in particular communities to citizenship.[56] In
this chapter, I can discuss only a handful of illustrative cases about marriage and
divorce and must direct readers elsewhere for a more complete survey of this body
of multicultural family law.[57]

Finding multiculturalism in the context of civil family law may come as a
surprise, even though, as Estin observes, it should not, given the religious heterogeneity within the United States and the migration of people across national
borders.[58] This "growing body of multicultural family law," she concludes, demonstrates the potential to embrace both "a number of fundamentally different
family law traditions" and "deeper values that structure and constrain the process of accommodation," such as "principles of due process, nondiscrimination,
and religious freedom" as well as family law's "protective policies."[59] Estin calls
for courts and lawmakers to develop a framework for a multicultural family law
that would "allow individuals greater freedom to express their cultural or religious identity and negotiate the consequences of these commitments," but also
"protect the rights of individuals to full membership and participation in the larger political community."[60]

This twin focus on expressing identity and safeguarding rights captures an important challenge posed to legal pluralism: how to provide space for living according

---

[56] On tensions between group membership and national citizenship, see Shachar, *Multicultural
Jurisdictions.*
[57] See, e.g., Estin, "Embracing Tradition: Pluralism in American Family Law"; Quraishi and Syeed-
Miller, "Islamic Family Law in US Courts." One important area of law that I omit is the care, custody,
and support of children.
[58] Estin, "Embracing Tradition: Pluralism in American Family Law," 540.
[59] Ibid., 603–604.
[60] Ibid., 542.

to and negotiating within the framework of religious law while also ensuring that membership in the political community is a source of entitlement and obligation that coexists with, and may put constraints on, other forms of affiliation. Bringing a feminist perspective – indeed a multicultural feminist perspective[61] – to bear on this challenge may fortify an analysis.

Because Nichols proposes a robust millet system of religious courts with civil government, upholding basic minimal guidelines, what civil courts have done may not be a useful model for what religious tribunals would do. But this case law is instructive on how civil family law's concerns for procedural and substantive fairness shape the accommodation now afforded to religious law. Religious family law often has gender asymmetries in the rights and duties of husbands and wives (including the power to initiate a divorce) and of fathers and mothers. Rules concerning the economic consequences of marriage and divorce also differ from the economic partnership model of civil family law. How have civil courts handled such tensions between civil and religious law?

Courts are sometimes asked to enforce – or to decline to enforce – terms of marriage contracts entered into pursuant to Jewish or Islamic marriages. In the instance of Jewish marriage contracts, these cases generally involve seeking to enforce an agreement to submit to religious arbitration.[62] This case law should be put in context of a general trend in family law away from hostility to premarital agreements about property distribution in the event of divorce – on the public policy ground that such agreements encourage divorce – to permitting parties to a marriage to make contracts with one another, that is, to engage in private ordering. At the same time, these Jewish and Islamic marriage contracts are not technically premarital agreements, although courts sometimes mistakenly treat them as such.[63]

Another relevant trend in family law is to allow, and sometimes require, arbitration and other alternatives to divorce litigation. However, there are limits to private ordering, rooted in process concerns and in substantive concerns about fairness or protection of vulnerable or dependent parties. When private ordering also entails religious law, courts face additional questions about whether enforcing such agreements excessively entangles a civil court with religion, in contravention of the First Amendment.

[61] Ayelet Shachar, "Feminism and Multiculturalism: Mapping the Terrain," in *Multiculturalism and Political Theory*, eds. Anthony Simon Laden and David Owen (Cambridge: Cambridge University Press, 2007) 115–147.

[62] See Michael J. Broyde, "New York's Regulation of Jewish Marriage: Covenant, Contract, or Statute?" (in this volume).

[63] Quraishi and Syeed-Miller, "Islamic Family Law in US Courts," 202 (critiquing *Dajani v. Dajani*, 204 Cal. App. 3d 1587 [Cal. App. 4th Dist. 1988]).

A. *Religious Marriage Contracts, Religious Arbitration,*
and the Get *Statutes*

A leading case for the proposition that a civil court may properly exercise jurisdiction in an action arising out of a religious marriage contract is *Avitzur v. Avitzur*.[64] In that case, New York's highest court held that secular terms of a religious marriage contract, the Jewish *ketubah*, may be enforceable as a contractual obligation. Relying on U.S. Supreme Court precedents, the court said it could apply "neutral principles of contract law" and need not consider religious doctrine.[65] The specific contract term was an agreement to appear before the *beth din*, a Jewish religious tribunal, to allow it to "advise and counsel the parties" in matters concerning their marriage. The wife had already obtained a civil divorce but, under Jewish law, was not religiously divorced and was therefore unable to remarry and have legitimate children until her husband granted her a Jewish divorce decree, a *get*.[66]

Jewish tradition refers to women whose husbands do not give them a *get* as an *agunah*, a chained woman (chained to the dead marriage).[67] Jewish tradition has developed ways to address this problem, such as putting a clause in the *ketubah* to agree to arbitration. *Avitzur* rationalized enforcing such an agreement as simply compelling a husband "to perform a secular obligation to which he contractually bound himself."[68] As Michael Broyde discusses in this volume, the New York legislature subsequently enacted two statutes aimed at addressing the plight of the *agunah*.[69]

Nichols offers the *get* statutes as an example of multi-tiered marriage,[70] but I think *Avitzur* and these statutes could better be understood as an attempt by civil government to remedy a disadvantage arising out of gender asymmetry in religious law that disproportionately affects religious women and has troubling spillover effects in the civil realm, such as unequal bargaining power and one-sided settlements.[71] Broyde, in this volume, suggests that these statutes seek to harmonize civil and religious divorce law, with the encouragement of religious leaders, based on advancing the

---

[64] *Avitzur v. Avitzur*, 446 N.E.2d 136 (N.Y. 1983).
[65] Ibid., 138 (citing to *Jones v. Wolf*, 443 U.S. 595, 602 [1979]).
[66] Ibid.
[67] Broyde, "New York's Regulation" (in this volume).
[68] *Avitzur*, 446 N.E.2d at 139.
[69] "Removal of Barriers to Marriage," N.Y. Dom. Rel. L. § 253(6), *McKinney's Consolidated Laws of New York Annotated* (Thomson-West, 2008); "Special Controlling Provisions; Prior Actions or Proceedings; New Actions or Proceedings," N.Y. Dom. Rel. L. § 236(6)(d), *McKinney's Consolidated Laws of New York Annotated* (Thomson-West, 2008). See Broyde, "New York's Regulation" (in this volume).
[70] Nichols, "Multi-Tiered Marriage," 163.
[71] Estin, "Embracing Tradition: Pluralism in American Family Law," 583–584.

"purpose and function of the secular divorce law" – that its citizens "are in fact free to remarry after they receive a civil divorce."[72]

Thus, civil law's attempt to solve the *get* problem seems less an argument for civil government ceding more authority to religious tribunals than for shared or cooperative jurisdiction: religious and secular authorities cooperate to solve a problem that neither can solve entirely on its own.[73] Analysis of Canada's *get* statutes suggests a similar concern on the part of civil authority both to ameliorate disadvantages for religious women and to cooperate with religious authorities to solve the problem.[74]

B. *Adjudication of Islamic Marriage Contracts: The* Mahr

Scholars of Islamic family law describe the marriage contract as a protective mechanism that affords a Muslim woman a chance to customize her marriage through provisions that guarantee her rights with regard to her spouse (for example, to work outside the home without her husband's permission, to initiate divorce, or not to clean the house). Many Muslim women, unaware of their rights, underutilize this protective device.[75]

Some state courts (including New York) have enforced a wife's right in Islamic marriage contracts to *mahr*, a bridal gift or dower.[76] *Mahr* is customarily divided into two parts: one "payable immediately on the marriage ... sometimes only a token amount or symbol," and a second part, which is "deferred to a later date, either specified or more usually payable on the termination of the marriage by death or divorce."[77] Islamic traditions regarding whether a woman is entitled to *mahr* at divorce are complex and differ based on who initiates divorce, the type of divorce at issue, and the school of interpretation.[78] Nonetheless, some civil courts have stated

---

[72] Broyde, "New York's Regulation" (in this volume).

[73] Ibid.

[74] Lisa Fishbayn, "Gender, Multiculturalism and Dialogue: The Case of Jewish Divorce," *Canadian Journal of Law and Jurisprudence* 21 (January 2008): 71–96. The Supreme Court of Canada recently spoke of how the *get* problem impinged on the dignity and equality interests of religious Jewish Canadian women. *Marcovitz v. Bruker*, 2007 SCC 54.

[75] Haddad, Smith, and Moore, *Muslim Women in America*, 114 (discussing the work of Azizah al-Hibri and her organization, KARAMAH: Muslim Women Lawyers for Human Rights, in educating women about marriage contracts).

[76] *Aziz v. Aziz*, 488 N.Y.S.2d 123 (Sup. Ct. Queens County 1985). For this definition, see Welchman, *Women's Rights and Islamic Family Law*, 188. In the case law I discuss, courts sometimes refer to *mahr* as "dowry," or "postponed dowry," rather than "dower."

[77] Welchman, *Women's Rights and Islamic Family Law*, 188–189.

[78] See Pascale Fournier, "In the (Canadian) Shadow of Islamic Law: Translating Mahr as a Bargaining Endowment," *Osgoode Hall Law Journal* 44 (Winter 2006): 649–677. See also Fadel, "Political Liberalism" (in this volume).

that the fact that these contracts were entered into in the context of Islamic religious ceremonies does not render them unenforceable.

An illustrative case is *Odatalla v. Odatalla*.[79] In that case, a New Jersey court rejected the husband's argument that the court could not order specific performance of his obligation to pay $10,000 in postponed dower because: (1) the First Amendment doctrine of separation of church and state precluded a civil court's review of the agreement; and (2) the agreement was not a valid contract under New Jersey law. Instead, the court ruled that it could specifically enforce the terms of the agreement, which was entered into during an Islamic marriage ceremony. The court reasoned that the agreement could be enforced "based upon 'neutral principles of law' and not on religious policy or theories."[80] Applying those neutral principles, the court held that the agreement had the elements of a valid contract. Rejecting the husband's argument that the term "postponed" made the contract too vague, the court found persuasive the wife's offer of testimony concerning Islamic custom in which the sum could be demanded by the wife at any time, although it usually is not unless there is a death of the husband or a divorce.[81] The court also suggested that interpreting the demands of the First Amendment requires attending to the contrast between the more religiously homogenous community of the late 1700s "when our Constitution was drafted" and the more religiously and ethnically diverse "community we live in today."[82]

A Florida appellate court, in *Akileh v. Elchahal*,[83] similarly looked to New York precedents and to testimony about Islamic law to uphold a husband's agreement in an Islamic marriage contract to pay his wife a "postponed dowry" of $50,000. The wife demanded payment in a divorce proceeding brought in civil court. The court concluded that the *sadaq*, the postponed dowry incorporated into the couple's marriage certificate when they married in Florida in an Islamic ceremony, could be enforced using principles of Florida contract law. The court heard four witnesses, including Islamic experts, regarding the meaning of *sadaq* and was persuaded that the parties understood the *sadaq's* protective function and that the wife's right to receive it was not negated if she filed for divorce.

Some courts, by contrast, have declined to enforce the obligation to pay *mahr*. One ground has been that, although in principle such an obligation could be enforced by a civil court, a particular contract failed to satisfy general contract principles such as stating the material terms of the agreement.[84] A different ground is

---

[79] *Odatalla v. Odatalla*, 810 A.2d 93 (N.J. Super. 2002).
[80] Ibid., 95–96 (citing *Jones v. Wolf*, 443 U.S. 595 (1979)).
[81] Ibid., 97–98.
[82] Ibid., 96.
[83] *Akileh v. Elchahal*, 666 So. 2d 246 (Fla. Dist. App. 1996).
[84] See, e.g., *Habibi-Fahnrich v. Fahnrich*, 1995 WL 507388 (Sup. Ct. Kings County 1995) (not reported in N.Y.S.2d).

that the *mahr* agreement offends public policy because it provides an incentive for the wife to seek divorce. In *Dajani v. Dajani*, the California court declined, on public policy grounds, to enforce a foreign proxy marriage contract (entered into in Jordan) involving what the court called a "foreign dowry agreement," under which the husband was obliged to pay the balance of the wife's dowry either when the marriage was dissolved or the husband died. The court bypassed the conflicting expert testimony over whether the husband had an obligation to pay if the wife initiated the divorce, and, analogizing the contract to a premarital agreement, ruled that it "clearly provided for [the] wife to profit by a divorce."[85]

The court found "apt" the rationale of the earlier California case, *In re the Marriage of Noghrey*,[86] in which the court declined on public policy grounds to enforce an agreement entered into before a Jewish religious ceremony that the husband would give his wife a house and $500,000 or "one-half of my assets, whichever is greater, in the event of a divorce." The *Dajani* court noted that in *Noghrey* the protective function of the *ketubah* – to discourage divorce by making it costly for the husband and to provide economic security for the wife because the husband "could apparently divorce his wife at will" – did not matter to the holding.[87] In effect, both the *ketubah* term in *Noghrey* and the Islamic dower agreement in *Dajani* encouraged divorce "by providing wife with cash and property in the event the marriage failed."[88]

These cases raise difficult questions about how civil courts should grapple with a religious tradition's protective devices adopted in light of vulnerabilities that women face due to gender asymmetry in religious law and broader cultural norms. For example, in *Noghrey*, the wife testified that this economic protection was necessary because "it is hard for an Iranian woman to remarry after a divorce because she is no longer a virgin."[89] She testified that in return for the agreement, she gave the groom "assurances that she was a virgin and was medically examined for that purpose."[90] Like Estin,[91] I wonder if the courts in these cases were too inattentive to this protective function and whether they couldn't find an analogy to protective measures of U.S. divorce law. Furthermore, as some Muslim scholars point out, had the *Dajani* court not taken such a "superficial" approach to Islamic law, it

[85] *Dajani v. Dajani*, 251 Cal. Rptr. 871, 872 (Cal. App. 4th Dist. 1988). The court used the term "dowry" to refer to "a bride's portion on her marriage," explaining that the state of California no longer recognized the "estate of dower," a widow's provision on her husband's death. Ibid., 871.
[86] *In re the Marriage of Noghrey*, 215 Cal. Rptr. 153 (Cal. App. 6th Dist. 1985).
[87] *Dajani*, 251 Cal. Rptr. at 872.
[88] Ibid.
[89] *Noghrey*, 215 Cal. Rptr. at 154.
[90] Ibid., 154–155.
[91] Estin, "Embracing Tradition: Pluralism in American Family Law," 584–585.

might have recognized that its "profiteering" assumptions about *mahr* did not apply uniformly to the rules about the wife's entitlement to *mahr*.[92]

C. Resolving Conflicts Between Civil and Religious Divorce Law: Two Contrasting Cases

How would a modern millet system handle clashes between civil and religious laws concerning the process due when spouses seek to divorce one another? Or concerning whether divorcing spouses have a right to support or to equitable distribution of property? Would civil family law's protective rules be part of a "minimum" insisted on by civil law or would private ordering prevail? For example, in Islamic family law, husband and wife generally maintain their separate property and, unless the contract specifies, there is no presumption of property division.[93] This contrasts with notions in civil family law either of community property during marriage and equal or equitable division of such property at divorce (in community property states) or, in common law states, of deferred community property in the form of equitable distribution at divorce.

To explore these questions and to illustrate how challenging questions about the interplay of religious and civil law intertwine with geographical location, family mobility, and citizenship, I will discuss two contrasting cases. In *Chaudry v. Chaudry*,[94] the wife filed suit in New Jersey civil court for separate maintenance and child support, alleging unjustified abandonment by her husband. The husband's defense was that he had obtained a valid divorce in Pakistan in accordance with Pakistani law. Both husband and wife were Pakistani citizens; the wife and children resided in Pakistan (but had lived in the United States for a few years early in the marriage), and the husband resided and practiced medicine in New Jersey.

The appellate court held there was not an "adequate nexus" between the marriage and the state of New Jersey to justify a New Jersey court awarding the wife alimony or equitable distribution. Second, it saw "no reason of public policy" not to interpret and enforce the marriage contract in accordance with the law of Pakistan "where it was freely negotiated and the marriage took place."[95] Expert testimony established that alimony "does not exist under Pakistan law" and that providing for it by contract is "void as a matter of law" in Pakistan. Conversely, the agreement could have given the wife an interest in her husband's property, but it did not.

---

[92] Quraishi and Syeed-Miller, "Islamic Family Law in US Courts," 202.
[93] See Fadel, "Political Liberalism" (in this volume).
[94] *Chaudry v. Chaudry*, 388 A.2d 1000 (N.J. Super. App. Div. 1978).
[95] Ibid., 1006.

Had there been a sufficient nexus, the court observed, a New Jersey court could consider a claim for alimony or equitable distribution, even though such relief could not be obtained in the state or country granting a divorce. Location is of obvious significance for jurisdiction: The wife's insufficient connection to the state of New Jersey (evidently due in part to the husband's conduct) barred relief. Husband and wife remained citizens of Pakistan, and expert testimony indicated that such citizenship was a "sufficient basis" for a divorce judgment in Pakistan. In concluding that the lower court should have applied comity to recognize the decree, the reviewing court stressed: "The need for predictability and stability in status relationships requires no less."[96]

An instructive example of when such a nexus *does* exist, also involving the law of Pakistan and a mobile family, is *Aleem v. Aleem*.[97] There, a Maryland appellate court upheld a lower court's ruling that it need not give comity to a Pakistani *talaq* divorce and was not barred from ruling that a wife receive equitable distribution of her husband's pension. The appellate ruling was affirmed by Maryland's highest court. This case illustrates how migration gives rise to jurisdictional questions and the possibility of forum shopping. Husband, twenty-nine, and wife, eighteen, married in Pakistan after their families arranged a meeting. They never lived together in Pakistan and had been living in Maryland more than twenty years at the time the wife initiated a civil divorce proceeding. They had two children, both born in the United States and thus U.S. citizens.

When the wife filed for divorce, the husband moved to dismiss on the ground that "all issues have already been decided in Pakistan." He referred to the parties' marriage contract, entered into in Pakistan, which called for a deferred dowry of about $2,500 (U.S.). He also informed the court that, subsequent to the wife filing her action, he obtained a *talaq* divorce at the Pakistani Embassy in Washington, DC, by pronouncing three times that he divorced his wife. The wife was served with the "Divorce Decree" and an attached notice from the "Union Council" (inquiring whether the parties wanted to reconcile).

The lower court declined to give comity to the divorce, stating that it "offends the notions of this Court in terms of how a divorce is granted."[98] On appeal, Maryland's highest court (the Court of Appeals of Maryland) invoked Maryland's Equal Rights Amendment to indicate that "a foreign *talaq* divorce provision ... where only the male, i.e., husband, has an independent right to utilize *talaq* and the wife may utilize it only with the husband's permission, is contrary to Maryland's constitutional provisions and ... to the public policy of Maryland."[99] Moreover,

---

[96] Ibid., 1005.
[97] *Aleem v. Aleem*, 931 A.2d 1123 (Md. Spec. App. 2007), *aff'd*, 947 A.2d 489 (Md. 2008).
[98] *Aleem*, 931 A.2d at 1127.
[99] *Aleem*, 947 A.2d at 500–501.

allowing such strategic forum shopping by the husband would defeat the local civil law's protective purposes:

> a husband who is a citizen of any country in which Islamic law, *adopted as the civil law*, prevails could go to the embassy of that country and perform *talaq*, and divorce her (without prior notice to her) long before she would have any opportunity to fully litigate, under Maryland law, the circumstances of the parties' dissolution of their marriage.[100]

Thus, public policy – including concern for due process – justified denial of comity to the foreign divorce.

The conflict between Maryland and Pakistan's rules concerning post-divorce property distribution afforded the ground for a second ruling: that, as a form of spousal support, the husband must pay his wife 50 percent of his monthly pension benefit until the death of either party. The husband argued that, by virtue of the marriage contract and the governing Pakistani law, his wife was not entitled to any portion of his pension. Both reviewing courts upheld the pension award and concluded that comity should be denied because Pakistani statutes were in conflict with Maryland's public policy about property distribution.[101] Under Pakistani law, the "default" was that the wife had no rights to property titled in a husband's name, whereas under Maryland law, the "default" is that she has such rights. The Court of Special Appeals also cautioned against equating the Pakistani marriage contract with "a premarital or post-marital agreement that validly relinquished, under Maryland law, rights in marital property."[102]

In *Aleem*, location of the family anchored the judicial assertion that "it is clear that this State has a sufficient nexus with the marriage to effect an equitable distribution of marital property."[103] By contrast to the facts in *Chaudry*, the *Aleem* court noted the couple's long residence in Maryland, the birth and rearing of their children in Maryland, and the permanent resident status of the wife, who sought the equitable distribution. There was also no plausible basis for Pakistani personal jurisdiction over the wife with respect to the *talaq* divorce. The decisions in *Aleem* express a public policy against strategic forum shopping – which would allow a domiciliary, while continuing that domicile, to seek to "'avoid the incidents of his domiciliary law and to deprive the other party to the marriage of her rights under that law'" and of due process by traveling elsewhere to invoke another state's jurisdiction.[104]

[100] Ibid., 501 (italics in original).
[101] *Aleem*, 931 A.2d at 1130; 947 A.2d at 502.
[102] Ibid., 1134.
[103] Ibid., 1131.
[104] Ibid., 1135 (quoting *Chaudhary v. Chaudhary*, [1985] 2 W.L.R. 350, [1984] 3 All E.R. 1017, [1985] Fam. 19, 1984 WL 282941 (CA (Civ. Div.)).

The link between the protections, benefits, and obligations of civil marriage and domicile seems important to a consideration of marriage pluralism in which a religious tribunal might not be in another country, but within the territorial boundaries of the state of which the party is a resident. How might this concern for strategic exploitation of nationality and of favorable religious law apply in a millet system within the United States? Would a new system of personal law mean that persons, no matter where they were located as citizens or resident aliens, would carry on their backs the religious law applicable to them? Would this regime resemble the legal pluralism of an earlier Europe, of which a ninth-century bishop observed that "[i]t often happened that five men were present or setting together, and not one of them had the same law as another"?[105]

One criticism of the traditional millet system and its contemporary vestiges is the lack of choice in jurisdiction. One's religious affiliation determines the religious court to which one may go. In a more contemporary system of legal pluralism, to what extent would people who are members of religious communities have rights, in terms of being free to leave that community or to stay but seek the protection of civil law? When adults exercise those exit rights, what is the impact on the rights of their children?[106] Shachar proposes that what is needed is a form of multiple jurisdiction that attempts to respect membership in religious communities as well as rights of citizenship and resists affording religious tribunals a monopoly.[107] Considering the recent controversy in Ontario, Canada, over so-called *shari'a* arbitration may help to elaborate the challenges of finding a useful model of contemporary legal pluralism.

IV. INTERNATIONAL MODELS?

A. *Assessing Multi-Tiered Marriage Through a Gender Equality Lens*

Training a gender lens on the comparative enterprise that the Multi-Tiered Marriage Project proposes would better inform the national conversation it invites. A significant body of feminist work identifies problems of gender inequality and discrimination in legal systems that cede jurisdiction to religious tribunals or apply religious and customary family law. As Helen Irving's recent comparative study of

---

[105] Tamanaha, "Understanding Legal Pluralism," 6 (quoting Bishop Agobard of Lyons, as quoted in John B. Morrall, *Political Thought in Medieval Times* [Toronto: University of Toronto Press, 1980]).

[106] One critical question is how robust legal pluralism would reconcile civil law's commitments to equal parental rights and responsibilities with religious law systems that have asymmetrical treatment of the rights of fathers and mothers.

[107] Shachar, *Multicultural Jurisdictions*. See also Ayelet Shachar, "Faith in Law? Diffusing Tensions Between Diversity and Equality" (in this volume).

constitutional design concludes, when women have participated in the process of constitution making in societies adopting new constitutions, they have "consistently asked" for constitutional equality and full citizenship, including "the supremacy of the constitution over tradition and custom, including over customary laws that perpetuate subordination."[108] In another comparative work on gender and constitutions, Beverley Baines and Ruth Rubio-Marin, speaking of Israel, India, and South Africa (three of Nichols's examples), note that governmental decisions "to recognize customary or religious jurisdiction over certain relationships, often including those which are the most intimate and intense, such as marriage, divorce, custody, property, and succession," have been of particular concern to feminists.[109] In that volume, Shachar and comparative constitutional law scholar Ran Hirschl argue: "A major obstacle to establishing women's full participation as equals in all spheres of life in Israel ... continues to be the intersection of gender and religious/national tensions."[110] Israel's contemporary millet system, they contend elsewhere, grants religious communities "a license to maintain intragroup practices that disproportionately injure vulnerable group members, such as women," for example through "gender discrimination in the religious divorce process."[111] To afford redress, Israel has made recent efforts "to enforce secular and gender egalitarian norms over the exercise of religious tribunals."[112] In the constitution-building process of various nations, bringing constitutional commitments to sex equality to bear on family law has been viewed as a sign of progressive change.[113]

As the ongoing debate about accommodation of multiculturalism reveals, "the status of women in distinct cultural communities" is often at stake because "[w]omen and their bodies are the symbolic-cultural site upon which human societies inscribe their moral bodies."[114] Calls to preserve religious or cultural autonomy

---

[108] See Helen Irving, *Gender and the Constitution: Equity and Agency in Comparative Constitutional Design* (Cambridge: Cambridge University Press, 2008), 21.

[109] Beverley Baines and Ruth Rubio-Marin, "Introduction: Toward a Feminist Constitutional Agenda," in *The Gender of Constitutional Jurisprudence*, eds. Beverley Baines and Ruth Rubio-Marin (Cambridge: Cambridge University Press, 2005), 1–21, 12.

[110] Ran Hirschl and Ayelet Shachar, "Constitutional Transformation, Gender Equality, and Religious/National Conflict in Israel: Tentative Progress through the Obstacle Course," in Baines and Rubio-Marin, *The Gender of Constitutional Jurisprudence*, 205–229, 220.

[111] Ran Hirschl, "Constitutional Courts vs. Religious Fundamentalism: Three Middle Eastern Tales," *Texas Law Review* 82 (June 2004): 1819–1860, 1840 (citing Shachar, *Multicultural Jurisdictions*, 57–60).

[112] Shachar, "Feminism and Multiculturalism: Mapping the Terrain," 134.

[113] Linda C. McClain and James E. Fleming, "Constitutionalism, Judicial Review, and Progressive Change," *Texas Law Review* 84 (December 2005): 433–470 (reviewing Ran Hirschl, *Toward Juristocracy: The Origins and Consequences of the New Constitutionalism* [Cambridge, MA: Harvard University Press, 2004]).

[114] Seyla Benhabib, *The Claims of Culture: Equality and Diversity in the Global Era* (Princeton, NJ: Princeton University Press, 2002), 83–84.

often target the family and women's roles as core features that must be preserved, even as other aspects of religion and culture adapt to modernization.[115] In response, some women and women's groups (such as Women Living Under Muslim Laws) contest patriarchal interpretations of culture and religion and reveal the actual diversity of religious laws and customs and the possibility for greater equality within particular traditions.[116]

If civil government is to cede authority to religious tribunals, who within the religious tradition has authority to say what constitutes religious law, and what room will there be for dissenting voices that contest the most patriarchal interpretations of religious family law?[117] A millet system that relegates religious women to the primary or exclusive jurisdiction of religious tribunals is not likely to facilitate such dissent, by contrast to a jurisdictional model that attempts to secure women's rights both as members of religious communities and as citizens. Shachar proposes a form of "multicultural feminism" that "treats women as *both* culture-bearers and rights-bearers."[118] It is attentive to the risks to women's rights to equality and full citizenship that arise both from privatizing family law (e.g., through such devices as private arbitration) and from granting public and binding authority to religious codes. These risks inform my own concerns about developing a millet system in the United States.

B. Canada: Membership and Citizenship in Ontario's Faith-Based Arbitration Controversy

Among his examples of alternative ways to arrange jurisdiction over marriage, Professor Nichols briefly mentions the recent controversy in Ontario over family law allowing individuals to "'opt' into an arbitral board of their choosing to resolve disputes – including a religious arbitral board with binding authority."[119] In Ontario, pursuant to the Arbitration Act of 1991, parties could choose the law under which the arbitration would be conducted. The law referred to the law of Ontario or of another Canadian jurisdiction, but was interpreted, in practice, to mean that "Christians, Jews, Muslims, and people of other faith traditions could

---

[115] See Uma Narayan, *Dislocating Cultures: Identities, Traditions, and Third World Feminism* (New York and London: Routledge, 1997); Shachar, *Multicultural Jurisdictions*.

[116] See Linda C. McClain, "Negotiating Gender and (Free and Equal) Citizenship: The Place of Associations," *Fordham Law Review* 72 (April 2004): 1569–1698; Madhavi Sunder, "Piercing the Veil," *Yale Law Journal* 112 (April 2003): 1399–1472.

[117] See Sunder, "Piercing the Veil."

[118] Shachar, "Feminism and Multiculturalism: Mapping the Terrain," 126 (italics in original). See also Shachar, "Faith in Law?" (in this volume).

[119] Nichols, "Multi-Tiered Marriage," 193.

Linda C. McClain

arbitrate their disputes according to the principles of their faith."[120] Nichols further explains that Ontario courts were required to "uphold arbitrators' decisions if both sides enter the process voluntarily and if results are fair, equitable, and do not violate Canadian law."[121]

My discussion of the religious arbitration controversy draws on the detailed report, *Dispute Resolution in Family Law: Protecting Choice, Promoting Inclusion* ("Boyd Report"), written by Marion Boyd, a former attorney general, at the request of the attorney general and the Minister Responsible for Women's Issues.[122] A trigger of the controversy was when, in 2003, Syed Mumtaz Ali, a retired Ontario lawyer, announced the establishment of the new Islamic Institute of Civil Justice, which would conduct arbitrations according to Islamic personal law.[123] As Boyd notes, Ali's statements about the obligations of "good Muslims" to use these tribunals and of the secular court to enforce their decisions "raised acute alarm." The Boyd Report notes "intense fear that the kind of abuses, particularly against women, which have been exposed in other countries where 'Sharia Law' prevails ... could happen in Canada," and that "[t]he many years of hard work, which have entrenched equality rights in Canada, could be undone through the use of private arbitration, to the detriment of women, children, and other vulnerable people."[124]

Given a mandate "to explore the use of private arbitration to resolve family and inheritance cases, and the impact that using arbitrations may have on vulnerable people," Boyd conducted an extensive, several-month review.[125] The Boyd Report recommended that "arbitration should continue to be an alternative dispute resolution option that is available in family and inheritance law cases," and that "[t]he Arbitration Act should continue to allow disputes to be arbitrated using religious law." However, it qualified its support by insisting that arbitration be subject to various "safeguards," not only those already in the act but also many others.[126]

The Boyd Report sparked protest. Ultimately, as Nichols recounts, Ontario's premier made a public announcement that "[t]here will be no sharia law in Ontario. There will be no religious arbitration in Ontario. There will be one law for all

---

[120] Ibid., 193–194 (citing Arbitration Act, 1991, S.O. 1991, c. 17 (Can.)).
[121] Ibid., 194 (citing Arbitration Act, 1991).
[122] Marion Boyd, *Dispute Resolution in Family Law: Protecting Choice, Promoting Inclusion* (2004) [hereinafter *Boyd Report*], available at http://www.attorneygeneral.jus.gov.on.ca/english/about/pubs/boyd/fullreport.pdf. For additional discussion of this controversy, see Daniel Cere, "Canadian Conjugal Mosaic: From Multiculturalism to Multi-Conjugalism?" (in this volume); Fadel, "Political Liberalism" (in this volume); Shachar, "Faith in Law?" (in this volume); Robin Fretwell Wilson, "The Perils of Privatized Marriage" (in this volume).
[123] *Boyd Report*, 3.
[124] Ibid.
[125] Ibid., 5.
[126] Ibid., 133.

Ontarians."[127] The legislature amended the Arbitration Act so that "[i]n a family arbitration, the arbitral tribunal shall apply the substantive law of Ontario, unless the parties expressly designate the substantive law of another Canadian jurisdiction, in which case that substantive law shall be applied."[128] An explanatory note to the amendment states: "The term 'family arbitration' is applied only to processes conducted exclusively in accordance with the law of Ontario or of another Canadian jurisdiction. Other third-party decision-making processes in family matters are not family arbitrations and have no legal effect."[129]

Presumably, from the perspective of a call to a more robust legal pluralism, this outcome is regrettable. Nichols comments: This "effectively cut off not only the rights of Muslims to settle disputes in family matters under Islamic law, but ... the rights of other religious traditions as well, including the rabbinic courts present and practicing in Ontario since 1889."[130] How does this controversy and its resolution look from a feminist perspective, particularly a multicultural one that aims to honor both community membership and citizenship?

A thorough evaluation of this controversy is beyond the scope of this chapter. My aim is to consider some salient themes in the Boyd Report and commentary on it (particularly by Canadian feminists) with a view to what light this sheds on the likely tension between gender equality as a core commitment of civil family law and religious jurisdiction in a system of multi-tiered marriage.

One notable feature of the Boyd Report is its presentation of a diversity of views among Canadian Muslims, including women's groups, about the desirability of religious arbitration and its appropriate jurisdictional limits. Concern about the status of women in various interpretations of Islam is featured in many of Boyd's interviews, particularly when women had emigrated to Canada from nations in which Islamic law was applied in family law matters. Respondents also worried about women being pressured into choosing religious arbitration.

Canadian feminist scholar Audrey Macklin observes that, with one exception, all the women's groups of self-identified Muslim women opposed religious arbitration. Indeed, the Canadian Council of Muslim Women, "the dominant institutional voice opposing Muslim arbitration," successfully formed an alliance with Women Living Under Muslim Laws (WLUML), a transnational network: "With the benefit of personal experience living in Islamic states and through the global clearinghouse of data gathered by WLUML, local opponents of Muslim arbitration tacitly encouraged the public to situate the Ontario proposal against a transnational landscape

---

[127] Nichols, "Multi-Tiered Marriage," 194.
[128] Ibid., 194–195 (citing to Family Statute Law Amendment Act, R.S.O. 2006, ch. 1, s. 2.2. (Can.)).
[129] Ibid. (citing to explanatory note).
[130] Ibid., 194.

of Muslim governance."[131] This was a "politically astute and effective tactic" (albeit "arguably somewhat inattentive to national context") because "it appealed to the fears of an uninformed public that enforcement of faith-based dispute resolution would somehow push Canada onto a slippery slope toward theocracy."[132]

The Boyd Report's handling of this issue of theocracy is also notable. Although some of Ali's statements suggest a model of religious authority independent of state review, most Muslim groups with whom Boyd spoke stressed that Muslims have a religious duty to obey the secular law in the nation in which they reside.[133] Moreover, the Boyd Report characterized any demand for Muslim political supremacy or a separate Muslim state within Canada as off the table:

> [U]nder the current legal structure, establishing a separate legal regime for Muslims in Ontario is not possible. Creating a separate legal stream for Muslims would require change to our justice system on a level not easily contemplated from a practical, social, legal, or political point of view. In addition, it must be clearly understood that arbitration is not a parallel system, but a method of alternative dispute resolution that is subject to judicial oversight, and is thus subordinate to the court system.[134]

A millet system that relegates people of particular religious faiths to religious tribunals is also inconsistent with the Canadian Charter of Rights and Freedoms:

> Ontarians do not subscribe to the notion of "separate but equal" when it comes to the laws that apply to us. ... A policy of compelling people to submit to different legal regimes on the basis of religion or culture would be counter to *Charter* values, values which Ontarians hold dear, and which the government is bound to follow. Equality before and under the law, and the existence of a single legal regime available to all Ontarians are the cornerstones of our liberal democratic society.[135]

This reasoning insists that membership in a polity must not be trumped by membership in particular religious and cultural communities. A number of the individual Muslims and Muslim groups that Boyd interviewed similarly resisted any advent of a personal law system, arguing that it would deprive them of the benefits and protections of citizenship.[136] Similarly, Macklin notes how "encultured women" managed to express political citizenship in the sphere of law reform, insisting that their rights as members of the broader polity be protected.[137]

---

[131] Macklin, "Particularized Citizenship," 284–285; see *Boyd Report*, 42 (discussing WLUML).
[132] Macklin, "Particularized Citizenship," 285.
[133] *Boyd Report*, 54.
[134] Ibid., 88.
[135] Ibid. (italics in original).
[136] Ibid., 42–55.
[137] Macklin, "Particularized Citizenship," 276.

The Boyd Report thoughtfully discusses membership and citizenship in a multicultural and democratic society in which individuals are "at the intersection of various identities."[138] Drawing on Shachar's work, it states that it is of "crucial importance" to recognize that persons are "always caught at the intersection of multiple affiliations" – members of groups and citizens of the state.[139] "It is citizenship that allows membership in the minority community to take shape," the report declares, and "the foremost political commitment of all citizens, particularly those who wish to identify at a cultural or religious level with a minority outside of the mainstream, must be able to respect the rights accorded to each one of us as individual Canadians and Ontarians."[140]

Women's rights are a particular concern. This focus is not accidental. Much of the public reaction to Ali's announcement concerned the possible negative impact on women. Boyd's mandate was to explore the impact of arbitration on vulnerable people. Ontario's statutes, and in particular the preamble of its Family Law Act, include, Boyd notes, "some of the strongest legislative statements about gender equality in Canadian law."[141]

The report "did not find any evidence to suggest that women are being systematically discriminated against as a result of arbitration of family law issues."[142] This conclusion, however, seems contradicted by various testimonies that Marion Boyd heard about gender disadvantage and pressures on women to participate in such tribunals.[143]

Another striking feature of the Boyd Report is its discussion of what role the Canadian Charter of Rights and Freedoms, with its comparatively robust commitment to equal citizenship and religious and cultural rights, played in this debate. Boyd concludes that the Charter's important guarantees are limits on public power, not private power, and that "[a]greeing to be bound by an arbitrator's decision falls into the category of an action that is private and therefore, in my view, is not subject to *Charter* scrutiny."[144] Government has an obligation to ensure that the legal rules concerning the breakdown of private relationships do not perpetuate gender

---

[138] *Boyd Report*, 91.

[139] Ibid., 92 (quoting Ayelet Shachar, "Group Identity and Women's Rights in Family Law: The Perils of Multicultural Accommodation," *Journal of Political Philosophy* 6:3 [1998]: 285, 296). Shachar's ideas about multiple jurisdiction and citizenship are featured in the Archbishop of Canterbury's recent lecture, in which he pondered a more accommodationist stance in Britain toward Muslim law. See Dr. Rowan Williams, "Civil and Religious Law in England: A Religious Perspective" Feb. 7, 2008, available at http://www.archbishopofcanterbury.org/1575.

[140] *Boyd Report*, 92.

[141] Ibid., 19 (quoting Family Law Act, R.S.O., 1990, ch. F.3, "Preamble" (Can.)).

[142] Ibid., 133.

[143] Ibid., 39–55.

[144] Ibid., 72 (italics in original).

roles and stereotypes; however, "if the participants choose not to follow that law, and instead make private arrangements, the government is not required to interfere."[145] She further observes: "Nothing in the *Charter* requires an equal result of private bargaining. Parties may choose an apparently unequal result for many reasons and may think a deal fair that outsiders think is unfair."[146]

The Boyd Report also notes that the Charter's commitment to freedom of religion is to be interpreted to enhance the multicultural heritage of Canadians. Some respondents argued that Section 27 of the Charter not only permits but demands that multicultural communities be allowed "to use their own form of personal law to resolve disputes."[147] Boyd states that a commitment to enhancing the multicultural heritage "suggests respect for people's choices as long as those choices or the results are not illegal."[148] In a move familiar to liberalism, she continues: "People are entitled to make choices that others may perceive not to be correct, as long as they are legally capable of making such choices and the choice is not prohibited by law. In the areas where the state has chosen to allow people to order their lives according to private values, the state has no place enforcing any particular set of values, religious or not."[149]

These strong assumptions about choice made in "private" have drawn thoughtful criticism by Canadian feminists. For example, Pascale Fournier critiques the Boyd Report's "neo-liberal vision" of choice – that Muslim women "should be free to live as they wish in the private sphere" – because it "disregards the overall socioeconomic and distributive background of Muslim women living in Canada."[150] She notes such factors as Muslim women's "susceptibility to marriage at a younger age, the precariousness of immigration status, the higher rate of unemployment, and the segregation into sectors of low-income jobs."[151] She faults the Boyd Report's "abstract vision of multiculturalism," which is attentive to issues of identity and religious freedom but inattentive to the broader landscape in which religious subjects live. Lost in the celebration of "protecting choice" is attention to "the distributive stakes involved for Muslim women in allowing religious law through the Arbitration Act" and issues of gender equality and economic fairness.[152]

Fournier's critique invites attention to the relationship between family law's default rules and the scope of private choice. In the United States, for example,

---

[145] Ibid.
[146] Ibid., 73 (italics in original).
[147] Ibid., 72.
[148] Ibid., 74.
[149] Ibid., 75. Ronald Dworkin's account of liberalism is one example.
[150] Fournier, "In the (Canadian) Shadow of Islamic Law," 659.
[151] Ibid.
[152] Ibid., 677.

current constitutional law bars states from enacting laws that require a gendered division of labor in the home or return to the common law's model of marriage as a gender hierarchy. However, U.S. constitutional law does not bar individuals from choosing to order their family life a particular way, subject, of course, to legal protections against violence, child abuse, and neglect.[153] At the same time, family law has adopted default rules that reflect an ideal of marriage as an economic partnership and, through doctrines like equitable distribution of property at divorce, serve (not always very well) to alleviate some of the economic vulnerability that women who choose more traditional gender roles may suffer at divorce.

A similar dilemma arises in the arbitration context: What if people, in dissolving their marriages, choose not to avail themselves of the economic protections of civil family law's rules concerning property distribution and spousal support? Macklin argues that the controversy over faith-based arbitration needs to be understood in the broader context of the extent to which Canadian law allows parties to "opt out" of family law's default positions of protecting the vulnerable and promoting gender equality when it allows; encourages parties to arbitrate and to make domestic contracts concerning matters relating to property and support.[154] It is important not to exaggerate the protection that civil law's default rules afford, in view of this ability to opt out.[155]

The broader move to look to the relationship between default rules and the latitude for opting out is a cogent one because it invites attention to whether courts may compromise default rules of gender equality in the name of upholding freedom of contract.[156] This move helps guard against an automatic assumption that civil law is more protective of gender equality and fairness than religious law. At the same time, Shachar cautions that the analogy between religious tribunals and secular courts upholding freedom of contract may be overly simple if it suggests "that religious pressures are no different in kind than economic or related pressures imposed on women in our society."[157] It may discount "the communal pressures that may be imposed on a devout believer to comply with what is presented as a *religious* duty."[158]

[153] McClain, *Place of Families*, 78–79.
[154] See Audrey Macklin, "Privatization Meets Multiculturalism: The Case of Faith-Based Arbitration," (unpublished paper presented at Annual Meeting of the Canadian Political Science Association).
[155] She writes critically (as have other Canadian feminists) of the recent Canadian Supreme Court decision *Hartshorne v. Hartshorne*, 1 S.C.R. 550, 2004 SCC 22 (2004), in which the court upheld a marital agreement concerning property distribution that independent legal counsel advised the wife-to-be was "grossly unfair," and the record, the dissent argued, suggested the wife was more vulnerable and in a position of relative dependence.
[156] Shachar, "Feminism and Multiculturalism: Mapping the Terrain," 139.
[157] Ibid.
[158] Ibid. (italics in original).

All of this feminist commentary offers useful avenues of inquiry for considering possible models of legal pluralism in the United States. Within the United States, standards for when to uphold a premarital or marital contract vary considerably, with a robust commitment to freedom of contract (even in the face of substantive unfairness) on one end of the spectrum and a protective regime that insists on both procedural and substantive unfairness (or at least a very informed waiver of rights) on the other.[159]

What might be said in favor of Boyd's report? Would the safeguards have been sufficient? A liberal model that recognizes agency by allowing choice, even incorrect ones, puts a high premium on fostering informed choice. Thus, the Boyd Report recommended many safeguards to facilitate informed choice.[160] The report also calls for a legal education campaign to inform the public in general, and vulnerable women in particular, about their legal options for resolving disputes. Such a campaign would include education about "general rights and obligations under the law," "family law issues," alternative dispute resolution (ADR), the Arbitration Act, "immigrant law issues," and "community support."[161] All of these measures aim to ensure that choice is both informed and voluntary. These assumptions about the power of Muslim women's groups to carry out such educational efforts and the likely impact of such a campaign may be too robust, as some feminist commentators note.

Would it have been better, from the perspective of fostering equal citizenship and religious freedom, if the Boyd Report had been adopted? Should the state have tried to harness religion by allowing religious arbitration that is subject to state-imposed procedural and substantive limits? What if, Beverley Baines asks, Canadian feminists, particularly Muslim feminists, had "expended more energy on the question: What is needed to safeguard faith-based arbitration for women?"[162] The fact that Ontario law now specifies that arbitration that takes place pursuant to religious law is not family law arbitration (that is, it does not carry any civil effects) does not mean that parties will not pursue religious arbitration.[163] It will, instead, as Estin notes in this volume,

---

[159] For a robust freedom of contract approach, see *Simeone v. Simeone*, 581 A.2d 162 (Pa. 1990); by contrast, California's statutory law and the American Law Institute's *Principles of the Law of Family Dissolution: Analysis and Recommendations* (Newark, NJ: LexisNexis, 2002) take a more protective approach. The ALI rejects a contract analysis because intimate bargaining is different from other sorts of bargaining. For further discussion of the ALI, see Bix, "Pluralism and Decentralization" (in this volume).

[160] *Boyd Report*, 21 (citing Family Law Act, R.S.O. 1990, ch. F.3, s. 56(4), "Domestic Contracts" (Can)); see Macklin, "Privatization Meets Multiculturalism," 133–136.

[161] Macklin, "Privatization Meets Multiculturalism," 138.

[162] Beverley Baines, "Must Feminists Identify as Secular Citizens?" in *Gender Equality: Dimensions of Women's Equal Citizenship*, eds. Linda C. McClain and Joanna L. Grossman (Cambridge: Cambridge University Press, 2009) (noting that the Canadian feminist group Women's Legal Education and Action Fund [LEAF] and some Canadian Muslim feminists did pursue this strategy).

[163] See Shachar, "Feminism and Multiculturalism: Mapping the Terrain"; Estin, "Unofficial Family Law" (in this volume).

be "unofficial family law" and the parties will lack whatever protections they would have had if Boyd's recommendations were adopted.[164] These mediated solutions, Shachar argues, may "never be subject to regulation by state norms if they remain unchallenged by the parties." A cost of this outcome is that it leaves "extremely vulnerable precisely those women who may be most in need of joint-governance in the regulation of family affairs," women who "for either economic or cultural reasons might feel obliged to have at least some aspects of their marriage and divorce regulated by religious principles." By contrast, a "joint governance" solution might have helped address this vulnerability by facilitating a process of reform from within a religious tradition. She explains:

> The decision of the tribunal will not become legally binding and enforceable if it breaches the basic protections to which each woman is entitled by virtue of her equal citizenship status.... [T]his resolution may eventually prove to offer effective, non-coercive measures to encourage a process of "change from within" the religious tradition.[165]

V. CONCLUSION

In this chapter, I have argued that the call for multi-tiered marriage, or a "robust" modern millet system, in the United States should be resisted. I have raised questions about whether there actually is such a demand in the United States. I contrasted two possible strategies for giving more voice to religious models of marriage: securing congruence between religious and civil law by instantiating religious law in civil law or recognizing the binding authority of religious tribunals to adjudicate family law. Normative pluralism is indeed everywhere, including in the "unofficial" family law that shapes many people's lives. Translating this into more legal pluralism, however, warrants concern. U.S. courts already give official, or civil, effect to certain aspects of religious family law. However, they also decline to do so based on certain limiting principles rooted in concerns for due process and for the substance of civil family law's commitments.

Civil law's concerns for gender equality and for protecting vulnerable parties are salient reasons to be cautious about new forms of legal pluralism. Any system of "multi-tiered marriage" that does not attend adequately to the equal protection and equal citizenship of women as well as men conflicts with the commitments of the U.S. family law system and constitutional principles. Moreover, lending the state's imprimatur to models of family based on male authority and female submission or

---

[164] Estin, "Unofficial Family Law" (in this volume).
[165] Shachar, "Feminism and Multiculturalism: Mapping the Terrain," 142. See also Shachar, "Faith in Law?" (in this volume).

on other forms of gender privilege and preference may educate children as to the legitimacy of those models in broader society. This implicates the state's interest in children as future citizens. As the recent controversy over faith-based arbitration in Ontario suggests, what is needed is a model of legal pluralism that holds fast both to the value of religious membership and to the rights and duties of equal citizenship.

13

Faith in Law? Diffusing Tensions Between Diversity and Equality

Ayelet Shachar

How should a democratic state and its public law system respond to claims by members of religious minorities seeking to establish private faith-based arbitration tribunals to resolve family disputes? Classic liberals and civic republicans would have had a quick response to such a query. They favored a strict separation between state and religion, as part of their support for drawing a plain and clean line between the public and private spheres. Be a citizen in public, a Jew (or a Catholic or a Muslim, and so on) in private, remains the favored mantra, dating back to as early as the 1791 French National Assembly's decree admitting Jews as individuals to the rights of citizenship, after they had "freed" themselves from any communal semi-autonomous governance institutions.

But the world now is a very different place. My aim in this chapter is to highlight the centrality of women, gender, and the family in renewed state and religion contestations that inject new meanings into the traditional categories of "private" and "public." This chapter focuses exclusively on the situation of members of minority religions living in otherwise secularized societies. My interest, more specifically, lies in exploring how different legal arrangements between secular and religious jurisdictions shape and affect women's rights to religious freedom and equality. Of special interest here are those situations in which renegotiated relations between state and religion intersect and interact with public concerns about power disparities between men and women in the resolution of family law disputes.[1]

At present, the bulk of the theoretical literature on citizenship and multiculturalism engages in intricate attempts to delineate the boundaries of *public*, state-sponsored accommodation of diversity, as exemplified by the veiling controversies.

---

[1] In addressing these weighty issues, my departure point is a deep commitment toward respecting women's identity and membership interests, as well as promoting their equality both within and across communities. I am also guided by an understanding of culture and religion as amenable to change and open to a plurality of interpretations.

As if these charged dilemmas currently playing out in the courts do not present enough of a hurdle, we are also starting to see a new type of challenge on the horizon: the request by members of religious minorities to *privatize diversity*. By this I refer to the recent proposals raised by self-proclaimed "guardians of the faith" to establish private arbitration tribunals in which consenting members of the group will have their legal disputes resolved in a binding fashion – according to religious principles – under the secular umbrella of alternative dispute resolution (ADR). While formally deploying the logic of ADR, this new development is potentially far-reaching: The main claim raised by advocates of privatized diversity is that respect for religious freedom or cultural integrity does not require inclusion in the public sphere, but *exclusion* from it. This leads to a demand that the state adopt a hands-off, noninterventionist approach, placing civil and family disputes with a religious or cultural aspect "outside" the official realm of equal citizenship. This potential storm must be addressed head on. This is the case because privatized diversity mixes three inflammatory components in today's political environment: religion, gender, and the rise of a neoliberal state. The volatility of these issues is undisputed; they require a mere spark to ignite.

Privatized diversity's potentially dramatic alterations to the legal system increasingly revolve around the regulation of women and the family, placing them at the center of larger debates about citizenship and identity. These challenges cannot be fully captured by our existing legal categories; they require a new vocabulary and a fresh approach. I will begin to sketch here the contours of such an approach by asking what is owed to women whose legal dilemmas (at least in the family law arena) arise from the fact that their lives have already been affected by the interplay between overlapping systems of identification, authority, and belief: in this case, religious and secular law.

The standard legal response to this challenge is to seek shelter behind a formidable "wall of separation" between state and religion, even if this implies turning a blind eye to the concerns of religious women – especially those caught in the uncoordinated web of secular and religious marriage bonds. I will advance a different approach. By placing these once-ignored agents at the center of analysis, this chapter explores the idea of permitting a degree of *regulated interaction* between religious and secular sources of obligation, so long as the baseline of citizenship-guaranteed rights remains firmly in place.[2] Despite the understandable desire to "disentangle" law from religion by metaphorically "caging" each in its appropriate sphere or domain, it is worth contemplating whether a carefully regulated recognition of multiple legal affiliations (and the subtle interactions among them) can allow

---

[2] The term "citizenship rights" here applies to anyone who resides in the territory, regardless of her or his formal membership status.

devout women to benefit from the protections offered by the state to other citizens –
yet without abandoning the tenets of their faith. I will demonstrate the possibility of
implementing such a vision by reference to a recent decision of the Supreme Court
of Canada, *Bruker v. Marcovitz*, which breaks new ground.[3]

Finally, I will revisit an acrimonious controversy that broke out in Canada following a proposal by a communal Muslim organization in Ontario to establish a
private "Islamic Court of Justice" (*darul qada*) to resolve family law disputes among
consenting adults, known as the "*shari'a* tribunal" debate. I will reflect on the government's chosen policy to ban any type of family arbitration by such faith-based
tribunals, thus reaffirming the classic secular–religious divide. While this decision
is politically defensible and symbolically astute, it does not necessarily provide adequate protection for those individuals most vulnerable to their community's formal
and informal pressures to push them to accept "unofficial" dispute-resolution forums
in resolving marital issues. The decision may instead thrust these tribunals underground where no state regulation, coordination, or legal recourse is made available
to those who may need it most.

I. PRIVATIZED DIVERSITY

Before we turn to alternative remedies, it is important to first articulate the privatized diversity challenge in greater detail. In discussions about citizenship, we
repeatedly come across the modernist and liberal schema of separate spheres: We
are expected to act as citizens in the public sphere, but remain free to express our
distinct cultural or religious identities in the private domain of family and communal life. Yet multiple tensions have exposed cracks in this separate-spheres formula.
For example, where precisely does the "private" end and the "public" begin? Who
is to bear the burdens if the modern state's desire to keep religion out of the public
sphere indirectly inspires calls to limit access to citizenship, or conversely, to create
unregulated "islands of jurisdiction" that immunize the practices of certain religious communities because they occurred under the cover of privatized diversity?
By focusing on these topical issues, we are faced with a larger puzzle: What might
the new engagement between state and religion in the twenty-first century look like?
Would it permit a path to accommodating diversity *with* equality? In the remainder of this chapter I will try to provide some concrete institutional answers to this
query by reliance on recent and quite creative attempts by courts and legislatures
to forge ahead.

Family law serves as an excellent illustration to these simmering gender and
religion tensions. It demonstrates that for some observant women, the claim for

[3] *Bruker v. Marcovitz*, 2007 3 SCR 607.

achieving greater equality and legal protection as female citizens may in part be informed by their claim for religious recognition and accommodation. Consider, for example, the situation of observant religious women who may wish (or feel bound) to follow their faith community's divorce requirements in addition to the rules of the state that remove barriers to remarriage. Without the removal of such barriers, women's ability to build new families, if not their very membership status (or that of their children), may be adversely affected. This is particularly true for observant Jewish and Muslim women living in secular societies who have entered marriage through a religious ceremony – as permitted by law in many jurisdictions.[4] For them, a civil divorce – which is all that a secular state committed to a separation of state and church can provide – is simply part of the story; it does not, and cannot, dissolve the religious aspect of the relationship. Failure to recognize their "split-status" position – of being legally divorced according to state law, but still married according to their faith tradition – may leave these women prone to abuse by recalcitrant husbands. These men are often well aware of the adverse effect this split-status situation has on their wives, women who fall between the cracks of the civil and religious jurisdictions.[5]

Add to this the recognition that, for a host of complex historical, political, and institutional path-dependency reasons, family law has become crucial for minority religions in maintaining their definition of membership. Religious minorities in secularized democracies are typically nonterritorial entities; unlike certain national or linguistic communities (think of the Québécois in Canada, the Catalans in Spain, and so on). They have no semiautonomous subunit in which they constitute a majority, nor have they power to define the public symbols that manifest, and in turn help preserve, their distinctive national or linguistic heritage. Religious minorities, as nonterritorial communities, are thus forced to find other ways to sustain their distinct traditions and ways of life. With no authority to issue formal documents of membership, regulate mobility, or hold the power to collect mandatory taxes, religious personal laws that define marriage, divorce, and lineage have come to serve an

---

4 Even in France, which does not permit entry into marriage through the religious route (only a civil marriage is visible to the eyes of the state), we find growing attention paid to the effects of religious marriage and divorce on women. The concern is this: If the parties have not married in a civil fashion but have entered a "halâl marriage" in France, the state will not recognize the religious marriage and therefore cannot provide a divorce. Because there are no religious institutions to turn to, the wife can then remain trapped in an unsuccessful marriage, without an ability to free herself. See, e.g., John R. Bowen, *Can Islam Be French? Pluralism and Pragmatism in a Secularist State* (Princeton, NJ: Princeton University Press, 2009), 158–178.

5 Related legal dilemmas can also arise for Roman Catholic couples in the context of a civil divorce. In certain cases, the Catholic Church has nullified the religious marriage bond so as to avoid the split-status situation.

important role in regulating membership boundaries. These laws demarcate a pool of individuals endowed with the collective responsibility to maintain the group's values, practices, and distinct ways of life (if they maintain their standing as members in that community). I have elsewhere labeled this family law's *demarcating* function. For some religious minorities it comes close to serving the same core purposes as citizenship law does for the state. It delineates who is legally affiliated to the community and thus strengthens the bonds of continuity between past and future by identifying who is considered part of the tradition. This is why gaining control over the religious aspects of entry into (or exit from) marriage matters greatly to these communities; it is part of a membership demarcation and intergenerational project. At the same time, family law is also the area in which women have historically and traditionally been placed at a disadvantage by both states and religious communities, in part because the recognition of female members plays a crucial role in "reproducing the collective" – both literally and figuratively. Although this core contribution to the collective could, in theory, have empowered them, in most places and legal traditions it led to tight control and regulation of women, treating them, by law, as less than equal.

With this background in mind, we can now see more clearly why the *shari'a* tribunal controversy in Canada has provoked such an unwieldy storm of response, as did the Archbishop of Canterbury's lecture on civil and religious law in England, which contemplated the option of allowing British Muslim communities the freedom to regulate certain functions (especially those dealing with family law) according to faith-based principles tamed by state-defined baseline protections. In Ontario, a bitter debate erupted after a small and relatively conservative organization, the Canadian Society of Muslims, declared in a series of press releases its intention to establish a faith-based tribunal that would operate as a forum for binding arbitration on consenting parties. The envisioned tribunal (which never came into operation) would have permitted consenting parties not only to enter a less adversarial, out-of-court, dispute-resolution process, but also to use choice-of-law provisions to apply religious norms to resolve family disputes, according to the "laws (*fiqh*)" of any Islamic school, for example, Shia or Sunni (Hanafi, Shafi'i, Hanbali, or Maliki).

The proposal to establish a tribunal of this kind was perceived as challenging the normative and juridical authority, not to mention legitimacy, of the secular state's asserted mandate to represent and regulate the interests and rights of *all* its citizens in their family matters, irrespective of communal affiliation. In this respect, it raised profound questions concerning hierarchy and lexical order in the contexts of law and citizenship: Which norms should prevail, and who, or what entity, ought to have the final word in resolving any value-conflicts between equality and diversity. No less significant for our discussion is the recognition that the proposal to establish a non-state arbitration tribunal of this kind does not by itself provide a conclusive answer to determining how secular and religious norms should interact in governing the family. To the contrary, it serves to provoke just such a debate. As an analytical matter, secular and religious norms may stand in tension with one another, point in different directions, lead to broadly similar results, or directly contradict one another. It is the latter outcome that is seen to pose the greatest challenge to the superiority of secular family law by its old adversary: religion.

If the only choice on offer were between rejecting or accepting such a tribunal (as a concrete illustration of privatized diversity comprising "enclaves" or "islands" of unregulated jurisdictions) I would strongly oppose it. I would hold this position even if we accept the force of the argument for nonintervention on the grounds of allowing communities as much associational freedom as possible to pursue their own visions of the good in a diverse society. The reason is as simple as it is powerful: Hardly anyone suggests that religious liberty is absolute; it may be overridden or restricted by other liberties or compelling state interests. Without such limitations in place, the state becomes an implicit accomplice in potentially tolerating infringements of women's basic citizenship protections in the name of respecting cultural and religious diversity.

Furthermore, the privatized-diversity framework relies on an artificial and oversimplified distinction between private and public, culture and citizenship, contractual and moral obligation. This vision is not only inaccurate on a descriptive level; it is normatively unattractive as well. It is blind to the intersection of overlapping affiliations in individuals' lives. These parallel "belongings" are often the significant source of meaning and value for religious women; at the same time, they may also make them vulnerable to a double or triple disadvantage, especially in a legal and governance system that permits little interaction and dialogue between their overlapping sources of obligation. Women situated in minority religious communities are often especially hard hit by the privatized-diversity framework and are left to fend for themselves under structurally unfavorable conditions.

II. THE PREDICAMENT FACING VULNERABLE MEMBERS OF RELIGIOUS COMMUNITIES

The established strict-separation approach asks religious women to adhere to the civil rules on the dissolution of marriage and divorce, leaving it up to each individual woman to somehow negotiate a termination of the religious aspect of the relationship – a task that may prove extremely difficult if the husband is recalcitrant. Another response, often presented by well-meaning philosophers and political theorists, is to recommend that these members simply "exit" their home communities if they experience injustice within.[6] However, this recommendation provides little solace. If pious women wanted to leave their communities, the central legal dilemmas that haunt them – the challenge of adhering to both secular and non-state religious requirements of forming and dissolving marriage – would not have arisen in the first place.

Into this vacuum enters the privatized-diversity approach. It takes a diametrically opposed path to that of strict separation, placing the need to address the religious side of the marriage at the heart of the non-statist legal response: for instance, by recommending that parties move the "full docket" of their disputes from public state-provided courtrooms to private faith-based tribunals that may (or may not) comply with statutory and constitutional protections of rights and obligations that citizens hold as members of the larger political community. Blanket acceptance of privatized diversity would thus amount to a dramatic redefinition of the relationship between state and religion under the guise of mere procedural reliance on private alternative dispute-resolution mechanisms. The price to be paid for such a move might prove dangerously high: forfeiting the hard-won protections that women won through democratic and equity-enhancing legislation, itself achieved as a result of significant social mobilization by women's groups and other justice-seeking individuals and communities. While offering opposing solutions, the strict-separation and privatized-diversity approaches rely on a common matrix of denying their *shared* responsibility and obligation to assist women whose marriage regulation is grounded in an uneasy amalgam of secular and religious traditions. Between them, the two approaches compel devout women to make an all-or-nothing choice between these sources of law and identity.

This punishing dilemma can be avoided if the option of regulated interaction is contemplated. The core issue for us to assess is whether, and under what conditions, women's freedom and equality can be promoted (rather than inhibited) by law's recognition of certain faith-based obligations that structure marriage and divorce for religious citizens. The additional challenge is to develop a legal approach that can foster viable institutional paths for cooperation that begin to match the actual complexity of women's lived experience. Instead of assuming that gender equality and religious pluralism inevitably pull in contrasting directions, the recognizing of the actual dilemmas and claims raised by women embedded in religion (as in the split-status example) call for new approaches that incorporate state and communal input into the regulation of faith-based dispute-resolution processes in the family law

---

[6] For a critical discussion of the exit option, see Susan Moller Okin, "'Mistresses of Their Own Destiny': Group Rights, Gender, and Realistic Rights of Exit," *Ethics* 112(2) (January 2002): 205–230; Anne Phillips, *Multiculturalism* Without *Culture* (Princeton, NJ: Princeton University Press, 2007), 133–157.

arena as an opportunity to both empower women and to encourage transformation from within the tradition and by its authorized interpreters. This kind of regulated interaction promotes the intersection of religion with state oversight, ideally encouraging the participation of those long excluded from the "temple" of formal religious knowledge and the work of interpreting the faith's sacred texts. This is done with an eye to increasing new voices and re-readings of the tradition in a more egalitarian and inclusive fashion, but still within its permissible decision-making and interpretative techniques.

The standard legal response to such dilemmas is of course different. It tends to relegate civil and family disputes with certain religious aspects *beyond* the reach of the secular courts – and thus outside the realm of provision of the safeguards provided by the state to other litigants or vulnerable parties. This need not, however, be the sole or even primary response to such dilemmas, especially when "nonintervention" effectively translates into immunizing wrongful behavior by more powerful parties. In the deeply gendered world of intersecting religious and secular norms of family law, these more powerful parties are often husbands who may refuse to remove barriers to religious remarriage (as in the Jewish *get* [bill of divorcement], elaborated later) or who may seek to retract a financial commitment undertaken as part of the religious marriage contract (as might be the case with deferred *mahr* in certain Islamic marriages). Such retaliation impairs the woman's ability to build a new family or establish financial independence after divorce. The broader concern here is that while their multiple affiliations might offer religious women a significant source of meaning and value, they may also make them vulnerable to a double or triple disadvantage, especially in a legal system that categorically denies cooperation between their overlapping sources of obligation.

Is it possible to find a more fruitful engagement that overcomes this predicament by placing the interests of these historically marginalized participants at the center of the analysis? Arguably, the obligation to engage in just such renegotiation is pressing in light of growing global demands to reevaluate the crucial social arena of family law. From the perspective of women caught in the web of overlapping and potentially competing systems of secular and sacred law, the almost automatic rejection of any attempt to establish a forum for resolving standing disputes that address the religious dimension of their marriage might respect the protection-of-rights dimension of their lived experience, but unfortunately does little to address the cultural or religious affiliation issue. The latter may well be better addressed by attending to the removal of religious barriers to remarriage, obstacles that do not automatically disappear following a civil divorce. This is particularly true for observant women who have solemnized marriage according to the requirements of their religious tradition, and who may now wish – or feel obliged – to receive the blessing of this tradition for the dissolution of that relationship.

In the Canadian debate, this constituency also reflected a *transnational* element. In families with roots in more than one country, a divorce agreement that complies with the demands of the faith (as a nonterritorial identity community) – in addition to those of the state of residence – is perceived as more "transferable" across different Muslim jurisdictions.[7] In technical terms, this need not be the case – private international law norms are based on the laws of states, *not* of religions. But what matters here is the perception that a faith-based tribunal may provide a valuable legal service to its potential clientele, a service that the secular state, by virtue of its formal divorce from religion, simply cannot provide.

I believe we also face the urgent task of investigating and highlighting the importance of state action (or *in*action) in shaping, through law and institutional design, the context in which women can pursue their claims for equity and justice. Viewed through this perspective, the rise of privatized diversity mechanisms to implement religious principles should rightly be perceived with a healthy dose of skepticism, particularly if the parties lose the background protections and bargaining chips they are otherwise entitled to under secular law. One may well wonder whether this development represents a whole new and convenient way for the neoliberal state (and its "rolled-back" public institutions) to avoid taking responsibility for protecting the rights of more vulnerable parties precisely in that arena of social life, the family, that is most crucial for realizing both gender equality and collective identity.

In order to militate against such a result, it is high time to search for new terms of engagement between the major players. They have a stake in finding a viable path that accommodates diversity *with* equality, a path that includes the faith community, the state, and the individual. Any tractable solution, however, must do so in ways that will benefit religious women, while duly acknowledging they are members of intersecting (and potentially conflicting) identity- and law-creating jurisdictions.

III. FORGING A NEW PATH

Any new path requires a delicate balance. On the one hand, it demands vigilance to address the serious communal pressures that make "free consent" to arbitration a code name for thinly veiled coercion. On the other hand, it requires avoidance of any hasty conclusion that the answer to such complex legal and identity challenges lies in turning a blind eye to the severe implications of the split-status problem confronting women who wish to maintain good standing in both their religious and nonreligious communities. A number of alternative ideal-type responses present

---

[7] Similar misconceptions are traced in England as well. See Lucy Carroll, "Muslim Women and 'Islamic Divorce' in England," *Journal of Muslim Minority Affairs* 17(1) (April 1997): 97–115.

themselves. I will discuss just two promising alternatives: democratic deliberation
and intercultural dialogue in civil society; and changing the background conditions
that influence such intra- and inter-cultural negotiations.[8]

The democratic deliberation path emphasizes the importance of dialogue in civil
society and involves formal and informal intercultural exchanges. This route permits revealing the internal diversity of opinions and interpretations of the religious
and secular family law traditions in question. Deliberation and contestation can also
promote agency and direct empowerment through political participation and social
mobilization.

While I fully endorse and support these civil society avenues, something else
might be required in terms of institutional design to address situations of negotiation
breakdown, imbalance of power, and restoration or establishment of rights. That
"something else" translates into a focus on legal-institutional remedies that respond
to the fact that erosion of women's freedom and autonomy is increasingly the "col-
lateral damage" of charged state–religious "showdowns." To avert this disturbing
result, I will briefly explore how, despite the fact that the strict-separation approach
still remains the standard or default response, courts and legislatures have recently
broken new ground by adopting what we might refer to as "intersectionist" or "joint
governance" remedies.

One example is the case I mentioned earlier, *Bruker v. Marcovitz*,[9] in which the
Canadian Supreme Court explicitly rejected the simplistic "your culture or your
rights" formula. Instead, it ruled in favor of "[r]ecognizing the enforceability by civil
courts of agreements to discourage religious barriers to remarriage, addressing the
gender discrimination those barriers may represent and alleviate the effects they
may have on extracting unfair concessions in a civil divorce."[10] In the *Marcovitz*
case, a Jewish husband made a promise to remove barriers to religious remarriage
in a negotiated, settled agreement, which was incorporated into the final divorce
decree between the parties. He said he would give his wife a *get*, a bill of divorcement. This contractual obligation thus became part of the terms that enabled the
civil divorce to proceed. Once the husband had the secular divorce in hand, however, he failed to honor the signed agreement to remove the religious barriers to
his wife's remarriage, claiming that he had undertaken a moral rather than legal

[8] This categorization fits well with Seyla Benhabib's "dual track" approach. See Seyla Benhabib, *The
Claims of Culture: Equality and Diversity in the Global Era* (Princeton, NJ: Princeton University Press,
2002), 130–132. A similar distinction between the "legal track" and "citizen track" is found in a major
report recently published in Quebec about the boundaries of reasonable accommodation. Gérard
Bouchard and Charles Taylor, *Building the Future: A Time for Reconciliation*, (Quebec: Commission
de Consultation surles Pratiques d'Accommodement reliées aux Différences Culturelles, 2008),
1–370.

[9] *Bruker v. Marcovitz*, 2007 3 SCR 607.

[10] Ibid., 3, 92.

obligation. The Supreme Court was not in a position to order specific performance (forcing the husband to grant a *get*); instead, the court ordered the husband to pay monetary damages for breach of the contractual promise, a breach that had harmed the wife personally and the public interest generally. What *Marcovitz* demonstrates is the possibility of employing a standard legal remedy (damages for breach of contract, in this example) in response to specifically gendered harms that arise out of the intersection between multiple sources of authority and identity – religious and secular – in the actual lives of women.

The significance of the *Marcovitz* decision lies in its recognition that both the secular and religious aspects of divorce matter greatly to observant women if they are to enjoy gender equality, articulate their religious identity, enter new families after divorce, or rely on contractual ordering just like any other citizen. This joint-governance framework offers us a vision in which the secular law may be invoked to provide remedies for religious women to protect them from husbands who might otherwise "cherry-pick" their religious and secular obligations. This is a clear rejection of a punishing "either/or" approach, and instead offers a more nuanced and context-sensitive analysis that begins from the "ground up." It identifies who is harmed and why, and then proceeds to find a remedy that matches, as much as possible, the need to recognize the (indirect) intersection of law and religion that contributed to the creation of the very harm for which legal recourse is now sought.

IV. REGULATED INTERACTION

The last set of issues that I wish to address relates to the thorny challenge of tackling the potential conflict between secular and religious norms governing family disputes. The fear that religious law represented a rival normative system that resisted and challenged the paramount constitutional principle of the rule of law clearly played a significant part in the anxiety surrounding the *shari'a* tribunal debate in Canada.[11] Given the deference typically afforded to out-of-court arbitration procedures, critics of the proposal charged that nothing less than an attempt to use a technique of privatized diversity to redefine the relationship between state and religion was underway. This posed an existential threat that no secular state authority was likely to accept with indifference – not even in tolerant, multicultural Canada. And so, after much contemplation, the chosen response to the challenge was to quash the proposed tribunal with all the legal force the authorities could muster. This took the shape of an absolutist solution: prohibiting by decree the operation of any religious arbitration

---

[11] Ran Hirschl and Ayelet Shachar, "The New Wall of Separation: Respecting Diversity, Prohibiting Competition," *Cardozo Law Review* 30 (2009): 2535–2560.

process in the family law arena.[12] This response, which relies on imposition by state fiat, sends a strong symbolic message of unity, although it is a unity achieved by prohibition instead of dialogue. This universal ban effectively shuts down, rather than encourages, coordination between civil and religious authorities.

A less heavy-handed approach might have been worth exploring, especially once the idea of granting unrestricted immunity in the name of religious freedom to *any* kind of dispute-resolution forum is rejected. The alternatives include a range of options that permit a mixture of ex ante and ex post regulatory oversight in the service of human rights protections, mandatory provisions that no party is permitted to waive, and enhanced access to whatever public-sponsored resources are normally available to anyone facing a family breakdown. Regulated interaction envisions a new way of allocating and sharing jurisdiction between states and religious minorities.

The major insight here is that today's most contested social arenas – family law, education, criminal justice, and immigration, to mention but a few key examples – are internally divisible into parts or "submatters": multiple, separable yet complementary, legal components. Existing legal and normative models rarely recognize that most contested social arenas encompass multiple functions, or diverse submatters. Rather, they operate on the misguided assumption that each social arena is internally *indivisible* and thus should be under the full and exclusive jurisdiction of one authority, either the state or faith community. On this account, there is always a winner and loser in the jurisdictional contest between state and religion. But if power can be divided into submatters within a single social activity, it becomes possible to have a more creative, nuanced, and context-sensitive basis for coordination.[13]

Take marriage. Here at least two submatters should be identified. There is a *demarcating* function mentioned earlier, which regulates, among other things, the change of one's marital status or one's entitlement to membership in a given community. And then there is a *distributing* function, which covers, among other things, the definition of the rights and obligations of married spouses, together with a determination, in the event of divorce or death, of the property and economic consequences of this change in marital status. These demarcation and distributive submatters parallel the two key legal aspects of marriage and divorce rules: status and property relations. This division permits ample room for legal creativity. Recent studies have shown, for example, that Muslim women in Britain have turned to non-state institutions in order to gain a religious-authorized release from a dead marriage, one

---

[12] The government adopted this solution with the enactment of the Family Statute Law Amendment Act, 2005 (amending The Arbitration Act, 1991) and the subsequent regulations that followed in 2007: Family Arbitration, Ontario Regulation 134/07.

[13] For further discussion, see Ayelet Shachar, *Multicultural Jurisdictions: Cultural Differences and Women's Rights* (Cambridge: Cambridge University Press, 2001), 117–145.

that, in certain cases, no longer legally existed because a state divorce decree had already been granted.[14] For these women, the religious councils were performing the crucial communal demarcating function of removing religious barriers to remarriage. These "end users" were seeking specialized religious-oriented divorce services that the secular state is, by definition, barred from supplying. At the same time, the women who turned to these faith-based councils expressed no interest in (and indeed, some explicitly rejected) the idea of delegating control over the distributive components of their fractured marriage. They did not want their post-divorce property relations (controlling matters such as the rights and obligations owed by each former spouse to the other, to the children (if any), and to various third parties) determined by these non-state institutions.[15] Such division of responsibility fits well with the idea of submatter jurisdictions. It rejects transferring the "full docket" or "package" to privatized-diversity entities and, instead, demands some degree of coordination occur between religious and civil institutions in any initial allocation of shared responsibility and its subsequent implementation.[16]

In addition to the recommended division of authority according to component functions, the literature on institutional design distinguishes between different forms or techniques of oversight. The classic approach envisages minimal oversight: The rationale here is that the consenting parties intentionally removed their dispute from the public system, preferring instead an out-of-court process. In the case of severe breaches of procedural justice, however, laws governing ADR routinely permit the arbitrating parties to seek judicial review.[17] This is characterized in the literature as the "fire alarm" response (a decentralized and ex post review initiated by individual complainants or public interest groups) as opposed to "police control" (a more centralized, governmental ex ante mode of oversight).[18] These combined protections

---

[14] Samia Bano, "In Pursuit of Religious and Legal Diversity: A Response to the Archbishop of Canterbury and the 'Sharia Debate' in Britain," *Ecclesiastical Law Journal* 10(3) (September 2008): 283–309.

[15] Ibid.

[16] Presently, these non-state entities operate outside the official system of law in England and Wales – remaining "nonexistent" from the state's perspective, notwithstanding the fact that they operate within its territory and affect its citizens. This situation spells trouble for women and their hard-won equality rights. Why? Because there is no guarantee that the unregulated religious councils will not try to extend their reach beyond pure status or demarcation decisions to certain "ancillary" distributive issues, even where the latter have already been dealt with by civil courts. This concern is exacerbated, ironically, where there is no regulation, coordination, or even mere knowledge of what occurs behind the closed doors of privatized-diversity institutions. This represents precisely the kind of deleterious situation that the regulated-interaction approach seeks to prevent.

[17] See, e.g., the provisions (prior to its amendment in 2006) of *The Arbitration Act, 1991*, S.O. 1991 c. 17, §§ 6, 19, 45–7.

[18] These two models are described in Mathew McCubbins and Thomas Schwartz, "Congressional Oversight Overlooked: Police Patrols Versus Fire Alarms," *American Journal of Political Science* 28(1) (February 1984): 165–179.

are designed to assist individuals by reducing information asymmetries and power imbalances, as well as providing a check on the exercise of authority by arbitrators or any other independent third-party decision makers.[19] However, just like any other legal measure that respects individual choice, they may fall short of providing a *full* guarantee that no communal (or other) pressure was imposed on those utilizing an alternative dispute resolution forum. To address these real concerns, any principled scheme of regulation must also include a robust commitment to ensure that women are not dispossessed of whatever equal rights and protections they have as citizens when they raise a legal claim that incorporates the religious dimension as well. The possibility of implementing precisely such an "intersectionist" commitment was exemplified by the *Marcovitz* ruling.

With these conditions firmly in place, we can appreciate the dynamism and behavior-alteration potential of the regulated-interaction approach. For instance, communal decision makers (ideally trained in *both* civil and religious law) have the opportunity to enjoy the benefits of state recognition of their decisions – including the coveted public enforcement of their awards – when dissolving a religious marriage in accordance with the tenets of the relevant faith. The state retains the power to issue a civil divorce and to define the thresholds or default rules in matters such as the post-divorce distribution of matrimonial and other property, matters that inevitably concern *all* citizens facing a marriage breakdown. These safeguards typically establish a baseline or "floor" of protection, above which significant room for variation is permitted. These protections were designed, in the first place, to address concerns about power and gender inequities in family relations – concerns that are not absent from religious communities either. If anything, these concerns probably apply with equal force in the religious context as in the individualized, secular case.

This then is the regulated-interaction model, one that offers an alternative to the "top-down" prohibition model that was eventually chosen by the government in the Canadian debate. Provided the resolution by a non-state "arbitration" body falls within the reasonable margin of discretion permitted a family law judge or secular arbitrator, there is no reason to discriminate against that tribunal *solely* for the reason that it was guided by, and applied, religious norms and principles. The operative assumption here is that, in a diverse society, we can safely assume that at least some individuals might wish to turn to their "communal" institutions, knowing that their basic state-backed rights are still protected by these alternative fora.

---

[19] The distinction between ex ante and ex post regulation is addressed at greater length in Ayelet Shachar, "Privatizing Diversity: A Cautionary Tale from Religious Arbitration in Family Law," *Theoretical Inquiries in Law* 9(2) (July 2008): 573–607.

Under these conditions, the option of turning to a *regulated* non-state tribunal may, perhaps paradoxically, nourish the development of a more dynamic, context-sensitive, and moderate interpretation of the faith tradition. Why? Because it may transform the standing of non-state sources of authority from the realm of unofficial, nonbinding advice to that of potentially compelling decisions over consenting parties. The proviso that comes with such revamped jurisdictional authority is that actors cannot breach the basic protections to which each woman is entitled by virtue of her equal citizenship status. If they ignore these entitlements, religious authorities risk depriving themselves of the ability to provide relevant legal services to the very members of the community they most dearly care about. If they wish to see their faith community survive (and indeed, flourish), and if they wish to continue to define who belongs within the faith community's membership boundaries, these basic protections cannot be spurned.[20]

As we have seen earlier, religious marriage and divorce rules play a crucial role in fulfilling this identity-demarcating function. The obligation to comply with minimal standards defined by the larger community in governing the distributive obligations between the separated or divorced parties (and toward relevant third parties) does not have to cripple the new-found authority gained by the religious community and its tribunals. They may maintain their identity through control over the demarcating aspect of marriage and divorce (for those members who desire such an affiliation). By ensuring that incidents of "split status" are reduced within a diverse plural society (one that retains the option of secular divorce), both the community at large and the specific women involved benefit by having all barriers to remarriage removed in a conclusive and nonambivalent manner. Such processes could plant the seeds for meaningful reform that falls within the interpretative margins and methodologies for innovation permitted by the religious tradition *and* improves women's bargaining position and rights protection. This creates an alignment of interests between the group, the state, and the individuals at risk. In this fashion, regulated interaction can address the multiple aspects of the marriage and its breakdown, generating conditions that permit an effective, noncoercive encouragement of more egalitarian and reformist changes from *within* the tradition itself.

The state system, too, is transformed from strict separation by regulated interaction. It is no longer permitted to categorically relegate competing sources of authority to the realm of unofficial, exotic, if not outright dangerous, "non-law." The regulated-interaction approach discourages an underworld of unregulated religious

---

[20] Such a result is unattractive for religious authorities, who strive to provide distinct legal services that no other agency can offer, as well as for the individual who turns to this specialized forum in order to bring closure to a charged marital or family dispute that bears a religious aspect that simply cannot be fully addressed by the secular court system.

tribunals. It offers a path to transcend the "either/or" choice between culture and rights, family and state, citizenship and islands of "privatized diversity."

V. CONCLUSION

The familiar and almost automatic response of insisting on the *dis*entanglement of state and church (or mosque, synagogue, and so forth) in regulating the family may not always work to the benefit of female religious citizens, persons who are deeply attached to, and influenced by, *both* systems of law and identity. Their complex claim for inclusion in both the state and their faith group as full members derives from women's multilayered connections to each system. Some insight into this complex phenomenon was evident in the *Marcovitz* case, where the Supreme Court challenged the very assumption that it is impossible to grant consideration to religious diversity and gender equality at the same time.

While some, perhaps many, are accustomed to seek shelter behind a high "wall of separation" between state and religion, a qualified yet dynamic "entanglement" between these old rivals – under a combined ex ante and ex post regulatory framework (coupled with due recognition of interlocking and complementary submatters) – may present the best hope for expanding recognition to, and equal citizenship for, once-marginalized and voiceless religious women. Existing legal strategies offer a false sense of confidence. They draw uncompromising lines that aim to compartmentalize sacred from secular, private from public – despite the fact that the social reality they regulate no longer fits this bill (if it ever did).

To overcome this impasse, we must recognize the limits of our existing legal vocabulary: It relies upon, and replicates, a polarized, oppositional dichotomy between either promoting (gender) equality or promoting (religious) liberty. But this misses the mark: It provides no remedies or answers for religious women who seek to find recognition as *both* culture bearers *and* rights bearers. This new terrain is admittedly rugged and yet uncharted. It is worth exploring, however, because it holds significant moral and legal promise. It envisions the once-vulnerable becoming potential agents of renewal of both their own religious traditions and the larger political communities in which they strive to belong as equal citizens.

14

The Frontiers of Marital Pluralism

An Afterword

John Witte Jr. and Joel A. Nichols

I. INTRODUCTION

Anglican Archbishop Rowan Williams set off an international firestorm on February 7, 2008, by suggesting that some "accommodation" of Muslim family law was "unavoidable" in England.[1] His speech itself was nuanced and qualified, carefully discussing the "growing challenge" of "the presence of communities which, while no less 'law-abiding' than the rest of the population, relate to something other than the British legal system alone." Nonetheless, his public reflection on "what degree of accommodation the law of the land can and should give to minority communities with their own strongly entrenched legal and moral codes" gave rise to more than 250 articles in the world press within a month – with the vast majority denouncing his remarks. England, his critics charged, will be beset by "licensed polygamy," barbaric procedures, and brutal violence against women encased in suffocating burkas if official sanction is given to *shari'a* courts.[2] Despite the fact that religious citizens already turn to informal religious adjudication of family law and other disputes, critics proclaimed that giving legal sanction to such adjudications would create unequal citizenship and foster enclaves of legally ghettoized Muslim courts immune from civil appeal or constitutional challenge. Other critics pointed to Nigeria, Pakistan, and other former English colonies that have sought to balance *shari'a* with the common law. The horrific excesses and chronic human rights violations of their religious courts – even ordering the faithful to stone innocent rape victims for dishonoring their families – prove that religious laws and state laws on the family simply cannot coexist, they said. Case closed.

---

[1] Dr. Rowan Williams, "Archbishop's Lecture – Civil and Religious Law in England: A Religious Perspective," Feb. 7, 2008, available at http://www.archbishopofcanterbury.org/1575#.

[2] See, e.g., Catherine Bennett, "It's One Sharia Law for Men and Quite Another for Women," *The Observer (The Guardian (U.K.))*, Feb. 10, 2008, available at http://www.guardian.co.uk/commentisfree/2008/feb/10/religion.law ("licensed polygamy").

This case won't stay closed for long, however. The Archbishop was not calling for the establishment of a parallel system of independent Muslim courts in England, and certainly not the direct enforcement of *shari'a* by English civil courts. He was, instead, raising a whole series of hard but "unavoidable" questions about marital, cultural, and religious identity and practice in Western democratic societies committed to human rights for all.[3] What forms of marriage should citizens be able to choose, and what forums of religious marriage law should state governments be required to respect? How should Muslims and other religious groups with distinctive family norms and cultural practices that vary from those espoused by the liberal state be accommodated in a society dedicated to religious liberty and equality, to self-determination and nondiscrimination? Are legal pluralism and even "personal federalism" necessary to protect Muslims and other religious believers who are conscientiously opposed to the liberal values that inform modern state laws on sex, marriage, and family? Or must there instead be "legal universalism" with its attendant "exclusionary consequences"?[4] Are these really the only options – or instead is something more akin to a "dance" between religious and civil law more appropriate and necessary?[5]

These and other hard questions are indeed becoming "unavoidable" for many modern Western democracies with growing and diverse Muslim communities, each making new and ever louder demands. If current growth rates of Muslim communities in the West continue, a generation from now the Danish cartoon "crisis" is going to seem like child's play.[6] These are not at all new questions for Orthodox Jewish communities, who have long had to strike the balance between their own distinctive religious practices and the demands of the civil state.[7] In addition, the questions are increasingly relevant for more traditional Christian communities in Western liberal democracies as the norms of marriage are diverging in important ways from some of their core principles.[8]

[3] Williams, "Archbishop's Lecture."
[4] See Jean-Francois Gaudreault-Desbiens, "Shari'a, Federalism and Legal Transplants," in *Shari'a in the West*, eds. Rex Ahdar and Nicholas Aroney (Oxford: Oxford University Press, 2010). Compare Mohammad H. Fadel, "Political Liberalism, Islamic Family Law, and Family Law Pluralism" (in this volume).
[5] See Michael J. Broyde, "New York's Regulation of Jewish Marriage: Covenant, Contract, or Statute?" (in this volume). See also the complex interrelationship described in Ayelet Shachar, "Faith in Law? Diffusing Tensions Between Diversity and Equality" (in this volume), described in greater detail in Ayelet Shachar, *Multicultural Jurisdictions: Cultural Differences and Women's Rights* (Cambridge: Cambridge University Press, 2001), 88–150.
[6] See Paul Belien, "Jihad Against Danish Newspaper," *The Brussels Journal*, Oct. 22, 2005, available at http://www.brusselsjournal.com/node/382; Robert A. Kahn, "The Danish Cartoon Controversy and the Rhetoric of Libertarian Regret," *University of Miami International and Comparative Law Review* 16 (2009): 151–181.
[7] See Broyde, "New York's Regulation" (in this volume).
[8] See, e.g., Stephen B. Presser, "Marriage and the Law: Time for a Divorce?" (in this volume); Daniel Cere, "Canadian Conjugal Mosaic: From Multiculturalism to Multi-Conjugalism?" (in this volume).

The authors in this volume have begun to unpack these and related questions with candor and with awareness of the high stakes involved.[9] Some investigate the contours of existing pluralism in family law and question whether additional, or different, pluralism would be beneficial.[10] Others provide striking comparative analyses about extant pluralism in legal systems outside the United States.[11] Others provide enlightening descriptions of some of the nuances and diversity of religious systems and the culture-specific ways in which norms are instantiated.[12] Still others offer trenchant analyses of the serious constitutional and cultural implications of accommodating faith-based family laws like *shari'a*, warning of the real dangers of maintaining dual religious and political sovereigns to govern domestic life.[13]

As the chapters in this volume illustrate, modern liberal democratic systems have thus far taken varying approaches to addressing such questions, despite their often common legal heritage and their shared commitment to human rights.[14] England, with large groups of Muslim minorities, has been particularly accommodating of Muslim schools, charities, and banks – and especially Muslim religious councils that govern (or provide advice to) the family, financial, and other private issues of their voluntary faithful.[15] Jewish law courts (*beth din*) similarly function to decide the rights of religious adherents, and there is a general solicitude among English courts to respect the decision making of these and similar religious "tribunals," provided they meet minimum norms such as mutual consent to participation and

[9] See Joel A. Nichols, "Multi-Tiered Marriage: Reconsidering the Boundaries of Civil Law and Religion" (in this volume). See also Joel A. Nichols, "Multi-Tiered Marriage: Ideas and Influences from New York and Louisiana to the International Community," *Vanderbilt Journal of Transnational Law* 40 (2007): 135–196 (raising similar questions and calling for a conversation about them).

[10] See, e.g., Brian H. Bix, "Pluralism and Decentralization in Marriage Regulation" (in this volume); Ann Laquer Estin, "Unofficial Family Law" (in this volume).

[11] See, e.g., Werner Menski, "Ancient and Modern Boundary Crossings Between Personal Laws and Civil Law in Composite India" (in this volume); Johan D. van der Vyver, "Multi-Tiered Marriages in South Africa" (in this volume); Fadel, "Political Liberalism" (in this volume).

[12] See, e.g., Broyde, "New York's Regulation" (in this volume); Fadel, "Political Liberalism" (in this volume).

[13] See, e.g., Linda C. McClain, "Marital Pluralism in the United States: On Civil and Religious Jurisdiction and the Demands of Equal Citizenship" (in this volume); Robin Fretwell Wilson, "The Perils of Privatized Marriage" (in this volume).

[14] Werner Menski helpfully cautions against insisting on a one-size-fits-all model for all cultures and all systems. See Menski, "Ancient and Modern Boundary Crossings" (in this volume). John Bowen has pointed out that Muslims in civil law countries, like France, at times have different discussions than common law countries regarding the level of integration regarding religious law. See, e.g., John R. Bowen, *Why the French Don't Like Headscarves: Islam, the State, and Public Space* (Princeton, NJ: Princeton University Press, 2007).

[15] See David Pearl and Werner F. Menski, *Muslim Family Law* (London: Sweet & Maxwell, 3d ed. 1998), 65–83; John R. Bowen, "Private Arrangements: 'Recognizing Sharia' in England," *Boston Review* (March/April 2009), available at http://bostonreview.net/BR34.2/bowen.php; Samia Bano, "In Pursuit of Religious and Legal Diversity: A Response to the Archbishop of Canterbury and the 'Sharia Debate' in Britain," *Ecclesiastical Law Journal* 10 (2008): 283–309, 294–299.

freedom from physical coercion or threat (and so long as child custody matters are not involved). Canada, although constitutionally liberal, debated seriously the official recognition of *shari'a* arbitration tribunals in Ontario but ultimately rejected religious arbitration in favor of exclusive application of Ontarian and Canadian marriage law for all its citizens in arbitral matters.[16] This occurred despite the calls for a more interconnected relationship by former Attorney General Marion Boyd, and despite the fact that Jewish and Islamic religious councils had been functioning and resolving disputes for some time in Ontario.[17] Nonetheless, Canadian Muslims and Jews retain religious freedom to engage in their own worship, education, banking, and religious rituals and apparel.[18] And South Africa has intentionally sought to accommodate and incorporate minority groups as a key part of its recent constitutional undertakings, although it continues to struggle with striking the right balance between universal norms and cultural and religious distinctives regarding marriage and family law.[19]

The United States, like other Western democracies, faces two questions about the intersection of religious and civil law. First, how are the norms of minority religious groups (whether traditional minorities like Orthodox Jews or the newer, rapidly growing Muslim populations) to be accommodated? Second, how are religious norms of historically majority groups such as conservative Christians to be accommodated (if at all) when those norms seem to be out of step with liberal notions of gender equality or, increasingly, the ability of same-sex individuals to marry?

On the first question, American Muslims have uniformly not fared well of late when they have challenged state denials of charters or exemptions for their schools, charities, or mosques. Nor have they often succeeded in challenging prohibitions to wear traditional religious apparel while in public spaces or in winning accommodations for Muslim family law, let alone *shari'a* courts. State courts have only sporadically upheld private Muslim marriage contracts, often siding with non-Muslim spouses in divorce and child custody cases involving mixed marriages while also holding a firm line against Muslim polygamy.[20] Jewish parties, by contrast, have

---

[16] Family Statute Law Amendment Act, S.O. 2006, ch. 1 (Ont.) (assented to Feb. 23, 2006). The act and new regulations came into force on April 30, 2007. Ministry of the Attorney General, http://www.attorneygeneral.jus.gov.on.ca/english/family/arbitration. See Shachar, "Faith in Law?" (in this volume); Cere, "Canadian Conjugal Mosaic" (in this volume); Fadel, "Political Liberalism" (in this volume); Estin, "Unofficial Family Law" (in this volume).

[17] See generally Marion Boyd, Office of Canadian Attorney General, *Dispute Resolution in Family Law: Protecting Choice, Promoting Inclusion* (2004), available at http://www.attorneygeneral.jus.gov.on.ca/english/about/pubs/boyd/fullreport.pdf [hereinafter *Boyd Report*].

[18] See *Belonging? Diversity, Recognition and Shared Citizenship in Canada*, eds. Keith Banting, Thomas J. Courchene, and F. Leslie Seidle (Montreal: Institute for Research and Public Policy, 2007).

[19] See van der Vyver, "Multi-Tiered Marriages in South Africa" (in this volume).

[20] See Pascale Fournier, *Muslim Marriage in Western Courts* (Burlington, VT: Ashgate Publishing, 2010); Gregory C. Sisk and Michael Heise, "Muslims and Religious Liberty in the Post-9/11 Era: Empirical

fared better – especially in marriage and divorce matters in the state of New York. Since the 1980s, New York's *get* statutes have been the bridge between religious and civil law in that state, facilitating a delicate dance between the civil and religious judges in divorce matters.[21] Other U.S. states, however, with smaller concentrations of Orthodox Jews, have uniformly rejected similar *get* statutes. Their courts evaluate Jewish marriage contracts as prenuptial agreements, which are often deemed unenforceable entirely because of their religious nature.

On the second question, the rise of no-fault divorce (on a unilateral basis, in most states) over the past forty years has sparked concern in a number of conservative Christian quarters. Some commentators, like Katherine Shaw Spaht, have developed covenant marriage statutes designed to shore up marriage formation requirements and to reintroduce "fault" into divorce law, at least when agreed upon in advance by both parties.[22] Others, especially in light of the legalization of same-sex marriage in a few states, have called for a "divorce" between marriage and civil law instead of pressing for legal reforms.[23] Still others have mobilized to defeat same-sex marriage movements at the polls and to pass new state statutes or constitutional provisions that define marriage as a presumptively lifelong and heterosexual monogamous union. While traditional Christian commentators differ widely about the relationship between civil and religious law, many decry the modern privatization, liberalization, and secularization of marriage and family law.

II. THE EVOLUTION OF THE (WESTERN) LAW OF MARRIAGE

Given that marriage has long been regarded as both a legal and spiritual institution – subject at once to special state laws of contract and property, as well as to special religious canons and ceremonies – it is no surprise that the law of marriage and family life has triggered this renewed contest between law and religion in Western democracies. Marriage has long been regarded as the most primal institution of Western society and culture. Aristotle and the Roman Stoics called the marital household the "foundation of the republic" and "the private font of public virtue." The Church Fathers and medieval Catholics called it "the seedbed of the city" and "the force that welds society together." Early modern Protestants called it a "little church," a "little state," a "little seminary," and "the first school" of love and justice, charity and citizenship. John Locke and the Enlightenment philosophers called marriage "the

---

Evidence from the Federal Courts," (forthcoming 2012); McClain, "Marriage Pluralism in the United States" (in this volume); Estin "Unofficial Family Law" (in this volume).

[21] See Broyde, "New York's Regulation" (in this volume).

[22] See, e.g., the discussion of covenant marriage laws in Katherine Shaw Spaht, "Covenant Marriage Laws: A Model for Compromise" (in this volume).

[23] See Presser, "Marriage and the Law" (in this volume).

first society" to be formed as men and women moved from the state of nature to an organized society dedicated to the rule of law and the protection of rights. And as Justice Joseph Story remarked in 1841, marriage was regarded as "more than a mere contract" in America (and in the common law generally) because of its mixture of covenantal and contractual, communal and individual elements.[24]

Because of its cultural importance, marriage was also one of the first institutions to be reformed during the divisive battles between church and state in the history of the West. In the fourth century, when Constantine and his imperial successors converted the Roman Empire to Christianity, they soon passed new and comprehensive marriage and family laws predicated directly on Christian teachings.[25] In the later eleventh and twelfth centuries, when Pope Gregory VII and his successors threw off their civil rulers and established the Catholic Church as an independent legal authority, the Church seized jurisdiction over marriage, calling it a sacrament subject to Church courts and to the Church's canon laws. In the sixteenth century, when Martin Luther, Henry VIII, and other Protestants called for reforms of church, state, and society, one of their first acts was to reject the Catholic canon law of marriage and the sacramental theology that supported it, and to transfer principal legal control over marriage to the Christian magistrate. In the later eighteenth century, when the French revolutionaries unleashed their fury against traditional institutions they took early aim at the Catholic Church's complex marital rules, roles, and rituals, consigning marriage to the realm of secular state authorities. And, in the early twentieth century, when the Bolsheviks completed their revolution in Russia, one of Lenin's first acts was to abolish the legal institution of marriage as a bourgeois impediment to the realization of true communism.[26]

Modern Western democracies have not (to date) abolished marriage as a legal category, but they have dramatically privatized it, thinned out many of its traditional elements, and tried to make any regulation of it the sole province of the state. Half a century ago, most Western states treated marriage as a public institution in which church, state, and society were all deeply invested. With ample variation across

---

[24] See generally John Witte Jr., *From Sacrament to Contract: Marriage, Religion, and Law in the Western Tradition* (Louisville, KY: Westminster John Knox Press, 1997); John Witte Jr. and Don S. Browning, *Christian Marriage and Modern Marriage Law* (Cambridge: Cambridge University Press) (forthcoming); John Witte Jr. and Joel A. Nichols, "More than a Mere Contract: Marriage as Contract and Covenant in Law and Theology," *University of St. Thomas Law Journal* 5 (2008): 595–615. For more on the history of marriage and divorce in America, see Nichols, "Reconsidering the Boundaries" (in this volume); Presser, "Marriage and the Law" (in this volume).

[25] See Judith Evans-Grubbs, "Marrying and Its Documentation in Later Roman Law," in *To Have and to Hold: Marrying and Its Documentation in Western Christendom, 400–1600*, eds. Philip L. Reynolds and John Witte Jr. (Cambridge: Cambridge University Press, 2007), 43–94.

[26] See John Witte Jr., *God's Joust, God's Justice: Law and Religion in the Western Tradition* (Grand Rapids, MI: William B. Eerdmans Publishing Company, 2006), 11–18, 114–142.

jurisdictions, most Western states still generally defined marriage as a presumptively permanent monogamous union between a fit man and a fit woman with freedom and capacity to marry each other. A typical state law required that engagements be formal and that marriages be contracted with parental consent and witnesses after a suitable waiting period. It required marriage licenses and registration and solemnization before civil and/or religious authorities. It prohibited sex and marriage between couples related by various blood or family ties identified in the Mosaic Law. It discouraged, and sometimes prohibited, marriage where one party was impotent or had a contagious disease that precluded procreation or endangered the other spouse. Couples who sought to divorce had to publicize their intentions, petition a court, show adequate cause or fault, and make provision for the dependent spouse and children. Criminal laws outlawed fornication, adultery, sodomy, polygamy, contraception, abortion, and other perceived sexual offenses. Tort laws held third parties liable for seduction, enticement, loss of consortium, or alienation of the affections of one's spouse. Churches and other religious communities were given roles to play in the formation, maintenance, and dissolution of marriage, as well as in the physical, educational, and moral nurturing of children.[27]

Today, by contrast, a private contractual view of sex, marriage, and family life has come to dominate the West, with little constructive role left to play for parents, peers, or religious or political authorities. Marriage is now generally treated as a private bilateral contract to be formed, maintained, and dissolved as the couple sees fit (although only along such standard minimum baselines as the state dictates). Prenuptial, marital, and separation contracts, which allow parties to define their own rights and duties within the marital estate and thereafter, have gained increasing acceptance.[28] Some states impute implied marital contracts to longstanding lovers, upon which claims for maintenance and support during and after the relationship may be based. Surrogacy contracts are executed for the rental of wombs. Medical contracts are executed for the introduction of embryos or the abortion of fetuses. Traditional prohibitions against contraception and abortion have been held to violate the constitutional right of privacy. No-fault divorce statutes have reduced the divorce proceeding to an expensive formality and largely obliterated the complex procedural and substantive distinctions between annulment and divorce. Payments of alimony and other forms of post-marital support to dependent spouses are giving way to lump-sum property exchanges providing a clean break for parties to remarry. The functional distinctions between the rights of the married and the unmarried couple, and the straight and the gay partnership, have been considerably narrowed by an array of new statutes and constitutional cases. Marriages, civil unions, and

[27] See generally ibid., 295–363.
[28] See Bix, "Pluralism and Decentralization" (in this volume).

domestic partnerships have become veritable legal equivalents in many states. And the roles of the church, other religious organizations, and even the broader community have been gradually truncated in marriage formation, maintenance, and dissolution – in deference to constitutional principles of sexual autonomy, laïcité, or church-state separation.[29]

These and other exponential legal changes in the past half century have, in part, been efforts to bring greater equality and equity within marriage and society, and to stamp out some of the patriarchy, paternalism, and prudishness of the past. These legal changes are also, in part, simple reflections of the exponential changes that have occurred in the culture and condition of Western families – the stunning advances in reproductive and medical technology; the exposure to vastly different perceptions of sexuality and kinship born of globalization; the explosion of international and domestic norms of human rights; and the implosion of the traditional nuclear family born of new economic and professional demands on wives, husbands, and children. More fundamentally, however, these legal changes represent the rise of individual autonomy exemplified by increased private ordering in the domestic sphere, coupled with the simultaneous (and paradoxical) advance of the state's assertion of exclusive jurisdiction over family law matters as a way to enforce laudable liberal norms of autonomy, equality, and nondiscrimination.

III. RELIGION, FAMILY, AND THE STATE

A wide range of literature – jurisprudential, theological, ethical, political, economic, sociological, anthropological, and psychological – has emerged in the past four decades vigorously describing, defending, or decrying these legal changes. The contributors to the present volume join that discussion in an interdisciplinary dialogue as they offer a variety of perspectives on these important issues. The contributions, international in scope, raise foundational questions about the present and future interaction of the civil state and religious bodies regarding marriage and divorce: Is separation of church and state an ultimate goal in matters of family law, or one of several goals? What is the actual capacity of the civil state to set and enforce baseline norms of equal citizenship for marriage and divorce matters? What may the role of religious values be in setting baseline norms for family law matters? And how should the state deal with the fact that some of its citizens have allegiances to other communities that may be stronger than their allegiances to the civil state?

As several of the chapters in this volume illustrate, one emerging response of various Christians, Jews, Muslims, Hindus, and others is a call to withdraw from the state family law system and to operate their own internal religious legal systems for

---

[29] See generally Witte, *From Sacrament to Contract*.

their voluntary faithful. These groups believe the state has betrayed the essentials of marriage by adopting this new easy-in/easy-out private ordering scheme. They effectively want to contract out of the state's thin family law into their own thicker religious family law system. They want this faith-based family law system to be respected and supported by the state. They want a new division between the secular public and the religious private.

The flashpoint for these controversies to date, especially in Canada and the United Kingdom, has been for practicing Muslims – many of whom decry the massive changes to prevailing state laws of sex, marriage, and family. Some Muslims have just returned to their Muslim-majority homelands, shaking their heads in dismay at what Western libertinism has wrought. Others have remained and quietly ignored the state's marriage and family law, using the shelter of constitutional laws of privacy and sexual autonomy to become, in effect, a law unto themselves. Others have sought to draw upon the increasingly contractual nature of family law by developing elaborate premarital contracts that purport to exempt Muslim couples from much of the state law in favor of the internal norms and practices of their religious communities. Still others have led bicultural lives, dividing their time between Western homes and Muslim-majority lands that allow them to form Muslim marriages and families, including those that license polygamy, patriarchy, and primogeniture.

All of these informal methods of cultural and legal coexistence, however, can only be temporary expedients. Not only do some of these arrangements jeopardize many of the state's rights and privileges for spouses and children that depend on a validly contracted marriage, but these creaky accommodations and concessions that now exist in various Western lands can easily fall apart. Eventually a Muslim citizen will appeal to the state for relief from a marriage contract, religious family practice, or worship community that he or she cannot abide but cannot escape. Eventually an imam or (shadow) *shari'a* court will overstep by using force or issuing a fatwa that draws the ire of the media and the scrutiny of state courts. Eventually, an aggressive state caseworker or prosecutor will move upon a Muslim household, bringing charges of coerced or polygamous marriage. Eventually, a Muslim school or charity will find itself in court faced with a suit for gender discrimination or with child abuse owing to its practice of single-sex education and corporal punishment. Eventually, another major media event like that surrounding the Ontario *shari'a* controversy of 2005 or Archbishop Williams's comments of 2008 will bring a bright spotlight back on the family law of Western Muslim communities. Once such a major case or controversy breaks and the international media gets involved, many of these informal and temporary arrangements might well unravel – particularly given the current cultural backlash against Muslims in the West.

It is precisely this vulnerability that advocates of faith-based family law and *shari'a* councils want to avert. They want to put *shari'a*, and its voluntary use by Muslim faithful, on firmer constitutional and cultural ground in the West. Rather than denouncing Western liberalism, however – and the sexual, moral, and marital lassitude it has occasioned – sophisticated advocates now press their case for *shari'a* in and on the very terms of Western constitutionalism and political liberalism.

A. *The Case for* Shari'a *Councils*

Part of the case for *shari'a* is an argument for religious freedom. Both Western constitutional laws and international human rights norms give robust protection to the religious freedom of individuals and groups. Why should peaceable Muslim citizens not have the freedom to choose to exercise their domestic lives in accordance with the norms of their own voluntary religious communities? Why doesn't freedom of religion provide a sincere Muslim with protection against a unilateral divorce action or a child custody order by a state court that directly contradicts the rules of *shari'a*? Why doesn't freedom of religious exercise empower a pious Muslim man to take four wives into his loving permanent care in imitation of the Prophet, particularly when his secular counterpart can consort and cavort freely with four women at once and then walk out scot free? In turn, why shouldn't Muslim religious authorities enjoy the autonomy and freedom to apply their own internal laws and procedures for guiding and governing the private domestic lives of their voluntary faithful? Religious groups in the West have long enjoyed the corporate free exercise rights to legal personality, corporate property, collective worship, organized charity, parochial education, freedom of press, and more. Why can't Muslim (and other) religious groups also have the right to govern the marriage and family lives of their voluntary members – particularly when such domestic activities have such profound religious and moral dimensions for Islamic life and identity?

Part of the case for *shari'a* is an argument from political liberalism. One of the most basic teachings of classic liberalism is that marriage is a pre-political and pre-legal institution. It comes before the state and its positive laws, both in historical development and in ontological priority. As John Locke put it famously in *Two Treatises of Government* (1689), the marital contract was "the first contract" and "the first society" to be formed as men and women came forth from the state of nature.[30] The broader social contract came later, presupposing stable marital contracts. And contracts to form state governments, churches, and other voluntary associations within this broader society came later still. Why, on this simple contractarian logic, should the state get exclusive jurisdiction over marriage? After all, it was sixteenth-century Protestants, not eighteenth-century Enlightenment philosophers, who first vested the state with marital jurisdiction. Why is state jurisdiction over marriage mandatory,

---

[30] John Locke, *Two Treatises of Government*, II: 77–83 (1689).

or even necessary? Before the sixteenth-century Protestant Reformation – and in many Catholic lands well after the Reformation, too – the Catholic canon law and Catholic Church courts governed marriage. Moreover, even in Protestant England until the nineteenth century, the state delegated to ecclesiastical courts the power to treat many questions relating to marriage and the family. There is evidently nothing inherent in the structure and history of Western marriage and family law that requires it to be administered by the state. Moreover, there is nothing ineluctable in liberalism's contractarian logic that requires marital couples to choose the state rather than their own families or their own religious communities to govern their domestic lives – particularly when the state's liberal rules diverge so widely from their own beliefs and practices.

And part of the case for *shari'a* is an argument for religious equality and nondiscrimination. After all, many Western Christians have religious tribunals to govern their internal affairs, including some of the family matters of their faithful, such as annulments, and state courts will respect their judgments even if their cases are appealed to Rome or Canterbury, Moscow or Constantinople. No one is talking of abolishing these church courts or trimming their power, even after recent discoveries of grave financial abuses and cover-ups of clerical sexual abuse of children in some churches. No one seems to think these Christian tribunals are illegitimate when some of them discriminate against women in decisions about ordination and church leadership. Similarly, Jews are given wide authority to operate their own Jewish law courts to arbitrate marital, financial, and other disputes among the Orthodox Jewish faithful. Indeed, already in New York State by statute, and in several European nations by custom, courts will not issue a civil divorce to a Jewish couple unless and until the *beth din* issues a religious divorce, even though Jewish law systematically discriminates against the wife's right to divorce. If Christians can have their canon laws and consistory courts, if Jews can have their *halacha* and *beth din*, and if even indigenous peoples can have their ancestral laws and tribal rulers, why can't Muslims be treated equally in their use of *shari'a* and Islamic courts?

B. The Case Against Shari'a Councils

The problem with the pro-*shari'a* argument from religious freedom is that, in its strongest form, it falsely assumes that claims of conscience and freedom of religious exercise must always trump. But this is hardly the case in modern democracies, even though religious freedom is cherished.[31] Even the most sincere and zealous conscientious objectors must pay their taxes, register their properties, answer their

[31] See generally Robert K. Vischer, *Conscience and the Common Good* (Cambridge: Cambridge University Press, 2010).

subpoenas, obey their court orders, swear their oaths (or otherwise prove their verac-
ity), answer their military conscriptions (even if by noncombat duty), and abide by
many other general laws for the common good that they may not in good conscience
wish to abide. Their eventual choice if they persist in their claims of conscience is
to leave the country or go to prison for contempt. Even the most devout religious
believer has no claim to exemptions from criminal laws against activities like polygamy, child marriage, female genital mutilation, or corporal discipline of wives, even
if their particular brand of religion commends or commands it. The guarantee of
religious freedom is not a license to engage in crime. Muslims who are conscientiously opposed to liberal Western laws of sex, marriage, and family are certainly free
to ignore them. They can live chaste private lives in accordance with *shari'a* and not
register their religious marriages with the state. That choice will be protected by the
constitutional rights of privacy and sexual autonomy so long as their conduct is truly
consensual. That choice, however, also leaves their family entirely without the protections, rights, and privileges available through the state's complex laws and regulations of marriage and family, marital property and inheritance, social welfare, and
more. And if minor children are involved, the state will intervene to ensure their
protection, support, and education, and will hear nothing of free exercise objections
from their parents or community leaders. Western Muslims enjoy the same religious
freedom as everyone else, but some of the special accommodations pressed by some
Muslim advocates and others today in the name of religious freedom are simply
beyond the pale.

Even further beyond the pale is the notion of granting a religious group actual sovereignty over the sex, marriage, and family lives of their voluntary faithful. Allowing
religious officials to officiate at weddings, testify in divorce cases, assist in the adoption of a child, facilitate the rescue of a distressed family member, and the like are
one thing. Most Western democracies readily grant Muslims and other peaceable
religious communities those accommodations.[32] But that is a long way from asking
the state to delegate to a religious group the full legal power to govern the domestic
affairs of their voluntary faithful in accordance with their own religious laws. No
democratic state can readily accommodate a competing sovereign to govern such
a vital area of life for its citizens – especially because family law is so interwoven
with other state public, private, procedural, and penal laws, and especially because
so many other rights and duties of citizens turn on a person's marital and familial
status.[33] Surely a democratic citizen's status, entitlements, and rights cannot turn on
the judgments of a religious authority that has none of the due process and other
procedural constraints of a state tribunal.

---

[32] See Estin, "Unofficial Family Law" (in this volume).
[33] See Wilson, "The Perils of Privatized Marriage" (in this volume).

The pro-*shari'a* argument from liberal contractarian logic – that marital contracts are pre-political and thus parties should be free to choose whose laws and which tribunals govern them – is clever but incomplete. It ignores another elementary teaching of classical liberalism, namely that only the state and no other social or private unit can hold the coercive power of the sword. The civil state will only grant the use of this power in exchange for strict guarantees of due process of law, equal protection under the law, and respect for fundamental rights. A comprehensive system of marriage and family law – let alone the many correlative legal systems of inheritance, trusts, family property, children's rights, education, social welfare, and more – cannot long operate without coercive power. It needs police, prosecutors, and prisons; subpoenas, fines, and contempt orders; and material, physical, and corporal sanctions. Moral suasion, example, communal approbation, and censure can certainly do part of the work. But a properly functioning marriage and family law system requires resort to all these coercive instruments of government. Indeed, it is precisely the coercive power that religious tribunals seek when moving for official state sanction. Only the state, however, and not a religious body, can properly use these instruments in a modern democracy.[34]

The pro-*shari'a* argument from religious equality and nondiscrimination takes more effort to parry. A useful starting point is the quip of United States Supreme Court Justice Oliver Wendell Holmes Jr.: "The life of the law has not been logic but experience."[35] This adage has bearing on this issue. The current accommodations made to the religious legal systems of Christians, Jews, First Peoples, and others in the West were not born overnight. They came only after decades, even centuries, of sometimes hard and cruel experience, with gradual adjustments and accommodations on both sides.

The accommodation of and by Jewish law to Western secular law is particularly instructive. It is discomfiting but essential to remember that Jews were the perennial pariahs of the West for nearly two millennia, consigned at best to second-class status and periodically subject to waves of brutality – whether imposed by Germanic purges, medieval pogroms, early modern massacres, or the twentieth-century Holocaust. Jews have been in perennial diaspora after the destruction of Jerusalem in 70 C.E., living in a wide variety of legal cultures in the West and well beyond. After the third century C.E., the diaspora Jews developed the important legal concept of *dina d'malkhuta dina* ("the law of the community is the law").[36] This meant that Jews accepted the law of the legitimate and peaceful secular ruler who hosted them

---

[34] See, e.g., *Boyd Report*, 75–76.
[35] Oliver Wendell Holmes Jr., *The Common Law* (1881), 1–2.
[36] See Rabbi Dr. Dov Bressler, "Arbitration and the Courts in Jewish Law," *Journal of Halacha and Contemporary Society* 9 (1985): 105–117.

as the law of their own Jewish community, to the extent that it did not conflict with core Jewish laws.[37] This technique allowed Jewish communities to sort out which of their own religious laws were indispensable and which more discretionary; which secular laws and practices could be accommodated and which had to be resisted even at the risk of life and limb. This technique led to ample innovation and diversity of Jewish law over time and across cultures, and it also gave the Jews the ability to survive and grow legally, even in the face of persecution.

Western democracies, in turn – particularly in the aftermath of the Holocaust and in partial recompense for the horrors it visited on the Jews – have gradually come to accommodate core Jewish laws and practices. It is only in the past two generations, however, and only after endless litigation and lobbying in state courts and legislatures, that Western Jews have finally gained legal ground to stand on – and even that ground is still thin and crumbles at the edges sometimes. Today, Western Jews generally have freedom to receive Sabbath day accommodations; to gain access to kosher food; to don yarmulkes, distinctive grooming, and other forms of religious dress in most public places; to gain zoning, land use, and building charters for their synagogues, charities, and Torah schools; to offer single-sex and bilingual education; and more. Additionally, Jewish law courts have gained the right to decide some of the domestic and financial affairs of their faithful who voluntarily elect to arbitrate their disputes before them rather than suing in secular courts. These Jewish law courts are attractive to Jewish disputants because they are staffed by highly trained jurists who are conversant with both Jewish and secular law and sensitive to the bicultural issues that are being negotiated. Unlike their medieval and early modern predecessors, these modern Jewish law courts do not claim full authority over Jewish sex, marriage, and family life, but leave many such issues to the state. These Jewish law courts have also abandoned their traditional authority to impose physical coercion or sanctions on the disputants.[38]

C. Lessons and Analogies

The modern lessons in this story for *shari'a* advocates are four. First, it takes time and patience for a secular legal system to adjust to the realities and needs of new religious groups and to make the necessary legal accommodations. The hard-won accommodations that modern Jewish law and culture now enjoy are not fungible commodities that Muslims or any others can claim with a simple argument from

---

[37] Ibid. See generally David Novak, "Law and Religion in Judaism," in *Christianity and the Law: An Introduction*, eds. John Witte Jr. and Frank S. Alexander (Cambridge: Cambridge University Press, 2008), 33–52.

[38] See generally Broyde, "New York's Regulation" (in this volume).

equality. They are individualized, equitable adjustments to general laws that each community needs to earn for itself based on its own needs and experiences. Muslims simply do not have the same history of persecution that the Jews have faced in the West, and they simply do not yet have a long enough track record of litigation and lobbying. Concessions and accommodations will come, but only with time, persistence, and patience.

Second, it takes flexibility and innovation on the part of a religious community to win accommodations from secular laws and cultures. Not every religious belief can be claimed as central, and not every religious practice can be worth dying for. Over time, and of necessity, diaspora Jewish communities learned to distinguish between what was core and what was more penumbral to their faith, and what was essential and what was more discretionary to Jewish legal and cultural identity. Over time, and only grudgingly, Western democracies learned to accommodate the core religious beliefs and practices of Jewish communities. Diaspora Muslim communities in the West will need to do the same. Modern day Islam now features immense variety in its legal, religious, and cultural practices. That diversity provides ample opportunity and incentive for Muslim diaspora communities to make the necessary adjustments to Western life and to sort out for themselves what is core and what is more discretionary in their religious lives.

Third, religious communities, in turn, have to accommodate, or at least tolerate, the core values of their secular host nations if they expect to win concessions for their religious courts and other religious practices. No Western nation will long countenance a religious community that cannot accept its core values of liberty, equality, and fraternity, or of human rights, democracy, and the rule of law. So far, only a small and brave band of mostly Western-trained Muslim intellectuals and jurists have called for the full embrace of democracy and human rights in and on Muslim terms. These are highly promising arguments, but so far they are still hard to hear amidst the loud, competing denunciations from more traditional Muslims in and beyond the West. Moreover, even liberal Muslims remain hard pressed to point to modern examples of a *shari'a*-based legal system that consistently maintains core democratic and human rights values. Until that case can be reliably made, deep suspicion will remain the norm. Western-based Muslims have an ideal opportunity to show that *shari'a* and democracy can coexist and complement each other. And it is certainly possible that things will evolve more quickly than one might expect, because the new and complex diaspora communities of Western Muslims are currently in the midst of a very dynamic period of development.

Finally, Muslim tribunals must be perceived as routinely legally sophisticated and procedurally equitable to be both attractive to voluntary Muslim disputants and acceptable to secular state courts. Like the Jewish *beth din* that sits in New York or London, the Muslim law court needs to be staffed by jurists who are well trained both in religious law and secular law, and who maintain basic standards of due process and representation akin to those in secular courts or arbitration tribunals. A single imam pronouncing legal judgments in an informal proceeding at the local mosque will get no more deference from a state court than a single priest or rabbi making legal pronouncements in a church or synagogue. Moreover, Western state courts will suspect that the disputing parties who appeared before the imam either did not understand the full legal options available to them at state law or were coerced to participate in the internal religious procedures. It is much harder and much less appropriate for a court to have such suspicions when educated Muslim parties, eyes wide open, voluntarily choose a legally sophisticated Muslim arbitration tribunal over a secular court that does not share their core values but still offers them a serious jurisprudential option to state marriage law.

Lest the foregoing sound like an unduly patronizing argument that Muslims and other religious groups just need to "wait and see" or "change and hope for the best" regarding religious and civil family law, it is worth remembering that religion and the state have already undertaken a similar jurisdictional dance in the area of religion and education, especially in the United States. In the later nineteenth century, a number of American states wanted a monopoly on education in public (that is, state-run) schools. Some of this agitation was driven by anti-Catholicism and some by more general anti-religious animus. For half a century, churches, schools, and religious parents struggled earnestly to protect their rights to educate their children in their own private religious schools. In the landmark case of *Pierce v. Society of Sisters* (1925), the United States Supreme Court finally held for the churches and ordered American states to maintain parallel public and private education options for their citizens.[39] But in a long series of cases thereafter, courts also made clear that states could set basic educational requirements for all schools – mandatory courses, texts, and tests; minimal standards for teachers, students, and facilities; and common requirements for laboratories, libraries, and gymnasia. Religious schools could add to the state's minimum requirements, but they could not subtract from them. Religious schools that sought exemptions from these requirements found little sympathy from the courts, which instructed the schools either to meet the standards or lose their accreditation and licenses to teach.

This compromise on religion and education, forged painfully over more than half a century of wrangling, has some bearing on questions of religion and marriage – and may help lead to swifter changes than could be predicted otherwise. Marriage, like education, is not a state monopoly, even if marriage law must be a state prerogative. Religious parties in the West have long had the right to marry in a religious sanctuary, following their religious community's preferred wedding

---

[39] 268 U.S. 510 (1925).

liturgy. Religious officials have long had the right to participate in the weddings, annulments, divorces, and custody battles of their voluntary members. But the state has also long set the threshold requirements of what marriage is and who may participate. Religious officials may add to these threshold state law requirements on marriage but not subtract from them. A minister may insist on premarital counseling before a wedding, even if the state will marry a couple without it. But if a minister bullies a minor to marry out of religious duty, the state could throw him in jail. A rabbi may encourage a bickering couple to repent and reconcile, but he cannot prevent them from filing for divorce. An imam may preach of the beauties of polygamy, but if he knowingly presides over a polygamous union he is an accessory to crime.

If religious councils or tribunals do eventually get more involved in marriage and family law, states might well build on these precedents and set threshold requirements in the form of a license – formulating these license rules through a democratic process in which all parties of every faith and nonfaith participate. Among the most important license rules to consider: There may be no child or polygamous marriages or other forms of marital union not recognized by the state.[40] There may be no compelled marriages or coerced conversions before weddings that violate elementary freedoms of contract and conscience. There may be no threats or violations of life and limb, or provocations of the same. There may be no blatant discrimination against women. There may be no violation of basic rules of procedural fairness. Religious tribunals may add to these requirements but not subtract from them. Those who fail to conform will lose their licenses and will find little sympathy when they raise religious liberty objections.

Such an arrangement of state minimums but not exclusive state control worked well to resolve some of the nation's hardest questions of religion and education, and something similar holds comparable promise for questions of religion and marriage. It not only prevents a descent to "licensed polygamy" and other ills that the Archbishop's critics feared, but it encourages today's religious tribunals to reform themselves and the marital laws that they offer while also respecting demands for pluralism by adherents with dual allegiances and citizenships.

IV. FIRST AMENDMENT CONSIDERATIONS

In the United States, however, these are not only cultural but also constitutional issues. The First Amendment of the U.S. Constitution provides: "Congress shall make no law respecting an establishment of religion, or prohibiting the free exercise

---

[40] For the case against religiously based polygamy, see John Witte Jr., "The Legal Challenges of Polygamy in the USA," *Ecclesiastical Law Journal* 11 (2009): 72–75.

thereof."[41] The Supreme Court now also applies the First Amendment to the actions of states and localities.[42] Just as all state laws on education and religion have to comport with the First Amendment's dictates, so too must all state laws of marriage, divorce, and contract. And just as the courts have long had to decide First Amendment questions regarding religious schools and the state to ensure free exercise and avoid the establishment of religion, so too will the courts have to address First Amendment questions in the ongoing dance of religion and the state in marriage law. At least three major areas of constitutional concern are implicated by the questions raised in this chapter (and, indeed, in this volume).

First, advocates of faith-based family laws could bring claims of constitutional entitlement to an alternate system under the First Amendment's Free Exercise Clause, notwithstanding general norms about marriage and divorce law set by the state. Current Supreme Court free exercise law does not leave much room for such an "opt-out" claim. Free exercise litigants generally will lose if they seek an exemption from an otherwise neutral and generally applicable law like general state family laws. Such stand-alone free exercise claims are assessed under the "rational basis test," whereby a court will ask if the legislature had a rational basis for passing the law and whether the law reasonably achieves the legislature's objectives. Litigants almost always lose under such a test. Claimants are not entitled to a higher standard of review, with an attendant higher likelihood of success, unless the law in question specifically discriminates against religion or implicates "hybrid rights."[43] Even if minority religions could claim that their internal group norms are being discriminated against by the application of majority family law norms, this is not the kind of direct "targeting" of religious beliefs and practices that triggers higher levels of judicial scrutiny of a free exercise claim. Claimants could also try to assert a hybrid right of religious belief coupled with free speech, free association, or the implication of a fundamental right (such as the right to marry or the right to raise children as one sees fit), but these also seem unlikely as stand-alone claims. Courts have been generally reluctant to find hybrid rights that would trigger higher judicial scrutiny. Even if a court did apply stricter scrutiny, a state would likely show a strong enough interest in uniformity of its family law (including protection of women's rights to equal citizenship and the state's *parens patriae* status respecting children) to justify its rejection of a party's claim for a free

---

[41] U.S. Constitution, Amend. I. See generally John Witte Jr. and Joel A. Nichols, *Religion and the American Constitutional Experiment* (Boulder, CO: Westview Press, 3d ed. 2011).

[42] See *Cantwell v. Connecticut*, 310 U.S. 296 (1940); *Everson v. Board of Education*, 330 U.S. 1 (1947).

[43] See *Employment Division v. Smith*, 494 U.S. 872 (1990); *Church of Lukumi Babalu Aye v. City of Hialeah*, 508 U.S. 520 (1993). See also Witte and Nichols, *Religion and the American Constitutional Experiment*, 131–167.

exercise exemption from its system of marriage law. Even so, the state may have a harder time justifying uniform laws if the asserted religious exemption was the ability of a couple to impose stricter guidelines on when they could be divorced (e.g., limiting themselves to divorce on fault bases only instead of the lesser no-fault regime mandated by the state) than if the desired exemption was to apply a property distribution scheme that was less favorable to a divorcing woman than the state's default civil property regime.

A subset of free exercise issues relate to potential claims by a religious group *qua* group to operate a faith-based family law system for its voluntary members. Such a claim would rest on a growing modern literature, albeit with deep historical roots, about religious group autonomy and the "freedom of the church" to practice its corporate faith in ways consistent with its beliefs. Although historically in the United States religious group autonomy claims have arisen almost solely over property disputes, there are instances where religious groups have claimed (and received) the authority to hire and fire their own employees and set their own internal terms of membership.[44] It is not too far a stretch to think that matters of marriage, divorce, and family should be deemed central enough to a religion to merit good-faith claims about the need for some modicum of internal group control over such issues if the religious adherents desire it.

Second, different First Amendment issues will arise if it is state legislatures, rather than the courts, that allow religious tribunals to serve as official decision makers regarding marriage and divorce matters. The Supreme Court has stated that there is "play in the joints" in the First Amendment – that is, there is space between what government *must* permit per the Free Exercise Clause and that which government *may not* under the Establishment Clause.[45] Some state laws touching religion, such as tax exemptions for religion, have long been permissible under the Free Exercise Clause and not forbidden by the Establishment Clause. After *Employment Division v. Smith* (1990), Congress and many state legislatures passed numerous laws that gave discrete benefits and protections to religion and accorded higher levels of protection for religious exercise and autonomy than that mandated by the Free Exercise Clause. These laws have been upheld when challenged under the Establishment Clause. Were a state legislature to pass a law that required its state courts to defer to the decisions of religious tribunals for their voluntary faithful, the hard constitutional question would be whether this was just another permissible accommodation of religion or an impermissible delegation of core governmental powers in contravention

---

[44] See, e.g., *Presiding Bishop v. Amos*, 483 U.S. 327 (1987); Witte and Nichols, *Religion and the American Constitutional Experiment*, 241–262. But see *Christian Legal Society v. Martinez* 561 U.S. ___, 130 S.Ct. 2971 (2010).

[45] E.g., *Locke v. Davey*, 540 U.S. 712 (2004).

of the Establishment Clause.[46] Courts and legislatures would have to face head-on the complicated question of whether the state *may* get out of the marriage business if it so desires, or whether instead marriage is so central to human flourishing, and so within the unique ambit of the state, that it is a quintessential state function (even if it can be limited at the edges by private ordering).

A third set of concerns will arise if state legislatures wish to refrain from "privatizing diversity" by granting jurisdiction to religious bodies[47] and instead choose to offer their citizens several models of marriage within their civil marriage law, one of which is more consistent with traditional religious norms. Although some might assert that the Establishment Clause does not allow a state to ground its civil family law in religious principles at all, courts and most commentators agree that a state's marriage and divorce laws may be consonant with traditional religious (Christian) norms and mores.[48] It would be a closer constitutional case if the state were to proclaim more explicitly the linkage between the civil law and its religious inspiration. Having two forms of marriage and divorce law – such as contract laws and the covenant marriage laws in Louisiana, Arizona, and Arkansas, which follow earlier common law norms – should be permissible under current First Amendment doctrine because those covenant marriage laws merely grant couples an option of more stringent norms and have safeguards to ensure voluntariness and escape from the stringent norms in the event of abuse, habitual intemperance, or after a period of separation.[49] Other laws that are more particular to specific religions, such as New York's *get* statutes, which effectively grant Orthodox Jewish rabbis the power to determine the civil divorce rights of Orthodox Jewish citizens, are much more vulnerable to constitutional challenge on grounds of unduly entangling government and religion, or unduly favoring or singling out one religion.[50] Even so, the Supreme Court has indicated that not all entanglement is constitutionally problematic, but only "entanglement" that is truly "excessive" and that

[46] *Larkin v. Grendel's Den*, 459 U.S. 116 (1982) (holding that a state may not effectively give "veto power" over state decisions regarding liquor licenses to nearby establishments); *Bd. of Educ. of Kiryas Joel School Dist. v. Grumet*, 512 U.S. 687 (1994) (holding that a state may not delegate its "discretionary authority over public schools to a group defined by its character as a religious community").

[47] See Ayelet Shachar, "Privatizing Diversity: A Cautionary Tale from Religious Arbitration in Family Law," *Theoretical Inquiries in Law* 9:2 (2008): 573–607.

[48] But see Justice Scalia's concern that the Supreme Court has removed or severely reduced the role that morality can play in undergirding a law. *Lawrence v. Texas*, 539 U.S. 558 (2003) (Scalia, J., dissenting).

[49] See the detailed constitutional analysis in Joel A. Nichols, "Louisiana's Covenant Marriage Law: A First Step Toward a More Robust Pluralism in Marriage and Divorce Law?," *Emory Law Journal* 47 (1998): 929–1001.

[50] See, e.g., discussion and sources in Broyde, "New York's Regulation" (in this volume).

involves more than the "administrative cooperation" of civil law and ecclesiastical officials.[51] Moreover, the Court now permits increased interaction and cooperation between religion and the government in matters of funding for faith-based organizations and even vouchers for school children (so long as the funding is done on an equal basis).[52] Both lines of cases leave open the possibility that state laws allowing for more formal interplay between religious and civil officials in family law matters would not be as readily stricken down as some opponents might suggest.

[51] *Agostini v. Felton*, 521 U.S. 203 (1997). See also discussion in Witte and Nichols, *Religion and the American Constitutional Experiment*, 180–181, 214–216.
[52] *Bowen v. Kendrick*, 487 U.S. 589 (1988); *Zelman v. Simmons-Harris*, 536 U.S. 639 (2002).

Index

CPSIA information can be obtained at www.ICGtesting.com
Printed in the USA
LVOW080105081112

306372LV00001B/4/P